EVALUATION

To the memory of *Donald T. Campbell*—
architect of modern evaluation theory and practice;
mentor, directly and indirectly, to all evaluators

PETER H. ROSSI
HOWARD E. FREEMAN
MARK W. LIPSEY

EVALUATION
A SYSTEMATIC APPROACH

SIXTH EDITION

SAGE Publications
International Educational and Professional Publisher
Thousand Oaks   London   New Delhi

For information:

SAGE Publications, Inc.
2455 Teller Road
Thousand Oaks, California 91320
E-mail: order@sagepub.com

SAGE Publications Ltd.
6 Bonhill Street
London EC2A 4PU
United Kingdom

SAGE Publications India Pvt. Ltd.
M-32 Market
Greater Kailash I
New Delhi 110 048 India

Printed in the United States of America

Library of Congress Cataloging-in-Publication Data

Rossi, Peter Henry, 1921-
    Evaluation: a systematic approach / by Peter H. Rossi,
Howard E. Freeman, and Mark W. Lipsey. — 6th ed.
       p.   cm.
    Includes bibliographical references and index.
    ISBN 0-7619-0893-5 (acid-free paper)
    1. Evaluation research (Social action programs).   I. Freeman,
Howard E.   II. Lipsey, Mark W.   III. Title.
    H62.R666   1998
    361.6'1'072—dc21   98-40244

This book is printed on acid-free paper.

99 00 01 02 03 04 10 9 8 7 6 5 4 3 2 1

Acquiring Editor:	C. Deborah Laughton
Editorial Assistant:	Eileen Carr
Production Editor:	Astrid Virding
Designer/Typesetter:	Janelle LeMaster
Cover Designer:	Ravi Balasuriya

CONTENTS

PREFACE

Throughout the six editions of this book, its objectives have remained constant. It provides an introduction to the range of research activities used in appraising the design, implementation, and utility of social programs. That set of research procedures known as evaluation has become solidly incorporated into the routine activities of all levels of government throughout the world, into the operations of nongovernmental organizations, and into the discussions of social issues. We believe that evaluation research has influenced social policies and other efforts to improve the social conditions of the citizens of many communities. It is also an exciting professional role providing opportunities to advance social well-being along with the exercise of technical skills.

Evaluation: A Systematic Approach has strong ambitions to communicate the technical knowledge and collective experiences of practicing evaluators to those who might consider engaging in evaluation and to those who need to know what evaluation is all about. Our intended audiences are students, practitioners, novice social researchers, public officials, sponsors of social programs, social commentators, and the legendary intelligent layperson. Although some very experienced evaluators might find our book too elementary, we hope that reading it will help others at earlier stages of their encounters with evaluation. We also provide references to more advanced discussions of critical topics for those readers who want to pursue some topic in greater depth.

When Howard Freeman died suddenly and prematurely shortly before the fifth edition was published, I was quite sure that there would never be a sixth edition of which I would be a living coauthor. Howard Freeman had been a person of great knowledge, experience, and wit, working with whom was most of the reward of collaboration. Without Howard to work with, the prospect of yet another revision seemed painfully unrewarding.

However, it became increasingly clear after a few years had passed that the fifth edition was rapidly becoming out of date. Our noble Sage senior editor, C. Deborah Laughton, started to urge me to consider a major revision. At first I resisted on the grounds that I had no collaborator with whom to work. Working with great subtlety, stealth, and a bit of benign deception, she told Mark Lipsey that I was interested in having him as coauthor at the same time telling me that Mark was interested in becoming a coauthor. Knowing the high quality of Mark Lipsey's evaluation work, I was quite flattered at his interest. He tells me that he was also pleased that I was interested in working with him. And so a new collaboration was forged. Mark cannot replace Howard: He brings to the collaboration a different background and set of experiences, equal to Howard's in depth and sophistication but different in content in ways that enrich the sixth edition. Working with him has been a great pleasure, greatly enhanced by his sense of proportion and ready humor. I am grateful to C. Deborah Laughton for her skillful matchmaking and for the improvements in this edition that it made possible.

Most of the new material that appears in this revision is Mark Lipsey's contribution. The previous edition covered quite sketchily evaluation diagnostic procedures and how evaluations should be tailored to fit programs and social contexts. The current version has greatly expanded coverage of those topics, adding important detailed material on explicating program theory. The treatment in the first five chapters of this version carries the reader through a sequence that follows more closely the typical steps that the development of evaluations take. Lipsey has also updated the exhibits that appear in this edition, often with examples of evaluations currently under way or very recently completed.

We are grateful to the following reviewers for their comments: Jack McKillip, Ron Andersen, Melissa Jonson-Reid, David MacPhee, and William Shadish. A special acknowledgment is also extended to Kate Peterson for her extensive copyediting efforts.

We have dedicated this edition to the memory of Donald T. Campbell. In our view, there is no one who more deeply influenced the development of evaluation. Not only are his publications cited in all major works on evaluation, but he was also an important mentor. Several generations of his students now are leading figures in the field and their students are rising quickly to prominence. His influence on this volume can be seen in the discussion of impact assessment, which follows rather closely his exposition of research designs laid down in his 1966 publication (Campbell and Stanley, 1966). All evaluators can see farther because we stand on his shoulders: Campbell was a giant who gave us a lofty perspective on how social science can advance the improvement of the human condition.

—P.H.R.

Social program; social intervention	An organized, planned, and usually ongoing effort designed to ameliorate a social problem or improve social conditions.
Program evaluation	The use of social research procedures to systematically investigate the effectiveness of social intervention programs that is adapted to their political and organizational environments and designed to inform social action in ways that improve social conditions.
Social research methods	Procedures for studying social behavior devised by social scientists that are based on systematic observation and logical rules for drawing inferences from those observations.
Comprehensive evaluation	An assessment of a social program that covers the need for the program, its design, implementation, impact, and efficiency.
Evaluation sponsor	The person(s), group, or organization that requests or requires the evaluation and provides the resources to conduct it.
Stakeholders	Individuals, groups, or organizations having a significant interest in how well a program functions, for instance, those with decision-making authority over it, funders and sponsors, administrators and personnel, and clients or intended beneficiaries.

CHAPTER 1

PROGRAMS, POLICIES, AND EVALUATIONS

This chapter introduces program evaluation as a robust arena of activity directed at collecting, analyzing, interpreting, and communicating information about the effectiveness of social programs undertaken for the purpose of improving social conditions. Evaluations are conducted for a variety of practical reasons: to aid in decisions concerning whether programs should be continued, improved, expanded, or curtailed; to assess the utility of new programs and initiatives; to increase the effectiveness of program management and administration; and to satisfy the accountability requirements of program sponsors. Evaluations also may contribute to substantive and methodological social science knowledge.

Understanding evaluation in contemporary context requires some appreciation of its history, its distinguishing concepts and purposes, and the inherent tensions and challenges that shape its practice. Program evaluation represents an adaptation of social research methods to the task of studying social intervention in its natural political and organizational circumstances so that sound judgments can be drawn about the need for intervention and the design, implementation, impact, and efficiency of programs that address that need. Individual evaluation studies, and the cumulation of knowledge from many such studies, can make a vital contribution to informed social action aimed at improving the human condition.

The principal purpose of program evaluation, therefore, is to provide valid findings about the effectiveness of social programs to those persons with responsibilities or interests related to their creation, continuation, or improvement.

Long before Sir Thomas More coined the word *utopia* in 1516, many persons had tried to envision a perfect world. That their aspirations, and ours, have not been realized is evident in the social problems and attendant personal problems that confront every country in the world. True, how we define social problems and estimate their scope and which problems are salient to us have changed over time with shifts in values and lifestyles. And it is equally true that communities, societies, and cultures differ widely in the attention they pay to particular problems. But now, as ever, to borrow from Charles Dickens, these are the best of times for some of us and the worst of times for others.

Since antiquity, organized efforts have been undertaken to describe, understand, and ameliorate the defects in the human condition. This book is rooted in the tradition of scientific study of social problems—a tradition that has aspired to improve the quality of our physical and social environments and enhance our individual and collective well-being through the systematic creation and application of knowledge. Although the term *evaluation research* is a relatively recent invention, the activities that we will consider under this rubric are not. They can be traced to the very beginnings of modern science. Three centuries ago, as Cronbach and colleagues (1980) point out, Thomas Hobbes and his contemporaries endeavored to devise numerical measures to assess social conditions and identify the causes of mortality, morbidity, and social disorganization.

Even social experiments, the most technically challenging form of contemporary evaluation research, are hardly a recent invention. One of the earliest "social experiments" took place in the 1700s when a British ship's captain observed the lack of scurvy among sailors serving on the naval ships of Mediterranean countries. He noticed, too, that citrus fruit was part of their rations. Thereupon he made half his crew consume limes while the other half continued with their regular diet. Despite much grumbling among the crew in the "treatment" group, the experiment was a success—it showed that consuming limes prevented scurvy.

The good captain probably did not know that he was evaluating a demonstration project nor did he likely have an explicit *impact theory* (a term we will discuss later), namely, that scurvy is a consequence of a vitamin C deficiency and that limes are rich in vitamin C. Nevertheless, the intervention worked and British seamen eventually were compelled to consume citrus fruit regularly, a practice that gave rise to the still-popular label *limeys*. Incidentally, it took about 50 years before the captain's "social program" was widely adopted. Then, as now, diffusion and acceptance of evaluation findings did not come easily.

WHAT IS EVALUATION RESEARCH?

Although the broadest definition of evaluation includes all efforts to place value on events, things, processes, or people, we will be concerned here with the evaluation of social programs. For purposes of orientation, we offer a preliminary definition of social program evaluation now and will present and discuss a more complete version later in this chapter: *Program evaluation is the use of social research procedures to systematically investigate the effectiveness of social intervention programs.* More specifically, evaluation researchers (evaluators) use social research methods to study, appraise, and help improve social programs in all their important aspects, including the diagnosis of the social problems they address, their conceptualization and design, their implementation and administration, their outcomes, and their efficiency.

At various times, policymakers, funding organizations, planners, program managers, taxpayers, or program clientele need to distinguish worthwhile programs from ineffective ones and launch new programs or revise existing ones so as to achieve certain desirable results. To do so, they must obtain answers to questions such as the following:

- What are the nature and scope of the problem? Where is it located, whom does it affect, and how does it affect them?

- What is it about the problem or its effects that justifies new, expanded, or modified social programs?

- What feasible interventions are likely to significantly ameliorate the problem?

- What are the appropriate target populations for intervention?

- Is a particular intervention reaching its target population?

- Is the intervention being implemented well? Are the intended services being provided?

- Is the intervention effective in attaining the desired goals or benefits?

- How much does the program cost?

- Is the program cost reasonable in relation to its effectiveness and benefits?

Exhibit 1-A conveys the views of one feisty senator about the need for evaluation evidence on program effectiveness. Answers to questions such as those above are necessary for local or specialized programs, such as job training in a small town, a new mathematics curriculum for elementary schools, or the outpatient services of a community mental health clinic, as well as for broad national or state programs such as health care, family preservation, or educational reform. Providing those answers is the work of persons in the program evaluation field.

Although this text emphasizes the evaluation of social programs, especially human service programs, program evaluation is not restricted to that arena. An excellent example of the broad scope of program evaluation is provided by the work of the Program Evaluation Methodology Division of the U.S. General Accounting Office (GAO). This unit was established in 1980 to foster the application of evaluation research to the program and policy review functions that the GAO performs for Congress. During its history, it has evaluated such endeavors as the procurement and testing of military hardware, quality control for drinking water, the maintenance of major highways, the use of hormones to stimulate growth in beef cattle, and other organized activities far afield from human services.

Indeed, the techniques described in this text have utility to virtually all spheres of activity in which issues of the effectiveness of organized social action are raised. For example, the mass communication and advertising industries use fundamentally the same approaches in developing media programs and marketing products; commercial and industrial corporations evaluate the procedures they use in selecting, training, and promoting employees and organizing their workforces; political candidates develop their campaigns by evaluating the voter appeal of different strategies; consumer products are tested for performance, durability, and safety; and administrators in both the public and private sectors often assess the clerical, fiscal, and personnel practices of their organizations.

The distinctions among these various applications of evaluation lie primarily in the nature and goals of the endeavors being evaluated. Our emphasis in this text is on the evaluation of programs designed to benefit the human condition rather than with such purposes as increasing profits or amassing influence and power. This choice of focus stems not from a sense of righteousness about the proper application of social research methods but from a desire to concentrate on a particularly significant and active area of evaluation combined with a practical need to limit the scope of the book.

※ EXHIBIT 1-A   Veteran Policymaker Wants to See the Evaluation Results

But all the while we were taking on this large—and, as we can now say, hugely successful—effort [deficit reduction], we were constantly besieged by administration officials wanting us to *add* money for this social program or that social program. . . . *My* favorite in this miscellany was something called "family preservation," yet another categorical aid program (there were a dozen in place already) which amounted to a dollop of social services and a press release for some subcommittee chairman. The program was to cost $930 million over five years, starting at $60 million in fiscal year 1994. For three decades I had been watching families come apart in our society; now I was being told by seemingly everyone on the new team that one more program would do the trick. . . . At the risk of indiscretion, let me include in the record at this point a letter I wrote on July 28, 1993, to Dr. Laura D'Andrea Tyson, then the distinguished chairman of the Council of Economic Advisors, regarding the Family Preservation program:

Dear Dr. Tyson:

You will recall that last Thursday when you so kindly joined us at a meeting of the Democratic Policy Committee you and I discussed the President's family preservation proposal. You indicated how much he supports the measure. I assured you I, too, support it, but went on to ask what evidence was there that it would have any effect. You assured me there were such data. Just for fun, I asked for two citations.

The next day we received a fax from Sharon Glied of your staff with a number of citations and a paper, "Evaluating the Results," that appears to have been written by Frank Farrow of the Center for the Study of Social Policy here in Washington and Harold Richman at the Chapin Hall Center at the University of Chicago. The paper is quite direct: "Solid proof that family preservation services can affect a state's overall placement rates is still lacking."

Just yesterday, the same Chapin Hall Center released an "Evaluation of the Illinois Family First Placement Prevention Program: Final Report." This was a large scale study of the Illinois Family First initiative authorized by the Illinois Family Preservation Act of 1987. It was "designed to test effects if this program on out-of-home placement and other outcomes, such as subsequent child maltreatment." Data on case and service characteristics were provided by Family First caseworkers on approximately 4,500 cases: approximately 1,600 families participated in the randomized experiment. The findings are clear enough.

Overall, the Family First placement prevention program results in a slight increase in placement rates (when data from all experimental sites are combined). This effect disappears

---

The importance of evaluating social programs—both those currently in effect and those in various stages of design and pilot testing—should not be underestimated. The continuing challenge of devising ways to remedy the deficiencies in the quality of human life, both in industrialized countries and in less developed nations, needs no elaboration here. But along with the need for purposeful, practical, and well-organized efforts to implement new initia-

🎴 EXHIBIT 1-A   Continued

once case and site variations are taken into account. In other words, there are either negative effects or not effects.

This is nothing new. Here is Peter Rossi's conclusion in his 1992 paper, "Assessing Family Preservation Programs." Evaluations conducted to date "do not form a sufficient basis upon which to firmly decide whether family preservation programs are either effective or not."

May I say to you that there is nothing in the least surprising in either of these findings? From the mid-60s on this has been the repeated, I almost want to say consistent, pattern of evaluation studies. Either few effects or *negative* effects. Thus the negative income tax experiments of the 1970s appeared to produce an *increase* in family breakup.

This pattern of "counterintuitive" findings first appeared in the '60s. Greeley and Rossi, some of my work, and Coleman's. To this day I cannot decide whether we are dealing here with an artifact of methodology or a much larger and more intractable fact of social programs. In any event, by 1978 we had Rossi's Iron Law. To wit: "If there is any empirical law that is emerging from the past decade of widespread evaluation activity, it is that the expected value for any measured effect of a social program is zero."

I write you at such length for what I believe to be an important purpose. In the last six months I have been repeatedly impressed by the number of members of the Clinton administration who have assured me with great vigor that something or other is known in an area of social policy which, to the best of my understanding, is not known at all. This seems to me perilous. It is quite possible to live with uncertainty, with the possibility, even the likelihood that one is wrong. But beware of certainty where none exists. Ideological certainty easily degenerates into an insistence upon ignorance.

The great strength of political conservatives at this time (and for a generation) is that they are open to the thought that matters are complex. Liberals got into a reflexive pattern of denying this. I had hoped twelve years in the wilderness might have changed this; it may be it has only reinforced it. If this is so, current revival of liberalism will be brief and inconsequential.

Respectfully,

Senator Daniel Patrick Moynihan

SOURCE: Adapted, with permission, from D. P. Moynihan, *Miles to Go: A Personal History of Social Policy* (Cambridge, MA: Harvard University Press, 1996), pp. 47-49.

tives and improve existing ones comes the need for evaluation to determine if those efforts are worthwhile. Limited resources for social programs in every country, including the United States, make it critical that such investments yield demonstrable and proportionate social benefits. Moreover, experiences of the past several decades have highlighted the barriers to successful implementation of social programs and, correspondingly, the importance of assessing the practicality of program design and the effectiveness of program operations.

To "put some meat on the bones" and make the notion of program evaluation more concrete, we offer below examples of social programs that have been evaluated under the sponsorship of local, state, and federal governmental agencies, international organizations, private foundations and philanthropies, and both nonprofit and for-profit associations and corporations.

• With support from the U.S. Department of Justice, the cities of Houston and Newark instituted community policing on a trial basis. In Houston the police set up neighborhood substations, conducted door-to-door surveys of citizen problems, started newsletters, and held community meetings. In Newark the police established local walking police beats, dispersed groups of loiterers, and conducted random checks of motor vehicles. In both cities the trial neighborhoods showed increases in citizen confidence in the police and slight reductions in crimes when compared with similar areas without community policing.

• In several major cities in the United States, a large private foundation provided the initial operating costs to establish community health centers in low-income areas. The centers were intended as an alternative way for residents to obtain ambulatory patient care otherwise available to them only from hospital outpatient clinics and emergency rooms at great public cost. It was further hoped that by improving access to such care, the clinics might increase timely treatment and thus reduce the need for lengthy and expensive hospital care. Evaluations indicated that some of these centers were cost-effective in comparison with hospital clinics.

• A small number of philanthropic advocates of school vouchers have initiated a privately funded program in New York City for poor families with children in the first three grades of more disadvantaged public schools. In spring 1997, scholarships of $1,400 for a period of three years were offered to eligible families to go toward tuition costs in the private schools of their choice. Some 14,000 scholarship applications were received, and 1,500 successful candidates were chosen by random selection. Taking advantage of this mode of selection, Mathematica Policy Research is regarding the program as a randomized experiment and intends to compare educational outcomes among those selected and attending private schools with outcomes among those who were not selected. The evaluation will be conducted over a three-year period.

• A community mental health center in a medium-sized New England city developed an extensive program using local community members to counsel teenagers and adults about their emotional, sexual, and educational problems. Compared with persons treated by psychiatrists and social workers, the clients of the indigenous counselors did as well in terms of need for hospitalization, maintenance of treatment, and self-reports of satisfaction with the center.

• In the past decade, the federal government has allowed states to modify their welfare programs provided that the changes were evaluated for their effects on clients and costs. Some states instituted strong work and job training requirements, others put time limits on benefits, and a few prohibited increases in benefits for children born while on the welfare rolls. Evaluation research showed that such policies were capable of reducing welfare rolls and increasing employment. Many of the program features studied were incorporated in the federal welfare reforms passed in 1996 (Personal Responsibility and Work Opportunity Reconciliation Act).

• Fully two-thirds of the world's rural children suffer mild to severe malnutrition, with serious consequences for their health, physical growth, and mental development. A major demonstration of the potential for improving children's health status and mental development by providing dietary supplements was undertaken in Central America. Pregnant women, lactating mothers, and children from birth through age 12 were provided with a daily high-protein, high-calorie food supplement. Results showed major gains in physical growth and modest increases in cognitive functioning.

• Over the past two decades, the number of reported cases of child abuse and neglect has more than doubled in the United States. As a consequence more than half a million children are in foster or group care. Concerned that removal from their families might be harmful, many child welfare agencies have provided short-term intensive services to families with abused or neglected children with the goal of preventing removal of the children from their families while keeping them safe from further abuse or neglect. Several evaluation studies have been undertaken in which children at risk of being removed from their homes were randomly assigned to "family preservation" programs or to the usual service. Those assigned to family preservation programs were no less likely to end up being removed from their homes, showing that these programs were ineffective.

• In an effort to increase worker satisfaction and product quality, a large manufacturing company reorganized its employees into independent work teams. Within the teams, workers designated and assigned tasks, recommended productivity quotas to management, and voted on the distribution of bonuses for productivity and quality improvements. Information from an assessment of the program revealed that it reduced days absent from the job, turnover rates, and similar measures of employee inefficiency.

These short examples illustrate the diversity of social interventions that have been systematically evaluated. However, all of them involve one particular evaluation activity: the assessment of program outcomes. As we will discuss later, evaluation may also focus on the need for a program, its design, operation and service delivery, or efficiency. Before moving ahead to more fully describe the nature and range of program evaluation, we provide a brief history of the development of the field to convey a sense of the traditions in which current work is rooted.

A BRIEF HISTORY OF EVALUATION RESEARCH

As we have noted, evaluation research is one facet of the general use of social research for understanding and addressing social problems. However, despite historical roots that extend to the 17th century, systematic evaluation research is a relatively modern development. The application of social research methods to program evaluation coincides with the growth and refinement of the methods themselves as well as with ideological, political, and demographic changes that have occurred during this century. Of key importance were the emergence and increased standing of the social sciences in

---

※ EXHIBIT 1-B   An Early (1930s) Argument for Studying Social Program

---

No one can deny the progress in the social sciences. But with all the exacting methods developed, the economists, sociologists, and political scientists have suffered from a lack of large-scale experimental set-ups to match the everyday resources of the scientists in the laboratory.

The current enthusiasm over planning schemes now being devised by the alphabetical corporations of the federal government furnishes some hope that this deficiency may be partially remedied. The blueprints of these agencies and the carrying out of their plans may well be looked upon as the creation of experimental laboratories for the social scientists, and for the social workers, educators, and administrators who may profit from their research.

These laboratories, set up by the planning agencies of the New Deal, permit a more effective use of the experimental method in the research projects of the social scientists. This research, in turn, would not only be an addition to science but would also be a form of social auditing for the planning authorities in noting and accounting for the changes wrought by the programs.

SOURCE: Adapted, with permission, from A. S. Stephan, "Prospects and Possibilities: The New Deal and the New Social Research," *Social Forces*, May 1935, 13:515, 518.

---

universities and increased support for social research. Social science departments in universities became centers of early work in program evaluation and have continued to occupy an influential place in the field.

Evaluation Research as a Social Science Activity

Commitment to the systematic evaluation of social programs first became commonplace in education and public health. Prior to World War I, the most significant efforts were directed at assessing literacy and occupational training programs and public health initiatives to reduce mortality and morbidity from infectious diseases. By the 1930s, social scientists in various disciplines were advocating the use of rigorous research methods to assess social programs, and systematic evaluations became more frequent (Freeman, 1977). In sociology, for instance, Dodd's study of attempts to intro-

duce water boiling as a public health practice in villages in the Middle East is a landmark in the pre–World War II literature. And it was an Arkansas sociology professor who first pleaded for studies of President Roosevelt's New Deal programs (see Exhibit 1-B). It was also during this period that social experimentation emerged in psychology. Lewin's pioneering "action research" studies and Lippitt and White's work on democratic and authoritarian leadership, for example, were widely influential evaluative studies. The famous Western Electric experiments on worker productivity that contributed the term *Hawthorne effect* to the social science lexicon date from this time as well. (See Bernstein and Freeman, 1975, for a more extended discussion and Bulmer, 1982, Cronbach et al., 1980, and Madaus and Stufflebeam, 1989, for somewhat different historical perspectives.)

From such beginnings, applied social research grew at an accelerating pace, with a particular boost provided by its contributions during World War II. Stouffer and his associates worked with the U.S. Army to develop procedures for monitoring soldier morale and evaluate personnel policies and propaganda techniques, whereas the Office of War Information used sample surveys to monitor civilian morale (Stouffer et al., 1949). A host of smaller studies assessed the efficacy of price controls and media campaigns to modify American eating habits. Similar social science efforts were mounted in Britain and elsewhere.

The Boom Period in Evaluation Research

Following World War II, numerous major programs were launched to meet needs for urban development and housing, technological and cultural education, occupational training, and preventive health activities. It was also during this time that major commitments were made to international programs for family planning, health and nutrition, and rural development. Expenditures were very large and consequently were accompanied by demands for "knowledge of results."

By the end of the 1950s, program evaluation research was commonplace. Social scientists were engaged in assessments of delinquency prevention programs, psychotherapeutic and psychopharmacological treatments, public housing programs, educational activities, community organization initiatives, and numerous other such areas. Studies were undertaken not only in the United States, Europe, and other industrialized countries but also in less developed nations. Increasingly, programs for family planning in Asia, nutrition and health care in Latin America, and agricultural and community development in Africa included evaluation components (Freeman,

Rossi, and Wright, 1980; Levine et al., 1981). Expanding knowledge of the methods of social research, including sample surveys and advanced statistical procedures, and increased funding and administrative know-how, made possible even large-scale, multisite evaluation studies.

During the 1960s, the numbers of papers and books about evaluation research grew dramatically. Hayes's (1959) monograph on evaluation research in less developed countries, Suchman's (1967) review of evaluation research methods, and Campbell's (1969) call for social experimentation are a few illustrations. In the United States, a key impetus for the spurt of interest in evaluation research was the federal war on poverty, initiated under Lyndon Johnson's presidency. By the late 1960s, evaluation research had become, in the words of Wall Street, a growth industry.

In the early 1970s, evaluation research emerged as a distinct specialty field in the social sciences. A variety of books appeared, including the first texts (Weiss, 1972), critiques of the methodological quality of evaluation studies (Bernstein and Freeman, 1975), and discussions of the organizational and structural constraints on evaluation research (Riecken and Boruch, 1974). The journal *Evaluation Review* was established in 1976 and continues to be widely read by evaluators. Other journals followed in rapid succession, and today there are about a dozen devoted primarily to evaluation. During this period, special sessions on evaluation studies at the meetings of academic and practitioner groups became commonplace, and professional associations specifically for evaluation researchers were founded (see Exhibit 1-C for a listing of the major journals and professional organizations). By 1980, Cronbach and his associates were able to state, "Evaluation has become the liveliest frontier of American

---

EXHIBIT 1-C   Major Evaluation Journals and Professional Organizations

Journals devoted primarily to program and policy evaluation:

- *Evaluation Review: A Journal of Applied Social Research* (Sage Publications)
- *Evaluation Practice,* renamed (1998) *American Journal of Evaluation* (JAI Press)
- *New Directions for Evaluation* (Jossey-Bass)
- *Evaluation: The International Journal of Theory, Research, and Practice* (Sage Publications Ltd.)
- *Evaluation and Program Planning* (Pergamon)
- *Journal of Policy Analysis and Management* (John Wiley)
- *Canadian Journal of Program Evaluation* (University of Calgary Press)
- *Evaluation Journal of Australasia* (Australasian Evaluation Society)
- *Evaluation & the Health Professions* (Sage Publications)
- *Educational Evaluation and Policy Analysis* (American Educational Research Association)
- *Assessment and Evaluation in Higher Education* (Carfax Publishing Ltd.)

Professional organizations for program and policy evaluators:

- American Evaluation Association (Web page: http://www.eval.org/)
- Association for Public Policy Analysis and Management
      (Web page: http://qsilver.queensu.ca/appam/)
- Canadian Evaluation Association
      (Web page: http://www.unites.uqam.ca/ces/ces-sce.html)
- Australasian Evaluation Society
      (Web page: http://www.parklane.com.au/aes/)
- European Evaluation Society
      (Web page: http://www.europeanevaluation.org)
- UK Evaluation Society
      (Web page: http://www.evaluation.org.uk)
- German Evaluation Society
      (Web page: http://www.fal.de/tissen/geproval.htm)
- Italian Evaluation Society
      (Web page: http://www.valutazione.it/)

---

social science" (pp. 12-13). Although the period of rapid growth is over, evaluation continues to be an important specialty area within the social sciences and is widely supported by public and private agencies.

The development of the field of evaluation in the postwar years was made possible to a large extent by advances in research methods and statistics applicable to the study of social problems, social processes, and interpersonal relations. Conversely, the need for sophisticated methods for evaluating social programs stimulated methodological innovation. In particular, two essential inputs contributed to the evolution of the field: improvements in systematic data collection brought about by the refinement of measurement and survey research procedures, and the development of electronic computers that made it possible to analyze large numbers of variables by means of multivariate statistics. The computer revolution was an especially important stimulus to the growth of evaluation research (Nagel, 1986) and has facilitated not only data analysis but data collection as well (Gray, 1988). The close relationship between technological changes and technical developments in applied social research continues today.

But history can obscure as well as illuminate. Although there is continuity in the development of the evaluation field, a qualitative change occurred as it matured. In its early years, evaluation was an endeavor shaped mainly by the interests of social researchers. In later stages, however, the consumers of evaluation research have had a significant influence on the field. Evaluation is now sustained primarily by policymakers, program planners, and administrators who use the findings and believe in the worth of the evaluation enterprise. It is also supported by the interests of the general public and the clients of the programs evaluated. Evaluations may not make front-page headlines, but their findings are often matters of intense concern to informed citizens and those whose lives are affected, directly or indirectly, by the programs at issue. Over the years, these various consumers and sponsors of evaluation have played an increasingly large role in defining the nature of the field.

Incorporation of the consumer perspective into evaluation research has moved the field beyond the study of social programs by applied social researchers. It has also become a political and managerial activity, an input into the complex mosaic from which emerge policy decisions and resources for the planning, design, implementation, and continuance of programs

to better the human condition. In this regard, evaluation research must be seen as an integral part of the social policy and public administration movements.

Social Policy and Public Administration Movements

A full treatment of the development of the overlapping social policy and public administration movements would require tracing the remarkable growth of population and industrialization in the United States during the first part of this century. During this period, changing social values resulted in a shift of responsibility for community welfare from family members, church charities, and private philanthropy to government agencies. At least a few highlights are important here.

The Emergence of Government Programs

Social programs and the evaluation activities that accompanied them emerged from the relatively recent transfer of responsibility for the nation's social and environmental conditions, and the quality of life of its citizens, to governmental bodies. As Bremner (1956) has described, before World War I, except for war veterans, the provision of human services was seen primarily as the obligation of individuals and voluntary associations. Poor people, physically and mentally disabled persons, and troubled families were the clients of local charities staffed mainly by volunteers drawn from the ranks of the more fortunate. Our image of these volunteers as wealthy matrons toting baskets of food and hand-me-down clothing to give to the poor and unfortunate is only somewhat exaggerated. Along with civic associations and locally supported charity hospitals, county and state asylums, locally supported public schools, state normal schools, and sectarian old-age homes, volunteers were the bulwark of our human service "system."

Indeed, government was comparatively small before the 1930s, particularly the federal government. There were few national health, education, and welfare programs and no need for an army of federal employees. The idea of annual federal expenditures of billions of dollars for health research, for instance, would have completely bewildered the government official of the 1920s. The notion of more billions going to purchase medical care for the aged or for poor persons would have been even more mind-boggling. Federal fiscal support of public education was infinitesimal—more dollars for public education currently flow from Washington in six months than were spent in the entire first decade of this century. Moreover, the scope and use of social and economic information mirrored the sparseness of government program operations. Even in the late 1930s, federal expenditures for social science research and statistics were only $40-$50 million, as compared to 40 to 50 times that amount today (Lynn, 1980).

Finally, human services and government operated under different norms than today. Key government officials usually were selected without regard to objective competence criteria; indeed, there were few ways of objectively determining competence. The professional civil service was a fraction of the size it is today, most jobs did not require technical know-how, and formal training programs were not widely available. Moreover, because its activities and influence were comparatively small, there was relatively little interest in what went on in government, at least in terms of human service programs.

All this began to change in the 1930s. Human services grew at a rapid pace with the advent of the Great Depression, and, of course, so did government in general, especially during the period surrounding World War II. In part because of the unwieldiness that accompanied this accelerated growth, there was strong pressure to apply the concepts and techniques of so-called scientific management, which were well regarded in industry, to government programs and activities. These ideas first took hold in the Department of Defense and then diffused to other government organizations, including human service agencies. Concepts and procedures for planning, budgeting, quality control, and accountability, as well as later, more sophisticated notions of cost-benefit analysis and system modeling, became the order of the day in the human resource area.

The Development of Policy and Public Administration Specialists

During this same period, persons with social science training began to apply themselves to understanding the political, organizational, and administrative decision making that took place in executive departments and other governmental agencies. Also, economists were perfecting models for planning and refining theories of macroeconomic social processes (Stokey and Zeckhauser, 1978). In part, the interests of social scientists in government at this time were purely academic. They wanted to know how government worked. However, persons in leadership positions in governmental agencies, groping for ways to deal with their large staffs and full coffers of funds, recognized a critical need for orderly, explicit ways to handle their policy, administrative, program, and planning responsibilities. They became convinced that concepts, techniques, and principles from economics, political science, and sociology could be useful. The study of the public sector thus grew into the largely applied research specialty that is now most commonly called "policy science" or "policy analysis."

Moreover, as the federal government became increasingly complex and technical, its programs could no longer be adequately managed by persons hired as intelligent generalists or because of their connections with political patrons, relatives, or friends. Most midlevel management jobs and many senior executive positions required specific substantive and technical skills, and those who filled them needed either training or extensive experience to do their work competently (see Exhibit 1-D). The state and local counterparts of federal agencies expanded at a similar rate, stimulated in part by federal initiatives and funding, and they too required skilled staffs. In response, university social science departments mobilized to provide trained persons for government positions as well as training researchers. Graduate schools of management, public health, and social work began programs to meet the need for executives and technicians, and special schools, generally with "public administration" in their titles, were established or expanded.

In short, a new army of professionals emerged. Furthermore, the institutionalization of policy analysis and public administration programs in universities has maintained the momentum of the intertwined policy science and public administration movements. Concepts and methods from the social sciences have become the core of the educational programs from which are drawn many of our public officials and program managers as well as the staffs of foundations, public and private human service agencies, and international or-

ganizations. In particular, these training programs stress evaluation research, both as an assessment procedure and as a body of knowledge about the effectiveness of programs and practice in the sundry policy areas.

The importance of evaluation is now acknowledged by those in political as well as executive roles. For example, the GAO, Congress's "watchdog," made a major commitment to evaluation in 1980 in response to congressional interest in the assessment of government initiatives. In addition, many federal agencies have their own evaluation units, as do a large number of their state counterparts. Even more commonplace at federal, state, and local levels are procedures for commissioning program evaluation, as the need arises, on a contract basis from university researchers or research firms and consultants.

In short, although evaluation research continues to have an academic side oriented toward training, methodology, theory, and relatively detached study of the nature and effects of social programs, it is a field that now extends well beyond university social science departments. Evaluation is generally practiced in a context of policy making, program management, and client or consumer advocacy. Thus, not only is its history intertwined with the social policy and public administration movements, but its practice typically occurs in the same political and organizational arenas as policy analysis and public administration.

The Great Society and Its Aftermath: Political Ideology and the Evaluation Enterprise

Evaluation activities increased rapidly during the Kennedy and Johnson eras when social

✿ **EXHIBIT 1-D**   The Rise of Policy Analysis

The steady growth in the number, variety, complexity, and social importance of policy issues confronting government is making increasing intellectual demands on public officials and their staffs. What should be done about nuclear safety, teenage pregnancies, urban decline, rising hospital costs, unemployment among black youth, violence toward spouses and children, and the disposal of toxic wastes? Many of these subjects were not on the public agenda 20 years ago. They are priority issues now, and new ones of a similar character emerge virtually every year. For most elected and appointed officials and their staffs, such complicated and controversial questions are outside the scope of their judgment and previous experience. Yet the questions cannot be sidestepped; government executives are expected to deal with them responsibly and effectively.

To aid them in thinking about and deciding on such matters, public officials have been depending to an increasing extent on knowledge derived from research, policy analysis, program evaluations, and statistics to inform or buttress their views. More often than in the past, elected and appointed officials in the various branches and levels of government, from federal judges to town selectmen, are citing studies, official data, and expert opinion in at least partial justification for their actions. Their staffs, which have been increasing in size and responsibility in recent decades, include growing numbers of people trained in or familiar with analytic techniques to gather and evaluate information. Increasing

amounts of research, analysis, and data gathering are being done.

Because the power to influence policy is widely shared in our system of government, public officials seeking to influence policy—to play the policy game well—must be persuasive. Because of the changing character of policy issues, it is probably harder to be persuasive than it used to be. Seniority, affability, and clever "wheeling and dealing" may be relatively less influential than being generally knowledgeable and tough-minded, having the ability to offer ideas and solutions that can attract a wide following, or having a reputation as a well-informed critic. Increasingly, officials from the president on down lose influence in policy debates when they cannot get their numbers right or when their ideas and arguments are successfully challenged by opposing experts. Indeed, thorough and detailed command of an issue or problem is often mandatory. Legislatures are requiring executives to be experts in the programs and issues under their jurisdiction. Judges are requiring detailed proof that administrative decisions are not arbitrary and capricious. Budget officials demand positive program evaluations. The public demands accountability. Thus the dynamic processes whereby our political system confronts social problems are perceptibly, if not dramatically, raising the standards of substantive and managerial competence in the performance of public responsibilities.

SOURCE: Adapted, with permission, from Laurence E. Lynn, Jr., *Designing Public Policy* (Santa Monica, CA: Scott, Foresman, 1980).

⧉ EXHIBIT 1-E   The 1960s Growth in Policy Analysis and Evaluation Research

The year 1965 was an important one in the evolution of "policy analysis and evaluation research" as an independent branch of study. Two developments at the federal government level—the War on Poverty-Great Society initiative and the Executive Order establishing the Planning-Programming-Budgeting (PPB) system— were of signal importance in this regard. Both offered standing, legitimacy, and financial support to scholars who would turn their skills and interests toward examining the efficiency with which public measures allocate resources, their impacts on individual behavior, their effectiveness in attaining the objectives for which they were designed, and their effects on the well-being of rich versus poor, minority versus majority, and North versus South.

The War on Poverty-Great Society developments initiated in 1965 represented a set of social interventions on an unprecedented scale. All impacted by them wanted to know if they were working, and who was being affected by them and how. Those with the skills to answer these questions found both financial support and an interested audience for their efforts. And the social science community responded. The same year saw government-wide adoption of the formal evaluation and analysis methods that had earlier been applied in Robert McNamara's Defense Department in the Planning-Programming-Budgeting system. A presidential Executive Order gave employment and financial support to thousands who wished to apply their analytical skills to such efficiency, effectiveness, and equity questions.

SOURCE: Robert H. Haveman, "Policy Analysis and Evaluation Research After Twenty Years," *Policy Studies Journal,* 1987, 16:191-218.

programs undertaken under the rubrics of the War on Poverty and the Great Society provided extensive resources to deal with unemployment, crime, urban deterioration, access to medical care, and mental health treatment (see Exhibit 1-E). These programs were often hurriedly put into place, and at least a significant portion were poorly conceived, improperly implemented, and ineffectively administered. Findings of limited effectiveness and poor benefit-to-cost ratios for the large-scale federal initiatives of this era prompted widespread reappraisal of the magnitude of effects that can be expected from social programs. Social intervention all too often yields small gains, much to the chagrin of those who advocate them (Weick,

1984). But more realistic expectations for social programs only increase the importance of undertaking evaluation before putting programs into place on a permanent and widespread basis or making significant modifications to them.

Partly as a consequence of the apparent ineffectiveness of many initiatives, the decade of the 1970s was marked by increasing resistance to the continued expansion of government programs (Freeman and Solomon, 1979). The reaction was most clear in referenda such as California's Proposition 13, which limited real estate tax revenue, and in "sunset laws," which required the automatic shutdown of ineffective programs (Adams and Sherman, 1978). Of course, some of the attacks on big government were simply political campaign rhetoric. And although a number of states and major cities enacted sunset laws, in only a few instances have programs actually been shut down. More often, only superficial and symbolic assessments were undertaken or the programs were given extensions to allow them to develop documentation for their effectiveness.

Nevertheless, it is clear that the rise of fiscal conservatism in the 1970s resulted in a decline in governmental support for new social programs and, to some extent, private support as well. This, in turn, brought about a change in emphasis in the evaluation field. In particular, increased attention has been given to assessing the expenditures of social programs in comparison to their benefits and to demonstrating fiscal accountability and effective management. In the process, many fiscal and political conservatives, often skeptical about social science, have joined the advocates of social action programs in pressing for the information that evaluations provide.

In the 1980s, during both the Reagan and Bush administrations, domestic federal expenditures were curtailed in an attempt to control inflation and reduce the federal deficit. Many of the largest cutbacks were targeted on social programs. A similar posture was manifest in many states and cities; indeed, some of the local and state reactions to their deteriorating economic situations were particularly severe. These developments were partly a consequence of the distrust, hostility, and political actions of community members dismayed with the painful bite of income and property taxes. As we have indicated, however, they were also influenced by disenchantment with the modest effects and poor implementation of many of the programs most ardently championed by public officials, planners, and politicians in the past several decades.

As should be apparent, social programs and, consequently, the evaluation enterprise are shaped by the changing times. Political perspectives during the 1980s, not only in the United States but also in a number of Western European countries, have brought about increased concern with the balance of benefits and costs for social programs, even in social problem areas that receive generous funding. On the intellectual front, both conservative and liberal critique of the Great Society programs have had an impact on the evaluation field. Although these criticisms were sometimes based more on ideology than evidence, they nevertheless have drawn on evaluation results in condemning social programs. For instance, evaluation research has been used to argue that the major federal welfare program, Aid to Families With Dependent Children (AFDC), provides perverse incentives that increase the social problem it was intended to ameliorate (Murray, 1984). The evaluation field has thus been thrust into the middle of contentious debates about the very concept of social intervention and faced with new challenges to demonstrate that any major program initiative can be effective.

Meanwhile, new social problems are continually emerging on the political landscape, accompanied by demands that they receive programmatic attention and that the efforts made to ameliorate them be evaluated. A striking example is the issue of homelessness (Jencks, 1994; Rossi, 1989). At the time the first edition of this text was published (1979), there was little public notice of the homeless, little political activity to initiate and fund public programs to better their lot, and, consequently, little effort to estimate the number of such persons, their characteristics, or the reasons for their condition. Today, views on how to deal with the homeless range from an emphasis on institutionalization to efforts to increase tolerance for street people and make heavier commitments of resources for their medical care, shelter, food, and other necessities. Enumerations of the homeless, diagnoses of their conditions, and demonstration programs with accompanying evaluations are numerous and expanding, despite the budgetary shortfalls at all levels of government.

The Evaluation Field in the 1990s

Fiscal conservatism, the devolution of responsibility to the states, and skepticism about social programs dominate national policy making today. The Clinton Democratic presidency and the Republican majority Congress seem determined to cut federal spending and hand over major social programs to the administration of the states. For instance, welfare reform legislation, passed in 1996 (Personal Responsibility and Work Opportunity Reconciliation Act), that abolished the entitlement status of AFDC required the states to administer it under severe time eligibility restrictions and imposed an emphasis on moving beneficiaries into employment. Such changes have mixed implications for evaluation. On the one hand, these major revisions and reforms in social programs require evaluations if anything is to be learned about their fiscal and social impacts. On the other hand, much of the responsibility for conducting evaluation has devolved to the states along with the programs, and many states do not have the capabilities or the will to undertake the rigorous evaluation needed.

Fundamentally, however, whether there is a "liberal" or "conservative" outlook in government and among the public should not change the role of evaluation research in the social

program arena (Freeman, 1983). Rather, these different political conditions raise different sets of evaluation questions corresponding to the shifts in the concerns emphasized by the stakeholders. Regardless of political outlook, two matters are clear about the 1990s. First, restraints on resources will continue to require choosing the social problem areas on which to concentrate and the programs that should be given priority. Second, intensive scrutiny of existing programs will continue because of the pressure to curtail or dismantle those that do not demonstrate that their services are effective and efficient. Moreover, both dissatisfaction with existing programs and shifts in political currents will result in new and modified programs that come forward with promises of being more effective and less costly. All these circumstances will generate a need, and quite likely a demand, for evaluation research.

Major worldwide changes will also affect the evaluation field. The globalization of economic activities may force nations with generous social welfare programs to cut back their expenditures to remain competitive on world markets. Nations emerging from totalitarian socialist regimes, on the other hand, may have to launch new social initiatives. Indeed, in many developing nations throughout the world there is intense pressure to develop *and* evaluate social programs virtually overnight. At the same time, evaluation itself is becoming increasingly international (see Exhibit 1-F).

Perhaps more subtle, but at least as great a source of influence on programs and their evaluations, are shifts in the values and self-interests of community members and organizations. Surveys in the United States and a number of Western European countries, for instance, document a reduced emphasis among workers on earnings and an increased value placed on nonwork activities. As another illus-

---

✄ EXHIBIT 1-F   Evaluation Is Becoming Internationalized

Evaluation is becoming increasingly international, but in ways that go beyond previous conceptions of what *international* means. *International* is no longer used only to describe the efforts of particular evaluators in individual countries around the world—although it certainly is still used in this way. . . . Today, evaluation is also becoming international in the sense of being at the same time more indigenous, more global, and more transnational. By *indigenous,* we mean that evaluators in different countries around the world are developing their own infrastructures to support their endeavors as well as their own preferred theoretical and methodological approaches. By *global,* we mean that developments in one part of the globe frequently affect people, institutions, and programs all around the world. . . . By *transnational,* we mean that the problems and programs that we are called upon to evaluate today often extend beyond the boundaries of any one nation, any one continent, or even one hemisphere. . . . These include problems of pollution, of the economics of developing countries, and of the role of women in society. We cannot say exactly what the best responses to these internationalizing developments will be for evaluators, but we do know that recognizing the developments is the first step toward accommodating to them.

SOURCE: Quoted, with permission, from Eleanor Chelimsky and William R. Shadish, *Evaluation for the 21st Century: A Handbook* (Thousand Oaks, CA: Sage, 1997), pp. xi-xii.

---

tration, until this decade most large corporations opposed publicly funded national health insurance or governmental health subsidy programs for employed persons. But the extremely high cost of medical care and its impact on worker incomes has led to a decided change in outlook. Trends in values and self-interests quite likely will have much to do with the nature and scope of the social programs that are initiated and those that are continued, with corresponding implications for their assessment.

AN OVERVIEW OF PROGRAM EVALUATION

With the benefit of some historical context, we can attempt a more complete definition of program evaluation, as we wish to use the term,

than the preliminary version offered earlier: *Program evaluation is the use of social research procedures to systematically investigate the effectiveness of social intervention programs that is adapted to their political and organizational environments and designed to inform social action in ways that improve social conditions.* Elaborating on the various distinct components of this definition, in turn, will provide an introductory overview of the nature of program evaluation as presented in this book.

Application of Social Research Procedures

The concept of *evaluation* entails, on the one hand, a description of the performance of the entity being evaluated and, on the other, some standards or criteria by which that per-

> ### ▓ EXHIBIT 1-G   The Two Arms of Evaluation
>
> Evaluation is the process of determining the merit, worth, and value of things, and evaluations are the products of that process. . . . Evaluation is not the mere accumulation and summarizing of data that are clearly relevant for decision making, although there are still evaluation theorists who take that to be its definition. . . . In all contexts, gathering and analyzing the data that are needed for decision making—difficult though that often is—comprises only one of the two key components in evaluation; absent the other component, and absent a procedure for combining them, we simply lack anything that qualifies as an evaluation. *Consumer Reports* does not just test products and report the test scores; it (i) *rates or ranks* by (ii) *merit or cost-effectiveness.* To get to that kind of conclusion requires an input of something besides data, in the usual sense of that term. The second element is required to get to conclusions about merit or net benefits, and it consists of evaluative premises or standards. . . . A more straightforward approach is just to say that evaluation has two arms, only one of which is engaged in data-gathering. The other arm collects, clarifies, and verifies relevant values and standards.
>
> SOURCE: Quoted, with permission, from Michael Scriven, *Evaluation Thesaurus,* 4th ed. (Newbury Park, CA: Sage, 1991), pp. 1, 4-5.

formance is judged (see Exhibit 1-G). It follows that a central task of the program evaluator is to construct a valid description of those areas of program performance that are at issue in a form that permits incisive comparison with the applicable criteria. This task presents several challenges, some involving identification of the areas of performance at issue and the applicable criteria that we will address later. Here we focus on the problem of constructing a valid description of performance that is sufficiently distinct and precise to permit meaningful assessment.

A valid description of program performance is one that accurately represents what the program actually accomplishes. As should be obvious, it is a serious defect for an evaluation to fail to describe program performance with a reasonable degree of validity. Doing so is a misrepresentation of the facts that may distort a program's accomplishments, deny it credit for its successes, or overlook shortcomings for which it should be accountable. A distinct and precise description of program performance is one that is sufficiently definite and discriminating for meaningful variations in level of performance to be detected. An evaluation that produces an unduly vague or equivocal description of program performance may also fall short by making it impossible to determine with confidence whether program performance actually meets some appropriate standard.

Social research procedures and the accompanying standards of methodological quality have been developed and refined over the years explicitly for the purpose of constructing sound factual descriptions of social phenomena. In particular, contemporary social science techniques of systematic observation, measurement, sampling, research design, and data analysis represent rather highly evolved procedures for producing valid, reliable, and precise characterizations of social behavior. Because social programs are instances of organized social behavior, we take it as virtually self-evident that social research procedures offer the best approach to the task of describing program performance in ways that will be as credible and defensible as possible. Moreover, credibility and defensibility are important characteristics of the evidence evaluators put forward, both because of the practical importance of evaluation in most contexts of application and because of the disputatious reception often given to evaluation results when they do not conform to the expectations of significant stakeholders.

Regardless of the type of social intervention under study, therefore, we advocate evaluations that employ social research procedures for gathering evidence about program performance and analyzing and interpreting that evidence. This commitment to the rules of social research is at the core of our perspective on evaluation and is what we mean by the subtitle of this book, *A Systematic Approach*. This is not to say, however, that we believe evaluation studies must follow some particular social research style or combination of styles, whether quantitative or qualitative, experimental or ethnographic, "positivistic" or "naturalistic." Indeed, one of the principal characteristics of program evaluation is that its methods cover the gamut of prevailing social research paradigms. Nor does this commitment to the methods of social science mean that we think current methods are a finished piece of work beyond improvement. Evaluators must often innovate and improvise as they attempt to find ways to gather credible, defensible evidence about social programs. In fact, evaluators have been, and will likely continue to be, especially productive contributors to furthering methodological development in applied social research.

Finally, our view does not imply that methodological quality is necessarily the most important aspect of an evaluation nor that only the highest technical standards, without compromise, are appropriate for evaluation. As Carol Weiss (1972) once observed, social programs are inherently inhospitable environments for research purposes. The nature of program circumstances, and of the particular issues the evaluator is called on to address, frequently necessitates compromises and adaptations of textbook methodological standards. The challenges to the evaluator, as we see them, are to match the research procedures to the evaluation questions and circumstances as well as possible and, whatever procedures are used, to apply them at the highest possible standard feasible in those circumstances.

The Effectiveness of Social Intervention Programs

Any program evaluation worthy of the name must, of course, evaluate; that is, some assessment must be made of one or more aspects of the program. As indicated above, evaluating something requires that pertinent dimensions of its performance or characteristics be described and then judged against appropriate standards or criteria. Program evaluation generally involves assessment of one or more of five program domains: (a) the need for the program, (b) the design of the program, (c) the program implementation and service delivery, (d) the program impact or outcomes, and (e) program efficiency (cost-effectiveness). In some circumstances, an evaluation of a social program may encompass all these program domains;

evaluations that do so are termed *comprehensive evaluations.*

Evaluation methods can be applied to many kinds of programs, projects, and endeavors, but the domain of program evaluation orients chiefly to social programs and the focus of this book is primarily on that type of program. What we mean by a social program in this context is a planned, organized, and usually ongoing set of activities carried out for the purpose of improving some social condition. A social program thus is directed at ameliorating a social problem or responding to a social need, usually through the provision of some form of human services. As we are using the term, therefore, social programs are defined as entities whose principal reason for existing is to "do good," that is, to produce social benefits and improve social conditions. It follows that they are appropriately held accountable within an evaluative framework on the basis of their contribution to the social good. Most social programs will thus hold themselves accountable for producing positive social effects, at least to the extent of recognizing the legitimacy of that expectation. In addition, of course, many social programs will be held accountable for such results by those parties who invest in them, sponsor them, administer them, or are legally responsible for them, for instance, taxpayers, funders, boards of directors, agency heads, and legislators.

The importance of this issue is that it has critical implications for the question of what criteria or standards should be used to assess programs when conducting a program evaluation. Different values frameworks are appropriate for different types of programs. Many of the evaluation methods described in this book can be applied to programs in the business sector, for instance, but the applicable criteria for assessing performance will generally have more to do with "the bottom line" of profits and productivity than with amelioration of social problems. Similarly, evaluation methods could be applied to assess social clubs, professional organizations, and other such programs whose purposes are to provide certain benefits to their members. The criteria for assessing these programs would largely and appropriately relate only to the interests of the members. The goals of other types of programs are generally quite different from those of social programs and the criteria appropriate for assessing them will also be different.

Our focus on the large and important topic of evaluating social programs, therefore, carries with it a set of assumptions about the general value framework within which appropriate criteria and standards for assessing the various aspects of those programs will be defined. In particular, when we describe evaluation as investigating the *effectiveness* of social programs we are assuming that what effectiveness means for such programs relates ultimately to their contribution to improving social conditions. Of course, there may be ambiguity and dispute about just what contributions a program should be making and the implications for everyday program operations, which an evaluator will have to resolve before appropriate criteria can be defined and an evaluation can be conducted. These matters will be discussed in greater detail in other chapters of this book. Most of our discussion, advice, and illustrations, however, assumes that it is social programs that are being evaluated and that the foundation for judgments about how effective they are is some articulation of the social good they are expected to produce.

Adapting Evaluation to the Political and Organizational Context of the Program

Program evaluation is not a cut-and-dried activity like putting up a prefabricated house or checking a document with a word processor's spelling program. Rather, evaluation is a practice in which the initial evaluation plan must be tailor-made to the particular program circumstances and then typically requires revision and modification during its implementation. The specific form and scope of an evaluation depend primarily on its purposes and audience, the nature of the program being evaluated, and the political and administrative context within which the evaluation is conducted.

The evaluation plan is generally organized around the questions posed about the program by those who request and commission the evaluation (the *evaluation sponsor*) and other pertinent stakeholders. These questions may be stipulated in very specific, fixed terms that allow little flexibility, as in a detailed contract for evaluation services, but typically the evaluator must negotiate with the evaluation sponsors and stakeholders to develop and refine the questions. Although these parties presumably know their own interests and purposes, they will not necessarily formulate their concerns in ways that the evaluator can use to structure an evaluation plan. For instance, the initial questions may be vague, overly general, or phrased in program jargon that must be translated for more general consumption. Occasionally, the evaluation questions put forward are essentially pro forma (e.g., is the program effective?) and have not emerged from careful reflection regarding the relevant issues. In such cases, the evaluator must probe thoroughly to determine what this means to the evaluation sponsor and program stakeholders and why they are concerned.

As important to tailor-making an evaluation plan as the questions to be answered are the reasons why those questions are being asked and the use that will be made of the answers. Social programs consist of, and exist within, a swirl of individual, organizational, and political decisions dealing with a range of issues from the trivia of ordering paper clips to threat of termination. In such a context, an evaluation must deal with the issues that matter, provide information that addresses those issues, develop that information in a way that is timely and meaningful for the decisionmakers, and communicate it in a form that is usable for their purposes. An evaluation might be designed quite differently if it is to provide information about the quality of service as feedback to the program director for purposes of incremental program improvement than if it is to provide such information to an external funder who will use it to decide whether to renew the program's funding. In all cases, however, it must be sensitive to the political context within which it is planned and conducted (see Exhibit 1-H).

As a practical matter, of course, an evaluation must also be tailored to the organizational makeup of the program. The availability of administrative cooperation and support; the ways in which program files and data are kept and access permitted to them; the character of the services provided; the nature, frequency, duration, and location of the contact between program and client; and numerous other such matters must be taken into consideration in the evaluation design. In addition, once an evaluation is launched, it is common for changes and "in-flight" corrections to be required. Modifications, perhaps even compromises, may be necessary in the types, quantity, or quality of the data collected as a result of unanticipated practical or political obstacles.

EXHIBIT 1-H Where Politics and Evaluation Meet

Evaluation is a rational enterprise that takes place in a political context. Political considerations intrude in three major ways, and the evaluator who fails to recognize their presence is in for a series of shocks and frustrations:

First, the policies and programs with which evaluation deals are the creatures of political decisions. They were proposed, defined, debated, enacted, and funded through political processes, and in implementation they remain subject to pressures—both supportive and hostile—that arise out of the play of politics.

Second, because evaluation is undertaken in order to feed into decision making, its reports enter the political arena. There evaluative evidence of program outcomes has to compete for attention with other factors that carry weight in the political process.

Third, and perhaps least recognized, evaluation itself has a political stance. By its very nature, it makes implicit political statements about such issues as the problematic nature of some programs and the unchallengeability of others, the legitimacy of program goals and program strategies, the utility of strategies of incremental reform, and even the appropriate role of the social scientist in policy and program formation.

Knowing that political constraints and resistances exist is not a reason for abandoning evaluation research; rather, it is a precondition for usable evaluation research. Only when the evaluator has insight into the interests and motivations of other actors in the system, into the roles that he himself is consciously or inadvertently playing, the obstacles and opportunities that impinge upon the evaluative effort, and the limitations and possibilities for putting the results of evaluation to work—only with sensitivity to the politics of evaluation research—can the evaluator be as creative and strategically useful as he should be.

SOURCE: Quoted, with permission, from Carol H. Weiss, "Where Politics and Evaluation Research Meet," *Evaluation Practice*, 1993, 14(1):94, where the original 1973 version was reprinted as one of the classics in the evaluation field.

Moreover, adaptations may be required in the basic questions being addressed in response to shifts that occur in the operation of the program or the composition and interests of the stakeholders.

Informing Social Action to Improve Social Conditions

As indicated, this book is about the evaluation of social programs or, more generally, those programs whose mission, whether defined by the program itself or the expectations of the public that supports it, is to intervene in social conditions in ways that make them better. And if the purpose of these programs is in some way to improve the human condition, the purpose of evaluation, in turn, is to improve the programs.

In particular, the role of program evaluation is to provide answers. It answers questions about what the program is doing but, more important, about how well it is being done and whether it is worth doing. It is undertaken on the assumption that there is an audience with such questions and an interest in the answers. The concept of program evaluation presupposes more than a merely interested audience, however. It is characteristically designed to produce answers that will be useful and will actually be used. An evaluation study, therefore, primarily addresses the audience (or, more accurately, audiences) with the potential to make decisions and take action on the basis of the evaluation results. This point is fundamental to evaluation—its purpose is to inform social action.

In most instances, the main audiences to which an evaluation is directed are the sponsors of the evaluation and other program stakeholders. These are the individuals or groups with rather immediate interests in the particular program being evaluated and includes those with decision-making authority over the program or the capability to influence such decision making. Evaluation findings may assist such persons to make go/no-go decisions about specific program modifications or, perhaps, about initiation or continuation of entire programs. They may bear on political, practical, and resource considerations or make an impression on the views of individuals with influence. They may have direct effects on judgments of a program's value as part of an oversight process that holds the program accountable for results. Or they may have indirect effects in shaping the way program issues are framed and the nature of the debate about them. The evaluation sponsor and other such decisionmakers and stakeholders have a rather obvious primacy in these matters; however, they are not the only audience potentially interested in the evaluation nor are they necessarily the only agents whose actions may be influenced by the evaluation.

Programs, like people, have their unique profiles of characteristics but also share characteristics with others that make for meaningful categories and groupings. What is learned from an evaluation about one specific program, say, a drug use prevention program implemented at a particular high school, also tells us something about the whole category of similar programs. Many of the parties involved with social intervention must make decisions and take action that relates to categories or types of programs rather than individual instances. Policymakers, program planners, and program sponsors and funders, for instance, must often select, promote, or support a particular type of program rather than any one instance. A federal legislative committee may deliberate the merits of compensatory education programs, or a state correctional department may consider instituting boot camps for juvenile offenders, or a philanthropic foundation may decide to promote and underwrite programs that provide visiting nurses to single mothers. The body of evaluation findings for programs of each of these types is very pertinent to decisions and social actions of this sort. Each evaluation study, therefore, not only informs the immediate stakeholders but potentially informs those whose situations require decisions and action about different program concepts.

Indeed, one important form of evaluation research is that which is conducted on demonstration programs, that is, social intervention projects designed and implemented explicitly to test the value of an innovative program concept. In such cases, the findings of the evaluation are significant because of what they reveal about the program concept and are used primarily by those involved in policy making and program development at levels broader than any one program. Another significant evaluation-related activity is the integration of the findings of multiple evaluations of a particular type of program into a synthesis that can inform policy making and program planning. Some evaluation researchers, therefore, have been involved in the activities of systematic research synthesis or meta-analysis (Lipsey and Wilson, 1993).

Evaluations can thus inform social action by providing useful feedback for management and administrative purposes; by supporting the oversight functions of those funders, sponsors, and authorities to which the program is accountable; or by accurately depicting program activities and accomplishments to advocates, adversaries, clients, and other stakeholders. They may also contribute information for planning and policy purposes, indicate if innovative approaches to community problems are worth pursuing, or demonstrate the utility of some principle of professional practice. Evaluation research may even help shape our general understanding of how to bring about planned social change by testing social science hypotheses regarding the effects of certain broad forms of intervention. The common denominator is that evaluation research is intended to be useful and used, either directly and immediately or as an incremental contribution to a cumulative body of practical knowledge.

These assertions, of course, assume that an evaluation would not be undertaken unless there was an audience interested in receiving and, at least potentially, using the findings. Unfortunately, there are instances in which evaluations are commissioned without any intention of using their findings. Evaluations may be conducted only because they are mandated by program funders and then ignored when the findings are presented. Or an evaluation may be carried out because "everyone does it" without expectation of using the results

in any significant way. Responsible evaluators try to avoid being drawn into such situations of "ritualistic" evaluation. An early step in planning an evaluation, therefore, is a thorough inquiry into the motivation of the evaluation sponsors, the intended purposes of the evaluation, and the uses to be made of the findings.

EVALUATION RESEARCH IN PRACTICE

We have outlined the general considerations, purposes, and approaches that shape evaluation research and guide its application to any program situation. In actual practice, application of these concepts typically involves something of a balancing act between competing forces. Paramount among these is the inherent conflict between the requirements of systematic inquiry and data collection associated with evaluation research and the organizational imperatives of a social program devoted to delivery of service and maintenance of essential routine activities. The planning phase of evaluation, which is best accomplished in collaboration with program personnel and stakeholders, and, especially, the data collection phase necessarily place unusual and not altogether welcome demands on program personnel and program processes. Data collection, for instance, may require interaction with program files, clients, staff, and facilities that are disruptive of normal program processes and distract from and, in some cases, even compromise the service functions that are the program's primary obligation.

Every evaluation plan, therefore, must negotiate a middle way between optimizing the program circumstances for research purposes and minimizing the disruption caused to normal program operation. We use the word *nego-tiate* quite deliberately here, because the best approach to the inherent tension between the requirements of research and those of running a service program is for the evaluator to develop the evaluation plan collaboratively with program personnel. If the needs and purposes of the evaluation are spelled out in detail before the research begins, and those program personnel who will be affected (not just the administrators) are given an opportunity to react, make input, and otherwise help shape the data collection plan, the result is usually a more workable plan and better cooperation from program personnel in the face of the inevitable strains the evaluation will place on them.

In addition to the conflict between evaluation and program functions, there are other inherent tensions in the practice of evaluation that warrant comment. Here we introduce a few of the more notable dilemmas the evaluator must confront: the incompatibility of a fixed evaluation plan with the volatility of social programs; the strain between a press for evaluations to be scientific, on the one hand, and pragmatic, on the other; and the competing approaches to evaluation offered up by a field of great diversity and little consensus.

Evaluation and the Volatility of Social Programs

One of the most challenging aspects of program evaluation is the continually changing decision-making milieu of the social programs that are evaluated. In particular, the resources, priorities, and relative influence of the various sponsors and stakeholders of social programs are dynamic. These changes are frequently associated with the shifts in political context and social trends we noted earlier. For example, the

1996 welfare reform legislation has drastically altered the nature of income support for poor families. A program reconfiguration of this magnitude clearly requires evaluations of family income support programs to be defined differently than in the past with new outcomes and quite different program components at issue.

Priorities and responsibilities more specific to the organizations implementing a program can also change in significant ways. For example, a school system relieved by the courts from forced school busing may lose interest in its programs to increase white students' acceptance of attendance in predominantly minority schools. Or unanticipated problems with the intervention may require modifying the program and, consequently, the evaluation plan as well. For instance, a program to reduce the absence rates of low-income high school students by providing comprehensive medical care might be thwarted if a large proportion of the eligible students refused the services.

Somewhat ironically, preliminary findings from the evaluation itself may stimulate program changes that render the remainder of the evaluation plan obsolete. Consider, for example, a study of the impact of an alcohol treatment program that included six-month and one-year follow-ups of the clients. When the six-month follow-up revealed very high rates of drunkenness among the treatment group, the program staff markedly modified the intervention.

Not all social programs, of course, transform significantly while an evaluation is under way. Nonetheless, the evaluator must attempt to anticipate such changes and prepare for them to the extent possible. More important, perhaps, is to match the form of the evaluation to the program circumstances and prospects at the time the evaluation is planned. It would generally make little sense to design a rigorous impact assessment for a program under consideration for significant revision by relevant decisionmakers. Of equal importance, however, is the flexibility the evaluator brings to the evaluation task. Knowing the dynamic nature of programs, evaluators must be prepared to substantially modify an evaluation if it becomes apparent that the original plan is no longer appropriate to the circumstances. This often involves difficult issues associated with the availability of resources for the evaluation, the time lines for producing results, and the relationships with the program administrators and evaluation sponsors, so it is not to be taken lightly. Social programs are not research laboratories, however, and evaluators must expect to be buffeted about by forces and events outside their control.

The contrast between the image of a research laboratory and the reality of social programs as places to conduct social research leads us directly to another of the inherent tensions in evaluation, that between a scientific and a pragmatic perspective on the process.

Scientific Versus Pragmatic Evaluation Postures

Perhaps the single most influential article in the evaluation field was written by the late Donald Campbell and published in 1969. This article outlined a perspective that Campbell advanced over several decades: Policy and program decisions should emerge from continual social experimentation that tests ways to improve social conditions. Not only did he hold this position in principle, but he contended that the technology of social research made it feasible to actually develop the "experimenting society." Campbell, thus, sought to extend the

experimental model, as he learned and practiced it in social psychology, to evaluation research. Although he tempered his position in some of his later writing, it is fair to characterize him as fitting evaluation research into the scientific research paradigm (see Exhibit 1-I).

Campbell's position was challenged by Lee Cronbach, another giant in the evaluation field. While acknowledging that scientific investigation and evaluation may use some of the same logic of inquiry and research procedures, Cronbach argued that the purpose of evaluation sharply differentiates it from scientific research (Cronbach, 1982). In his view, evaluation is more art than science and every evaluation should be tailored to meet the needs of program decisionmakers and stakeholders. Thus, whereas scientific studies strive principally to meet research standards, evaluations should be dedicated to providing maximally useful information for decisionmakers given the political circumstances, program constraints, and available resources (see Exhibit 1-J).

One might be inclined to agree with both these views—that evaluations should meet high standards of scientific research quality *and* be fully dedicated to serving the information needs of program decisionmakers. The problem, of course, is that in practice these two goals often are not especially compatible. In particular, social research at a high scientific standard generally requires resources that exceed what is available in the typical program evaluation context. These resources include time, because high-quality research cannot be done quickly whereas program decisions often have to be made on short notice, and funding proportionate to the expertise, level of effort, and materials required for research to scientific standards. Moreover, research within the scientific framework may require structuring the

---

🕸 **EXHIBIT 1-I**   Reforms as Experiments

The United States and other modern nations should be ready for an experimental approach to social reform, an approach in which we try out new programs designed to cure specific social problems, in which we learn whether or not these programs are effective, and in which we retain, imitate, modify, or discard them on the basis of apparent effectiveness on the multiple imperfect criteria available.

SOURCE: Quoted from Donald Campbell, "Reforms as Experiments," *American Psychologist,* April 1969, 24:409.

🕸 **EXHIBIT 1-J**   Evaluators as Teachers

An evaluative study of a social program is justified to the extent that it facilitates the work of the polity. It therefore is to be judged primarily by its contribution to public thinking and to the quality of service provided subsequent to the evaluation. . . . An evaluation pays off to the extent that it offers ideas pertinent to pending actions and people think more clearly as a result. To enlighten, it must do more than amass good data. Timely communications—generally not "final" ones—should distribute information to the persons rightfully concerned, and those hearers should take the information into their thinking. To speak broadly, an evaluation ought *to inform and improve the operations of the social system.*

SOURCE: Quoted from Lee J. Cronbach and Associates, *Toward Reform of Program Evaluation* (San Francisco: Jossey-Bass, 1980), pp. 65-66.

---

inquiry in ways that do not mesh well with the perspectives of those who must make decisions about the program. For example, specifying variables so that they are well defined and measurable under scientific standards may fragment and, in some regards, trivialize what the policymakers see as complex and dynamic facets of the program. Similarly, meeting scientific standards for inferring causality, as when investigating program outcomes, may require such elaborate experimental controls that what is studied is no longer the program's services, but some contrived and constrained version of uncertain relevance to the actual program.

On the other hand, one cannot blithely dismiss scientific concerns in evaluation. Properly understood, what the scientific approach represents is a very considered attempt to produce conclusions that are valid and credible. Even when it falls short of this ideal, which is inevitable, such input makes a very important contribution to a decision-making context that otherwise is rife with self-interested perceptions and assertions, ideological biases, and undocumented claims about the way things are. But this statement, in turn, assumes that those conclusions meaningfully address aspects of the situation of concern to the decisionmakers; if not, they may be praiseworthy for their validity and credibility, but still irrelevant.

In practice, therefore, the evaluator must struggle to find a workable balance between the emphasis to be placed on procedures that help ensure the validity of the evaluation findings and those that make the findings timely, meaningful, and useful to the consumers. Where that balance point should be will depend on the purposes of the evaluation, the nature of the program, and the political or decision-making context. In many cases, evaluations will justifiably be undertaken that are "good enough" for answering relevant policy and program questions even though program conditions or available resources prevent them from being the best possible designs from a scientific standpoint. For example, program sponsors concerned about whether a rehabilitation treatment for alcoholics is effective may find six-month follow-up interviews showing that few clients report heavy drinking to be very useful even though the data lack the experimental controls that permit this result to be confidently attributed to the influence of the program.

What further complicates an already difficult situation for evaluation planning is that there is often ambiguity about the identity of the ultimate users of the evaluation and which of the potential users should be given priority in the design. An evaluation generally has various potential audiences, some with very immediate interests in particular aspects of the program under investigation, some with broader interests in the type of intervention the particular program represents, and others falling

somewhere in between. Occasionally, the purposes and priority users of an evaluation are defined so clearly and explicitly in advance that the evaluator has relatively little difficulty in balancing scientific and pragmatic considerations. For instance, an evaluation of a demonstration project on needle exchange to prevent AIDS among drug addicts funded by the National Institutes for Health may be clearly stipulated as a contribution to general policy-relevant knowledge about this intervention approach that should meet the highest possible scientific standards. On the other hand, an evaluator retained as a consultant by a program administrator to provide an assessment of a problematic unit in a community mental health center may understand quite clearly that the findings are for the sole purpose of informing certain decisions that administrator must make and, indeed, will not be reported outside the organization.

However, many program evaluation situations are not so clear-cut. Evaluation may be routinely required as part of funding or contract arrangements with the presumption that it will be generally informative to program managers, sponsors, and other interested parties. Or it may evolve from a collaboration between a service agency with a need for information for management purposes and a researcher with broader interests in the type of intervention that particular program provides. Indeed, given the effort and expense required for evaluation, there are probably more instances in which it is expected to be multipurpose than cases where the purpose and user are tightly specified. Unfortunately, the trade-offs between utility for program decisionmakers and scientific rigor are such that it is rarely possible to design an evaluation that serves both interests well. Thus, if evaluators choose to emphasize the needs of the immediate consumers, they must be prepared for the possibility that the findings will be criticized on methodological grounds by more remote audiences, for example, applied researchers, other evaluators, or sophisticated policymakers or service professionals. This carries with it the risk that the credibility of the evaluation will be undermined, perhaps even in the eyes of the immediate consumers to whom it was directed. But if the evaluation emphasizes methodological quality at the expense of utility, it may satisfy those knowledgeable about research standards but be assailed by program stakeholders as too academic, ivory tower, and even irrelevant to the "real" program issues.

Some evaluation theorists champion utilization as the overriding concern and advocate evaluation that is designed around the specific information needs of individually identified target consumers with whom the evaluator collaborates very closely (e.g., Patton, 1997). The authors of review articles in applied research journals who attempt to synthesize available research on the effectiveness of various interventions, on the other hand, regularly deplore the poor methodological quality of evaluation studies and urge a higher standard. Some commentators want to have it both ways and press the view that evaluations should strive to have utility to program stakeholders *and* contribute to cumulative knowledge about social intervention (Lipsey, 1997). Our outlook, for the didactic purposes of this book, is that all these options are defensible, but not necessarily equally defensible in any given evaluation situation. This, then, presents yet another issue for which the evaluator will be required to make a judgment call and must attempt to tailor the evaluation design to the particular purposes and circumstances presented in each application.

Diversity in Evaluation Outlooks and Approaches

As the preceding discussion illustrates, the field of evaluation is not monolithic in conceptual outlook or methodological approach. On the contrary, it is a contentiously diverse field. The fundamental difference represented historically by Campbell and Cronbach represents but one instance of this diversity. Evaluation practitioners are drawn from a wide range of academic disciplines and professions with different orientations and methods, and this multidisciplinary mix has contributed significantly to the multiplicity of perspectives. Other differences in outlook are related to the motivations of evaluators and the settings in which they work. The solo practitioner who undertakes short-term evaluations on contract with local agencies and the tenured professor with long-term foundation funding will likely have quite divergent views on their evaluation activities.

As the field of evaluation has matured and become institutionalized, interest has developed in explicating the different postures toward evaluation and the methods preferred by leaders in various "camps." In particular, there is a growing interest in identifying congruent elements among different perspectives to advance what is referred to as "evaluation theory" (Shadish, Cook, and Leviton, 1991). Advocates of the evaluation theory movement envision the development of a theory that will serve as the basis for decision making by evaluators as they proceed with their work (see Exhibit 1-K).

Virtually all experienced evaluators see the need for better formulated guidelines as they face the various decision points that come up in any evaluation. Also, there is a need for such guidelines so that training the fledgling evaluator is not so heavily dependent on trial-and-error experience. But not every evaluator sub-

---

✖ EXHIBIT 1-K   The Ideal Evaluation Theory

The ideal (never achievable) evaluation theory would describe and justify why certain evaluation practices lead to particular kinds of results across situations that evaluators confront. It would (a) clarify the activities, processes, and goals of evaluation; (b) explicate relationships among evaluative activities and the processes and goals they facilitate; and (c) empirically test propositions to identify and address those that conflict with research or other critically appraised knowledge about evaluation.

SOURCE: Quoted from William R. Shadish, Thomas D. Cook, and Laura C. Leviton, *Foundations of Program Evaluation: Theories of Practice* (Newbury Park, CA: Sage, 1991), pp. 30-31.

---

scribes to the view that the field of evaluation has sufficiently clear boundaries to distinguish it conceptually from what goes on generally in the policy sciences or procedurally from the "rules" that guide applied social research. There is probably as much diversity in outlook among evaluators about the utility of evaluation theory as there is about the right way of doing evaluations.

At present, therefore, we must acknowledge that evaluation is at least as much art as science, and perhaps should be and always will be. Inevitably, the evaluator's task is to creatively weave together many competing concerns and objectives into a tapestry in which different viewers can find different messages. We recognize, too, the difficulty of teaching an art form, especially via the written word. Teaching evaluation is analogous to training physicians to be diagnosticians. Any intelligent person can be taught to understand the results from laboratory tests, but a doctor becomes an astute diagnostician only through practice, experience, and attention to the idiosyncrasies of each individual case. In this sense, learning from a text can provide only part of the knowledge needed to become a capable evaluator.

WHO CAN DO EVALUATIONS?

Systematic evaluation is grounded in social science research techniques; hence, most evaluation specialists have had some social research training. But we should be quick to point out that there is great heterogeneity in the disciplinary and professional training of persons doing evaluations (see Exhibit 1-L). Ideally, every evaluator should be familiar with the full repertoire of social research methods. In practice, we can come close to this ideal only by continually broadening and deepening our technical knowledge by means all of us know about: keeping up with the literature, attending workshops and professional conferences, and learning from colleagues. Moreover, it would be deceptive to suggest that this or any textbook can teach someone how to *do* evaluations. There is no substitute for experience. What we do believe is that this book will provide an organized conceptual framework that identifies

> ### ❊ Exhibit 1-L   Diversity of the Members of the American Evaluation Association (in percentages)

Major Professional Responsibility		Organizational Setting		Primary Discipline	
Evaluation	28	College or university	40	Education	22
Research	19	Private business	12	Psychology	18
Administration	18	Nonprofit organization	11	Evaluation	14
Teaching	13	Federal government agency	10	Statistical methods	10
Consulting	8	State/local government agency	10	Sociology	6
Student	5	School system	4	Economics and political science	6
Other	9	Other	13	Organizational development	3
				Other	21

SOURCE: Adapted from *Evaluation Practice News* (October 1993); based on 2,045 AEA members as of June 1993.

the important issues and the options for addressing them.

Although knowledge of the concepts and methods instrumental to good program evaluation research is essential for conducting evaluations, it is important to note that a great deal of knowledge about the target problem area (e.g., crime, health, drug abuse) and the nature, range, and results of the interventions that have been used to address that problem are also required. This is necessary not only so the evaluator will understand the issues and context with which the program deals but so that an appropriate evaluation plan can be developed that reflects the reality of the program and existing knowledge relevant to such programs. At the most complex level, evaluation activities can be so technically complicated, sophisticated in conception, costly, and of such long duration that they require the dedicated participation of highly trained specialists at ease with the latest in social science theory, program knowledge, data collection methods, and statistical techniques. Such highly complex evalu-

ations are usually conducted by specialized evaluation staffs. At the other extreme, there are many evaluation tasks that can be understood easily and carried out by persons of modest expertise and experience.

It is the purpose of this book to provide an introduction to the field for those whose current positions, professional interests, or natural curiosity inspire them to want to learn how evaluations are conducted. Studying the book is, of course, only a start along the path to becoming an expert in evaluation. We also aim to provide persons responsible for administering and managing human resource programs with sufficient understanding of evaluation tasks and activities to be able to judge for themselves what kinds of evaluations are appropriate to their programs and projects and to comprehend the results of evaluation studies of their programs. In brief, we have tried to provide a text that is helpful to those who conduct evaluations, those who commission them, those who oversee evaluation staffs, and those who are consumers of evaluation research.

SUMMARY

- Program evaluation is the use of social research methods to systematically investigate the effectiveness of social intervention programs. It draws on the techniques and concepts of social science disciplines and is intended to be useful for improving programs and informing social action aimed at ameliorating social problems.

- Modern evaluation research grew from pioneering efforts in the 1930s and burgeoned in the postwar years as new methodologies were developed that could be applied to the rapidly growing social program arena. The social policy and public administration movements have contributed to the professionalization of the field and to the sophistication of the consumers of evaluation research.

- The need for program evaluation is undiminished in the 1990s and may even be expected to grow. Indeed, contemporary concern over the allocation of scarce resources makes it more essential than ever to evaluate the effectiveness of social interventions.

- Evaluation must be tailored to the political and organizational context of the program to be evaluated. It typically involves assessment of one or more of five program domains: (a) the need for the program, (b) the design of the program, (c) the program implementation and service delivery, (d) the program impact or outcomes, and (e) program efficiency. Evaluation requires an accurate description of the program performance or characteristics at issue and assessment of them against relevant standards or criteria.

- In practice, program evaluation presents many challenges to the evaluator. Program circumstances and activities may change during the course of an evaluation, an appropriate balance must be found between scientific and pragmatic considerations in the evaluation design, and the wide diversity of perspectives and approaches in the evaluation field provide little firm guidance about how best to proceed with an evaluation.

- Most evaluators are trained either in one of the social sciences or in professional schools that offer applied social research courses. Highly specialized, technical, or complex evaluations may require specialized evaluation staffs. A basic knowledge of the evaluation field, however, is relevant not only to those who will perform evaluations but also to the consumers of evaluation research.

KEY CONCEPTS FOR CHAPTER 2

Formative evaluation	Evaluative activities undertaken to furnish information that will guide program improvement.
Summative evaluation	Evaluative activities undertaken to render a summary judgment on certain critical aspects of the program's performance, for instance, to determine if specific goals and objectives were met.
Target	The unit (individual, family, community, etc.) to which a program intervention is directed. All such units within the area served by a program comprise its target population.
Stakeholders	Individuals, groups, or organizations having a significant interest in how well a program functions, for instance, those with decision-making authority over it, funders and sponsors, administrators and personnel, and clients or intended beneficiaries.
Evaluation sponsor	The person(s), group, or organization that requests or requires the evaluation and provides the resources to conduct it.
Independent evaluation	An evaluation in which the evaluator has the primary responsibility for developing the evaluation plan, conducting the evaluation, and disseminating the results.
Participatory or collaborative evaluation	An evaluation organized as a team project in which the evaluator and representatives of one or more stakeholder groups work collaboratively in developing the evaluation plan, conducting the evaluation, or disseminating and using the results.
Empowerment evaluation	A participatory or collaborative evaluation in which the evaluator's role includes consultation and facilitation directed toward the development of the capabilities of the participating stakeholders to conduct evaluation on their own, to use it effectively for advocacy and change, and to have some influence on a program that affects their lives.
Evaluation questions	A set of questions developed by the evaluator, evaluation sponsor, and other stakeholders; the questions define the issues the evaluation will investigate and are stated in terms such that they can be answered using methods available to the evaluator in a way useful to stakeholders.
Needs assessment	An evaluative study that answers questions about the social conditions a program is intended to address and the need for the program.
Assessment of program theory	An evaluative study that answers questions about the conceptualization and design of a program.
Assessment of program process	An evaluative study that answers questions about program operations, implementation, and service delivery. Also known as a process evaluation or an implementation assessment.
Impact assessment	An evaluative study that answers questions about program outcomes and impact on the social conditions it is intended to ameliorate. Also known as an impact evaluation or an outcome evaluation.
Efficiency assessment	An evaluative study that answers questions about program costs in comparison to either the monetary value of its benefits or its effectiveness in terms of the changes brought about in the social conditions it addresses.

CHAPTER 2

TAILORING EVALUATIONS

Every evaluation must be tailored to its program. The tasks that evaluators undertake depend on the purposes of the evaluation, the conceptual and organizational structure of the program, and the resources available. Formulating an evaluation plan therefore requires the evaluator to first explore these aspects of the evaluation situation with the evaluation sponsor and such other stakeholders as policymakers, program personnel, and program participants. Based on this reconnaissance and negotiation with the key stakeholders, the evaluator can then develop a plan that identifies the evaluation questions to be answered, the methods to be used to answer them, and the relationships to be developed with the stakeholders during the course of the evaluation.

No hard-and-fast guidelines direct the process of investigating the evaluation situation and designing an evaluation—it is necessarily a creative and collaborative endeavor. Nonetheless, achieving a good fit between the evaluation plan and the program circumstances usually involves attention to certain critical themes. It is essential, for instance, that the evaluation plan be responsive to the purposes of the evaluation as understood by the evaluation sponsor and other central stakeholders. An evaluation intended to provide feedback to program decisionmakers so that the program can be improved will take a different approach than one intended to help funders determine if a program should be terminated. In addition, the evaluation plan must reflect an understanding of how the program is designed and organized so that the questions asked and the data collection arranged will be appropriate to the circumstances. Finally, any evaluation, of course, will have to be designed within the constraints of available time, personnel, funding, and other such resources.

Although the particulars are diverse, the basic program circumstances for which evaluation is requested typically represent one of a small number of recognizable variations. Consequently, the evaluation designs that result from the tailoring process tend to be adaptations of one or more of a set of familiar evaluation approaches or schemes. In practice, therefore, tailoring an evaluation is often primarily a matter of selecting and adapting these schemes to the specific circumstances of the program to be evaluated. One set of evaluation approaches is defined around the nature of the evaluator-stakeholder interaction. Evaluators may function relatively independently or work quite collaboratively with stakeholders in designing and conducting the evaluation. Another distinct set of evaluation approaches is organized around common combinations of evaluation questions and the usual methods for answering them. Among these are evaluation schemes for assessing social problems and needs, program theory, program process or implementation, program impact or outcome, and program efficiency.

One of the most challenging aspects of evaluation is that there is no "one size fits all" approach. Every evaluation situation has its unique profile of characteristics, and the evaluation design must involve an interplay between the nature of the evaluation situation, on the one side, and the evaluator's repertoire of approaches, techniques, and concepts, on the other. A good evaluation design is one that fits the circumstances while yielding credible and useful answers to the questions that motivate it. This chapter provides an overview of the issues and considerations the evaluator should take into account when tailoring an evaluation plan to accomplish these purposes.

WHAT ASPECTS OF THE EVALUATION PLAN MUST BE TAILORED?

Evaluation designs may be quite simple and direct, perhaps addressing only one narrow question such as whether using a computerized instructional program helps a class of third graders read better. Or they may be prodigiously complex, as in a national evaluation of the operations and effects of a diverse set of programs for reducing substance abuse in multiple urban sites. Fundamentally, however, we can view any evaluation as structured around three issues:

The questions the evaluation is to answer. An endless number of questions might be raised about any social program by a wide range of interested parties. There may be concerns about such matters as the needs of the target population and whether they are being adequately reached and served, the management and operation of the program, the effectiveness

of services, whether the program is having its desired impact, and its costs and efficiency. No evaluation can, nor generally should, attempt to address all such concerns. A central feature of an evaluation design, therefore, is a specification of the guiding purpose of the evaluation and the corresponding questions on which it will focus. Later in this chapter, and in more detail in Chapter 3, we discuss the nature of evaluation questions, how they can be derived, and some of the factors that influence the priority they should be given.

The methods and procedures the evaluation will use to answer the questions. An important aspect of the evaluator's distinctive expertise is knowing how to obtain useful, timely, and credible information about the various dimensions of program performance that are to be evaluated. A large repertoire of social research techniques and conceptual tools are available for this task. An evaluation design must identify the methods that will be used to answer each of the questions at issue and organize them into a feasible work plan. Moreover, the methods selected must not only be capable of providing meaningful answers to the questions but also must be practical while still providing the degree of scientific rigor appropriate to the evaluation circumstances. Most of the rest of this book (Chapters 4-11) is devoted to consideration of evaluation methods and the circumstances in which they are applicable.

The nature of the evaluator-stakeholder relationship. One of the most important lessons from the first several decades of experience with systematic evaluation is that there is nothing automatic about the assimilation and use of evaluation findings by the stakeholders presumed interested in them. Part of an evaluation design, therefore, is a plan for effectively interacting with program stakeholders to identify and clarify the issues, conduct the evaluation, and make effective use of the evaluation findings. This interaction may be highly collaborative, with the evaluator serving as a consultant or facilitator to a group of stakeholders who take primary responsibility for planning, conducting, and using the evaluation. Or the evaluator may take that responsibility but seek essential guidance and information from the stakeholders. In addition, an evaluation plan should indicate which audiences are to receive which information at what times, what the nature and schedule of written reports and oral briefings will be, and how broadly findings are to be disseminated beyond the evaluation sponsor. The evaluator-stakeholder relationship is discussed later in this chapter and in Chapter 12.

WHAT CONSIDERATIONS SHOULD GUIDE EVALUATION PLANNING?

Many aspects of the program and the circumstances of the evaluation will necessarily shape the evaluation design. Some of these involve general considerations of almost universal relevance to evaluation planning, but others will be specific to the particular situation of each evaluation. Development of the evaluation plan, therefore, must be guided by a careful analysis of the evaluation context. The more significant considerations for that analysis can be organized into three categories, having to do with (a) the purposes of the evaluation, (b) the program structure and circumstances, and (c) the resources available for the evaluation. All these topics will receive later attention in the course of discussion about the specific as-

pects of the evaluation plan they most influence; an overview is provided here.

The Purposes of the Evaluation

Evaluations are initiated for many reasons and may have quite different purposes from one situation to another. They may be intended to help management improve a program; support advocacy by supporters or critics; gain knowledge about program effects; provide input to decisions about program funding, structure, or administration; respond to political pressures; or have any of a number of such purposes individually or in combination. One of the first determinations the evaluator must make, therefore, is just what those purposes are. This is not always a simple matter. Some statement of the purposes generally accompanies the initial request for an evaluation, but these announced purposes rarely tell the whole story and sometimes are only rhetorical. Furthermore, evaluations may be routinely required in a program situation or sought simply because it is presumed to be a good idea without any distinct articulation of its purposes or the sponsor's intent (see Exhibit 2-A).

The prospective evaluator determines the purposes of the evaluation by attempting to establish as firmly as possible who wants the evaluation, what they want, and why they want it. There is no cut-and-dried method for doing this, but it is usually best approached the way a journalist would try to dig out a story. That is, source documents should be examined, key informants with different vantage points on the situation should be interviewed, and pertinent history and background should be uncovered. Although the details will vary greatly, evaluations are generally done for one or more of the following broad reasons (Chelimsky, 1997):

>

EXHIBIT 2-A   Does Anybody Want This Evaluation?

Our initial meetings with the Bureau of Community Services administrators produced only vague statements about the reasons for the evaluation. They said they wanted some information about the cost-effectiveness of both New Dawn and Pegasus and also how well each program was being implemented. . . . It gradually became clear that the person most interested in the evaluation was an administrator in charge of contracts for the Department of Corrections, but we were unable to obtain specific information concerning where or how the evaluation would be used. We could only discern that an evaluation of state-run facilities had been mandated, but it was not clear by whom.

SOURCE: Quoted from Dennis J. Palumbo and Michael A. Hallett, "Conflict Versus Consensus Models in Policy Evaluation and Implementation," *Evaluation and Program Planning*, 1993, 16(1):11-23.

program improvement, accountability, knowledge generation, and political ruses or public relations.

Program improvement. The evaluation findings may be intended to furnish information that will guide program improvement. Such evaluation is often called *formative evaluation* (Scriven, 1991) because its purpose is to help form or shape the program to perform better (for an example, see Exhibit 2-B). The audiences for the findings of formative evaluation typically are the program planners (in the case of programs in the planning stage) or program administrators, oversight boards, or funders with an interest in optimizing program effectiveness. The information desired by these persons may relate to the need for the program, the program concept and design, its implementation, its impact, or its efficiency. Typically, the evaluator in this situation will work closely with program management and other stakeholders in designing, conducting, and reporting the evaluation. Evaluation for program improvement characteristically emphasizes findings that are timely, concrete, and immediately useful. Correspondingly, the communication between the evaluator and the respective audiences about the findings may occur regularly throughout the evaluation and be relatively informal.

Accountability. The use of social resources such as taxpayer dollars by human service programs is justified on the grounds that these programs make beneficial contributions to society. It follows that persons with significant responsibilities for such social investments will expect programs to manage resources effectively and efficiently and actually produce the intended benefits. Evaluation may be conducted, therefore, to determine if these expectations are met. Such evaluation is often called *summative evaluation* (Scriven, 1991) because its purpose is to render a summary judgment on certain critical aspects of the program's performance (Exhibit 2-C provides an example). The findings of summative evaluation are usually intended for decisionmakers with major roles in program oversight, for example, a

---

❦ EXHIBIT 2-B   A Stop-Smoking Telephone Help Line That Nobody Called

Formative evaluation procedures were used to help design a "stop smoking" hotline for 2,148 adult smokers in a cancer control project sponsored by a health maintenance organization (HMO). Phone scripts for use by the hotline counselors and other aspects of the planned services were discussed with focus groups of smokers and reviewed in telephone interviews with a representative sample of HMO members who smoked. Feedback from these informants led to refinement of the scripts, hours of operation arranged around the times participants said they were most likely to call, and advertising of the service through newsletters and "quit kits"

routinely distributed to all project participants. Despite these efforts, an average of less than three calls per month was made during the 33 months the hotline was in operation, about a 2.4% use rate by the target population. To further assess this disappointing response, comparisons were made with similar services around the country. This revealed that 1%-2% use rates were typical but the other hotlines served much larger populations and therefore received many more calls. The program sponsors concluded that to be successful, the smoker's hotline would have to be offered to a larger population and be intensively publicized.

SOURCE: Adapted from Russell E. Glasgow, H. Landow, J. Hollis, S. G. McRae, and P. A. La Chance, "A Stop-Smoking Telephone Help Line That Nobody Called," *American Journal of Public Health,* February 1993, 83:252-253.

❦ EXHIBIT 2-C   U.S. General Accounting Office Assesses Early Effects of the Mammography Quality Standards Act

The Mammography Quality Standards Act of 1992 required the Food and Drug Administration (FDA) to administer a code of uniform standards for mammogram-screening procedures in all the states. When the act was passed, Congress was concerned that access to mammography services might decrease because providers would choose to drop them rather than upgrade operations to comply with the new standards. The U.S. General Accounting Office (GAO) was asked to assess the early effects of implementing the act and report back to Congress. They found that the FDA had taken a gradual approach to implementing the act's requirements, which had

helped to minimize adverse effects on access. The FDA inspectors had not closed many facilities that failed to meet certification standards; rather, they had given them additional time to correct the problems found during inspections and to meet the new quality assurance requirements. Only a relatively small number of facilities had terminated their mammography services and those were generally small-volume providers located within 25 miles of another certified facility. The GAO concluded that the Mammography Quality Standards Act was having a positive effect on the quality of mammography services, as Congress had intended.

SOURCE: Adapted from U.S. General Accounting Office, *Mammography Services: Initial Impact of New Federal Law Has Been Positive.* Report 10/27/95, GAO/HEHS-96-17 (Washington, DC: General Accounting Office, 1995).

funding agency, governing board, legislative committee, political decisionmaker, or upper management, but may also be of interest to critics, constituents, and concerned citizens outside the formal decision-making channels. Summative evaluation may influence such significant decisions as program continuation, allocation of resources, restructuring, or legal action. For this reason, such evaluation often requires information of sufficient credibility under scientific standards to provide a confident basis for action and to withstand criticism aimed at discrediting it. The evaluator may be expected to function relatively independently in planning, conducting, and reporting the evaluation with input from, but no direct decision-making participation by, stakeholders. Similarly, it may be important to avoid premature or careless conclusions and, therefore, communication of the evaluation findings to the respective audiences may be relatively formal, rely chiefly on written reports, and occur primarily at the end of the evaluation.

Knowledge generation. Some evaluations are not intended to directly inform decisions related to specific programs in place or contemplated but, rather, mainly describe the nature and effects of an intervention for broader purposes and audiences. The intervention at issue, for instance, might be a demonstration configured expressly to try out a promising concept such as integrated services for children with mental health problems or monthly visits by nurses to pregnant women at risk of premature births (see Exhibit 2-D for another example). A similar situation occurs when an academic researcher arranges to study an intervention with interesting characteristics, for example, an innovative science curriculum, to contribute to knowledge about that particular form of inter-

vention. Because evaluations of this sort are intended to make contributions to the social science knowledge base, they are usually conducted in a scientific framework using the most rigorous methods feasible. The audience for the resulting findings may include the research sponsors in cases of demonstration projects or externally funded research. Beyond that, however, the audience is generally quite diffuse—all those interested in the particular type of program or, perhaps, the particular methods used to study it. Dissemination of the evaluation findings in these situations is most likely through scholarly journals, conferences, and other such professional outlets. These knowledge generation studies may turn out to be useful for the development of new public programs as program developers draw on social science research for program ideas.

Political ruses or public relations. Sometimes, the true purpose of the evaluation, at least for those who initiate it, has little to do with actually obtaining information about program performance. It is not unusual, for instance, for program administrators or boards to launch an evaluation because they believe it will be good public relations and might impress funders or political decisionmakers. Occasionally, an evaluation is commissioned to provide a public context for a decision that has already been made behind the scenes to terminate a program, fire an administrator, or the like. Or the evaluation may be a delaying tactic to appease critics and defer difficult decisions, rather like appointing a committee to study a problem rather than acting on the problem.

Virtually all evaluations have some elements of political maneuvering and public relations among their instigating motives, but when these are the principal purposes, the prospective evaluator is presented with a diffi-

⚜ EXHIBIT 2-D Testing an Innovative Treatment Concept for Pathological Gambling

Pathological gambling is characterized by a loss of control over gambling impulses, lies about the extent of gambling, family and job disruption, stealing money, and chasing losses with additional gambling. Though recent increases in the availability of gambling have led to corresponding increases in the prevalence of pathological gambling, few treatment programs have been developed to help the victims of this disorder. Research on the psychology of gambling has shown that problem gamblers develop an illusion of control such that they believe they can employ strategies that will increase their winnings despite the inherent randomness of games of chance. A team of clinical researchers in Canada hypothesized that a treatment based on "cognitive correction" of these erroneous beliefs would be an effective therapy. Because excessive gambling leads to financial problems and interpersonal difficulties, they combined their cognitive intervention with problem-solving and social skills training.

To test their treatment concept, the researchers used media advertisements and referrals from health providers to recruit 40 pathological gamblers willing to accept treatment. These were randomly assigned to the treatment or control group and measures of pathological gambling, perception of control, desire to gamble, self-efficacy perception, and frequency of gambling were taken at various intervals before and after the treatment period. The results showed significant changes in the treatment group on all outcome measures with maintenance of the gains at 6- and 12-month follow-up. However, the results may have been compromised by high attrition—8 of the 20 gamblers who began treatment and 3 of the 20 in the control group dropped out, a common occurrence during intervention for addictive problems. Despite this limitation, the researchers concluded that their results were strong enough to demonstrate the effectiveness of their treatment concept.

SOURCE: Adapted from Caroline Sylvain, Robert Ladouceur, and Jean-Marie Boisvert, "Cognitive and Behavioral Treatment of Pathological Gambling: A Controlled Study," *Journal of Consulting and Clinical Psychology*, 1997, 65(5):727-732.

cult dilemma. The evaluation must either be guided by the political or public relations purposes, which may compromise its integrity, or focus on program performance issues that are of no real interest to those commissioning the evaluation and may even be threatening. In either case, the evaluator would be well advised to try to avoid such situations. If a lack of serious intent becomes evident during the initial exploration of the evaluation context, proceeding with an evaluation plan would not generally be wise. Instead, the prospective evaluator may wish to assume an "evaluation consultant" role and assist the relevant parties to clarify the nature of evaluation, identify appropriate and realistic expectations, and redirect the effort toward more appropriate uses.

The Program Structure and Circumstances

No two programs are identical in their organizational structure and environmental, social, and political circumstances, even when they ostensibly provide the "same" service. The particulars of a program's structure and circumstances constitute major features of the evaluation situation to which the evaluation plan must be tailored. Although there is a myriad of such particulars, three broad categories are especially important to evaluators because of their pervasive influence on evaluation design and implementation:

■ The stage of program development— whether the program being evaluated is new or innovative, established but still developing or undergoing restructuring, or established and presumed stable.

■ The administrative and political context of the program, in particular, the degree of consensus, conflict, or confusion among stakeholders about the values or principles the program embodies, its mission and goals, or its social significance.

■ The structure of the program, including both its conceptual and organizational makeup. This involves the nature of the program rationale; the diversity, scope, and character of the services provided and of the target populations for those services; location of service sites and facilities; administrative arrangements; record-keeping procedures; and so forth.

The influence of these factors will be considered in relation to various specific aspects of evaluation design discussed throughout the remainder of this book; we provide a brief orientation here.

The Stage of Program Development

The life of a social program can be thought of as a developmental progression in which different questions are at issue at different stages and, therefore, different evaluation approaches must be applied to answer those questions (see Exhibit 2-E). Assessment of a program still in the early stages of planning will be a distinctly different endeavor than assessment of a well-established program. Similarly, assessment of an established program for which restructuring is contemplated or under way will raise different concerns than a program presumed stable in its basic operations and functions.

When new programs are initiated, especially innovative ones, evaluation is often requested to examine the social needs the program should address, the program design and objectives, the definition of its target population, the expected outcomes, and the means by which it assumes those outcomes can be attained. These issues are especially relevant during the planning phase when the basic design is being formulated and changes can be made relatively easily. The evaluator, therefore, may function as a planning consultant before the program is launched by helping to assess and improve the program design as it is developed. Assessment of the program conceptualization may also be the focal point of an evaluation after the planning phase when the program is in the early stage of implementation. Decisionmakers associated with young programs are often open to some amount of reformulation of the program model and may wish to have it assessed to ensure that their approach is as good as it can be.

The following examples illustrate the role of evaluators in the early stages of program development:

• A small New England city wanted to establish an emergency shelter for homeless persons. To determine how many beds should be provided, the city funded a nighttime survey,

> **EXHIBIT 2-E**   Stages of Program Development and Related Evaluation Functions

Stage of Program Development	¹Question to Be Asked	Evaluation Function
1. Assessment of social problems and needs	To what extent are community needs and standards met?	Needs assessment; problem description
2. Determination of goals	What must be done to meet those needs and standards?	Needs assessment; service needs
3. Design of program alternatives	What services could be used to produce the desired changes?	Assessment of program logic or theory
4. Selection of alternative	Which of the possible program approaches is best?	Feasibility study; formative evaluation
5. Program implementation	How should the program be put into operation?	Implementation assessment
6. Program operation	Is the program operating as planned?	Process evaluation; program monitoring
7. Program outcomes	Is the program having the desired effects?	Outcome evaluation
8. Program efficiency	Are program effects attained at a reasonable cost?	Cost-benefit analysis; cost-effectiveness analysis

SOURCE: Adapted from S. Mark Pancer and Anne Westhues, "A Developmental Stage Approach to Program Planning and Evaluation," *Evaluation Review*, 1989, 13(1):56-77.

attempting to count all persons sleeping in public places such as bus stations, parks, or store entrance ways.

• A program to increase public awareness of risk factors in cardiovascular diseases and encourage exercise and proper diet attempted to organize discussion groups among employees of local firms. The evaluators found that this approach was largely unsuccessful because workers were reluctant to form discussion groups. The evaluators suggested a more successful approach using existing organized groups such as churches, fraternal organizations, and clubs.

Sometimes evaluations of new programs are expected to address questions of impact and efficiency, but the unsettled nature of the programs in their beginning years most often makes those issues premature. It can easily take a year or more for a new program to establish facilities, acquire and train staff, make contact with the target population, and develop its services to the desired level. During this period, it may not be realistic to expect much impact on the social conditions toward which the program is directed. Formative evaluation aimed at clarifying target population needs, improving program operations, and enhancing the quality of service delivery, using approaches such as those discussed later in Chapters 4-6, is likely to be more apt in these cases.

Although the evaluation of new programs represents an important activity for the field, by far the greater effort goes into assessing established programs. Evaluating these programs requires first understanding their social and political history. Most well-established social programs have sprung from long-standing ameliorative efforts, and unless some crisis necessitates consideration of fundamental change, they are constrained to their traditional forms and approaches. Often there is considerable opposition from some stakeholders to any questioning of their fundamental assumptions or the ways they have been put into place. The value of such well-entrenched programs as Social Security pensions, guidance counselors in schools, vocational programs for disabled persons, parole supervision for released convicts, and community health education for the prevention of diseases is taken for granted.

Evaluation of established, stable programs, therefore, rarely focuses on assessing the underlying program conceptualization. It is more likely that attention will be directed toward such issues as coverage, effective service delivery, and the impact and efficiency of those services. However, if the program is very large and well established, it can be difficult to evaluate impact and efficiency, especially if it is a full-coverage program that provides services to virtually the entire eligible population. In such cases, the evaluator has limited ability to develop credible depictions of what things would be like in the absence of the program as a baseline for assessing its impact. Often, evaluation of such programs is directed toward assessing the extent to which the program objectives are explicit and relevant to the interests of program sponsors, staff, and other stakeholders, whether the program is conforming to

program plans, and whether it is reaching the appropriate target population. For example, the U.S. Department of Agriculture conducts periodic studies of participation in the food stamps program to measure the extent to which eligible households are enrolled and to guide outreach efforts to increase participation (Trippe, 1995).

Sometimes, however, evaluation is sought for established programs primarily because the program status quo has been called into question. This may be due to external pressures such as political attack, competition, mounting program costs, or dramatic changes in the target population served. Or it may occur because program sponsors and staff are dissatisfied with the effectiveness of their interventions and wish to bring about improvement. In either event, some restructuring may be considered, and evaluation is sought to guide that change. In circumstances such as these, the evaluation may focus on any and all aspects of the program. Questions might be raised about the need for the program, its conceptualization and design, its operations and implementation, and its impact and efficiency.

The federal food stamps program mentioned above, for instance, has been a national program for more than two decades. It is intended to increase the quantity and quality of food consumed by poor households by providing them with food stamps redeemable only by purchasing approved foods at grocery stores. The Department of Agriculture contemplated abandoning food stamps and issuing checks instead, thereby eliminating the high costs of printing, distributing, and redeeming an earmarked currency. To test the effects of cashing out food stamps, it started four experiments comparing the food consumption in households receiving food stamps with the food consumption of households receiving the same dollar amount of benefits in the form of checks

(Fraker, Martini, and Ohls, 1995). Significant differences were found: Households receiving checks purchased less food than those that received food stamps. The Department of Agriculture therefore decided to retain food stamps.

The Administrative and Political Context of the Program

Except possibly for academic researchers who conduct an evaluation study on their own initiative for knowledge generation purposes, evaluators are not free to establish their own definitions of what the program is about, its goals and objectives, and what evaluation questions should be addressed. The evaluator interacts with the evaluation sponsor, program personnel, and other program stakeholders to develop this essential background. Somewhat different perspectives from these various groups are to be expected and, in most instances, the evaluator will attempt to develop an evaluation plan that reflects all significant views and concerns or, at least, is compatible with the prevailing views among the major parties.

If significant stakeholders are in substantial conflict about the mission, goals, probity, procedures, or presenting issues for the program, it presents an immense difficulty for evaluation design (see Exhibit 2-F). The evaluator can attempt to incorporate the conflicting perspectives into the design, but this may not be an easy task. The evaluation sponsors may be unwilling to embrace the inclusion of issues and perspectives from groups they view as adversaries. Furthermore, the issues and perspectives may be so different that it is difficult to incorporate them in a single evaluation plan or to do so may require more time and resources than are available. For instance, it would be

challenging to design an evaluation that simultaneously addressed effectiveness questions generated by stakeholders who asserted that the purpose of a program for dysfunctional families was to protect the children from abuse and, therefore, should readily support removing them from the home if there is suspicion of abuse, and those generated by stakeholders insisting that the purpose was to keep families intact and help them work out their problems. Each of these perspectives entails different objectives, and procedures to attain those objectives, that have correspondingly different conceptions of program effectiveness associated with them. Although the evaluator might attempt to design an evaluation that would encompass these different perspectives and thus inform both sets of stakeholders, such an effort would require a careful balance in determining what data to collect and what criteria to apply to interpret them.

Alternatively, the evaluator could plan the evaluation from the perspective of one of the stakeholders, typically the evaluation sponsor or some other stakeholder designated by the evaluation sponsor. This, of course, will not be greeted with enthusiasm by stakeholders with conflicting perspectives and they may well oppose the evaluation and criticize the evaluator. The challenge to the evaluator is to be clear and straightforward about the perspective represented in the evaluation and the reasons for it, despite the objections. It is important to recognize that it is not necessarily wrong to plan and conduct an evaluation from the perspective of one stakeholder without giving strong representation to conflicting views. Nonetheless, evaluators generally solicit input from all the major stakeholders and attempt to incorporate their concerns so that the evaluation plan will be as comprehensive as possible and the results as useful as possible. Where there are conflict-

---

EXHIBIT 2-F   Stakeholder Conflict Over Home Arrest Program

In an evaluation of a home arrest program using electronic monitoring for offenders on parole, the evaluators made the following comments about stakeholder views:

> There were numerous conflicting goals that were considered important by different agencies, including lowering costs and prison diversion, control and public safety, intermediate punishment and increased options for corrections, and treatment and rehabilitation. Different stakeholders emphasized different goals. Some legislators stressed reduced costs, others emphasized public safety, and still others were mainly concerned with diverting offenders from prison. Some implementors stressed the need for control and discipline for certain "dysfunctional" individuals, whereas others focused on rehabilitation and helping offenders become reintegrated into society. Thus, there was no common ground for enabling "key policymakers, managers, and staff" to come to an agreement about which goals should have priority or about what might constitute program improvement.

SOURCE: Dennis J. Palumbo and Michael A. Hallett, "Conflict Versus Consensus Models in Policy Evaluation and Implementation," *Evaluation and Program Planning*, 1993, 16(1):11-23.

---

ing perspectives, however, it is not inappropriate for an evaluation sponsor to seek information relevant to its perspective or the evaluator to conduct such an evaluation even if some stakeholder views are given little or no influence.

Suppose, for instance, that the funding sponsors for a program to provide job training to the hard-core unemployed have concerns about whether a program is "creaming" the cases that are easy to work with, providing services that are more weighted toward vocational counseling than job skill training, and are inefficiently organized. They might quite appropriately commission an evaluation to examine these questions. Program managers and their advocates, on the other hand, may have a sharply conflicting perspective that justifies their selection of clients, training program, and management practices. A conscientious evaluator will listen to the managers' perspective and

encourage their input so that the evaluation design can be as sensitive as possible to the realities of the program and the legitimate concerns of management about misrepresentation of what they are doing and why. But the evaluation design should, nonetheless, be developed primarily from the perspective of the evaluation sponsors and the issues that concern them. The evaluator's primary responsibilities are simply to be clear about the perspective the evaluation takes, so there is no misunderstanding, and to treat the program personnel fairly and honestly.

Another approach to situations of stakeholder conflict is for the evaluator to attempt to design an evaluation that facilitates better understanding among the conflicting parties about the aspects of the program at issue. This might be done, for instance, by efforts to clarify the different concerns, assumptions, and perspectives of the parties; some portion of such conflicts often involves matters that the evaluator can examine and report on in ways that inform all parties. For instance, parents of special education children may believe that their children are stigmatized and discriminated against when mainstreamed in regular classrooms. Teachers may feel equally strongly that this is not true. A careful observational study of the interaction of regular and special education children conducted by the evaluator may reveal that there is a problem, but that it occurs outside the classroom on the playground and during other informal interactions among the children.

Where stakeholder conflict is deep and hostile, it may be based on such profound differences in political values or ideology that no matter how comprehensive and ecumenical, an evaluation cannot conjoin them. One school of thought in the evaluation field holds that all program situations are of this sort and that it is the central feature to which the evaluator must attend. In this view, the social problems that programs address, the programs themselves, and the meaning and importance of those programs are all social constructions that will inevitably differ for different individuals and groups. Thus, rather than focus on program objectives, decisions, outcomes, and the like, evaluators are advised to engage directly the diverse claims, concerns, issues, and values put forth by the various stakeholders.

Guba and Lincoln (1989), the leading proponents of this particular construction of the evaluation enterprise, have argued that the proper role of the evaluator is to facilitate interpretive dialogue among the program stakeholders. Correspondingly, the primary purpose of the evaluation is to facilitate a negotiation among the stakeholders from which a more shared construction of the value and social significance of the program can emerge that still respects the pluralism of ideologies and concerns represented by the different stakeholders. Additional discussions of this perspective can be found in Guba and Lincoln (1987, 1989, 1994). It may have particular appeal for the evaluator working in contexts where the evaluation is highly politicized or stakeholder values and views about the program are strongly divergent.

Finally, the evaluator must realize that despite best efforts to communicate effectively and develop an appropriate, responsive evaluation plan, program stakeholders owe primary allegiance to their own positions and political alignments. This means that sponsors of evaluation and other stakeholders may turn on the evaluator and harshly criticize the evaluation if the results contradict the policies and perspectives they advocate. Thus, even those evaluators who do a superb job of working with stakeholders and incorporating their views and concerns in the evaluation plan should not expect to be acclaimed as heroes when the results are in. The multiplicity of stakeholder perspectives makes it likely that no matter how the results come out, someone will be unhappy. Evaluators work in a political environment, and it is the nature of such environments that stakeholders will often react to evidence contrary to their interests with a vigorous attempt to discredit it and those who produced it. It may matter little that everyone agreed in advance on the evaluation questions and the plan for answering them or that each stakeholder group understood that honest results might not favor its position. Nonetheless, it is highly advisable for the evaluator to give early attention to the identification of stakeholders, working out a strategy for minimizing discord in the evaluation due to their different perspectives, and conditioning their expectations for the nature and significance of the evaluation results.

The Conceptual and Organizational
Structure of the Program

It is a simple truism that if authoritative stakeholders do not have a clear idea about what a program is supposed to be doing, it will be difficult to evaluate how well it is doing it. One factor that shapes the evaluation design, therefore, is the nature of the program conceptualization, that is, the distinctness and explicitness of its plan of operation, the logic that connects its activities to the intended outcomes, and the rationale provided for why it does what it does. This conceptual structure or *program theory* can itself be a focus of evaluation.

If there is significant uncertainty about whether the program conceptualization is appropriate for the social problem the program addresses, it may make little sense for the evaluation design to focus on how well those concepts are implemented. In such cases, the evaluation activities may be more usefully devoted to assessing and better developing the program plan.

In the planning stages of a new program, establishing the program design is a major activity and its nature and details are usually easily identified and articulated. The participation of an evaluator, however, often helps sharpen and shape the conceptualization to make it both more explicit and more useful for identifying key issues of program performance. After the planning stage, especially for well-established programs, program personnel or sponsors generally find little need or opportunity for identifying and reviewing basic assumptions and expectations in any systematic manner. Everyday practice and routine operating procedures tend to dominate, and personnel may find it difficult to articulate the underlying program rationale or agree on any single version of it. For instance, the personnel in a counseling agency under contract to the school district to work with children who are having academic problems may be quite articulate in describing their counseling theories, goals for clients, and therapeutic techniques. But they may have difficulty expressing and agreeing on a view of how their focus on improving family communication is supposed to translate into better grades. However, the evaluator needs some understanding of their assumptions on this matter to plan any assessment of the program's overt performance or outcomes. Correspondingly, the more explicit and cogent the program conceptualization, the less specific assessment it may require in the evaluation plan and the easier it will be to identify the program functions and effects on which the evaluation should focus.

At a more concrete level, the organizational structure of the program must also be taken into consideration when planning an evaluation. Such program characteristics as multiple services or target populations, distributed service sites or facilities, or extensive programmatic collaboration with other organizational entities have powerful implications for the nature and range of evaluation questions to be covered, data collection procedures, resources required for the evaluation, and stakeholder groups to involve. Organizational structures that are larger, more complex, more decentralized, and more geographically dispersed will present greater practical difficulties than their simpler counterparts. In such cases, a team of evaluators is often needed, with resources and time proportionate to the size and complexity of the program. The challenges of evaluation for complex, multisite programs are sufficiently daunting that planning and conducting

---

EXHIBIT 2-G Multisite Evaluations in Criminal Justice: Structural Obstacles to Success

Besides the usual methodological considerations involved in conducting credible evaluations, the structural features of criminal justice settings impose social, political, and organizational constraints that make multisite evaluations difficult and risky. To begin, the system is extremely decentralized. Police departments, for example, can operate within the province of municipalities, counties, campuses, public housing, mass transit, and the states. The criminal justice system is also highly fragmented. Cities administer police departments and jails; counties administer sheriffs' and prosecutors' offices, jails, and probation agencies; state governments run the prisons. Agencies are embedded in disparate political settings, each with its own priorities for taxing and spending. In addition, criminal justice agencies foster a subculture of secrecy concerning their work that has serious consequences for evaluators, who are readily seen as "snoops" for management, the courts,

or individuals with political agendas. Line staff easily adopt an "us against them" mentality toward outside evaluators. Also, criminal justice agencies generally exist in highly charged political environments. They are the most visible components of local government, as well as the most expensive, and their actions are frequently monitored by the media, who historically have assumed a watchdog or adversarial posture toward the system. Finally, the criminal justice system operates within a context of individual rights—legal constraint in procedural issues, an unwillingness to risk injustice in individual cases, and a stated (though not actually delivered) commitment to providing individualized treatment. This translates, for example, into a general aversion to the concept of random or unbiased assignment, the hallmark of the best designs for yielding interpretable information about program effects.

SOURCE: Adapted from Wesley G. Skogan and Arthur J. Lurigio, *Multisite Evaluations in Criminal Justice Settings: Structural Obstacles to Success,* New Directions for Evaluation, no. 50 (San Francisco: Jossey-Bass, summer 1991), pp. 83-96.

---

them are distinct topics of discussion in the evaluation literature (see Exhibit 2-G; Turpin and Sinacore, 1991).

Equally important is the nature and structure of the particular intervention or service the program provides. The easiest interventions to evaluate are those that are discrete, one-shot events (e.g., serving meals to homeless persons) expected to have relatively immediate observable effects (they are not hungry). The organizational activities and delivery systems for such

interventions are usually relatively straightforward (soup kitchen), the service itself is uncomplicated (hand out meals), and the outcomes are direct (people eat). These features greatly simplify the evaluation questions likely to be raised, the data collection required to address them, and the interpretation of the findings.

The most difficult interventions to evaluate are those that are diffuse in nature (community organizing), extend over long time periods (an elementary school math curriculum), vary widely across applications (eclectic psychotherapy), or have expected outcomes that are long term (preschool compensatory education) or indistinct (improved quality of life). For interventions of this sort, many evaluation questions dealing with program process and outcome can arise because of the differentiated nature of the services and their potential effects. Furthermore, the evaluator may have difficulty developing measures that cleanly capture critical aspects of program implementation and outcome when they are complex or diffuse. Actual data collection, too, may be challenging if it must take place over extended time periods or involve many different variables and observations. All these factors have implications for the particulars of the evaluation plan and, especially, for the effort and resources that will be required to complete the plan.

The Resources Available for the Evaluation

It requires resources to conduct a program evaluation. Some number of person-hours devoted to the evaluation activities and materials, equipment, and facilities to support data collection, analysis, and reporting must be available whether drawn from the existing resources of the program or evaluation sponsor or separately funded. An important aspect of planning an evaluation, therefore, is to break down the tasks and timelines so that a detailed estimate can be made of the personnel, materials, and expenses associated with completion of the steps essential to the plan. The sum total of the resources required must then, of course, fit within what is available or some changes in either the plan or the resources must be made. Useful advice on the practicalities of resource

planning, budgeting, and determining timelines can be found in Hedrick, Bickman, and Rog (1992), Card, Greeno, and Peterson (1992), and Fink (1995, chap. 9).

Although the available funding is, of course, one of the critical resource issues around which the evaluation must be planned, it is important to recognize that the dollar amount of that funding is not the only resource that will concern the evaluator. Evaluation is a specialized form of inquiry that takes place largely within the operating environment of the program being evaluated. This means, for instance, that pertinent technical expertise must be available if the evaluation is to be done well. In a large evaluation project, a number of proficient evaluators, data collectors, data managers, analysts, and assistants may be required to do a quality job. Even with generous funding, it will not always be easy to obtain the services of sufficient persons with the requisite expertise. This is why large, complex evaluation projects are often done through contracts with research firms with appropriate personnel on hand.

Another critical resource for an evaluation is support from program management, staff, and other closely related stakeholders. For instance, the degree of cooperation from program personnel on certain aspects of data collection such as opportunity to observe key program activities can have considerable influence on how much an evaluation can accomplish. Although these factors cannot be easily represented as dollar values, they are valuable resources for an evaluation. Barriers to access and lack of cooperation from the program, or worse, active resistance, are very expensive to the evaluation effort. It can take a considerable amount of time and effort to overcome these obstacles sufficiently to complete the evaluation, not to mention the associated stress for all concerned. In the most severe cases, such resistance may compromise the scope or validity of the evaluation or even make it impossible to complete.

An especially important interaction with the program involves access to and use of program records, documents, and other such internal data sources. It is a rare evaluation design that does not require at least some information from program records and many are based heavily on those records. Such records may be necessary to identify the number and characteristics of clients served, the type and amount of services they received, and the cost of providing those services. The scope, completeness, and quality of program records, as well as access to those records, thus are frequently major resource issues for an evaluation. Information that can be confidently obtained from program records need not be sought in a separate, and almost certainly more expensive, data collection administered by the evaluator. In some cases, program personnel may be provided to compile such data with, of course, appropriate monitoring from the evaluator to ensure their integrity. Indeed, evaluations conducted by evaluators internal to an organization, and therefore already on the payroll, that rely primarily on program records may be undertaken with very little direct funding. Evaluation sponsors and program managers are often quite unaware of what will be required of them in the course of an evaluation. They may, for instance, be surprised by an evaluator's request to have "hands on" access to records or to have program staff undertake activities in support of the evaluation.

Program records vary in how easy it is to use them. Records kept in writing are often difficult to use without considerable amounts of processing. In contrast, a management information system (MIS) consisting of records kept in machine-readable databases is usually easier to process. Increasingly, agency records are kept on computers, with duplicate copies obtainable for analysis. Of course, machine databases may contain missing information that reduces their utility, but in most cases, MIS data are valuable in evaluations.

The crucial point here is that the evaluator must view cooperation from program personnel, access to program materials, and the nature, quality, and availability of data from program records as major resource issues when planning an evaluation. The potential for misunderstanding and resistance can be lowered considerably if early discussions with evaluation sponsors, program personnel, and other relevant stakeholders spell out the resources and support needed for the various aspects of the evaluation. It follows that an important step in the planning process is to canvass such resources as thoroughly as possible so that realistic assumptions can be made about them in the evaluation design (Hatry, 1994). As early as possible during planning, therefore, the evaluator should meet with a range of program personnel and discuss their role in the evaluation and issues of access to staff, records, clients, and other pertinent information sources. It is also wise to determine what program records are kept, where and how they are kept, and what access will be permitted. It is advisable to actually inspect a sample of actual program records both to try out the procedures for accessing and working with them and to determine their completeness and quality. Because of the heavy workload demands often put on program personnel, record keeping is not always a high priority. A program may, therefore, have a very complete set of forms and procedures, but examining their files will reveal that they are used inconsistently or, perhaps, hardly at all.

Alongside adequate funding and cooperation from program personnel, experienced evaluators know that one of the most precious resources is time. The period of time allotted for completion of the evaluation and the flexibility of those time parameters are essential considerations in evaluation planning but are rarely determined by the evaluator's preferences. The decisions about the program that the evaluation is expected to inform follow the scheduling imperatives of the policy process. Evaluation results often have to be in the hands of certain decisionmakers by a certain date to have any chance of playing a role in a decision; after that they may be relatively useless. Such constraints often set very tight timelines for conducting an evaluation. Further complicating the situation is a pervasive underestimation among evaluation sponsors and decisionmakers of how long it takes to complete an evaluation. It is not uncommon for evaluation sponsors to request an evaluation that encompasses an imposing range of issues and requires considerable effort and then expect results in a matter of a few months.

The trade-offs here are quite significant. An evaluation can have breadth, depth, and rigor but will require proportionate funding and time. Or it can be cheap and quick but will, of necessity, either deal with a very narrow issue or be relatively superficial (or both). All but the most sophisticated evaluation sponsors usually want evaluations that have breadth, depth, and rigor *and* are cheap and quick. The result is all too often both overburdened evaluators working frantically against deadlines with inadequate resources and frustrated evaluation sponsors perturbed about shortfalls and delays in receiving the product they have paid for. An especially direct relationship exists between the time and technical expertise available for the evaluation and the methods and procedures that can be realistically planned. With few exceptions, the higher the scientific standard to be met by the evaluation findings, the greater the time, expertise, effort, and program cooperation that is required. Evaluations to which very limited resources are allocated of necessity must either focus on a circumscribed issue or rely on relatively informal procedures for obtaining pertinent information.

It takes careful planning to get the scope of work for the evaluation in balance with the funding, program cooperation, time, and other essential resources allocated to the project. Evaluation sponsors who insist on more work than available resources adequately support, or evaluators who overpromise what they can accomplish with those resources, are creating a situation that will likely result in shoddy work, unfulfilled promises, or both. It is generally better for an evaluation to answer a limited number of important questions well than a larger number poorly. Because evaluation sponsors and other stakeholders often do not have realistic notions of the amount of effort and expertise required to conduct quality evaluation, it is very easy for misunderstandings and conflicts to develop. The best way to prevent this is to negotiate very explicitly with the evaluation sponsor about the resources to be made available to the evaluation and the trade-offs associated with the inevitable constraints on resources.

THE NATURE OF THE EVALUATOR-STAKEHOLDER RELATIONSHIP

One of the matters requiring early attention in the planning of an evaluation is the nature of the relationship between the evaluator and the primary stakeholders. Every program is necessarily a social structure in which various individuals and groups engage in the roles and activities that constitute the program: Program managers administer, staff provide service, participants receive service, and so forth. In addition, every program is a nexus in a set of political and social relationships among those with an association or interest in the program, such as relevant policymakers, competing programs, and advocacy groups. These parties are typically involved in, affected by, or interested in the evaluation, and interaction with them must be anticipated as part of the evaluation. Who are the parties typically involved in, or affected by, evaluations? Listed below are some of the stakeholder groups that often either participate directly or become interested in the evaluation process and its results:

- *Policymakers and decisionmakers:* Persons responsible for deciding whether the program is to be started, continued, discontinued, expanded, restructured, or curtailed.

- *Program sponsors:* Organizations that initiate and fund the program. They may also overlap with policymakers and decisionmakers.

- *Evaluation sponsors:* Organizations that initiate and fund the evaluation (sometimes the evaluation sponsors and the program sponsors are the same).

- *Target participants:* Persons, households, or other units who receive the intervention or services being evaluated.

- *Program managers:* The personnel responsible for overseeing and administering the intervention program.

- *Program staff:* Personnel responsible for delivering the program services or in supporting roles.

- *Program competitors:* Organizations or groups who compete with the program for available resources. For instance, an educational program providing alternative schools will attract the attention of the public schools because they see the new schools as competitors.

- *Contextual stakeholders:* Organizations, groups, individuals, and other social units in the immediate environment of a program with interests in what the program is doing or what happens to it (e.g., other agencies or programs, public officials, or citizens' groups in the jurisdiction in which the program operates).

- *Evaluation and research community:* Evaluation professionals who read evaluations and pass judgment on their technical quality and credibility and academic and other researchers who work in areas related to a program.

Although other parties might be involved in the "politics of evaluation," this list represents the stakeholders who most often pay attention to an evaluation and with whom the evaluator may interact while the evaluation is being conducted or when its findings are reported. We emphasize *may:* these stakeholders are *potential* participants in one way or another in the evaluation process or *potential* audiences for the evaluation. In any given case, all these groups or only a few may be involved. But whatever the assortment of individuals and groups with significant interests in the evaluation, the evaluator must plan to interact with them in some fashion and be aware of their concerns. Consideration of the appropriate form of interaction for at least the major stakeholders thus should be part of evaluation planning (see Exhibit 2-H for one point of view on involving stakeholders).

✕ **EXHIBIT 2-H**   Stakeholder Involvement in Evaluation: Suggestions for Practice

Based on experience working with school district staff, one evaluator offers the following advice for bolstering evaluation use through stakeholder involvement:

- *Identify stakeholders:* At the outset, define the specific stakeholders who will be involved with emphasis on those closest to the program and who hold high stakes in it.

- *Involve stakeholders early:* Engage stakeholders in the evaluation process as soon as they have been identified because many critical decisions that affect the evaluation occur early in the process.

- *Involve stakeholders continuously:* The input of key stakeholders should be part of virtu-

ally all phases of the evaluation; if possible, schedule regular group meetings.

- *Involve stakeholders actively:* The essential element of stakeholder involvement is that it be active; stakeholders should be asked to address design issues, help draft survey questions, provide input into the final report, and deliberate about all important aspects of the project.

- *Establish a structure:* Develop and use a conceptual framework based in content familiar to stakeholders that can help keep dialogue focused. This framework should highlight key issues within the local setting as topics for discussion so that stakeholders can share concerns and ideas, identify information needs, and interpret evaluation results.

SOURCE: Adapted from Robert A. Reineke, "Stakeholder Involvement in Evaluation: Suggestions for Practice," *Evaluation Practice,* 1991, 12(1):39-44.

The process of considering the relationships with stakeholders necessarily starts with the evaluation sponsor. The sponsor is the agent who initiates the evaluation, usually provides the funding, and makes the decisions about how and when it will be done and who should do it. Various relationships with the evaluation sponsor are possible, and their particular form will largely depend on the sponsor's preferences and whatever negotiation takes place with the evaluator. A common situation is one in which the sponsor expects the evaluator to function as an independent professional practitioner who will receive guidance from the sponsor, especially at the beginning,

but otherwise take full responsibility for planning, conducting, and reporting the evaluation. For instance, government agencies and other program funders often commission evaluations by publishing a request for proposals (RFP) or request for applications (RFA) to which evaluators respond with statements of their capability, proposed design, budget, and time line, as requested. The evaluation sponsor then selects an evaluator from among those responding and establishes a contractual arrangement for the agreed-on work.

Other situations are configured so that the evaluator works more collaboratively with the evaluation sponsors. For instance, the sponsors may want to be involved in an ongoing way with the planning, implementation, and analysis of results, either to react step by step as the evaluator develops the project or to actually participate with the evaluator in each step. Variations on this form of relationship are typical for internal evaluators who are part of the organization whose program is being evaluated. In such cases, the evaluator generally works closely with management in planning and conducting the evaluation, whether management of the evaluation unit, the program being evaluated, someone higher up in the organization, or some combination. Or an evaluator from outside the organization may be retained as an evaluation consultant to assist the evaluation sponsors in planning and conducting the evaluation but not take the primary role in doing that work.

In some instances, the evaluation sponsor will ask that the evaluator work collaboratively but stipulate that the collaboration be with a stakeholder group other than the evaluation sponsors themselves. For instance, private foundations that fund social programs often want an evaluation to be developed in close interaction with the local stakeholders of the program. An especially interesting variant of this approach is when the evaluation sponsor requires that the evaluation be a collaborative venture in which the recipients of program services take the primary role in planning, setting priorities, collecting information, and interpreting the results. Part of the philosophy of the W. K. Kellogg Foundation, for instance, is to avoid being prescriptive in its approach to evaluation of the programs it funds. In the words of the foundation's director of evaluation, "We believe that people in the communities and institutions we serve are in the best position to make decisions, to implement the programs that are the best suited for their

circumstances at a given time, and to evaluate the lessons learned" (Millett, 1996, p. 68).

The evaluator's relationship to the evaluation sponsor or another stakeholder designated by the evaluation sponsor is so central to the evaluation context and planning process that a somewhat specialized, and not altogether systematic, vocabulary has arisen in the evaluation profession to describe various circumstances. Some of the major forms of evaluator-stakeholder relationships recognized in this vocabulary are as follows:

Independent evaluation. The evaluator takes the primary responsibility for developing the evaluation plan, conducting the evaluation, and disseminating the results. The evaluator may initiate and direct the evaluation quite autonomously, as when a social scientist undertakes an evaluation of an interesting program for purposes of knowledge generation under the researcher's own sponsorship or with research funding that leaves the particulars to the researcher's discretion. More often, the independent evaluator is commissioned by a sponsoring agency that stipulates the purposes and nature of the evaluation but leaves it to the evaluator to do the detailed planning and conduct the evaluation. In such cases, however, the evaluator generally confers with a range of stakeholders to give them some influence in shaping the evaluation.

Participatory or collaborative evaluation. This form of evaluation is organized as a team project with the evaluator and representatives of one or more stakeholder groups constituting the team (Greene, 1988; Mark and Shotland, 1985). The participating stakeholders are directly involved in planning, conducting, and analyzing the evaluation in collaboration with the evaluator whose function might range from team leader or consultant to that of a resource person to be called on only as needed. One particularly well-known form of participatory evaluation is Patton's (1986, 1997) "utilization-focused evaluation." Patton's approach emphasizes close collaboration with those specific individuals who will use the evaluation findings to ensure that the evaluation is responsive to their needs and produces information that they can and will actually use.

Empowerment evaluation. Various proponents have articulated a concept of evaluator-stakeholder interaction that emphasizes the initiative, advocacy, and self-determination of the stakeholder group (Fetterman, Kaftarian, and Wandersman, 1996). In this form of evaluation, the evaluator-stakeholder relationship is participatory and collaborative, as described above. In addition, however, the evaluator's role includes consultation and facilitation directed toward development of the capabilities of the participating stakeholders to conduct evaluation on their own, to use it effectively for advocacy and change, and to experience some sense of control over a program that affects their lives. The evaluation process, therefore, is not only directed at producing informative and useful findings but also at enhancing the self-development and political influence of the participants. As these themes imply, empowerment evaluation most appropriately involves those stakeholders who otherwise have little power in the program context, often the program recipients or intended beneficiaries.

A significant contribution of the participatory and empowerment perspectives is to call into question what might otherwise be a routine presumption that an independent evaluation is appropriate. There are, of course, many situations in which the evaluation sponsor explicitly wants an independent evaluation that will pursue that sponsor's concerns under expert guidance from a professional evaluator. This process assures that the perspective of the evaluation sponsor will have priority and, given a competent evaluator, that the results will have a certain credibility stemming from the evaluator's expertise and a decision-making process that filters the influence of the self-interests of the stakeholders.

There are other situations, however, where the advantages of independent evaluation are not relevant or are outweighed by the benefits of a more participatory process. Direct participation by the evaluation sponsors or one or more other stakeholder groups can ensure that the evaluation results will address their concerns and be useful and usable for them. Moreover, it can create a sense of ownership in the evaluation that amplifies the significance of its findings and reduces its potential to engender resistance. And as the empowerment theorists point out, when stakeholder groups with little formal power are able to conduct and use an evaluation, it can alter the balance of power in a program context by enhancing their influence and sense of efficacy. It is thus appropriate for the evaluation sponsors and the evaluator to give explicit consideration to the question of how the evaluation responsibilities are to be assigned and the arrangements for organizing the evaluator-stakeholder interactions. Where such deliberation has not already taken place or an arrangement stipulated, it may be constructive for the evaluator to raise the issue and suggest that it be a matter of discussion during the earliest phase of evaluation planning. Exhibit 2-I illustrates what might be in store for stakeholders who opt to participate in a collaborative evaluation.

Whether the evaluation is planned and conducted by an independent evaluator or by a team of stakeholders has considerable effect on

☒ EXHIBIT 2-I   Blueprint for a Participatory Evaluation Process

Two Canadian evaluators who were involved in a participatory evaluation of programs sponsored by a community economic development organization offered the following "blueprint" for the evaluation process they used:

Initiation phase:

- Presentation to the board of administrators for their approval.

- Identification of interested stakeholders.

Selecting the topics and questions to be addressed:

- Interested stakeholders meet several times in small groups, each centering on one of the services offered by the organization, to brainstorm ideas for questions; guidelines in Patton (1986) are followed to explain tasks such as focusing evaluation questions.

- Questions are rephrased clearly, regrouped for each program, and collated into one document.

- A general meeting of stakeholders is called to prioritize questions according to their potential utility and to plan how the evaluation results will be utilized once they are available.

Instrument design and data collection:

- Small groups are reconvened to decide on the final wording and format of questions retained at the general meeting.

- Data are collected by the program evaluator and other interested participants who are given appropriate training.

Data analysis and reporting:

- Data analysis proceeds in small groups, with the evaluator participating in all groups.

- Individual reports are drafted for each program; the evaluator is responsible for writing reports in consultation with stakeholders.

Strategic planning:

- A series of strategic planning meetings is convened to study the evaluation reports and decide on follow-up steps.

- The evaluation questions are revised for future use on an ongoing basis; program workers are expected to coordinate future evaluation efforts.

SOURCE: Adapted from Danielle Papineau and Margaret C. Kiely, "Participatory Evaluation in a Community Organization: Fostering Stakeholder Empowerment and Utilization," *Evaluation and Program Planning*, 1996, 19(1):79-93.

the nature of the decision making, the evaluator's role, and, most likely, the focus and character of the evaluation. The resulting project, nonetheless, should represent an applica-

tion of recognizable evaluation concepts and methods to a particular program. We thus distinguish the process of working with stakeholders, whether as an independent evaluator, collaborator, facilitator, or resource person, from the evaluation plan that results from that process. That plan may be developed and largely settled early in the process or may emerge piecemeal as the process develops and evolves, but the features of a good plan for the evaluation context and the program at issue can be considered separate from the process through which the planning and implementation is done. In the remainder of this chapter, therefore, we will discuss general planning issues and, when reference is made to the evaluator's role, assume that can mean either an independent evaluator or a collaborative team.

First, however, one other aspect of evaluator-stakeholder interaction must be addressed: the communication and dissemination of the evaluation findings. Even in the most participatory evaluation, there will be stakeholders who have not been directly involved who will want to know the results. For an independent evaluation, of course, the evaluation sponsor may be among those stakeholders. For evaluation to be useful, a necessary step is that its findings be communicated to those with interest in the program, especially to those with responsibility for making important decisions about the program. It is difficult to communicate evaluation findings in fine detail, and additionally, there is often inherent uncertainty about what information will be of most interest to stakeholders at the time the evaluation is completed. It is usually best, therefore, to discuss this issue with the major stakeholders and develop an organized communication and dissemination plan from the beginning.

As a general framework, the communication and dissemination plan should indicate what information from the evaluation is to be communicated to which stakeholders in what form and at which time. Different information may be relevant for different stakeholder groups, depending on their interest in the program and their decision-making roles. Moreover, that information might be communicated as soon as available or later when all phases of the evaluation are complete, and it might be communicated in writing or verbally and formally or informally. Typically, the evaluator should consider multiple communication events ranging from informal oral briefings to formal written reports. The objective of the communication and dissemination plan should be to report the findings of most interest to each stakeholder as soon as possible and proper and in forms that are easy to understand and use (see Exhibit 2-J).

Evaluation conducted for purposes of program improvement, for instance, might include regular briefings for the evaluation sponsor and program managers conducted as soon as each distinct data collection reaches a point where tentative analysis and interpretation are possible. These might be relatively informal briefings in which the evaluator presents a verbal summary with supporting handouts and encourages discussion. Other stakeholders might receive similar interim briefings in written or verbal format at less frequent intervals. At the conclusion of the evaluation, a written report might be prepared for the record and for the more peripheral stakeholders or might not if no use for it was apparent. Evaluation conducted for purposes of accountability, on the other hand, might properly involve a more formal communication and dissemination process throughout. Information might be released only after it was thoroughly verified and analyzed and primarily in carefully worded written form with verbal briefings used only as a supplement. This higher level of caution and formality would be justified if the stakes were high or the evaluation results were expected to

⬚ EXHIBIT 2-J   Successful Communication With Stakeholders

Torres, Preskill, and Piontek (1996) surveyed and interviewed members of the American Evaluation Association about their experiences communicating with stakeholders and reporting evaluation findings. The respondents identified the following elements of effective communication:

- Ongoing, collaborative communication processes were the most successful. Periodic meetings and informal conversations can be used to maintain close contact throughout the evaluation, and interim memos and draft reports can be used to convey findings as they develop.

- It is important to use varied formats for communication. These might include short reports and summaries, verbal presentations, and opportunities for informal interaction.

- The content of the communication should be tailored to the audience and be easy for them to understand. Communication should use clear language, graphs and charts, and vivid, concrete illustrations. It should present contextual information about the program and the evaluation, cover both positive and negative findings, and be specific about recommendations.

SOURCE: Adapted from Rosalie T. Torres, Hallie S. Preskill, and Mary E. Piontek, *Evaluation Strategies for Communicating and Reporting: Enhancing Learning in Organizations* (Thousand Oaks, CA: Sage, 1996), pp. 4-6.

---

be especially controversial. It should be noted that this approach does not necessarily mean being highly secretive about the evaluation findings until the final report is delivered. The process of verifying and analyzing the information in such formal circumstances might quite appropriately include soliciting the reactions of potential critics and other important stakeholders to the initial summaries of the major findings and incorporating their feedback in the final report.

Whatever the schedule, form, and audiences for evaluation findings, it is wise to include some consideration of the communication media and materials in the planning. Evaluation findings, like the programs they describe, are rarely simple and easily understood. Communication will often be most effective if it makes good use of graphical and

pictorial displays, uses engaging audiovisual materials, and personalizes portions of the story as much as possible through well-chosen anecdotes and case examples. To have such material available when needed, the evaluator must plan for its development during the course of the evaluation. For instance, it may be appropriate to make audio or video recordings of certain events or situations, systematically collect anecdotes and case examples from which to select representative instances, and make other such preparations for effective communication. Useful advice for planning effective communication and dissemination activities is found in Torres, Preskill, and Piontek (1996; also see Exhibit 2-J).

For many evaluations, it is also appropriate to allow stakeholders access to the database on which the evaluation was based, at the same time safeguarding the privacy of sources from whom the data were obtained. Making a dataset public signals to stakeholders that the evaluators have nothing to hide and allows them to try alternative modes of analysis to verify that the evaluator's findings were properly drawn. We believe that making data publicly available should be a routine procedure in evaluations of large-scale or very important programs.

EVALUATION QUESTIONS AND EVALUATION METHODS

A program evaluation is essentially an information-gathering and -interpreting endeavor that attempts to answer a specified set of questions about a program's performance and effectiveness. An important step in designing an evaluation, therefore, is determining the questions the evaluation must answer. This is sometimes done in a very perfunctory manner, but we advocate that it be given studious and detailed attention. A carefully constructed set of evaluation questions gives structure to the evaluation, leads to appropriate and thoughtful planning, and serves as a basis for informative discussions about who is interested in the answers and how they will be used. Indeed, constructing such questions and planning how to answer them is the primary way in which an evaluation is tailored to the unique circumstances associated with each program that comes under scrutiny.

Generally, the evaluation sponsor puts forward some initial evaluation questions when proposing or commissioning an evaluation or, in the case of a competition to select an evaluator, as part of the RFP or RFA that goes out to prospective evaluators. Those initial declarations are the obvious starting point for defining the questions around which the evaluation will be designed but usually should not be taken as final for purposes of evaluation planning. Often the questions presented at this stage are too general or abstract to function well as a basis for evaluation planning. Or the questions, as worded, may be beyond the capability of the evaluator to answer within the operative constraints on time, resources, available information, and organizational or political arrangements.

Any initial description of what the evaluation sponsors have in mind, therefore, must usually be further explored, refined, and augmented to obtain a set of meaningful, appropriate evaluation questions around which the evaluation can actually be planned. In addition, it is usually useful for the evaluator to analyze the program independently and derive evaluation questions that may not otherwise arise so that they too can be considered during the planning process. However accomplished, a thorough effort must be made to generate a set of candidate evaluation questions that covers all the issues of potential relevance to the concerns of the evaluation sponsor, the decisionmakers who will use the findings, and other significant stakeholders. This approach allows the evaluation design to be responsive to the needs of decisionmakers and offers the potential to involve stakeholders as collaborators in the evaluation process. It is relatively easy to generate questions, however, so the initial set resulting from a diligent effort will likely be too large for the evaluation to answer them all. The evaluator, evaluation sponsor, and other key stakeholders must therefore impose priorities to select a workable number dealing with the most important issues.

Because the evaluation questions to be addressed are so pivotal to evaluation planning,

Chapter 3 is devoted entirely to discussing the form they should take, how they are generated, and how they are winnowed, organized, and integrated to provide the structure for the evaluation design. For present purposes, we will assume that an appropriate set of evaluation questions has been identified and consider some of the broader implications of their character for tailoring and planning the evaluation.

In particular, the evaluation questions to be answered for a given program will, of necessity, be very specific to the idiosyncratic nature of that program. They will ask such things as "How many of the households that fall below the federal poverty line in the Fairview School District need afterschool care for school-aged children between 3 and 7 p.m. on weekdays?" "What proportion of the juveniles on probation have at least three contacts with their probation officer per month for the full six-month probationary period?" and "What nutritional benefits does the meals-on-wheels program at the senior citizens' center have for the housebound frail elderly in its catchment area?" Beyond the specifics, however, evaluation questions fall into recognizable types according to the program issues they address. Five such types are readily distinguished:

- Questions about the need for program services
- Questions about program conceptualization or design
- Questions about program operations and service delivery
- Questions about program outcomes
- Questions about program cost and efficiency

Evaluators have developed relatively distinct conceptual frameworks and associated methods to address each type of evaluation question. Evaluators use these schemes to organize their thinking about how to approach different program evaluation situations. For planning purposes, an evaluator will typically select the general evaluation approach that corresponds to the types of questions to be answered in an evaluation, then tailor the particulars to the specifics of the questions and the program situation. To complete our discussion of tailoring evaluations, therefore, we must introduce the common evaluation approaches or schemes and review the circumstances in which they are most applicable.

The common conceptual and methodological frameworks in evaluation correspond to the types of frequent evaluation questions, as follows:

- *Needs assessment:* answers questions about the social conditions a program is intended to address and the need for the program.

- *Assessment of program theory:* answers questions about program conceptualization and design.

- *Assessment of program process (or process evaluation):* answers questions about program operations, implementation, and service delivery.

- *Impact assessment (impact evaluation or outcome evaluation):* answers questions about program outcomes and impact.

- *Efficiency assessment:* answers questions about program cost and cost-effectiveness.

These forms of evaluation are discussed in detail in later chapters of this volume (Chapters 4-11). Here we will only provide some guidance regarding the circumstances for which each is most appropriate.

Needs Assessment

The primary rationale for initiating or maintaining a social program is a presenting or incipient social problem—by which we mean socially recognized deficiencies in the social conditions—that legitimate social agents endeavor to remedy. The impetus for a new program to increase literacy, for example, is likely to be recognition that a significant number of persons in a given population are deficient in reading skills. Similarly, an ongoing program may be justified by the persistence of a social problem: Driver education in high schools receives public support because of the continuing high rates of automobile accidents among adolescent drivers.

If there is no significant problem or no perceived need for intervention, there is generally no basis for affirming the value of a program that purports to address this nonproblem. One important form of evaluation, therefore, assesses the nature, magnitude, and distribution of a social problem; the extent to which there is a need for intervention to address it; and the implications of these circumstances for the conceptualization and design of the intervention. These diagnostic activities are often referred to as *needs assessment* in the evaluation field but overlap what is called social epidemiology and social indicators research in other fields (McKillip, 1987; Reviere et al., 1996; Soriano, 1995; Witkin and Altschuld, 1995). Needs assessment is often used as a first step in designing and planning a new program or restructuring an established program to provide information about what services are needed and how they might best be delivered to those who need them. Needs assessment is also often important for established, stable programs to examine whether they are responsive

to the actual needs of the target participants and to provide guidance for improvement.

Needs assessments may take the form of finding out the needs of a potential target population as they perceive them. For example, homeless persons may be queried about the kinds of services for which they feel the greatest need (e.g., see Exhibit 2-K). Alternatively, the objective of needs assessment may be to describe conditions in such a way that the services needed to alleviate them can be inferred.

Needs assessments may be conducted through surveys of knowledgeable informants, such as personnel of service agencies or potential service recipients, that focus on perceived problems and needs, services desired, and shortcomings of existing services. They may also analyze demographic and social indicator data from such sources as the U.S. Census or data from local agencies that describe the availability of services and patterns of current use. The resulting descriptions of social problems, service utilization, and perceived needs must then be assessed against some set of social norms or some view of desired conditions held by social agents or those experiencing the problems to evaluate their magnitude, seriousness, and actionable implications. Chapter 4 of this book discusses the various aspects of needs assessment in detail.

Assessment of Program Theory

Given a recognized problem and need for intervention, it does not follow that any program, willy-nilly, will be appropriate for the job. The conceptualization and design of the program must reflect valid assumptions about the nature of the target problem and represent a well-founded and feasible approach to resolving

---

✻ EXHIBIT 2-K   Needs for Help Among Homeless Men and Women

A representative sample of 1,260 homeless men and women were interviewed in New York City's municipal shelters for single adults to determine their perception of their needs. The interview covered 20 items, each indicating need for help in a particular area. Most respondents identified multiple needs, averaging 6.3. The need for help in finding a place to live and having a steady income were the most commonly cited needs overall, closely followed by the need for help in finding a job and improving job skills. Compared to women, men more often reported needs for help with drinking problems, drug problems, learning how to handle money, getting veterans benefits, problems with the police, getting along better with other people, and finding a place to live. Women more frequently reported needs for help with health and medical problems and learning self-protection skills. The evaluators pointed out that for programs to be truly responsive to these multiple needs, they must have the capacity to deliver or broker access to a comprehensive range of services.

SOURCE: Adapted by permission from Daniel B. Herman, Elmer L. Struening, and Susan M. Barrow, "Self-Reported Needs for Help Among Homeless Men and Women," *Evaluation and Program Planning*, 1994, 17(3):249-256. Copyright © 1998, John Wiley & Sons, Inc.

---

it. Put another way, every social program is based on some plan or blueprint that represents the way it is "supposed to work" according to those who understand its history, purposes, and activities the best. This plan is rarely written out in complete detail, and may not be written out at all, but exists nonetheless as a shared conceptualization among the principal stakeholders. Because this program plan consists essentially of a set of assumptions and expectations about how the program should conduct its business and attain its goals, we will refer to it as the program theory (discussed more fully in the next chapter). If this theory is faulty, the intervention will fail no matter how elegantly it is conceived or how well it is implemented (Chen, 1990; Weiss, 1972).

Assessment of the program theory involves, first, representing it in explicit and detailed written or graphical form. Then, various approaches can be used to examine how rea-sonable, feasible, ethical, and otherwise appropriate it is. Assessment of program theory is most essential to programs during their early stages, for example, when they are new or in pilot testing or even earlier when they are in the planning stage. However, it is also applicable to established programs, especially when questions arise about how well matched their services are to the social needs they are attempting to meet. The sponsors of this form of evaluation are generally those attempting to launch a new program, such as the funding agency or administrators, or those seeking assurance that the conceptualization and design of a program are appropriate for its purposes. Exhibit 2-L, for example, describes an examination of the conceptual foundation for family preservation programs, which indicated that they had little prospect for success.

Evaluation of program theory rests on the presumption that the need for the program and

---

✵ EXHIBIT 2-L A Flaw in the Design of Family Preservation Programs

---

As part of an evaluability assessment (see Chapter 5), evaluators working under contract to the U.S. Department of Health and Human Services reviewed the design of family preservation programs (FPPs). FPPs are time-limited, intensive home-based services to families in crisis that are intended to prevent the placement of children in foster care. The evaluators held discussions with the staff of federal and national private sector agencies about the definition of FPPs, reviewed available literature, obtained descriptions of state and local programs, and made site visits to four programs. From this information they developed "models" of how the programs were supposed to operate and then obtained the views of policymakers,

program managers, and operating-level staff on four key dimensions: (a) program goals, (b) aspects of the child welfare system that affect the programs, (c) the target population, and (d) the characteristics that distinguish FPPs from other home-based services. Based on their own analysis and discussions with an expert advisory committee, the evaluators concluded that as currently designed, family preservation programs could not achieve the policymakers' primary goal of preventing placement in foster care. The major flaw found in the program design was the practical difficulty of identifying children at "imminent risk" of placement; this meant that programs could not consistently target families with children truly at risk of placement.

SOURCE: Adapted from Joseph S. Wholey, "Assessing the Feasibility and Likely Usefulness of Evaluation," in *Handbook of Practical Program Evaluation*, ed. J. S. Wholey, H. P. Hatry, and K. E. Newcomer (San Francisco: Jossey-Bass, 1994), pp. 29-31. Wholey's account, in turn, is based on Kaye and Bell (1993).

---

adequate diagnosis of the problem the program is to address has already been established or can confidently be assumed. Also, because analysis of program design requires a close collaboration among the evaluator, program designers and managers, and other key stakeholders, it is most readily accomplished when all parties are willing to be fully engaged in the process and can establish constructive working relationships. Somewhat paradoxically, however, many of the techniques associated with the evaluation of program theory are applicable in situations of stakeholder conflict, for example, disagreement about program goals and objectives, appropriate priorities, and the nature of program activities. Assessment of program theory

involves making that theory explicit so there will be little uncertainty about significant aspects of the program concept and intended implementation. Stakeholder disagreement over such matters raises uncertainty and may also create a politically fluid situation in which fundamental program changes are possible. These conditions are sufficiently similar to those of a new program still under design to permit methods for assessing program theory to be potentially helpful. In this case, however, the context of application may be distinguished more by hostility among stakeholder groups than cooperative working arrangements, posing special challenges (and hazards) to the evaluator.

Assessment of Program Process

Given a plausible theory about how to favorably intervene to ameliorate accurately diagnosed social problems, a program must still be implemented well to have a reasonable prospect of actually affecting the target problem. Many programs are not implemented and executed according to their intended design. A program may simply be poorly managed or be compromised by political interference. Sometimes personnel are not available or facilities are in disrepair; sometimes project staff cannot carry out the program due to lack of motivation or expertise. Often the program design is not well structured, leaving much room for interpretation, or the original program plan may not be transmitted well to staff so that program activities drift over time. Possibly, the intended program participants do not exist in the numbers required, cannot be identified precisely, or are not cooperative. For example, some programs to serve children with congenital heart conditions found it so difficult and costly to locate potential clients that insufficient funds remained for providing the intended treatments.

A central and widely used form of evaluation, therefore, assesses the fidelity and effectiveness of program implementation. Implementation assessment evaluates program process, the activities and operations of the program. For this reason, it is commonly called *process evaluation* or, when it is an ongoing function, *program monitoring*. Process evaluation addresses questions related to how well the program is functioning. It might include assessment of how congruous the services are with the goals of the program, whether services are delivered as intended to appropriate recipients, how well service delivery is organized, the effectiveness of program management, the use of program resources, and other such matters (Exhibit 2-M provides an example).

In a typical process evaluation, criteria are developed for the program functions viewed as critical in two ways. These may be configured in the form of a "blueprint" of the intended program design that depicts the functions, activities, and service transactions that the program is supposed to accomplish in, perhaps, flowchart form (a version of program theory; see Chapter 3). Or the criteria may be stated in the form of specific administrative or service objectives, for example, to enroll 20 new clients each week, to provide a minimum of ten sessions of service to each client within the first three months, to have 90% of the clients receive the full term of service, and to make educational presentations to one community group each week. Such criteria can be developed in various ways: They may simply be stipulated by program administrators, they may be mandated by program funders, they may be derived from studies and reports of other programs or follow the specification of some model program, they may result from a process of reflection and goal setting by program personnel or other stakeholders, or they may be drawn from accepted principles of organizational effectiveness or professional practice.

With the critical program functions and corresponding performance criteria identified, the other component of process evaluation is the definition and operationalization of performance measures that describe program accomplishments in relation to the respective criteria. Thus, data collection procedures might be put in place to determine the number of new patients enrolled each week, the percentage who complete a full term of service, the number of presentations to community groups, and the like. Program performance can then be assessed by comparing what is found on these

---

⚉ EXHIBIT 2-M Failure on the Front Lines: Implementing Welfare Reform

Work Pays is a state-level welfare reform demonstration program in California designed to establish incentives to work and disincentives for staying on the AFDC welfare program. The program administrators recognized that to realize the policymakers' intent, the workers in local welfare offices would have to inform their clients about the new policy and present this information in a positive, individualized way that would reinforce clients' understanding of their obligations and choices about work and welfare. An implementation assessment was therefore conducted in which researchers interviewed welfare workers about the Work Pays program and observed a number of meetings with clients. This information revealed that the type of transaction expected between welfare workers and their clients under the new policy was exceedingly rare. In more than 80% of their interviews with clients, workers did not provide and interpret information about the new policy. Most workers continued their routine patterns of collecting and verifying eligibility information and providing scripted recitations of welfare rules. However, the evaluators also found that the workers had been given only minimal information about the Work Pays program and no additional time or resources for educating their large caseloads about the changes. These findings demonstrated that welfare reform was not fully implemented at the street level in California and revealed some of the reasons why it was not.

SOURCE: Adapted from Marcia K. Meyers, Bonnie Glaser, and Karin MacDonald, "On the Front Lines of Welfare Delivery: Are Workers Implementing Policy Reforms?" *Journal of Policy Analysis and Management,* 1998, 17(1):1-22.

---

measures with the criterion for desired performance on that program function.

Although process evaluation is often done as a one-shot evaluation study, say, for one cohort of program clients, it should be apparent that similar procedures can be used routinely as a management tool. When set up to provide periodic performance data for key program functions on a continuous basis, this form of assessment is generally known as program monitoring or performance monitoring. There are many good reasons for programs to institute monitoring schemes. For instance, monitoring provides a way for program managers to ensure that the day-to-day operations of a program are conducted appropriately and efficiently and thus helps them properly adminis-

ter the program. Managers who develop reputations for wasting funds, using staff resources inappropriately, and being inefficient in other regards frequently jeopardize not only their own positions but the futures of their programs.

Also, program monitoring information systems give program administrators a powerful tool for documenting for program sponsors and stakeholders the operational effectiveness of the organization, justifying the ways staff are deployed, requesting further support, and defending the program's performance compared with its competitors. Routinely collecting and reporting program performance information, therefore, makes the program accountable and provides evidence to funders and sponsors that what was paid for and deemed desirable was actually accomplished.

Process evaluation of some variant is the assessment approach most frequently applied to social programs. It is used both as a freestanding evaluation and in conjunction with impact evaluation as part of a more comprehensive evaluation. As a freestanding evaluation, it yields quality assurance information. That is, it assesses the extent to which a program is implemented as intended and operating up to the standards established for it. When the program model employed is one of established effectiveness, a demonstration that the model is well implemented is presumptive evidence that the expected outcomes are produced as well. When the program is new, a process evaluation provides invaluable feedback to administrators and other stakeholders about the progress that has been made operationalizing the program theory. From a management perspective, process evaluation provides the feedback that allows a program to be managed for high performance (Wholey and Hatry, 1992), and the associated data collection and reporting of key indicators may be institutionalized in the form of an MIS to provide routine, ongoing performance feedback.

In its other common application, process evaluation is an indispensable adjunct to impact evaluation. The information about program outcomes that impact evaluation provides is incomplete and ambiguous without knowledge of the program activities and services that produced those outcomes. When no impact is found, process evaluation has significant diagnostic value by indicating whether this result occurred because of *implementation failure*, that is, the intended services were not provided hence the expected benefits could not have occurred, or *theory failure*, that is, the program was implemented as intended but failed to produce the expected effects. On the other hand, when program effects are found, process evaluation helps confirm that they resulted from program activities, rather than spurious sources, and identify those aspects of service most instrumental to producing the effects so that program managers know where to concentrate their efforts.

As a general evaluation approach, process evaluation is widely applicable to social programs. For stable programs that have established operating procedures, personnel, and facilities, process evaluation may provide summative information relevant to both program accountability and knowledge generation. For new programs or those in flux, process evaluation may constitute a formative evaluation that provides useful feedback for program managers attempting to improve program operations. In either case, however, process evaluation requires a well-defined, consensual program theory that stipulates the "program as intended." If program managers and other pertinent stakeholders cannot delineate the program model that is supposed to be implemented, or cannot agree on the intended clientele, services, and procedures, then there is no defined process for the evaluator to observe and assess. In this case, the evaluator may adopt the techniques for assessing program theory and work with program managers, evaluation sponsors, and other stakeholders to better define the program conceptualization.

Process evaluation and its variants are described in greater depth in Chapter 6 of this volume. It is important to note here, however, that although it is widely used as a freestanding evaluation approach to give evaluation sponsors, program managers, and other stakeholders an assessment of how well the program is implemented, it is not a substitute for impact evaluation. Process evaluation does not address the question of whether a program produces the intended outcomes and benefits for its recipients. Even in cases where the program model is known to be effective in other applications and process evaluation demonstrates that it is well implemented, there remains a possibility that circumstances are sufficiently different in the program at issue to keep it from being effective there.

Impact Assessment

An impact assessment, sometimes called an impact evaluation or an outcome evaluation, gauges the extent to which a program produces the intended improvements in the social conditions it addresses. The evaluation questions around which impact assessment is organized relate to such matters as whether the desired program outcomes were attained, whether the program was effective in producing change in the social conditions targeted, and whether program impact included unintended side effects. These questions assume a set of operationally defined objectives and criteria of success. The objectives may be social-behavioral ones, such as lowering functional illiteracy or nutritional deficiencies among children; they may be community related, such as reducing the frequency of certain crimes; or they may be physical, such as decreasing water pollution or the amount of litter on city streets. Impact assessments are essential when there is an interest in determining if a program is effective in its efforts to ameliorate a target problem, comparing the effectiveness of different programs, or in testing the utility of new efforts to address a particular community problem.

Impact assessment has the basic aim of producing an estimate of the net effects of an intervention—that is, an estimate of the impact of the intervention uncontaminated by the influence of the other processes and events that also affect the conditions the program attempts to change. To conduct an impact assessment, the evaluator needs a plan for collecting data that will permit a persuasive demonstration that observed changes are a function of the intervention and cannot readily be accounted for in other ways. This requires a careful specification of the outcome variables on which program effects may occur, development of measures for those variables, and a research design that not only establishes the status of program recipients on those measures but also estimates what their status would be had they not received the intervention. Much of the complexity of impact assessment is associated with obtaining a valid estimate of the latter status, known as the *counterfactual* because it describes a condition contrary to what actually happened to program recipients. Specific impact assessment designs vary considerably. Sometimes it is possible to use classic experimental designs in which control and experimental groups are constructed by random assignment and receive different interventions. For practical reasons, however, it is often necessary to employ statistical approaches to isolating program effects rather than true experiments. Thus, nonrandomized quasi-experiments and other nonexperimental methods are commonly employed in impact assessments. With proper safeguards and appropriate qualifications, such nonexperimental designs may provide reasonable estimates of effects (Exhibit 2-N describes such a situation).

As mentioned above, impact assessment is often combined with process evaluation so that a linkage can be made between program implementation and the program outcomes observed. When an impact assessment is conducted without any semblance of a process

EXHIBIT 2-N   No Impact on Garbage

Taiwan is a high-density island country with a garbage problem. Garbage accumulation has increased exponentially in recent years, 26 rivers are polluted by garbage, and the number of landfill sites is increasingly limited. Consequently, in 1993 a demonstration garbage reduction program (GRD) was launched in Nei-fu, a suburb of Taipei, and evaluated for its impact on the amount of waste produced. Garbage is collected daily in Taiwan and the plan of the GRD was to disrupt this routine by suspending Tuesday collections. The theory was that requiring residents to store garbage one day a week in their homes, which are ill equipped for that function, would create sufficient inconvenience and unpleasantness to raise awareness of the garbage problem. As a result, it was expected that residents would make efforts to reduce the volume of garbage they produced. A process evaluation established that the program was implemented as planned.

The impact assessment was conducted by obtaining records of the daily volume of garbage for Nei-fu and the similar, adjacent suburb of Nan-kan for a period beginning four months prior to the program onset and continuing four months after. Analysis showed no reduction in the volume of garbage collected in Nei-fu during the program period relative to the preprogram volume or that in the comparison community. The evidence indicated that residents simply saved their customary volume of Tuesday garbage and disposed of it on Wednesday, with no carryover effects on the volume for the remainder of each week. Interviews with residents revealed that the program theory was wrong —they did not report the inconvenience or unpleasantness expected to be associated with storing garbage in their homes.

SOURCE: Adapted from Huey-Tsyh Chen, Juju C. S. Wang, and Lung-Ho Lin, "Evaluating the Process and Outcome of a Garbage Reduction Program in Taiwan," *Evaluation Review*, 1997, 21(1):27-42.

evaluation, it is often referred to as *black box evaluation* because the evaluator may learn what the program effects are but does not know anything about the program processes that produced those effects—the program is a black box into which the evaluation cannot (or does not) see.

Determining when an impact assessment is appropriate, and what evaluation design to use when it is, present considerable challenge to the evaluator. On the one hand, evaluation sponsors often believe that they need an impact evaluation and, indeed, it is the only way to determine if the program is having the in-tended effects. On the other hand, impact assessment is characteristically very demanding of expertise, time, and resources and is often very difficult to set up properly within the constraints of routine program operation. For these reasons, a full-blown impact assessment is not to be undertaken lightly. It is generally appropriate only when there is an important purpose to be served by learning about program effects. This may be because the program concept is innovative and promising or in circumstances where identifiable decisionmakers have a high likelihood of actually using evidence about program impact as a basis for significant action. Such conditions may occur, for instance, with a demonstration project set up to test a program concept that, if effective, will be disseminated to other sites. Or impact assessment may be called for in high-accountability contexts where, for instance, continued funding for a program depends on its ability to demonstrate impact.

If the need for outcome information is sufficient to justify the expense and effort of an impact assessment, there is still a question of whether the program circumstances are suitable for such an evaluation. For instance, it makes little sense to establish the impact of a program that is not well structured or cannot be adequately described. Even if positive effects are found under such circumstances, ambiguity remains about what program features caused them or how they would be replicated elsewhere. Impact assessment, therefore, is most appropriate for mature, stable programs with a well-defined program model and a clear use for the results that justifies the effort required to conduct this form of evaluation. The most useful impact assessment results are for well-structured, well-documented programs believed to have important effects that must be established to support important decisions about the program or the program model.

Chapters 7-10 of this volume discuss impact assessment and the various ways in which it can be designed and conducted. Although all such designs are demanding, some are easier to implement than others in typical program circumstances. For impact assessment, therefore, much of the tailoring that must be done for application to a particular program is determining just which design to use, how to configure it, and what problems are associated with any compromises.

Efficiency Assessment

Unless programs have a demonstrable impact, it is hard to defend implementing or maintaining them—hence the need for impact assessments. But knowledge of impact alone is often insufficient; program results must also be judged against their costs. This is especially true in the present political climate as the resources for supporting social programs are curtailed and competition among programs for funds is intensified. Some programs may not be supportable because of high costs relative to their impact. In the face of budget problems, for example, some universities have terminated their student counseling programs because costs are high and benefits slight. Other initiatives may be expanded, retained, or terminated on the basis of their comparative costs. For instance, findings about the impact of institutional versus community care for adolescent offenders suggest that community programs are preferable because of their markedly lower costs.

Taking account of the relationship between costs and effectiveness requires efficiency assessments (Exhibit 2-O provides an example). This form of evaluation builds on process and impact assessment. If it is established that a program is well implemented and produces the desired outcomes, questions related to efficiency become relevant. Typical questions of this sort include "Is a program producing sufficient benefits in relation to the costs incurred?" and "Does it produce a particular benefit at a lower cost per unit of outcome than other interventions or delivery systems designed to achieve the same goal?" The techniques for answering these types of questions are found in two closely related approaches: cost-benefit and

---

EXHIBIT 2-O The Cost-Effectiveness of Community Treatment for Persons
With Mental Disabilities

If provided with supportive services, persons with mental disabilities can often be maintained in community settings rather than state mental hospitals. But is such community treatment more costly than residential hospital care? A team of researchers in Ohio compared the costs of a community program that provides housing subsidies and case management for state-certified severely mentally disabled clients with the costs of residential patients at the regional psychiatric hospital. Program clients were interviewed monthly for more than two years to determine their consumption of mental health services, medical and dental services, housing services, and other personal consumption. Information on the cost of those services was obtained from the respective service providers and

combined with the direct cost of the community program itself. Costs for wards where patients resided 90 or more days were gathered from the Ohio Department of Mental Health budget data and subdivided into categories that corresponded as closely as possible to those tabulated for the community program participants. Mental health care comprised the largest component of service cost for both program and hospital clients. Overall, however, the total cost for all services was estimated at $1,730 per month for the most intensive version of community program services and about $6,250 per month for residential hospital care. Community care, therefore, was much less costly than hospital care, not more costly.

SOURCE: Adapted from George C. Galster, Timothy F. Champney, and Yolonda Williams, "Costs of Caring for Persons With Long-Term Mental Illness in Alternative Residential Settings," *Evaluation and Program Planning*, 1994, 17(3):239-348.

---

cost-effectiveness analyses. Cost-benefit analysis studies the relationship between program costs and outcomes, with both costs and outcomes expressed in monetary terms. Cost-effectiveness analysis examines the relationship between program costs and outcomes in terms of the costs per unit of outcome achieved. Efficiency assessment can be tricky and arguable because it requires making assumptions about the dollar value of program-related activities and, sometimes, imputing monetary value to program benefits. Nevertheless, such estimates are often essential for decisions about the allocation of resources to programs, identi-

fying the program models that produce the strongest results with a given amount of funding, and determining the degree of political support stakeholders provide to a program.

Like impact assessment, efficiency assessment is most appropriate for mature, stable programs with a well-structured and well-documented program model. In addition, as mentioned above, efficiency analysis builds on both process and impact assessment, so it is important that the nature and magnitude of program effects be determined in advance of, or parallel to, efficiency assessment. Given the specialized expertise required to conduct efficiency assessments, it is also apparent that it should be undertaken only when there is a clear need and an identified user for the information. With the high level of concern about program costs in many contexts, however, this may not be an unusual circumstance.

The procedures used for efficiency assessment are not as demanding of resources and program cooperation as are those of impact evaluation, but they are quite technical and require a high level of expertise. Chapter 11 discusses efficiency assessment methods in more detail.

STITCHING IT ALL TOGETHER

This chapter has reviewed the major considerations involved in tailoring an evaluation so that there is an appropriate fit between the evaluation plan and the circumstances of the program to be evaluated. However, it supplies few directly prescriptive injunctions that tell the prospective evaluator just what approach to take, what options to select, and how to go about putting the elements of an evaluation plan together. Designing an evaluation is not a mechanical activity that can be accomplished by applying a set of rules. A good evaluation plan is heavily contextualized by the political situation, the nature of the program, the interests of the stakeholders, and many other such specific features of the program landscape. It thus requires the evaluator to make many judgment calls based on a careful reconnaissance of that landscape. Moreover, experienced evaluators will disagree among themselves on what "call" should be made for many aspects of an evaluation plan for a given program situation. What we have tried to do in this chapter, therefore, is identify the major issues the evaluator

must engage, the main alternatives that might be contemplated, and the primary considerations involved in making choices that tailor an evaluation plan to the program circumstances (see Exhibit 2-P for a similar perspective from "down under").

It should be evident that there is a certain logic in the relationships among the various program issues and the evaluation approaches surveyed in this chapter. In that logic, the social conditions, target population, and associated service needs a program is intended to address must first be identified and assessed. With that assessment in hand, the evaluator can ask if the basic conceptualization of the program (the program as intended) represents a reasonable means for addressing those needs. Deficiencies in this domain must be remedied by reconceptualizing the program. If the program theory is reasonable, the next question in this evaluation logic is whether the program is actually implemented and operationalized as intended, that is, as stipulated by the theory. Shortcomings in implementation generally must be solved by managerial initiatives. If the program is implemented as intended, then it is meaningful to ask if it has the intended effects—this is impact evaluation. A program that does not have the intended impact is either not implemented as intended or the program theory on which the program's operational plan is based must be faulty. If the intended effects are produced, it is then especially germane for the evaluation to inquire into the costs associated with attaining those effects and, especially, the efficiency with which they were attained. Programs with costs judged to be disproportionately large relative to their benefits, or to alternate ways of attaining those benefits, may need to find more cost-effective approaches or be replaced with more cost-effective alternatives.

▓ **EXHIBIT 2-P** / An Australian Team's Ten-Step Approach to Program Evaluation

A systematic approach to evaluation planning developed by the Research and Evaluation Support Services Unit of the New South Wales Department of Education is organized around the following ten questions:

1. *What is the program to be evaluated?* A common problem for the evaluator is defining what constitutes the "program" for evaluation. Some educational programs consist of a set of initiatives that may not be closely integrated. In general, a program is defined as "the set of operations, actions, or activities designed to produce certain desired effects or outcomes."

2. *Why is the program being evaluated?* Evaluation may focus on information needs related to what should be done, what can be done, what is being done, or what has been done.

3. *How are people to be prepared for the evaluation?* Thought should be given to who is likely to feel threatened by the evaluation, whose acceptance of the evaluation is essential, and what might be done to provide reassurance and gain acceptance.

4. *What are the main issues/questions with which the evaluation is to deal?* In this step the evaluator expands on the decisions made at Step 2 and develops a list of major issues or questions that define the evaluation's focus.

5. *Who will do what?* The responsibilities of participants in the evaluation should be understood and agreed on before the project is started.

6. *What are the resources for the evaluation?* In addition to workers, the evaluation may need other resources including money, material, facilities, transportation, and the like.

7. *What data need to be collected?* Data collection activities should be planned in relation to the major issues/questions identified in Step 4. They should be specific with regard to from whom the data are to be collected, how they will be collected, and what information must be covered.

8. *How will the data be analyzed?* Before data are collected, consideration should be given to what ultimately will be done with them. The answers will influence decisions both about the information to be collected and the form in which it will be collected.

9. *What will be the reporting procedure?* In this step, decisions should be made about to whom the reports will be provided and the appropriate ways to do this (e.g., written report, group discussion, newspapers). A further consideration is who should be asked to respond to the evaluation report. This step is important both for maintaining support for the evaluation and for ensuring that the report is communicating effectively to the groups who need to know the results.

10. *How will the report be implemented?* Attention should be given to identifying who is to be responsible for making recommendations on the basis of the evaluation results and who is responsible for implementing the recommendations. It should not be automatically assumed that the evaluation team will be the ones formulating recommendations; the evaluation may inform relevant decisionmakers who assume that task.

SOURCE: Adapted from Linda J. Lee and John F. Sampson, "A Practical Approach to Program Evaluation," *Evaluation and Program Planning,* 1990, 13(2):157-164.

SUMMARY

▨ Every evaluation must be tailored to the circumstances of the program being evaluated so that the evaluation design will be capable of yielding credible and useful answers to the specific questions at issue while still being sufficiently practical to actually implement within the resources available.

▨ One important influence on an evaluation plan is the purpose the evaluation is intended to serve. Evaluations generally are initiated to either provide feedback for program improvement to program managers and sponsors, establish accountability to decisionmakers with responsibility to ensure that the program is effective, or contribute to knowledge about some form of social intervention. The overall purpose of the evaluation necessarily shapes its focus, scope, and construction.

▨ Another important factor in planning an evaluation is the nature of the program structure and circumstances. The evaluation design must be responsive to how new or open to change the program is, the degree of consensus or conflict among stakeholders about the nature and mission of the program, the values and concepts inherent in the program rationale and design, and the way in which the program is organized and administered.

▨ Evaluation planning must also accommodate to the inevitable limitations on the resources available for the evaluation effort. The critical resources include not only funding but also the amount of time allowed for completion of the work, pertinent technical expertise, program and stakeholder cooperation, and access to important records and program material. A balance must generally be found between what is most desirable from an evaluation standpoint and what is feasible in terms of available resources.

▨ The evaluation design itself can be structured around three issues: (a) the questions the evaluation is to answer, (b) the methods and procedures to be used to answer those questions, and (c) the nature of the evaluator-stakeholder interactions during the course of the evaluation.

▨ Deciding on the appropriate relationship between the evaluator and the evaluation sponsor, as well as other major stakeholders, is an often neglected, but critical aspect of an evaluation plan. An independent evaluation, in which the evaluator takes primary responsibility for designing and conducting the evaluation, is often expected. In some circumstances, however, a more participatory or collaborative interaction with stakeholders may be desirable, with the evaluation conducted as a team project. In the latter case, the evaluation may be designed to help develop the capabilities of the participating stakeholders in ways that enhance their skills or political influence.

※ The evaluation questions that are identified during planning, and the methods for answering them, generally fall into one or more recognizable categories having to do with (a) the need for services, (b) program conceptualization and design, (c) program implementation, (d) program outcomes, or (e) program efficiency. Evaluators have developed relatively distinct conceptual and methodological approaches for each of these different categories of issues that are referred to by such terms as *needs assessment*, *process evaluation*, and *impact assessment*. In practice, much of evaluation planning consists of identifying the evaluation approach corresponding to the type of questions to be answered in an evaluation, then tailoring the specifics to the program situation.

Evaluation questions	A set of questions developed by the evaluator, evaluation sponsor, and other stakeholders; the questions define the issues the evaluation will investigate and are stated in terms such that they can be answered in a way useful to stakeholders using methods available to the evaluator.
Program goal	A statement, usually general and abstract, of a desired state toward which a program is directed. Compare with **program objectives.**
Program objectives	Specific, operationalized statements detailing the desired accomplishments of a program.
Performance criterion	The standard against which a dimension of program performance is compared so that it can be evaluated.
Utilization of evaluation	The use of the concepts and findings of an evaluation by decisionmakers and other stakeholders whether at the day-to-day management level or at broader funding or policy levels.
Program theory	The set of assumptions about the manner in which the program relates to the social benefits it is expected to produce and the strategy and tactics the program has adopted to achieve its goals and objectives.
Impact theory	The beliefs, assumptions, and expectations inherent in a program about the nature of the change brought about by program action and how it results in the intended improvement in social conditions. Program impact theory is causal theory: It describes a cause-and-effect sequence in which certain program activities are the instigating causes and certain social benefits are the effects they eventually produce.
Service utilization plan	The assumptions and expectations about how the target population will make initial contact with the program and be engaged with it through the completion of the intended services. In its simplest form, a service utilization plan describes the sequence of events through which the intended clients are expected to interact with the intended services.
Organizational plan	The assumptions and expectations about what the program must do to bring about the transactions between the target population and the program that will produce the intended changes in social conditions. The program's organizational plan is articulated from the perspective of program management and encompasses both the functions and activities the program is expected to perform and the human, financial, and physical resources required for that performance.
Program process theory	The combination of the program's organizational plan and its service utilization plan into an overall description of the assumptions and expectations about how the program is supposed to operate.
Implementation failure	The program does not adequately perform the activities specified in the program design that are assumed to be necessary for bringing about the intended social improvements. It includes situations in which no service, not enough service, or the wrong service is delivered, or the service varies excessively across the target population.
Theory failure	The program is implemented as planned but its services do not produce the immediate effects on the participants that are expected or the ultimate social benefits intended or both.

CHAPTER 3

IDENTIFYING ISSUES AND FORMULATING QUESTIONS

The previous chapter presented an overview of the many considerations that go into tailoring an evaluation. Although all those matters are important to evaluation design, the essence of the evaluation enterprise is generating credible answers to questions about the performance of a social program. Good evaluation questions must address program issues that are meaningful in relation to the nature of the program and also of concern to key stakeholders. They must be answerable with the research techniques available to the evaluator, and they must be formulated so that the criteria by which the corresponding program performance will be judged are explicit or can be determined in a straightforward way.

A set of appropriate evaluation questions, therefore, is the hub around which evaluation revolves. It follows that a careful, explicit formulation of those questions greatly facilitates both the design of the evaluation and the subsequent use of its findings. Evaluation questions may take various forms, some of which are more useful and meaningful than others for stakeholders and program decisionmakers. Furthermore, some forms of the evaluation questions are more amenable to the evaluator's task of providing credible answers, and some address critical program effectiveness issues more directly than others. Careful development and formulation of the questions that the evaluation will be designed to answer are, therefore, crucial steps in conducting a program evaluation.

This chapter discusses practical ways in which effective evaluation questions can be fashioned from input by stakeholders and analysis by the evaluator. An essential procedure for this purpose is identification of the decisionmakers who will use the evaluation results, what information they need, and how they expect to use it. The evaluator's own analysis of the program is also important. One approach that is particularly useful for this purpose is articulation of the program theory, a detailed account of how and why the program is supposed to work. Consideration of program theory focuses attention on critical events and premises that may be candidates for inquiry in the evaluation.

Program evaluation is fundamentally an endeavor that gathers and interprets information about program performance to answer questions relevant to decision making or, at least, of appreciable interest to one or more program stakeholders. A critical phase in an evaluation, therefore, is the identification and formulation of the questions the evaluation is to address. One might assume that this step would be very straightforward, indeed, that the questions would be stipulated routinely as part of the process of commissioning the evaluation. As described in Chapter 2, however, it is rare for final, workable evaluation questions to be specified by the evaluation sponsor at the beginning of an evaluation. Nor can the evaluator usually step up and define the focal questions unilaterally on the basis of his or her professional expertise. That maneuver would increase the risk that the evaluation would not be responsive to stakeholder concerns, would not be useful or used, and would be attacked as irrelevant or inappropriate.

To ensure that the evaluation will attend to the matters of greatest concern to the pertinent decisionmakers and stakeholders, therefore, the initial evaluation questions are best formulated through interaction and negotiation with those decisionmakers and stakeholders. This, of course, helps direct the evaluation toward the most relevant practical issues. Of equal importance, however, is that such interaction engages key stakeholders in the process of defining the evaluation in a detailed and personal way that increases the likelihood that they will understand, appreciate, and make effective use of the findings when they become available.

Although stakeholder input is critical, the evaluator should not depend only on the decisionmakers and stakeholders to identify the issues the evaluation will address. Sometimes the evaluation sponsors are very knowledgeable about evaluation and will already have done the necessary background work and formulated a complete and workable set of questions to which the evaluation should attend. Such situations are not typical, however. More often, the evaluation sponsors and program stakeholders are not especially expert at evaluation or, if so, have not done all the groundwork needed to focus the evaluation. This means that the evaluator will rarely be presented at the outset with a finished list of every issue the evaluation should address for the results to be useful, interpretable, and complete. Nor will the issues and questions that are put forward generally be formulated in a manner that permits ready translation into research design.

Thus, although the specification of the evaluation questions must involve input from stakeholders, the evaluator's role is also crucial. The stakeholders will be the experts on the practical and political issues facing the program, but generally the evaluator will know the most about how to analyze a program and focus an evaluation. The evaluator, therefore, must be prepared to raise issues for consideration that otherwise might be overlooked, identify aspects of program operations and outcomes that might warrant inquiry, and work with stakeholders to translate their concerns into questions of a form that evaluation research can attempt to answer.

In all but the most routine situations, it is generally wise for the evaluator to construct a written statement of the specific questions that will guide the evaluation design. This provides a reference to consult while designing the evaluation and selecting research procedures that can be very useful. Perhaps more important, this written statement can be discussed with the evaluation sponsor and key stakeholders to ensure that it encompasses their concerns and defines a focus for the evaluation

---

⚝ EXHIBIT 3-A   What It Means to Evaluate Something

There are different kinds of inquiry across practice areas, such as that which is found in law, medicine, and science. Common to each kind of inquiry is a general pattern of reasoning or basic logic that guides and informs the practice. . . . Evaluation is one kind of inquiry, and it, too, has a basic logic or general pattern of reasoning [that has been put forth by Michael Scriven]. . . . This general logic of evaluation is as follows:

1. *Establishing criteria of merit.* On what dimensions must the evaluand [thing being evaluated] do well?

2. *Constructing standards.* How well should the evaluand perform?
3. *Measuring performance and comparing with standards.* How well did the evaluand perform?
4. *Synthesizing and integrating data into a judgment of merit or worth.* What is the merit or worth of the evaluand?

. . . To evaluate anything means to assess the merit or worth of something against criteria and standards. The basic logic explicated by Scriven reflects what it means when we use the term *to evaluate.*

SOURCE: Quoted from Deborah M. Fournier, *Establishing Evaluative Conclusions: A Distinction Between General and Working Logic,* New Directions for Evaluation, no. 68 (San Francisco: Jossey-Bass, 1995), p. 16.

---

acceptable to them. Such a procedure also can safeguard against later misunderstanding of what the evaluation was supposed to accomplish.

The remainder of this chapter examines the two most important topics related to specifying the issues and questions that will guide an evaluation: (a) how to formulate evaluation questions in such a way that they can be addressed using the research procedures available to the evaluator, and (b) how to determine the specific questions on which the evaluation should focus.

WHAT MAKES A GOOD EVALUATION QUESTION?

The form evaluation questions should take is shaped by the functions they must perform.

Their principal role is to focus the evaluation on those areas of program performance at issue for key decisionmakers and stakeholders and to facilitate development of a design for data collection that will provide meaningful information about how well the program is performing. A good evaluation question, therefore, must identify a distinct dimension of program performance that is at issue and do so in such a way that the quality of the performance can be credibly assessed. Such assessment, in turn, requires an accurate description of the nature of the performance and some standard by which it can be evaluated (see Exhibit 3-A). Thus a good evaluation question must specify some measurable or observable dimension of program performance in reference to the criterion by which that performance is to be judged. Each of these different aspects warrants further discussion.

Dimensions of Program Performance

Good evaluation questions will identify aspects of performance dimensions that are relevant to the expectations stakeholders hold for the program and represent domains in which the program can realistically hope to have accomplishments, but where effectiveness cannot necessarily be taken for granted. It would hardly be fair to ask if a low-income housing weatherization program reduced the prevalence of drug dealing in a neighborhood. Nor would it generally be useful to ask if the program got a good deal on its purchase of file cabinets for the office. Furthermore, the evaluation questions must involve performance dimensions that are sufficiently specific, concrete, and practical that meaningful information can be obtained about their status. An evaluator would have great difficulty determining if an adult literacy program improved a community's competitiveness in the global economy or if the counselors in a drug prevention program were sufficiently caring in their relations with clients.

Evaluation Questions Must Be Reasonable and Appropriate

Program advocates sometimes put forward grandiose goals (e.g., improve the quality of life for children), expect unrealistically large effects, or believe the program has accomplishments that are disproportionate to its actual capabilities. Good evaluation questions deal with performance dimensions that are appropriate and realistic for the program. This means that the evaluator must often work with relevant stakeholders to scale down and focus the evaluation questions. The manager of a community health program, for instance,

might initially ask, "Are our education and outreach services successful in informing the public about the risk of AIDS?" In practice, however, those services may consist of little more than occasional presentations by program staff at Rotary Clubs and health fairs. With this rather modest level of activity, it may not be realistic to expect the public at large to receive much AIDS information through this channel, much less for that information to lower the risk of AIDS in the community. If a question about this service is deemed important for the evaluation, a better version might be something such as "Do our education and outreach services raise awareness of AIDS issues among the audiences addressed?" and "Do those audiences represent community leaders who are likely to influence the opinions of significant others?"

There are two complementary ways for an evaluator, in collaboration with pertinent stakeholders, to assess how appropriate and realistic a candidate evaluation question is. The first is to examine the question in the context of the actual program activities related to it. In the example above, for instance, the low-key nature of the education and outreach services were clearly not up to the task of "informing the public about the risk of AIDS" and there would be little point in having the evaluation attempt to determine if this was accomplished. The evaluator and relevant stakeholders should identify and scrutinize the program components, activities, and personnel assignments that relate to program performance and formulate the evaluation question in a way that is reasonable given those characteristics.

Another form of review for candidate evaluation questions is to analyze them in relationship to the experience and findings reported in applicable social science and social service literature. Questions involving certain program performance dimensions would be assessed as more appropriate if they were consistent with experience in similar programs or studies of those programs. For instance, the sponsor of an evaluation of a program for juvenile delinquents might initially ask if the program increases the self-esteem of the delinquents, in the belief that increased self-esteem is a problem for these juveniles and improvements in self-esteem will lead to better behavior. Examination of the applicable social science research, however, will reveal that juvenile delinquents do not generally have problems with self-esteem and, moreover, that increases in self-esteem are not generally associated with reductions in delinquency. In light of this information, the evaluator and the evaluation sponsor may well agree that the question of the program's impact on self-esteem is not appropriate after all.

The foundation for formulating appropriate and realistic evaluation questions is detailed and complete program description. Early in the process, the evaluator should become thoroughly acquainted with the program—how it is structured, what activities take place, the roles and tasks of the various personnel, the nature of the participants, and the assumptions inherent in its principal functions. The stakeholder groups with whom the evaluator collaborates (especially program managers and staff) will also, of course, have knowledge about the program. Evaluation questions that are inspired by close consideration of actual program activities and assumptions will almost automatically be appropriate and realistic. And a clear understanding of the program operation and its rationale is a necessary prerequisite for entering the social science and social service literature to find relevant concepts and analogous situations. The investigation and articulation of the various components of program theory, described later in this chapter, generally provide a very effective approach to developing this detailed understanding of the program.

Evaluation Questions Must Be Answerable

It is rather obvious that the evaluation questions around which an evaluation plan is developed should be answerable. Questions that cannot be answered may be intriguing to philosophers but serve poorly the needs of evaluators and the decisionmakers who intend to use the evaluation results. What is not so obvious, perhaps, is how easy it is to formulate an unanswerable evaluation question without realizing it. This may occur because the terms used in the question, although seemingly commonsensical, are actually ambiguous or vague when the time comes for a definitive interpretation ("Does this program enhance family values?"). Or sensible-sounding questions may invoke issues for which there are so few observable indicators that little can be learned about them ("Are the case managers sensitive to the social circumstances of their clients?"). Also, some questions lack sufficient indication of the relevant criteria to be answered ("Is this program successful?"). Finally, some questions may be answerable but to do so would require more expertise, data, or resources than are available to the evaluation ("Do the prenatal services this program provides to high-risk women increase the chances that their children will complete college?").

For an evaluation question to be answerable, it must be possible to identify in advance some evidence or "observables" that can realistically be obtained and will be credible as the basis for an answer. This generally means developing questions that involve measurable performance dimensions, that are sufficiently unambiguous so that explicit, noncontroversial definitions can be given for each of their terms, and for which the relevant standards or criteria are specified or obvious. The best way for an evaluator to test whether a candidate question is answerable in these terms is to determine whether a realistically attainable, specific evaluation finding can be imagined such that the relevant decisionmakers and stakeholders agree that it constitutes a meaningful answer.

Suppose, for instance, that a proposed evaluation question for a compensatory education program like Head Start is, "Are we reaching the children most in need of this program?" To affirm that this is an answerable question, the evaluator should be able to

a. Define the group of children at issue (e.g., those in census tract such and such, age five years or less, living in households with annual income under 150% of the federal poverty level);

b. Identify the specific measurable characteristics and cutoff values that represent the greatest need (e.g., annual income below the federal poverty level, single parent in the household with educational attainment of less than high school);

c. Give an example of the evaluation finding that might result (e.g., 60% of the children currently served fall in the high-need category; 75% of the high-need children in the catchment area are not enrolled in the program);

d. Stipulate the evaluative criteria (e.g., to be satisfactory, at least 90% of the children in the program should be high need and at least 50% of the high-need chil-

dren in the catchment area should be in the program); and

e. Have the evaluation sponsors and other pertinent stakeholders (who should be involved in the whole process) agree that this would, indeed, answer the question.

If such conditions can be met and, in addition, the resources are available to collect, analyze, and report the applicable data, then the evaluation question can be considered answerable.

Criteria for Program Performance

Beginning a study with a reasonable, answerable question or set of questions, of course, is standard in the social sciences (although often framed as hypotheses). What distinguishes *evaluation* questions is that they have to do with performance and are associated, at least implicitly, with some criteria by which that performance can be judged. Identifying the relevant criteria was mentioned above as part of what makes an evaluation question answerable. However, this is such an important and distinctive aspect of evaluation questions that it warrants separate discussion.

When program managers or evaluation sponsors ask such things as "Are we targeting the right client population?" or "Do our services benefit the recipients?" they are not only asking for a description of the program's performance with regard to serving appropriate clients and providing services that yield benefits. They are also asking if that performance is good enough according to some standard or judgment. There is likely little doubt that at least a few of the "right client population" receive services or that some recipients receive some benefit from services. But is it enough? Some criterion level must be set by which the

> ### ▧ EXHIBIT 3-B   Many Criteria May Be Relevant to Program Performance
>
> The standards by which program performance may be judged in an evaluation include:
>
> - The needs or wants of the target population
> - Stated program goals and objectives
> - Professional standards
> - Customary practice; norms for other programs
> - Legal requirements
>
> - Ethical or moral values; social justice, equity
> - Past performance; historical data
> - Targets set by program managers
> - Expert opinion
> - Preintervention baseline levels for the target population
> - Conditions expected in the absence of the program (counterfactual)
> - Cost or relative cost

numbers and amounts can be evaluated on those performance dimensions.

One implication of this distinctive feature of evaluation is that good evaluation questions will, when possible, convey the performance standard that is applicable as well as the performance dimension that is at issue. Thus, evaluation questions should be much like this: "Is at least 75% of the program clientele appropriate for services?" (by some explicit definition of *appropriate*) or "Do the majority of those who receive the employment services get jobs within 30 days of the conclusion of training that they keep at least three months?" In addition, the performance standards represented in these questions should have some defensible, though possibly indirect, relationship to the social needs the program addresses. There must be some reason why attaining that standard is meaningful, and the strongest rationale is that it represents a level of performance sufficient for that program function to contribute effectively to the overall program purpose of improving the target social conditions.

A considerable complication for the evaluator is that there are many forms in which the applicable performance criteria may appear for various dimensions of program performance (see Exhibit 3-B), and indeed, it is not always possible to establish an explicit, consensual performance standard in advance of collecting data and reporting results. Nonetheless, to the extent that the formulation of the initial evaluation questions includes explicit criteria on which key stakeholders agree, evaluation planning is made easier and the potential for disagreement over the interpretation of the evaluation results is reduced. It is worth noting that the criterion issue cannot be avoided. An evaluation that only describes program performance, and does not attempt to assess it, is not truly an evaluation (by definition; see Exhibit 3-A) and, at most, only pushes the issue of setting criteria and judging performance onto the consumer of the information.

With these considerations in mind, we turn attention to the various kinds of performance criteria that appear in evaluation studies and may be relevant to formulation of useful evaluation questions. Perhaps the most common criteria are those based on program goals and objectives. In this case, certain desirable accomplishments are identified as the program aims by program officials and sponsors. Often these statements of goals and objectives are not very specific with regard to the nature or level of program performance they represent. One of the goals of a shelter for battered women, for instance, might be to "empower them to take control of their own lives." Although reflecting commendable values, this statement may leave the evaluator uncertain of the tangible manifestations of such empowerment or what level of empowerment constitutes attainment of this goal. Considerable discussion with stakeholders may be necessary to translate such statements into mutually acceptable terminology that describes the intended outcomes more concretely, identifies the observable indicators that correspond to those outcomes, and specifies the level of accomplishment on each that would be considered a success in accomplishing this goal.

Some program objectives, on the other hand, may be very specific. These often come in the form of administrative objectives adopted as targets for routine program functions. The target levels may be set according to past experience or the experience of comparable programs, judgment of what is reasonable and desirable, or maybe only on a "best guess" basis. Examples of administrative objectives may be to establish intake for 90% of the referrals within 30 days, to have 75% of the clients complete the full term of service, to have 85% "good" or "outstanding" ratings on the client satisfaction questionnaire, to provide at least three appropriate services to each person under case management, and the like. There is typically a certain amount of arbitrariness in these criterion levels, but if they are administratively stipulated or can be established through stakeholder consensus and are reasonable, they are quite serviceable in the formulation of evaluation questions and the interpretation of the subsequent findings. However, it is not generally wise for the evaluator to press for such specific statements of target performance levels if the program does not have them or cannot readily and confidently develop them. Setting such targets on a highly arbitrary basis only creates a situation in which they are arbitrarily revised when the evaluation results are in.

In some, albeit rare, instances there are established professional standards that can be invoked as program performance criteria. This is particularly likely in medical and health programs where various practice guidelines and managed care standards have developed and may be relevant for setting desirable performance levels for programs. Much more common, however, is the situation where there are no established criteria or even arbitrary administrative objectives to invoke. A typical situation is one in which the performance dimension itself is clearly recognized, but there is ambiguity about the criterion for good performance on that dimension. For instance, relevant stakeholders may agree that the program should have a low drop-out rate, a high proportion completing service, a high level of client satisfaction, and the like, but only nebulous ideas as to what level constitutes "low" or "high" on the respective dimensions. Sometimes the evaluator can make use of prior experience or find information in the evaluation and program literature that provides a reasonable basis for setting a criterion level. Another approach is to collect judgment ratings from relevant stakeholders to establish the criterion levels or, perhaps more appropriate in such circumstances, to identify broad criterion ranges that can be accepted to distinguish, say, high, medium, and low performance.

When the performance dimension in an evaluation question involves outcome or impact issues, establishing a criterion level can be particularly difficult. Program stakeholders and evaluators alike may have little idea about how much change on a given outcome variable (e.g., a scale of attitude toward drug use) is large and how much is small. By default, these judgments are often made on the basis of statistical criteria. For instance, any statistically significant improvement in an outcome dimension may be viewed as an indication of program success. This is a poor practice for reasons that will be more fully examined later in this volume when impact evaluation is discussed. Statistical criteria have no intrinsic relationship to the practical significance of a change on an outcome dimension and can be misleading. Thus, as much as possible, the evaluator should attempt to determine and specify in practical terms what "success" level is appropriate for judging the nature and magnitude of the program effects.

Typical Evaluation Questions

As should be evident from the discussions above, well-formulated evaluation questions are very concrete and specific to the program at issue and the circumstances of the prospective evaluation. It follows that the variety of questions that might be relevant to some social program or another is enormous. As noted in Chapter 2, however, evaluation questions typically deal with one of five general program issues. Some of the more common questions in each category, stated in summary form, are as follows.

Questions about the need for program services:

- What are the nature and magnitude of the problem to be addressed?
- What are the characteristics of the population in need?
- What are the needs of the population?
- What services are needed?
- How much service is needed, over what time period?
- What service delivery arrangements are needed to provide those services to the population?

Questions about program conceptualization or design:

- What clientele should be served?
- What services should be provided?
- What are the best delivery systems for the services?
- How can the program identify, recruit, and sustain the intended clientele?
- How should the program be organized?
- What resources are necessary and appropriate for the program?

Questions about program operations and service delivery:

- Are administrative and service objectives being met?
- Are the intended services being delivered to the intended persons?
- Are there needy but unserved persons the program is not reaching?

- Once in service, do sufficient numbers of clients complete service?

- Are the clients satisfied with the services?

- Are administrative, organizational, and personnel functions handled well?

Questions about program outcomes:

- Are the outcome goals and objectives being achieved?

- Do the services have beneficial effects on the recipients?

- Do the services have adverse side effects on the recipients?

- Are some recipients affected more by the services than others?

- Is the problem or situation the services are intended to address made better?

Questions about program cost and efficiency:

- Are resources used efficiently?

- Is the cost reasonable in relation to the magnitude of the benefits?

- Would alternative approaches yield equivalent benefits at less cost?

These families of evaluation questions are not mutually exclusive, of course. Questions in more than one category, and maybe in all the categories, could be relevant to a program for which an evaluation was being planned. To develop an appropriate evaluation plan, the many possible questions that might be asked about the program must be narrowed down to those that are most relevant to the program context and the information needs of the key stakeholders (see Exhibit 3-C for an example of evaluation questions for an actual program). We turn now to a discussion of how the evaluator can identify the critical evaluation questions.

DETERMINING THE QUESTIONS ON WHICH THE EVALUATION SHOULD FOCUS

Occasionally, the evaluator is also the evaluation sponsor and primary stakeholder in a program. For instance, an academic researcher who heads a university counseling clinic may have an innovative program concept, implement it in the university clinic, and then conduct an evaluation. It is far more typical, however, for persons other than the evaluator to be the ones who have responsibility for the program, initiate the evaluation, and use the findings. In such circumstances, the evaluation is a project of the sponsor and other involved stakeholders; the evaluator is only the instrument for accomplishing that project. Correspondingly, it is only fitting that the evaluation give central attention to the issues and questions of the evaluation sponsor and the other principal stakeholders. In the discussion that follows, therefore, we first examine the matter of obtaining appropriate input from the evaluation sponsor and relevant stakeholders prior to and during the design stage of the evaluation.

However, it is rarely appropriate for the evaluator to rely only on input from the evaluation sponsor and stakeholders to determine the questions on which the evaluation should focus. Because of their close familiarity with the program, stakeholders may overlook critical, but relatively routine, aspects of program performance. Also, the experience and knowledge of the evaluator may yield distinctive insights into program issues and their inter-

EXHIBIT 3-C   Evaluation Questions for a Neighborhood Afterschool Program

An afterschool program located in an economically depressed area uses the facilities of a local elementary school to provide free afterschool care from 3:30 to 6:00 for the children of the neighborhood. The program's goals are to provide a safe, supervised environment for latchkey children and to enhance their school performance through academic enrichment activities. The following are examples of the questions that an evaluation might be designed to answer for the stakeholders in this program:

Is there a need for the program?

Question: How many latchkey children reside within a radius of 1.5 miles of the school? Latchkey children are defined as those of elementary school age who are without adult supervision during some period after school at least once a week during the school year.

Standard: There should be at least 100 such children in the defined neighborhood. The planned enrollment for the program is 60, which should yield enough children in attendance on any given day for efficient staffing, and it is assumed that some eligible children will not enroll for various reasons.

Question: What proportion of the children enrolled in the program are actually latchkey children?

Standard: At least 75% of the enrolled children should meet the definition for latchkey children. This is an administrative target that reflects the program's intent that a large majority of the enrollees be latchkey children while recognizing that other children will be attracted to, and appropriate for, the program even though not meeting that definition.

Is the program well designed?

Question: Are the planned educational activities the best ones for this clientele and the purposes of enhancing their performance in school?

Standard: There should be indications in the educational research literature to show that these activities have the potential to be effective. In addition, experienced teachers for the relevant grade levels should endorse these activities.

Question: Is there a sufficient number of staff positions in the program?

Standard: The staff-student ratio should exceed the state standards for licensed child care facilities.

Is the program implemented effectively?

Question: What is the attendance rate for enrolled children?

Standard: All enrolled children should either be in attendance every afternoon for which they are scheduled or excused with parental permission.

Question: Is the program providing regular support for school homework and related tasks?

Standard: There should be an average of 45 minutes of supervised study time for completion of homework and reading each afternoon, and all the attending children should participate.

Does the program have the intended outcomes?

Question: Is there improvement in the attitudes of the enrolled children toward school?

(continued)

✂️ EXHIBIT 3-C   Continued

Standard: At least 80% of the children should show measurable improvement in their attitudes toward school between the beginning and end of the school year. Norms for similar students show that their attitudes tend to get worse each year of elementary school; the program objective is to reverse this trend, even if the improvement is only slight.

Question: Is there an improvement in the academic performance of the enrolled children in their regular school work?

Standard: The average term grades on academic subjects should be at least a half letter grade better than they would have been had the children not participated in the program.

Is the program cost-effective?

Question: What is the cost per child for running this program beyond the fixed expenses associated with the regular operation of the school facility?

Standard: Costs per child should be near or below the average for similar programs run in other school districts in the state.

Question: Would the program be equally effective and less costly if staffed by community volunteers (except the director) rather than paid paraprofessionals?

Standard: The annual cost of a volunteer-based program, including recruiting, training, and supporting the volunteers, would have to be at least 20% less than the cost of the current program with no loss of effectiveness to justify the effort associated with making such a change.

---

relations that are important for identifying relevant evaluation questions. Generally, therefore, it is desirable for the evaluator to make a relatively independent analysis of the program for the purpose of identifying areas of program performance that may be pertinent for investigation.

The second topic addressed in the discussion that follows, therefore, is how the evaluator can analyze a program in a way that will uncover potentially important evaluation questions for consideration in designing the evaluation. An especially useful tool for this purpose is the concept of *program theory*, a depiction of the significant assumptions and expectations on which the program depends for its success.

We therefore discuss the different components of program theory, how the evaluator can describe and represent it, and how it can be used diagnostically to identify those program functions that relate most directly to its effectiveness.

Representing the Concerns of the Evaluation Sponsor and Major Stakeholders

In planning and conducting an evaluation, evaluators usually find themselves confronted with multiple stakeholders who hold different

▧ EXHIBIT 3-D   Diverse Stakeholder Perspectives on an Evaluation of a Multiagency Program for the Homeless

The Joint Program was initiated to improve the accessibility of health and social services for the homeless population of Montreal through coordinated activities involving provincial, regional, and municipal authorities and more than 20 nonprofit and public agencies. The services developed through the program included walk-in and referral services, mobile drop-in centers, an outreach team in a community health center, medical and nursing care in shelters, and case management. To ensure stakeholder participation in the evaluation, an evaluation steering committee was set up with representatives of the different types of agencies involved in the program and which, in turn, coordinated with two other stakeholder committees charged with program responsibilities.

Even though all the stakeholders shared a common cause to which they were firmly committed —the welfare of the homeless—they had quite varied perspectives on the evaluation. Some of these were described by the evaluators as follows:

The most glaring imbalance was in the various agencies' different organizational cultures, which led them to experience their participation in the evaluation very differently. Some of the service agencies involved in the Joint Program and its evaluation were front-line public organizations that were accustomed to viewing their actions in terms of a mandate with a target clientele. They were familiar with the evaluation process, both as an administrative procedure and a measurement of accountability. Among the nonprofit agencies, however, some relative newcomers who had been innovators in the area of community-based intervention were hoping the evaluation would recognize the strengths of their approach and make useful suggestions for improvement. Other nonprofit groups were offshoots of religious or charitable organizations that had been involved with the homeless for a very long time. For those groups the evaluation (and the logical, planning-based program itself) was a procedure completely outside of anything in their experience. They perceived the evaluators as outsiders meddling in a reality that they had managed to deal with up until now, under very difficult conditions. Their primary concern was the client. More than the public agencies, they probably saw the evaluation as a waste of time, money, and energy. Most of the day centers involved in the program fell into this category. They were the ones who were asked to take part in a process with which they were unfamiliar, alongside their counterparts in the public sector who were much better versed in research procedures. (p. 471)

SOURCE: Quoted, with permission, from Céline Mercier, "Participation in Stakeholder-Based Evaluation: A Case Study," *Evaluation and Program Planning*, 1997, 20(4):467-475.

and sometimes conflicting views on the program or its evaluation and whose interests will be affected by the outcome (see Exhibit 3-D for an illustration). At the planning stage of an evaluation, the evaluator usually attempts to identify all the stakeholders with an important point of view on what questions should be addressed in the evaluation, set priorities among those viewpoints, and integrate as many of the relevant concerns as possible into the evaluation plan.

The starting point, of course, is with the evaluation sponsors. Those who have commissioned and funded the evaluation rightfully have priority in defining the issues it should address. Sometimes evaluation sponsors have stipulated the evaluation questions and methods completely and want the evaluator only to manage the practical details. In such circumstances, the evaluator should assess which, if any, stakeholder perspectives are excluded and whether they are sufficiently distinct and important that their omission compromises the evaluation. If so, the evaluator must then decide whether to conduct the evaluation under the specified constraints, reporting the limitations and biases along with the results, or attempt to negotiate an arrangement whereby the evaluation is broadened to include additional perspectives.

More often, however, the evaluation sponsors' initial specifications are not so constrained or nonnegotiable that the concerns of other stakeholders cannot be considered. In this situation, the evaluator typically makes the best attempt possible within the constraints of the situation to consult fully with all stakeholders, set reasonable priorities, and develop an evaluation plan that will enhance the information available about the respective concerns of all parties.

Given the usual multiplicity of program stakeholders and their perspectives, and despite an evaluator's efforts to be inclusive, there is considerable inherent potential for misunderstandings to develop between the evaluator and one or more of the stakeholders regarding what issues the evaluation should address. It is especially important, therefore, that there be full and frank communication between the evaluator and the pertinent stakeholder groups from the earliest possible point in the planning process. Along with obtaining critical input from the stakeholders about the program and the evaluation, this exchange should emphasize realistic, shared understanding of what the evaluation will and will not do, and why. Most essentially, the evaluator should strive to ensure that the key stakeholders understand, and find acceptable, the nature of the evaluation process, the type of information the evaluation will produce, what it might mean if the results come out one way or another, and what ambiguities or unanswered questions may remain.

Obtaining Input
From Stakeholders

The major stakeholders, by definition, have a significant interest in the program and the evaluation. It is thus generally straightforward to identify them and obtain their views about the issues and questions to which the evaluation should attend. The evaluation sponsor, program administrators (who may also be the evaluation sponsor), and intended program beneficiaries are virtually always major stakeholders. Identification of other important stakeholders can usually be accomplished by analyzing the network of relationships surrounding a program. The most revealing relationships involve the flow of money to or from the program, political influence on and by the program, those whose actions affect or are affected by the program, and the set of direct interactions between the program and its various boards, patrons, collaborators, competitors, clients, and the like.

A *snowball sampling* approach is often helpful in identifying the various stakeholder groups and persons involved in relationships with the program. As each such representative is identified and contacted, the evaluator asks for nominations of other persons or groups who have a significant interest in the program or are likely to have useful information about it. Those representatives, in turn, are asked the same question. When this process no longer produces consequential new nominations, the evaluator can be reasonably assured that all major stakeholders have been identified.

If the evaluation is structured as an explicitly collaborative or participatory endeavor so that certain stakeholders are directly involved in designing and conducting the evaluation (as described in Chapter 2), they will, of course, have a firsthand role in shaping the evaluation questions. Similarly, an internal evaluator who is part of the organization that administers the program will likely receive forthright counsel from program personnel. Even when such stakeholder involvement is built into the way the evaluation is organized, however, this arrangement is usually not sufficient to represent the full range of pertinent stakeholder perspectives. There may be important stakeholder groups that are not involved in the participatory structure but have distinct and significant perspectives on the program and the evaluation. Moreover, there may be a range of viewpoints among the members of those groups that are represented in a participatory evaluation process so that a broader sampling of opinion is needed than that brought by the designated participant on the evaluation team.

Generally, therefore, formulating responsive evaluation questions requires some discussion with members of stakeholder groups who are not directly represented on the evaluation team. Fewer such contacts may be needed by evaluation teams that already represent many stakeholders and more by those on which few or no stakeholders are represented. In cases where the evaluation has not initially been organized as a collaborative endeavor with stakeholders, the evaluator may wish to consider configuring such an arrangement to ensure engagement by key stakeholders and full representation of their views in the evaluation design and implementation. Similarly, various participatory arrangements might be made through stakeholder advisory boards, steering committees, or simply involvement of key stakeholder representatives in regular consultation with the evaluator. More information about the procedures and benefits of such approaches can be found in Fetterman, Kaftarian, and Wandersman (1996), Greene (1988), Mark and Shotland (1985), and Patton (1997).

Outside of organized arrangements, evaluators generally obtain stakeholder views about the important evaluation issues through personal or telephone interviews. Because these early contacts with stakeholders are primarily for orientation and reconnaissance, such interviews are typically unstructured or, perhaps, semistructured around a small set of themes of interest to the evaluator. Input from some number of individuals representing one or more stakeholder groups might also be obtained through focus groups (Krueger, 1988). Focus groups have the particular advantages of efficiency in getting information from a number of people and the facilitative effect of group interaction in stimulating ideas and observations. They also may have some disadvantages for this purpose, notably the potential for conflict in politically volatile situations and the lack of confidentiality in group settings. In some cases, therefore, stakeholder informants may speak more frankly about the program and the evaluation one-on-one with the evaluator than they will in a focus group.

The evaluator will rarely be able to obtain input from every member of every stakeholder group, nor will that ordinarily be necessary to identify the major issues and questions with which the evaluation should be concerned. A modest number of carefully selected stakeholder informants who are representative of significant groups or distinctly positioned in relation to the program is typically sufficient to identify the principal issues. When the evaluator no longer hears new themes in discussions with diverse stakeholders, the most significant prevailing issues have probably all been discovered.

Topics for Discussion
With Stakeholders

As mentioned in the previous chapter, the issues identified by the evaluation sponsor when the evaluation is requested usually need further discussion with the sponsor and other stakeholders to clarify what they mean to the various parties and what sort of information would usefully bear on them. This endeavor may then lead to refinement and revision of the questions the evaluation will address. The topics that should be addressed in these discussions will depend in large part on the particulars of the evaluation situation. We will review some of the general topics that are often relevant.

Why is an evaluation needed? It is usually worthwhile for the evaluator to probe the reasons an evaluation is desired with the evaluation sponsor and other stakeholders. The evaluation may be motivated by an external requirement, in which case it is important to know the nature of that requirement and what

use is likely to be made of the results. The evaluation may be desired by program managers to determine if the program is effective, to find ways to improve it, or to "prove" its value to potential funders, donors, critics, or the like. Sometimes the evaluation is politically motivated only, for example, as a stalling tactic for a controversial program. Whatever the reasons, they provide an important starting point for determining what questions will be most important for the evaluation to answer and for whom.

What are the program goals and objectives? Inevitably, whether a program achieves certain of the goals and objectives ascribed to it will be pivotal questions for the evaluation to answer. The distinction between goals and objectives is critical. *Goals* are typically stated by programs in broad and rather abstract terms. For evaluation purposes, such goal statements must be refined and restated in terms that can be measured. For example, a program for the homeless may have as its goal "the reduction of homelessness" in its urban catchment area. Although easily understood, such a goal is too vague to support agreement that it has or has not been met. Is a "reduction of homelessness" 5%, 10%, or 100%? Does it refer to only those who are homeless or also to those who are marginally housed and at imminent risk of homelessness? For evaluation purposes, these broad goals must be translated into concrete statements that specify the condition to be dealt with together with one or more measurable criteria of success. Evaluators generally refer to these more specific statements of measurable attainments as *objectives*. Exhibit 3-E presents helpful rules for specifying objectives.

An important task for the evaluator, therefore, is to collaborate with the evaluation sponsors, program managers, and other relevant

▩ EXHIBIT 3-E   Some Rules for Specifying Objectives

Four techniques are particularly helpful for writing useful objectives: (a) using strong verbs, (b) stating only one purpose or aim, (c) specifying a single end-product or result, and (d) specifying the expected time for achievement (Kirschner Associates, 1975).

A "strong" verb is an action-oriented verb that describes an observable or measurable behavior that will occur. For example, "to increase the use of health education materials" is an action-oriented statement involving behavior which can be observed. In contrast, "to promote greater use of health education materials" is a weaker and less specific statement. The term "promote" is subject to many interpretations. Examples of action-oriented, strong verbs include: "to write," "to meet," "to find," "to increase," and "to sign." Examples of weaker, nonspecific verbs include: "to understand," "to encourage," "to enhance," and "to promote."

A second useful suggestion for writing a clear objective is to state only a single aim or purpose. Most programs will, of course, have multiple objectives, but within each objective only a single purpose should be delineated. An objective that states two or more purposes or desired outcomes may well require different implementation and assessment strategies, making achievement of the objective difficult to determine. For example, the statement "to begin three prenatal classes for pregnant women and provide outreach transportation services to accommodate twenty-five women per class" creates difficulties. This objective contains two aims—to provide prenatal classes and to provide outreach services. If one aim is accomplished but not the other, to what extent has the objective been met?

Specifying a single end-product or result is a third technique contributing to a useful objective. For example, the statement "to begin three prenatal classes for pregnant women by subcontracting with City Memorial Hospital" contains two results, namely, the three classes and the subcontract. It is better to state these objectives separately, particularly since one is a higher-order objective (to begin three prenatal classes) which depends partly on fulfillment of a lower-order objective (to establish a subcontract).

A clearly written objective must have both a single aim and a single end-product or result. For example, the statement "to establish communication with the Health Systems Agency" indicates the aim but not the desired end-product or result. What constitutes evidence of communication—telephone calls, meetings, reports? Failure to specify a clear end-product makes it extremely difficult for assessment to take place.

Those involved in writing and evaluating objectives need to keep two questions in mind. First, would anyone reading the objective, with or without knowledge of the program, find the same purpose as the one intended? Second, what visible, measurable, or tangible results are present as evidence that the objective has been met? Purpose or aim describes what will be done; end-product or result describes evidence that will exist when it has been done. This is assurance that you "know one when you see one."

Finally, it is useful to specify the time of expected achievement of the objective. The statement "to establish a walk-in clinic as soon as possible" is not a useful objective because of the vagueness of "as soon as possible." It is far more useful to specify a target date, or in cases where some uncertainty exists about some specific date, a range of target dates—for example, "sometime between March 1 and March 30"—is also useful.

SOURCE: Adapted, with permission, from Stephen M. Shortell and William C. Richardson, *Health Program Evaluation* (St. Louis, MO: C. V. Mosby, 1978), pp. 26-27.

stakeholders to identify the program goals and transform overly broad, ambiguous, or idealized representations of them into clear, explicit, concrete statements of objectives. The more closely the objectives describe situations that can be directly and reliably observed, the more likely it is that a meaningful evaluation will result. Furthermore, it is essential that the evaluator, evaluation sponsors, and other pertinent stakeholders achieve a workable agreement on which program objectives are most central to the evaluation and the criteria to be used in assessing whether those objectives have been met. For instance, if one stated objective of a job training program is to maintain a low drop-out rate, the key stakeholders should agree to its importance before it is accepted as one of the focal issues around which the evaluation will be designed.

If consensus about an appropriate criterion is weak, or not attained at all, it may be wise for the evaluator to employ multiple criteria that reflect the interests of the various stakeholders concerned with a particular objective. If consensus is weak or nonexistent about which objectives are important, one solution is to include all those put forward by the various stakeholders and, perhaps, additional objectives drawn from current viewpoints and theories in the relevant substantive field (Chen, 1990). For example, the sponsors of a job training program may be interested solely in the frequency and duration of postprogram employment. But the evaluator may propose that stability of living arrangements, competence in handling finances, and efforts to obtain additional education be examined as program outcomes because these lifestyle features also may undergo positive change with increased employment and job-related skills.

What are the most important questions for the evaluation to answer? With an understanding of why an evaluation is desired and by whom, and a careful specification of the program objectives that key stakeholders agree are central to the evaluation, attention can be given to formulating the questions the evaluation will be designed to answer. We echo Patton's (1997) view that the delineation of priority evaluation questions should be organized around a concept that generally concerns evaluators very much: *utilization.* Evaluation results are rarely intended by evaluators or evaluation sponsors to be "knowledge for knowledge's sake." Rather, they are intended to be useful, and to be used, by those with responsibility for making decisions about the program, whether at the day-to-day management level or at broader funding or policy levels (see Exhibit 3-F for an evaluation manager's view of this process).

Unfortunately, the experience of evaluators is replete with instances of evaluation findings that were virtually ignored by those to whom they were reported. There are numerous reasons why this may happen, many of which are not within the control of the evaluator. Program circumstances may change, for instance, between the initiation of the evaluation and its completion in ways that make the evaluation results irrelevant when they are delivered. But lack of utilization may also occur because the evaluation does not actually provide information useful to the decisionmakers for the decisions they must make. Moreover, this can happen rather innocently as well as through ineptness. It may well be, for instance, that an evaluation plan looks like it will produce relevant information but, when that information is generated, it is not as useful as the recipients expected. It may also happen that those to

---

⟨⟨⟨ EXHIBIT 3-F   Lessons Learned About the Utilization of Evaluation

An evaluation manager for a social services organization summarized his observations about the use of evaluation findings by program decisionmakers as follows:

1. The utilization of evaluation or research does not take care of itself. Evaluation reports are inanimate objects, and it takes human interest and personal action to use and implement evaluation findings and recommendations. The implications of evaluation must be transferred from the written page to the agenda of program managers.

2. Utilization of evaluation, through which program lessons are identified, usually demands changed behaviors or policies. This requires the shifting of priorities and the development of new action plans for the operational manager.

3. Utilization of evaluation research involves political activity. It is based on a recognition and focus on who in the organization has what authority to make x, y, or z happen. To change programs or organizations as a result of some evaluation requires support from the highest levels of management.

4. Ongoing systems to engender evaluation use are necessary to legitimate and formalize the organizational learning process. Otherwise, utilization can become a personalized issue and evaluation advocates just another self-serving group vying for power and control.

SOURCE: Quoted, with permission, from Anthony Dibella, "The Research Manager's Role in Encouraging Evaluation Use," *Evaluation Practice*, 1990, 11(2):119.

---

whom the evaluation results are directed are not initially altogether clear in their own minds about what information they need for what purposes.

With these considerations in mind, we advocate that the development of evaluation questions involve *backward mapping*, which starts with a specification of the desired endpoint then works backward to determine what must be done to get there (Elmore, 1980). Taking this approach, the essential discussion with the evaluation sponsor and other key stakeholders must establish who will use the evaluation results and for what purposes. Note that the question is not who is *interested* in the evaluation findings. Although relevant, that question does not probe the matter of what

actions or decisions are potentially affected. The evaluator wants to come as close as possible to understanding, in an explicit, detailed fashion, who specifically will use the evaluation and what specifically they will use it for. For instance, the administrator and board of directors of the program may intend to use the evaluation results to set administrative priorities for the next fiscal year. Or the legislative committee that oversees a program area may desire the evaluation as input to their deliberations about continued funding for the program. Or the program monitors in the government agency that has initiated the program may want to know if it represents a successful model that should be disseminated to other sites.

In each case, the evaluator should work with the respective evaluation users to describe the range of potential decisions or actions that they might consider taking and the form and nature of information that they would find pertinent in their deliberation. To press this exercise to the greatest level of specificity, the evaluator might even generate dummy information of the sort that the evaluation might produce, for example, "20% of the clients who complete the program relapse within 30 days," and discuss with the prospective users what this would mean to them and how they would use such information.

A careful specification of the intended use of the evaluation results and the nature of the information that is expected to be useful leads directly to the formulation of questions the evaluation must attempt to answer (e.g., "What proportion of the clients who complete the program relapse during the first month?") and provides a context within which to set priorities for which questions are most important. At this juncture, consideration must also be given to matters of timing. It may be that some questions must be answered before others can be asked, or users may need answers to some questions before others because of their own timetable for decision making. The important questions can then be organized into related groups, combined and integrated as appropriate, sequenced in appropriate time lines, and worked into final form in consultation with the designated users. With this in hand, developing the evaluation plan is largely a matter of working backward to determine what measures, observations, procedures, and the like must be undertaken to provide answers to the important questions in the form that the users require by the time they are needed.

Analysis of Program Assumptions and Theory

Evaluation is about assessing how the program is performing, whether at some global level or with regard to specific functions and aspects. Most evaluation questions, therefore, are variations on the theme of "Is what's supposed to be happening actually happening?" for example, "Are the intended target participants being reached?" "Are the services adequately delivered?" or "Are the goals being met?" A very useful analysis of a program for purposes of identifying relevant and important evaluation questions is to delineate in some detail just what it is that is supposed to be happening in a program. The evaluator can construct a representation, a conceptual model, of how the program is expected to work and the connections presumed between its various activities and functions and the social benefits it is intended to produce. This representation of the program assumptions and expectations can then be used to identify those aspects of the program most essential to effective performance. These, in turn, raise evaluation-related questions about whether the key assumptions and expectations are reasonable and appropriate and, if so, whether the program is enacting them in an effective manner.

What we are describing here is an explication of the program theory, the set of assumptions about the relationships between the strategy and tactics the program has adopted and the social benefits it is expected to produce. *Theory* has a rather grandiose sound to it and few program directors would claim that they were working from any distinct theory. Among the dictionary definitions of theory, however, we find "a particular conception or view of

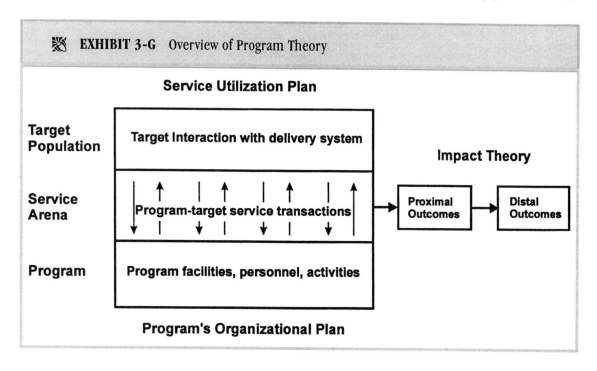

EXHIBIT 3-G   Overview of Program Theory

something to be done or of the method of doing it." It is generally this sense of the word that evaluators mean when they refer to program theory. It might alternatively be called the program conceptualization or, perhaps, the program plan, blueprint, or design.

Evaluators have long recognized the importance of program theory as a basis for formulating and prioritizing evaluation questions, designing evaluation research, and interpreting evaluation findings (Bickman, 1987; Chen and Rossi, 1980; Weiss, 1972; Wholey, 1979). It is, however, described and used under various different names, for example, logic model, program model, outcome line, cause map, action theory, and so forth. Moreover, there is no general consensus about how best to depict or represent program theory, and many different versions can be found in the evaluation litera-

ture, although all show common elements. Consequently, we will describe representations of several separate components of program theory that we have found useful in our own evaluation activities and that illustrate themes found in most variations of this type of analysis.

For this purpose, we depict the typical social program as centering on a set of program-target transactions, those points of direct contact between program operations and the target population the program serves that occur in some service arena (see Exhibit 3-G). These might involve counseling sessions for women with eating disorders in therapists' offices, recreational activities for high-risk youths at a community center, educational presentations to local citizens' groups, nutrition posters in a clinic, informational pamphlets about empowerment zones and tax law mailed to potential investors, delivery of meals to the front doors of elderly persons, or any such point of service contact. On one side of this program-target transaction, we have the program as an organizational entity, with its various facilities, personnel, resources, activities, and so forth. On the other side, we have the target participants in their lifespaces with their various situations and behaviors, including their circumstances and experiences in relation to the service delivery system that provides them with points of contact with the program.

For purposes of explicating and analyzing program theory, this simple scheme highlights three different, but interrelated, theory components, each of which focuses attention on an important facet of program performance. Most important are the program-target transactions, for they constitute the means by which the program expects to bring about its intended effects. These transactions are thus operationalizations of the program's *impact theory*, the assumptions about the change process actuated or facilitated by the program and the improved conditions expected to result from inducing that change. This impact theory may be as simple as presuming that exposure to information about the negative effects of drug abuse will motivate high school students to abstain or as complex as the ways in which an eighth-grade science curriculum will lead to deeper understanding of natural phenomena. It may be as informal as the commonsense presumption that providing hot meals to elderly persons improves their nutrition or as formal as classical conditioning theory adapted to treating phobias. Whatever its nature, however, an impact theory of some sort constitutes the essence of a social program. If the assumptions embodied in that theory about how desired changes are brought about by program action are faulty, or if they are valid but not well operationalized

by the program, the intended social benefits will not be achieved.

To instigate the change process posited in the program's impact theory, the program must first provide the intended services to the target population. If we view the program from the perspective of the target population, attention focuses on the points of service delivery and their accessibility, whether the services are actually delivered to the intended targets, and the extent to which targets complete the full sequence of services. Every program works within a framework of assumptions and expectations about how to reach the target population, provide and sequence service contacts with those designated as clients, and conclude the relationship when services are no longer needed or appropriate. These assumptions and expectations constitute an important part of program theory that we will call the program's *service utilization plan*.

In simplest form, a service utilization plan proposes that if the intended targets experience particular encounters and opportunities provided by the program's service delivery system, they will receive the intended services. For a program to increase awareness of AIDS risk, for instance, the service utilization plan may be simply that appropriate persons will read informative posters if they are put up in subway cars. A multifaceted AIDS prevention program, on the other hand, may be organized on the assumptions that if high-risk drug abusers in specified neighborhoods encounter outreach workers and are referred to clinics, and if streetfront clinics are available nearby, and if clients receive encouragement from case managers to maintain continuing program contact, and if they receive testing and information at the clinics, then high-risk drug abusers will have received the preventive service package the program intends to deliver.

EXHIBIT 3-H The Three Components of Program Theory

Program theory

Process theory

Organizational plan
How to garner, configure, and deploy resources, and organize program activities so that the intended service delivery system is developed and maintained.

Service utilization plan
How the intended target population receives the intended amount of the intended intervention through interaction with the program's service delivery system.

Impact theory
How the intended intervention for the specified target population brings about the desired social benefits.

The program, of course, must be organized in such a way that it can, indeed, actually provide the intended services, which, in turn, are expected to produce the desired benefits. The third component of program theory, therefore, has to do with the nature of the program resources, personnel, administration, and general organization. It might be called the program's *organizational plan*. It can generally be represented as a set of propositions: If the program has such and such resources, facilities, personnel, and so on, is organized and administered in such and such a manner, and engages in such and such activities and functions, then a viable organization will result with the capability of developing and/or maintaining the intended service delivery system and corresponding service utilization. Elements of programs' organizational theories include such presumptions as that case managers should have master's degrees in social work and at least five years' experience, that at least 20 case managers should be employed, that the agency should have an advisory board that represents local business owners, that there should be an administrative coordinator assigned to each site,

that working relations should be maintained with regard to referrals from the Department of Public Health, and so forth.

Adequate resources and effective organization, in this scheme, are the factors that make it possible to develop and maintain a service delivery system that enables utilization of the services so that the target population receives the intervention. Program organization and the service delivery system it supports are the parts of the program most directly under the control of program administrators and staff. These two aspects together are often referred to as *program process*, and correspondingly, the assumptions and expectations on which program process is based may be called the program's *process theory*.

The intervention the program implements as a result of its organizational and service delivery activities, in turn, is the means by which the program expects to bring about the desired changes in the target population or social conditions. Thus, all three theory components are closely interrelated and, collectively, can be viewed as constituting the overall program theory (Exhibit 3-H gives a summary of the theory components). With this overview, we turn now to a more detailed discussion of each of these theory components with particular attention to how the evaluator can construct a workable representation of program theory and use it to analyze the program and generate potentially important evaluation questions.

The Program Impact Theory

The central premise of any social program is that the services it delivers to the target population induce some change that improves social conditions. The program impact theory is the set of assumptions embodied in the program about how its services actuate or facilitate the intended change. Program impact theory, therefore, is causal theory: It describes a cause-and-effect sequence in which certain program activities are the instigating causes and certain social benefits are the effects they eventually produce. Evaluators, therefore, typically represent program impact theory in the form of a causal diagram showing the pattern of cause-and-effect linkages presumed to connect the program activities with the expected outcomes (Chen, 1990; Lipsey, 1993; Martin and Kettner, 1996). Because programs rarely exercise complete, direct control over the social conditions they are expected to improve, they must generally work indirectly by attempting to alter some critical but manageable aspect of the situation, which, in turn, is expected to lead to more far-reaching improvements. For instance, a program cannot make it impossible for people to abuse alcohol, but it can attempt to change their attitudes and motivation toward alcohol in ways that help them avoid abuse. Similarly, a program may not be able, at a stroke, to eliminate poverty in a target population, but it may be able to help unemployed

persons prepare for and find jobs that pay a living wage.

The simplest program impact theory, therefore, is generally the basic "two step" in which services change some intermediate condition such as motivation or employability that, in turn, helps ameliorate the social conditions of concern, for example, by reducing alcohol abuse or unemployment (Lipsey and Pollard, 1989). More complex program theories may have more steps along the path between program and social benefit and, perhaps, involve more than one distinct path. Exhibit 3-I illustrates causal diagrams for several different program impact theories. The distinctive features of any representation of program impact theory are that each element is either a cause or an effect and that the causal linkages between those elements show a chain of events that begins with program actions and ends with change in the social conditions the program ultimately intends to improve.

Depiction of the program's impact theory has considerable power as a framework for analyzing a program and generating significant evaluation questions. First, the process of making that theory explicit brings a sharp focus to the nature, range, and sequence of program outcomes that are reasonable to expect and may be appropriate for the evaluator to investigate. Every event following the instigating program activity in the causal diagram representing a program's impact theory is an outcome. Those following directly from the instigating program activities are the most direct outcomes, often called *proximal* or immediate outcomes, whereas those further down the chain constitute the more *distal* or ultimate outcomes. Program impact theory highlights the dependence of the more distal, and generally more important, outcomes on successful attainment of the more proximal ones. For a

EXHIBIT 3-I   Diagrams Illustrating Program Impact Theories

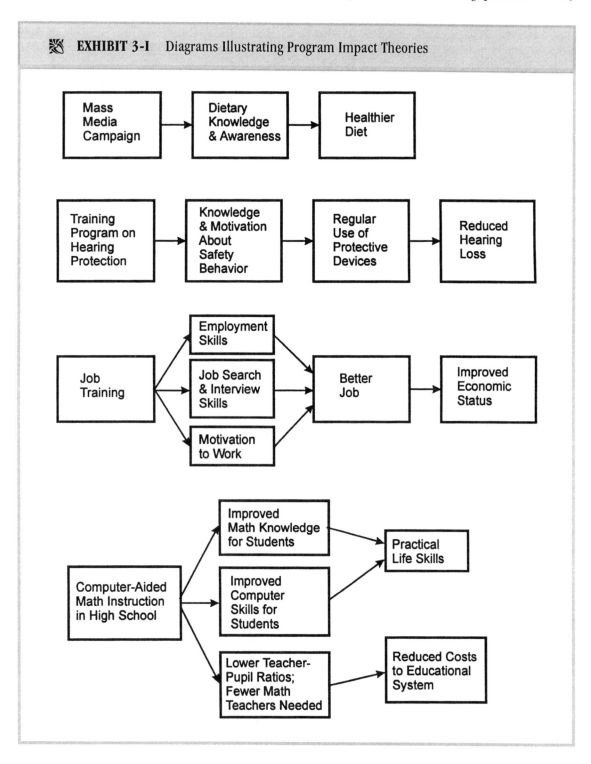

full understanding of program impact, therefore, it may be important for the evaluation to examine the proximal outcomes even when they are not themselves the accomplishments for which the program will be held accountable.

A second, and related, contribution of program impact theory to formulation of key evaluation questions is the distinction it reveals between two rather different sets of assumptions inherent in the program. The first set of assumptions represents the expectation that the program actions will have the intended effects on the proximal or immediate outcomes. For instance, a mass media campaign about AIDS must assume that the public service announcements, billboards, and other promotion it does (program actions) will result in heightened awareness and knowledge of the risk of unsafe sex practices (proximal outcomes). This set of assumptions thus links program actions to the immediate outcomes expected to follow from them and has been referred to as the program's "action theory" (Chen, 1990; see also Exhibit 3-J). Because it is only one link in the impact theory, however, we would prefer to call it the *action hypothesis*. Articulating the action hypothesis allows the evaluator to identify the important evaluation questions that relate to it, particularly with regard to whether the intended actions were implemented and the expected proximal effects achieved.

The second set of assumptions inherent in program impact theory connects the proximal outcomes with the distal ones. In the mass media campaign, for instance, it is expected that if knowledge and awareness are heightened (proximal outcomes), appropriate safe-sex behavior will follow with corresponding decreases in AIDS transmission (distal outcomes). This part of the process is completely out of the control of the program; it is only

assumed that if the program does its part by implementing the campaign in such a way that knowledge and awareness are heightened, the intended social benefits will follow. These assumptions have been referred to as the program's "conceptual theory" (Chen, 1990; see also Exhibit 3-J), although, again, we would prefer *conceptual hypothesis*. This hypothesis is the part of the impact theory that assumes that success in changing the targeted aspect of the problem (proximal outcomes) will, in turn, result in the desired social benefits (distal outcomes).

This aspect of impact theory, of course, draws the evaluator's attention to another set of linkages that might bear investigation and helps formulate questions about whether, given proximal outcome A, distal outcome B actually follows. The evaluator, therefore, might find it important not only to ask if awareness and knowledge of AIDS risk increased, but if such increases were further associated with changed behavior and reduced incidence of AIDS. This line of analysis helps identify the full set of outcome variables potentially relevant to an impact evaluation.

Of course, the intended outcomes may not be achieved by a program and the evaluator will generally want to be in a position to explain why unfavorable results occurred. One of the useful applications of program impact theory is for identification of the various points in the anticipated chain of events where things may not happen as expected. At a minimum, evaluators may wish to distinguish *implementation failure* from *theory failure*.

Implementation failure is the failure of the program to adequately deliver the services or perform the actions that are supposed to start off the change process expected to lead to improved social conditions (Exhibit 3-K provides an example). Obviously, if the program is not

EXHIBIT 3-J   Program Impact Theory: The Action and Conceptual Hypotheses

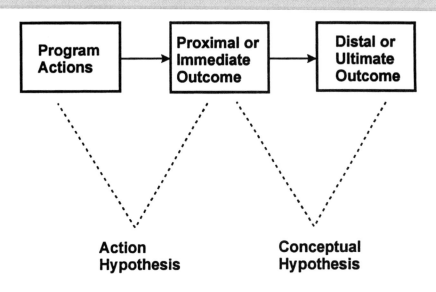

Example:

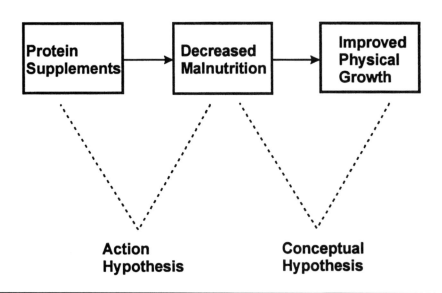

SOURCE: Adapted from Huey-Tsyh Chen, *Theory-Driven Evaluations* (Newbury Park, CA: Sage, 1990).

✖ EXHIBIT 3-K Implementation Failure: A Case Study of a School Not Ready to Support Change

---

A team of administrators and staff from a Southern school district worked with evaluators to plan a program to reduce problem behaviors—including drug and alcohol use, delinquent behavior, pregnancy, nonattendance, and misconduct—in a middle school with a large proportion of high-risk students. A program theory was developed on the basis of research showing that improvements in social bonding, social competency skills, and school success should result in a reduction in problem behaviors. Funding was obtained to support a four-year program with the following components:

- *Instructional improvement:* Cooperative learning techniques were to be used school-wide. In addition, for high-risk students, one-on-one tutoring was to be provided by community volunteers.

- *Mentoring:* High-risk students were to be paired with teachers who volunteered as "academic godparents" to tutor them, monitor their progress, and share in recreational activities.

- *Social competency promotion:* The Botvin life skills training (LST) and Manning's cognitive self-instruction (CSI) curriculum were to be implemented schoolwide. These were augmented with a social problem solving (SPS) course for seventh graders, a violence prevention (VP) curriculum for eighth graders, and a career and educational decision skills (CED) class for sixth and eighth graders.

Assessment of the implementation of this multicomponent program revealed the following:

- The first school year was largely a start-up period. A group of teachers was trained to use cooperative learning techniques, but only 13 actually used them. The CED course was implemented but not all the lessons were covered. Several teachers were trained to teach the LST course and a portion of it was taught in health classes.

- During the second school year, cooperative learning was implemented by more than half the teachers but in fewer than half their lessons. The CED course was provided to most of the eighth graders with about half the intended number of sessions. Seventh-grade high-risk students received the SPS course but eighth graders got neither the LST nor VP modules. About one-third of the high-risk students received tutoring, but the average was only five sessions for the year.

- In the third year, all the program components except tutoring and mentoring were incorporated into a single life focus course adapted to each grade level. Not all the intended material was covered, however, so some students did not get some of the components and, in other cases, received fewer lessons than intended. The mentoring component improved from the previous year, but the high-risk tutoring component deteriorated. Cooperative learning was implemented more fully but still at only about two-thirds the intended level.

- During the final year of the program, implementation of a few of the components improved but, in general, the overall level of the program declined.

In summary, the program was never implemented according to the initial intentions of the team that developed it. The outcome evaluation examined change in measures of problem behavior and antisocial attitudes, positive school adjustment, and school attendance. Not surprisingly, the results showed no reductions on any of these variables.

SOURCE: Adapted from Denise C. Gottfredson, Carolyn M. Fink, Stacy Skroban, and Gary D. Gottfredson, "Making Prevention Work," in *Establishing Preventive Services*, eds. R. P. Weissberg, T. P. Gullotta, R. L. Hampton, B. A. Ryan, and G. R. Adams (Thousand Oaks, CA: Sage, 1997), pp. 219-252.

implemented, or implementation is incomplete or weak, we would not expect it to be very successful in producing the intended outcomes, either the most immediate proximal outcomes or the ultimate outcomes to which it aspires. Evaluators gather information on this aspect of program performance through assessments of program process, including attention to both service utilization and program organizational issues.

Programs can also fail when the intended program activities are implemented but those activities do not actually have the intended effects. In the example of the mass media campaign on AIDS risk, the campaign may be implemented just as planned but may not be widely noticed and, therefore, not result in any heightened awareness or greater knowledge of AIDS risk. This is one form of theory failure, in particular, a failure of the action hypothesis—the program services do not bring about the immediate outcomes that are expected.

Another form of theory failure involves the conceptual hypothesis. This form of theory failure occurs when the program implements the intended services and, indeed, achieves the expected proximal outcomes, but those, in turn, do not lead to the expected distal outcomes. Thus, a mass media campaign may be hugely successful in raising awareness and knowledge about AIDS risk and how to reduce it, but people may not translate that knowledge into changed sexual behavior (one of the distal outcomes expected), and consequently, there will be no reduction in the incidence of AIDS (the social benefit the program ultimately hopes to produce). Exhibit 3-L provides an example of theory failure.

Although it simplifies considerably, we might liken the causal sequence embodied in program impact theory to the assumption that flipping a switch turns on a light. If we analyze this situation closely, it first requires moving one's hand to properly manipulate the switch, then having the switch activate a flow of current that causes the light to illuminate. Our assumptions about the relationship between moving our hand and the position of the switch are the action hypothesis. We can fail to change the position of the switch because we do not move our hands at all, or not the way we intended (implementation failure), or because we move them exactly the way we intend but somehow those moves are not successful in flipping the switch (failure of the action hypothesis). If the switch is flipped, our assumption that the light will come on represents our conceptual hypothesis. We can quite successfully manipulate the switch and still get no light if that part of the impact theory is in error, for example, the circuit is broken or the switch is not hooked up to a circuit (failure of the conceptual hypothesis).

The concept of program impact theory, the distinctions between proximal and distal outcomes, and the related distinctions between the program's action and conceptual hypotheses, therefore, can alert the evaluator to different aspects of program performance that may be appropriate to assess. It is for this reason that articulation of program impact theory during the planning stage of an evaluation is an important form of analysis for the evaluator to undertake. That exercise almost always yields very relevant evaluation questions regarding whether key program actions were implemented as intended and, if so, whether they produced the expected effects. Of course, the evaluator must also identify those key program activities in some detail so that appropriate questions can be raised about program implementation. This is where program process theory, encompassing service utilization and program organization, can be helpful.

※ EXHIBIT 3-L   Theory Failure: A Children's Mental Health Demonstration Project

Mental health services for children are often underfunded, fragmented, and limited in variety. The five-year, $80 million Fort Bragg Demonstration Project was designed to test an innovative alternative to traditional mental health systems for children. Developed around the concept of a "continuum of care," the Demonstration Project was organized to deliver needed services on an individualized basis at all levels of severity using case management and interdisciplinary treatment teams to integrate and coordinate care. This variant of managed care was expected to result in improved treatment outcomes and lower cost of care per client.

The Demonstration Project was set up for the 42,000 military dependents under age 18 in the vicinity of the Fort Bragg military base in North Carolina. For evaluation purposes, two comparison sites were selected—Fort Campbell, Kentucky, and Fort Stewart, Georgia. Dependent children in those areas received mental health care under a conventional health insurance plan in which parents used independent practitioners or agencies and were reimbursed, subject to deductibles, by CHAMPUS, the military insurance provider.

The evaluators identified critical implementation and outcome issues with the aid of a carefully developed program theory description. To assess implementation, the program-as-implemented was compared with the program-as-planned. The results showed that, as intended, the demonstration had implemented a single point of entry to services for the target population, provided a comprehensive range of services, and established case management and treatment teams to coordinate services. Moreover, relative to the comparison sites, the services the children received in the Demonstration

Project began sooner, were more individualized, had more variety, lasted longer with fewer dropouts, showed greater continuity and more parent involvement, and represented better matches between treatment and needs as judged by parents. The conclusion of the evaluators was that "the Demonstration was executed with sufficient fidelity to provide an excellent test of the program theory—the continuum of care."

The impact evaluation examined parents' satisfaction, treatment costs, and mental health outcomes with the following results:

- Parents were more satisfied with the services from the Demonstration Project than in the comparison sites.

- The costs per treated child were substantially higher in the Demonstration Project, not lower as expected.

- Mental health data collected on 984 children and families within 30 days after entry into the system and in two follow-up waves six months apart showed essentially no differences in clinical outcomes between the Demonstration and comparison sites. Of 116 distinct comparisons representing general and individualized measures reported by children, parents, therapists, and trained raters, 101 show no significant difference, 7 favored the comparison, and 8 favored the Demonstration.

In short, the continuum of care concept was well implemented but did not produce the effects that were expected on the basis of the program theory. Or, as the evaluators put it, "Commonly accepted wisdom about what is a better quality system of care is called into question."

SOURCE: Adapted from Leonard Bickman, "Implications of a Children's Mental Health Managed Care Demonstration Evaluation," *Journal of Mental Health Administration*, 1996, 23(1):107-118.

*The Program Service
Utilization Plan*

Whereas program impact theory describes the chain of events leading from program-target transactions to the intended improvements in social conditions, the service utilization plan describes the sequence of events through which clients engage in those transactions. The service utilization plan is the set of assumptions and expectations about how the targets will make initial contact with the program and be engaged with it through the completion of the intended services. Its distinctive theme is that it describes the program-target transaction from the perspective of the targets and their experience and history of engagement with the program. An explicit, even if relatively informal, service utilization plan pulls into focus the critical assumptions about how and why the intended recipients of service will actually become engaged with the program and follow through to the point of receiving sufficient services to initiate the change process represented in the program impact theory. In the example of a mass media campaign to reduce AIDS risk, the service utilization plan would describe how persons at risk for AIDS will encounter the communications disseminated by the program and engage them sufficiently for their message to be received. Or, for another example, the service utilization plan for a neighborhood afterschool program for latchkey children would describe how parents are expected to learn of the program and enroll their children as well as how the children are expected to get to the program regularly and return home again afterward.

A program's service utilization plan can be usefully depicted in a flowchart that tracks the various paths program targets can follow from some appropriate point prior to first program contact through a point where there is no longer any contact. Exhibit 3-M shows an example of a simple service utilization flowchart for a hypothetical aftercare program for released psychiatric patients. One of the desirable features of such charts is the identification of possible situations in which the program targets are *not* engaged with the program as intended. For instance, for the community aftercare program in Exhibit 3-M, we see that formerly hospitalized psychiatric patients in the target population may not receive the planned visit from a social worker or referrals to community agencies and, as a consequence, may receive no service at all. The size of this group will be a function of how vigorously the program contacts potentially eligible cases and establishes case management for them. Similarly, a service utilization flowchart can highlight such issues as insufficient referrals from gateway agencies, program dropouts, early terminations prior to receiving the full-service package intended, and other such issues of incomplete service or service not offered or not delivered. Of course, at the same time, it portrays the pattern of outreach, intake, receipt of service, and exit from service that represents the program's scheme for making services available to the targets.

As a tool for program analysis and formulation of evaluation questions, articulating the service utilization plan contributes an important perspective on how the program is designed and what assumptions are made about the ways in which the target population is expected to engage the program services. That perspective facilitates the identification of important questions of program performance related to whether the appropriate target population is being served and in sufficient numbers,

EXHIBIT 3-M Service Utilization Flowchart for an Aftercare Program for Formerly Hospitalized Psychiatric Patients

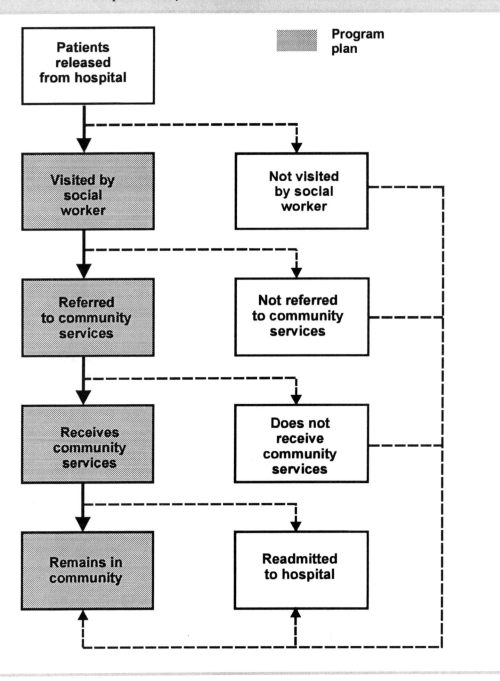

what barriers there may be to entry into the program, the extent to which full and appropriate service is completed by an acceptable proportion of those beginning service, and whether desirable follow-up contact is made following service completion. An evaluator who has made the effort to explicate the program's service utilization plan and analyze its implications for program performance will be able to raise many important issues for consideration in developing the questions around which the evaluation will be designed.

The Program's Organizational Plan

The organizational arrangements and program operations that constitute the routine functions of the program are based on a set of beliefs, assumptions, and expectations about what the program must do to bring about the intended target-program service transactions. These beliefs, assumptions, and expectations are what we call the program's organizational plan. The organizational plan is articulated from the perspective of program management and encompasses both the functions and activities the program is expected to perform and the human, financial, and physical resources required for that performance. Central to this scheme are the program services, those specific activities that constitute the program's role in the target-program transactions expected to lead to social benefits. However, it also must include those functions that provide essential preconditions and ongoing support to the organization's ability to provide its primary services, for instance, fund-raising, personnel management, facilities acquisition and maintenance, political liaison, and the like.

There are many ways the evaluator may depict the program's organizational plan. To be consistent with the schemes we have presented for impact theory and the service utilization plan, it is desirable to adopt a form that centers on those target-program service transactions that constitute the major points of contact between the program and the target population. The first element of the organizational plan, then, will be a description of the program's objectives with regard to the particular services it will provide: what those services are, how much is to be provided, to whom, and on what schedule. The next element of the organizational plan might then describe the resources and prior functions necessary to engage in those critical service activities. For instance, sufficient personnel with appropriate credentials and skills will be required as will logistical support, proper facilities and equipment, funding, supervision, clerical support, and so forth.

As with the other portions of program theory, it is often useful to describe a program's organizational plan with a chart or diagram. Exhibit 3-N presents an example in that form that describes the major organizational components of the hypothetical aftercare program for psychiatric patients whose service utilization scheme is depicted in Exhibit 3-M. A rather common way of depicting the organizational plan of a program is in terms of *inputs*, representing the resources and constraints applicable to the program, and *activities*, indicating the services the program is expected to provide. When included in a full *logic model*, these schemes typically represent receipt of services (service utilization) as program *outputs*, which, in turn, are related to the desired outcomes. Exhibit 3-O shows such a scheme, drawn from a widely used workbook prepared by the United Way of America.

Naturally, a description of program organization and articulation of the underlying as-

EXHIBIT 3-N Organizational Schematic for an Aftercare Program for Formerly Hospitalized Psychiatric Patients

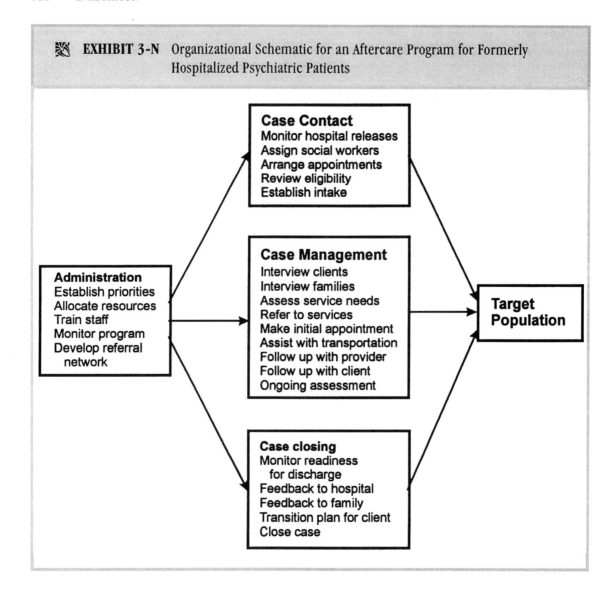

sumptions, expectations, and intentions reveal many aspects of the program related to how effectively it performs its various functions. Thus, the evaluator can use the organizational plan to generate evaluation questions that may be relevant to the design and planning of the evaluation. One major category of issues, for instance, relates to whether the program is actually implementing the functions and activities that are intended and in the intended way. Questions on this topic can be rather general or, more often, quite specific and detailed, for instance, whether the case managers are contacting the teachers about the child's

⚜ EXHIBIT 3-O A Logic Model for a Teen Mother Parenting Education Program

| | | | Outcomes | | |
Inputs	Activities	Outputs	Initial	Intermediate	Longer Term
Agency provides MSW program manager, part-time RN instructor, nationally certified education manuals, videos, and other teaching tools.	Program provides parenting classes on prenatal-through-infant nutrition, development, safety, and caretaking delivered in high schools twice a week for one hour to teen mothers from three months prior, to one year after, delivery of a child.	Pregnant teens attend program.	Teens are knowledgeable about prenatal nutrition and health guidelines.	Teens follow proper nutrition and health guidelines. Teens deliver healthy babies.	Babies achieve appropriate 12-month milestones for physical, motor, verbal, and social development.
Agency and high school identify pregnant teens to participate in program.			Teens are knowledgeable about proper care, feeding, and social interaction with infants.	Teens provide proper care, feeding, and social interaction to their babies.	

SOURCE: Adaped from United Way of America, *Measuring Program Outcomes: A Practical Approach.* Alexandria, VA: Author, 1996, p. 42. Used by permission, United Way of America.

schoolwork for every child in every family assigned to their caseload. A related question is whether those functions and activities are optimally configured for their purposes, represent appropriate standards of professional practice, are adequately supervised, and so forth.

Another set of important organizational questions relates to program resources. An evaluation may encompass questions about whether the personnel are sufficient in numbers or credentials for their assigned tasks, the adequacy of program funding, availability of the requisite facilities and equipment, and many other such matters. Still another category of organizationally important issues has to do with the administration, management, and governance of the program. Questions might

be raised about specific managerial functions or the effectiveness of overall program administration. Similarly, the nature and relationship of governing and advisory boards may be of interest as well as relations with other agencies, superordinate organizational structures, political entities, and so on.

How to Articulate Program Theory

Program theory in the detail indicated above is rarely written down in the documentation the program has on hand for the evaluator to examine, although the broad outlines will likely appear in statements of the program's mission and services or in funding proposals and annual reports. Typically, then, the evaluator must articulate the program theory on the basis of an initial investigation of the program being evaluated. Once articulated in a form endorsed by key program stakeholders, the program theory can itself be an object of evaluation. That is, an important evaluation question may relate to how well conceptualized the program is, and the evaluator may conduct an explicit assessment of the program theory. Chapter 5 of this volume describes in some detail how program theory can be evaluated. Because program theory must first be articulated before it can be evaluated, Chapter 5 also describes the ways the evaluator can reveal and express program theory. When program theory is formulated for the purpose of analyzing a program to identify pertinent evaluation questions, as discussed in this chapter, the same procedures are applicable. Because a full discussion is provided in Chapter 5, we will mention only a few general points here.

It is, for instance, important to recognize that articulation of program theory should be mainly a process of discovery and not one of invention. The evaluator is rarely the authoritative voice with regard to how the program is expected to work. The understandings of those persons who originate, plan, administer, and staff a social program are the primary source of information on this matter. The evaluator, of course, may play a large and creative role in interpreting and organizing that information. Moreover, few programs are so unique that they bear no resemblance to at least some other programs whose funders, administrators, staff, and so forth can be consulted by the evaluator for additional perspectives on how such programs should work. There may also be pertinent information available from professional

and research literature about that type of program and sources of expertise and experience among the members of the professions involved, for example, social work, nursing, psychiatry, or teaching.

The greatest difficulty the evaluator will encounter is that the various components of program theory often are implicit rather than explicit and may be in the form of tacit knowledge that is so routinized in the program context that it is rarely thought about or discussed. The evaluator attempting to describe the program theory, therefore, must generally draw it out piecemeal from program informants, available documents, and the professional and research literature, and then attempt to synthesize the pieces into a coherent whole. This exercise must involve considerable interaction with program stakeholders, especially administrators, who should provide both critical input and feedback on each iteration the evaluator produces. A useful way to approach this task is to draw figures and charts such as those shown in Exhibits 3-I, 3-M, 3-N, and 3-O for the various components of program theory, then go over them in detail with program informants to obtain feedback for refinement.

It is wise to avoid evaluation jargon in this task. Most program administrators will have little notion of what is meant by "program theory" if asked outright and are likely to assume it means something more formal and abstract than it does in this context. On the other hand, inquiries about how the program works, what various personnel do and why, and other such questions at a practical level generally lead to fruitful and often lengthy discussions that can be very informative. It does sometimes happen, nonetheless, that the effort to explicate program theory will reveal that there are important areas of the program conceptualization that are vague, undetermined, or inconsistent. In such cases, it may be appropriate for the evaluation itself to encompass a systematic assessment of the program theory aimed at identifying weaknesses and assisting program personnel in clarifying and refining their understanding of what the program should be doing and why (Chapter 5, on assessing program theory, describes how this might be done).

COLLATING EVALUATION QUESTIONS AND SETTING PRIORITIES

The evaluator who thoroughly explores stakeholder concerns and conducts an analysis of program issues guided by carefully developed descriptions of program theory will turn up many questions that the evaluation might address. The task at this point becomes one of organizing those questions according to distinct themes and setting priorities among them.

Organization is generally rather straightforward. Evaluation questions tend to cluster around different program functions (e.g., recruitment, services, outcomes) and, as noted earlier, around different evaluation issues (need, design, implementation, impact, efficiency). In addition, evaluation questions tend to show a natural hierarchical structure with many very specific questions (e.g., "Are elderly homebound persons in the public housing project aware of the program?") nested under broader questions ("Are we reaching our target population?").

Setting priorities to determine which questions the evaluation should be designed to answer can be much more challenging. Once articulated, most of the questions about the program that arise during the planning process are likely to seem interesting to some stakeholder or another, or to the evaluators themselves. Rarely will resources be available to address them all, however. At this juncture, it is especially important for the evaluator to focus on the purpose of the evaluation and the expected uses to be made of its findings. There is little point to investing time and effort in developing information that is of little use to any stakeholder.

That said, we must caution against an overly narrow interpretation of what information is useful. Evaluation utilization studies have shown that practical, instrumental use, for example, for program decision making, is only one of the contributions evaluation information makes (Leviton and Hughes, 1981; Rich, 1977; Weiss, 1988). Equally important in many cases are conceptual and persuasive uses—the contribution of evaluation findings to the way in which a program and the social problems to which it responds are understood and debated. Evaluations often identify issues, frame analysis, and sharpen the focus of discussion in ways that are influential to the decision-making process even when there is no direct connection evident between any evaluation finding and any specific program decision. A fuller discussion of this issue is presented in Chapter 12; our purpose here is only to point out the possibility that some evaluation questions may be important to answer even though no immediate use or user is evident.

With the priority evaluation questions for a program decided on through some reasonable process, the evaluator is ready to design that substantial part of the evaluation that will be devoted to trying to answer them. Most of the remainder of this book discusses the approaches, methods, and considerations related to that task. That discussion is organized to follow the natural logical progression of evaluation questions and thus addresses, in turn, how to assess the need for a program, the program theory or plan for addressing that need, the implementation of the program plan and the associated program process, the impact or outcome of the program implementation on the social need, and the efficiency with which the program attains its outcomes.

SUMMARY

- A critical phase in evaluation planning is the identification and formulation of the questions the evaluation will address. Those questions focus the evaluation on the areas of program performance most at issue for key stakeholders and guide the design so that it that will provide meaningful information about program performance. Good evaluation questions, therefore, must identify clear, observable dimensions of program performance that are relevant to the program's goals and represent domains in which the program can realistically be expected to have accomplishments.

- What most distinguishes evaluation questions, however, is that they involve criteria by which the identified dimensions of program performance can be judged. If the formulation of the evaluation questions can include performance standards on which key stakeholders agree, evaluation planning will be easier and the potential for disagreement over the interpretation of the results will be reduced.

- To ensure that the matters of greatest significance are covered in the evaluation design, the evaluation questions are best formulated through interaction and negotiation with the evaluation sponsors and other stakeholders representative of significant groups or distinctly positioned in relation to program decision making.

- Although stakeholder input is critical, the evaluator must also be prepared to identify program issues that might warrant inquiry. This requires that the evaluator conduct a somewhat independent analysis of the assumptions and expectations on which the program is based.

- One useful way to reveal aspects of program performance that may be important to assess in an evaluation is to make the program theory explicit. Program theory describes the assumptions inherent in a program about the activities it undertakes and how those relate to the social benefits it is expected to produce. It encompasses impact theory, which links program actions to the intended outcomes, and process theory, which describes a program's organizational plan and scheme for ensuring utilization of its services by the target population.

✖ When these various procedures have generated a full set of candidate evaluation questions, the evaluator must organize them into related clusters and draw on stakeholder input and professional judgment to set priorities among them. With the priority evaluation questions for a program determined, the evaluator is then ready to design the part of the evaluation that will be devoted to answering them.

KEY CONCEPTS FOR CHAPTER 4

Needs assessment
An evaluative study that answers questions about the social conditions a program is intended to address and the need for the program. Needs assessment may also be used to determine whether there is a need for a new program and to compare or prioritize needs within and across program areas.

Key informants
Persons whose personal or professional position gives them a perspective on the nature and scope of a social problem or a target population and whose views are obtained during a needs assessment.

Survey
Systematic collection of information from a defined population, usually by means of interviews or questionnaires administered to a sample of units in the population.

Focus group
A small panel of persons selected for their knowledge or perspective on a topic of interest that is convened to discuss the topic with the assistance of a facilitator. The discussion is usually recorded and used to identify important themes or to construct descriptive summaries of views and experiences on the focal topic.

Social indicator
Periodic measurements designed to track the course of a social condition over time.

Incidence
The number of new cases of a particular problem or condition that arise in a specified area during a specified period of time.

Prevalence
The number of existing cases with a particular condition in a specified area at a specified time.

Population at risk
The individuals or units in a specified area with characteristics judged to indicate that they have a significant probability of having or developing a particular condition.

Population in need
The individuals or units in a specified area that currently manifest a particular problematic condition.

Sensitivity
The extent to which the criteria used to identify a target population result in the inclusion of individuals or units that actually have or will develop the condition to which the program is directed.

Specificity
The extent to which the criteria used to identify the target population result in the exclusion of individuals or units who do not have or will not develop the condition to which the program is directed.

Rate
The occurrence or existence of a particular condition expressed as a proportion of units in the relevant population (e.g., deaths per 1,000 adults).

CHAPTER 4

ASSESSING THE NEED
FOR A PROGRAM

Previous chapters provided an overview of evaluation and an orientation to the critical themes in tailoring an evaluation to program circumstances and formulating the specific questions an evaluation will be designed to answer. Beginning with this chapter, we turn to fuller discussion of the various methods and approaches evaluators use to address different categories of evaluation questions.

The category of evaluation questions that is logically most fundamental to program evaluation has to do with the nature of the social problem the program is expected to ameliorate and the needs of the population experiencing that problem. These questions follow from the assumption that the purpose of social programs is to bring about improvement in problematic social conditions and that they are accountable to those who fund and support them for making a good faith effort to do so.

Needs assessment, in general, is a systematic approach to identifying social problems, determining their extent, and accurately defining the target population to be served and the nature of their service needs. From a program evaluation perspective, needs assessment is the means by which an evaluator determines if, indeed, there is a need for a program and, if so, what program services are most appropriate to that need. Such an assessment is critical to the effective design of new programs. However, it is equally relevant to established programs because there are many circumstances in which it cannot merely be assumed that the program is needed or that the services it provides are well suited to the nature of the need.

What makes the assessment of the need for a program so fundamental, of course, is that a program cannot be effective at ameliorating a social problem if there is no problem to begin with or if the program services do not actually relate to the problem. The concepts and procedures an evaluator can use to conduct this critical investigation of the nature and extent of the need for a program are discussed in this chapter.

As we described in Chapter 1, a fundamental premise of program evaluation within the human service domain is that effective programs are instruments for improving social conditions. Indeed, bringing about such improvement is the primary mission and reason for being of social programs (which is not to say that they are not also influenced by other political and organizational imperatives). Whether a program addresses a significant social need in a plausible way and does so in a manner that is responsive to the circumstances of those in need, therefore, are essential questions for evaluating the effectiveness of a social program.

Answering these questions for a given program first requires a description of the social problem the program intends to ameliorate. With that description in hand, the evaluator can ask if the program theory embodies a valid conceptualization of the problem and an appropriate means of remedying it. If that question is answered in the affirmative, attention can turn to whether the program is actually implemented in line with the program theory and, if so, whether the intended improvements in the social conditions actually result and at what cost. Thus, the logic of program evaluation builds upward from careful description of the social problem the program is expected to ameliorate.

Thorny issues in this domain revolve around deciding just what is meant by a need in contrast, say, to a want or desire, and what ideals or expectations should provide the benchmarks for distinguishing a need (cf. McKillip, 1998; Scriven, 1991). We will not attempt to resolve these issues here, if indeed they can be resolved, but will be content with the notion that a need is a social construction negotiated between a set of social agents with responsibility for social programs and policy and a set of claimants and their advocates who assert that a problem exists that warrants intervention.

The family of procedures used by evaluators and other social researchers to systematically describe and diagnose social needs is generally referred to as *needs assessment*. Its purpose is to determine if there is a need or problem and, if so, what its nature, depth, and scope are. In addition, needs assessment often encompasses the process of comparing and prioritizing needs according to how serious, neglected, or salient they are.

Within the context of program evaluation, however, the primary focus of needs assessment is not on human needs broadly defined but, rather, on social conditions deemed unsatisfactory through some process of social judgment and presumed remediable by social programs. The essential tasks for the program evaluator as needs assessor are to identify the decisionmakers and claimants who constitute the primary stakeholders in the program domain of interest, describe the "problem" that concerns them in a manner that is as careful, objective, and meaningful to both groups as possible, and help draw out the implications of that diagnosis for structuring effective intervention, whether through new or ongoing programs.

THE ROLE OF EVALUATORS IN DIAGNOSING SOCIAL CONDITIONS AND SERVICE NEEDS

In the grand scheme of things, evaluators' contributions to the identification and alleviation of social problems are modest compared with the weightier actions of political bodies, advocacy groups, investigative reporters, and sundry charismatic figures. The impetus for attending to social problems most often comes from political and moral leaders and community advocates who have a stake, either personally or professionally, in dealing with a particular condition. Thus, the post-World War II attention to mental illness was heavily influenced by the efforts of a single congressman; federal programs for mental retardation received a major boost during John F. Kennedy's presidency because he had a sibling with mental retardation; improved automobile safety can be credited to a considerable degree to Ralph Nader's advocacy; and efforts to control illegal and improper delivery of health and welfare services have most often come about because of exposés in the mass media and the activities of interest and pressure groups, including the organized efforts of those in need themselves.

Nevertheless, evaluators do contribute significantly to efforts to improve the human and social condition, though not by mobilizing the disaffected, storming the barricades, or shooting from the lip. Rather, they contribute in mundane but essential ways by applying their repertoire of research techniques to systematically describe the nature of social problems, gauge the appropriateness of proposed and established intervention programs, and assess the effectiveness of those programs for improving social conditions.

This chapter focuses on the role of evaluators in diagnosing social problems through systematic and reproducible procedures in ways that can be related to the design and evaluation of intervention programs. The importance of the resulting diagnostic information cannot be overstated. Speculation, impressionistic observations, political pressure, and even deliberately biased information may spur policymakers, planners, and funding organizations to initiate action, support ongoing programs, or withdraw support from programs. But if sound judgment is to be reached about such matters, it is essential to have an adequate understanding of the nature and scope of the problem the program is meant to address as well as precise information about the corresponding program targets and the context in which the intervention operates or will operate. Here are a few examples of what can happen when adequate diagnostic procedures are ignored:

- The problem of high unemployment rates in inner-city neighborhoods frequently has been defined as reflecting the paucity of employment opportunities in those neighborhoods. Programs have therefore been established that provided substantial incentives to businesses for locating in inner-city neighborhoods. Subsequent experiences often found that most of the workers these businesses hired came from outside the neighborhood that was supposed to be helped.

- After a social intervention designed to prevent criminal behavior by adolescents was put in place in a Midwestern suburb, it was discovered that there was a very low rate of juvenile crime in the community. The program planners had assumed that because juvenile delinquency was a serious problem nationally, it was a problem in their community as well.

- Planners of many of the urban renewal projects undertaken during the 1960s assumed that persons living in what the planners regarded as dilapidated buildings also viewed their housing as defective and would therefore support the demolition of their homes and accept relocation to replacement housing. In city after city, however, residents of urban renewal areas vigorously opposed these projects.

- Media programs designed to encourage people to seek physical examinations to detect early signs of cancer had the effect of swamping health centers with more clients than they could handle. The media effort stimulated many hypochondriacal persons without cancer symptoms to believe they were experiencing warning signs.

• In an effort to improve the clinical identification of AIDS, community physicians were provided with literature about the details of diagnosing the syndrome among high-risk patients using blood tests. Only after the materials had been disseminated was it recognized that few physicians take sex histories as a routine practice and thus they were unlikely to know which of their patients were high risk. Consequently, the only way they could make use of their new knowledge was by testing all their patients. The result was an excessive amount of testing, at high cost and some risk to the patients.

• A birth control project was expanded to reduce the reportedly high rate of abortion in a large urban center, but the program failed to attract many additional participants. Subsequently, it was found that most of the intended urban clients were already being adequately served and a high proportion practiced contraception. The high abortion rate was caused mainly by young women who came to the city from rural areas to have abortions.

• The problem of criminal use of handguns has led to legislative proposals to forbid the sale of such guns to persons convicted of felony offenses. However, most criminals do not purchase their guns from legitimate gun dealers, nor do dealers have reliable ways of ascertaining whether purchasers have criminal records.

In all of these examples, a good needs assessment would have provided information leading to a valid description of the problem that would have prevented programs from implementing inappropriate or unneeded services. In some cases, unnecessary programs were designed because the problem did not exist. In others, the intervention was not effective because the target population did not desire the services provided, was incorrectly identified, or was unlikely or unable to act in the way the program expected.

All social programs rest on a set of assumptions and representations of the nature of the problem they address and the characteristics, needs, and responses of the target population they intend to serve. Any evaluation of a plan for a new program, a change in an existing program, or the effectiveness of an ongoing program must necessarily engage those assumptions and representations. Of course, the problem diagnosis and target population description may already be well and convincingly established, in which case the evaluator can move forward with that as a given. Or the nature of the evaluation task may be stipulated in such a way that the need for the program and the nature of that need is not a matter for independent investigation. Indeed, program personnel and sponsors often believe they know the social problems and target population needs so well that further inquiry is a waste of time. Such situations must be approached cautiously. As the examples above show, it is remarkably easy for a program to be based on faulty assumptions, either through insufficient initial problem diagnosis, changes in the problem or target population since the program was initiated, or selective exposure or stereotypes that lead to distorted views.

In all instances, therefore, the evaluator should scrutinize the assumptions about the

---

EXHIBIT 4-A   The Rise and Fall of the Government's Role in Educational Needs Assessment

The widespread use of needs assessment (NA) as a systematic, rational means of determining goals and priorities for program planning and evaluation in the United States dates from 1965, with the passage of the Elementary and Secondary Education Act (ESEA, PL 89-10). In the next 15 years over 35 titles in the 54 largest grants-in-aid programs in health, education, and social services required applicants for categorical and competitive grants to document their needs.

Although satisfying granting agencies was not the only reason for needs assessment, the social legislation was a powerful stimulus to the development of models and the conduct of exemplary studies. The period of 1966-1981 was characterized by the conduct of large-scale needs assessments of whole systems, the dissemination of kits of materials and survey instruments (Witkin, 1977), the spread of NA to city planning and the private sector, and some development of theoretical perspectives.

With the passage of the Omnibus Budget Reconciliation Act of October 1981, about 90 percent of the legislation that included mandates for NA was eliminated. In the following year, there was an abrupt drop in NAs, especially in local education agencies. Although applications for categorical grants such as ESEA Chapter 1 (compensatory education) still required evidence of need, those NAs often consisted merely of reporting demographic data and test scores of the students to be served.

SOURCE: Quoted, with permission, from Belle Ruth Witkin, "Needs Assessment Since 1981: The State of the Practice," *Evaluation Practice*, 1994, 15(1):17.

---

target problem and population that shape the nature of a program. Where there is any ambiguity, it may be advisable for the evaluator to work with key stakeholders to formulate those assumptions explicitly so that they may serve as touchstones for assessing the adequacy of the program design and theory. Often it will also be useful for the evaluator to conduct at least some minimal independent investigation of the nature of the program's target problem and population. For new program initiatives, or established programs whose utility has been called into question, it may be essential to conduct a thorough assessment of the social need and target population to be served by the program at issue. In other cases, a needs assess-

ment may be virtually mandated. For example, the 1974 community mental health legislation called for periodic community mental health needs assessments, and the 1987 McKinney Act indicated that states and local communities should use needs assessments as the basis for planning programs for the homeless. The role of the federal government in fostering needs assessment for educational programs is described in Exhibit 4-A.

It should be noted that needs assessment is not always done with reference to a specific social program or program proposal. The techniques of needs assessment are also used as planning tools and decision aids for policymakers who must prioritize among competing

---

✦ EXHIBIT 4-B   Steps in Analyzing Need

1. *Identification of users and uses.* The users of the analysis are those who will act on the basis of the results and the audiences who may be affected by it. The involvement of both groups will usually facilitate the analysis and implementation of its recommendations. Knowing the uses of the need analysis helps the researcher focus on the problems and solutions that can be entertained, but also may limit the problems and solutions identified in Step 3, below.

2. *Description of the target population and service environment.* Geographic dispersion, transportation, demographic characteristics (including strengths) of the target population, eligibility restrictions, and service capacity are important. Social indicators are often used to describe the target population either directly or by projection. Resource inventories detailing services available can identify gaps in services and complementary and competing programs. Comparison of those who use services with the target population can reveal unmet needs or barriers to solution implementation.

3. *Need identification.* Here problems of the target population(s) and possible solutions are described. Usually, more than one source of information is used. Identification should include information on expectations for outcomes; on current outcomes; and on the efficacy, feasibility, and utilization of solutions. Social indicators, surveys, community forums, and direct observation are frequently used.

4. *Need assessment.* Once problems and solutions have been identified, this information is integrated to produce recommendations for action. Both quantitative and qualitative integration algorithms can be used. The more explicit and open the process, the greater the likelihood that results will be accepted and implemented.

5. *Communication.* Finally, the results of the need analysis must be communicated to decisionmakers, users, and other relevant audiences. The effort that goes into this communication should equal that given the other steps of the need analysis.

SOURCE: Adapted from Jack McKillip, "Need Analysis: Process and Techniques," in *Handbook of Applied Social Research Methods,* eds. L. Bickman and D. J. Rog (Thousand Oaks, CA: Sage, 1998), pp. 261-284.

---

needs and claims. For instance, a regional United Way or a metropolitan city council might commission a needs assessment to help them determine how funds should be allocated across various service areas. Or a state department of mental health might assess community needs for different mental health services to distribute resources optimally among its service units. Although different in scope and purpose from the assessment of the need for a particular program, whether existing or proposed, the methods for these broader needs assessments are much the same, and they also are generally conducted by evaluation researchers. Exhibit 4-B provides an overview of the general steps in a needs assessment. Useful book-length discussion of needs assessment applications and techniques can be found in

McKillip (1987), Reviere et al. (1996), Soriano (1995), and Witkin and Altschuld (1995).

As the examples and commentary above indicate, needs assessment has a number of facets and applications relevant to program evaluation. The next sections discuss the evaluator's role in identifying social problems, analyzing their location and scope, defining the targets of proposed interventions, and describing the nature of the associated service needs.

DEFINING SOCIAL PROBLEMS

Proposals for policy changes, new or modified programs, or evaluation of existing programs generally arise out of the dissatisfaction of one or more groups of stakeholders with the effectiveness of existing policies and programs or realization that a new social problem is emerging. Either case assumes that a social problem has been identified, a matter that is not as straightforward as it may seem. Indeed, the question of what defines a social problem has occupied spiritual leaders, philosophers, and social scientists for centuries. For our purposes, the key point is that social problems are not themselves objective phenomena. Rather, they are social constructions that emerge from the interests of the parties involved as they relate to observed conditions. In this sense, community members, together with the stakeholders involved in a particular issue, literally create the social reality that constitutes a recognized social problem (Miller and Holstein, 1993; Spector and Kitsuse, 1977).

It is generally agreed, for example, that poverty is a social problem. The observable facts are the statistics on the distribution of income and assets. However, those statistics do not define poverty; they merely permit one to determine how many are poor when a definition is given. Nor do they establish poverty as a social problem; they only characterize a situation that individuals and social agents may view as problematic. Moreover, both the definition of poverty and the goals of programs to improve the lot of the poor vary over time, between communities, and among stakeholders. Initiatives to reduce poverty, therefore, may range from increasing employment opportunities and reducing barriers to economic mobility to simply lowering the expectations of those persons with low income.

Defining a social problem and specifying the goals of intervention are thus ultimately political processes that do not follow simply from the inherent characteristics of the situation. This circumstance is illustrated nicely, for instance, in an analysis of legislation designed to reduce adolescent pregnancy that was conduced by the U.S. General Accounting Office (GAO, 1986). The GAO found that none of the pending legislative proposals defined the problem as involving the fathers of the children in question; every one addressed adolescent pregnancy as an issue of young mothers. Although this view of the problem of adolescent pregnancy may lead to effective programs, clearly there are alternative definitions that include the adolescent fathers.

Indeed, the social definition of a problem is so central to the political response that the preamble to proposed legislation usually shows some effort to specify the conditions for which the proposal is designed as a remedy. For example, two contending legislative proposals may both be addressed to the issue of homeless persons, but one may identify the homeless as needy persons who have no kin on whom to be dependent, whereas the other defines homelessness as the lack of access to conventional shelter. The first definition centers attention primarily on the social isolation of potential clients; the second focuses on housing arrangements. The ameliorative actions that are justified in terms of these definitions will likely be different as well. The first definition, for instance, would support programs that attempt to reconcile homeless persons with alienated relatives; the second, subsidized housing programs.

It is usually informative, therefore, for an evaluator to determine what the problem a program addresses is thought to be in its particular political context. To investigate this, the evaluator might, for instance, study the implicit or explicit definitions that appear in policy and program proposals. Revealing information may also be found in legislative proceedings, including committee hearings and floor debates, journals of opinion, newspaper and magazine editorials, and other sources in which discussions of the problem appear. The operative definition of the problem a particular program addresses can usually be found in program documents, newspaper accounts of its launch, proposals for funding it, and the like. Such materials may explicitly describe the nature of the problem and the program's plan of attack, as in funding proposals, or implicitly define the problem through the assumptions that underlie statements about program activities, successes, and plans.

This inquiry will almost certainly turn up information that will be useful for a preliminary description of the social need to which the program is presumably designed to respond. As such, it can guide a more probing needs assessment, both with regard to how the problem is defined and what alternative perspectives might be applicable. If the evaluation circumstances do not permit further systematic investigation, this information can nonetheless be the basis for a thoroughgoing discussion with

stakeholders about their perceptions and assumptions about the nature of the social conditions the program addresses. This, then, provides the evaluator with some basis for analyzing the structure and goals of the program and assessing its design.

Also, an important role evaluators may play at this stage is to provide policymakers and program managers with a critique of the problem definition inherent in their policies and programs and propose alternative definitions that may be more serviceable. For example, evaluators could point out that a definition of the problem of teenage pregnancies as primarily one of illegitimate births ignores the large number of births that occur to married teenagers and suggest program implications that follow from that definition.

SPECIFYING THE EXTENT OF THE PROBLEM: WHEN, WHERE, AND HOW BIG?

The design and funding of a social program should be geared to the size, distribution, and density of the problem it addresses. In assessing, say, emergency shelters for homeless persons in a community, it makes a very significant difference whether the total homeless population is 350 or 3,500. It also makes a big difference whether the problem is located primarily in poor neighborhoods or affluent ones and how many of the homeless suffer from mental illness, chronic alcoholism, and physical disabilities.

It is much easier to establish that a problem exists than to develop valid estimates of its density and distribution. Identifying a handful of battered children may be enough to convince a skeptic that child abuse exists. But specifying the size of the problem and where it is located geographically and socially requires detailed knowledge about the population of abused children, the characteristics of the perpetrators, and the distribution of the problem throughout the political jurisdiction in question. For a problem like child abuse, which is not generally public behavior, this can be difficult. Such social problems are mostly "invisible," so that only imprecise estimates of their rates of occurrence are possible. In such cases, it is often necessary to use data from several sources and use different approaches to estimating rates of occurrence (e.g., Ards, 1989).

It is also generally important to have at least reasonably representative samples to estimate rates of occurrence. It can be especially misleading to draw estimates from at-risk populations, such as those found in service programs, when general population estimates are needed to determine the extent of a problem. Estimation of the rate of spousal abuse during pregnancy based on women in shelters, for instance, results in considerable overestimation of the frequency of occurrence in the general population of pregnant women. An estimate from a more representative sample still indicates that battering of pregnant women is a serious problem, but places the extent of the problem in a realistic perspective (see Exhibit 4-C).

Using Existing Data Sources to Develop Estimates

Through their knowledge of existing research and data sources and their understanding of which designs and methods lead to conclusive results, evaluation researchers are in a good position to collate and assess what-

ever information already exists on a given social problem. Here we stress both *collate* and *assess*—unevaluated information can be as bad as no information at all.

For some social issues, existing data sources may be of sufficient quality to be used with confidence. For example, accurate and trustworthy information can usually be obtained about issues on which measures are routinely collected either by the Current Population Survey or the decennial U.S. Census. Moreover, through the census tract coding, that information can be disaggregated to state and local levels. As an illustration, Exhibit 4-D describes the use of vital statistics records and census data to assess the nature and magnitude of the problem of poor birth outcomes in a Florida county. This needs assessment was aimed at estimating child and maternal health needs so that appropriate services could be planned. Even when such direct information about the problem of interest is not available from existing records, indirect estimates may be possible if the empirical relationships between available information and problem indicators are known (e.g., Ciarlo et al., 1992).

In addition to the decennial census, data available in many of the statistical series routinely collected by federal agencies are often trustworthy. There are, unfortunately, exceptions. For example, it is widely acknowledged that the U.S. Census undercounts the numbers of African Americans and Hispanics and, to a considerable extent, the number of homeless. For the nation as a whole, these undercounts are relatively small and for many purposes can be ignored. For jurisdictions with large populations of African Americans and Hispanics, however, these undercounts may result in significant misestimation of the size of certain target populations relevant to assessing the need for social programs.

❋ EXHIBIT 4-C   Estimating the Frequency of Domestic Violence Against Pregnant Women

All women are at risk of battering; however, pregnancy places a woman at increased risk for severe injury and adverse health consequences, both for herself and her unborn infant. Local and exploratory studies have found as many as 40%-60% of battered women to have been abused during pregnancy. Among 542 women in a Dallas shelter, for example, 42% had been battered when pregnant. Most of the women reported that the violence became more acute during the pregnancy and the child's infancy. In another study, interviews of 270 battered women across the United States found that 44% had been abused during pregnancy.

But most reports on battering during pregnancy have been secured from samples of battered women, usually women in shelters. To establish the prevalence of battering during pregnancy in a representative obstetric popu-lation, McFarlane and associates randomly sampled and interviewed 290 healthy pregnant women from public and private clinics in a large metropolitan area with a population exceeding three million. The 290 black, white, and Latina women ranged in age from 18 to 43 years; most were married, and 80% were at least five months pregnant. Nine questions relating to abuse were asked of the women, for example, whether they were in a relationship with a male partner who had hit, slapped, kicked or otherwise physically hurt them during the current pregnancy and, if yes, had the abuse increased. Of the 290 women, 8% reported battering during the current pregnancy (one out of every twelve women interviewed). An additional 15% reported bat-tering before the current pregnancy. The fre-quency of battering did not vary as a function of demographic variables.

SOURCE: Adapted from J. McFarlane, "Battering During Pregnancy: Tip of an Iceberg Revealed," *Women and Health,* 1989, 15(3):69-84.

Because many federal programs are tied to the size of particular populations, such under-counting can also translate into substantial losses of federal funds for those jurisdictions. This circumstance has led to a stream of law-suits by cities and states, and to advocacy of statistical adjustments of the undercount. Al-though many statisticians regard such adjust-ments as a sound approach, adjustments have been rejected in the 1980 and 1990 censuses. In planning for the 2000 census, the Bureau of the Census has formulated a plan for statistical adjustments based on sampling nonrespon-dents. These plans are quite controversial, however, and Congress is considering legisla-tion that would instruct the Bureau of the Census to conduct a "complete census" and abandon any plans to adjust census returns on the basis of sampling.

As this example illustrates, it is often diffi-cult to separate technical decisions from politi-cal interests in diagnosing social problems. Ad-justing for the undercount of African American and, particularly, Hispanic persons would in-crease the amount of resources allocated to them under many federal programs. At the

✳ EXHIBIT 4-D   Using Vital Statistics and Census Data to Assess Child and Maternal Health Needs

The Healthy Start Initiative in Florida, a series of legislative measures intended to improve pregnancy and birth outcomes within the state, provides for the establishment of community-based prenatal and infant health care coalitions composed of health care providers, representatives of state and local government, community alliances, maternal and child health organizations, and consumers of family planning, prenatal care, and primary care services. Each coalition is required to conduct a needs assessment within its service delivery area and develop a service delivery plan. The needs assessment of the Gadsden Citizens for Healthy Babies, Inc., representing a small, primarily rural, majority African American county in north Florida, used existing data from the State of Florida vital statistics records and the U.S. Census of Population and Housing to estimate the magnitude and distribution of child and maternal health problems in the county.

First, pregnancy outcomes and related maternal characteristics within the county were investigated using data from the *Florida Vital Statistics* volumes, which report birth and death information collected annually within the state. In particular, the following indicators were examined:

- *Infant mortality.* The county's rate was far higher than national or state rates.
- *Fetal mortality.* The overall rate for the county was higher than the state goal and the rate for African American mothers was higher than for white mothers.
- *Neonatal mortality.* The rates were higher than the state goal for white mothers but below for African American mothers.
- *Postneonatal mortality.* The rates were below state goals.

- *Low birth rate babies.* There was a higher incidence for adolescents and women over age 35.
- *Very low birth weight births.* The overall rate was twice that for the whole state and exceeded state goals for both African American and white mothers.
- *Adolescent pregnancy.* The proportion of births to teens was over twice the state average; the rate for African American teens was more than twice that for white teens of the same age.
- *Age of mother.* The infant mortality and low birth rates were highest among children born to mothers 16-18 years of age.
- *Education of mother.* Mothers with less than high school education were slightly more likely to have low birth weight newborns but almost eight times more likely to have newborns identified as high risk on infant screening measures.

Based on these findings, three groups were identified with high risk for poor birth outcomes:

- Mothers less than 19 years of age
- Mothers with less than a high school education
- African American mothers

U.S. Census data on CD-ROM discs available from the Bureau of Census were then used to identify the number of women of childbearing age in each of these risk categories, the proportions who were in various low-income strata, and their geographical concentrations within the county according to census tract and zip code. This information was used by the coalition to identify the major problem areas in the county, set goals, and plan services.

SOURCE: Adapted from E. Walter Terrie, "Assessing Child and Maternal Health: The First Step in the Design of Community-Based Interventions," in *Needs Assessment: A Creative and Practical Guide for Social Scientists,* eds. R. Reviere, S. Berkowitz, C. C. Carter, and C. G. Ferguson (Washington, DC: Taylor & Francis, 1996), pp. 121-146.

same time, however, it would modify the distribution of congressional seats from state to state and, within states, result in the need to redraw electoral boundaries. Thus, although social researchers advise assessing the quality of data in terms of their measurement properties, the political implications of estimates of social problems and the distribution of the affected population may play a large role in the procedures used to collect the data.

When sources are used whose validity is not as widely recognized as that of the census, it is always necessary to examine carefully how the data were collected. A good rule of thumb is to anticipate that, on any issue, different data sources will provide disparate or even contradictory estimates. For needs assessment purposes, sometimes data on the same topic collected by opposing stakeholders can be especially useful. For example, both the Coalition Against Handguns and the National Rifle Association (NRA) have sponsored sample surveys of the U.S. population concerning approval or disapproval of gun control legislation. Although their reports differed widely in their conclusions—the one finding popular support for gun control measures and the other the opposite—close inspection of the data showed that many of the specific findings were nearly identical in the two surveys (Wright, Rossi, and Daly, 1983). Both surveys found that guns were owned by about half of U.S. households, for instance. Findings on which different surveys substantially agree can be regarded as having greater credibility.

Using Social Indicators
to Identify Trends

On some topics, existing data sources will provide periodic measures that can be used to chart historical trends in the society. For example, the Current Population Survey of the Bureau of the Census collects data annually on the characteristics of the U.S. population using a large household sample. The data include measures of the composition of households, individual and household income, and household members' age, sex, and race. The regular Survey of Income and Program Participation provides data on the extent to which the U.S. population participates in various social programs: unemployment benefits, Aid to Families With Dependent Children, food stamps, job training programs, and so on. The National Crime Survey compiles annual data on crime victimization from a national survey of households (see Exhibit 4-E).

These regularly occurring measures, called *social indicators*, can provide important information for assessing social problems and needs in several ways. First, when properly analyzed, the data can often be used to estimate the size and distribution of the social problem whose course is being tracked over time. Second, the trends shown can be used to alert decisionmakers to whether certain social conditions are improving, remaining the same, or deteriorating. Finally, the social indicator trends can be used to provide a first, if crude, estimate of the effects of social programs that have been in place. For example, the Survey of Income and Program Participation can be used to estimate the coverage of such national programs as food stamps or job training.

Similarly, the proportions of U.S. households at or below the poverty level can be followed from year to year over the post-World War II years through data obtained by the Current Population Survey. The question whether there was more or less poverty in the 1980s than in the preceding decades can thus be answered by referring to this social indicator. This is not to say that the trend data provided

---

☒ EXHIBIT 4-E Tracking Crime Victimization Trends Using Social Indicators

Since 1973 the Bureau of Justice Statistics in the Department of Justice has conducted an annual survey of a national sample of households that asks if each person in the household has been the victim of a crime during the year prior to the interview, whether reported to the police or not. The table below charts the ten-year trends in crimes with persons or households as their victims.

Victimization Rates per 1,000 Persons Age 12 and Older or per 1,000 Households

	1987	1988	1989	1990	1991	1992	1993	1994	1995	1996
Crimes of violence[a]	43.7	44.1	44.4	44.1	48.0	49.3	49.9	51.8	46.6	42.0
Property crimes[b]	298.4	295.3	295.3	276.5	282.3	325.3	318.9	310.2	290.5	266.3

NOTE: The 1987-1992 figures incorporate a statistical adjustment for a change in survey methodology.
a. Rape, robbery, assault.
b. Burglary, theft, auto theft.

SOURCE: U.S. Department of Justice, Bureau of Justice Statistics, *Criminal Victimization in the United States: 1973-92 Trends* (Washington, DC: U.S. Department of Justice, July 1994). U.S. Department of Justice, Bureau of Justice Statistics, *Criminal Victimization 1996* (Washington, DC: U.S. Department of Justice, November 1997).

---

by the Current Population Survey are without controversy; many believe that they underestimate the current level of poverty, whereas others believe the opposite (Ruggles, 1990).

Considerable effort is currently going into the collection of social indicator data on poor households in an effort to judge whether their circumstances have worsened or improved after the radical reforms in welfare enacted in the Personal Responsibility and Work Opportunity Reconciliation Act of 1996. Special surveys, concentrating on the well-being of children, are being conducted by the Urban Institute and the Manpower Development Research Corporation. In addition, the Bureau of the Census has extended the Survey of Income and Program Participation to constitute a panel of households repeatedly interviewed before and after the welfare reforms were instituted.

Unfortunately, the social indicators currently available are limited in their coverage of social problems, focusing mainly on issues of poverty and employment, criminal victimization, national program participation, and household composition. For many social problems, no social indicators exist or those that do support analysis of national trends but cannot be broken down to provide useful indicators of local trends.

Estimating Problem Parameters Through Social Research

In many instances, no existing data source will provide estimates of the extent and distribution of a problem of interest. For example, there are no ready sources of information about household pesticide misuse that would indicate whether it is a problem, say, in households with children. In other instances, good information about a problem may be available for a national or regional sample that cannot be disaggregated to a relevant local level. The National Survey of Household Drug Use, for instance, uses a nationally representative sample to track the nature and extent of substance abuse. However, the number of respondents from most states is not large enough to provide good state-level estimates of drug abuse, and no valid city-level estimates can be derived at all.

When pertinent data are nonexistent or insufficient, the evaluator must consider collecting new data. There are several ways of making estimates of the extent and distribution of social problems, ranging in increasing degrees of effort from relying on "expert" testimony to conducting large-scale sample surveys. Decisions about the kind of research effort to undertake must be based in part on the funds available and in part on how important it is to have precise estimates. If, for legislative or program design purposes, it is critical to know the number of malnourished infants in a political jurisdiction, a carefully planned health interview survey may be necessary. In contrast, if the need is simply to determine whether there is any malnutrition among infants, input from knowledgeable informants may be all that is required. This section describes the various procedures that can be used to determine the size of a social problem and its geographical and social distribution.

Agency Records

Records of organizations that provide services to the population in question are information sources that may be useful for estimating the extent of a social problem (Hatry, 1994). Some agencies keep excellent records on their clients, but others do not keep records of high quality or do not keep records at all. When an agency's clients include all the persons manifesting the problem in question and records are faithfully kept, then the evaluator need not search any further. Unfortunately, these conditions do not occur often.

It would be tempting to try to estimate, say, the extent of drug abuse by extrapolating from the records of persons treated in drug abuse clinics. To the extent that the drug-using community is fully covered by existing clinics, such estimates may be quite accurate. However, if drug abuse clinics did cover all or most of the drug-abusing population, drug abuse treatment programs might not be problematic. Hence, to the extent that a problem is being adequately handled by existing programs, data from such programs may be useful and accurate, but that is not the situation in which data are usually needed. In the case of drug abuse clinics, of course, it is doubtful that all drug abusers are in fact served by the clinics. (The different prevalence estimates obtained from a served population and a sample survey of the general population are illustrated in the example of battered pregnant women in Exhibit 4-C.)

Surveys and Censuses

When it is necessary to get very accurate information on the extent and distribution of a problem and there are no existing credible data, the evaluator may need to undertake original research using sample surveys or complete enumerations. Because they come in a variety of sizes and degrees of technical complexity, either of these techniques can involve considerable effort and skill, not to mention a substantial commitment of resources.

To illustrate one extreme, Exhibit 4-F describes a needs assessment survey undertaken

EXHIBIT 4-F   Using Sample Surveys to Study the Chicago Homeless

Most sample surveys are based on the assumption that all persons can be enumerated and surveyed in their dwellings, an assumption that fails by definition in any study of the homeless. The strategy devised for the Chicago study therefore departed from the traditional survey in that persons were sampled from non-dwelling units and interviews were conducted at times when the separation between the homed and homeless was at a maximum. Two complementary samples were taken: (1) a probability sample of persons spending the night in shelters provided for homeless persons, and (2) a complete enumeration of persons encountered between the hours of midnight and 6 a.m. in a thorough search of non-dwelling-unit places in a probability sample of Chicago census blocks. Taken together, the shelter and street surveys constitute an unbiased sample of the homeless of Chicago.

A person was classified as homeless at the time of the survey if that person was a resident of a shelter for homeless persons or was encountered in the block searches and found not to rent, own, or be a member of a household renting or owning a conventional dwelling unit. Conventional dwelling units included apartments, houses, rooms in hotels or other structures, and mobile homes.

In the street surveys, teams of interviewers, accompanied by off-duty Chicago policemen, searched all places on each sampled block to which they could obtain access, including all-night businesses, alleys, hallways, roofs and basements, abandoned buildings, and parked cars and trucks. All persons encountered in the street searches were awakened if necessary and interviewed to determine whether or not they were homeless. In the shelter samples, all persons spending the night in such places were assumed to be homeless. Once identified, homeless persons were interviewed to obtain data on their employment and residence histories as well as their sociodemographic characteristics. All cooperating respondents were paid $5.00.

SOURCE: Adapted from P. H. Rossi, *Down and Out in America: The Origins of Homelessness* (Chicago: University of Chicago Press, 1989).

to estimate the size and composition of the homeless population of Chicago. The survey covered both persons in emergency shelters and homeless persons who did not use shelters. Surveying the latter involved searching Chicago streets in the middle of the night. The survey was undertaken because the Robert Wood Johnson Foundation and the Pew Memorial Trust were planning a program for increasing the access of homeless persons to medical care. Although there was ample evidence that

serious medical conditions existed among the homeless populations in urban centers, there was virtually no precise, reliable information on either the size of the homeless population or the extent of medical problems in that population. Hence, the foundations funded a research project to collect the missing information. Although many regard the effort as less than satisfactory, this research stimulated further efforts to count the homeless and improve data collection procedures. For example, the

EXHIBIT 4-G   Assessing the Extent of Knowledge About HIV Prevention

To gauge the extent of knowledge about how to avoid HIV infection, a sample of Los Angeles County residents was interviewed on the telephone. They were asked to rate the effectiveness of four methods that "some people use to avoid getting AIDS through sexual activity" (see table). Their highest rating was for monogamous sex between HIV-negative people, although 12% felt that even in these circumstances there were no assurances of safety. Condom use, despite reported problems with breakage, leakage, and misuse, was rated as very effective by 42% of the respondents and as somewhat effective by another 50%. Respondents were much less certain about the effectiveness of spermicidal agents, regardless of whether they were used in conjunction with an alternative method.

Percentage Distribution of Ratings of the Effectiveness of Different Prevention Methods

Prevention Method	Very Effective	Somewhat Effective	Not at All Effective	Don't Know
Monogamous sex between HIV-negative individuals	73	14	12	1
Using a condom alone	42	50	7	1
Using a diaphragm with spermicide	9	35	50	6
Using spermicide alone	7	32	53	8

SOURCE: Adapted from D. E. Kanouse et al., *AIDS-Related Knowledge, Attitudes, Beliefs, and Behaviors in Los Angeles County* R-4054-LACH (Santa Monica, CA: RAND, 1991).

1990 census gave special attention to counting the homeless. One learning experience from subsequent research is the need to take into account the differences in the ways the homeless spend their time from community to community and the extent to which they are found in shelters, indoor settings that provide meals, on the streets, and in other outside areas.

Although time-consuming and costly, such extensive efforts are sometimes required for diagnostic purposes. To illustrate, Burnam and Koegel (1988) made a strenuous effort to obtain a representative sample and found that 44% of Los Angeles' homeless spent the night before being interviewed in a shelter bed and 26% slept on the street. An earlier study, with a poorer quality sample, had resulted in estimates of 66% in shelter beds and 14% sleeping on the streets. Given the costs of shelter care and the hostility of residents to persons sleeping on the streets in their neighborhoods, accurate estimates were worth obtaining for both program planning and political reasons.

Usually, however, needs assessment research is not as elaborate as that described in Exhibit 4-F. In many cases, conventional sample surveys can provide adequate information. If, for example, reliable information is required about the number and distribution of children needing child care so that new facilities can be planned, it will usually be feasible to obtain it from sample surveys conducted on the telephone. To illustrate, Exhibit 4-G describes a telephone survey conducted with more than

1,100 residents of Los Angeles County to ascertain the extent of public knowledge concerning the effectiveness of different AIDS prevention behaviors. For mass media educational programs aimed at increasing awareness of ways to prevent AIDS, a survey such as this identifies both the extent and the nature of the gaps in public knowledge.

Many survey organizations have the capability to plan, carry out, and analyze sample surveys for needs assessment. In addition, it is often possible to add questions to regularly conducted studies in which a number of organizations buy "time," thereby reducing costs. Whatever the approach, it must be recognized that designing and implementing sample surveys can be a complicated endeavor requiring quite specific skills. For discussion of the various aspects of sample survey methodology, see Fowler (1993), Henry (1990), Rossi, Wright, and Anderson (1983), and Sudman and Bradburn (1982).

Key Informant Surveys

Perhaps the easiest approach to obtaining estimates of the extent of a social problem is to ask *key informants*, those persons whose position or experience should give them some perspective on the magnitude and distribution of the problem. Unfortunately, such reports are generally not especially accurate. Although key informants can often provide very useful information about the characteristics of certain target populations and the nature of service needs, as we will discuss later in this chapter, few are likely to have a vantage point or information sources that permit very good estimation of the number of persons affected by a social condition or the demographic and geographical distribution of those persons.

Consider, for example, the task of estimating the number of homeless persons in a community. Although well-placed key informants may have experience with some subset of that population, it will be difficult for them to extrapolate from that experience to an estimate of the size of the total population. Indeed, it can be shown that selected informants' guesses about the numbers of homeless in their localities vary widely and tend to be overestimates, sometimes quite large overestimates (see Exhibit 4-H).

On the grounds that key informants' reports of the extent of a problem are better than no information at all, evaluators may wish to conduct a key informant survey when no other research is possible or when available funds are insufficient to support a better approach. Given those circumstances, evaluators must take care to ensure that the key informant survey is of the highest quality. The researchers should choose the persons to be surveyed very carefully, attempting to ensure that they have the necessary expertise, that they are questioned in a careful manner, and that any qualifications they may have about their reports are obtained (Averch, 1994).

Forecasting Needs

Both in formulating policies and programs and evaluating them, it is often important to be able to estimate what the magnitude of a social problem is likely to be in the future. A problem that is serious now may become more or less serious in later years, and program planning must attempt to take such trends into account. Yet the forecasting of future trends can be quite risky, all the more so as the time horizon lengthens.

EXHIBIT 4-H Using Key Informant Estimates of the Homeless Populations

To ascertain how close "expert" estimates of the number of homeless persons in downtown Los Angeles came to actual counts of homeless persons "on the streets," in shelters, or in single-room occupancy (SRO) hotels, a team of researchers asked eight service providers in the Skid Row area—shelter operators, social agency officials, and the like—to estimate the total homeless population in that 50-block area. The estimates obtained were as follows:

- Provider 1: 6,000 to 10,000
- Provider 2: 200,000
- Provider 3: 30,000
- Provider 4: 10,000

- Provider 5: 10,000
- Provider 6: 2,000 to 15,000
- Provider 7: 8,000 to 10,000
- Provider 8: 25,000

Clearly, the estimates were all over the map. Two providers (4 and 5) came fairly close to what the researchers estimated as the most likely number, based on shelter, SRO, and street counts.

SOURCE: Adapted from Hamilton, Rabinowitz, and Alschuler, Inc., *The Changing Face of Misery: Los Angeles' Skid Row Area in Transition—Housing and Social Services Needs of Central City East* (Los Angeles: Community Redevelopment Agency, July 1987).

There are a number of technical and practical difficulties in forecasting that derive in part from the necessary assumption that the future will be much like the past. For example, at first blush a projection of the number of persons in the population aged 18 to 30 a decade from now seems easy to construct from current data—it is almost completely determined by the present age structure of the population. However, had demographers made forecasts ten years ago for central Africa, they would have been substantially off the mark because of the unanticipated and tragic impact of the AIDS epidemic, which is most prevalent among young adults. Projections with longer time horizons would be even more problematic because they would have to take into account trends in fertility as well as mortality.

We are not arguing against the use of forecasts in a needs assessment. Rather, we wish to warn against accepting forecasts uncritically without a thorough examination of how they were produced. Moreover, such critical examination may itself involve some difficulty. For simple extrapolations of existing trends, the assumptions on which a forecast is based may be relatively few and easily ascertained. Even if the assumptions are known, however, it may not be easy to determine whether they are reasonable. For sophisticated projections such as those developed from multiple-equation, computer-based models, examining the assumptions may require the skills of an advanced programmer and the expertise of an experienced statistician. In any event, it must be recognized that all but the simplest forecasts are technical activities that require specialized knowledge and procedures.

DEFINING AND IDENTIFYING THE TARGETS OF INTERVENTIONS

Correctly defining and identifying the targets for intervention is crucial to the success of social programs from the very early stage when stakeholders begin to converge in their definition of a social problem to the extended period over which the program is operated. Specifying those targets is complicated by the fact that the definition and corresponding estimates of the size of the population may shift over this period. As a new social problem emerges or becomes increasingly visible, one definition of the targets of an intervention may be adopted; as stakeholders plan and eventually implement a program initiative, however, that definition may well be modified or abandoned.

As an illustration, during the early 1980s the problem of homelessness became extremely salient. Initially, the homeless were identified as those individuals who lived in streets and alleyways or in shacks they constructed for themselves. As advocates of the homeless became increasingly active, however, the targets of interventions began to also include persons who spent periods of time sleeping in shelters (sensibly so, because many persons who sleep in shelters also sleep out on the streets, and vice versa). Then, as programs began to emerge, some of them took the view that persons who had no regular place to live but moved in for brief periods with various relatives, friends, and sometimes strangers should be included. For some stakeholders and programs, the homeless population also encompassed the large number of individuals who lived in single rooms, usually paying for them daily or weekly and without the protection of leases or other contractual arrangements. (For further discussion of the technical and policy issues in homeless research, see Carr, 1991.)

As we will discuss shortly, the targets of an intervention need not be persons or groups of persons: They can also be organizations or "conditions." Here the same point about shifts in target definition applies. The target of a social intervention might be defective housing, which, at first, might be defined in terms of serious violations of the building code and later come to also include, for instance, buildings that are not earthquake proof.

Although the definition and estimated number of targets for a program are always in flux to some degree, they are critically important at two points in time. First, in the predesign phase of laying out policy and program alternatives, it is important to clearly identify the intended targets. Obviously, this is necessary so that the size and character of the social problem as a basis for realistic planning can be estimated. In addition, how the targets are defined will affect the potential effectiveness of a policy or program because that definition will shape the program emphasis and approach. For these reasons, new legislation and program proposals ordinarily contain statements about who or what the targets are to be.

Second, the issue of target definition is critical during the course of designing the specific content and structure of a program. Although targets may be initially defined in legislation or program proposals, in practice, programs often have to limit the targets to which they actually direct an intervention to some portion of those defined targets. This often happens simply because the funds provided are insufficient to cover all the originally intended targets or because the nature of the program is such that it cannot be appropriately provided to all those in the initially defined target population.

Sometimes the reverse is true and, in operation, the program is directed at a broader or larger group than originally planned. For example, health clinics set up in shelters for the homeless were initially intended to provide services for persons sleeping there and in the streets. However, when poor persons housed in the same neighborhoods learned of the clinics, some of them began to use them too and were accepted as patients.

What Is a Target?

The targets of social programs are usually individuals. But they also may be groups (families, work teams, organizations), geographically and politically related areas (such as communities), or physical units (houses, road systems, factories). Whatever the target, it is imperative at the outset of a needs assessment to define the units in question clearly.

In the case of individuals, targets are usually identified in terms of social and demographic characteristics, location, or their problems, difficulties, and conditions. Thus, targets of an educational program may be designated as children aged 10 to 14 who are between one and three years below their normal grade in school. Or targets of a maternal and infant care program may be pregnant women and mothers of infants with annual incomes less than 150% of the poverty line.

When aggregates (groups or organizations) are targets, they are often defined in terms of the characteristics of the individuals that constitute them: their informal and formal collective properties and their shared problems. An

organizational-level target for an educational intervention might be elementary schools (kindergarten to eighth grade) with at least 300 pupils in which at least 30% of the pupils qualify for the federal free lunch program.

Direct and Indirect Targets

Targets may also be regarded as direct or indirect depending on whether services are delivered to them immediately (directly) or eventually (indirectly). Most programs specify direct targets. This is clearly the case in medical interventions, for example, where persons with a given affliction directly receive medical treatments. However, in some cases, either for economic or feasibility reasons, planners may design programs to affect a target population indirectly by acting on an intermediary population or condition that will, in turn, have an impact on the intended target population. In a rural development project, for example, influential farmers were selected from small communities for intensive training programs. The intention was that afterward they would return to their communities and communicate their new knowledge to other farmers, the indirect targets of the program. Similarly, a project that identifies substandard dwelling units as its direct targets may be intended to benefit (indirectly) the current and future occupants of those dwellings.

When targets are defined as indirect, the program's effectiveness depends to a large extent on whether the pathways leading from immediate to ultimate targets are correctly identified in the program theory. The effectiveness of the project that used influential farmers, for instance, depended heavily on the ability and motivation of those farmers to communicate their knowledge persuasively to other farmers in their communities. Similarly, if there is a strong relationship between housing quality and health, investing in the physical improvement of housing to indirectly promote householders' well-being may be justified, but if the correlation is low or zero, the investment is likely to be ineffective for that purpose.

Specifying Targets

At first glance, specification of the size and distribution of target populations may seem simple. Although target definitions may be easy to write, however, it is often difficult to employ such definitions in the more precise work of needs assessment and program design. There are few human and social problems that can be easily and convincingly described in terms of simple, unambiguous characteristics of the individuals experiencing that problem.

Take a single illustration: What is the population of persons with cancer in a given community? The answer depends, first, on whether one counts only permanent residents or includes temporary ones as well (a decision that would be especially important in any community with a large number of vacationers such as Orlando, Florida). Second, are "recovered" cases to be counted, or are those without a relapse for, say, five years to be eliminated from the estimate? Third, is having cancer to be defined only as diagnosed cases or does it also include those persons whose cancer had not yet been detected? Finally, the estimate must take into account the purpose for which it is being used. If it is to be used in designing a special nursing-home program, for instance, persons with skin cancer should not be included because their condition rarely requires inpatient services.

An illustration of the considerations that go into specifying targets is provided in Exhibit 4-I, which is extracted from a landmark article that greatly influenced the development of the "poverty line" concept, a definition of poverty that is still employed today, adjusted to the current value of the dollar. Note that Orshansky's (1969) article dealt both with technical issues, such as the availability of appropriate data, and with substantive issues, such as trying to arrive at a definition that would satisfy stakeholders and social scientists. It is a tribute to her skill in balancing those objectives that the poverty-level concept she developed is still in use more than two decades later. The Orshansky measures have been heavily criticized, however, and several alternatives have been proposed (Ruggles, 1990).

Benchmarks for the size of major problem populations, such as the poor, and the definition underlying their identification have important consequences for the way governmental and private resources are allocated. For example, federal officials use the poverty-level approach just discussed in determining how much to appropriate for food stamp, medical care, and housing assistance programs.

Target Boundaries

Adequate target specification establishes boundaries, that is, rules determining who or what is included and excluded when the specification is applied. One risk in specifying target populations is to make a definition too broad or overinclusive. For example, specifying that a criminal is anyone who has violated any law or administrative regulation is useless; only saints have not at one time or another violated some law or regulation, wittingly or otherwise. This definition of criminal is too inclusive, lumping together in one category trivial and serious offenses and infrequent violators with habitual felons.

✺ EXHIBIT 4-I   Defining a Target Population: How Poverty Is Measured

---

Counting the poor is an exercise in the art of the possible. For deciding who is poor, prayers are more relevant than calculation because poverty, like beauty, lies in the eye of the beholder. . . . To say who is poor is to use all sorts of value judgments. The concept has to be limited by the purpose which is to be served by the definition. There is no particular reason to count the poor unless you are going to do something about them. When it comes to defining poverty, you can only be more subjective or less so. You cannot be nonsubjective.

Defining the Issue

We wanted to be sure that every family or consumer unit had its fair chance to be numbered among those who would be considered as needing attention. Indeed, it was precisely to ensure consideration of the needs of large families as well as small, and of young people as well as old, that we refined the initial standard developed by the Council of Economic Advisers. Their standard said that any family of two or more with less than $3,000 annual income, and any single person living alone with less than $1,500, would be considered poor for purposes of antipoverty program planning—but not for program eligibility. This original standard led to the odd result that an elderly couple with $2,900 income for the year would be considered poor, but a family with a husband, wife, and four little children with $3,100 income would not be.

Moreover, when we looked at the poor distributed demographically, by comparison with the total population, we made some unusual discoveries. For example, the percentage of the families classified as poor who had no children was higher than that for the population as a whole, and to make it even more unrealistic, the percentage of the poor families with four children or more was actually less than the representation of such families in the population. We did not think this was correct, so we tried to vary the poverty line—the necessary minimum of resources—with the size and composition of the family.

Setting the Benchmark

A concept which can help influence public thinking must be socially and politically credible. We need benchmarks to distinguish the population group that we want to worry about. A benchmark should neither select a group so small, in relation to all the population, that it hardly seems to deserve a general program, nor so large that a solution to the problem appears impossible. For example, in the 1930s, President Roosevelt said, "I see before me one-third of a nation ill-clothed, ill-housed, and ill-fed." This fraction is now part of our history. No matter how we get our numbers today, if more than a third of the population is called poor, it will lose value as a public reference point.

Definitions may also prove too restrictive, or underinclusive, sometimes to the point that almost no one falls into the target population. Suppose that the designers of a program to

rehabilitate released felons decided to include only those who have never been drug or alcohol abusers. The prevalence of substance abuse is so great among released prisoners that only a

EXHIBIT 4-I   Continued

At the Social Security Administration, we decided that we would develop two measures of need, and state, on the basis of the income sample of the Current Population Survey, how many and what kinds of families these measures delineated. It was not the Social Security Administration that labeled the poverty line. It remained for the Office of Economic Opportunity and the Council of Economic Advisers to select the lower of the two measures and decide they would use it as the working tool. The best you can say for the measure is that at a time when it seemed useful, it was there. It is interesting that few outside the Social Security Administration ever wanted to talk about the higher measure. Everybody wanted only to talk about the lower one, labeled the "poverty line," which yielded roughly the same number of people in poverty as the original $3,000 measure did, except that fewer families with more children were substituted for a larger number of older families without children.

Thresholds of Poverty

We have developed two poverty thresholds, corresponding to what we call the "poor" and "near-poor." These thresholds are set separately for 124 different kinds of families, based on the sex of the head, the number of children under 18, the number of adults, and whether or not the household lives on a farm. The threshold is defined as an attempt to "specify the minimum money income that could support an average family of given composition at the lowest level consistent with the standards of living prevailing in this country. It is based on the amount needed by families of different size and type to purchase a nutritionally adequate diet on the assumption that no more than a third of the family income is used for food." The two thresholds were developed from food consumption surveys conducted by the Department of Agriculture. . . . These revealed that the average expenditure for food by all families was about one-third of income.

An assumption was made that the poor would have the same flexibility in allocating income as the rest of the population but that, obviously, their margin for choice would be less. The amount allocated to food from the average expenditure was cut to the minimum that the Agriculture Department said could still provide American families with an adequate diet. We used the low-cost plan to characterize the near-poor and for the poor an even lower one, the economy food plan.

SOURCE: Quoted, with permission, from Mollie Orshansky, "Perspectives on Poverty: How Poverty Is Measured," *Monthly Labor Review*, 1969, 92(2):37-38.

---

small proportion would be eligible given this exclusion. In addition, because persons with long arrest and conviction histories are more likely to be substance abusers, this definition may eliminate those most in need of rehabilitation as targets of the proposed intervention.

In addition to specifying appropriate boundaries, useful target definitions must be feasible to apply. A specification that hinges on a characteristic that is difficult to observe or for which existing data contain no measures—for example, a definition of the targets of a job training program as persons who hold favorable attitudes toward accepting job training—may be virtually impossible to put into practice. Overly complex definitions requiring much detailed information are similarly difficult to apply. The data required to select targets defined as "farmer members of producers' cooperatives who have planted barley for at least two seasons and have an adolescent son" would be difficult, if not impossible, to gather. Moreover, in general the more criteria a definition has, the smaller the number of units that can qualify for inclusion in the target population. (The farmers satisfying the criteria just given would be a small group indeed.) Complex specifications are therefore kin to narrow ones and carry the same risks.

Varying Perspectives
on Target Specification

Another issue in the definition of target populations arises from the differing perspectives of professionals, politicians, and the other stakeholders involved—including, of course, the potential recipients of services. During all phases of intervention, beginning with the emergence of a social problem, there can be differences in opinion as to the exact parameters of the target population.

Discrepancies may exist, for instance, between the views of legislators at different levels of government. At the federal level, Congress may plan to alleviate the financial burden on the government for natural disasters by encouraging states to invest in such disaster-mitigating measures as improved land-use management of flood plains and building codes that

lower risks of damage and injury. From the federal perspective, the target population would be viewed as all those areas in which 100-year floods may occur. Because the federal government must be concerned with all the flood plains in the United States, their perspective recognizes that such a flood may occur somewhere as often as once every few days. True to their name, however, 100-year floods occur in any one place only once in every century (on average). From the local perspective, therefore, a given flood plain may not be viewed as a reasonable target at all and local governments may object strongly to the burdens of a program targeted on their flood plains.

Differences in perspective can arise in program design as well. The planners of programs concerned with improving the quality of housing available to poor persons may have a conception of housing quality much different from those of the people who will live in those dwellings. Their definition of what constitutes the target population of substandard housing for renewal, therefore, may result in a great outcry from residents of those dwellings who find them adequate.

Although needs assessment cannot establish which perspective on program targets is "correct," it can help eliminate conflicts that might arise from groups talking past each other. This is accomplished by investigating the perspectives of all the significant stakeholders on target definition and helping ensure that none is left out of the decision process through which the program focus is determined. Information collected about needs from varying perspectives may lead to a reconceptualization of the target population or of the prospective intervention, or even indicate the advisability of abandoning the program (especially if the different perspectives turn out to be contradictory and intensely held by the various stakeholders).

Useful Concepts in Target Definition

Understanding the nature of a social problem and estimating the size and characteristics of a target population are prerequisite to documenting the need for a program. Delivering service to a target population, however, requires that the definition of the target population permit targets to be distinguished from nontarget units in a relatively unambiguous and efficient manner as part of the program's normal operating procedures. To be effective, a program must not only know what its target population is but also be able to readily direct its services to that population and screen out individuals who are not part of that population. This section discusses a number of concepts that underlie appropriate target definition and selection.

Incidence and Prevalence

A useful distinction is the difference between *incidence* and *prevalence*. Incidence refers to the number of *new* cases of a particular problem that are identified or arise in a specified geographical or otherwise defined area during a specified period of time. Prevalence refers to the number of *existing* cases in a particular area at a specified time. These concepts are derived from the field of public health where generally they are sharply distinguished. For example, the incidence of influenza during a particular month is defined as the number of new cases reported during the month; its prevalence during that month is the number of afflicted people at any given time, regardless of when they were first stricken. In the health sector, project planners generally are interested in incidence when dealing with disorders of short duration, such as upper-respiratory infec-

tions and minor accidents. They are more interested in prevalence when dealing with problems that cannot be eradicated quickly but require long-term management and treatment efforts, including chronic diseases such as cancer and clinically observable long-term illnesses such as severe malnutrition.

The concepts of incidence and prevalence have been adapted to the study of social problems. In studying the impact of crime on victims, for instance, the critical measure is the incidence of victimization: the numbers of new cases (or persons victimized) per interval of time in a given area. Similarly, in programs aimed at lowering drunken-driver accidents, the incidence of accidents involving a drunken driver in a specified area and period of time may be the best measure of the need for intervention. But for chronic conditions such as low educational attainment, criminality, or poverty, prevalence is generally the appropriate measure. In the case of poverty, for instance, prevalence may be defined as the number of poor individuals or families in a community at a given time, regardless of when they became poor.

For other social problems, it is often unclear whether one should define target populations in terms of prevalence or incidence. In dealing with the problem of unemployment, it is important to know its prevalence, the numbers or proportions of the total population unemployed at a particular time. If the concern is with providing financial support for the unemployed, however, it is not clear whether the definition should refer to persons who are unemployed at a particular time or those who become unemployed in a given period. The principle involved centers on the issue of whether one is concerned with detecting and treating new cases as they appear or with existing cases whatever their time of origin.

Population at Risk

Another public health concept, *population at risk*, is helpful in specifying targets, particularly in projects that are preventive in character. Population at risk refers to that group of persons or units that has a significant probability of developing a given condition. Thus, the population at risk in fertility control programs is usually defined as women of childbearing age. Similarly, projects designed to mitigate the effects of typhoons and hurricanes may define targets as communities located in the typical paths of such storms and, hence, at risk of experiencing a disaster.

A population at risk can be defined only in probabilistic terms. Women of childbearing age may be the population at risk in a fertility control project, but a given woman may or may not conceive a child within a given period of time. In this instance, specifying the population at risk simply in terms of age results unavoidably in overinclusion; that is, the definition includes many women as targets who may not be in need of family planning efforts because they are not sexually active or are otherwise incapable of getting pregnant.

Sensitivity and Specificity

The *sensitivity* of a criterion for target identification refers to the likelihood of correctly selecting those targets who should be in a program in contrast to those who might also be selected by the criterion but not be appropriate for the program. If the program is designed to serve those with a specified condition, sensitivity is the ability of a screening or selection procedure to identify *true positives*, that is, those who actually have the condition. *Specificity*, on the other hand, refers to correctly excluding those persons or units who do not

have the relevant condition, that is, *false positives*. A program that selects its clientele with poor sensitivity overlooks many who need and qualify for service. A program that selects with poor specificity uses its resources to serve many who do not need or qualify for service. Ideally, both high sensitivity and high specificity are desired in defining a target population and selecting individuals for a program.

Need and Demand

Whereas a population at risk includes all those with a high probability of having or acquiring a given condition, a *population in need* is a group of potential targets who currently manifest the condition. A population in need can usually be defined rather exactly; that is, one can identify a precise criterion for including a unit among targets (e.g., a screening technique). For instance, there are reliable and valid tests for determining an individual's degree of literacy. These tests can be used to specify a target population of functionally illiterate persons. For projects directed at alleviating poverty, one may define the population in need as families whose income, adjusted for family size, is below a certain minimum.

Just because individuals constitute a population in need by some criteria representing the social construction of need used in program or policy context, however, does not mean that they necessarily want the program or service at issue. Desiring service or being willing to participate in a program defines *demand* for service, a concept that usually only partially overlaps the applicable criteria of need. Community leaders and service providers, for instance, may quite reasonably define a "need" for overnight shelter among homeless persons sleeping on the streets but may find that some of these persons will not use such facilities. Thus, there may be a need but not a demand.

Some needs assessments undertaken to estimate the extent of a problem and serve as the basis for designing programs are actually *at-risk assessments* or *demand assessments* according to the definitions just offered. Such assessments may do duty for true needs assessments either because it is technically infeasible to measure need or because it is impractical to implement a program that deals only with the at-need population. For example, although only sexually active females may require family planning information, the target population for most such programs is those women assumed to be at risk, generally defined by an age span such as 15 to 50, because it would be difficult to identify and designate only those who are sexually active. Similarly, whereas the in-need group for an evening educational program may be all nonliterate adults, only those who are willing or who can be persuaded to participate can be considered the target population (an "at demand" definition). Clearly, the distinctions between populations at risk, in need, and at demand are important for estimating the scope of a problem, anticipating the size of the target population, and subsequently designing, implementing, and evaluating the program.

Rates

In addition to estimating the size of a problem group, it is generally also important to know the proportion of a population with a particular problem. Many times it is critical to be able to express incidence or prevalence as a *rate* to compare areas or problem groups. Thus, the number of new cases of unemployment or underemployment during a given period in an area (incidence) might be described per 100 or per 1,000 of a population (e.g., 133 new unemployed persons per 1,000 population).

Rates or percentages are especially critical in identifying the characteristics of the target population. For example, in describing the population of crime victims, it is important to have estimates by sex and age group. Although almost every age group is subject to some kind of crime victimization, young people are much more likely to be the victims of robbery and assault, whereas older persons are more likely to be the victims of burglary and larceny; men are considerably less likely than women to be the victims of sexual abuse; and so on. The ability to estimate targets by various characteristics allows a program to be planned and developed in ways that maximize opportunities to include the most appropriate participants and to tailor the program to the particular characteristics of sizable groups.

Estimates of target populations and their characteristics may be made at several levels of disaggregation. For example, illiteracy rates, calculated by dividing the number of functionally illiterate persons in various age groups by the total number of persons in each group, allow one to estimate the target populations that can be reached by tailoring a project to specific age cohorts. More powerful statistical techniques may usefully be employed to take into account additional sociodemographic variables simultaneously.

In most cases, it is not only traditional but also useful to specify rates by age and sex. In communities in which there are marked subcultural differences, racial, ethnic, and religious groups also become important denominators for the disaggregation of characteristics. Other variables useful in identifying characteristics of the target population include socioeconomic status, geographic location, and residential mobility. (See Exhibit 4-J for an example of crime

✖ **EXHIBIT 4-J**   Rates of Violent Crime Victimization, by Sex, Age, and Race

Victimization per 1,000 Persons Age 12 or Older: 1996

Characteristic of Victim	All Violent Crimes	Rape; Sexual Assault	Robbery	Aggravated Assault	Simple Assault
Sex					
Male	49.9	0.4	7.2	11.6	30.8
Female	34.6	2.3	3.4	6.2	22.7
Age					
12-15	95.0	2.6	10.0	15.6	66.8
16-19	102.7	4.9	12.0	25.3	60.4
20-24	74.3	2.1	10.0	15.9	46.4
25-34	51.1	1.8	7.1	9.8	32.4
35-49	32.8	1.3	3.8	7.4	20.3
50-64	15.7	0.1	1.8	3.8	10.0
65+	4.9	0.0	1.1	0.8	3.0
Race					
White	40.9	1.3	4.2	8.2	27.2
Black	52.3	1.8	11.4	13.4	25.6
Hispanic	44.0	1.2	8.4	10.6	23.9
Other	33.2	2.1	7.4	7.2	16.6

SOURCE: U.S. Department of Justice, Bureau of Justice Statistics, *Criminal Victimization 1996* (Washington, DC: U.S. Department of Justice, November 1997).

victimization rates disaggregated by sex, age, and race.)

DESCRIBING THE NATURE OF SERVICE NEEDS

As described above, a central function of needs assessment research is to develop estimates of the extent and distribution of a given problem and the associated target population. However, it is also often important for such research to yield useful descriptive information about the specific character of the need within that population. This is important because it is often not sufficient for a social program to merely deliver some standard services in some standard way

presumed to be responsive to a given problem or need. To be effective, a program may need to adapt its services to the local nature of the problem and the distinctive circumstances of the persons in need. This, in turn, requires information about the way in which the problem is experienced by those in need, their perceptions and attributions about relevant services and programs, and the barriers and difficulties they encounter in attempting to access services.

A needs assessment might, for instance, probe into the matter of why the problem exists and what other problems are linked with it. For example, a search for information on how many high school students study a non-English language may reveal that many schools do not offer such courses; thus, part of the problem turns out to be that opportunities to learn foreign languages are insufficient. Similarly, the fact that many primary school children of low socioeconomic backgrounds appear to be tired and listless in class may be explained with a finding that many regularly do not eat breakfast, which, in turn, reflects their families' economic problems. Of course, different stakeholders are likely to have different views about the nature and source of the problem so it is important that the full range of perspectives be represented (see Exhibit 4-K for an example of diverse stakeholder perspectives).

Cultural factors or perceptions and attributions that characterize a target population may be especially relevant to the effectiveness of a program's outreach to members of the target population and the way in which it delivers its service. A thorough needs assessment on poverty in Appalachian mountain communities, for instance, should reflect the sensitivities of the target population about their self-sufficiency and independence. Programs that are construed as charity or that give what are perceived as handouts are likely to be shunned by needy but proud families.

Another important dimension of service needs may involve difficulties some members of the target population have in using services. This may result from transportation problems, limited service hours, lack of child care, or a host of similar such obstacles. The difference between a program with an effective service delivery to needy persons and an ineffective one is often chiefly a matter of how much attention is paid to overcoming these barriers. Job training programs that provide child care to the participants, nutrition programs that deliver meals to the homes of elderly persons, and community health clinics that are open during evening hours all illustrate approaches that

have based service delivery on a recognition of the complexity of their clients' needs.

Qualitative Methods for Describing Needs

Qualitative research can be especially useful for obtaining detailed, textured knowledge of the specific needs in question. Such research can range in complexity from interviews of a few persons or group discussions to elaborate ethnographic research such as that employed by anthropologists. As an example of the utility of such research, qualitative data on the structure of popular beliefs can contribute substantially to the effective design of educational campaigns. What, for instance, are the trade-offs people believe exist between the pleasures of cigarette smoking and the resulting health risks? A good educational program must be adapted to those perceptions.

Carefully and sensitively conducted qualitative studies are particularly important for uncovering process information of this sort. Thus, ethnographic studies of disciplinary problems within high schools may not only provide some indication of how widespread disciplinary problems are but also suggest why some schools have fewer disciplinary problems than others. The findings on how schools differ might have implications for the ways programs are designed. Or consider the qualitative research on household energy consumption that revealed the fact that few householders had any information about the energy consumption characteristics of their appliances. Not knowing how they consumed energy, these householders could not very well develop effective strategies for reducing their consumption.

A popular and useful technique for obtaining rich information about a social problem is the *focus group* approach made popular in the

---

✵ EXHIBIT 4-K   Stakeholders Have Different Perceptions of the Problems With Local Health Services

---

Telephone interviews were conducted in three rural Colorado communities to identify health service problems related to cancer. In each community the study participants included (a) health care providers (physicians, nurses, public health personnel), (b) community influentials (teachers, librarians, directors of community agencies, business leaders), and (c) patients or family members of patients who had a cancer experience. While there was general agreement about problems with availability and access to services, each stakeholder group had somewhat different perceptions of the nature of the problems:

Physicians and health care providers:

- Regional facilities only accept paying patients or close down.

- The remoteness of the community creates a lack of services.

- Physician shortage exists because of low salaries, large workloads, and difficult patients.

- We don't have training or equipment to do high-tech care.

Community influentials:

- People are on waiting lists for services for several months.

- There are not enough professionals or volunteers here.

- There is inadequate provider knowledge about specialized services.

Patients and family members:

- A time or two we have had no doctor here.

- We have a doctor here now but his patients have no money and I hear he's going to leave.

- We need treatment locally.

- I was on a waiting list for three weeks before the mammography van got here.

SOURCE: Adapted from Holly W. Halvorson, Donna K. Pike, Frank M. Reed, Maureen W. McClatchey, and Carol A. Gosselink, "Using Qualitative Methods to Evaluate Health Service Delivery in Three Rural Colorado Communities," *Evaluation & the Health Professions*, 1993, 16(4):434-447.

---

past several presidential elections when small panels of voters were assembled to provide perceptions of how the campaign rhetoric was being received (Morgan, 1988). Focus groups bring together selected knowledgeable persons for a discussion of a particular topic or theme under the supervision of a facilitator (Dean, 1994; Krueger, 1988). With a careful selection and grouping of individuals, a modest number of focus groups can provide a wealth of descriptive information about the nature and nuances of a social problem and the service needs of those who experience it (Exhibit 4-L provides a helpful protocol for a needs assessment focus

---

EXHIBIT 4-L   Sample Protocol for a Needs Assessment Focus Group

A focus group protocol is a list of topics or open-ended questions to be covered in a focus group session that is used to guide the group discussion. The protocol should (a) cover topics in a logical, developmental order so that they build on one another; (b) raise open-ended issues that are engaging and relevant to the participants and that invite the group to make a collective response; and (c) carve out manageable "chunks" of topics to be examined one at a time in a delimited period. For example, the following is a protocol for use in a focus group with low-income women to explore the barriers to receiving family support services:

- Introduction—greetings; explain purpose of the session; fill out name cards; introduce observers, ground rules and how the focus group works (10 minutes).

- Participant introductions—give first names only; where participants live, age of children; which family support services are received

and for how long, and other services received (10 minutes).

- Introduce idea of barriers to services—ask participants for their views on what have been the most important barriers to receipt of family support services (probe regarding transportation, treatment by agency personnel, regulations, waiting lists); have they discontinued any services or been unable to get ones they want? (30 minutes).

- Probe for reasons behind their choices of most important barriers (20 minutes).

- Ask for ideas on what could be done to overcome barriers in the future—what would make it or would have made it easier to enter and remain in the service loop? (30 minutes).

- Debrief and wrap up—moderator summary, clarifications, and additional comments or questions (10 minutes).

SOURCE: Adapted from Susan Berkowitz, "Using Qualitative and Mixed-Method Approaches," in *Needs Assessment: A Creative and Practical Guide for Social Scientists,* eds. R. Reviere, S. Berkowitz, C. C. Carter, and C. G. Ferguson (Washington, DC: Taylor & Francis, 1996), pp. 121-146.

---

group). A range of other group techniques for eliciting information for needs assessment can be found in Witkin and Altschuld (1995).

Appropriate participants in focus groups would generally include various knowledgeable community leaders, directors of service agencies, the line personnel in those agencies who deal firsthand with clients, representatives of advocacy groups, persons experiencing the social problem or service needs directly, and other such stakeholders. Of course, for these interactions to be productive and comfortable for the

participants, care must be taken in mixing some of these stakeholders in the same focus group.

Any use of key informants in needs assessment must, therefore, involve a careful selection of the persons or groups whose perceptions are going to be taken into account. A useful approach to identifying key informants for a needs assessment is *snowball sampling*. This technique requires that an initial set of appropriate informants be located through some reasonable means and surveyed. They are then

---

⚶ EXHIBIT 4-M Homeless Men and Women Report Their Needs for Help

As efforts to help the homeless move beyond the provision of temporary shelter, it is important to understand homeless individuals' perspectives on their needs for assistance. Responses from a representative sample of 1,260 homeless men and women interviewed in New York City shelters revealed that they had multiple needs not easily met by a single service. The percentage reporting a need for help on each of 20 items was as follows:

Finding a place to live	87.1	Problems with drugs	18.7
Having a steady income	71.0	Learning to get along better with other people	18.5
Finding a job	63.3	Nerves and emotional problems	17.9
Improving my job skills	57.0	Learning how to protect myself	17.6
Learning how to get what I have coming from agencies	45.4	Learning how to read and fill out forms	17.3
Getting on public assistance	42.1	Legal problems	15.0
Health and medical problems	41.7	Drinking problems	13.0
Learning how to manage money	40.2	Getting around town	12.4
Getting along with my family	22.8	Getting veteran's benefits	9.6
Getting on SSI/SSD	20.8	Problems with the police	5.1

SOURCE: Adapted from Daniel B. Herman, Elmer L. Struening, and Susan M. Barrow, "Self-Reported Needs for Help Among Homeless Men and Women," *Evaluation and Program Planning,* 1994, 17(3):249-256.

---

asked to identify other informants whom they believe are knowledgeable about the matter at issue. These other informants are then contacted and asked, in turn, to identify still others. When this process no longer produces relevant new names, it is likely that most of those who would qualify as key informants have been identified. Because those persons active and involved in any matter of public interest in a community tend to know of each other, snowball sampling works especially well for key informant surveys about social problems.

An especially useful group of informants that should not be overlooked in a needs assessment consists of a program's current clientele or, in the case of a new program, representatives of its potential clientele. This group, of course, is especially knowledgeable about the characteristics of the problem and the associated needs as they are experienced by those whose lives are most affected by the problem. Although they are not necessarily in the best position to report on how widespread the problem is, they are the key witnesses with regard to how seriously the problem affects individuals and what dimensions of it are most pressing. Exhibit 4-M illustrates the unique perspective of potential service beneficiaries.

Because of the distinctive advantages of qualitative and quantitative approaches, a useful and frequently used strategy is to conduct needs assessment in two stages. The initial, exploratory stage uses qualitative research approaches to obtain rich information on the nature of the problem (e.g., Mitra, 1994). The second stage, estimation, builds on this information to design a more quantitative assessment that provides reliable estimates of the extent and distribution of the problem.

SUMMARY

▧ Within evaluation research, needs assessment attempts to answers questions about the social conditions a program is intended to address and the need for the program, or to determine whether a new program is needed. More generally, it may be used to identify, compare, and prioritize needs within and across program areas.

▧ Adequate diagnosis of social problems and identification of the target population for interventions are prerequisites to the design and operation of effective programs. Nonetheless, it must be recognized that social problems cannot be objectively defined but, rather, are social constructions that emerge from the interests and political actions of the parties involved.

▧ To specify the size and distribution of a problem, evaluators may gather and analyze data from existing sources, such as the U.S. Census, or use ongoing social indicators to identify trends. Because the needed information often cannot be obtained from such sources, however, evaluators frequently conduct their own research on a social problem. Useful approaches include studies of agency records, surveys, censuses, and key informant surveys. Each of these has its uses and limitations; for example, key informant surveys may be relatively easy to conduct but of doubtful reliability; agency records generally represent persons in need of services but may be incomplete; surveys and censuses can provide valid, represen- tative information but can also be expensive and technically demanding.

▧ Forecasts for future needs are often very relevant to needs assessment but are complex and technical activities ordinarily performed by specialists. In using forecasts, evaluators must take care to examine the assumptions on which the forecasts are based.

▧ Appropriate definitions and accurate information about the numbers and characteristics of the targets of interventions are crucial throughout the intervention process, from initial planning through all the stages of program implementation. Targets may be individuals, groups, geographical areas, or physical units, and they may be defined as direct or indirect objects of an intervention.

🕱 Good target specifications establish appropriate boundaries, so that an intervention correctly addresses the target population, and are feasible to apply. In defining targets, care must be taken to allow for the varying perspectives of different stakeholders. Useful concepts in target definition include incidence and prevalence, population at risk, sensitivity and specificity, need and demand, and rates.

🕱 For purposes of program planning or evaluation, it is important to have detailed information about the local nature of a social problem and the distinctive circumstances of those in need of program services. Such information is usually best obtained through qualitative methods such as ethnographic studies or focus groups with selected representatives of various stakeholders and observers.

KEY CONCEPTS FOR CHAPTER 5

Program theory	The set of assumptions about the manner in which the program relates to the social benefits it is expected to produce and the strategy and tactics the program has adopted to achieve its goals and objectives. Within program theory we can distinguish *impact theory,* relating to the nature of the change in social conditions brought about by program action, and *process theory,* which depicts the program's organizational plan and service utilization plan (see Chapter 3 for fuller descriptions).
Articulated program theory	An explicitly stated version of program theory that is spelled out in some detail as part of a program's documentation and identity or as a result of efforts by the evaluator and stakeholders to formulate the theory.
Implicit program theory	Assumptions and expectations inherent in a program's services and practices that have not been fully articulated and recorded.
Evaluability assessment	Negotiation and investigation undertaken jointly by the evaluator, the evaluation sponsor, and possibly other stakeholders to determine if a program meets the preconditions for evaluation and, if so, how the evaluation should be designed to ensure maximum utility.
Black box evaluation	Evaluation of program outcomes without the benefit of an articulated program theory to provide insight into what is presumed to be causing those outcomes and why.

CHAPTER 5

EXPRESSING AND ASSESSING PROGRAM THEORY

Mario Cuomo, former governor of New York, once described his mother's rules for success as (a) figure out what you want to do and (b) do it. These are pretty much the same rules that social programs must follow if they are to be effective. In the last chapter, we discussed how the evaluator could assess the need for a program. Given an identified need, program decisionmakers must (a) conceptualize a program capable of alleviating that need and (b) implement it. In this chapter, we review the concepts and procedures an evaluator can apply to the task of assessing the quality of the program conceptualization. In the next chapter, we describe the ways in which the quality of the program implementation can be assessed.

The social problems that programs address are often so complex and difficult that bringing about even marginal improvement may pose formidable challenges. The foundation on which every program rests is some conception of what must be done to bring about the intended social benefits, whether that conception is expressed in a detailed program plan and rationale or is only implicit in the program's structure and activities. That conception is what we have referred to as the program theory.

A program's theory can be a good one, in which case it represents the "know-how" necessary for the program to attain the desired results, or it can be a poor one that would not produce the intended effects even if implemented well. One aspect of evaluating a program, therefore, is to assess how good the program theory is—in particular, how well it is formulated and whether it presents a plausible and feasible plan for improving the target social conditions. For program theory to be assessed, however, it must first be expressed clearly and completely enough to stand for review. This chapter describes how evaluators can tease out the theory implicit in a program and then, after it has been made explicit, assess how good it is.

In Chapter 3, we advocated that evaluators analyze a program's critical assumptions and expectations about the way in which it is intended to improve social conditions as an aid to identification of potentially important evaluation questions. This advice was presented in the context of planning an evaluation and setting priorities for the issues it would address. In this chapter, we return to the topic of program theory, not as a framework for identifying important evaluation questions, but as a constituent part of the program itself.

Every program embodies a conception of the structure, functions, and procedures appropriate to attain its goals. This conception constitutes the "logic" or plan of the program, which we have called *program theory*. The program theory explains why the program does what it does and provides the rationale for expecting that doing things that way will achieve the desired results.

Evaluators and other informed observers recognize that there is little basis for presuming that program theory is universally sound and thus warrants little concern. There are many poorly designed social programs in operation with faults that reflect deficiencies in their underlying conception of how the desired social benefits can be attained. This circumstance stems in large part from the fact that careful, explicit conceptualization of program objectives and how they are supposed to be achieved is often not given sufficient attention during planning for new programs. Sometimes the political context within which programs originate does not permit extensive planning, but even when that is not the case, conventional practices for designing programs are not very probing with regard to the nature and plausibility of the underlying theory. The human service professions operate with repertoires of established modes and types of intervention associated with their respective specialty areas. As a result, program design is often principally a matter of configuring a variation of familiar "off the shelf" services into a package that seems appropriate for a social problem without a close analysis of the match between those services and the nature of the problem.

For example, many social problems that involve deviant behavior among the target population, such as alcohol and drug abuse,

criminal behavior, early sexual activity, or teen pregnancy, are addressed by programs that provide some mix of counseling and educational services. Although rarely made explicit during planning, these programs are based on the assumption that people will change their problem behavior if given information and interpersonal support for doing so. Such theories may seem reasonable in the general case, but experience and research provide ample evidence that many such behaviors are very resistant to change despite knowledge by the participants about how to change and strong encouragement from loved ones to do so. Thus, the theory that education and supportive counseling will reduce deviant behavior may not be a sound basis for program design.

The rationale and conceptualization on which a program is based, therefore, should be subject to critical scrutiny within an evaluation just as any other important aspect of the program. If the program's goals and objectives do not relate in a reasonable way to the social conditions the program is intended to improve, or the assumptions and expectations embodied in a program's functioning do not represent a credible approach to bringing about that improvement, there is little prospect that the program will be effective. Evaluations of program process, impact, and efficiency thus ride on the presumption that the program theory is sound. Accordingly, evaluators must often make some assessment of the quality of a program's theory. Evaluating program theory, however, is not an easy task and certainly does not lend itself to structured and formalistic procedures. It is an important task, nonetheless, and one the evaluator must be prepared to undertake in many situations.

The first step in assessing program theory is to articulate it, that is, produce an explicit description of the conceptions, assumptions, and expectations that constitute the rationale for the way the program is structured and operated. It is rare for a program to be able to immediately provide the evaluator with a statement of its program theory in a sufficiently explicit and detailed form to allow meaningful assessment. Although always implicit in program structure and operations, a full description of the program theory is seldom written down and available in program documents. Moreover, when some write-up of program theory is available, it is often in material that has been prepared for funding proposals or public relations purposes and may not correspond well with actual program practice.

Assessment of program theory, therefore, almost always requires that the evaluator first draw on program sources to synthesize and articulate the theory in a form amenable to analysis. Accordingly, the discussion in this chapter is organized around two themes: (a) how the evaluator can explicate and express program theory in a form that will be representative of key stakeholders' actual understanding of the program and workable for purposes of evaluation, and (b) how the quality of the articulated program theory can then be evaluated.

THE EVALUABILITY ASSESSMENT PERSPECTIVE

One of the earliest systematic attempts to describe and assess program theory arose from the experiences of an evaluation research group at the Urban Institute in the 1970s (Wholey, 1979). They found it often difficult, sometimes impossible, to undertake evaluations of public programs and began to analyze the obstacles.

This led to the view that a qualitative assessment of whether minimal preconditions for evaluation were met should precede most evaluation efforts. Wholey and his colleagues termed the process *evaluability assessment* (see Exhibit 5-A).

Evaluability assessment generally involves three primary activities: (a) description of the "program model" with particular attention to defining the program goals and objectives, (b) assessment of how well defined and evaluable that program model is, and (c) identification of stakeholder interest in evaluation and the likely use of the findings. Evaluators conducting evaluability assessments operate much like program ethnographers. They seek to describe and understand the program through interviews and observations that will reveal its "social reality" as viewed by program personnel and other significant stakeholders. The evaluator begins with the conception of the program presented in documents and official information, but then tries to see the program through the eyes of those closest to it. The intent is to end up with a description of the program as it exists and an understanding of the program issues that really matter to the various parties involved. Although this process clearly involves considerable judgment and discretion on the part of the evaluator, various practitioners have attempted to codify its procedures so that evaluability assessments will be reproducible by other evaluators (see Rutman, 1980; Smith, 1989; Wholey, 1994).

A common outcome of evaluability assessments is that program managers and sponsors recognize the need to modify their programs. The evaluability assessment may reveal faults in a program's delivery system, that the program's target population is not well defined, or that the intervention itself needs to be reconceptualized. Or there may be few program

---

✵ EXHIBIT 5-A The Rationale for Evaluability Assessment

If evaluators and intended users fail to agree on program goals, objectives, information priorities, and intended uses of program performance information, those designing evaluations may focus on answering questions that are not relevant to policy and management decisions. If program goals and objectives are unrealistic because insufficient resources have been applied to critical program activities, the program has been poorly implemented, or administrators lack knowledge of how to achieve program goals and objectives, the more fruitful course may be for those in charge of the program to change program resources, activities, or objectives before formal evaluation efforts are undertaken. If relevant data are unavailable and cannot be obtained at reasonable cost, subsequent evaluation work is likely to be inconclusive. If policymakers or managers are unable or unwilling to use the evaluation information to change the program, even the most conclusive evaluations are likely to produce "information in search of a user." Unless these problems can be overcome, the evaluation will probably not contribute to improved program performance.

These four problems, which characterize many public and private programs, can be reduced and often overcome by a qualitative evaluation process, *evaluability assessment,* that documents the breadth of the four problems and helps programs—and subsequent program evaluation work—to meet the following criteria:

- Program goals, objectives, important side effects, and priority information needs are well defined.

- Program goals and objectives are plausible.

- Relevant performance data can be obtained.

- The intended users of the evaluation results have agreed on how they will use the information.

Evaluability assessment is a process for clarifying program designs, exploring program reality, and—if necessary—helping redesign programs to ensure that they meet these four criteria. Evaluability assessment not only shows whether a program can be meaningfully evaluated (any program can be evaluated) but also whether evaluation is likely to contribute to improved program performance.

SOURCE: Quoted, with permission, from Joseph S. Wholey, "Assessing the Feasibility and Likely Usefulness of Evaluation," in *Handbook of Practical Program Evaluation,* eds. J. S. Wholey, H. P. Hatry, and K. E. Newcomer (San Francisco: Jossey-Bass, 1994), p. 16.

---

objectives that stakeholders agree on or no feasible performance indicators for the objectives. In such cases, the evaluability assessment has uncovered problems with the program design, which program managers must correct before any meaningful performance evaluation can be undertaken.

The aim of evaluability assessment is thus to create a climate favorable to evaluation work and an agreed-on understanding of the nature and objectives of the program that will facilitate evaluation design. As such, it can be integral to the approach the evaluator employs to tailor an evaluation and formulate evaluation questions

> ### 🐾 EXHIBIT 5-B   Evaluability Assessment for the Appalachian Regional Commission
>
> Evaluators from the Urban Institute worked with managers and policymakers in the Appalachian Regional Commission (ARC) on the design of their health and child development program. In this evaluability assessment, the evaluators
>
> - Reviewed existing data on each of the 13 state ARC-funded health and child development programs;
>
> - Made visits to five states and then selected two states to participate in evaluation design and implementation;
>
> - Reviewed documentation related to congressional, commission, state, and project objectives and activities (including the authorizing legislation, congressional hearings and committee reports, state planning documents, project grant applications, ARC contract reports, local planning documents, project materials, and research projects);
>
> - Interviewed approximately 75 people on congressional staffs and in commission headquarters, state ARC and health and child development staffs, local planning units, and local projects;
>
> - Participated in workshops with approximately 60 additional health and child development practitioners, ARC state personnel, and outside analysts.
>
> Analysis and synthesis of the resulting data yielded a *logic model* that presented program activities, program objectives, and the assumed causal links between them. The measurability and plausibility of program objectives were than analyzed and new program designs more likely to lead to demonstrably effective performance were presented. These included both an overall ARC program model and a series of individual models, each concerned with an identified objective of the program.
>
> In reviewing the report, ARC staff were asked to choose explicitly among alternative courses of action. The review process consisted of a series of intensive discussions in which ARC and Urban Institute staff focused on one objective and program model at a time. In each session, the evaluators and staff attempted to reach agreement on the validity of the flow models presented, the importance of the respective objective, and the extent to which any of the information options ought to be pursued.
>
> ARC ended up adopting revised project designs and deciding to systematically monitor the performance of all their health and child development projects and to evaluate the effectiveness of the "innovative" ones. Twelve of the 13 ARC states have since adopted the performance monitoring system. Representatives of those states report that project designs are now much more clearly articulated and that they believe the projects themselves have improved.
>
> SOURCE: Adapted from Joseph S. Wholey, "Using Evaluation to Improve Program Performance," in *Evaluation Research and Practice: Comparative and International Perspectives,* eds. R. A. Levine, M. A. Solomon, G.-M. Hellstern, and H. Wollmann (Beverly Hills, CA: Sage, 1981), pp. 92-106.

(see Chapters 2 and 3). To illustrate the typical procedure, Exhibit 5-B presents an example of an evaluability assessment.

Evaluability assessment requires program stakeholders to articulate the program design and logic (the program model); however, it can also be carried out for the purposes of describing and assessing program theory (Wholey, 1987). Indeed, the evaluability assessment approach represents the most fully developed set of concepts and procedures available in the evaluation literature for describing and assessing a program's conceptualization of what it is supposed to be doing and why. We turn now to a more detailed discussion of procedures for identifying and evaluating program theory, drawing heavily on the writings associated with the practice of evaluability assessment.

ELICITING AND EXPRESSING PROGRAM THEORY

Sometimes, though not often, a program's theory is spelled out in some detail in program documents and well understood by staff and stakeholders. In this case, we might say the program is based on an *articulated theory* (Weiss, 1997). This is most likely to occur when the original planning and design of the program are theory based. For instance, the design and delivery of a school-based drug use prevention program that features role-playing of refusal behavior in peer groups may be derived directly from social learning theory and its implications for peer influences on adolescent behavior.

In many cases, however, programs involve services and practices that are viewed as reasonable for the purposes of the program but the underlying assumptions and explanations of just how they are presumed to accomplish those purposes has not been fully articulated and recorded. In these cases, we might say that the program has an *implicit theory* or, as Weiss (1997) put it, a *tacit theory*. This might be the case for a counseling program to assist couples

with marital difficulties. Although it may be reasonable to assume that discussing marital problems with a trained professional would be helpful, the way in which such interaction translates into improvements in the marital relationship is not described by an explicit theory nor would different counselors necessarily agree about that process.

When a program's theory is implicit rather than articulated, the evaluator must extract and describe it through some appropriate means before it can be analyzed and assessed. The first topics we must discuss, therefore, are how program theory can be elicited if it is not already fully articulated, how it might most usefully be expressed, and how it can be validated to ensure that it is an accurate representation of a program's actual working assumptions.

The evaluation literature presents diverse ways of defining and depicting program theory and thus muddies the waters for anyone wanting to see clearly to the bottom of this issue (Weiss, 1997). As indicated in Chapter 3, we view program theory as a relatively detailed description of the relationships between program resources, program activities, and program outcomes that shows how the program is supposed to work and, in particular, how it is supposed to bring about the intended outcomes. The objective for an articulation of program theory is to depict the "program as intended," that is, the actual expectations held by program decisionmakers about what the program is supposed to do and what results are expected to follow.

For expository purposes, we highlighted two components of a complete program theory: program impact theory (consisting of an action hypothesis and a conceptual hypothesis) and program process theory (consisting of the service utilization plan and the organizational plan). A brief review of these basic theory components may be helpful at this point.

Program impact theory delineates the cause-and-effect sequence through which the program is expected to bring about change in the social conditions it addresses. An agricultural extension program to increase the use of disease-resistant seeds among corn growers, for instance, may consist of distribution of educational materials, promotional talks with farmers' groups, and supply of seeds at discount prices. The presumptions that information, persuasion, and financial incentives will influence farmers' motivation (the action hypothesis) and that increased motivation will lead them to use the new seeds (conceptual hypothesis) constitute the program's impact theory.

Program process theory provides an account of how the program intends to bring about the desired interactions with the target population and provide the planned services. The service utilization plan describes how the target population will be engaged with the program from initial contact to completion of the intended services. For the agricultural extension program outlined above, the service utilization plan would lay out the sequence of interactions the target farmers are expected to have with the educational materials, the agricultural extension agents, and the suppliers of the disease-resistant seeds. The organizational plan would describe the program activities and resources and how they are to be organized and managed. To effectively promote the new seeds, for instance, the agricultural extension program would have to prepare and distribute educational materials, train agents and arrange promotional opportunities for them, acquire sufficient quantities of the new seeds, and organize distribution and the cost subsidy through, say, local commercial suppliers.

With this review as background, we turn to consideration of the concepts and procedures an evaluator can use to extract and articulate program theory as a prerequisite for assessing it.

What Is a Program for Purposes of Program Theory?

A crucial early step in articulating program theory is to define the boundaries of the program at issue (Smith, 1989). A human service agency may have many programs and provide multiple services; a regional program may have many agencies and sites. Depicting program theory thus almost always requires a clear definition of which components, activities, objectives, and target populations are encompassed in the program at issue. There is usually no one correct definition of a program for this purpose and the boundaries that the evaluator applies will depend, in large part, on the scope of the evaluation sponsor's concerns and the program domains to which they apply.

One way to circumscribe the program entity at issue is to work from the perspective of the decisionmakers expected to act on the evaluation findings and the nature of the decisions they are expected to make. What constitutes the program for which theory is to be articulated, then, should at minimum represent the relevant jurisdiction of those decisionmakers and the organizational structures and activities about which decisions are likely to be made. If the evaluation sponsor is the director of a single local community mental health agency, for instance, the decisions at issue and, hence, the boundaries of the program to be assessed may be defined primarily around one of the distinct combinations of service packages and target patients administered by that agency, such as outpatient counseling for eating disorders. When the evaluation sponsor is the state director of mental health, however, the relevant program boundaries may be defined around effectiveness questions that relate to outpatient counseling services statewide, that is, the outpatient counseling component of all the local mental health agencies in the state.

Because program theory deals mainly with means-ends relations, the most critical aspect of defining program boundaries is to ensure that they encompass all the important activities, events, and resources linked to one or more outcomes recognized as central to the endeavor. This involves a form of backward mapping in which the point of departure is a set of well-defined program objectives relating to the social benefits the program intends to produce. From there, all the activities and resources under the relevant organizational auspices that are presumed to contribute to attaining those objectives are identified as part of the program. From this perspective, the eating disorders program at either the local or state level would be defined as the set of activities organized by the respective mental health agency that have an identifiable role in attempting to alleviate eating disorders for the eligible population in the respective jurisdiction.

Note, however, that although these approaches to defining a program for purposes of articulating program theory are straightforward in concept, they can be problematic in practice. Not only can programs be complex, with crosscutting resources, activities, and goals, but the characteristics described above as linchpins for program definition can themselves be difficult to establish. Thus, in this matter, as with so many other aspects of evaluation, the evaluator must be prepared to negotiate a program definition agreeable to the evaluation sponsor and key stakeholders and be flexible about modifications as the evaluation progresses.

Procedures for Explicating Program Theory

For a program in the planning stage, theory might be derived from prior practice and research. For an existing program, however, the appropriate task is to describe the theory that is actually embodied in the program structure and operation. To accomplish this, the evaluator must interact with the program stakeholders to draw out their implicit program theory, that is, the theory represented in their actions and assumptions.

The Implicit Theory of Program Personnel and Other Stakeholders

The most straightforward approach to developing a description of a program's theory is to obtain it from program personnel and other pertinent stakeholders. The general procedure for this involves successive iteration. Draft descriptions of the program theory are generated, usually by the evaluator, and discussed with knowledgeable stakeholder informants to get feedback. The draft is then refined on the basis of their input and shown again to appropriate stakeholders. This process continues until the stakeholders find little to criticize in the description. The theory description developed in this fashion may involve impact theory or process theory or any components or combination deemed relevant to the evaluation purposes. Exhibit 5-C presents one evaluator's account of how a program process theory was formulated.

The primary sources of information for developing and differentiating descriptions of program theory are (a) review of program documents; (b) interviews with program personnel, stakeholders, and other selected informants; and (c) site visits and observation of various

---

🕮 EXHIBIT 5-C   Formulating Program Process Theory for Adapted Work Services

---

Adapted Work Services (AWS) was initiated at the Rochelle Center in Nashville, Tennessee, to provide low-stress, paid work and social interaction to patients in the early stages of Alzheimer's disease. It was based on the belief that the patients would benefit emotionally and cognitively from working in a sheltered environment and their family members would benefit from being occasionally relieved of the burden of caring for them. The evaluator described the procedures for formulating a program process theory for this program as follows:

The creation of the operational model of the AWS program involved using Post-it notes and butcher paper to provide a wall-size depiction of the program. The first session involved only the researcher and the program director. The first question asked was, "What happens when a prospective participant calls the center for information?" The response was recorded on a Post-it note and placed on the butcher paper. The next step was then identified, and this too was recorded and placed on the butcher paper. The process repeated itself until all (known) activities were identified and placed on the paper. Once the program director could not identify any more activities, the Post-it notes were combined into clusters. The clusters were discussed until potential component labels began to emerge. Since this exercise was the product of only two people, the work was left in an unused room for two weeks so that the executive director and all other members of the management team could react to the work. They were to identify missing, incorrect, or misplaced activities as well as comment on the proposed components. After several feedback sessions from the staff members and discussions with the executive director, the work was typed and prepared for presentation to the Advisory Board. The board members were able to reflect on the content, provide further discussion, and suggest additional changes. Several times during monthly board meetings, the executive director asked that the model be revisited for planning purposes. This helped further clarify the activities as well as sharpen the group's thinking about the program.

SOURCE: Quoted, with permission, from Doris C. Quinn, "Formative Evaluation of Adapted Work Services for Alzheimer's Disease Victims: A Framework for Practical Evaluation in Health Care" (doctoral diss., Vanderbilt University, 1996), pp. 46-47.

---

program functions and circumstances. Each of these warrants some discussion.

Documents. Some written description of the program or crucial aspects of it will almost always be available. However, the form, variety, and amount of such documentation will vary considerably depending on the nature of the program. For programs with legislative origins, there will likely be pertinent information in the authorizing legislation or legislative history and there may be accompanying regulations and guidelines. Descriptive information for programs is often found in conjunction with fund-raising and fiscal accountability. For example, grants, grant applications, contract documents, budget justifications, audit reports, and annual financial reports may provide information about program goals and characteristics. Similarly, documents delineating formal commitments with other agencies or groups, for instance, interagency agreements to provide certain services, often include descriptive information about clients, services, and program objectives. Internal documents involving formal commitments, such as mission or vision statements, manuals of operating procedures, contracts with clients, job descriptions, and other such material, may also be informative.

In addition, many programs prepare and distribute promotional material. This may include flyers, brochures, newsletters, reports of program accomplishments, and listings in service and agency directories. Finally, any available management reports, organization charts, flowcharts, program monitoring documents, or evaluation studies relating to the program are good prospects for providing important descriptive information. Even though all these various sources of written information are not necessarily available or useful to the evaluator, thorough canvassing will generally turn up enough documentation to permit creation of a first approximation to a program theory description.

Although program documents can be informative for the evaluator attempting to describe the program and articulate the components of program theory, their limitations must be kept in mind. All program documents are prepared for some purpose, and that purpose will rarely be to present program theory in a valid and straightforward manner. The most descriptive documents are usually written to persuade some outside party to support the program and, naturally, have a self-serving bias. Others may describe an official or historical view of the program that does not coincide well with the program reality as it exists at the time of an evaluation. Thus, although program documents can be very illuminating to an evaluator attempting to understand and describe a program, their original context and purposes must be taken into account when they are interpreted.

Interviews. The most important sources of information describing a program and contributing to the articulation of program theory are those persons with firsthand knowledge and experience of the program. Generally, the best way for the evaluator to interact with these informants is through face-to-face discussion, individually or in small groups. Whereas written surveys and questions might be useful for some limited purposes, that approach lacks the flexibility to tailor the line of discussion to the expertise of the individual, probe and explore issues in depth, and engage the informant in careful reflection.

Central among the informants whose input is needed to properly depict program theory are the various members of the program staff in positions to know about key aspects of the program. Program managers and administrators, of course, are especially relevant because of their positions of oversight and responsibility. Line personnel should not be neglected when selecting informants, however. They often have the most detailed firsthand knowledge of how things actually work and generally are the personnel most closely in contact with the target population the program serves. Unique vantage points are also held by the program sponsors, funders, and policymakers, who often have a broader view of the objectives and goals of a program and its significance to the community than program personnel.

Critical sources of information related to the various components of program theory are members of the target population the program serves. Surprisingly often this group is overlooked by evaluators formulating program descriptions and depicting program theory, perhaps because they are generally less accessible than program personnel and other such stakeholders. Nonetheless, representatives of the target population will generally have a unique perspective on the program, sometimes one at variance from that of other informants. They can be especially helpful to the process of formulating the service utilization plan by reporting on the nature of their contact and access to the program. As the recipients of a program's attempts to bring about change, their stories are also frequently illuminating for purposes of articulating the program's impact theory.

Finally, of course, the evaluator should obtain input from representatives of major stakeholders outside of the circle of persons directly involved with the program. This might include informants from other agencies, advocacy groups, community leaders, professional groups, and the like who have some interest in the program and some awareness of its purposes and activities. Many informants from these groups will not possess detailed knowledge of the program but may, nonetheless, provide useful insights about the perception of the program's purposes in the informed community, its relationships with other agencies and programs, and how it relates to social conditions and social needs recognized in that community.

Because theory description is worked out chiefly with stakeholders, evaluators experienced with evaluability assessment recommend that one or more stakeholder groups be organized to facilitate interaction for this purpose (e.g., Smith, 1989; Wholey, 1994). For example, Wholey (1994) reports that in many evaluability assessments it has proven useful to organize two groups, a policy group and a

work group. A work group consists of program managers, staff, and representatives of stakeholders who are knowledgeable about program details and interact extensively with the evaluator to fashion a valid and useful rendition of program theory. The policy group, on the other hand, is composed of upper-level administrators, policymakers, and significant stakeholder representatives in decision-making roles whose feedback and endorsement are important to the acceptability and credibility of the theory description. This group is convened periodically for briefing and discussion as the work progresses.

Observation. Although program documents and stakeholder interviews will usually prove very informative, an evaluator is wise not to rely exclusively on them for describing the program and the theory it embodies. Documents and informants both have inherent limitations resulting from their partisan role in relationship to the program and the particular purposes and vantage points of their accounts. Based on experience with evaluability assessment, Wholey (1994) recommends that evaluators "explore program reality" firsthand through site visits and direct observation. In particular, evaluators should observe what they can of the program resources and routine operations so that they may make independent input to the formulation of program theory and so that they can be assured that the input from other sources is realistic with relation to the program capability.

The articulation of program theory necessarily and appropriately represents the program as intended more than the program as it actually is. Program managers and policymakers will generally think of the idealized program as the "real" one with various shortfalls from that ideal as glitches that do not represent what the program is really about. Those further away from the day-to-day operations, on the other hand, may be unaware of such shortfalls and will naturally describe what they presume the program to be even if in actuality it does not quite live up to that image.

Some discrepancy between program theory and program reality is therefore natural. Indeed, examination of the nature and magnitude of that discrepancy is the task of process or implementation evaluation, as discussed in the next chapter. However, if the discrepancy is so great that the program theory describes activities and accomplishments that the program clearly cannot attain given its actual nature and resources, then the theory is overblown and cannot be realistically held up as a depiction of what is supposed to happen in the program context. For instance, suppose that a job training program's service utilization plan calls for monthly contacts between each client and a case manager. If the program resources are insufficient to support case managers, and none are employed by the program, this part of the theory is fanciful and should be revised to more realistically depict what the program might actually be able to accomplish.

The purpose of supplementing the accounts from program documents and stakeholders with direct observation, therefore, is not for the evaluator to verify that the program actually lives up to the intentions represented in its various theory components, but to ascertain that those intentions are generally realistic. When the program reality falls well short of the design envisioned by the key stakeholders, and that shortfall is readily apparent, there is little point in pursuing assessment of the theory or the details of how well the program implements the theory. Program redesign or reconceptualization is more in order, and the

evaluator should provide that feedback to the pertinent stakeholders.

Collating information from different sources. Evaluators typically handle the information gleaned from program documents, interviews, and observations with some form of informal content analysis. Summaries or transcripts are made from the source material and then reviewed so that ambiguous or incomplete portions can be clarified with appropriate informants. The evaluator next extracts the pertinent information from each document in the form of thematic notes or excerpts and sorts them according to the aspect of the program to which they relate, such as goals, services, clients, personnel, program components, and resources. The information in each category is then used, along with other available information, to depict program theory in whatever representational form is preferred, for instance, a chart or graphic. Discussions of the general nature of this process can be found in Boyatzis (1998), Miles and Huberman (1994), Patton (1990), and Strauss and Corbin (1990). Exhibit 5-D reveals something of what the evaluator must bring to this process.

Topics for Attention During Document Review, Interviews, and Observations

Above, we reviewed the common sources of information useful to the task of articulating program theory but gave little attention to what information the evaluator might attempt to obtain from those sources. In this section, we turn attention to that matter.

Program goals and objectives. Perhaps the most important matter to be determined from program sources relates to the goals and objectives

---

✵ **EXHIBIT 5-D**   Theoretical Sensitivity

Theoretical sensitivity is the ability to recognize what is important in data and to give it meaning. It helps to formulate theory that is faithful to the reality of the phenomena under study. Theoretical sensitivity has two sources. First, it comes from being well grounded in the technical literature as well as from professional and personal experience. You bring this complex knowledge into the research situation. However, theoretical sensitivity is also acquired during the research process through continual interactions with the data—through your collection and analyses of the data. While many of the analytic techniques that one uses to develop theoretical sensitivity are creative and imaginative in character, it is important to keep a balance between that which is created by the researcher and the real. You can do so by (a) asking, what is really going on here? (b) maintaining an attitude of skepticism toward any categories or hypotheses brought to or arising early in the research, and validating them repeatedly with the data themselves; and (c) by following the data collection and analytic procedures as discussed in this book. Good science (good theory) is produced through this interplay of creativeness and the skills acquired through training.

SOURCE: Quoted, with permission, from Anselm Strauss and Juliet Corbin, *Basics of Qualitative Research: Grounded Theory Procedures and Techniques* (Newbury Park, CA: Sage, 1990), pp. 46-47.

---

of the program; these are necessarily an integral part of program theory, especially impact theory. The goals and objectives that must be represented in program theory, however, are not necessarily the same as those identified in program mission statements or in response to questions about goals to stakeholders. To be meaningful within an evaluation context, program goals must identify a state of affairs that could realistically be attained as a result of program actions; that is, there must be some reasonable connection between what the program does and what it intends to accomplish. Smith (1989) suggests that the evaluator use a line of questioning that does not ask about goals directly but, rather, about consequences. For instance, in a review of major program activities, the evaluator might ask about each, "Why do it? What are the expected results?

How could you tell if those results actually occurred?" This approach attempts to keep the discussion concrete and specific rather than abstract and general as is typically the case if program goals are asked about directly (see Exhibit 5-E).

Given a set of relatively concrete and realistic goal statements, they must be integrated into the descriptions of program theory in a meaningful way. Within the context of the division of program theory into impact theory and process theory used here, the first distinction to be made is between goals appropriate to these different theory components. The ultimate goal of any social program should always be a specifiable improvement in the social conditions the program addresses. Thus, the goals and objectives that describe the outcome of the change process the program aims to bring about

---

✎ EXHIBIT 5-E   Asking About Program Goals and Objectives

The Illinois Cooperative Extension Service's teleconferencing network (TeleNet) was initiated to provide information and educational assistance to public officials, civic organizations, planning groups, and the general public on locally identified issues such as county jails, collective bargaining, and financial and personnel management. In an evaluability assessment, Midge Smith developed the following interview questions for program staff to help formulate program goals and objectives and the program activities and resources associated with them:

Goals and objectives:

- What do you think the TeleNet programs are trying to accomplish?
- What changes or differences, if any, is this program making with regard to participants, county advisors, the community, and the county?
- What negative effects, if any, might the program have or be having? (If some are mentioned, ask: What do you think could/should be done to avoid these negative effects?)

Tasks and activities:

- What tasks do you perform with the program?
- How does each of these tasks contribute to accomplishing the objectives?
- What problems, if any, do you face in performing these tasks?
- To what extent do you feel you reach the target audience?

Resources:

- What resources are used or are available at the local level to carry out the different program activities?
- How adequate are these resources?

Performance indicators:

- What are some of the indicators of success that the evaluation might try and measure? When could they be measured?
- Are there any questions or concerns about the program operation or results that you would like to see addressed by an evaluation?

SOURCE: Adapted from Midge F. Smith, *Evaluability Assessment: A Practical Approach* (Norwell, MA: Kluwer, 1989), p. 91.

---

in social conditions relate to program impact theory. Also associated with impact theory are any intermediate objectives that represent steps along the pathway leading from program services, on one end, to the improved social conditions that are the program's ultimate goal, at the other.

In contrast to the program goals and objectives related to effects on social conditions are those related to program activities and service delivery. These, in turn, are relevant to program process theory. For instance, "to provide case management" is a service objective but not an outcome goal because it describes action the program will take, not the effect of those actions on the social conditions the program aims to improve. An objective that might appear in the description of a program's service utilization plan, for instance, could be "all persons released from mental institutions are contacted and offered services" or "80% of the clients are retained in service for the full ten-week duration." These statements describe program accomplishments related to service delivery in terms of what happens to members of the target population, but do not address the benefits of those services for those persons. Similarly, the goals and objectives related to the program's organizational plan would deal with performing certain program functions, for instance, "to prepare curricular materials" or "to offer literacy classes four times a week."

One other consideration is important for the evaluator who is attempting to ascertain the various program goals and objectives and organize them into a description of program theory. The inquiry should attend to possible side effects and unintended outcomes that may be important for understanding the program as well as to the intended effects. Thus, a program "accomplishment" may be to have some impact that was not desired and may not be desirable. A mandatory job training program for women on welfare, for instance, may have the effect of increasing the number of children in substandard child care arrangements (Exhibit 5-F provides another example). Although such unintended effects cannot be said to be program goals, they follow from program activities in the same way as goal attainment and should be represented in program theory as possible outcomes.

Program functions, components, and activities. Program process theory mainly represents distinct program functions and how they relate to each other and to the participation of the targets in the program services. To properly describe this part of program theory, it is important for the evaluator to carefully identify each distinct program component, its functions, and the particular activities and operations associated with those functions. For this purpose, it is usually most instructive to view the program as a process rather than as an entity and describe it with verbs rather than nouns (Weick, 1982). An organization chart reveals little about how a program actually operates to achieve its objectives; that information appears in a description of what the program does. Thus, an essential part of describing program theory is to identify all the important program functions that must be performed for the program to operate as intended.

Program functions include such operations as "assess client need," "complete intake," "assign case manager," "recruit referral agencies," "train field workers," and the like. Viewed from the clients' perspective as part of a description of a service utilization plan, these functions appear in such forms as "receive referral for services," "contacted by case manager," "participate in group counseling sessions," and so forth. Each such function, whether represented from the program or the client perspective, will consist of various specific activities and will be associated with certain program personnel or components and resources. Full description of the program functions, therefore, also entails some level of description of the constituent activities and the program components and resources that support those activities (an example appears in Exhibit 5-G).

Logic or sequence linking program functions, activities, and components. A critical aspect of program theory is how the various steps and functions relate to each other. Sometimes those relationships involve only the temporal sequencing of key program activities and their effects; for instance, prison officials must notify the program that a convict has been released

---

☒ **EXHIBIT 5-F**   Unintended Effects of "Getting Tough" on Drunken Driving

California's drunk-driving laws were revised in 1982 to impose mandatory jail sentences and license suspension, even for first offenders, and to restrict plea-bargaining aimed at avoiding penalty. This new policy was intended to deter the practice of driving under the influence of alcohol (DUI) and reduce alcohol-related accidents.

However, subsequent research and anecdotal reports indicated that, whatever the positive effects of this policy, it also had a number of unintended and largely undesirable outcomes:

- An increase in court workloads. These changes resulted from an increased arrest rate for DUI and, also, because more defendants contested their arrest. There was a general decrease in the number of guilty pleas, an increase in the desire for attorney representation, an increase in the number of trials demanded by defendants (most noticeably for jury trials), and, because of the increased use of probation, an increase in probation revocation hearings.

- Increased cost for counties to provide defense and prosecuting attorneys. Because of the demands for more jury trials and the various avenues of postponement available to defendants, the cost of the time for publicly funded attorneys skyrocketed and some

county boards of supervisors had to allot emergency funds to provide proper legal counsel to the influx of defendants.

- An increase in the need for new programs and facilities to deal with the DUI offenders. These offenders often served their sentences in areas or buildings apart from the mainstream jail populations or in special programs, for example, home monitoring systems to enforce house arrest or distinctive treatment, educational, or guidance programs.

- A strain on the correctional system. The increased numbers of DUI incarcerates caused a significant increase in the jail populations in all jurisdictions. Also, the DUI offenders occupied expensive space; due to overcrowding, many had to be housed in maximum and medium security space rather than minimum security. Probation populations also increased in the state.

- An upsurge in jail suicides. Individuals with drinking problems, who otherwise view themselves as law-abiding citizens, can feel stigmatized by incarceration; this apparently pushes some to take their own lives. Overcrowding exacerbates this problem by disallowing adequate prisoner supervision.

SOURCE: Adapted from Patrick T. Kinkade, Matthew C. Leone, and Wayne N. Welsh, "Tough Laws: Policymaker Perceptions and Commitment," *Social Science Journal*, 1995, 32(2):157-178.

---

before the program can initiate contact to arrange aftercare services. In other cases, these relationships have to do with activities or events that must be coordinated, as when child care and transportation must be arranged in conjunction with job training sessions, or with supportive functions, like training the instructors who will conduct in-service classes for nurses. Other relationships entail logical or conceptual linkages, especially those repre-

✄ EXHIBIT 5-G   Program Functions for the Adapted Work Services Program

Exhibit 5-C earlier introduced the Adapted Work Services program, developed to provide low-stress, paid work and social interaction to patients in the early stages of Alzheimer's disease. The formulation of the program process theory that resulted from the procedures summarized in Exhibit 5-C was presented to stakeholders in the form of an "operational model" that described the following program functions:

Marketing	Case Finding	Responding to Inquiries	Hosting Initial Contacts
Compile data on community need	Develop referral sources Family members	Answer questions from families, referral services, and participants	Introduction to staff, peers Observe work in progress Staff observation of
Educate public and referral sources	EAPs Health providers	Provide current cost schedule	participant and family Information sheet
Advertise program	Assisted living facilities Hospital discharge Church leaders Senior citizen centers Maintain referral network	Complete screening Obtain referral form Invite program visits	

Conducting Assessments	Intake and Assignment	Providing Service	Arranging Transitions
Arrange trial period	Analysis of assessment	Transportation	Plan with caregiver for transitions
Observe Work competence Motivation Behavior	Testing Family dynamics Trial period Enrollment	Coffee and socialization Work periods Training Support	Monitor criteria for discharge Self-select out
Conduct testing Mini-mental exam Depression scale	Application form Agreement form Billing information	Case management Ongoing evaluation Functional status	Review transportation, health, family Discuss with participant
Assess family Supportness Ability to pay	Waiver form Nonenrollment Referral to other services	Health Communication Progress reports	Feedback to Physician Referral source
Communicate with Referral source Family Physician	Documentation	Caregivers Physicians Referral sources	Families Follow-up Family Next service provider

SOURCE: Adapted from Doris C. Quinn, "Formative Evaluation of Adapted Work Services for Alzheimer's Disease Victims: A Framework for Practical Evaluation in Health Care" (doctoral diss., Vanderbilt University, 1996), pp. 81-82.

sented in program impact theory. Thus, the connection between mothers' knowledge about how to care for their infants and the actual behavior of providing that care assumes a psychological process through which information influences behavior (Exhibit 5-H describes some of the relationships that are basic to program logic).

Describing program theory, therefore, requires an understanding of how different events, persons, functions, and the other elements represented in the theory are presumed

---

✳ **EXHIBIT 5-H** The Components of a Program Logic

A program logic consists of seven components, including

1. *An outcomes hierarchy.* This is a cause-effect hierarchy of desired outputs (e.g., the number of members of the target group serviced by a program), which lead to immediate impacts (e.g., changes in knowledge and skills of the target group), which in turn lead to outcomes (e.g., clients live an independent lifestyle, safer roads).

For each output, impact, and outcome in the hierarchy there should be

2. *Success criteria and definitions of terms* (e.g., what are the desired types of clients, what is meant by an independent lifestyle, what is meant by safer roads?).
3. *Factors that are within the control or influence of the program and are likely to affect the extent to which the outcome is achieved* (e.g., quality of service delivery, the way in which priorities are set).

4. *Factors that are outside the control or influence of the program and are likely to affect the extent to which the outcome is achieved* (e.g., the demographics of the target group, competing programs, past experiences of program clients).
5. *Program activities and resources used to control or influence both types of factors* (e.g., training given to staff to improve service quality, risk management strategies to respond to factors outside control).
6. *Performance information required to measure the success of the program in achieving desired outcomes* (e.g., the percentage of clients who show improved knowledge, information about the way in which the program is being implemented as a prerequisite for testing causal links between program activities and observed results).
7. *Comparisons required to judge and interpret performance indicators* (e.g., comparisons with standards to make judgments, comparisons with control conditions, pre-post comparisons to interpret performance and attribute it to the program).

SOURCE: Adapted from Sue Funnell, "Program Logic: An Adaptable Tool for Designing and Evaluating Programs," *Evaluation News and Comment: The Magazine of the Australasian Evaluation Society,* 1997, 6(1):5-17.

---

to be related. Because the number and variety of such relationships are often appreciable, evaluators typically construct charts or graphical displays to describe them (examples were shown in Chapter 3 and might be appropriately reexamined at this point). These may be configured as lists, flowcharts, hierarchies, or in any number of creative forms designed to identify the key elements and relationships in a program's theory. Such displays not only portray program theory but also provide a way to make it sufficiently concrete and specific for program personnel and stakeholders to engage. Working collaboratively with stakeholders to draft, differentiate, and discuss displays of program theory can be a very effective way for the evaluator to draw out the implicit knowledge of those informants.

*Corroborating and Using
Theory Description*

Confirmation of a program theory description is chiefly a matter of demonstrating that pertinent program personnel and stakeholders endorse it as a meaningful account of how the program is intended to work. If it is not possible to generate a theory description that all relevant stakeholders accept as reasonable, this is diagnostic of a poorly defined program, conflicting perspectives among stakeholders about what the program is supposed to be doing and why, or competing program philosophies embodied in the same program. In such cases, the most appropriate response for the evaluator may be to take on a consultant role and assist the program in clarifying its assumptions and intentions to yield a theory description that will be acceptable to all key stakeholders.

Even when all pertinent stakeholders generally agree on a description of the program theory, they sometimes find parts of it questionable. Depicting the theory explicitly often surfaces assumptions and expectations inherent in a program that do not seem very plausible when laid out in black and white. This reaction may motivate program personnel and other stakeholders to pursue changes in program design. When this results from their involvement in the theory description process or from insights gained when the results of that process are reviewed, it demonstrates the utility of the theory description.

For the evaluator, the end result of the theory description exercise is a relatively detailed and complete statement of the program as intended that can then be analyzed and assessed as a distinct program evaluation function. Note that stakeholder agreement on the theory description serves only as confirmation that the description does, in fact, represent their understanding of how the program is supposed to work. This does not necessarily mean that the theory is a good one. To determine the soundness of a program theory, it must not only be described well but evaluated carefully. The procedures that evaluators use to assess program theory are described in the next section.

ASSESSING PROGRAM THEORY

Assessment of some aspect of a program's theory is relatively common in evaluation, often in conjunction with an evaluation of program process or impact. Nonetheless, outside of the modest evaluability assessment literature, remarkably little has been written of a specific nature about how this should be done, especially when the program design itself is the primary focus of the assessment. Our interpretation of this relative neglect is not that theory assessment is unimportant or unusual, but that it is typically done in an informal manner that relies on commonsense judgments, which, for most commentators, may not seem to require much explanation. Undeterred by the limited attention elsewhere, in this section we attempt to pull together a perspective on how to assess program theory, drawing from diverse sources and our own experience.

Frameworks for Assessing Program Theory

It is seldom possible or useful to individually appraise each distinct assumption and expectation represented in a program theory. But there are certain critical tests that can be conducted to provide general assurance that the program conceptualization is sound. Depending on how significant the questions about the program theory are judged to be, a more or less stringent assessment may be appropriate. When there is little reason to believe that the program theory is problematic, its validity may be accepted on the basis of limited evidence or on commonsense judgment and "face validity." This is most likely to be the situation for programs whose services are directly related to straightforward objectives. A meals-on-wheels service, for instance, that brings hot meals to homebound elderly persons to improve their nutritional intake would be such a program.

Many programs are not based on presumptions as simple as the notion that delivering food to elderly persons improves their nutrition. A family preservation program that assigns case managers to coordinate community services for parents deemed at risk of having their children placed in foster care, for instance, involves many assumptions about exactly what it is supposed to accomplish and how. In such cases, the program theory might easily be faulty, and correspondingly, a rather probing evaluation of it may be warranted. The various procedures the evaluator might use for conducting that assessment are summarized below.

Assessment in Relation to Social Needs

The most important framework for assessing program theory builds on the results of needs assessment, as discussed in the previous chapter. Or, more generally, it is based on a thorough understanding of the social problem the program is intended to address and the service needs of the relevant target population, whether based on a formal needs assessment or not. A program theory that does not embody a conceptualization of program activities and outcomes that relate in an appropriate and effective manner to the actual nature and circumstances of the social conditions at issue will yield an ineffective program no matter how well implemented and administered. It is fundamental, therefore, to assess program theory in relationship to the needs of the target population the program is intended to serve.

There is no push-button procedure that an evaluator can use to assess program theory against social needs to determine if it describes a suitable conceptualization of how those needs should be met. Inevitably, this assessment requires a series of judgment calls. When the assessment is especially critical, its validity is strengthened if those judgments are made collaboratively with relevant experts and stakeholders to broaden the range of perspectives and expertise on which they are based. Such collaborators, for instance, might include social scientists knowledgeable about research and theory related to the intervention, administrators with long experience managing such programs, representatives of advocacy groups associated with the target population, and policymakers or policy advisers highly familiar with the program and problem area.

Whatever the nature of the group that contributes to the assessment, the crucial aspect of the process is *specificity*. When program theory and social needs are described in general terms, there often appears to be more correspondence than is evident when the details are examined. To illustrate, consider a curfew program prohibiting juveniles under age 18 from being outside their homes after midnight that is initiated in a metropolitan area to address the problem of skyrocketing juvenile crime. The program theory, in general terms, is that the curfew will keep the youths home at night and, if they are at home, they are unlikely to commit crimes. Because the general social problem the program addresses is juvenile crime, the program theory does seem responsive to the social need.

A more detailed problem diagnosis and service needs assessment, however, might show that the bulk of juvenile crimes are residential burglaries committed in the late afternoon when school lets out. Moreover, it might reveal that the offenders represent a relatively small proportion of the juvenile population who have a disproportionately large impact because of their high rates of offending. Furthermore, it might be found that these juveniles are predominantly latchkey youths who have no supervision during after school hours. When the program, in turn, is examined in some detail, it is apparent that it assumes that significant juvenile crime occurs late at night and that potential offenders will know about and obey the curfew. Furthermore, it depends on enforcement by parents or the police if compliance does not occur voluntarily.

Although more specificity than this would be desirable, even this much detail illustrates how program theory can be compared with need to discover shortcomings in the theory. In this example, examining the particulars of the program theory and the social problem it is intended to address reveals a large disconnect. The program blankets the whole city rather than targeting the small group of problem juveniles and focuses on late night activity rather than early afternoon when most of the crimes occur. In addition, it makes the questionable assumptions that youths already engaged in more serious lawbreaking will comply with a curfew, that parents who leave their delinquent children unsupervised during the early part of the day will be able to supervise their later behavior, and that the overburdened police force will invest sufficient effort in arresting juveniles who violate the curfew to enforce compliance. Careful review of these particulars

alone would raise serious doubts about the validity of the program theory for addressing the social problem at issue (Exhibit 5-I presents another example).

One useful approach to comparing program theory with what is known (or assumed) about the respective social needs is to separately assess impact theory and program process theory. Each of these relates to the social problem in a different way and, as each is differentiated, specific questions can be asked about how compatible the assumptions of the theory are with the nature of the social circumstances to which it applies. We will briefly describe the main points of comparison for each of these theory components.

Program impact theory involves the sequence of causal links between program services and outcomes that improve the targeted social conditions. The key point of comparison between program impact theory and social needs, therefore, relates to whether the effects the program is expected to have on the social conditions according to the theory correspond to what the needs assessment indicates are required to improve those conditions. Consider, for instance, a school-based educational program aimed at getting elementary school children to learn and practice good eating habits. The problem this program attempts to ameliorate is poor nutritional choices among school-aged children, especially those in economically disadvantaged areas. The program impact theory would show a sequence of links between the planned instructional exercises and the children's awareness of the nutritional value of foods, culminating in healthier selections and improved nutrition.

Now, suppose a thorough needs assessment shows that the children's eating habits are, indeed, poor but their nutritional knowledge is not especially deficient. The needs as-

---

EXHIBIT 5-I   The Needs of the Homeless as a Basis for Assessing Program Theory

Exhibit 4-M in the prior chapter on needs assessment described the responses of a large sample of homeless men and women to a needs assessment survey. The largest proportions identified a place to live and having a job or steady income as their greatest need. Fewer than half, but significant proportions, also said they needed help with medical, substance abuse, psychological, and legal problems. The evaluators reported that among the service delivery implications of the needs assessment were indications that this population needs interventions that provide ongoing support in a range of domains at varying degrees of intensity. Thus, to be responsive, programs must have the capacity to deliver or broker access to a comprehensive range of services.

These findings offer two lines of analysis for assessment of program theory. First, any program that intends to alleviate homelessness must provide services that address the major problems the homeless persons experience. That is, the expected outcomes of those services (impact theory) must represent improvements in the most problematic domains if the conditions of the homeless are to be appreciably improved. Second, the design of the service delivery system (process theory) must be such that multiple services can be readily and flexibly provided to homeless individuals in ways that will be accessible to them despite their limited resources and difficult circumstances. Careful, detailed comparison of the program theory embodied in any program for this homeless population with the respective needs assessment data, therefore, will reveal how sound that theory is as a design for effective intervention.

SOURCE: Daniel B. Herman, Elmer L. Struening, and Susan M. Barrow, "Self-Reported Needs for Help Among Homeless Men and Women," *Evaluation and Program Planning*, 1994, 17(3):249-256.

---

sessment further shows that the foods served at home and even those offered in the school cafeterias provide limited opportunity for healthy selections. Against this background, it is evident that the program impact theory is flawed. Even if the program successfully imparts additional information about healthy eating, the children will not be able to act on that information because they have little control over the selection of foods available to them. Thus, the proximal outcomes the program impact theory describes may be achieved, but they are not what is needed to ameliorate the problem at issue.

Program process theory, on the other hand, describes the interactions expected between the target population and the program (service utilization plan) and the functions the program is expected to perform (organizational plan). A sound process theory thus will make assumptions about the capability of the program to provide services accessible to the target population and compatible with their needs. These assumptions, in turn, can be compared with needs assessment information relating to the target population's opportunities to obtain service and the barriers that inhibit their service use.

As an example, consider an adult literacy program that offers classes in the evenings at the local high school. Its process theory incorporates significant instructional and advertising functions and it provides an appropriate selection of courses for the target population. The details of this scheme can be compared with needs assessment data that show what logistical and psychological support the target population requires to make effective use of the program. For instance, child care and transportation may be critical for many potential participants. Also, illiterate adults may be reluctant to enroll in courses without more personal encouragement than they would receive from advertising. Cultural and personal affinity with the instructors may be important factors in attracting and maintaining participation from the target population as well. The intended program process can thus be assessed in terms of how responsive it is to these dimensions of the needs of the target population.

Assessment of Logic and Plausibility

A thorough job of articulating program theory should reveal for inspection the critical assumptions and expectations inherent in the program's design. The program's goals and objectives will be specified and the primary program components and functions will be identified. The significant relationships among program functions and the nature of the expected interactions with the target population will be delineated. Most important, the description of the program's theory should lay out the cause-and-effect sequence through which program actions are presumed to ultimately produce the intended social benefits. One essential form of assessment is simply a critical review of the logic and plausibility of these various aspects of the program theory.

The appropriate questions to ask of the theory and its different aspects are basically of two sorts. First, "Is it well defined?" The theory in all its parts should be sufficiently specific, concrete, and clear to minimize ambiguity about what is supposed to be done and what is supposed to happen. Second, "Is it reasonable?" Informed reviewers should find it plausible that what is supposed to be done can be done and that what is expected to happen will happen. This judgment, in turn, will depend on an analysis of such matters as how logical the relationships are, what resources are available, what is viewed as realistic and practical within the organizational, political, and community context of the program, and assorted other such considerations. Exhibit 5-J describes such a review conducted as part of an evaluability assessment.

As should be apparent, assessing whether a program theory is well defined and reasonable requires considerable judgment and expertise. Although the evaluator will have a distinctive perspective on the issues and should be able to contribute importantly to the assessment, it would be rare for the evaluator to have the depth and breadth of knowledge about the program and its circumstances to be able to conduct a good assessment of its theory without assistance. As in the case of assessing the "fit" between a program's theory and the needs it addresses, discussed above, it may be appropriate to involve other knowledgeable persons in the review.

Commentators familiar with assessing program theory generally suggest that a panel of reviewers be organized for that purpose (Chen, 1990; Rutman, 1980; Smith, 1989; Wholey, 1994). This process may follow directly from the formulation of the program

---

⚆ EXHIBIT 5-J   Assessing the Clarity and Plausibility of the Program Theory for Maryland's 4-H Program

---

An evaluability assessment of Maryland's 4-H youth program based on program documents and interviews with 96 stakeholder representatives included a review of key facets of the program's theory with the following results:

Question: Are the mission and goals clear?

Conclusion: There is a lack of clarity about the overall mission of 4-H and some lack of agreement among the stakeholders and between persons directly involved in implementing the program and those not. Among the statements of mission were "introduce youth to farm life," develop "sense of responsibility in agriculture and home economics," and "developing life skills."

Question: Is it clear who is to be affected, who is the audience?

Conclusion: There is some lack of agreement between 4-H faculty and the other stakeholders about the audience of 4-H. Written documents identified the audience as youth and adults; any youth between age 8 and 18 was viewed as the traditional audience for the program; recently, 6- and 7-year-olds have been targeted; some informants viewed the adult volunteers who assist with the program as one audience.

Question: Is there agreement about intended effects?

Conclusion: Social, mental, and physical development were listed as the program objectives in the state program direction document. There was agreement among all groups and in written documents that the effects of 4-H are primarily social in nature, for example, self-confidence/self-esteem, leadership, citizenship. There was less agreement about its effects on mental development and no agreement about its impact on physical development.

Question: Is it plausible that the program activities would achieve the intended effects?

Conclusion: Even if all the activities identified in the program model were implemented according to plan, the plausibility of these leading to the intended program effects is questionable. A link appears to be missing from the program logic—something like "Determine the Curriculum." Lack of such a link prevents plausible activities in the initial program events, that is, without a curriculum plan, how can county faculty know what types of leaders to recruit, what to train volunteers to do, and what they and the volunteers should implement?

SOURCE: Adapted from Midge F. Smith, *Evaluability Assessment: A Practical Approach* (Norwell, MA: Kluwer, 1989), p. 91.

---

theory and involve the groups organized for that purpose, such as the work group or policy group associated with an evaluability assessment. Certainly, an expert review panel should include selected representatives of the program staff and other major stakeholders as well as the evaluator. By definition, however, stakeholders have some direct stake in the program at issue. To balance the assessment and expand the available expertise, it may be advisable to bring in informed persons with no direct relationship to the program. Such outside experts might include experienced administrators of similar programs, social researchers with relevant specialties, representatives of advocacy groups or client organizations, and the like.

A review of the logic and plausibility of program theory will necessarily be a relatively unstructured and open-ended process. Many different aspects of the theory may be questioned in different ways, and there will be numerous particulars distinctive to the program and its context. Nonetheless, there are some general issues such reviews should be expected to address and that provide guidance for the assessment. These are briefly described below in the form of questions reviewers can ask. Additional useful detail can be found in Rutman (1980), Smith (1989), and Wholey (1994).

- Are the program goals and objectives well defined? The outcomes for which the program is to be accountable should be stated in sufficiently clear and concrete terms that it is possible to determine if they have been attained. One line of inquiry on this issue is to ask if there are observable implications of the goals and objectives such that meaningful measures and indicators of success could be defined. Goals such as "introducing students to computer technology" are not well defined in this sense whereas "increasing student knowledge of the ways computers can be used" is well defined and measurable.

- Are the program goals and objectives feasible; is it realistic to assume that they can actually be attained as a result of program action? Program theory should specify expected outcomes that are of a nature and scope that might reasonably follow from a successful program and should not be grandiose or represent unrealistically high expectations. Moreover, the stated goals and objectives should involve conditions the program might actually be able to affect in some meaningful fashion, not those that are largely beyond its influence. For instance, "eliminating poverty" is grandiose whereas "decreasing the unemployment rate" is not, but might be unrealistic for a program located in a chronically depressed labor market.

- Is the change process presumed in the program theory plausible? The presumption that a program will create benefits for the intended target population depends on the occurrence of some cause-and-effect chain that begins with the targets' interaction with the program and ends with the improved circumstances in the target population that the program expects to bring about (program impact theory). Every step of this causal chain should at least be plausible. Because the validity of this impact theory is the key to the program's ability to produce the intended effects, it is best if it is also supported by evidence that the assumed links and relationships do actually occur. A program based on the presumption that exposure to literature about the health hazards of drug abuse will motivate long-term heroin addicts to renounce drug use, for instance, does not present a plausible change process, nor is it supported by any research evidence.

- Are the program procedures for identifying members of the target population, delivering service to them, and sustaining that service through completion well defined and sufficient? The program theory should involve specific procedures and functions for locating potential service recipients, determining their eligibility, delivering service, and most important, handling all likely contingencies in this process. Moreover, those procedures should be adequate for the purposes, viewed both from the perspective of the program's ability to perform them and the target population's likelihood of being engaged by them. Consider, for example, health screenings for high blood pressure among poor and elderly populations. It is reasonable to ask if these are provided in locations members of these groups frequent and if there is an effective means of locating those with uncertain addresses so that feedback can be provided. Absent these characteristics, it is unlikely that many persons from the target groups will receive the intended service.

• Are the constituent components, activities, and functions of the program well defined and sufficient? Program structure and process should be specific enough to permit orderly operations, effective management control, and monitoring using attainable, meaningful performance measures. Most critical, the program components and activities should be sufficient and appropriate to attain the intended program goals and objectives. Such functions as "client advocacy" have little practical significance if no personnel are assigned to it or there is no common understanding of what it means operationally. Similarly, providing a "supportive milieu" is not very convincing as the centerpiece of a program for emotionally disturbed adolescents.

• Are the resources allocated to the program and its various components and activities adequate? Program resources include funding, of course, but also personnel, material, equipment, facilities, relationships, reputation, and other such assets. There should be some reasonable correspondence between the program as intended that is described in program theory and the resources presumed (or known) to be available for operating the program. A program

theory that calls for activities and outcomes that are unrealistic relative to available resources cannot be said to be a good theory. For a program to be conducted as expected and have the intended consequences, the assumptions made about how it will operate and what it will accomplish should be scaled to the resources available. For example, a management training program too short-staffed to initiate more than a few brief workshops cannot expect to have a significant impact on management skills in the organization.

Assessment Through Comparison With Research and Practice

Although every program is distinctive in some ways, few are based entirely on unique presumptions about how to engender change, deliver service to the target population, and perform major program functions. It follows that some information applicable to assessing the various components of program theory is likely to appear in the social science and human services research literature. In most program areas, there is also significant information available describing the experience of various programs with different practices, program approaches, and the like. One useful approach to assessing program theory once it is articulated, therefore, is to find out if it is congruent with research evidence and practical experience elsewhere (Exhibit 5-K summarizes one example of this approach).

There are several ways in which program theory might be compared with findings from research and practice. The most straightforward approach is to examine evaluations of programs based on similar concepts. The results will give some indication of the likelihood that such programs will be successful and per-

◼ EXHIBIT 5-K   GREAT Program Theory Is Consistent With Criminological Research

In 1991 the Phoenix, Arizona, Police Department initiated a program with local educators to provide youths in the elementary grades with the tools necessary to resist becoming gang members. Known as GREAT (Gang Resistance Education and Training), the program has attracted federal funding and is now distributed nationally. The program is taught to seventh graders in schools over nine consecutive weeks by uniformed police officers. It is structured around detailed lesson plans that emphasize teaching youths how to set goals for themselves, how to resist peer pressure, how to resolve conflicts, and how gangs can affect the quality of their lives.

The program has no officially stated theoretical grounding other than Glasser's (1975) reality therapy, but GREAT training officers and others associated with the program make reference to sociological and psychological concepts as they train GREAT instructors. As part of an analysis of the program's impact theory, a team of criminal justice researchers identified two well-researched criminological theories relevant to gang participation: Gottfredson and Hirschi's self-control theory (SCT) and Akers's social learning theory (SLT). They then reviewed the GREAT lesson plans to assess their consistency with the most pertinent aspects of these theories. To illustrate their findings, a summary of Lesson 4 is provided below with the researchers' analysis in italics after the lesson description:

Lesson 4. Conflict Resolution: Students learn how to create an atmosphere of understanding that would enable all parties to better address problems and work on solutions together. *This lesson includes concepts related to SCT's anger and aggressive coping strategies. SLT ideas are also present: Instructors present peaceful, nonconfrontational means of resolving conflicts. Part of this lesson deals with giving the student a means of dealing with peer pressure to join gangs and a means of avoiding negative peers with a focus is on the positive results (reinforcements) of resolving disagreements by means other than violence. Many of these ideas directly reflect constructs used in previous research on social learning and gangs.*

Similar comparisons showed good consistency between the concepts of the criminological theories and the lesson plans for all but one of the eight lessons. The reviewers concluded that the GREAT curriculum contained implicit and explicit linkages both to self-control theory and social learning theory.

SOURCE: Adapted from L. Thomas Winfree, Jr., Finn-Aage Esbensen, and D. Wayne Osgood, "Evaluating a School-Based Gang-Prevention Program: A Theoretical Perspective," *Evaluation Review*, 1996, 20(2):181-203.

haps identify some of the critical problem areas. Evaluations of very similar programs, of course, will be the most informative in this regard. However, evaluation results for programs that are similar only in terms of general theory, even if different in other regards, might also be instructive.

This approach can be illustrated by considering a mass media campaign in a metropolitan area to encourage women to have mammogram screening for early detection of breast cancer. The impact theory for this program presumes that exposure to TV, radio, and newspaper messages will stimulate a reaction that will eventuate in increased rates of mammogram screening. Whatever the impact theory assumed to link exposure and increases in testing, its credibility is enhanced by evidence that similar media campaigns in other cities have resulted in increased mammogram testing. Moreover, if the evaluations or descriptive information for the campaigns in other cities shows that the program functions and scheme for delivering messages to the target population were similar to that intended for the program at issue, then the program's process theory also gains some support.

Suppose, however, that no evaluation results or practical descriptive accounts are available about media campaigns to increase rates of mammogram screening in other cities. It might still be informative to examine information about other media campaigns more or less analogous to the one at issue. For instance, reports may be available about the nature and results of media campaigns to promote immunizations, dental checkups, or other such actions that are health related and require a visit to a provider. The success of such programs, and different variations of such programs, might well be relevant to assessing the program theory on which the mammogram campaign is based so long as they involve similar principles.

In many program areas, numerous competing program approaches are directed toward accomplishing the same, or very similar, outcomes. Various different programs have been implemented for the treatment of alcoholism, for instance. In such cases, there are likely to be research reviews or meta-analyses that examine the existing evaluation research and summarize what has been learned about more and less promising program approaches. Consideration of how the program theory being assessed compares to those represented in the different program approaches covered in a research review often will support a convincing assessment.

In some instances, behavioral or social science research on the social and psychological processes central to the program will be available as a framework for assessing the program theory, particularly impact theory. From the perspective of the evaluation field, it is unfortunate that relatively little "basic" research has been done on many of the social dynamics that are common and important to intervention programs, because the results can be very useful. For instance, a mass media campaign to encourage mammogram screening, as in the example above, inherently involves persuasive messages intended to change attitudes and behavior. The large body of basic research on attitude change and its relationship to behavior in social psychology provides some basis for assessing the impact theory for any media campaign. One established finding, for instance, is that messages designed to raise fears are generally less effective than those providing positive reasons for a behavior. Thus, an impact theory based on the presumption that increasing awareness of the dangers of breast cancer will prompt increased mammogram screening may not be a good one.

There is also a large applied research literature on media campaigns and related approaches in the field of advertising and marketing. Although this literature largely has to do with selling products and services, it too may provide some basis for assessing the program theory for the breast cancer media campaign. Market segmentation studies, for instance, may show what media and what times of the day are best for reaching women with various demographic profiles. This information can then be used as part of the assessment of the program's service utilization plan to examine whether the media plan is optimal for communicating with women whose age and circumstances put them at the highest risk for breast cancer.

Fortunately, use of the research and practice literature to help with assessment of program theory is not limited to situations of relatively good overall correspondence between the programs or processes the evaluator is investigating and those represented in the literature. Often there is little or no literature dealing with programs or processes sufficiently similar to the ones under study to be applicable. An alternate approach for assessing program theory against existing research is to break the theory down into its component parts and linkages and search for research evidence relevant to each component.

Much of program theory can be stated as "if-then" propositions: If case managers are assigned, then more services will be provided; if school performance improves, then delinquent behavior will decrease; if teacher-to-student ratios are higher, then students will receive more individual attention. Frequently, research can be found that aids in appraising the plausibility of the individual propositions of this sort that are most fundamental to the program theory. The results of these appraisals, in turn, provide a basis for a broader assessment of the theory with the added advantage of potentially identifying any especially weak links. This approach was pioneered by the Program Evaluation and Methodology Division of the U.S. General Accounting Office as a way to provide rapid review of program proposals arising in the congress (Cordray, 1993; U.S. General Accounting Office, 1990).

Assessment Via Preliminary Observation

Program theory, of course, is inherently conceptual and not something that can be observed directly. However, program theory does involve many assumptions about how things are supposed to work that can be assessed by observing the program in operation, talking to staff and service recipients, and other such inquiries focused specifically on the program theory. Indeed, a thorough assessment of program theory description should incorporate some firsthand observation of the program and its circumstances and not rely entirely on logical analysis and similar "armchair" reviews. Direct observation provides something of a "reality check" to assess the concordance between the program theory and the program it is supposed to describe.

Consider a program theory that presumes that distributing brochures about good nutrition to senior citizens centers will influence the attitudes and eating behavior of elderly persons. Observations revealing that the brochures are rarely read by anyone attending the centers would certainly raise a question about a key assumption of the theory. In particular, this observation challenges the presumption that the target population will be exposed to the information in the brochures, which is a precondition for any attitude or behavior change. In this regard, it is the plausibility of the program theory, or a portion of it, that is being assessed, as discussed above. Rather than being assessed on the basis of informed judgment by the evaluator or other knowledgeable informants, however, it is checked directly through observation of the circumstances at issue or, perhaps, interviews with persons in close contact with those circumstances.

To assess program impact theory, observations and interviews might be focused on the intended program outcomes and the interactions between program services and the target population that are expected to produce those outcomes. This inquiry might look into the question of whether the intended outcomes are appropriate for the program circumstances and whether they are realistically attainable. For example, the presumption that a welfare-to-work program can enable a large proportion of welfare clients to find and maintain employment might be investigated by examining the local job market, the work readiness of the welfare population (number physically and mentally fit, skill levels, work histories, motivation), and the relative economic benefits of work to gauge how realistic the intended program outcomes are. At the service end of the change process, the job training activities might be observed and interviews with participants conducted to assess the plausibility that the intended changes would occur.

Inquiry aimed at testing the service utilization component of a program's process theory would examine the circumstances of the target population to better understand how and why they might become engaged with the program and, once engaged, continue until the intended services had been received. This information would permit some assessment of the quality of the program's service delivery plan for locating, engaging, and serving the intended target population. To assess the service utilization plan of a midnight basketball program to reduce delinquency among high-risk youths, for instance, the evaluator might observe the program in action and interview participants, program staff, and neighborhood youths about who participates and how regularly. The program's service utilization assumptions would be supported by indications that the most delinquent-prone youths participate regularly in the program.

Indications of the plausibility of the organizational component of the program's process theory might be developed through observations and interviews relating to program activities and the supporting resources. Critical here is evidence that the program can actually perform the intended functions. Consider, for instance, a program plan that calls for the sixth-grade science teachers throughout the school district to take their classes on two science-related field trips per year. The evaluator could probe the presumption that this would be done by interviewing a number of teachers and principals to find out if this was broadly feasible in terms of scheduling, availability of buses, funding, and other such matters.

Any assessment of the practicality of program theory or its appropriateness for the program circumstances that involves the collection of new data could easily turn into a full-scale investigation of the program aimed at determining if what was presumed in the theory actually happened. And, indeed, an empirical "theory testing" study is one obvious approach to assessing program theory, an approach that emphasizes descriptive and predictive accuracy (see, e.g., Bickman, 1990; also, Exhibit 5-L gives an example). As later chapters in this volume will discuss, many aspects of the evaluation of program process and impact take on this character when the evaluation design is guided by a detailed analysis of program theory, as we advocated in Chapter 3.

In this chapter, however, our focus is on the task of assessing the soundness of the program theory description as a plan, that is, as a statement of the program as intended rather than as a statement of what is actually happening (that assessment comes later). By recognizing the role of observation and interview in the

---

EXHIBIT 5-L   Testing a Model of Patient Education for Diabetes Self-Care Management

The daily management of diabetes involves a complex interaction of metabolic variables, self-care behaviors, and psychological and social adjustments to having the disease. An important component of treatment for diabetes, therefore, is the instruction of patients so that they have the skills and knowledge required to do their part. A team of university medical researchers with a particular interest in the personal meaning to patients of having diabetes formulated an impact theory for the effects of patient education, which they diagramed as follows:

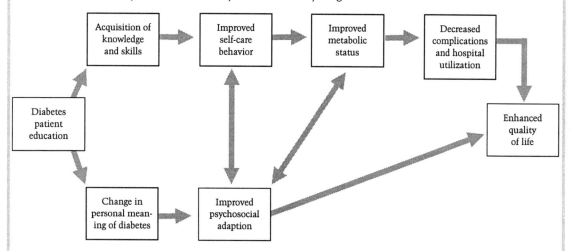

The researchers investigated this model by examining the correlations representing some of the key hypotheszed relationships on survey data collected from a sample of 220 people with diabetes recruited from clinics in several states. The data were analyzed using a structural equation analysis which showed only an approximate fit to the model. The relationships between the "personal meaning of diabetes" variables and "psychosocial adaptation" were strong, as were those between knowledge and self-care behavior. However, other relationships in the model were eqivocal. The researchers' conclusion: "While the results showed that the data did not fit the proposed model well enough to allow for definitive conclusions, the results are generally supportive of the original hypothesis that the personal meaning of diabetes is an important element in the daily management of diabetes and the psychosocial adjustment to the disease."

SOURCE: Adapted from George A. Nowacek, Patrick M. O'Malley, Robert A. Anderson, and Fredrick E. Richards, "Testing a Model of Diabetes Self-Care Management: A Causal Model Analysis With LISREL," *Evaluation & the Health Professions,* 1990, 13(3):298-314.

---

process, therefore, we are not suggesting that theory assessment as a distinct evaluation activity necessarily requires a full evaluation of the program. Instead, we are suggesting that some appropriately configured contact with the program activities, target population, and related situations and informants can provide the evaluator with valuable information about how plausible and realistic the program theory is.

Outcomes and Responses to the Results of Program Theory Assessment

A program whose conceptualization is weak or faulty has little prospect for success even if it adequately operationalizes that conceptualization. Thus, if the program theory is not sound, there is little justification for attempting to assess other evaluation issues, such as program implementation, impact, or efficiency. Within the framework of evaluability assessment, finding that the program theory is poorly defined or seriously flawed indicates that the program is not evaluable.

When assessment of program theory reveals deficiencies in the program theory, one appropriate response is for the responsible parties to redesign the program. This would involve carefully working out a well-defined impact theory, program process theory, or whatever components of those theories are deficient. Program reconceptualization may include (a) clarification of goals and objectives and identification of the observable implications of attaining them; (b) restructuring program components for which the intended activities are not happening, are not needed, or are not reasonable; and (c) working with stakeholders to obtain consensus on program objectives and the logic that connects program activities with the desired outcomes. The evaluator may help in this process as a consultant.

If an evaluation of program process or impact goes forward without articulation of a well-defined and credible program theory, then a certain amount of ambiguity will be inherent in the results. This ambiguity is potentially twofold. First, if program process theory is not well defined and explicit, there is ambiguity about what the program is expected to be doing operationally. This complicates the matter of identifying criteria by which to judge how well it is implemented. Such criteria must then be established individually for the various key program functions through some piecemeal process. For instance, administrative criteria may be stipulated regarding the number of clients to serve, the amount of service to provide, and the like, but they will not be integrated into an overall plan for the program.

The second form of ambiguity is introduced into an evaluation when there is no adequate specification of the program impact theory. Impact evaluation may be able to determine whether certain outcomes were produced (see Chapters 7-10), but without a guiding theory it will be difficult to explain why or—often more important—why not. Poorly specified impact theory limits the ability to identify or measure the intervening variables on which the outcomes may depend and, correspondingly, the ability to explain what went right or wrong in producing the expected outcomes. If program process theory is also poorly specified, it will not even be possible to describe very distinctly the nature of the program that produced, or failed to produce, the outcomes of interest. Evaluation under these circumstances is often referred to as *black box evaluation* to indicate that assessment of outcomes is made without much insight into what is causing those outcomes.

If program theory is well defined and well justified, the articulation of that theory permits ready identification of critical program functions and effects and defines what the program is expected to do and what is supposed to happen as a result. This structure provides meaningful benchmarks against which actual program performance can be compared by both managers and evaluators. The framework of program theory, therefore, gives the program a blueprint for effective management and gives the evaluator guidance in designing process, impact, and efficiency evaluations, as the subsequent chapters in this volume will discuss.

SUMMARY

- Every program embodies a program theory, a set of assumptions and expectations that constitute the logic or plan of the program and provide the rationale for what the program does and why. These assumptions may be well formulated and explicitly stated, representing an *articulated* program theory, or they may be inherent in the program but not overtly stated, thus comprising an *implicit* program theory.

- Program theory is an aspect of a program that can be evaluated in its own right. Such assessment is important because a program based on weak or faulty conceptualization has little prospect of achieving the intended results.

- The most fully developed approaches to evaluating program theory occur in the context of *evaluability assessment*, a preevaluation appraisal of whether a program's performance can be evaluated and, if so, whether it should be.

- Evaluability assessment involves describing program goals and objectives, assessing whether the program is well enough conceptualized to be evaluable, and identifying stakeholder interest in evaluation findings. Evaluability assessment may result in efforts by program managers to better conceptualize their program. It may indicate that the program is too poorly defined for evaluation or that there is little likelihood that the findings will be used. Alternatively, it could find that the program theory is well defined and plausible, that evaluation findings will likely be used, and that a meaningful evaluation could be done.

- To assess program theory, it is necessary for the evaluator to articulate the theory, that is, state it in a clear, explicit form acceptable to stakeholders. The aim of this effort is to describe the "program as intended" and its rationale, not the program as it actually is, although, of course, some resemblance is expected.

- The evaluator describes program theory by collating and integrating information from program documents, interviews with program personnel and other stakeholders, and observations of program activities. It is especially important that clear, concrete statements of the program's goals and objectives be formulated as well as an account of how the desired outcomes are expected to result from program action. Also, the relationships expected among program functions, components, and activities must be described.

※ The most important assessment of program theory the evaluator can make is based on a comparison of the intervention specified in the program theory with the social needs the program is expected to address. Examining critical details of the program conceptualization and the social problem indicates whether the program represents a reasonable plan for ameliorating the target problem. This analysis is facilitated when a needs assessment has been conducted to systematically diagnose the problematic social conditions (Chapter 4).

※ A complementary approach to assessing program theory uses stakeholders and other informants to appraise the clarity, plausibility, feasibility, and appropriateness of the program theory as formulated. This review can often be usefully supplemented with direct observations by the evaluator to further probe critical assumptions in the program theory.

※ Program theory also can be assessed in relation to the support for its critical assumptions found in research or documented program practice elsewhere. Sometimes findings are available for similar programs, or programs based on similar theory, so that an overall comparison can be made between a program's theory and relevant evidence. If the research and practice literature does not support overall comparisons, however, evidence bearing on specific key relationships assumed in the program theory may still be obtainable.

※ Assessment of program theory yields findings that can help improve the conceptualization of a program or, possibly, affirm its basic design. Such findings are an important evaluation product in their own right and can be informative for program stakeholders. In addition, a sound program theory provides a basis for evaluation of how well that theory is implemented, what outcomes are produced, and how efficiently they are produced, topics to be discussed in subsequent chapters of this volume.

KEY CONCEPTS FOR CHAPTER 6

Program monitoring	The systematic documentation of aspects of program performance that are indicative of whether the program is functioning as intended or according to some appropriate standard. Monitoring generally involves program performance related to program process, program outcomes, or both.
Accountability	The responsibility of program staff to provide evidence to stakeholders and sponsors that a program is effective and in conformity with its coverage, service, legal, and fiscal requirements.
Administrative standards	Stipulated achievement levels set by program administrators or other responsible parties, for example, intake for 90% of the referrals within one month. These levels may be set on the basis of past experience, the performance of comparable programs, or professional judgment.
Process evaluation	A form of program monitoring designed to determine whether the program is delivered as intended to the targeted recipients. Also known as implementation assessment.
Management information system (MIS)	A data system, usually computerized, that routinely collects and reports information about the delivery of services to clients and, often, billing, costs, diagnostic and demographic information, and outcome status.
Performance measurement	The collection, reporting, and interpretation of performance indicators related to how well programs perform, particularly with regard to the delivery of service (outputs) and achievement of results (outcomes).
Outcome monitoring	The measurement and reporting of indicators of the status of the social conditions the program is accountable for improving.
Implementation failure	The program does not adequately perform the activities specified in the program design that are assumed to be necessary for bringing about the intended social improvements. It includes situations in which no service, not enough service, or the wrong service is delivered, or the service varies excessively across the target population.
Accessibility	The extent to which the structural and organizational arrangements facilitate participation in the program.
Coverage	The extent to which a program reaches its intended target population.
Bias in coverage	The extent to which subgroups of a target population participate differentially in a program.

CHAPTER 6

MONITORING PROGRAM PROCESS AND PERFORMANCE

In previous chapters, we discussed the ways in which evaluators can assess the nature of the social problem targeted by a program and the quality of the theory inherent in a program about how the program activities will ameliorate that problem. To be effective in bringing about the desired improvements in social conditions, of course, a program needs more than a good plan of attack, although that is an essential precondition. Most important, the program must implement its plan; that is, it must actually carry out the intended functions in the intended way.

Although implementing a program concept may seem straightforward, in practice it is often very difficult. Social programs typically must contend with many adverse influences that can compromise even well-intentioned attempts to conduct program business appropriately. The result can easily be substantial discrepancies between the program as intended and the program actually implemented.

An important evaluation function, therefore, is to assess program implementation: the program activities that actually take place and the services that are actually delivered in routine program operation. Program monitoring and related procedures are the means by which the evaluator investigates these issues.

Program monitoring is usually directed at one or more of three key questions: (a) whether a program is reaching the appropriate target population, (b) whether its service delivery and support functions are consistent with program design specifications or other appropriate standards, and (c) whether positive changes appear among the program participants and social conditions the program addresses. Monitoring may also examine what resources are being, or have been, expended in the conduct of the program.

Program monitoring is an essential evaluation activity. It is the principal tool for formative evaluation designed to provide feedback for program improvement and is especially applicable to relatively new programs attempting to establish their organization, clientele, and services. Also, adequate monitoring (process evaluation) is a vital complement to impact evaluation, helping distinguish cases of poor program implementation from ineffective intervention concepts.

Program monitoring also informs policymakers, program sponsors, and other stakeholders about how well programs perform their intended functions. Increasingly, some form of program performance monitoring is being required by government and nonprofit agencies as a way of demonstrating accountability to the public and the program stakeholders.

After signing a new bill, President Kennedy is reputed to have said to his aides, "Now that this bill is the law of the land, let's hope we can get our government to carry it out." Both those in high places and those on the front lines are often justified in being skeptical about the chances that a social program will be appropriately implemented. Many steps are required to take a program from concept to full operation, and much effort is needed to keep it true to its original design and purposes. Thus, whether any program is fully carried out as envisioned by its sponsors and managers is always problematic.

One important and useful form of evaluation, therefore, is devoted to describing how a program is operating and assessing how well it is performing its intended functions. This form of evaluation does not represent a single distinct evaluation procedure but, rather, a family of approaches, concepts, and methods that are used in different contexts and for different purposes. The defining theme of this form of evaluation is a focus on the enacted program itself—its operations, activities, functions, performance, component parts, resources, and so forth. There is no widely accepted label for this family of evaluation approaches, but because it mainly involves measuring and recording information about the operation of the program, we will refer to it generally as program monitoring.

WHAT IS PROGRAM MONITORING?

Program monitoring is the systematic documentation of key aspects of program performance that are indicative of whether the program is functioning as intended or according to some appropriate standard. It generally involves program performance in the domain of service utilization, program organization, and/or outcomes. Monitoring service utilization consists of examining the extent to which the intended target population receives the intended services. Monitoring program organization requires comparison of the plan for what the program should be doing, especially with regard to providing services, and what is actually done. Monitoring program outcome entails a survey of the status of program participants after they have received service to determine if it is in line with what the program intended to accomplish.

In addition to these primary domains, program monitoring may include information about resource expenditures that bear on whether the benefits of a program justify its cost. Monitoring also may include an assessment of whether program activities comply with legal and regulatory requirements—for example, whether affirmative action requirements have been met in the recruitment of staff.

More specifically, program monitoring schemes are designed to answer such evaluation questions as these:

How many persons are receiving services?

Are those receiving services the intended targets?

Are they receiving the proper amount, type, and quality of services?

Are there targets who are not receiving services?

Are members of the target population aware of the program?

Are necessary program functions being performed adequately?

Is program staffing sufficient in numbers and competencies for the functions that must be performed?

Is the program well organized? Do staff work well with each other?

Does the program coordinate effectively with the other programs and agencies with which it must interact?

Are program resources, facilities, and funding adequate to support important program functions?

Are program resources used effectively and efficiently?

Are costs per service unit delivered reasonable?

Is the program in compliance with requirements imposed by its governing board, funding agencies, and higher-level administration?

Is the program in compliance with applicable professional and legal standards?

Is program performance at some program sites or locales significantly better or poorer than at others?

Are participants satisfied with their interactions with program personnel and procedures?

Are participants satisfied with the services they receive?

Do participants engage in appropriate follow-up behavior after service?

Are participants' conditions, status, or functioning satisfactory in areas the service addresses after service is completed?

Do participants retain satisfactory conditions, status, or functioning for an appropriate period after completion of services?

For any particular program, of course, more specialized versions of these questions will be at issue. In a Head Start early education program, for instance, the questions would involve pertinent characteristics of the target children,

the teachers and aides, the classroom facilities and materials, the instructional and recreational activities, the parents' attitudes toward the program, the language and social skills of the children, and so forth. Nonetheless, this list of questions serves to characterize the general nature of the issues that program monitoring typically investigates.

It is especially important to recognize the evaluative themes in program monitoring questions such as those listed above. Virtually all involve words such as *appropriate, adequate, sufficient, satisfactory, reasonable, intended*, and other phrasing that indicates that an evaluative judgment is required. To answer these questions, therefore, the evaluator or other responsible parties must not only describe the program performance but assess whether it is satisfactory. This, in turn, requires that there be some basis for making a judgment, that is, some defensible criteria or standards to apply. In situations where such criteria are not already articulated and endorsed, the evaluator may find that establishing workable criteria is as difficult as determining program performance on the pertinent dimensions.

There are several approaches to the matter of setting criteria for program performance. Moreover, different approaches will likely apply to different dimensions of program performance because the considerations that go into defining, say, what constitutes an appropriate number of clients served are quite different from those pertinent to deciding what constitutes adequate program resources. This said, however, the approach to the criterion issue that has the broadest scope and most general utility in program monitoring is the application of program theory as described previously in Chapter 3.

Recall that program theory, as we presented it, is divided into program process theory and program impact theory. Program process theory is formulated to describe the program as intended in a form that virtually constitutes a plan or blueprint for what the program is expected to do and how, as a result, targets will receive appropriate services. Program impact theory is formulated to describe what outcomes are expected to follow from effective service and why. Furthermore, these formulations, properly done, build on a needs assessment (whether systematic or informal) and thus connect the program design with the social conditions the program is intended to ameliorate. And, of course, the process through which they are derived and adopted usually involves both input and ultimate endorsement by the major stakeholders. Program theory thus has a certain authority in delineating what a program "should" be doing and, correspondingly, what constitutes adequate performance.

Program monitoring, therefore, can be built on the scaffolding of program theory, especially process theory. Program process theory describes the critical components, functions, and relationships that are assumed to be necessary for an effective program, because that is its primary purpose. This information identifies the aspects of program performance that are most important to monitor. As a program blueprint, however, process theory also gives some indication of what level of performance is intended and, thus, provides some basis for assessing whether actual performance measures up.

An example will perhaps clarify the relationship between program process theory and the assessment of program performance through a monitoring scheme. Exhibit 3-M in Chapter 3 illustrated the service utilization component of program process theory for an aftercare program for released psychiatric pa-

tients. For convenience, this is reproduced in this chapter as Exhibit 6-A. This flowchart depicts, step by step, the interactions and experiences patients released from the hospital are supposed to have as a result of program service.

A thorough monitoring procedure should report on each important aspect of service utilization. The first role of the service utilization flowchart in Exhibit 6-A, therefore, is to identify the important events so that information can be collected about them. Program monitoring would then document in some systematic manner what actually happened at each step. A monitoring procedure for this aftercare program, for instance, might report how many patients were released from the hospital each month, what proportion were visited by a social worker, how many were referred to services and which services, how many actually received those services, and so forth.

The second function of the service utilization flowchart is to indicate just what *should* happen at each step. If what is supposed to happen does not happen, that indicates poor program performance. In practice, of course, the critical events will not occur in an all-or-none fashion but will be attained to some higher or lower degree. Thus some, but not all, of the released patients will receive visits from the social worker, some will be referred to services, and so forth. Moreover, there may be important quality dimensions. For instance, it would not represent good program performance if a released patient was referred to several community services but they were not appropriate to his or her needs.

The service utilization plan in Exhibit 6-A only tells us categorically what is supposed to happen, which provides some basis for assessing performance but does not tell us how much must be done, or how well, to constitute good

EXHIBIT 6-A   Service Utilization Flowchart for an Aftercare Program for Formerly Hospitalized Psychiatric Patients

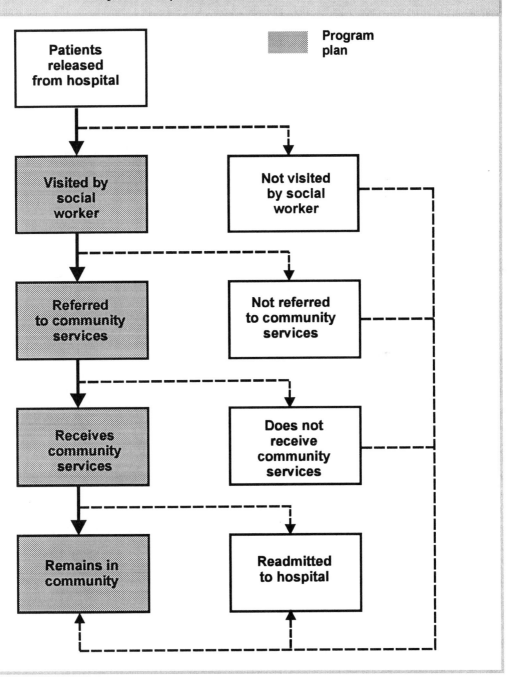

performance. For that, we need additional criteria that parallel the information the monitoring procedure provides. That is, if the monitoring procedure reports that 63% of the released patients are visited by a social worker within two weeks of release, we cannot evaluate that performance without some standard that tells us what percentage is "good." Is 63% a poor performance, given that we might expect 100% to be desirable, or is it a very impressive performance with a clientele that is difficult to locate and serve?

The most common and widely applicable criteria for such situations are simply *administrative standards* or objectives, that is, stipulated achievement levels set by program administrators or other responsible parties. For example, a program director and staff may commit to attaining 80% completion rates for services or to having 60% of the program participants permanently employed six months after receiving the program's job training. For the aftercare program above, it might be that the administrative target is to have 75% of the patients visited within two weeks of hospital release. Thus, the 63% found with program monitoring shows a subpar performance that, nonetheless, is not too far below the mark.

Administrative standards and objectives for program performance may be set on the basis of past experience, the performance of comparable programs, or simply the professional judgment of program managers or advisers. If reasonably justified, however, they can provide meaningful standards against which to assess observed program performance. In a related vein, some aspects of program performance may fall under applicable legal, ethical, or professional standards. The "standards of care" adopted in medical practice for treating common ailments, for instance, provide an essential set of criteria against which to assess program performance in health care settings. Similarly, a program of children's protective services has legal requirements to meet with regard to how it handles cases of possible child abuse or neglect.

Some recognition must also be given to the fact that, in practice, the assessment of particular dimensions of program performance is often not based on specific, predetermined criteria but represents an after-the-fact judgment call. This is the "I'll know it when I see it" school of thought on what constitutes good program performance. An evaluator who collects program monitoring data on, say, the proportion of high-risk adolescents who recall seeing program-sponsored antidrug media messages may find program staff and other key stakeholders rather vague and inconsistent in their views of what an acceptable proportion would be. If the results come in at 50%, however, a consensus may arise that this is rather good considering the nature of the population, even though some stakeholders might have reported much higher expectations prior to seeing the data. On the other hand, 5% might strike all stakeholders as distressingly low.

The example above makes use of the service utilization component of program process theory. Very similar considerations apply to the organizational component of the process theory. A depiction of the organizational plan for the aftercare program was presented in Exhibit 3-N in Chapter 3. Looking back at it will reveal that it, too, identifies dimensions of program performance that can be monitored and assessed against appropriate standards. Under that plan, for instance, case managers are expected to interview clients and families, assess service needs, make referrals to services, and so forth. A program monitoring procedure would document what was done under each of those categories and provide that information for assessment.

Program impact theory, on the other hand, serves a somewhat different role in relation to program monitoring than program process theory. Impact theory identifies the outcomes that are expected to result from the program and, therefore, gives guidance to any attempt to monitor the status, condition, or functioning of program participants on relevant outcome dimensions. Not all program monitoring schemes include outcome indicators, in part because the data can be difficult to collect. Moreover, describing service recipients with regard to their status on relevant outcome indicators does not tell us what effects (or impact) the program has had on those dimensions, only what participants' overall level is on them. (The next four chapters of this volume discuss the special demands of impact assessment.) Nonetheless, as will be discussed later in this chapter, there are good reasons for some program monitoring schemes to track outcome data and assess them, like process data, against administrative objectives and other such applicable standards.

Common Forms of Program Monitoring

Monitoring and assessment of program performance are quite common in program evaluation, but the approaches used are rather varied and there is little uniformity in the terminology for the different variants. The commonality among these variants is a focus on indicators (qualitative or quantitative) of how well the program performs its critical functions. An assessment of this sort may be conducted as a one-shot endeavor or may be continuous so that information is produced regularly over an extended period of time. It may be conducted by an outside evaluator or an evaluator employed within the program agency and may, indeed, be set up as a management tool with little involvement by professional evaluators. Moreover, its purpose may be to provide feedback for managerial purposes, to demonstrate accountability to sponsors and decisionmakers, to provide a freestanding process evaluation, or to augment an impact evaluation. Amid this variety, we distinguish three principal forms of program monitoring, which are described briefly below.

Process or Implementation Evaluation

Evaluators often distinguish between process (or implementation) evaluation and outcome (or impact) evaluation. *Process evaluation*, in Scheirer's (1994) words, "verifies what the program is and whether or not it is delivered as intended to the targeted recipients." It does not, however, attempt to assess the effects of the program on those recipients—that is the province of impact evaluation. Process evaluation is typically conducted by evaluation specialists as a separate project that may involve program personnel but is not integrated into their daily routine. When completed and, often, while under way, process evaluation generally provides information about program performance to program managers and other stakeholders, but is not a regular and continuing part of management information systems (MISs). Exhibit 6-B describes a process evaluation of an integrated services program for children.

As an evaluation approach, process evaluation plays two major roles. First, it can stand alone as an evaluation of a program in circumstances where the only questions at issue are

---

✦ EXHIBIT 6-B   Process Evaluation to Assess Integrated Services for Children

Many analysts have observed that the traditional system of categorical funding for children's services, with funds allocated to respond to specific problems under strict rules regarding eligibility and expenditures, has not served children's needs well. The critics argue that this system fragments services and inhibits collaboration between programs that might otherwise lead to more effective services.

In 1991 the Robert Wood Johnson Foundation launched the Child Health Initiative to test the feasibility of achieving systemic changes through the integration of children's services and finances. Specifically, the initiative called for the development of the following components:

- A decategorization mechanism that would pool existing categorical program funds and create a single children's health fund.

- A care coordination procedure using case management that would use the pooled funds to provide comprehensive and continuous care for needy children.

- A monitoring system that would identify the health and related needs of children in the community and the gaps in existing services.

Nine sites across the country were selected to launch demonstration programs. The Institute for Health Policy Studies, University of California, San Francisco conducted an evaluation of these programs with two major goals: (a) to gauge the degree to which the implementation of the projects was consistent with the original planning objectives (fidelity to the model), and (b) to assess the extent to which each of the major program components was implemented.

In the first year, the evaluation focused on the political, organizational, and design phase of program development. During subsequent years, the focus turned to implementation and preliminary outcomes. A combination of methods was used, including site visits, written surveys completed by the program managers, in-depth interviews of key participants, focus groups of service providers and clients, and reviews of project-related documents.

The evaluation found that most of the nine sites experienced some degree of success in implementing the monitoring and care coordination components, but none was able to implement decategorization. The general findings for each component were as follows:

- Decategorization—several sites successfully created small pools of flexible funds but these were from sources other than categorical program funds. No site was able to fully implement decategorization under the definitions originally adopted.

- Care coordination—was implemented successfully by most of the sites at the client level through case management but there was generally less coordination at the system level.

- Monitoring—the sites encountered a number of barriers in successfully completing this task but most instituted some appropriate process.

SOURCE: Adapted from Claire Brindis, Dana C. Hughes, Neal Halfon, and Paul W. Newacheck, "The Use of Formative Evaluation to Assess Integrated Services for Children," *Evaluation & the Health Professions,* 1998, 21(1):66-90.

about the effectiveness of program operations, service delivery, and other such matters. A stand-alone process evaluation might be appropriate for a relatively new program, for instance, to answer questions about how well it has established its operations and services. Program process is often the focus of formative evaluation designed to provide useful feedback to managers and sponsors of new programs. A process evaluation might also be called for in the case of a more established program when questions arise about how well it is organized, the quality of its services, or the success with which it is reaching the target population. A process evaluation may also constitute the major evaluation approach to a program charged with delivering a service known or presumed effective so that the most significant performance issue is whether that service is being delivered properly. In a managed care environment, for instance, process evaluation may be employed to assess whether the prescribed medical treatment protocols are being followed for patients in different diagnostic categories.

Process or implementation evaluation is also often carried out in conjunction with an impact evaluation. Indeed, it is generally not advisable to conduct an impact evaluation without including at least a minimal process evaluation. A precondition for impact on the social conditions a program addresses is that the program actually be implemented in a manner that could plausibly affect those conditions. Because maintaining an operational program and delivering appropriate services on an ongoing basis are formidable challenges in many human service arenas, it is not generally wise to take program implementation for granted. A full impact evaluation, therefore, generally includes a process component to determine what quality and quantity of services the program

provides so that this information can be integrated with findings on what impact those services have.

Routine Program Monitoring and Management Information Systems

Continuous monitoring of indicators of selected aspects of program process can be a useful tool for effective management of social programs by providing regular feedback about how well the program is performing its critical functions. Such feedback allows managers to take corrective action when problems arise and can also provide stakeholders with regular assessments of program performance. For these reasons, a form of process assessment is often integrated into the routine information systems of social programs so that appropriate data are obtained, compiled, and periodically summarized for review. In such cases, process evaluation becomes coextensive with the MISs in human service programs. Exhibit 6-C describes an MIS that was developed for a marital and family counseling program.

MISs routinely provide information on a client-by-client basis about services provided, staff providing the services, diagnosis or reasons for program participation, sociodemographic data, treatments and their costs, outcome status, and so on. Some of the systems bill clients (or funders), issue payments for services, and store other information, such as a client's treatment history and current participation in other programs. MISs have supplanted process evaluations in many instances because much of the information that would be gathered for process evaluation is available in the program's MIS. Even when a program's MIS is not configured to completely fulfill the requirements of a thoroughgoing process evalu-

**⚑ EXHIBIT 6-C   An Integrated Information System for a Family and Marriage
Counseling Agency in Israel**

The Marital and Family Counselling Agency is run under the joint auspices of the Welfare Department of the Tel Aviv municipality and the Bob Shapell School of Social Work at Tel Aviv University. The agency provides marital and family counseling and community services for the Jewish, Moslem, and Christian residents of one of the poorest sections of Tel Aviv.

The integrated information system developed for the agency is designed to follow up clients from the moment they request help to the end of treatment. It is intended to serve the agency and the individual counselors by monitoring the process and outcomes of treatment and providing the data needed to make organizational and clinical decisions. To accomplish this, data are collected on three forms and then programmed into the computerized information system. The data elements include

- Background data provided by the client, for example, sociodemographic characteristics, medical and psychological treatment history, the problems for which they are seeking help, the urgency of those problems, their expectations from treatment, and how they found out about the clinic.

- The McMaster Clinical Rating Scale, a standardized scale that monitors families on the basis of six dimensions of family functioning and overall family health; the counselors fill out this form once a month for each client.

- A retrospective evaluation form filled out after treatment is completed, one by the

counselors and another by the clients. This includes, for example, factual questions about the treatment such as its duration, the problems dealt with, the degree to which the client and counselor agreed on the problems, whether there were issues not addressed and why, retrospective assessments of the process and evaluations of improvement in the presented problems and the McMaster areas of functioning, client and counselor satisfaction with the process and outcomes.

The counselors can enter and retrieve data from this system whenever they wish and are given a graph of each client's status every three months to support clinical decisions. Also, reports are generated for the clinic management. For example, a report of the distribution of clients by ethnic group led to the development of a program located within Arab community centers to better reach that population. Other management reports describe the ways and times at which treatment is terminated, the problems that brought clients to the agency, and the percentage of people who applied for treatment but did not show up for the first session. The information system has also been used for research purposes. For example, studies were conducted on the predictors of treatment success, the comparative perceptions by clients and counselors of the treatment process and outcomes, and gender differences in presenting problems.

SOURCE: Adapted from Rivka Savaya, "The Potential and Utilization of an Integrated Information System at a Family and Marriage Counselling Agency in Israel," *Evaluation and Program Planning*, 1998, 21(1):11-20.

ation, it may nonetheless provide a large portion of the information an evaluator needs for such purposes. MISs can thus supply data that can be used by both managers and evaluators.

Performance Measurement and Monitoring

Increased public and political demands for accountability from social service agencies in recent years have brought forth a variety of initiatives to require such agencies to demonstrate that their programs accomplish something worthwhile. The most far-reaching of these initiatives is the Government Performance and Results Act of 1993 (GPRA), which requires federal agencies to identify the goals of their programs and report on their results in attaining those goals. Recognizing that this will be difficult for many agencies, GPRA provided for a seven-year implementation period with all agencies required to institute regular reporting by fiscal year 2000. More than 70 pilot projects have been launched under this act to provide experience with the concepts and procedures involved (Martin and Kettner, 1996; U.S. General Accounting Office, 1997).

In addition, many of the federal block grant programs require performance measurement and reporting, and a number of state legislatures have imposed similar requirements on their state agencies (Hatry, 1997). In the 1990s, the Governmental Accounting Standards Board (GASB), a private organization that sets the accounting standards for state and local governments, began working on "service efforts and accomplishments" (SEA) reporting. If such reporting becomes mandatory, as is expected within several years, all state and local government agencies will be required to identify measures of performance and report results on them (Martin and Kettner, 1996). Many major

nonprofit agencies are also pressing forward with performance measurement initiatives (Plantz, Greenway, and Hendricks, 1997). The United Way of America has produced materials for its regional chapters and member agencies to use in developing performance monitoring, and similar efforts have been made by such organizations as Boy Scouts of America, Girls Incorporated, the Family Services Association of America, and Goodwill Industries International. Managed care agencies in health and mental health services have been particularly active in developing performance monitoring systems as part of their cost-control and quality assurance efforts.

The performance measurement schemes emerging from these various initiatives (also known as performance monitoring and outcome monitoring) have much in common with those for process evaluation and MISs. Like process evaluation, they involve collection, reporting, and interpretation of information relevant to how well programs perform certain critical functions, particularly the delivery of service. And, like MISs, performance measurement is intended to be a routine and continuing program activity that will improve management and yield regular reports of program accomplishments. Compared with these other program monitoring approaches, however, performance measurement strategies orient especially toward assessment of program outcomes, that is, the results of services. An example of performance measurement for a family crisis program appears in Exhibit 6-D.

In particular, performance measurement schemes distinguish program *outcomes* from program *outputs*. Program outputs are the products or services delivered to program participants or other such activities viewed as part of the program's contribution to society. Measures of output, for example, would relate to

---

✵ EXHIBIT 6-D   Outcome Monitoring for a Family Crisis Program

Many states buy crisis intervention services. The concept is to identify and help families where child abuse or neglect has occurred as a result of a temporary crisis. Florida began an Intensive Crisis Counseling Program (ICCP) as a demonstration in one site more than ten years ago. Under contract, professional counselors enter the home and work intensively with the family for relatively short periods to resolve the crisis, to remove the risk of subsequent or continued abuse or neglect, and thereby to avert a placement in emergency shelter or foster care.

Florida has used an outcome monitoring system for ICCP since its inception. The most significant outcome indicators are counts of the families that remain intact at case closures and those for which children were removed and placed in shelter or foster care. Overall, these data showed that 80% or more of the families served remained intact at case closure. This apparent

success was one of the factors that has encouraged Florida to gradually expand ICCP over the years.

The ICCP outcome monitoring system recently began to report data by individual contract providers. This has shown that there is much variation in performance—from 70% to 93% of the families served by different providers remained intact at case closure and even wider variation was found for family status three months after cases were closed.

One use of the findings from the outcome monitoring system was that administrative staff decided to investigate providers showing poorer outcomes. In the case of one of the poorest performers, for instance, they discovered that the program had evolved into a service where the provider was available 24 hours via a telephone hotline but no longer provided in-home service beyond an initial assessment.

SOURCE: Adapted from Dennis P. Affholter, "Outcome Monitoring," in *Handbook of Practical Program Evaluation*, eds. J. S. Wholey, H. P. Hatry, and K. E. Newcomer (San Francisco: Jossey-Bass, 1994), pp. 96-118.

---

such things as the number of clients served, the number of service units provided, cost per service unit, the quality of services provided, the nature and volume of advocacy or promotional efforts made by the program, and so forth. In contrast, program outcomes represent the results of those activities, such as improved health for the individuals served, increased community awareness of AIDS risk, better reading skills, and other such social benefits. Performance measurement is generally intended to encompass the quantity and quality of both outputs and outcomes.

An important distinction must be made here between *measuring or monitoring* the social conditions that programs aim to affect and assessing the *impact* of programs on those conditions. Measuring program outcomes means describing social conditions on some set of indicators that represent the nature or extent of those conditions. The number of homeless families who obtain housing, the unemployment rate, the reported quality of life among frail elderly persons, and the average math achievement scores of sixth-grade students are all measures of conditions that some program may strive to change. An effective program might hope to find that regular measurement reveals improved conditions or, at worst, no deterioration in them.

Measuring and monitoring the target social conditions, however, are not sufficient to show that the program activities have actually been the source of any changes observed. To demonstrate program impact on the conditions, the effects of the program must be distinguished from the effects of other influences on those conditions, such as outside social forces, natural trends, and ameliorative actions taken by other social programs or policies or by members of the target population themselves. Chapters 7-10 of this volume discuss the demanding nature of impact evaluation and the special methods required to isolate the cause-and-effect relationship between program action and the resulting outcomes. These methods are typically beyond the scope of performance measurement schemes. The monitoring of outcome conditions in such schemes is aimed at providing feedback about how bad those conditions are and whether they are changing in favorable directions, not at assessing the distinct impact of the program on those conditions.

This is not to say that outcome monitoring provides no useful information about program effects. Outcome measures that focus specifically on the recipients of program service, and are collected periodically so that the status of those recipients prior to service and after service can be ascertained, can be very revealing. A treatment program for alcoholism that shows that 80% of its clients no longer drink six months after the program ends presents evidence more consistent with effectiveness than one showing only 25% abstaining. Of course, neither may, in fact, have real effects because the severity of their cases may differ and other

independent influences on drinking may override any program effects. A good monitoring scheme, however, will also include indicators of the severity of the initial problem, exposure to other important influences, and the like. Although falling short of formal impact assessment, reasonable interpretation and comparison of patterns of such indicators and, especially, trends in those indicators as programs attempt to improve their effectiveness can provide useful indications of program performance.

PERSPECTIVES ON PROGRAM MONITORING

There is and should be considerable overlap in the purposes of program monitoring whether they are driven by the information needs of evaluators, program managers and staff, or policymakers, sponsors, and stakeholders. Ideally, the monitoring activities undertaken as part of evaluation should meet the information needs of all these groups. In practice, however, limitations on time and resources may require giving priority to one set of information needs over another. At the risk of overemphasizing the differences in outlook, for didactic purposes it is useful to delineate the perspectives of the three key "consumer groups" on the purposes of program monitoring.

Monitoring From the Evaluator's Perspective

A number of practical considerations underlie the need for evaluation researchers to monitor programs. All too often a program's impact is sharply diminished and, indeed, sometimes reduced to zero because the appropriate intervention was not delivered, was not delivered to the right targets, or both. In our estimation, more program failures are due to such implementation problems than to lack of potentially effective services. Monitoring studies, therefore, are essential to understanding and interpreting impact findings. Knowing what took place is a prerequisite for explaining or hypothesizing why a program did or did not work. Without monitoring, the evaluator is engaged in "black box" research with no basis for speculating whether a larger dose of the program or a different means of delivering the intervention would have changed the impact results.

Also, for program staff to improve a program, secure support (particularly for expanding a program), and counter critics, evaluations that demonstrate effective performance are often required. Many program evaluations, therefore, will be process evaluations that focus on service utilization and organizational issues. For evaluators who work within a social program or agency, developing and maintaining program monitoring systems are likely to be their major responsibility.

Finally, monitoring provides information necessary for program dissemination. The essential features of an effective intervention can be reproduced elsewhere only if the evaluation documentation can describe the program in operational detail. The critical points in implementation need to be identified, solutions to managerial problems outlined, qualifications of successful program personnel documented, and so on. Sound program development and evaluation include communicating these features in detail. The results of program monitoring at the development stage can be profitably used in the diffusion of effective and efficient programs.

Monitoring From an Accountability Perspective

Monitoring information is also critical for those who sponsor and fund programs. Program managers have a responsibility to inform their sponsors and funders of the activities undertaken, the degree of implementation of programs, the problems encountered, and what the future holds (see Exhibit 6-E for one perspective on this matter). However, evaluators frequently are mandated to provide the same or similar information. Indeed, in some cases the sponsors and funders of programs perceive program evaluators as "their eyes and ears," as a second line of information on what is going on in a particular program.

Government sponsors and funding groups, including Congress, operate in the glare of the mass media. Their actions are also visible to the legislative groups who authorize programs and to governmental "watchdog" organizations. For example, at the federal level, the Office of Management and Budget, part of the executive branch, wields considerable authority over program development, funding, and expenditures. The U.S. General Accounting Office, an arm of Congress, advises members of the House and Senate on the utility of programs and in some cases conducts its own evaluations. Both state governments and those of large cities have analogous oversight groups. No social program that receives outside funding, whether public or private, can expect to avoid scrutiny and escape demand for accountability.

In addition to funders and sponsors, other stakeholders may press for program accountability. In the face of taxpayers' reservations about spending for social programs, together with the increased competition for resources resulting from cuts in available funding, all

⁂ EXHIBIT 6-E   Program and Service Utilization Studies

Any service organization, especially in an era of shrinking resources, needs to evaluate its services and activities. Through these evaluative activities, an organization can develop and maintain the flexibility needed to respond to an ever-changing environment. It has been suggested that, even in an ideal world, an organization needs to be self-evaluating. Self-evaluation requires an organization continually to review its own activities and goals and to use the results to modify, if necessary, its programs, goals, and directions.

Within the agency, the essential function of evaluation is to provide data on goal achievement and program effectiveness to a primary audience consisting of administration, middle management, and governing board. This primary audience, especially the administration and board, is frequently confronted with inquiries from important sources in the external environment, such as legislators and funding agencies. These inquiries often focus on issues of client utilization, accessibility, continuity, comprehension, outcome or effectiveness, and cost.

The building block of this information is the *patterns of use* or *client utilization* study. The patterns of use study, whether it consists of simple inquiries or highly detailed, sophisticated investigations, is basically a description. It describes who uses services and how, and it becomes evaluative when it is related to the requirements or purposes of the organization.

SOURCE: Adapted from G. Landsberg, *Program Utilization and Service Utilization Studies: A Key Tool for Evaluation,* New Directions for Program Evaluation, no. 20 (San Francisco: Jossey-Bass, December 1983), pp. 93-103.

stakeholders are scrutinizing both the programs they support and those they do not. Concerned parties use monitoring information to lobby for the expansion of programs they advocate or find congenial with their self-interests and the curtailment or abandonment of those programs they disdain. Stakeholders, it should be noted, include the targets themselves. A dramatic illustration of their perspective occurred when President Reagan telephoned an artificial heart transplant patient to wish him well and, with all of the country listening, the patient complained about not receiving his Social Security check.

Clearly, social programs operate in a political world. It could hardly be otherwise, given the stakes involved. The human and social service industry is not only huge in dollar volume and number of persons employed but is also laden with ideological and emotional baggage. Programs are often supported or opposed by armies of vocal community members; indeed, the social program sector is comparable only to the defense industry in its lobbying efforts, and the stands that politicians take with respect to particular programs often determine their fates in elections. Accountability information is the major weapon that stakeholders use in their battles as advocates and antagonists.

Monitoring From a Management Perspective

Management-oriented monitoring (including use of MISs) often is concerned with the same questions as evaluation and program accountability studies; the differences lie in the purposes to which the findings are to be put. Evaluators' interest in monitoring data generally centers on determining how a program's impact is related to its implementation. Accountability studies primarily provide information that decisionmakers, sponsors, and other stakeholders need to judge the appropriateness of program activities and to decide whether a program should be continued, expanded, or contracted. Such studies may use the same information base employed by program management staff, but they are usually conducted in a critical spirit. In contrast, management-oriented monitoring activities are concerned less with making decisive judgments and more with incorporating corrective measures as a regular part of program operations.

Monitoring from a management perspective is particularly vital during the implementation and pilot testing of new programs, especially innovative ones. No matter how well planned such programs may be, unexpected results and unwanted side effects often surface early in the course of implementation. Program designers and managers need to know rapidly and fully about these problems so that changes can be made as soon as possible in the program design. Suppose, for example, a medical clinic intended to help working mothers is open only during daylight hours. Monitoring may disclose that however great the demand is for clinic services, the clinic's hours of operation effectively screen out most of the target population. Or suppose that a program is predicated on the assumption that severe psychological problems are prevalent among children who act out in school. If it is found early on that most such children do not in fact have serious disorders, the program can be modified accordingly.

For programs that have moved beyond the development stage to actual operation, pro-

gram monitoring serves management needs by providing information on coverage and process, and hence feedback on whether the program is meeting specifications. Fine-tuning of the program may be necessary when monitoring information indicates that targets are not being reached, that the implementation of the program costs more than initially projected, or that staff workloads are either too heavy or too light. Managers who neglect to monitor a program fully and systematically risk the danger of administering a program that is markedly different from its mandate.

Where monitoring information is to be used for both managerial and evaluation purposes, some problems must be anticipated. How much information is sensible to collect and report, in what forms, at what frequency, with what reliability, and with what degree of confidentiality are among the major issues on which evaluators and managers may disagree. For example, the experienced manager of a nonprofit children's recreational program may feel the highest priority is weekly information on attendance, which is added to graphs for the program's governing board. The evaluator, however, may be comfortable with aggregating the data monthly or even quarterly, but may believe that before being reported they should be adjusted to take into account variations in the weather, occurrence of holidays, and so on—even though the necessary adjustments require the use of sophisticated statistical procedures.

A second concern is the matter of proprietary claims on the data. For the manager, monitoring data on, say, the results of a program innovation should be kept confidential until discussed with the research committee of the board of directors and presented at the board meeting. The evaluator may wish immediately to write a paper for publication in the *American*

Journal of Evaluation. Or a serious drop in clients from a particular ethnic group may result in the administrator of a program immediately replacing the director of professional services, whereas the evaluator's reaction may be to do a study to determine why the drop occurred. As with all relations between program staff and evaluators in general, negotiation of these matters is essential.

A warning: There are many aspects of program management and administration (such as complying with tax regulations and employment laws or negotiating union contracts) that few evaluators have any special competence to assess. In fact, evaluators trained in social science disciplines and (especially) those primarily involved in academic careers may be unqualified to manage anything. It is wise to keep in mind that the evaluator's role, even when sharing information from an MIS, is not to join the administrators in the running of the organization.

In the remainder of this chapter, we concentrate on the concepts and methods pertinent to monitoring program process and program outcome. It is in these areas that the competencies of persons trained in social research are most relevant. Because most program monitoring approaches emphasize process information, we give it especial attention by separately discussing the service utilization component and the organizational component of program process, drawing on the distinctions we have used for defining program theory.

MONITORING SERVICE UTILIZATION

In Chapter 4, we discussed how essential it is to define target populations carefully in planning, designing, and implementing programs.

But, having done so, it is also important to know the extent to which the intended targets actually receive program services. Target participation concerns both program managers and sponsors. Managing a project effectively requires that target participation be kept at an acceptable level and corrective action be taken if it falls below that level. From the viewpoint of program sponsors, target participation is a key measure of a program's vitality and the demand for its services.

Monitoring of service utilization is particularly critical for interventions in which program participation is voluntary or in which participants must learn new procedures, change their habits, or take instruction. For example, community mental health centers designed to provide a broad range of services often fail to attract a significant proportion of those persons who may benefit from their services. Even patients who have been recently discharged from psychiatric hospitals and encouraged to make use of the services of community mental health centers often fail to contact the centers (Rossi, Fisher, and Willis, 1986). Similarly, a program designed to provide information to prospective home buyers might find that few persons seek the services offered. Hence, program developers need to be concerned with how best to motivate potential targets to seek out the program and participate in it. Depending on the particular case, they might, for example, need to build outreach efforts into the program or pay special attention to the geographical placement of program sites (Boruch, Dennis, and Carter-Greer, 1988).

One of the most useful tools in designing a scheme for monitoring service utilization is a careful description of the program's service utilization plan, as described above (see Exhibit 6-A). The service utilization plan, recall, is a detailed depiction of the sequence of events through which the target population is expected to make contact with the program, become engaged, and maintain involvement through completion of the intended services. A full articulation of a program's service utilization plan will identify the junctures in the process that are most critical to the program's success in serving the target population and, therefore, most important to monitor for purposes of evaluation, management, or accountability. Moreover, a good service utilization plan will be sufficiently specific about what is expected to happen at each juncture, and what the undesirable alternatives are, to guide the selection of measures or performance indicators that can be used to monitor those events.

Coverage and Bias

Service utilization issues typically break down into questions about *coverage* and *bias*. Whereas coverage refers to the extent to which participation by the target population achieves the levels specified in the program design, bias is the degree to which some subgroups participate in greater proportions than others. Clearly, coverage and bias are related. A program that reaches all projected participants and no others is obviously not biased in its coverage. But because few social programs ever achieve total, exact coverage, bias is typically an issue.

Bias can arise out of self-selection; that is, some subgroups may voluntarily participate more frequently than others. It can also derive from program actions. For instance, a program's personnel may react favorably to some clients while rejecting or discouraging others. One temptation commonly faced by programs is to select the most "success prone" targets. Such "creaming" frequently occurs because of the self-interests of one or more stakeholders (a dramatic example is described in Exhibit

6-F). Finally, bias may result from such unforeseen influences as the location of a program office, which may encourage greater participation by a subgroup that enjoys more convenient access to program activities.

It is usually thought desirable that a program serve a large proportion of the intended targets. The exceptions are those projects whose resources are too limited to provide the appropriate services to more than a portion of the potential targets. In such cases, however, the target definition established during the planning and development of the program probably was not specific enough. Program staff and sponsors may correct this problem by defining the characteristics of the target population more sharply and by using resources more effectively. For example, establishing a health center to provide medical services to persons without regular sources of care may result in such an overwhelming demand that many of those who want services cannot be accommodated. The solution might be to add eligibility criteria that weight such factors as severity of the health problem, family size, age, and income to reduce the size of the target population to manageable proportions while still serving the neediest persons.

The opposite effect, overcoverage, also occurs. For instance, the TV program *Sesame Street* has consistently captured audiences far exceeding the original targets—disadvantaged preschoolers—including children who are not at all disadvantaged and even adults. Because these additional audiences are reached at no additional cost, this overcoverage is not a financial drain. It does, however, thwart one of *Sesame Street's* original goals, which was to lessen the gap in learning between advantaged and disadvantaged children.

In other instances, overcoverage can be costly and problematic. The bilingual programs

---

🎗 **EXHIBIT 6-F** "Creaming" the Unemployed

When administrators who provide public services choose to provide a disproportionate share of program benefits to the most advantaged segment of the population they serve, they provide grist for the mill of service utilization research. The U.S. Employment Service (USES) offers a clear and significant example of creaming, a practice that has survived half a century of USES expansion, contraction, and reorganization. The USES has as its major aim to provide employers with workers, downplaying the purpose of providing workers with work. This leads the USES to send out the best prospects among the unemployed and to slight the less promising.

It is hardly surprising that USES administrators, a generation after the establishment of the program, stressed the necessity rather than the desirability of an employer-centered service. Its success, by design, depended on serving employers, not the "hard-core" unemployed. As President Johnson's task force on urban employment problems noted some two weeks before the 1965 Watts riots, "We have yet to make any significant progress in reaching and helping the truly 'hard-core' disadvantaged."

SOURCE: Adapted from David B. Robertson, "Program Implementation Versus Program Design," *Policy Study Review*, 1984, 3:391-405.

---

sponsored by the Department of Education, for instance, have been found to include many students whose primary language is English. Some school systems whose funding from the program depends on the number of children enrolled in bilingual classes have inflated attendance figures by registering inappropriate students. In other cases, schools have used assignment to bilingual instruction as a means of ridding classes of "problem children," thus saturating bilingual classes with disciplinary cases.

The most common coverage problem in social interventions, however, is the failure to achieve full target participation, either because of bias in the way participants are recruited or retained or because potential clients are unaware of the program, unable to use it, or reject it. For example, in most employment training programs only small minorities of those eligible by reason of unemployment ever attempt to join the programs. Similar situations occur in mental health, substance abuse, and numerous other programs (see Exhibit 6-G). We turn now to the question of how program coverage might be measured as a part of program monitoring.

Measuring and Monitoring Coverage

Program managers and sponsors alike need to be concerned with both undercoverage and overcoverage. Undercoverage is measured by the proportion of the targets in need of a program that actually participates in it. Overcoverage is sometimes expressed as the number of program participants who are not in need, compared with the total number not in need in a designated population, and sometimes as the

---

✺ EXHIBIT 6-G   The Coverage of the Food Stamp Program for the Homeless

Based upon a rigorously designed survey of homeless persons sampled from shelters and food kitchens in American cities with a population of 100,000 and over, Burt and Cohen gave some precise dimensions to what we know is true virtually by definition: The homeless live on food intakes that are inadequate both in quantity and in nutritional content. There is no way that a demographic group whose incomes hover slightly above zero can have adequate diets. That the homeless do not starve is largely a tribute to the food kitchens and shelters that provide them with meals at no cost.

Because most homeless persons are eligible by income for food stamps, their participation rates in that program should be high. But they are not—Burt and Cohen reported that only 18% of the persons sampled were receiving food stamps and almost half had never used them. This is largely because certification for food stamps requires passing a means test, a procedure that requires some documentation. This is not easy for many homeless who may not have the required documents, an address to receive the stamps, or the capability to fill out the forms.

Moreover, the food stamp program is based on implicit assumptions that participants can readily acquire their foodstuffs in a local food store, prepare servings on a stove, and store food supplies in their dwellings. These assumptions do not apply to the homeless. Of course, food stores do sell some food items that can be consumed without preparation and, with some ingenuity, a full meal of such foods can be assembled. So some benefit can be obtained by the homeless from food stamps, but for most homeless persons food stamps are relatively useless.

Legislation passed in 1986 allows homeless persons to exchange food stamps for meals offered by nonprofit organizations and made shelter residents in places where meals were served eligible for food stamps. By surveying food providers, shelters, and food kitchens, however, Burt and Cohen found that few meal providers had applied for certification as receivers of food stamps. Of the roughly 3,000 food providers in the sample, only 40 had become authorized.

Furthermore, among those authorized to receive food stamps, the majority had never started to collect food stamps or had started and then abandoned the practice. It made little sense to collect food stamps as payment for meals that otherwise were provided free so that, on the same food lines, food stamp participants were asked to pay for their food with stamps while nonparticipants paid nothing. The only food provider who was able to use the system was one that required either cash payment or labor for meals; for this program, food stamps became a substitute for these payments.

SOURCE: Based on Martha Burt and Barbara Cohen, *Feeding the Homeless: Does the Prepared Meals Provision Help?* Report to Congress on the Prepared Meal Provision, vols. I and II (Washington, DC: Urban Institute, 1988). Reprinted with permission.

---

number of participants not in need compared with the total number of participants in the program. Generally, it is the latter figure that is important; efficient use of program resources requires both maximizing the number served who are in need and minimizing the number served who are not in need. Efficiency of coverage may be measured by the following formula:

$$\begin{array}{c} \text{Coverage} \\ \text{efficiency} \end{array} = 100 \times \left[\begin{array}{cc} \dfrac{\text{Number in}}{\text{need served}} & \dfrac{\text{Number not}}{\text{in need served}} \\ \dfrac{}{\text{Total number}} - \dfrac{}{\text{Total number}} \\ \text{in need} & \text{served} \end{array} \right]$$

This formula yields a positive value of 100 when the actual number served equals the designated target population in need and no inappropriate targets are served. A negative value of 100 occurs if only inappropriate targets are served. Positive and negative values between +100 and −100 indicate the degree of coverage efficiency. For example, if 100 targets need a program in a particular geographical area, and 100 persons are served but only 70 are among those in need, the value obtained by the formula would be +40. If 100 targets need a program, and only 10 of the 100 actually served are appropriate targets, the value obtained would be −80.

This procedure provides a means of estimating the trade-offs in a program that includes inappropriate as well as appropriate targets. The manager of a hypothetical program confronted with a −80 value might, for instance, impose additional selection criteria that eliminated 70 of the 90 inappropriate targets and secure 70 appropriate replacements through an extensive recruitment campaign. The coverage efficiency value would then increase to +60. If the program was inexpensive or if it was either politically unwise or too difficult to impose additional selection criteria to eliminate undercoverage, the manager might elect the option of expanding the program to include all appropriate targets. Assuming the same proportion of inappropriate targets are also served, however, the total number of participants would increase to 1,000!

The problem in measuring coverage is almost always the inability to specify the number in need, that is, the magnitude of the target population. The needs assessment procedures described in Chapter 4, if carried out as an integral part of program planning, usually minimize this problem. In addition, three sources of information can be used to assess the extent to which a program is serving the appropriate target population: program records, surveys of program participants, and community surveys.

Program Records

Almost all programs keep records on targets served. Data from well-maintained record systems—particularly from MISs—can often be used to estimate both program coverage and program bias. For instance, information on the various screening criteria for program intake may be tabulated to determine whether the units served are the ones specified in the program's design. Suppose the targets of a family planning program are women less than 50 years of age who have been residents of the community for at least six months and who have two or more children under age ten. Records of program participants can be examined to see whether the women actually served are within the eligibility limits and the degree to which particular age or parity groups are under- or overrepresented. Such an analysis might also disclose bias in program participation in terms of the eligibility characteristics or combinations of them. Another example involving public shelter utilization by the homeless is described in Exhibit 6-H.

However, programs differ widely in the quality and extensiveness of their records and in the sophistication involved in storing and maintaining them. Moreover, the feasibility of maintaining complete, ongoing record systems for all program participants varies with the nature of the intervention and available resources. In the case of medical and mental

> ### ▓ EXHIBIT 6-H   Public Shelter Utilization Among Homeless Adults in New York and Philadelphia
>
> The cities of Philadelphia and New York have standardized admission procedures for persons requesting services from city-funded or -operated shelters. All persons admitted to the public shelter system must provide intake information for a computerized registry that includes the client's name, race, date of birth, and gender and must be assessed for substance abuse and mental health problems, medical conditions, and disabilities. A service utilization study conducted by researchers from the University of Pennsylvania analyzed data from this registry for New York City for 1987-1994 (110,604 men and 26,053 women) and Philadelphia for 1991-1994 (12,843 men and 3,592 women).
>
> They found three predominant types of users: (a) the chronically homeless, characterized by very few shelter episodes, but which might last as long as several years; (b) the episodically homeless, characterized by multiple, increasingly shorter stays over a long period; and (c) the transitionally homeless who had one or two stays of short duration within a relatively brief period of time.
>
> The most notable finding was the size and relative resource consumption of the chronically homeless. In New York, for instance, 18% of the shelter users stayed 180 days or more in their first year, consuming 53% of the total number of system days for first-time shelter users, triple the days for their proportionate representation in the shelter population. These long-stay users tended to be older people and to have mental health, substance abuse, and, in some cases, medical problems.
>
> SOURCE: Adapted by permission from Dennis P. Culhane and Randall Kuhn, "Patterns and Determinants of Public Shelter Utilization Among Homeless Adults in New York City and Philadelphia," *Journal of Policy Analysis and Management*, 1998, 17(1):23-43. Copyright © 1998, John Wiley & Sons, Inc.

health systems, for example, sophisticated, computerized management and client information systems have been developed for managed care purposes that would be impractical for many other types of programs.

In measuring target participation, the main concerns are that the data are accurate and reliable. It should be noted that all record systems are subject to some degree of error. Some records will contain incorrect or outdated information, and others will be incomplete. The extent to which unreliable records can be used for decision making depends on the kind and degree of their unreliability and the nature of the decisions in question. Clearly, critical decisions involving significant outcomes require better records than do less weighty decisions. Whereas a decision on whether to continue a project should not be made on the basis of data derived from partly unreliable records, data from the same records may suffice for a decision to change an administrative procedure.

If program records are to serve an important role in decision making on far-reaching issues, it is usually desirable to conduct regular audits of the records. Such audits are similar in intent to those that outside accountants conduct on fiscal records. For example, records might be sampled to determine whether each target has a record, whether records are complete, and whether rules for completing them have been followed.

Surveys

An alternative to using program records to assess target participation is to conduct special surveys of program participants. Sample surveys may be desirable when the required data cannot be obtained as a routine part of program activities or when the size of the target group is large and it is more economical and efficient to undertake a sample survey than to obtain data on all the participants.

For example, a special tutoring project conducted primarily by parents may be set up in only a few schools in a community. Children in all schools may be referred, but the project staff may not have the time or the training to administer appropriate educational skills tests and other such instruments that would document the characteristics of the children referred and enrolled. Lacking such complete records, an evaluation group could administer tests on a sampling basis to estimate the appropriateness of the selection procedures and assess whether the project is serving the designated target population.

When projects are not limited to selected, narrowly defined groups of individuals but instead take in entire communities, the most efficient and sometimes the only way to examine whether the presumed population at need is being reached is to conduct a community survey. Various types of health, educational, recreational, and other human service programs are often community-wide, although their intended target populations may be se-

lected groups, such as delinquent youths, the aged, or women of childbearing age. In such cases, surveys are the major means of assessing whether targets have been reached.

The evaluation of the *Feeling Good* television program illustrates the use of surveys to provide data on a project with a national audience. The program, an experimental production of the Children's Television Workshop (the producer of *Sesame Street*), was designed to motivate adults to engage in preventive health practices. Although it was accessible to homes of all income levels, its primary purpose was to motivate low- income families to improve their health practices. The Gallup organization conducted four national surveys, each of approximately 1,500 adults, at different times during the weeks *Feeling Good* was televised. The data provided estimates of the size of the viewing audiences as well as of the viewers' demographic, socioeconomic, and attitudinal characteristics (Mielke and Swinehart, 1976). The major finding was that the program largely failed to reach the target group, and the program was discontinued.

To measure coverage of Department of Labor programs, such as training and public employment, the department started a periodic national sample survey. The Survey of Income and Program Participation is now carried out by the Bureau of the Census and measures participation in social programs conducted by many federal departments. This large survey, now a three-year panel covering 21,000 households, ascertains through personal interviews whether each adult member of the sampled households has ever participated or is currently participating in any of a number of federal programs. By contrasting program participants with nonparticipants, the survey provides information on the programs' biases in coverage.

In addition, it generates information on the uncovered but eligible target populations.

Assessing Bias: Program Users, Eligibles, and Dropouts

An assessment of bias in program participation can be undertaken by examining differences between individuals who participate in a program and either those who drop out or those who are eligible but do not participate at all. In part, the drop-out rate, or attrition, from a project may be an indicator of clients' dissatisfaction with intervention activities. It also may indicate conditions in the community that militate against full participation. For example, in certain areas lack of adequate transportation may prevent those who are otherwise willing and eligible from participating in a program.

It is important to be able to identify the particular subgroups within the target population who either do not participate at all or do not follow through to full participation. Such information not only is valuable in judging the worth of the effort but also is needed to develop hypotheses about how a project can be modified to attract and retain a larger proportion of the target population. Thus, the qualitative aspects of participation may be important not only for monitoring purposes but also for subsequent program planning.

Data about dropouts may come either from service records or from surveys designed to find nonparticipants. However, community surveys usually are the only feasible means of identifying eligible persons who have not participated in a program. The exception, of course, is when adequate information is available about the entire eligible population prior to the implementation of a project (as in the case of data from a census or screening interview). Comparisons with either data gathered for project-planning purposes or community surveys undertaken during and subsequent to the intervention may employ a variety of analytical approaches, from purely descriptive methods to highly complex models.

In Chapter 11, we describe methods of analyzing the costs and benefits of programs to arrive at measures of economic efficiency. Clearly, for calculating costs it is important to have estimates of the size of populations at need or risk, the groups who start a program but drop out, and the ones who participate to completion. The same data may also be used in estimating benefits. In addition, they are highly useful in judging whether a project should be continued and whether it should be expanded in either the same community or other locations. Furthermore, project staff require this kind of information to meet their managerial and accountability responsibilities. Although data on project participation cannot substitute for knowledge of impact in judging either the efficiency or the effectiveness of projects, there is little point in moving ahead with an impact analysis without an adequate description of the extent of participation by the target population.

MONITORING ORGANIZATIONAL FUNCTIONS

Monitoring the critical organizational functions and activities of a program focuses on whether the program is performing well in managing its efforts and using its resources to accomplish its essential tasks. Chief among those tasks, of course, is delivering the intended services to the target population. In addition, programs have various support functions that must be carried out to maintain the viability and effectiveness of the organization, for example, fund-raising, promotion, advocacy, and governance and management. Program process monitoring seeks to determine whether a program's actual activities and arrangements sufficiently approximate the intended ones.

Once again, program process theory as described in Chapter 3 is a useful tool in designing monitoring procedures. In this instance, what we called the organizational plan is the relevant component (see Exhibit 3-N in Chapter 3). A fully articulated process theory will identify the major program functions, activities, and outputs and show how they are related to each other and to the organizational structures, staffing patterns, and resources of the program. This depiction provides a map to guide the evaluator in identifying the significant program functions and the preconditions for accomplishing them. Program process monitoring then becomes a matter of identifying and measuring those activities and conditions most essential to a program's effective performance of its duties.

Service Delivery Is Fundamental

As mentioned earlier in this chapter, for many programs that fail to show impacts, the problem is a failure to deliver the interventions specified in the program design, a problem generally known as *implementation failure.* There are three kinds of implementation failures: First, no intervention, or not enough, is delivered; second, the wrong intervention is delivered; and third, the intervention is unstandardized or uncontrolled and varies excessively across the target population. In each instance,

monitoring the actual delivery of services to identify faults and deficiencies is essential.

"Nonprograms" and Incomplete Intervention

Consider first the problem of the "nonprogram" (Rossi, 1978). McLaughlin (1975) reviewed the evidence on the implementation of Title I of the Elementary and Secondary Education Act, which allocated billions of dollars yearly to aid local schools in overcoming students' poverty-associated educational deprivations. Even though schools had expended the funds, local school authorities were unable to describe their Title I activities in any detail, and few activities could even be identified as educational services delivered to schoolchildren. In short, little evidence could be found that a program existed.

The failure of numerous other programs to deliver services has been documented as well. Datta (1977), for example, reviewed the evaluations on career education programs and found that the designated targets rarely participated in the planned program activities. Similarly, an attempt to evaluate PUSH-EXCEL, a program designed to motivate disadvantaged high school students toward higher levels of academic achievement, disclosed that the program consisted mainly of the distribution of buttons and hortative literature and little else (Murray, 1980).

Instead of not delivering services at all, a delivery system may dilute the intervention so that an insufficient amount reaches the target population. Here the problem may be a lack of commitment on the part of a front-line delivery system, resulting in minimal delivery or "ritual compliance," to the point that the program does not exist. Exhibit 6-I, for instance, expands on an exhibit presented in Chapter 2 to

🕸 EXHIBIT 6-I   On the Front Lines: Are Welfare Workers Implementing Policy Reforms?

In the early 1990s the state of California initiated the Work Pays demonstration project, which expanded the state job preparation program (JOBS) and modified AFDC welfare policies to increase the incentives and support for finding employment. The Work Pays demonstration was designed to "substantially change the focus of the AFDC program to promote work over welfare and self-sufficiency over welfare dependence."

The workers in the local welfare offices were a vital link in the implementation of Work Pays. The intake and redetermination interviews they conducted represent virtually the only in-person contact that most clients have with the welfare system. This fact prompted a team of evaluators to study how welfare workers were communicating the Work Pays policies during their interactions with clients.

Using "backwards mapping," the evaluators reasoned that worker-client transactions appropriate to the policy would involve certain "information content" and "use of positive discretion." Information content refers to the explicit messages delivered to clients; it was expected that workers would notify clients about the new program rules for work and earnings, explain opportunities to combine work and welfare to achieve greater self-sufficiency, and inform them about available training and supportive services. Positive discretion relates to the discretion workers have in teaching, socializing, and signaling clients about the expectations and opportunities associated with welfare receipt. Workers were expected to emphasize the new employment rules and benefits during client interviews and communicate the expectation that welfare should serve only as temporary assistance while recipients prepared for work.

To assess the welfare workers' implementation of the new policies, the evaluators observed and analyzed the content of 66 intake or redetermination interviews between workers and clients in four counties included in the Work Pays demonstration. A structured observation form was used to record the frequency with which various topics were discussed and to collect information about the characteristics of the case. These observations were coded on the two dimensions of interest: (a) information content, and (b) positive discretion.

The results, in the words of the evaluators:

In over 80% of intake and redetermination interviews workers did not provide and interpret information about welfare reforms. Most workers continued a pattern of instrumental transactions that emphasized workers' needs to collect and verify eligibility information. Some workers coped with the new demand by providing information about work-related policies, but routinizing the information and adding it to their standardized, scripted recitations of welfare rules. Others were coping by particularizing their interactions, giving some of their clients some information some of the time, on an ad hoc basis.

These findings suggest that welfare reforms were not fully implemented at the street level in these California counties. Worker-client transactions were consistent with the processing of welfare claims, the enforcement of eligibility rules, and the rationing of scarce resources such as JOBS services; they were poorly aligned with new program objectives emphasizing transitional assistance, work, and self-sufficiency outside the welfare system. (pp. 18-19)

SOURCE: Adapted by permission from Marcia K. Meyers, Bonnie Glaser, and Karin MacDonald, "On the Front Lines of Welfare Delivery: Are Workers Implementing Policy Reforms?" *Journal of Policy Analysis and Management,* 1998, 17(1):1-22. Copyright © 1998, John Wiley & Sons, Inc.

describe the implementation of welfare reform in which welfare workers communicated little to clients about the new policies.

Wrong Intervention

The second category of program failure—namely, delivery of the wrong intervention—can occur in several ways. One is that the mode of delivery negates the intervention. An example is the Performance Contracting experiment, in which private firms contracted to teach mathematics and reading were paid in proportion to pupils' gains in achievement. The companies faced extensive difficulties in delivering the program at school sites. In some sites the school system sabotaged the experiments, and in others the companies were confronted with equipment failures and teacher hostility (Gramlich and Koshel, 1975).

Another way in which wrong intervention can result is when it requires a delivery system that is too sophisticated. There can be a considerable difference between pilot projects and full-scale implementation of sophisticated programs. Interventions that work well in the hands of highly motivated and trained deliverers may end up as failures when administered by staff of a mass delivery system whose training and motivation are less. The field of education again provides an illustration: Teaching methods such as computer-assisted learning or individualized instruction that have worked well within the experimental development centers have not fared as well in ordinary school systems.

The distinction made here between an intervention and its mode of delivery is not always clear-cut. The difference is quite clear in income maintenance programs, in which the "intervention" is the money given to beneficiaries and the delivery modes vary from automatic deposits in savings or checking accounts to hand delivery of cash to recipients. Here the intent of the program is to place money in the hands of recipients; the delivery, whether by electronic transfer or by hand, has little effect on the intervention. In contrast, a counseling program may be handled by retraining existing personnel, hiring counselors, or employing certified psychotherapists. In this case, the distinction between treatment and mode of delivery is fuzzy, because it is generally acknowledged that counseling treatments vary by counselor.

Unstandardized Intervention

The final category of implementation failures includes those that result from unstandardized or uncontrolled interventions. This problem can arise when the design of the program leaves too much discretion in implementation to the delivery system, so that the intervention can vary significantly across sites. Early programs of the Office of Economic Opportunity provide examples. The Community Action Program (CAP) gave local communities considerable discretion in choosing among a variety of actions, requiring only "maximum feasible participation" on the part of the poor. Because of the resulting disparities in the programs of different cities, it is almost impossible to document what CAP's programs accomplished (Vanecko and Jacobs, 1970).

Similarly, Project Head Start gave local communities funds to set up preschool teaching projects for underprivileged children. Across the country, centers varied by sponsoring agencies, coverage, content, staff qualifications, objectives, and a host of other characteristics (Cicirelli, Cooper, and Granger, 1969). Because there is no specified Head Start design, it is not possible to conclude from an evaluation of a sample of projects whether the Head Start concept works. The only generalization that can be made is that some projects are effective and some are ineffective and, among the effective ones, some are more successful than others.

The Delivery System

A program's delivery system can be thought of as a combination of pathways and actions undertaken to provide an intervention (see Chapter 3). It usually consists of a number of separate functions and relationships. As a general rule, it is wise to assess all the elements unless previous experience with certain aspects of the delivery system makes their assessment unnecessary. Two concepts are especially useful for monitoring the performance of a program's delivery system: *specification of services* and *accessibility.*

Specification of Services

For both planning and monitoring purposes, it is desirable to specify the actual services provided in operational (measurable) terms. The first task is to define each kind of service in terms of the activities that take place and the providers who participate. When possible, it is best to separate the various aspects of a program into separate, distinct services. For example, if a project providing technical education for school dropouts includes literacy training, carpentry skills, and a period of on-the-job apprenticeship work, it is advisable to separate these into three services for monitoring purposes. Moreover, for estimating program costs in cost-benefit analyses and for fiscal accountability, it is often important to attach monetary values to different services. This step is impor-

tant when the costs of several programs will be compared or when the programs receive reimbursement on the basis of the number of units of different services that are provided.

For program monitoring, simple, specific services are easier to identify, count, and record. However, complex elements often are required to design an implementation that is consistent with a program's objectives. For example, a clinic for children may require a physical exam on admission, but the scope of the exam and the tests ordered may depend on the characteristics of each child. Thus, the item "exam" is a service but its components cannot be broken out further without creating a different definition of the service for each child examined. The strategic question is how to strike a balance, defining services so that distinct activities can be identified and counted reliably while, at the same time, the distinctions are meaningful in terms of the program's objectives.

In situations where the nature of the intervention allows a wide range of actions that might be performed, it may be possible to describe services primarily in terms of the general characteristics of the service providers and the time they spend in service activities. For example, if a project places master craftspersons in a low-income community to instruct community members in ways to improve their dwelling units, the craftspersons' specific activities will probably vary greatly from one household to another. They may advise one family on how to frame windows and another on how to shore up the foundation of a house. Any monitoring scheme attempting to document such services could only describe the service activities in general terms and by means of examples. It is possible, however, to specify the characteristics of the providers—for example, that they should have five years of experience in home construction and repair and knowledge of carpentry, electrical wiring, foundations, and exterior construction—and the amount of time they spend with each service recipient.

Indeed, services are often defined in terms of units of time, costs, procedures, or products. In a vocational training project, service units may refer to hours of counseling time provided; in a program to foster housing improvement, they may be defined in terms of amounts of building materials provided; in a cottage industry project, service units may refer to activities, such as training sessions on how to operate sewing machines; and in an educational program, the units may be instances of the use of specific curricular materials in classrooms. All these examples require an explicit definition of what constitutes a service and, for that service, what units are appropriate for describing the amount of service.

Accessibility

Accessibility is the extent to which the structural and organizational arrangements facilitate participation in the program. All programs have a strategy of some sort for providing services to the appropriate target population. In some instances, being accessible may simply mean opening an office and operating under the assumption that the designated participants will "naturally" come and make use of the services provided at the site. In other instances, however, ensuring accessibility requires outreach campaigns to recruit participants, transportation to bring persons to the intervention site, and efforts during the intervention to minimize dropouts. For example, in many large cities, special teams are sent out into the streets on very cold nights to persuade homeless per-

sons sleeping in exposed places to spend the night in shelters.

A number of evaluation questions arise in connection with accessibility, some of which relate only to the delivery of services and some of which have parallels in relation to the previously discussed topic of service utilization. Primary is the issue of whether program actions are consistent with the design and intent of the program with regard to facilitating access. For example, is there a Spanish-speaking staff member always available in a mental health center located in an area with a large Hispanic population?

Also, are potential targets matched with the appropriate services? It has been observed, for example, that community members who originally make use of emergency medical care for appropriate purposes may subsequently use them for general medical care. Such misuse of emergency services may be costly and reduce their availability to other community members. A related issue is whether the access strategy encourages differential use by targets from certain social, cultural, and ethnic groups, or is there equal access for all potential targets?

Program Support Functions

Although providing the intended services is presumed to be a program's main function, and one essential to monitor, most programs also perform important support functions that are critical to their ability to maintain themselves and continue to provide service. These functions are of interest to program administrators, of course, but often are also relevant to monitoring by evaluators or outside decision-makers. Vital support functions may include such activities as fund-raising; public relations to enhance the program's image with potential sponsors, decisionmakers, or the general public; staff training including, possibly, the training of the direct service staff; recruiting and retention of key personnel; developing and maintaining relationships with affiliated programs, referral sources, and the like; obtaining materials required for services; and general advocacy on behalf of the target population served.

Program monitoring schemes can, and often should, incorporate indicators of vital program support functions along with indicators relating to service activities. In form, such indicators and the process for identifying them are no different than for program services. The critical activities first must be identified and described in specific, concrete "output" terms resembling service units, for example, units of fund-raising activity and dollars raised, training sessions, advocacy events, and the like. Measures are then developed that are capable of differentiating good from poor performance and that can be regularly collected. These measures are then included in the program monitoring procedures along with those dealing with other aspects of program performance.

MONITORING PROGRAM OUTCOMES

Outcome monitoring is the routine measurement and reporting of indicators of the results of a program's efforts in the social domain it is accountable for improving (Affholter, 1994). It is important in this context to distinguish between the program's efforts and the resulting improvements (if any) in the target domain. Program outcomes are changes in the social conditions the program addresses that are pre-

sumed to result from program actions but are not themselves the program actions. Thus, providing meals to 100 housebound elderly persons is not a program outcome, it is service delivery encompassed within program process. The nutritional effect of those meals on the health of the elderly persons, however, is an outcome, as are any improvements in their morale, perceived quality of life, and risk of injury from attempting to cook for themselves.

A prerequisite for outcome monitoring is identification of the outcomes the program can reasonably be expected to produce. Here, again, a careful articulation of program theory is a very useful tool. In this instance, it is the program impact theory that is relevant. A good impact theory, as described in Chapter 3, will display the chain of outcomes expected to result from program services and be based on detailed input from major stakeholders, consideration of what results are realistic and feasible, and efforts to describe those outcomes in concrete, measurable terms. Another useful feature of well-developed impact theory is that it will distinguish proximal outcomes, those expected to result most immediately from program action, from more distal outcomes that may require more time or a greater cumulation of program effects to attain.

Program outcome monitoring requires that indicators be identified for important program outcomes, starting with the most proximal and covering as many of the more distal ones as is feasible (Exhibit 6-J gives some examples of outcome indicators). This means finding or developing measures that are practical to collect routinely and informative with regard to program performance. The latter requirement is particularly difficult. It is often relatively easy to find indicators of the status of the relevant social condition or target population on an outcome dimension, for instance, the number

EXHIBIT 6-J   Examples of Quality-of-Life Changes in Program Participants

Examples of movement toward some desirable change:
- Condition   A homeless client finding shelter
- Status   An unemployed client getting a job
- Behavior   An increase in a juvenile's school attendance
- Functioning   An increase in a client's coping skills
- Attitude   An increase in a juvenile's valuing of education
- Feeling   An increase in a client's sense of belonging
- Perception   An increase in a client's self-esteem

Examples of movement away from some undesirable change:
- Condition   Number of nights a homeless person spends on the streets
- Status   Number of days of work missed by substance-abusing client
- Behavior   A decrease in the number of times a juvenile skips school
- Functioning   A decrease in the incidence of a client's fighting with spouse
- Attitude   A decrease in a juvenile's number of acting-out incidents
- Feeling   A decrease in a client's feeling of powerlessness over his or her environment
- Perception   A decrease in a client's negative perception about another ethnic group

SOURCE: Adapted from Lawrence L. Martin and Peter M. Kettner, *Measuring the Performance of Human Service Programs* (Thousand Oaks, CA: Sage, 1996), p. 52.

of children in poverty, the prevalence of drug abuse, the unemployment rate, the reading skills of elementary school students, and the like. The difficulty is in linking *change* in that status specifically with the efforts of the program so that the indicators bear some relation to whatever outcomes the program has actually produced.

The source of this difficulty, as mentioned earlier in this chapter, is that there are usually many influences on a social condition that are not under the program's control. Thus, poverty rates, drug use, unemployment, reading scores, and so forth may change for any number of reasons related to the economy, social trends, and the effects of other programs and policies.

Under these circumstances, finding outcome indicators that do a reasonable job of isolating the results attributable to the program in question is often not an easy matter (U.S. General Accounting Office, 1997). Indeed, to isolate program effects in a convincing manner from other influences that might have similar effects requires the special techniques of impact evaluation discussed in Chapters 7-10 of this volume. Because the techniques of impact evaluation are rarely practical for routine, continuing use, outcome monitoring generally will rely on outcome indicators that, at best, are only "outcome related" and, as such, respond to other social influences as well as to the outcomes actually produced by the program.

Guidelines for Outcome Indicators

Nonetheless, there are some guidelines for developing outcome indicators that are as responsive as possible to program effects. One simple point, for instance, is that outcome indicators should be measured only on the members of the target population who actually receive the program services. This means that readily available social indicators for the catchment area served by the program are not good choices for outcome monitoring if they encompass an appreciable number of persons not actually served by the program (although they may be informative supplements to outcome indicators). It also means that those initial program participants who do not actually complete the full prescribed service package should be excluded from the indicator. This is not to say that drop-out rates are unimportant as a measure of program performance, only that they should be assessed as a service utilization issue, not an outcome issue.

Perhaps the most useful technique for focusing outcome indicators on program results is to develop indicators of preprogram to postprogram change whenever possible. For example, it is less informative to know that 40% of the participants in a job training program are employed six months afterward than to know that this represents a change from a preprogram status in which 90% had not held a job for the previous year. One approach to outcome indicators is to define a "success threshold" for program participants and report how many moved from below that threshold to above it after receiving service. Thus, if the threshold is defined as "holding a full-time job continuously for six months," a program might report the proportion of participants falling below that threshold for the year prior to program intake

and the proportion of those who were above that threshold during the year after completion of services.

A particularly difficult case for developing outcome indicators with some responsiveness to program-induced change is for preventive programs, whose participants initially are only at risk for a problem rather than actually manifesting the problem. Family preservation programs that intervene when children are judged at risk for being removed from the home illustrate this point. If, after service, 90% of the children are still with their family instead of in foster care, this might appear to indicate a good program outcome. What we do not know is just how much risk there was in the first place that the child would be removed. Perhaps few of these children would actually have been removed from the home in any event, hence the "change" associated with intervention is trivial.

The most interpretable outcome indicators, absent an impact evaluation, are those that involve variables that only the program can affect to any appreciable degree. When these variables also represent outcomes central to the program's mission, they make for an especially informative outcome-monitoring system. Consider, for instance, a city street-cleaning program aimed at picking up litter, leaves, and the like from the municipal streets. Simple before-after photographs of the streets that independent observers rate for cleanliness would yield convincing results. Short of a small hurricane blowing all the litter into the next county, there simply is not much else likely to happen that will clean the streets.

The outcome indicator easiest to link directly to the program's actions is client satisfaction, increasingly called customer satisfaction even in human service programs. Direct ratings by recipients of the benefits they believe

> ### ▨ EXHIBIT 6-K   Client Satisfaction Survey Items That Relate to Specific Benefits
>
> Client satisfaction surveys typically focus on satisfaction with program services. While a satisfied customer is one sort of program outcome, this alone says little about the specific program benefits the client may have found satisfactory. For client satisfaction surveys to go beyond service issues, they must ask about satisfaction with the *results* of service, that is, satisfaction with particular changes the service might have brought about. Martin and Kettner suggest adding items such as the following to routine client satisfaction surveys:
>
> *Service:* Information and referral
>
> *Question:* Has the information and referral program been helpful to you in accessing needed services?
>
> *Service:* Home-delivered meals
>
> *Question:* Has the home-delivered meals program been helpful to you in maintaining your health and nutrition?
>
> *Service:* Counseling
>
> *Question:* Has the counseling program been helpful to you in coping with the stress in your life?
>
> ---
>
> SOURCE: Adapted from Lawrence L. Martin and Peter M. Kettner, *Measuring the Performance of Human Service Programs* (Thousand Oaks, CA: Sage, 1996), p. 97.

the program provided to them are one form of assessment of outcomes. In addition, creating feelings of satisfaction about the interaction with the program among the participants is a form of outcome, although not one that, in itself, necessarily improves the participants' lives. The more pertinent information comes from participants' reports of whether very specific benefits resulted from program service (see Exhibit 6-K). The limitation of such indicators is that program participants are not always in a position to recognize or acknowledge program benefits, such as drug addicts encouraged to use sterile needles. Alternatively, participants may be able to report on benefits but be reluctant to appear critical and thus overrate them, as might elderly persons asked about the visiting nurses who come to their homes.

Pitfalls in Outcome Monitoring

Because of the dynamic nature of the social conditions typical programs attempt to affect, the limitations of outcome indicators described above, and the pressures on program agencies, there are many pitfalls that are associated with program outcome monitoring. This is not to say that such indicators cannot be a valuable source of information about program performance for program decisionmakers, only that they must be developed and used very carefully.

One important consideration is that any outcome indicator to which program funders or other influential decisionmakers give serious attention will also inevitably receive emphasis from program staff and managers. Thus, if the outcome indicators are not appropriate or fail to cover all important outcomes, program efforts to improve the performance they reflect may distort program activities. Affholter (1994), for instance, describes a situation in which a state used the number of new foster homes licensed as an indicator of increased placements for children with multiple problems. Workers responded by vigorously recruiting and licensing new homes even when the foster parents lacked the specialized skills needed to take hard-to-place children or were not appropriate at all for such children. Thus, the indicator continued to move upward but the actual placement of children in the target population did not actually improve. In education, this is called "teaching to the test." Good outcome indicators, by contrast, must "test to the teaching."

A related problem is the "corruptibility of indicators." This refers to the natural tendency for those whose performance is being evaluated to fudge and pad the indicator whenever possible to make their performance look better than it is. In a program for which the rate of post-program employment among participants is a major outcome indicator, for instance, consider the pressure on the program staff who telephone the participants six months after completion of the program to ascertain their job status. Even with a reasonable effort at honesty, ambiguous cases will be far more likely to be recorded as employment than not. It is usually best for such information to be collected by persons independent from the program if possible. If it is collected internal to the program, it is especially important that careful procedures be used and the results verified in some convincing manner.

Another potential problem area has to do with the interpretation of results on outcome indicators. Given a range of factors other than program performance that may influence those indicators, interpretations made out of context can be very misleading and, even with proper context, can be difficult. To provide suitable context for interpretation, outcome indicators must generally be accompanied by other information that provides a relevant basis for comparison or helps explain potentially anomalous results on the indicator. Outcome indicators are more informative, for instance, if they are examined as part of a time series that shows how the current situation compares with prior periods. It is also pertinent to have information about changes in client mix, demographic trends, and the like as part of the package. Decreased job placement rates, as one example, are more accurately interpreted as a program performance indicator if accompanied by summaries indicating the seriousness of the unemployment problems of the program participants. It may be no reflection on program performance if the placement rate decreases so long as it is clear that the program is working with clients who have fewer job skills and longer unemployment histories.

Similarly, outcome information is often more readily interpreted when accompanied by program process and service utilization information. A favorable job placement rate for clients completing training may, nonetheless, be a matter for concern if, at the same time, monitoring of service utilization shows that training completion rates have dropped to very low levels. The favorable placement rates may only reflect the dropout of all the clients with serious problems, leaving only the "cream of the crop" for the program to place. Incorporating process and utilization information into the interpretation of outcome indicators is especially important when different units, sites, or programs are being compared. It would be neither accurate nor fair to form a negative judgment of one program unit that was lower on an outcome indicator than other program units without considering whether it was dealing with more difficult cases, maintaining lower drop-out rates, or coping with other extenuating factors.

The upshot of these various considerations is that a weak showing on an outcome indicator is not usually a sufficient basis for concluding that program performance is poor. Rather, it should be a signal that further inquiry is needed to determine why the outcome indicator is low. In this way, outcome monitoring is not a substitute for impact evaluation but a preliminary outcome assessment that is capable of giving informative feedback to program decisionmakers, holding programs accountable for showing outcomes, and highlighting where a more probing evaluation approach is needed to contribute the most to program improvement.

COLLECTING DATA FOR MONITORING

A variety of techniques may be used singly and in combination to gather data on program implementation (see King, Morris, and Fitz-Gibbon, 1987; Martin and Kettner, 1996). As in all aspects of evaluation, the particular approaches used must take into account the resources available and the expertise of the evaluator. There may be additional restrictions on data collection, however. One concerns issues of privacy and confidentiality. Program services that depend heavily on person-to-person delivery methods, such as mental health, family planning, and vocational education, cannot be directly observed without violating privacy. In other contexts, self-administered questionnaires might, in theory, be an economical means of studying a program's implementa-

tion, but functional illiteracy and cultural norms may prohibit their use.

Several data sources should be considered for program monitoring purposes: data collected directly by the evaluator, program records, and information from program participants or their associates. The approaches used to collect and analyze the data overlap from one data source to the next. A comprehensive monitoring evaluation might include data from all three sources.

Data Collected by the Evaluator

Often critical program monitoring information can be obtained by direct observation of service delivery or other important program functions (Exhibit 6-I, presented earlier, provides an example). Observational methods are feasible whenever the presence of an observer is not obtrusive and the matter at issue is directly observable. In some cases, it can be useful for observers to become, at least for a time, full or partial program participants. Reiss (1971), for example, placed observers in police patrol cars and had them fill out systematic reports of each encounter between the police and citizens in a sample of duty tours. A similar approach was used in the Kansas City Preventive Patrol experiment (Kelling et al., 1974). It is always a question, however, how much the presence of participant observers alters the behavior of program personnel or program participants. Impressionistic evidence from the police studies does not indicate that observers affected the delivery system, because police in the patrol cars soon become accustomed to being observed. Nonetheless, participant-observation methods should be sensitive to the problem of observer effects.

An essential part of any observation effort is a plan for systematically recording the observations made (see Miles and Huberman, 1994, and Patton, 1990, for guidance on observational methods). Observers must be trained in how to make observations and how to record them uniformly. There are three common ways of making systematic observations. The first approach, known as the narrative method, involves the least structuring: The observer is simply asked to record events in as much detail as possible and in the order in which they occur. Typically, observers are provided with a list of important types of activities to which their attention should be directed.

A more structured approach is to provide observers with a data guide: a set of questions they are required to answer from their observations or a checklist on which to record the different activities observed. A data guide physically can resemble a survey instrument. For example, a data guide for observers attending technical training classes may have questions such as "How did the instructor make use of available training aids?" Or it may call for ratings, for instance, regarding the clarity of the instructor's presentation. Some ratings may be purely descriptive. Others may call for expert judgments, such as a scale to assess the way a police officer handles an encounter with a suspect. Structured recording instruments simplify analysis considerably and increase the likelihood that observers will provide consistent information.

Evaluators may also arrange for program staff to generate monitoring data according to the evaluator's specifications. Sometimes staff are asked to provide narrative reports in the form of diaries; sometimes they are asked to complete data forms or questionnaires for the evaluator. The evaluator may also survey or interview staff about certain aspects of their experiences, observations, or activities. The most efficient approach is to use a structured questionnaire or data form that can be completed by interview or by the staff person alone. As with observational data, structured instruments lend themselves readily to tabulation. It is also generally wise to organize the data collection so as to minimize the work demanded by program staff and, correspondingly, their resistance to cooperating with the data collection.

In some circumstances, it is possible to reduce the data collection burden by developing adequate sampling approaches. This may allow one or a few observers to record project activities in an economical fashion or an efficient number of staff persons to provide data. Sometimes sampling is done by randomly selecting time periods for observation; in other instances, it is more appropriate to sample persons or events. In doing so, it is important to ensure that a representative sample is employed to avoid intentional or unintentional bias in the information obtained.

Service Record Data

We have already seen how program records can be used to assess the participation of targets in a program. Often the delivery of project services can also be monitored from service records. Exhibit 6-L, for example, describes the use of medical charts to track service delivery in a program providing primary medical care to homeless individuals; the information gathered was also useful for several other purposes.

Service records vary; they can be the equivalent of narrative reports or highly structured data forms on which project personnel check which services were given, how they were received, and the observable results. Their level of detail is related to the complexity of the project and to the number of alternatives that can be specified in advance. Often service rec-

---

⚝ EXHIBIT 6-L   Using Clinic Encounter Records to Track Delivery of Medical Services to the Homeless

In the mid-1980s the Robert Wood Johnson Foundation and the Pew Memorial Trust funded 19 medical clinical programs serving homeless persons in as many cities throughout the country. To keep track of the medical problems encountered and the services delivered, each time a client was served, the attending medical person filled out a standard "encounter" record, with information about the person served, the medical condition, and the treatment prescribed. The encounter sheets also contained identifying information enabling the tracking of specific individuals throughout any number of subsequent clinic visits.

The records were sent each month to the Social and Demographic Institute at the University of Massachusetts where they were entered into a database. At the end of three years of clinic operation, more than 290,000 encounters had been entered into the database, pertaining to almost 94,000 individual clients served.

The database was used to document the incidence of various medical conditions as well as variations among sites and to identify the medical care needs of the homeless. In addition, the records were also used by each of the sites to monitor clinic activities.

SOURCE: Adapted from James D. Wright and Eleanor Weber, *Homelessness and Health* (New York: McGraw-Hill, 1987).

---

ord systems have serious limitations for monitoring purposes. In record systems designed primarily to serve administrative needs, the records are often not filled in completely if parts are viewed as irrelevant to staff for their purposes. If monitoring components are added, they may seem overly burdensome to program staff and they may not cooperate.

On the other hand, record information is inexpensive and efficient to obtain and analyze. Its use for monitoring depends on adequately training program staff, on providing the staff with motivation to complete records properly, and on incorporating quality-control checks to ensure that they follow through. A few items of data gathered consistently and reliably are generally much better for monitoring purposes than a more comprehensive set of information of doubtful reliability collected inconsistently.

It is also usually helpful if the record forms are structured as checklists whenever possible so that program staff can simply check off various items rather than provide narrative information. This procedure not only minimizes the time required of project staff but also yields data in a form convenient for analysis. In addition, if completed records are reviewed carefully as soon as possible for consistency and accuracy, omissions and inconsistencies can be caught in a timely way.

Again, it is important to recognize the risks involved in using service records as the only data source. Program staff, intentionally or unintentionally, may exaggerate the extent to which program elements are being delivered to targets because they are overly zealous about maintaining appearances of effectiveness or are simply displaying ritual compliance in what they record. There are also occasions when the project staff's interpretation of a particular service differs from that of the program's designers or evaluators.

Management Information Systems

The introduction of MISs into the social program arena provides new opportunities for effective monitoring. In a sense, all record systems are MISs. However, the concept is usually reserved for those systems that organize information using computers and allow it to be accumulated and displayed in a variety of ways at specified periods or on demand. An MIS thus provides information on an ongoing basis that can be used for program managers' decision making, for reports produced for stakeholders, and for evaluation purposes.

For example, a community mental health center may have 5,000 clients, see 600 patients a week, provide 15 services, refer patients to 12 providers outside the center, and have 22 professionals treating patients within the center, including psychiatrists, social workers, psychologists, psychiatric nurses, and vocational counselors. The patients may vary in age, sex, ethnicity, length and outcome of treatment, diagnoses, and a host of other characteristics. Program managers might well be interested in ascertaining any or all of these features and their interrelationships. They may want to know on a monthly basis the average number of patient visits by diagnosis, ethnicity, sex, or age. They might want to know what types of patients are being treated by which types of personnel or what types are receiving which kinds of services. The number of permutations of even these few measures is huge. Thus, MISs require computers for storing data and retrieving information in a variety of combinations.

Typically, computer-based MISs produce tables periodically (e.g., monthly) containing information regularly used by staff and management. They may produce other tables on different schedules for sponsors and stakeholders. For example, a mental health center's MIS may produce a second set of tables quarterly to send to the county agency that provides its support and an annual set of tables to send to the National Institute of Mental Health in Washington. These tables may differ in the ways the data are accumulated, the summary statistics provided, and so on.

In addition, an MIS can be used to answer specific management and research questions. For example, the mental health center's director may become uneasy about the proportion of patients who drop out of treatment. She might want to see whether the dropouts cluster by ethnicity, by the provider treating them, or some other characteristic. Or suppose a university-based clinical psychologist has secured funds to undertake an innovative demonstration program with depressive young adults and wants to include the center as one of the sites if it has a large enough target population. The MIS could provide the needed information by reporting diagnoses by age. Similarly, the MIS can supply information requested by stakeholders; for example, the local mental health association may want to know whether elderly patients are provided with psychotherapy and rehabilitation services rather than drug therapy.

From the evaluator's perspective, two aspects of MISs can present problems. First, it is essential that the system include the information that will be required by the various users, including researchers and evaluators. For example, information about the full mix and amount of services for each patient will be important for evaluation and obviously must be entered into the system to be available. The task involves more than simply identifying the information components, however; each must be operationally defined and rules must be developed for entering and accessing information. If 97% of a center's patients receive three or fewer distinct services, the system may store only three service codes per patient. In this case, a rule must be stated that specifies which three are entered for those few patients who have four or more.

The second and perhaps more critical consideration is that all the persons who provide and enter data must understand the utility of the system, its rules and definitions, and their responsibility to collaborate in its implementation. The finest hardware and software and the most sophisticated, well-conceptualized system will be useless if service providers do not take the time to enter the required data after seeing each patient. If providers wait until the end of the day to put in what they remember, for instance, the result will be what those in the business refer to as a "gigo" system ("garbage in, garbage out"). A combination of lack of training, apathy, fear of the system's revealing negative information, and occasional sheer malice need to be overcome if the organization is to reap the benefits of a properly functioning MIS. Thus, realizing the potential of the system requires training, oversight, regular quality control procedures, sanctions, and tender loving care.

Program Participant Data

The final approach to collecting monitoring information is to obtain data about program performance directly from participants themselves. Such information is valuable for a number of reasons, among them the distinctive perspective participants often have on a program. Securing participant data may be necessary for providers to know what is important to clients, including their satisfaction with and understanding of the intervention. Moreover, it may be the only way of finding out what was actually delivered.

In many programs, the services provided are not identical with those actually received and used by the participants. The literature on family planning has shown, for example, that participants may receive study guides, exercises, manuals, and equipment for use outside the classroom that are not used as intended. Thus, it may be critical to query participants to find out whether specific services were used or even received. For interventions involving complex interventions, it may also be important to ascertain participants' understanding of the interventions, the program's operating rules, and so on. In short, it is necessary to establish not only that designated services have been delivered but also that they were received, used, and understood as intended.

In our discussion of access earlier in this chapter, we pointed out that there are times when participants' satisfaction with a program is a key indicator in monitoring program implementation. Clearly, in this case the participant is the appropriate and sole information source. Information from participants must necessarily be obtained by interviews or self-administered questionnaires. Participants may be sampled in some systematic way, or an entire census may be conducted.

ANALYSIS OF MONITORING DATA

Data, of course, are useful only when they have been appropriately analyzed. In general, the analysis of monitoring data addresses the following three issues: description of the project, comparison between sites, and conformity of the program to its design.

Description of the Program Performance

Assessing the extent to which a program as implemented resembles the program as designed depends on having a full and accurate description of how the program actually operated. A description derived from monitoring data would cover the following topics: estimates of coverage and bias in participation, the types of services delivered, the intensity of services given to participants of significant kinds, and the reactions of participants to the services delivered. Descriptive statements might take the form of narrative accounts, especially when monitoring data are derived from qualitative sources, or quantitative summaries in the form of tables, graphs, and the like.

Comparison Between Sites

When a program includes more than one site, a second question concerns differences in program implementation between the sites.

Comparison of sites permits an understanding of the sources of diversity in program implementation and outcomes, such as differences in staff, administration, targets, or surrounding environments, and it also can facilitate efforts to achieve standardization. In addition, between-site differences may provide clues as to why programs at some sites are more effective than those at others.

Conformity of the Program to Its Design

The third issue is the one with which we began: the degree of conformity between a program's design and its implementation. Shortfalls may occur because the program is not performing functions it is expected to or because it is not performing them as well as expected. Such discrepancies may lead to efforts to move the implementation of a project closer to the original design or to a respecification of the design itself. Such analysis also provides an opportunity to judge the appropriateness of impact evaluation and, if necessary, to opt for more formative evaluation to develop the desired convergence of design and implementation.

SUMMARY

- Program monitoring is a form of evaluation designed to describe how a program is operating and assess how well it performs its intended functions. It builds on program theory, which identifies the critical components, functions, and relationships assumed necessary for the program to be effective.

- The results of program monitoring allow performance to be assessed against the stipulations of program theory, administrative standards, applicable legal, ethical, or professional standards, and after-the-fact judgment calls.

- The common forms of program monitoring include process (or implementation) evaluation, management information systems (MISs), and performance measurement.

- Process evaluation assesses whether the program is delivered as intended to the targeted recipients and is typically conducted as a separate project by evaluation specialists. It may constitute a stand-alone evaluation when the only questions are about implementation of program operations, service delivery, and other such matters. Process evaluation is also often carried out in conjunction with an impact evaluation to determine what services the program provides to complement findings about what impact those services have.

- When program monitoring is integrated into a program's routine information collection and reporting, it constitutes an MIS. In such systems, data relating to program process and service utilization is obtained, compiled, and periodically summarized for review.

- Performance measurement refers to various program monitoring schemes developed in response to demands for accountability from public and nonprofit agencies. The most far-reaching of these is the Government Performance and Results Act of 1993 (GPRA), which requires federal agencies to identify their program goals and report on their results in attaining those goals.

- Performance measurement distinguishes program *outputs*, the products or services delivered to program participants, from program *outcomes*, the results of those activities, such as improved health for the individuals served. Performance measurement is designed to periodically report results on indicators of the quantity and quality of both outputs and outcomes.

- Program monitoring takes somewhat different forms and serves different purposes when undertaken from the perspectives of evaluation, accountability, and program management, but the types of data required and the data collection procedures used generally are the same or overlap considerably. In particular, it generally involves one or more of three relatively distinct domains of program performance: service utilization, organizational functions, or program outcomes.

⬚ Service utilization issues typically break down into questions about coverage and bias. Coverage relates to how fully the target population participates in the program and bias relates to differential participation among those with different characteristics, for example, resistance to service, sociodemographic attributes, diagnosis, or location. The sources of data useful for assessing coverage are program records, surveys of program participants, and community surveys. Bias in program coverage can be revealed through comparisons of program users, eligible nonparticipants, and dropouts.

⬚ Monitoring a program's organizational functions focuses on how well the program is organizing its efforts and using its resources to accomplish its essential tasks. Particular attention is given to identifying shortcomings in program implementation that prevent a program from delivering the intended services to the target population. Three sources of such implementation failures are incomplete interventions, delivery of the wrong intervention, and unstandardized or uncontrolled interventions.

⬚ Program outcome monitoring is the routine measurement and reporting of indicators of the results of a program's efforts in the social domain it is accountable for improving. Outcome monitoring requires that indicators be identified that are practical to collect routinely and informative with regard to program results. Because there are usually many influences on a social condition that are not under the program's control, finding outcome indicators that isolate results attributable to the program is often difficult without the special techniques of impact evaluation.

⬚ Because of the dynamic nature of the social conditions typical programs attempt to affect, the limitations of outcome indicators, and the pressures on program agencies, there are many pitfalls associated with program monitoring. These include program distortions resulting from attempts to look good on inappropriate indicators, corruption of the indicators so they overstate performance, and misinterpretation of what indicators reveal about actual program performance.

⬚ The data used for monitoring purposes are generally collected from three sources: data collected directly by the evaluator, service records, and program participants. In recent years, MISs have become an essential tool for organizing, storing, and retrieving data from program records in ways that serve the needs of multiple users.

⬚ The analysis of monitoring data typically addresses such issues as description of program operations, comparison of sites, conformity of a program to its design, and program performance relative to standards or expectations.

KEY CONCEPTS FOR CHAPTER 7

Impact	The net effects of a program (see **net effects**).
Gross outcomes	The overall outcome subsequent to intervention, only part of which might actually be caused by the intervention.
Net effects	The effects of an intervention that can be attributed uniquely to it, that is, with the influence of confounding effects from other sources controlled or removed. Also called net outcomes and net impact.
Confounding factors	Extraneous variables resulting in observed effects that obscure or exaggerate the true effects of an intervention.
Selection bias	A confounding effect produced by preprogram differences between program participants and eligible targets who do not participate in the program.
Design effects	The influence of the research methods and procedures on the estimate of the net effects of a program.
Measurement validity	The extent to which a measure reflects the concept it is intended to measure.
Reliability	The extent to which scores obtained on a measure are reproducible in repeated administrations (provided that all relevant measurement conditions are the same).
Stochastic effects	Measurement fluctuations attributable to chance.
Proxy measure	A variable used to stand in for one that is difficult to measure directly.
Randomized experiment	An impact research design in which experimental and control groups are formed by random assignment.
Quasi-experiment	An impact research design in which "experimental" and "control" groups are formed by a procedure other than random assignment.
Reproducibility	The extent to which the findings of a study can be reproduced by other researchers in replications.
Generalizability	The extent to which an impact assessment's findings can be extrapolated to similar programs or from the program as tested to the program as implemented.

CHAPTER 7

STRATEGIES FOR IMPACT ASSESSMENT

The ultimate purpose of a social program is to ameliorate some social problem or improve some social condition. If the program theory is sound and the program plan is well implemented, those social benefits are expected to follow. Rarely are those benefits assured, however. Practical and conceptual shortcomings combined with the intractable nature of many social problems all too easily undermine the effectiveness of social programs.

Impact assessments are undertaken to find out whether interventions actually produce the intended effects. Such assessments cannot be made with certainty but only with varying degrees of plausibility. A general principle applies: The more rigorous the research design, the more plausible the resulting estimate of intervention effects.

The design of impact evaluations needs to take into account two competing pressures: On the one hand, evaluations should be undertaken with sufficient rigor that relatively firm conclusions can be reached; on the other hand, practical considerations of time, money, cooperation, and protection of participants limit the design options and methodological procedures that can be employed.

Ordinarily, evaluators assess the effects of social programs by comparing information about outcomes for participants and nonparticipants, by making repeated measurements on participants before and after intervention, or by other methods that attempt to achieve the equivalent of such comparisons. The basic aim of an impact assessment is to produce an estimate of the net effects of an intervention—that is, an estimate of the impact of the intervention uncontaminated by the influence of other processes and events that also may affect the behavior or conditions at which a program is directed. The strategies available for isolating the effects attributable to an intervention and estimating their magnitude are introduced in this chapter, together with issues surrounding their use.

Impact assessment can be relevant at many points throughout the life course of social programs. At the stage of policy and program

formation, impact assessments of pilot demonstrations are sometimes commissioned to determine whether the proposed program would have the intended effects. At the stage of program design, impact evaluations may be undertaken to test for the most effective ways to develop and integrate the various program elements. For example, the relative impact of different durations of service, of one type of practitioner versus another, and of providing follow-up services or not to targets are all issues that can be addressed through impact assessment.

When a new program is authorized, it is often started initially in a limited number of sites. Obviously, it is unwise to implement a new program widely without some knowledge of its effects. Impact assessments may be called for to show that the program has the expected effects before extending it to broader coverage. Furthermore, in many cases the sponsors of innovative programs, such as private foundations, implement programs on a limited scale with a view to promoting their adoption by government agencies if their effects can be demonstrated. Moreover, knowledge of program effects is critical to decisions about whether a particular initiative should be supported in preference to competing social action efforts.

Also, programs may be modified and refined to enhance effectiveness or to accommodate revised program goals. Sometimes the changes made are major and the assessments of the modified program resemble those of innovative programs. At other times, the modifications are modest "fine-tuning" efforts and the skeleton of the program remains fundamentally the same. In either case, the modifications can be subjected to impact assessments.

Finally, many established programs can be subjected to impact assessments, either continually or periodically. For example, the high costs of certain medical treatments make it essential that their efficacy be continually evaluated and compared with other means of dealing with the same medical problem. In other cases, long-established programs are evaluated at regular intervals either because of "sunset" legislation requiring demonstration of effectiveness if funding is to be renewed or as a means of defending the programs against attack by supporters of alternative interventions or other uses for the public funds involved.

KEY CONCEPTS IN IMPACT ASSESSMENT

All impact assessments are comparative (see Exhibit 7-A). Determining impact requires comparing, with as much rigor as is practicable, the conditions of targets who have experienced an intervention with those of equivalent targets who have experienced something else. There may be one or more groups of targets receiving "something else," and "something else" may mean receiving alternative services or simply going untreated. The "equivalent" targets for comparison may be selected in a variety of ways or comparisons may be made between information about the behavior or condition being examined and similar information from the same targets taken at an earlier time, or between measures of outcomes and conjectures about what would have occurred in the absence of the intervention.

The Experimental Model

Although there are many ways in which impact assessments can be conducted, the options available are not equal: Some characteristically produce more credible estimates of

---

⚝ EXHIBIT 7-A The General Problem of Assessing Program Effects

Estimating the effect of a new social or educational program requires comparing the condition of the individuals who have received the new service against the condition they would have been in had they not received the service. At times, their condition in the absence of the service is predictable; often, however, predicting how a group of individuals would have fared without the new service is difficult or impossible. A forecast of a group's behavior would, for example, have to take into account ordinary growth, cyclical or seasonal variations in behavior and the environment, and ordinary random fluctuations. Such a forecast also would need to determine whether the group might have received no services or services other than the new one, then somehow predict the effect of these unreceived services or alternative services.

In the absence of reliable predictions about a group's behavior, it is natural to construct a comparison group that has not received the new service. For a comparison to be fair, the comparison group must not differ systematically from new service recipients in any respect that would affect their future state. That is, the groups must be such that an unbiased estimate of the relative effect of the service is possible. More precisely, a fair comparison requires that the characteristics of individuals who receive services, or those who do not, be independent of the response variable used to make judgments about relative effectiveness. In other words, how people are selected for groups, or select themselves into groups, must not depend on factors that could influence outcome.

SOURCE: Quoted, with permission, from Robert F. Boruch, *Randomized Experiments for Planning and Evaluation: A Practical Guide* (Thousand Oaks, CA: Sage, 1997), pp. 1-2.

---

impact than others. The options also vary in cost and level of technical skill required. As in other matters, the better approaches to impact assessment generally require more skills and more time to complete, and they cost more.

In this and subsequent chapters, our discussion of the available options is rooted in the view that the optimal way to establish the effects caused by an intervention is a randomized field experiment. The laboratory model of such experiments is no doubt familiar. Subjects in laboratory experiments are randomly sorted into two or more groups. One group is designated the control group and receives no intervention or an innocuous one; the other group

or groups, called the experimental group(s), are given the intervention(s) being tested. Outcomes are then observed for both the experimental and the control groups, with any differences being attributed to the experimental intervention.

This research model underlies impact evaluations as well, because such evaluations, like laboratory experiments, are efforts to establish whether certain effects are caused by the intervention. Sometimes impact evaluations closely follow the model of randomized experiments; at other times, practical circumstances, time pressures, and cost constraints necessitate compromises with the ideal. This chapter provides an overview of impact evaluations and the alternative ways of estimating the effects of social programs; the three following chapters go into detail about undertaking such evaluations.

Prerequisites for Assessing Impacts

In earlier chapters, we have outlined the two prerequisites for assessing the impact of an intervention. First, the program's objectives must be sufficiently well articulated to make it possible to specify credible measures of the expected outcomes or the evaluator must be able to establish such a set of measurable outcomes. Second, the intervention should be sufficiently well implemented that there is no question that its critical elements have been delivered to appropriate targets. It would be a waste of time, effort, and resources to attempt to estimate the impact of a program that lacks measurable outcomes or that has not been properly implemented. An important implication of this last consideration is that interventions should be evaluated for impact only when they have been in place long enough to have ironed out implementation problems.

We cannot overemphasize the technical and managerial difficulties involved in undertaking the more rigorous forms of impact evaluation. The targets of social programs are often persons and households who are difficult to reach or from whom it is hard to obtain outcome and follow-up data. In addition, the more credible impact designs are demanding in both their technical and practical dimensions. Finally, as we discuss in detail in Chapter 12, evaluation research has its political dimensions as well. The evaluator must constantly cultivate the cooperation of program staff and target participants to conduct impact assessment while contending with inherent pressures to produce timely and unambiguous findings.

Linking Interventions to Outcomes

The problem of establishing a program's impact is identical to the problem of establishing that the program is a cause of some specified effect. Hence, establishing impact essentially amounts to establishing causality. There are many deep and thorny issues surrounding the concept of causality that need not concern us here. Rather, we shall accept the view that the world is sufficiently orderly for research to yield valid statements such as "*A* is a cause of *B* in circumstances *C*." Note, however, that this statement recognizes that a given social phenomenon may have more than one cause, and usually does.

In the social sciences, causal relationships are ordinarily stated in terms of probabilities. Thus, the statement "*A* is a cause of *B*" usually means that if we introduce *A*, *B* is more likely to result than if we do not introduce *A*. This statement does not imply that *B* *always* results if *A* is introduced, nor does it mean that *B* occurs *only* if *A* is introduced. To illustrate, consider a program designed to reduce unemployment, such as job training. If successful, it will increase the probability that participating targets will subsequently be employed. However, the likelihood of finding a job is related to many factors other than amount of training, including conditions and processes that have nothing to do with training programs, such as the economic condition of the community. Thus, although the introduction of a voluntary employment training program for unskilled adults should raise the level of participants' technical skills and thereby increase the likelihood that they will find employment, no training program, no matter how well designed, will completely eradicate unemployment. Some target adults will simply refuse to take advantage of the opportunity offered, and some willing participants will be unable to benefit for a variety of reasons, not least the number of vacancies in the labor market.

By the same token, other factors besides the training program might be responsible for reducing the unemployment rate of the program targets. Economic conditions may take a strong turn for the better so that more jobs open up; employers may decide to take on new workers with limited skills, experience, or questionable work records, perhaps because they think they can pay them lower wages than more highly trained workers; new firms with strong needs for unskilled workers may start up; other programs may be initiated that provide hiring incentives.

Assessment of a program's real effects is complicated further by biases in the selection of participants. For programs in which participation is voluntary, there is always the possibility that those who choose to participate will be the ones most likely to improve whether or not they receive the services of the program. Men and women who enter employment training programs are often those persons who are most motivated to obtain employment and thus are more likely to reach that goal than less motivated targets whether or not they receive the training program. Similarly, students awarded scholarships may do better academically than other students, but they may well have been more likely to succeed even if they had not received the scholarships. Other factors favoring the selection of some targets into a program may not reflect motivation or ability

so much as opportunity. For example, those living near a well-baby clinic may be more likely to use it, or persons with good literacy skills may be more easily reached by printed publicity. In short, the same factors that lead to self-selection by some participants into a program may also account for their subsequent improvement, a change that can easily be mistaken as an outcome of the program.

Still another confounding factor is that other social programs might be in effect at the same time as the one under examination. While a job training program is being implemented, for example, other initiatives may provide special incentives for employers to hire the unemployed, on-the-job training opportunities may become more available, or special "sheltered" jobs may be created to enable workers to gain experience while learning. Thus, the assessment of whether a specific intervention produces the desired effect is complicated by the many other factors besides the program itself that affect the condition in question.

The critical issue in impact evaluation, therefore, is whether a program produces desired effects over and above what would have occurred either without the intervention or, in some cases, with an alternative intervention.

"Perfect" Versus "Good Enough" Impact Assessments

In many circumstances, it is difficult or impossible to conduct impact evaluations using what is, in ideal terms, the best possible research design. In some instances, the available design options are so far from the ideal that the evaluator must question whether to undertake the assessment at all, especially if meaningful results are unlikely.

Unfortunately, evaluators are confronted all too frequently with situations where it is difficult to implement the "very best" impact evaluation design. First, as we explain later in this chapter, sometimes the designs that are best in technical terms cannot be applied because the intervention or target coverage does not lend itself to that sort of design. For example, the circumstances in which randomized experiments can be ethically and practicably carried out with human subjects are limited, and evaluators must often use less rigorous designs. Second, time and resource constraints always limit design options. Third, the justification for using the best design, which often is the most costly one, varies with the importance of the intervention being tested and the intended use of the results. Other things equal, an important program—one that is of interest because it attempts to remedy a very serious condition or employs a controversial intervention—should be evaluated more rigorously than other programs. At the other extreme, some trivial programs probably should not have impact assessments at all.

Our position is that evaluators must review the range of design options to determine the most appropriate one for a particular evaluation. The choice always involves trade-offs; there is no single, always-best design that can be used universally as the "gold standard." Rather, we advocate using what we call the "good enough" rule in formulating research designs. Stated simply, the good enough rule is that the evaluator should choose the best possible design from a methodological standpoint after having taken into account the potential importance of the results, the practicality and feasibility of each design, and the probability that the design chosen will produce useful and credible results.

The application of this rule is discussed in greater detail at several points in later chapters. For the purposes of presenting an overview of research designs in this chapter, we will discuss them as if there were no constraints on the choice of design. It should be borne in mind that this perspective generally needs to be modified in practice.

Gross Versus Net Outcomes

As we noted earlier, the starting point for impact assessment is the identification of one or more measurable outcomes that represent the objectives of the program. Thus, in studying a program designed to increase adult literacy, the objectives of the program may be stated as increasing reading-level scores on a standard reading skills test. The program may be considered successful if, after the program, the participants' scores are higher than what would be expected had they not received the program.

A critical distinction must be made at this point between *gross outcomes* and *net outcomes*, more aptly called *net effects*. The gross outcome consists of *all the change* in an outcome measure that is observed when assessing a program. Gross outcomes are usually easily measured and ordinarily consist of the differences between pre- and postprogram values on outcome measures. A gross outcome in an adult literacy program, for instance, would be any change in participants' reading level when measured just before participation in the program compared with measures afterward. In some cases in which preprogram values cannot be measured, gross outcomes may be measured in terms of postprogram values only.

Net effects are much more difficult to measure. Net effects are the changes on outcome measures that can be reasonably attributed to the intervention, free and clear of the influence of any other causal factors that may also influence outcomes. Gross outcomes, of course, include net effects but also include other effects that are not produced by the intervention. In symbolic terms, the relationship between gross outcomes and net effects can be expressed as follows:

$$
\begin{bmatrix} \text{Gross} \\ \text{outcome} \end{bmatrix} = \begin{bmatrix} \text{Effects of} \\ \text{intervention} \\ \text{(net effect)} \end{bmatrix} + \begin{bmatrix} \text{Effects of} \\ \text{other} \\ \text{processes} \\ \text{(extraneous} \\ \text{confounding} \\ \text{factors)} \end{bmatrix} + \begin{bmatrix} \text{Design} \\ \text{effects} \end{bmatrix}
$$

Thus, a gain in literacy in before-and-after measurements of a group of participants in an adult literacy program (gross outcome) is composed of three parts: first, the effects of the program (net effect); second, the effects of extraneous confounding factors (consisting of selection effects and other events, experiences, or processes that influenced literacy during the period in question); and third, design effects (artifacts of the research process itself, including such factors as errors of measurement, sampling variations, and inconsistency in data collection).

Of course, impact assessments are concerned primarily with net effects. In the following two sections, we first discuss the problem of extraneous confounding factors and then turn attention to design effects.

EXTRANEOUS CONFOUNDING FACTORS

Given that gross effects reflect not only the effects of an intervention but also the effects of other processes occurring at the same time and already under way at the start of the intervention, the primary challenge of impact assessment is to arrive at an estimate of net intervention effects. To accomplish this, the evaluator must exclude or purge the confounding factors from the gross effects. That is, the influence of any extraneous factors that explain, in whole or in part, the observed changes in the target problem or population must somehow be removed from the estimates of the intervention effects. Note that these confounding factors are extraneous only in the sense that they are not wanted in the estimate of net effects. In other regards, they are often the factors that ordinarily produce the outcome, for example, natural recovery processes, changes in the economy, and the like.

Confounding factors vary according to the social phenomenon in question. An intervention designed to improve the nutritional habits of families will compete with processes quite different from those affecting a program to improve young people's occupational skills. Despite the idiosyncratic features of programs and their target populations, however, certain processes are general enough to be identified as potential competitors with almost any intervention. Some of the most important of these are outlined below.

Uncontrolled Selection

By *uncontrolled selection* we mean processes and events not under the researcher's control that lead some members of the target population to be more likely than others to participate in the program under evaluation. When there are preexisting differences between those who receive a program and otherwise eligible persons who do not, differences in the outcomes for these respective groups may be accounted for by selection and not be attributable to the intervention. Such preexisting differences, when related to outcome variables, are known as *selection bias*.

Uncontrolled selection is among the most difficult of the extraneous confounding factors. Even if some person or agency deliberately chooses the targets for participation, such selection is still uncontrolled in the sense that the evaluator cannot account for it in a manner that allows its influence to be differentiated from true intervention effects. If the participants in a program are volunteers, uncontrolled selection is almost inevitable because those who volunteer almost certainly are more interested, more motivated, more appropriate or otherwise importantly different in relation to the program than those who do not volunteer.

Although the most familiar uncontrolled selection process is self-selection by targets who choose, of their own accord, to participate in a program, selection may come about in a variety of ways. As noted earlier, program location and access often play a role, as do motivation and such factors as whether prospective targets read newspapers and so learn about programs described there. In some "voluntary" programs, selection into a program may involve little choice from the viewpoint of participants as a result of political or administrative actions. Consider a community that through its municipal government, "volunteers" for a program to improve sewage disposal infrastructure. Although individual community members do not volunteer to participate, all persons living in the area are subject to the program and its potential benefits. A community in which officials are more likely to volunteer may be more progressive, more affluent, or otherwise different from other communities in ways that affect outcome measures. Similarly, when a new textbook is adopted for use in elementary schools,

individual pupils ordinarily do not choose to use the book; the volunteering is done by the school system. Nevertheless, from the standpoint of impact assessment, this is a form of selection.

Similarly, "deselection" processes work in the opposite direction to bring about differential attrition in program participation. Seldom is the participation of everyone who begins a program carried through to the end. Drop-out rates vary from program to program but are almost always disturbingly large. The individuals who leave a program may well be different in significant and relevant ways from those who remain. For one thing, those who are clearly benefiting from the intervention are likely to remain, whereas those who find it unrewarding or difficult are more likely to drop out. The consequence of attrition often is that the participants who stay with a program are those who may have needed the program least and were most likely to have improved on their own.

At the beginning of this chapter, we discussed the experimental model that underlies impact evaluations. To have a true experiment, evaluators must control the assignment of targets to participant and comparison groups and, indeed, make that assignment on the basis of a random process. Random assignment under the researcher's control is not only the optimal way to equate experimental and comparison groups but may vitiate the need to adjust for extraneous confounding effects altogether.

Endogenous Change

Social programs operate in environments in which ordinary or "natural" sequences of events inevitably influence the outcomes of interest. Such naturally occurring effects are termed *endogenous changes*. For example, most persons who recover from acute illnesses do so naturally, because ordinary body defenses typically are sufficient to overcome such illnesses. Thus, medical experiments testing a treatment for some pathological condition—influenza, say—must distinguish the effects of the intervention from the changes that would have occurred without the treatment. Because almost all influenza sufferers recover from the illness, an effective treatment may be defined as one that accelerates the recovery that would have occurred anyway.

The situation is similar for social interventions. A program for training young people in particular occupational skills must contend with the fact that some people will obtain the same skills in ways that do not involve the program. Likewise, assessments of a program to reduce poverty must consider that some families and individuals will become better off economically without outside help.

Secular Drift

Relatively long-term trends in the community, region, or country, often termed *secular drift*, may produce changes in gross effects that enhance or mask the net effects of a program. In a period when a community's birth rate is declining, a program to reduce fertility may appear effective because of that downward trend. Similarly, a program to upgrade the quality of housing occupied by poor families may appear to be effective because of upward national trends in real income that enable everyone to put more resources into their housing, thereby producing gross effects that favor the program.

Secular trends can also mask the impact of programs by producing contrary effects that cancel out an intervention's positive net effects.

Thus, an effective project to increase crop yields may appear to have no impact when gross effects are observed if unfavorable weather during the program period created poor growing conditions. Similarly, a program to provide employment opportunities to released prisoners may appear to have no effects if it coincides with a depressed period in the labor market.

Interfering Events

Like long-term secular trends, short-term events can produce changes that artificially enhance or mask net program effects. A power outage that disrupts communications and hampers the delivery of food supplements may interfere with a nutritional program. A natural disaster may make it appear that a program to increase community cooperation has been effective, when in reality it is the crisis situation that has brought community members together.

Maturational Trends

Evaluations of programs designed to produce changes in a target population must cope with the fact that maturational and developmental processes can produce considerable change that mimics or masks program effects. For example, the evaluation of an educational program designed to increase the language skills of small children must take into account the natural increases in such skills that occur with age. Similarly, the effectiveness of a campaign to increase interest in sports among young adults may be masked by a general decline in such interest that occurs when they enter the labor force. Maturational trends can affect older adults as well: A program to improve preventive health practices among adults may seem ineffective because health generally declines with age.

Although several commentators have identified additional extraneous confounding factors (for classic discussions, see Campbell and Stanley, 1966; Cook and Campbell, 1979; Kish, 1987), these factors either are applicable primarily to laboratory conditions or are encountered rarely. The extraneous confounding factors we have listed are those to which evaluators must be particularly alert in designing impact assessment research. Strategies for isolating the effects of extraneous factors are discussed later in this chapter.

DESIGN EFFECTS

The obstacles to estimating net effects described so far are a consequence of the nature of the social problem involved, participant selection processes, and endogenous changes taking place in participants and in the program's social and historical context. These confounding factors are neither equally nor uniformly distributed across all impact evaluations. Thus, maturational effects may be of little concern in a study of the potential work disincentives of unemployment benefits, because the program is relatively short in duration and is directed at adults who are in the prime of their working lives. On the other hand, maturational effects are undoubtedly much more important in the study of the impact of long-term programs directed at preschool children or other age groups that naturally are changing rapidly.

Design effects, in contrast, result from the research process itself and thus are always present and always threaten the validity of impact assessments. Fortunately, our knowledge of many design effects is more complete than our understanding of extraneous confounding factors. Hence, whereas adjusting for extraneous confounding effects is always problematic, estimating and compensating for design effects are only sometimes problematic.

Stochastic Effects

The end product of an impact assessment is an estimate of net program effects based on empirical data. For example, a carefully controlled study of the impact of a teaching method may find that a class learning with that method increased its scores on an achievement test by 7.8 points more than a control group taught by conventional methods. The issue then becomes whether 7.8 points is a large enough difference to indicate a decided advantage to the tested teaching method, or whether a difference of this magnitude could be due to chance fluctuations.

Judgments about the sizes of differences between experimental and control groups are not easy to make, mainly because some differences can be expected independently of the effects of an intervention. An experimental class is likely to differ to some degree from its control even if both are taught in exactly the same way by the same teacher. Just as any random sample from a deck of cards in which there is exactly the same number of red and black cards will, through chance, often have an uneven number of reds and blacks, so too any two classes of students will differ from each other in learning when measured at any given point in time. Such chance-produced fluctuations, called *stochastic effects*, complicate the task of assessing the net effects of interventions.

Given the inherent instability of measures taken from samples, how can we judge whether a given difference is large enough that we would be safe believing it is not a chance fluctuation? Fortunately, mathematical models of sampling variation enable us to make that judgment rather precisely. Sampling variations are dependent mainly on two characteristics of the set of observations made: First, the larger the sample, the smaller the sample-to-sample variation; second, the more variable the individuals in a sample, the larger the sample-to-sample variation (in other words, the larger the standard deviation, or variance, the greater the sampling variability). Other factors, such as the expected shape of the distribution of sample-to-sample measures, also may play a role that is too complex to discuss in detail here. (Readers interested in pursuing this topic further should consult any of the many standard texts on statistical methods, such as Hays, 1990, or Myers and Well, 1995.)

For example, suppose that scores on an achievement test used to evaluate the effects of a teaching method had a normal distribution with an overall standard deviation of 10. If we use the test on two classes of 100 pupils each, sampling theory tells us that for two-thirds of classes of that size, sampling variations would lead to differences of between +0.7 and –0.7. Furthermore, only 1 comparison in 1,000 would show chance differences greater than +1.4 or less than –1.4. Given these considerations, it would be safe to assume that a difference of 7.8 score points between the two classes indicates an effect larger than can be reasonably attributed to the chance element in sampling variability. Such effects are said to be *statistically significant*, and this line of reasoning is known as *statistical inference*, that is, using what is known about the expected sizes of

sampling variations to infer the likelihood that a given observation is due to chance.

Whereas chance fluctuations could lead us to conclude wrongly that an intervention had a certain effect, they may also make interventions appear ineffective when in fact they were effective. Thus, chance differences may make the impact seem larger or smaller than it actually is. The concept of *statistical power* is useful in understanding the issues involved here. Statistical power refers to the likelihood that a given impact evaluation design will detect a net effect of a given size, taking into account the statistical properties of the samples used and the statistical procedures employed to test for effects. For example, given an estimated value for the difference between posttest scores for experimental and control groups and the size of the sample, the probability of detecting the effect at a statistically significant level can be calculated. This is known as the power of the statistical analysis. Conversely, if an appraisal can be made of how large the net effects are expected to be, statistical power calculations can indicate how large the experimental and control groups must be for such effects to be detected reliably. These calculations are fairly straightforward; details and useful tables can be found in Cohen (1988), Kraemer and Thiemann (1987), and Lipsey (1990).

Using statistical inference to account for stochastic effects in impact evaluation involves making judgments about the relative importance of two types of error:

- Type I error (false positive): Making a positive decision when the correct decision is a negative one, that is, concluding that a program has an effect when it actually does not.
- Type II error (false negative): Making a negative decision when the correct decision is

positive, that is, failing to detect a real program effect.

The probability of making a Type I error is equal to the level of significance set for the statistical test used in the analysis. Thus, in testing a program that is in fact ineffective, one risks declaring it effective (false positive) 5 times in 100 trials if the significance level is set at .05. One can minimize false positives by setting a very strict criterion for statistical significance, but that increases the probability of making a Type II (false negative) error, for the two types of errors are inversely related for a given sample size. It is possible to minimize both types of errors simultaneously only by increasing the number of observations (sample size) or decreasing the variability in the observations through such techniques as statistically controlling the influence of covariates (Lipsey, 1990).

In every impact evaluation, the evaluator should decide a priori the importance of each of the two types of errors and then design the study and choose statistical analysis procedures accordingly. The judgment of whether it is more important to minimize false positives or false negatives should be based on substantive and practical grounds, not on theory or statistics. In testing the equipment of an airplane for safety, for example, it is clear that false positives are more serious than false negatives. That is, it is more important to avoid certifying as safe an airplane that might fail than it is to avoid rejecting as unsafe one that would not fail. One can make this judgment on the grounds that preserving life is more important than manufacturing airplanes inexpensively. Evaluating the safety of many medical interventions requires similar weighting of false positives.

In contrast, the opposite situation may apply in a relatively low-cost program, such as an educational television intervention. Effective educational programs of any type are difficult to design, and the negative effects of adopting an ineffective low-cost program are not very serious (especially in the absence of other educational alternatives known to be effective). It follows that false positives are less problematic than false negatives. It may be better to adopt a set of educational programs that, in statistical terms, are uncertain in their effectiveness in the hope that at least some actually are effective.

Tests of statistical significance are not the only basis for making judgments about the effects of an intervention. It is also useful to take into account evidence from other studies. Evidence from only one of several studies is less impressive than evidence that is consistent across studies. Indeed, replicating impact evaluations to determine whether the same effects are found is recommended when it is deemed important to be certain about effectiveness. In addition, it should be kept in mind that large samples can make small differences statistically significant when they are substantively unimportant and, conversely, small samples can make important effects statistically undetectable. These considerations have led to several suggestions to supplement statistical tests with other measures of intervention effects. For a discussion of these issues, see Browner and Newman (1989), Jacobson and Truax (1992), Kirk (1996).

Chapter 12 will take up the issue of judging evaluation results in greater detail. As we will see in that chapter, there are additional considerations, also based on value judgments, that should be taken into account. The important point here is that stochastic effects can be minimized to some extent by modifications in design. If evaluators anticipate small but important net effects, then sample sizes can and should be enlarged and variance control techniques applied so that the sampling variation will be smaller than the anticipated effects. If the new teaching method used as an illustration earlier was expected to produce average gains on an achievement test of between 0.5 and 1.0, and this range was meaningful in practical terms, statistical power should be high enough to ensure that they would be detected. This could be accomplished by increasing the numbers of students used in the design or by measuring and statistically controlling for variation from influential covariates, such as IQ, or both (see Lipsey, 1990). Because program stakeholders generally overestimate program effects, we recommend that considerable effort be made to ensure that impact designs have sufficient statistical power to detect statistically modest effects that may nonetheless be of substantive importance.

In this discussion, we have touched on only the barest essentials of the principles of statistical inference. Anyone planning to conduct impact evaluation should become familiar with the main issues and methods of statistical analysis, especially considerations of statistical power.

Measurement Reliability

A measure is reliable to the extent that, in a given situation, it produces the same results repeatedly. No measuring instrument, classification scheme, or counting procedure is perfectly reliable. Measurement error, or the extent to which a measuring instrument produces results that vary from administration to administration when applied to the same (or comparable) objects, plagues all measurement, whether of physical or social objects.

Although all measurement is subject to reliability problems, measures have such problems to varying degrees. Measurements of height and weight as obtained from standard devices and scales, for example, will be more consistent from one administration to another than measurements produced by repeated application of an intelligence test. By the same token, IQ tests have been found to be more reliable than reports of household expenditures for consumer goods, which, in turn, have been found to be more reliable than typical attitude scales.

For evaluators, a major source of unreliability lies in the nature of the measurement instruments used, many of which are based on participants' responses to written or oral questions posed to them by researchers. Differences in the testing or measuring situation, observer or interviewer differences in measure administration, and even participants' mood swings contribute to unreliability.

The effect of unreliability in measures is to dilute and obscure real differences. A truly effective intervention, the outcome of which is measured unreliably, generally will appear to be less effective than it actually is. An illustration of the effect of unreliability is shown in Exhibit 7-B. The table in that exhibit compares two measures of differing reliability in a hypothetical example of an educational intervention designed to raise levels of cognitive achievement among children from a disadvantaged background. The true outcome of the program is as shown in the top panel, labeled I. Forty out of 50 children (80%) in the participating group reached high achievement levels at the end of the program, but only 25 out of 50 (50%) of the nonparticipating or control individuals reached those levels. These are the results we would

---

⚜ **EXHIBIT 7-B**   Hypothetical Example of Attenuation Effects of Measurement Unreliability on Intervention Outcomes

I. True outcome without measurement error

	Participants	Nonparticipants
High achiever	40 (80%)	25 (50%)
Low achiever	10 (20%)	25 (50%)
True program effect =	30%	

II. Comparison of results of measures of achievement that vary in reliability

	Correct Classifications			
	Measure A		Measure B	
	High	Low	High	Low
High achiever	60%	40%	90%	10%
Low achiever	40%	60%	10%	90%

III. Measured outcomes using Measure A and Measure B

	Measure A		Measure B	
	Participants	Nonparticipants	Participants	Nonparticipants
High achiever	28 (56%)	25 (50%)	37 (74%)	25 (50%)
Low achiever	22 (44%)	25 (50%)	13 (26%)	25 (50%)
Measured effect =	6%		24%	

---

observe if we had a perfectly reliable test of cognitive achievement, that is, a test that made no classification errors.

The reliability of two measures, A and B, is compared in the middle panel (II). Measure A is less reliable than Measure B. Note that whether a child is truly a high achiever or a low achiever, Measure A correctly classifies the child only 60% of the time. In contrast, Measure B correctly classifies 90% of the individuals measured. This means, also, that Measure A makes mistakes in classification 40% of the time, whereas Measure B makes such mistakes only 10% of the time.

The bottom panel (III) shows the different effects of the application of the two unreliable measures on the assessed outcome of the intervention. With Measure A, we find that, in total, 28 children (56%) are identified as high achievers. These 28 high achievers include 60% of the 40 children correctly classified as high achievers (i.e., 24 children) plus 40% of the 10 low achievers incorrectly classified as high achievers (or 4 children).

In contrast, with Measure B, 37 children are identified as high achievers (74%). They are composed of 90% of the 40 children correctly identified as high achievers (or 36 children) plus 10% of the 10 children (or 1 child) incorrectly so identified.

Using Measure A, we get a contrast between the nonparticipating and the participating groups of only 6%, whereas for Measure B the contrast is 24%. Obviously, the more reliable Measure B comes closer to showing the actual extent to which the program was effective (30%).

Note that neither measure provides an accurate estimate of the hypothetical true program effect; both underestimate the true effect. This problem is known as "attenuation due to unreliability" and is well documented (Muchinsky, 1996; Schmidt and Hunter, 1996). In most cases, it is impossible to eradicate unreliability completely, although it is possible to make adjustments in results that take it into account if the degree of unreliability is known. The point of the example in Exhibit 7-B is to emphasize the importance of care in both the construction and the application of measurement procedures.

There are no hard-and-fast rules about acceptable levels of reliability. Measures generally lose their utility, however, when their reproducibility falls below 75% to 80%—that is, when less than 75%-80% of objects measured on two occasions with the same instrument are given the same scores (see, e.g., Mehrens and Lehmann, 1991, and Suen, Ary, and Covalt, 1990, for ways to estimate reliability).

Measurement Validity

The issue of measurement validity is more difficult to deal with than the problem of reliability. A measure is valid to the extent that it measures what it is intended to measure. Although the concept of validity is easy to comprehend, it is difficult to test whether a particular instrument is valid because for many, if not most, social and behavioral variables, no agreed-on standard exists. For example, an attitude scale measuring "attachment to employment" ideally might require as a validity test some behavioral measure of the extent to which an individual remains employed when working and seeks employment when unemployed, a measure that clearly would involve long-term observations. To complicate the issue, employment and job seeking are affected by other variables besides attachment, including employers' decisions and workers' health. As a result, neither steady employment nor long-term unemployment always reflects degrees of attachment to employment. Any measure based on long-term observations would have to take involuntary employment changes into account. This adjusted measure would also have to be one on which most social scientists concerned with studying labor force attachment could agree.

Although in principle it may be possible to collect the behavioral data needed to provide a benchmark against which to validate a measure, to do so is ordinarily impractical in view of the time and costs involved. Furthermore, not all social scientists who are concerned with a topic would accept any proposed standard as appropriate. For the concept of attachment to employment, for example, some would perhaps argue that expressed willingness to work overtime was a more appropriate standard.

In practice, there are usually a number of ways a given characteristic might be measured; for example, many different questions could be asked that would be related, at least conceptually, to the idea of attachment to employment. If everyone could agree on the best method of measuring it, then potential measures could be compared with this best measure. In the absence of a best measure, the question of whether a particular measure or set of measures is valid is usually a matter of case-by-case argument.

With outcome measures used for impact evaluation, validity turns out to depend very much on whether a measure is accepted as valid by the appropriate stakeholders, including members of the scientific community. Among social researchers, there is general agreement that one or more of the following criteria must be met for a measure to be considered valid:

1. *Consistency with usage.* A valid measure of a concept must be consistent with past work using that concept. Hence, if one develops a new scale to measure attachment to employment, it should not contradict the usual ways the concept has been used in previous studies.

2. *Consistency with alternative measures.* A valid measure must be consistent with alternative measures that have been used effectively by other evaluators. That is, it must produce roughly the same results as these established measures or have sound reasons for producing different ones.

3. *Internal consistency.* A valid measure must be internally consistent. That is, if several data items are used to measure a concept, the several measures should produce similar results, as if they were alternative measures of the same thing.

4. *Consequential predictability.* Some measures implicitly or explicitly entail predictions. For example, a measure of "propensity to move" implies by its name alone that it predicts whether or not a person or household will move. For such a measure to be judged valid, it should in fact predict moving behavior. Although not all measures have such clearly implied predictability, many do, and such measures ought to be tested for an adequate degree of predictability.

These criteria are clearly conservative in the sense that they stress the use of existing measures as reference points and discourage innovation in measurement. This conservative bent, however, is mitigated somewhat by the last criterion, consequential predictability. If a proposed new measure can be shown to be a better predictor than a previously accepted measure, then it may justifiably supplant the earlier one.

Clearly, a useful measure must be both valid and reliable; reliability alone is a necessary but not sufficient criterion for selecting measures. However, because a measure cannot be valid unless it is also reliable, assessment of reliability can be a first test of a measure's validity.

Choice of Outcome Measures

A critical measurement problem in evaluations is that of selecting the best measures for assessing outcomes (Rossi, 1997). We recommend that evaluators invest the necessary time and resources to develop and test appropriate outcome measures (Exhibit 7-C provides an instructive example). A poorly conceptualized outcome measure may not properly represent the goals and objectives of the program being evaluated, leading to questions about its validity. An unreliable outcome measure is likely to underestimate the effectiveness of a program and could lead to incorrect inferences about the program's impact. In short, an irrelevant or unreliable measure can completely undermine the worth of an impact assessment by producing misleading estimates. Only if outcome measures are valid and reliable can impact

⚅ EXHIBIT 7-C   Reliability and Validity of Self-Report Measures With Homeless Mentally Ill Persons

Evaluations of programs for homeless mentally ill people typically rely heavily on self-report measures. But how reliable and valid are such measures, particularly with persons who have psychiatric problems? One group of evaluators built a measurement study into their evaluation of case management services for homeless mentally ill clients. They focused on self-report measures of psychiatric symptoms, substance abuse, and service utilization information.

Psychiatric symptoms. Self-report on the Brief Symptom Inventory (BSI) was the primary measure used in the evaluation to assess psychiatric symptoms. Internal consistency reliability was examined for five waves of data collection and showed generally high reliabilities (.76-.86) on the scales for anxiety, depression, hostility, and somatization but lower reliability for psychoticism (.65-.67). To obtain evidence for the validity of these scales, correlations were obtained between them and comparable scales from the Brief Psychiatric Rating Schedule (BPRS), rated for clients by master's-level psychologists and social workers. Across the five waves of data collection, these correlations showed modest agreement (.40-.60) for anxiety, depression, hostility, and somatization. However, there was little agreement regarding psychotic symptoms (–.01 to .22).

Substance abuse. The evaluation measure was clients' estimation of how much they needed treatment for alcohol and other substance abuse using scales from the Addiction Severity Index

(ASI). For validation, interviewers rated the clients' need for alcohol and other substance abuse treatment on the same ASI scales. The correlations over the five waves of measurement showed moderate agreement, ranging from .44 to .66 for alcohol and .47 to .63 for drugs. Clients generally reported less need for service than the interviewers.

Program contact and service utilization. Clients reported how often they had contact with their assigned program and whether they had received any of 14 specific services. The validity of these reports was tested by comparing with case managers' reports at two of the waves of measurement. Agreement varied substantially with content area. The highest correlations (.40-.70) were found for contact with the program, supportive services, and specific resource areas (legal, housing, financial, employment, health care, medication). Agreement was considerably lower for mental health, substance abuse, and life skills training services. The majority of the disagreements involved a case manager reporting service and the client reporting none.

The evaluators concluded that the use of self-report measures with homeless mentally ill persons was justified but with caveats: Evaluators should not rely solely on self-report measures for assessing psychotic symptoms, nor for information concerning the utilization of mental health and substance abuse services, since clients provide significant underestimates in these areas.

SOURCE: Adapted from Robert J. Calsyn, Gary A. Morse, W. Dean Klinkenberg, and Michael L. Trusty, "Reliability and Validity of Self-Report Data of Homeless Mentally Ill Individuals," *Evaluation and Program Planning,* 1997, 20(1):47-54.

estimates be regarded as credible. Bausell (1992) identifies some useful resources for locating existing assessment instruments.

In addition to being reliable and directly enough related to the goals of the program to be valid, a good outcome measure is one that is feasible to employ, given the constraints of time and budget. Suppose, for example, that a family planning program, whose goal is to reduce average family size in the community, considers the following alternatives for measuring outcomes:

- Proportion of couples adopting effective contraceptive practices

- Average desired number of children

- Average number of children in completed families

- Attitudes toward large families

These four possibilities do not exhaust all the measures that can reasonably be viewed as relevant to the goal of reducing fertility. But even among the four, there are variations in terms of ease of measurement, cost of data collection, and probable validity. Thus, although a reduction in the average number of children in completed families (i.e., those past childbearing) may be the best expression of the eventual goal of a program to reduce fertility, the use of that measure to define the outcome implies a long-term evaluation of considerable complexity and cost. In contrast, it may be easy to measure attitudes toward large families, proceeding on the assumption that the impact of a fertility reduction program will be reflected in low approval of large families. However, given what is known about the often weak and erratic relationship between attitudes and behavior, a downward shift in the average desirability of

large families is likely to be a remote measure of the program's goals. Because changes in attitude may occur without a corresponding shift in fertility practices, the "consequential predictability" of such a measure is not likely to be very high.

Of our four alternative ways of measuring the outcomes of a family planning program, shifts in contraceptive practices may, on balance, be the best choice. The relevant behavior can be studied over a relatively short period of time, there are ample precedents for adequate measurements in previous research, and shifts in contraceptive practices are known to be directly related to fertility. As a further illustration, Exhibit 7-D displays a variety of outcome measures that were established for a program designed to prevent adolescents from initiating the use of tobacco.

As illustrated above, often the most valid outcome measures either cannot be obtained directly at all or can be obtained only at prohibitive expense. Under such circumstances, indirect measures, generally referred to as *proxy measures*, must be substituted. A proxy measure is one that is used as a stand-in for an outcome that is not measured directly. The selection of a proxy measure is clearly a critical decision. Ideally, a proxy measure should be closely related to the direct measure of the program objectives but be much easier to obtain. In practice, it is often necessary to accept proxy measures that are less than ideal. Although there are no firm rules for selecting appropriate proxy measures, there are some guidelines.

First, for objectives that are measurable in principle but too costly to measure in practice, previous research may include studies that test the worth of alternatives. For example, suppose we wanted to assess whether the jobs obtained

EXHIBIT 7-D   Program Outcome Measures

A community intervention to prevent adolescent tobacco use in Oregon included youth anti-tobacco activities (e.g., poster and T-shirt giveaways) and family communication activities (e.g., pamphlets to parents). In the impact assessment the outcomes were measured in a variety of ways:

Outcomes for Youths

- Attitudes toward tobacco use
- Knowledge about tobacco
- Reports of conversations about tobacco with parents

- Rated intentions to smoke or chew tobacco
- Whether smoked or chewed tobacco in last month and, if so, how much

Outcomes for Parents

- Knowledge about tobacco
- Attitudes toward community prevention of tobacco use
- Attitudes toward tobacco use
- Intentions to talk to their children about not using tobacco
- Reports of talks with their children about not using tobacco

SOURCE: Adapted from A. Biglan, D. Ary, H. Yudelson, T. E. Duncan, D. Hood, L. James, V. Koehn, Z. Wright, C. Black, D. Levings, S. Smith, and E. Gaiser, "Experimental Evaluation of a Modular Approach to Mobilizing Antitobacco Influences of Peers and Parents," *American Journal of Community Psychology*, 1996, 24(3):311-339.

by persons completing training programs are better than those the trainees would have found otherwise as part of a broad evaluation of the quality of life of families participating in a comprehensive program that had a large number of intervention elements and outcomes. In principle, the quality of jobs could be measured by some weighted combination of earnings, wage rates, steadiness of employment, working conditions, and other measurable attributes. To do so might require surveying the former trainees and their comparison group peers and developing an extensive battery of survey items. Instead of this long and expensive procedure, the family member who was going to be interviewed anyway by telephone might be asked one or two items about the job satisfaction of

targets of the training program. This procedure might be justified by previous research showing satisfaction to be highly correlated with the other attributes of "good jobs."

Second, objectives that are expected to be reached in the far future can be represented by proxy measures that reflect intermediate steps toward those goals. For example, although the objective of a program on family fertility is to reduce average family size, that goal can be measured definitively only after the women in those families have passed through their childbearing years. Proxy measures that center on the adoption of practices that will reduce completed fertility are reasonable surrogates—for example, adoption of contraceptive practices or changes in desired family size.

Third, when proxy measures, or any outcome measures of uncertain validity, must be used, it is wise to use several such measures when possible. Multiple measurement of important outcomes potentially provides for broader coverage of the concept and allows the strengths of one measure to compensate for the weaknesses of another. It may also be possible to statistically combine multiple measures into a single, more robust and valid composite measure that is better than any of the individual measures taken alone. In a program to reduce family fertility, for instance, changes in desired family size, adoption of contraceptive practices, and average desired number of children might all be measured and used in combination to assess outcome.

The Hawthorne Effect and Other Delivery System Contaminants

In a famous "before and after" study conducted in the 1930s, researchers attempted to determine the effects of varying illumination on the productivity of women assembling small electronic parts (Roethlisberger and Dickson, 1939). It was discovered that any change in the intensity of illumination, positive or negative, brought about a rise in worker productivity. The researchers interpreted this effect as an artifactual result of conducting the research and it has since been dubbed the *Hawthorne effect* after the site where the study was conducted. Ostensibly, the researchers were studying the effects of varying illumination levels, but during the research, there was continuous observation of work-group members by researchers stationed in the assembly room. Roethlisberger and Dickson reasoned that the workers took the fact that they were being given so much attention by the researchers as a sign that the firm was interested in their personal welfare. The workers' response was to develop a high level of work-group morale and increase their productivity. Thus, the measured gross effect was a combination of the effects of the intervention (varying illumination), the delivery of that intervention (apparent concern on the part of management and the presence of researchers in the workplace), and the constant observation. Because productivity continued to increase throughout the duration of the study even though the workplace illumination was first increased and later decreased, the researchers concluded that the workers' increased productivity could not be a response to variations in the levels of lighting but was due to the continuous presence of the researchers themselves.

The Hawthorne effect is not specific to any particular research design; it may be present in any study involving human subjects. For example, in medical experiments, especially those involving pharmacological treatments, the Hawthorne effect is known as the placebo effect. This is why the evaluation of the effectiveness of a new drug usually involves both a placebo control, consisting of a group of patients who are given essentially neutral medication (sugar pills), and a control given the standard pill commonly prescribed. The effectiveness of the new drug is measured by how much more relief is reported from it in comparison to that reported by those who received either the placebo or the standard pill. The placebo group is required for comparison because participants are often affected simply by the knowledge that they are receiving treatment, irrespective of the efficacy of the treatment itself. The placebo control enables the researchers to identify and allow for this artifact of the research process.

It is possible to exaggerate the importance of the Hawthorne effect. Reanalyses of the original study (e.g., Franke and Kaul, 1978) have cast doubt on whether the data actually demonstrate any Hawthorne effect at all, and it may, in fact, be less important than once thought. One competing explanation is that the Hawthorne research occurred during the Great Depression, a time of severe unemployment and layoffs. Workers may have perceived the research activity as evidence that they were not going to be fired and thus worked enthusiastically and unusually productively. The important point, however, is that an intervention consists not just of the intervention administered but of everything that is done to the targets involved. Evaluation researchers must allow that the act of research itself is an intervention.

Our discussion of the Hawthorne effect underscores the fact that an intervention is rarely delivered in a pure form; it can rarely be separated from its context. Thus, counseling therapy for juvenile delinquents involves not only the therapist but also other personnel (e.g., the intake clerks), a setting in which the therapy is conducted, the reactions of the juveniles' peers who know of the therapy, and so on. Every aspect of the intervention delivery system, including the physical plant, rules and regulations, and the labeling of targets, can affect the outcome of the intervention, so much so that monitoring of the delivery of interventions almost always is a necessary adjunct to impact assessments.

Missing Information

No data collection plan is ever fulfilled to perfection. For a variety of reasons, almost all data sets are "perforated"; that is, they have gaps in them consisting of entirely missing cases or ones for which some portion of the required measures do not exist. In studies that follow up participants after intervention, for instance, some respondents move away and cannot be located, others refuse to provide more information, others become too sick or disabled to participate, and some may die—all events that result in missing data for some individuals. Even for individuals who have consistently participated, some parts of the data are often missing: Interviewers forget to ask questions, or respondents inadvertently skip over items on questionnaires or refuse to answer questions they regard as intrusive, irrelevant, or ambiguous.

Were missing data randomly spread across observations, their main effect would be similar to that of unreliability, namely, to obscure differences. But ordinarily that is not the case; persons lost to a study through attrition are often different from those who remain in ways that are related to the intervention outcome. For example, in experiments on the effects of welfare payments, families in the control group, who receive no payments, will be more likely to drop out. Similarly, persons who refuse to answer questions are often different in outcome-relevant ways from those who answer. For example, high-income respondents are more likely than low-income ones to refuse to answer questions about income. As Exhibit 7-E describes, high school students whose parents do not consent to their participation in data collection are also different from those who do.

To reduce these biases, alternative survey items or unobtrusive measures may be used. Also, various analytical procedures are available to estimate the extent of missing data biases and to impute estimates for purposes of analysis (Foster and Bickman, 1996; Little and Rubin, 1987).

✺ EXHIBIT 7-E   Missing Data Bias Related to Parental Consent in School-Based Surveys

The evaluators of a major community health promotion initiative in the western United States were presented with an informative opportunity to investigate the differences in evaluation outcome data associated with different forms of parental consent for surveys of high school students. Seventeen schools in six California communities either received the program or were in the control condition. Even though all the students in each school were thus research subjects, outcome data could be collected only on those students whose parents gave consent for them to complete surveys. Most school districts require one of two forms of parental consent. Active parental consent requires the parents to sign a consent form that is returned to the school. Passive consent involves notifying the parents of the survey and asking them to return a signed form only if they do *not* want their child to participate.

The California educational code requires active parental consent prior to asking students sex-related questions. The outcome survey for the evaluation covered a broad range of health-related topics, including sexual activity and contraception. Parents were sent a consent form via first-class mail that explained the study and gave them three response options: (a) Sign and return the form indicating permission for their child to be given a complete survey (active consent); (b) not return the form, which would indicate willingness to have their child be given a version of the survey that excluded the sex-related questions (passive consent); or (c) sign and return the form declining to give permission for their child to participate in the survey at all (fewer than 2% elected this option). This provided the opportunity to compare the characteristics of student respondents available for research through active consent with those available through passive consent on all survey items except the sex-related ones.

In both grades surveyed (9th and 12th), students with active parental consent were significantly more likely to be white, female, have a grade point average of B or above, live in two-parent households, have college-educated parents, and be involved in extracurricular activities. With respect to health status and risk-taking behavior, a significantly smaller proportion of students with active parental consent reported their health as less than "very good" and fewer reported irregular seat belt use. Among 9th graders the prevalence of current cigarette smoking was significantly lower in the active consent group. These latter differences remained after controlling for demographic variables. In addition, students with active consent were significantly more likely to report having seen the health promotion information from the intervention.

Thus, data from adolescents whose parents gave active consent for their participation in research involving sensitive subjects were not representative of all those who were exposed to the intervention. Evaluation research that was restricted to collecting data under active consent would therefore lose, as missing data, responses from students with distinctive characteristics whose parents do not provide active consent but would accept passive consent.

SOURCE: Adapted from C. Anderman, A. Cheadle, S. Curry, P. Diehr, L. Shultz, and E. Wagner, "Selection Bias Related to Parental Consent in School-Based Survey Research," *Evaluation Review,* 1995, 19(6):663-674.

Sample Design Effects

Most evaluation research is carried out on samples of potential or actual targets and non-participant controls. Findings from such research can be generalized to other groups—for example, all targets—only if the samples are properly designed and the design is then carried out with fidelity. Designing samples is a technical task, and most evaluators faced with a sampling issue of any magnitude would be well advised to involve a sampling statistician for the purpose.

The goal of a sampling strategy is to select an unbiased sample of the universe of interest. The first task is to identify a relevant sensible universe, that is, a population that includes those units (persons, households, firms, etc.) that are actual or potential targets of the program in question. Thus, a program designed to provide benefits to young males between the ages of 16 and 20 needs to be tested on a sample of that group.

The second task is to design a means of selecting a sample from the identified universe in an unbiased fashion. An unbiased selection procedure is one that gives each unit in the universe a known, nonzero probability of being selected. In practice, this often means that every member of the universe has an equal chance of being selected. There are many ways of designing such a selection strategy; additional details can be found in standard textbooks on the sampling of human populations (e.g., Henry, 1990; Kish, 1995).

The final task is to implement a sample selection strategy with fidelity; that is, persons who are supposed to be selected for the sample should in fact be selected. Rarely, if ever, is a sample of noninstitutionalized persons carried out without some selected individuals being missed. Indeed, most survey researchers are pleased when they are able to obtain cooperation from 75% or more of a designated sample. The Current Population Survey, administered by the Bureau of the Census, is reputed to have the highest response rates of all continuing surveys. It routinely gets cooperation rates in the high 90s, but this record is very exceptional. Cooperation rates can be affected strongly by the effort put into achieving contact with designated participants and by ardent persuasion, but such efforts add to the research expenses (see Ribisl et al., 1996, for useful tips on minimizing attrition).

Minimizing Design Effects

As we have seen, design effects are aspects of research design whose influence ordinarily is to diminish the capability of a given study to discern net effects when they actually exist. Careful planning of evaluations is the best antidote to design effects. In some cases—for example, when evaluations are planned that involve developing new measures—pretesting may be advisable to ensure that any outcome measures are sufficiently reliable and valid to respond to intervention effects. Attention must also be given to selecting representative samples that are large enough to provide adequate statistical power, measuring those target characteristics that may be appropriate for statistical control during analysis, and minimizing missing data problems.

DESIGN STRATEGIES FOR ISOLATING THE EFFECTS OF EXTRANEOUS FACTORS

As we noted earlier, the task of impact assessment is to estimate the difference between two conditions: one in which the intervention is present and one in which it is absent. The strategic issue, then, is how to isolate the effects of extraneous factors so that observed differences can safely be attributed to the intervention.

Ideally, the conditions being compared should be identical in all respects, save for the intervention. There are several alternative (but not mutually exclusive) approaches to approximating this ideal that vary in effectiveness. All involve establishing *control conditions*, groups of targets in circumstances such that they do not receive the intervention being assessed. The following common approaches to establishing control conditions are discussed in detail in this and the next three chapters:

- *Randomized controls:* Targets are randomly assigned to an experimental group, to which the intervention is administered, and a control group, from which the intervention is withheld. There are sometimes several experimental groups, each receiving a different intervention or variation of an intervention, and sometimes several control groups, each also receiving a different variant, for instance, no intervention, placebo intervention, and "treatment as usual."

- *Regression-discontinuity controls:* Targets are assigned to an intervention group or a control group on the basis of measured values on a precisely identified selection instrument. Because the basis for selection is explicitly known, its relationship to outcome measures can be statistically modeled and separated from any remaining differences between experimental and control groups.

- *Matched constructed controls:* Targets to whom the intervention is given are matched on selected characteristics with individuals who do not receive the intervention to construct an "equivalent" group, not selected randomly, that serves as a control.

- *Statistically equated controls:* Participant and nonparticipant targets, not randomly assigned, are compared with differences between them on selected characteristics adjusted by statistical means.

- *Reflexive controls:* Targets who receive the intervention are compared with themselves using measurement before and after the intervention.

- *Repeated measures reflexive controls:* Also called *panel studies*, this technique is a special case of reflexive controls in which the same targets are observed repeatedly over time both before and after the intervention.

- *Time-series reflexive controls:* This technique is a special case of reflexive controls in which rates of occurrence of some event or other such social indicators are compared at frequent time points before and after the intervention.

- *Generic controls:* Intervention effects among targets are compared with established norms about typical changes in the target population.

Full- Versus Partial-Coverage Programs

The most severe restriction on the choice of an impact assessment strategy is whether the intervention in question is delivered to all (or virtually all) members of a target population. For programs with total coverage, such as long-standing, ongoing, fully funded programs, it is usually impossible to identify anyone who is not receiving the intervention and who in essential ways is comparable to the individuals who are receiving it. In such circumstances, the main strategy available is to use reflexive controls, that is, some form of before-and-after comparison. In contrast, some interventions will not be delivered to all the potential target population. Programs may lack the resources to serve the entire target population or their activities may be restricted to certain jurisdictions or geographical areas. Also, new programs or those that are to be tested on a demonstration basis ordinarily have only partial coverage, at least during their early stages.

In all likelihood, no program has ever achieved total coverage of its intended target population. Even in the best of programs, some persons refuse to participate, others are not aware that they can participate, and still others are declared ineligible on technicalities. Nevertheless, many programs achieve nearly full coverage. The Social Security Administration's retirement payments, for example, reach most eligible retired people. As a rule of thumb, when programs reach as many as four of five eligible units (80% coverage), a program has "full coverage" for the purposes of the present discussion.

The smaller the proportion of the target population that is not reached, the greater the differences are likely to be between those individuals who are covered and those who are not. For all practical purposes, almost all children between the ages of 6 and 14 attend school; those who do not suffer from temporary or permanent disabilities, receive tutoring at home from parents or private tutors, or are members of migratory worker families who move constantly from work site to work site. Hence, children who at any point in time are not enrolled in school are likely to be so different from those who are enrolled that no amount of matching or use of statistical controls will produce comparability of the sort needed for meaningful comparisons. Similarly, a recent report on Head Start evaluation strategies recommended that no randomized experiments be done on that program because so large

a proportion of its target population is now covered by the program (Collins Management Services, 1990).

Nonetheless, some aspects of the impact of full-coverage programs can be evaluated, especially if the programs are not uniform over time or over localities. These differences provide the evaluator with some limited opportunities to assess the effects of variations in the program. Thus, evaluators might not be able to assess what the net impact of elementary schooling is (as compared to no schooling at all), but they can assess the differential impact of various kinds of schools and of changes in schools over time. Because most educational policy issues revolve around improving the existing school system, impact assessments of proposed changes in that system may be exactly what is needed to inform policy decisions.

These variations in ongoing, established programs occur in a variety of ways. Policies change over time, along with their accompanying programs. Program administrators institute modifications to meet some new condition or to make administration easier. Thus, from time to time, Social Security benefits have been increased to take into account new conditions or to add new services (e.g., Medicare). Similarly, sufficient local autonomy may be given to states and local governments that a program (e.g., Temporary Assistance to Needy Families [TANF]) may vary from place to place. With proper precautions, such "natural variation" can provide a point of leverage for estimating some program effects.

For partial-coverage programs, a greater variety of strategies is available. If it is practical, as may be the case especially in new or prospective programs, the ideal solution is to use randomized controls. In this strategy, a set of potential targets, representative of those who might be served if the program goes full scale, is selected by an unbiased procedure and randomly assigned to an experimental group and a control group. With sufficient numbers of persons, the process of randomization maximizes the probability that the groups are equivalent; that is, individual variations in extraneous variables are likely to be distributed across the groups in such a way that the experimental and control groups will not differ materially in ways related to the intervention outcome. When an evaluator cannot use randomization procedures in forming experimental and control groups or conditions, other types of control groups often may be formed from uncovered targets, provided that proper procedures are used.

A CATALOG OF IMPACT ASSESSMENT DESIGNS

The simultaneous consideration of control conditions, intervention features, and data collection strategies produces the schematic classification of impact assessment research designs shown in Exhibit 7-F. The designs are classified into those that are appropriate primarily for impact assessments of partial-coverage programs and those that are useful primarily for full-coverage programs. The following discussion examines each of the research designs shown in that exhibit.

Designs for Partial-Coverage Programs

Design IA: Randomized Experiments

The essential feature of true experiments is random assignment of targets to treated and untreated groups constituting, respectively, the experimental and control groups. In evaluation efforts, randomized experiments are applicable only to partial-coverage programs. Randomized experiments can vary greatly in complexity, as the following examples illustrate:

- Alarmed by a rapid rise in the number of children placed in foster care after being abused or neglected, the state of Illinois instituted a family preservation program consisting of intensive casework with families of abused and neglected children and contracted with the Chapin Hall Center for Children at the University of Chicago to evaluate its effects. Families at risk of having their children placed in foster care were randomly assigned to an experimental group who experienced the family preservation program or a control group who experienced "ordinary" child protective services, typically a much less intensive case work regimen. Both experimental and control families were tracked through repeated interviews and administrative records to ascertain subsequent foster care placement and abuse or neglect complaints (Schuerman, Rzepnicki, and Littell, 1994).

- To assess the impact of enriched preschool experience on school performance and adult functioning, in 1962 researchers randomly assigned low-socioeconomic-status three- and four-year-old children to an experimental group, who were enrolled in an intensive preschool enrichment program, and a control group, who were not enrolled. The members of both groups were studied throughout their schooling and into adulthood with the latest observations made when the participants were age 27. In their young adulthood, members of the experimental group were found to have higher incomes, more steady employ-

⬥ EXHIBIT 7-F   A Typology of Research Designs for Impact Assessment

Research Design	Intervention Assignment	Type of Controls Used	Data Collection Strategies
I. Designs for partial-coverage programs			
A. Randomized or "true" experiments	Random assignment controlled by researcher	Experimental and control groups randomly selected	Minimum data needed are after-intervention measures; typically consist of before, during, and after measures
B. Quasi-experiments			
1. Regression-discontinuity	Nonrandom but fixed and known to researcher	Selected targets compared to unselected targets, holding selection constant	Typically consists of multiple before- and after-intervention outcome measures
2. Matched controls	Nonrandom and unknown	Intervention group matched with controls selected by researcher	Typically consists of before- and after-intervention measures
3. Statistically equated controls	Nonrandom and often nonuniform	Exposed and unexposed targets compared by means of statistical controls	Before-and-after or after-only intervention outcome measures and control variables
4. Generic controls	Nonrandom	Exposed target compared with outcome measures available on general population	After-intervention outcome measures on targets plus publicly available "norms" of outcome levels in general population
II. Designs for full-coverage programs[a]			
A. Simple before-and-after studies	Nonrandom and uniform	Targets measured before and after intervention	Outcome measured on exposed targets before and after intervention
B. Cross-sectional studies for nonuniform programs	Nonrandom and nonuniform	Targets differentially exposed to intervention compared with statistical controls	After-intervention outcome measures and control variables
C. Panel studies: Several repeated measures for nonuniform programs	Nonrandom and nonuniform	Targets measured before, during, and after intervention	Repeated measures of exposure to intervention and of outcome
D. Time series: Many repeated measures	Nonrandom and uniform	Large aggregates compared before and after intervention	Many repeated before- and after-intervention outcome measures on large aggregates

a. Many of these designs are also used for impact assessments of partial-coverage programs. This use is not recommended.

ment, and fewer arrests (Schweinhart and Weikart, 1998).

The critics of Aid to Families With Dependent Children (AFDC) have maintained that the incremental payments given to poor families for each child enticed them to have additional children. The state of New Jersey introduced a "family cap" modification to its AFDC rules in 1992, which prohibited increases in payments for children born after enrollment. To test the effectiveness of this rule, a randomized experiment was started in which a control group of about 3,000 families was subject to the old AFDC rules that increased payments for additional children, and an experimental group of about 6,000 families were subject to the family-cap rules. Births and abortions occurring to both groups were followed using administrative records (Camasso, Harvey, and Jaganathan, 1996).

- The effects of an HIV prevention program in New York City were examined by randomly assigning 151 adolescents to seven sessions, three sessions, or no sessions of small group instruction and role-play. The intervention procedures involved learning cognitive-behavioral strategies, social skills, and HIV-related information. Over the subsequent three months, the evaluators tracked the number of unprotected risk acts and number of sexual partners for respondents in each group (Rotheram-Borus et al., 1998).

- To test the effectiveness of reemployment training and job search programs to help workers whose jobs had been eliminated in industrial restructuring, more than 2,000 displaced workers at several sites in Texas were randomly assigned to job search programs, to combined job search and retraining programs, or to control conditions. The workers were followed over a period of time to ascertain subsequent employment and earnings experiences (Bloom, 1990).

- The Big Brothers and Big Sisters program pairs adult volunteers with youths from single-parent households for purposes of forging a friendship through which the adult mentor can support and aid the youth. During 1991-1993, all youths who came to eight selected agencies were randomly assigned to receive a Big Brother or Big Sister mentor or go into a waiting list control group. Both groups were followed for the next 18 months and assessed with regard to use of alcohol and drugs, aggressive behavior, theft, property destruction, school grades, and school attendance (Grossman and Tierney, 1998).

The most elaborate field experiments to assess program effects are longitudinal studies consisting of a series of periodic observations of experimental and control groups extending, in some cases, over years. For example, the largest field experiments every conducted, the negative income tax studies in the late 1960s and early 1970s, all employed the same basic longitudinal design while varying in the kinds of interventions tested and the length of time over which they were given, ranging from three to ten years. One of these, the New Jersey Income Maintenance Experiment (Kershaw and Fair, 1976; Rossi and Lyall, 1976), was designed with eight experimental groups, each of which was offered a slightly different income maintenance plan, and one control group. Eligible families were randomly assigned to one of the nine groups. Each participating family was studied over a three-year period through monthly income-reporting requirements, quarterly and annual interviews, and special reviews of income tax returns. Of course, during the three-year period, the experimental group families were given cash benefits as part of the income maintenance intervention; in addition, both experimental and control families were paid fees for completing interviews.

It must be noted that large-scale field experiments generally involve testing prospective national policies and hence are concerned with generalizability to the nation as a whole. Small-scale field experiments, less concerned with national generalizability, are appropriate and, as some of the examples above demonstrate, have frequently been used to assess the effects of more localized interventions.

Most randomized experiments are designed with at least preintervention and postintervention measurement of outcome. The main reason for using both measures is to hold the starting points of targets constant in subsequent analyses of experimental effects. (There are also important statistical reasons for doing so, as is explained more fully in Chapter 8.) However, preintervention measures often are impossible to obtain. For example, prisoner rehabilitation experiments designed to affect recidivism can be based only on postintervention measures, because recidivism cannot be identified before release from prison. Similarly, intervention efforts designed to reduce the incidence of disease or accidents have undefined preintervention outcome measures. Several examples of post-only experiments are given in Chapter 8.

Design IB: Quasi-Experiments

A large class of impact assessment designs consists of nonrandomized quasi-experiments in which comparisons are made between targets who participate in a program and nonparticipants who are presumed similar to participants in critical ways. These techniques are called quasi-experimental because, although they use "experimental" and "control" groups, they lack the random assignment to conditions essential for true experiments. The following examples of quasi-experiments illustrate some of the nonrandomized controls to be discussed in this section:

• The Personal Responsibility and Work Opportunity Reconciliation Act of 1996 (PRWORA) profoundly changed public welfare, abolishing AFDC and substituting TANF. TANF is limited to five years of lifetime participation, emphasizes moving adult participants into employment, and is administered as block grants to states with wide discretion given to states to define their own programs. To monitor the effects of the program on poor families, the Urban Institute has instituted a telephone survey of some 50,000 households to be undertaken before and after the implementation of TANF that oversamples poor households and households with children. An additional survey is planned for 1999. Contrasting the findings of the two surveys provides a basis for assessing the effects of the changes from AFDC to TANF in the well-being of poor families and their children (Urban Institute, 1998).

• Births to poor women historically have been characterized by high incidences of neonate mortality, low birth weights, and high medical costs. The Special Supplemental Nutrition Program for Women, Infants, and Children (WIC), administered by the Department of Agriculture, provides supplemental food to pregnant women to help counter these adverse birth outcomes. To assess the effects of the program, more than 100,000 women who were Medicaid participants in five states during 1988 were studied. Using WIC and Medicaid records, the birth outcomes for women enrolled in WIC were compared with those who were not, statistically controlling for differences in age, education, marital status, and race of mother. Births to women enrolled in WIC were found to have a significantly higher average birth weight, lower mortality, and smaller Medicaid expenditures (Devaney, Bilheimer, and Schore, 1991).

• Using data on high school juniors and seniors gathered in a national sample of high schools in 1981, Coleman and his colleagues (Coleman, Hoffer, and Kilgore, 1981) found that students in Catholic high schools had higher achievement scores in mathematics and English than those in public schools. Using these data supplemented by a follow-up survey in 1983, and qualitative surveys conducted in a small sample of Catholic schools, Bryk and his colleagues were able to show that the advantages of Catholic high schools were due to the distinctive community climates of those schools and their uniform curricula. Furthermore, minority students enrolled in Catholic high schools did much better than their counterparts in the public schools (Bryk, Lee, and Holland, 1993).

• Success for All (SFA) is a program to improve instruction in the early grades so that all preschool and elementary students will have the skills necessary to succeed later in school. Its basic components include reading instruction, periodic assessments and regrouping for instruction, reading tutors, and family support. Students in one SFA school in Charleston, South Carolina were compared with those of another school chosen to be similar in student demographics and history of performance on district standardized tests. The scores on reading and math tests showed a positive effect for the SFA kindergarten program but inconsistent and small effects for the later grades (Jones, Gottfredson, and Gottfredson, 1997).

• A 15-week cognitive-behavioral skills training program for male spouse abusers was tested for effectiveness by comparing the 32 men who completed the program with the 36 who dropped out. Those who completed showed a lower rate of subsequent abuse than the controls (Hamberger and Hastings, 1988).

Four quasi-experimental designs are commonly used: regression-discontinuity designs, matched constructed control groups, statistically equated constructed controls, and designs using generic outcome measures as controls.

Regression-discontinuity designs. Evaluations that are based on regression-discontinuity designs come closest to the randomized experiment in ability to produce unbiased estimates of net intervention effects. Regression-discontinuity designs use a selection variable that must be strictly applied to determine placement in the intervention or control group. For instance, a *cutting point* may be defined on a pretest measure of reading ability to divide a sample into those with scores above that point and those with scores below. Those below (the poorest readers) are then given the reading program, and those above the cutting point are used as controls. The postintervention reading scores for the two groups are then compared while statistically controlling for the selection variable, leaving the groups otherwise comparable except for the intervention.

Regression-discontinuity analyses can be employed only for the assessment of programs in which the targets are selected, or can be selected, for intervention according to a sharp cutting point applied to scores on an explicit selection variable. For example, some college fellowship programs allocate awards on the basis of scores received on a standardized test (e.g., the National Merit Scholarship Competition). If the cut-off point is applied to those scores with reasonable consistency, good estimates of the net effects of receiving a fellowship can be derived by means of statistical analyses of differences in outcome measures around the cutting point, statistically adjusted for the relationship to the original selection variable.

Although this approach to studying impact is free of many of the problems associated with nonexperimental designs, its applicability is limited to those programs that can select participants on the basis of explicit, uniform, quantitative criteria. In addition, the statistical analysis required is sufficiently sophisticated that it cannot be used by persons without a relatively advanced knowledge of statistics. Chapter 9 discusses this design further; more discussion can be found in Trochim (1984) and Reichardt, Trochim, and Cappelleri (1995).

Matched "constructed" control groups. Historically, the "constructed" control approach has been the most frequently used quasi-experimental design. When two nonrandomly assigned groups are to be compared, it is generally better to use statistical controls to equate them rather than trying to match the groups case by case. However, the constructed control group might be used in circumstances where statistical control procedures cannot be undertaken because of untrained staff or unavailability of computer resources, or where insufficient data are available to support statistical controls. In the latter case, of course, the data deficiencies are also likely to make matching difficult.

Typically, in this design a group of targets is selected to receive an intervention, usually through normal program processes. To provide estimates of what their outcomes would be without intervention, the evaluator selects matching, unserved targets as controls who resemble the treated targets as much as possible in relevant ways. Relevant resemblance, in this case, refers to similarity on variables with important relationships to the selected outcome variables. The matched constructed control groups may be chosen from among existing groups, as when school classes are selected to match, in age and grade, a group of classes that are to receive a new educational program. Or they may be aggregates of individuals who are comparable to the targets receiving the intervention as when probationers receiving an intensive supervision program are matched with cases drawn from the files who did not receive that program.

Statistically equated constructed controls. A more sophisticated alternative to matching is provided by procedures that equate participants and nonparticipants by statistically "controlling" the role of variables on which they show initial differences in the analysis of outcome data. Typically, the equating is accomplished by using one of several multivariate statistical procedures, such as multiple regression, log-linear models, or analysis of covariance.

Typically, in this design a survey is undertaken of the target population or some sample of that population to identify targets who have and have not participated in a program and to obtain the data that will be used in statistically adjusting the two groups. To measure program impact, the researchers compare outcomes for participants and nonparticipants, statistically controlling for differences between the groups as identified by the control variables. Very sophisticated analyses of cross-sectional surveys, for instance, may attempt to model the processes by which participants are selected (or select themselves into programs, a topic dealt with in greater detail in Chapter 9).

Regression discontinuity, matched constructed control designs, and statistically equated constructed control designs are alternatives when the evaluator is unable to randomize. Under favorable circumstances, they have the capability of removing the selection biases resulting from uncontrolled selection so that experimental and control groups can be meaningfully compared. In this regard, therefore, they resemble true experiments. They rely much more heavily than experiments on statistical models, and the assumptions required to apply those models, however, and thus are more vulnerable to error if those models or assumptions are not adequate.

Impact assessments using matching and statistical equating designs are also susceptible to whatever errors may be made in selecting the variables that are to be taken into account (i.e., adjusted for) in the comparisons between participants and nonparticipants. If important variables that differentiate the groups in relation to their likely status on outcome variables are not included in the statistical models, or are included but in distorted form because of poor measurement, the results may be biased. Thus, differences between the experimental and control groups on outcome might be due to inadequate statistical adjustments rather than to the effects of intervention.

Generic outcome measures as controls. Generic controls usually consist of measurements purporting to represent the typical performance of untreated targets or the population from which targets are drawn. Thus, in judging the performance of schoolchildren enrolled in a new learning program, the participants' scores on a standardized achievement test may be compared to published norms for schoolchildren of that age or grade. Although generic controls are widely available for certain subjects—IQ and academic achievement, for example—ordinarily they are not easily at hand.

Furthermore, as discussed further in Chapter 9, generic controls are very often not suitable because targets are selected precisely because of the ways in which they differ from the general population on which the norms are based.

Designs for Full-Coverage Programs

Full-coverage programs present special difficulties to evaluators attempting impact assessments, because there are no unserved targets available to use as controls. As we discuss in more detail in Chapter 10, the only comparisons available to the researcher are between the same targets before and after exposure to the intervention, which are called reflexive controls, and between natural variations in such aspects as the activities, intensity, or duration of the program.

Although the designs discussed in the last section cannot be used for full-coverage programs, those discussed in this section could be employed to study programs with partial coverage. In particular, before-and-after designs without comparison or control groups are commonplace for partial-coverage programs. However, evaluators are strongly advised not to use them for that purpose. In most circumstances, the resulting impact estimates will not be credible because of the possibilities for bias resulting from various confounding effects such as maturation and secular drift.

Design IIA: Simple Before-and-After Studies

Although few designs have as much intuitive appeal as simple before-and-after studies, they are among the least valid of the impact assessment approaches. The essential feature of this design is a comparison of the same targets at two points in time, separated by a period of participation in a program. The differences between the two measurements are taken as an estimate of the net effects of the intervention. The main deficiency of such designs is that ordinarily they cannot disentangle the effects of extraneous factors from the effects of the intervention. Consequently, estimates of the intervention's net effects are dubious at best.

An additional complication is that when programs have been in place for a period of time, "before" measures normally can be gathered only by asking participating targets to reconstruct retrospectively what they were like before the intervention. In such studies, the unreliability of recall can be a serious design effect.

Design IIB: Cross-Sectional Studies for Nonuniform Programs

Although many full-coverage programs deliver a uniform intervention to all their targets, there are many in which the intervention varies. For example, all states have welfare programs, but the eligibility requirements and payment levels vary widely from state to state; indeed, the difference between payment levels in the least and most generous states is more than five magnitudes. The effects of these variations can be estimated using cross-sectional surveys that measure how much of an intervention is received (program dosage) and then contrasting measures of outcome for targets receiving different levels of intervention, perhaps with statistical controls for any important differences other than the program level.

Design IIC: Panel Studies (several repeated measures) for Nonuniform Programs

Panel studies are based on repeated measures of targets exposed to the intervention. Although panel studies appear to be a simple extension of before-and-after designs, the addition of more data collection points gives the results of these studies considerably more plausibility. The additional data at different time points, properly employed, allow the researcher to begin to specify the processes by which an intervention has impacts on targets.

This design is especially important in the study of full-coverage programs in which targets are differentially exposed to the intervention. In Chapter 10, we provide an example of how this design was used to study the impact of children's viewing of violence and aggression in television programs on their own aggressive behavior toward their classmates. Given the circumstance of almost universal television viewing among children and hence the virtual impossibility of establishing control groups who do not view TV, the best approach was to study how varying amounts of violent-TV viewing affected displays of aggression at subsequent points in time.

Design IID: Time-Series Analyses (many repeated measures)

Time-series consist of repeated measures taken on an *aggregate unit* with many data points preceding and following the point in time at which a new full-coverage intervention was introduced or an old program was substantially modified. By an aggregate unit, we mean periodic measures taken on a relatively large population or parallel samples of it, as, for example, vital statistical series (births, deaths, migrations), crime rates, and economic indicators.

Although the technical procedures involved in time-series analysis are complicated, the ideas underlying them are quite simple. The researcher analyzes the trend before an intervention was enacted to obtain a projection of what would have happened without the intervention. This projection is then compared with the actual trend after the intervention. Statistical tests are used to determine whether or not the observed postintervention trend is sufficiently different from the projection to justify the conclusion that the intervention had an effect. For example, evaluators used a time-series analysis to study the effects of introducing community policing in Houston on calls for service, crime rates, and narcotics cases by analyzing the trends in these variables before community policing began and comparing them with the trends afterward (Kessler and Duncan, 1996).

Time-series analysis is especially important for estimating the net impacts of changes in full-coverage programs, particularly those that are delivered uniformly. In many full-coverage programs, every eligible target is given the same amount of the intervention. For example, most legislation, such as criminal codes, applies uniformly to all of its targets (i.e., all residents) in a given jurisdiction. Similarly, Social Security retirement payments are uniform for all persons with the same preretirement employment records. If retirement payments or sanctions for convicted felons are changed at some point in time, the impact of those changes can be studied through time-series analyses.

Time-series designs are the strongest way of examining full-coverage programs, provided that the requirements for their use are met.

Some of the limitations of time-series analysis are detailed in Chapter 10. Perhaps the most serious limitation of time-series designs is the large number of preintervention observations needed to model preintervention trends accurately (more than 30 data points are recommended).

Indeed, a time-series analysis can be performed only if extensive before-enactment and after-enactment observations on outcome measures exist. Thus, it may be possible to study the effect of the enactment of a gun control law in a particular jurisdiction, but only if the evaluator has access to a sufficiently long-term series consisting of crime statistics that track trends in gun-related offenses over a long period of time. Of course, for many ongoing interventions such long-term measures do not exist. For example, there are no long-term, detailed time series on the incidence of certain acute diseases, making it difficult to assess the impact of Medicare or Medicaid on them. For this reason, time-series analyses are usually restricted to outcome concerns for which governmental or other groups routinely collect and publish statistics.

JUDGMENTAL APPROACHES TO IMPACT ASSESSMENT

Impact assessments using the designs outlined in Exhibit 7-F are often expensive and time-consuming. It is therefore tempting to turn to approaches that do not involve collecting new data or analyzing masses of existing data. In addition, circumstances may be such that none of the designs discussed can be used, especially when time pressures require net effect estimates within a month or two.

In this section, we discuss some of the major alternatives to the approaches presented so far. In these alternative approaches, the judgments of presumed experts, program administrators, or participants play the major roles in estimates of net impact.

Connoisseurial Impact Assessments

In connoisseurial impact assessments, an expert, or connoisseur, is employed to examine a program, usually through visits to the site of the program. The expert gathers data informally and renders a judgment. The judgment may be aided by the use of generic controls, that is, existing estimates of what the population as a whole usually experiences, or "shadow" controls, more or less educated guesses about what normal progress would be (see Chapter 10). Needless to say, connoisseurial assessments are among the shakiest of all impact assessment techniques.

Administrator Impact Assessments

Equally suspect are impact assessments that rely on the judgments of program administrators. Because of their obvious interest in making their efforts appear successful, such judgments are far from disinterested and impartial. Exhibit 7-G reports the findings of a team of evaluators who made an explicit comparison between the impressions of program staff about program impact and the results of an experimental impact assessment. Not surprisingly, staff viewed the program as having greater impact than the empirical evidence indicated.

Participants' Judgments

In the assessment of some programs, participants' judgments of program success have been used. These judgments have some validity, especially for programs in which increasing participant satisfaction is a stated goal. However, it is usually difficult, if not impossible, for participants to make judgments about net impact because they ordinarily lack appropriate knowledge for making such judgments.

The Use of Judgmental Assessments

Despite their obvious limitations, we do not mean to argue that judgmental assessments should never be used in estimating the impact of programs. In some circumstances, the evaluator can do nothing else. Although some might then advise against undertaking any assessment at all, we believe that some assessment is usually better than none. Evaluators may need to resort to judgmental designs when very limited funds are available, when no preintervention measures exist so that reflexive controls cannot be used, or when everyone is covered by a program and the program is uniform over places and time so that neither randomized nor constructed controls can be used.

QUANTITATIVE VERSUS QUALITATIVE DATA IN IMPACT ASSESSMENTS

Our discussion of research designs has so far been almost exclusively in terms of quantitative studies. Whether the data collected for an impact assessment should be qualitative or quantitative is a separate issue.

⚜ EXHIBIT 7-G Do Program Staff Have Exaggerated Impressions of Program Impact on Participants?

While evaluating drug education and prevention programs in junior high schools attended by students from high-risk neighborhoods, a team of evaluators interviewed program staff about their impressions of the programs' impacts on drug use behavior and risk factors related to drug use. On the drug use items, the overall staff response revealed some uncertainty about the impact of the programs—the majority indicated that they did not have a confident judgment about effects on youths' actual drug use. Still, rather substantial proportions said they believed that the programs had delayed clients' first use of drugs (25%-39%) and had generally prevented use of drugs by their clients (18-33%).

Staff views on the impact of the program on risk factors for drug use, however, were very positive. A majority (60%-90%) answered that the program had a distinct effect on participants' school attendance and performance, self-esteem, anger control, and peer and adult relations. Moreover, while most staff felt they had little opportunity to observe the youths' actual drug use, they did believe they were in a position to directly observe changes on these risk factors.

The impact assessment of the programs relied on self-report information gathered from program participants and control participants who attended comparable schools in the same communities. The evaluation results did not support the staff impressions about program effects. Responses from the participants showed that, relative to controls, there was little impact on their use of drugs, their attitudes toward use of drugs, or the various risk factors believed to be related to drug use.

Faced with this disparity, the evaluators considered two possibilities: Either there were program effects that the evaluation failed to detect but that were seen by staffers from their different vantage point, or there were in fact less substantial program effects than the staffers believed. Their conclusion was that the latter of these two possibilities was more likely. They found strong indications in their interviews that staff impressions were based mainly on anecdotal evidence of positive change in a few problem cases with which they were acquainted, change that may not even have been induced by the program.

Moreover, in this age group the actual rates of drug use and related problems are relatively low but staff nonetheless believed that the client population was at great risk for problematic behavior. The staff's faith in the efficacy of the program, therefore, might lead them to believe that these low rates were the result of the program's efforts. The evaluators noted that, in the interviews, staffers often asserted that without the ministrations of the program, many of their youthful clients would be using drugs.

SOURCE: Adapted from Steven A. Gilham, Wayne L. Lucas, and David Sivewright, "The Impact of Drug Education and Prevention Programs: Disparity Between Impressionistic and Empirical Assessments," *Evaluation Review*, 1997, 21(5):589-613.

Quantitative data are those observations that readily lend themselves to numerical representations: answers to structured questionnaires, pay records compiled by personnel offices, counts of speech interactions among co-workers, and the like. In contrast, qualitative data, such as protocols of unstructured interviews and notes from observations, tend to be less easily summarized in numerical form. Obviously, these distinctions are not hard and fast; the dividing line between the two types of data is fuzzy.

The relative advantages and disadvantages of the two types of data have been debated at length in the social science literature (Cook and Reichardt, 1979; Guba and Lincoln, 1994). Critics of quantitative data decry the dehumanizing tendencies of numerical representation, claiming that a better understanding of causal processes can be obtained from intimate acquaintance with people and their problems and the resulting qualitative observations (Guba and Lincoln, 1989; Lincoln and Guba, 1985; Patton, 1990). The advocates of quantitative data reply that qualitative data are expensive to gather on an extensive basis, are subject to misinterpretation, and usually contain information that is not uniformly collected across all cases and situations.

We cannot here resolve the debate surrounding data preferences. As we have indicated in previous chapters, qualitative observations have important roles to play in certain types of evaluative activities, particularly in the assessment of program theory and the monitoring of ongoing programs. However, it is true that qualitative procedures are difficult and expensive to use in many of the designs described in Exhibit 7-F. For example, it would be virtually impossible to meld a long-range randomized experiment with qualitative observations at any reasonable cost. Similarly, large-scale surveys or time series are not ordinarily built on qualitative observations.

In short, although in principle impact assessments of the structured variety shown in Exhibit 7-F could be conducted qualitatively, considerations of cost and human capital usu-

ally rule out such approaches. Furthermore, assessing impact in ways that are scientifically plausible and that yield relatively precise estimates of net effects requires data that are quantifiable and systematically and uniformly collected.

INFERENCE VALIDITY ISSUES IN IMPACT ASSESSMENT

The paramount purpose of an impact assessment is to arrive at valid inferences about whether a program has significant net effects of the desired sort. To accomplish this end, an impact assessment must have two characteristics: *reproducibility* and *generalizability*.

Reproducibility refers to the ability of a research design to produce findings that are robust enough that another researcher using the same design in the same setting would achieve substantially the same results. Generalizability refers to the applicability of the findings to similar situations that were not studied, for instance, similar programs in comparable settings.

Reproducibility

The reproducibility of an impact assessment is largely a function of the power of the research design, the fidelity with which the design was implemented, and the appropriateness of the statistical models used to analyze the resulting data. Impact assessments that use powerful research designs with large numbers of observations and that are analyzed correctly will tend to produce similar results whoever conducts the research. In this regard, randomized controlled experiments ordinarily can be expected to have high reproducibility, whereas impact assessments conducted with cross-sectional surveys or using expert judgments and shadow controls (see Chapter 10) can be expected to have low reproducibility.

Generalizability

In evaluation research, generalizability is as important a characteristic as reproducibility. Indeed, one classic evaluation text (Cronbach, 1982) asserts that generalizability is at least as important as any other design feature in applied social research. For example, a well-conducted impact assessment that tests a demonstration program under conditions that would not be encountered in the program's actual operation may show that the program would be effective under those special conditions, but these findings may not be applicable to realistic program circumstances. In practice, the problem of generalizability is an especially critical one in the assessment of a prospective program, because such evaluations are usually conducted with a trial version of the program administered by the researchers.

The generalizability of an impact assessment is affected by a number of factors. To begin with, the sample of target units should be an unbiased sample of the targets that will be or actually are the clients of the enacted program. It would make little sense to test a new method of teaching mathematics on classes consisting of gifted children if the program is being designed for use in average classes. Obviously, a method that produces fine results with gifted children may not work as well with children of lesser ability. Similarly, a program to help the unemployed that is tested only on unemployed white-collar workers may yield findings that are not generalizable to other types of unemployed workers.

Assessments of ongoing programs may likewise be faulty if they are based on an inappropriate sample of the population of clients. The testing of gun control measures in a state such as Massachusetts, where gun ownership in the general population is quite low, may not generalize to states such as Texas or Arizona, where levels of gun ownership are very high.

Issues of generalizability also concern the variants of the programs being tested in an impact assessment. Assessments of a test program administered by highly dedicated and skillful researchers may not be generalizable to programs administered by government workers who do not have the same levels of commitment and skill. For example, a randomized experiment run by researchers to test the effectiveness of a prospective program providing limited unemployment benefit coverage to released prisoners produced results that were quite favorable to the prospective policy. Unfortunately, replications of the experiment in Georgia and Texas that used state agencies to administer the payment program produced results considerably at variance with the earlier, experimental findings (Rossi, Berk, and Lenihan, 1980). In short, for impact assessments to be generalizable, the interventions tested must be faithful reproductions of the programs as they actually are or will be implemented.

Other aspects of impact assessments also involve issues of generalizability. Often impact assessments are made in settings that may not closely resemble those that will characterize the enacted program. If an income maintenance program is evaluated on a sample of poor clients in an economically depressed community, it may produce effects that reflect the community setting as well as the program and hence lack generalizability to other types of communities. Likewise, the results of an impact assessment of an educational program may reflect the environment of the particular school used in the evaluation.

Whether or not an impact assessment will have high generalizability is always an issue in the assessment of prospective programs. The program when enacted may have only slight resemblance to the program that was tested, or the coverage of an enacted program may emphasize clients that are different from those used in the evaluation. Changes of this sort sometimes occur because in drawing up the appropriate legislation lawmakers may seek to find a program definition that will be supported by a variety of interests, and hence incorporate features that the evaluators did not test. The best an evaluator can do is to test a range of prospective programs and hope that the enacted program will fall within the range tested.

Some commentators on evaluation design issues have suggested that there is an inherent trade-off between reproducibility and generalizability, arguing that powerful, reproducible designs often cannot be conducted at reasonable cost on a large enough scale to meet high generalizability requirements. Thus, evaluation researchers may have to choose between reproducibility and generalizability. In such cases, reproducibility has been suggested as the more appropriate goal. Other evaluation experts (Cronbach, 1982) accept the trade-off but emphasize generalizability as the more important form of validity for evaluations. Cronbach asserts that less rigorous impact assessment designs of high generalizability are more relevant for policy purposes than very rigorous designs with low generalizability.

Our own inclination is to question whether the alleged trade-off is always a constraint in the design of impact assessments. We believe that the trade-off constraint will vary with the kind of program being tested. An evaluator must assess in each case how strong the trade-off constraint is and make decisions appropriately. For example, a program that has a very robust intervention (e.g., transfer payments) need not be nearly so concerned with the generalizability of the intervention as a program of human services whose interventions are tailored to individual clients, a variety of intervention that tends to be much less robust. Similarly, reproducibility goals may be judged as more important for interventions that are controversial or that may have undesirable side effects.

Perhaps the best strategy is to envisage the assessment of prospective programs as proceeding through several stages, with the early stages stressing reproducibility and the later ones stressing generalizability. This strategy in effect presumes that it is initially important to identify programs that work under at least some conditions. Having found such programs, it is then necessary to find out whether or not they will work under the conditions normally to be encountered under enactment.

Pooling Evaluations: Meta-Analysis

In some program areas, the existing evaluation literature is so extensive that it may be possible to examine reproducibility and generalizability empirically. To the extent that evaluations of very similarly configured programs yield convergent results, reproducibility is demonstrated. To the extent that similar program effects are found over a range of program variations, types of targets, settings, sites, and the like, generalizability is demonstrated (Cook, 1993).

A systematic approach to representing and analyzing evaluation findings across studies is meta-analysis. Meta-analysis involves coding the estimates of program effects and various descriptive information about the programs and methods involved in producing those effects for each of a number of comparable studies. This information is then compiled into a database that can be analyzed in various ways. Most relevant for the present discussion is analysis of the variation in program effects across different evaluations. Such analyses can not only show the degree of convergence or divergence of findings but can examine the relationships between observed program effects and the characteristics of the programs and methods involved in the evaluations (Lipsey and Wilson, 1996).

Meta-analysis has increasingly been used to summarize and analyze findings across large numbers of evaluation studies. Lipsey and Wilson (1993) reported on 300 meta-analyses of programs based on psychological, behavioral, or educational interventions. Major meta-analyses have been conducted in such program areas as marital and family therapy (Shadish, Ragsdale, et al., 1995), prevention in mental health (Durlak and Wells, 1997), Title I educa-

tion (Borman and D'Agostino, 1996), juvenile delinquency (Lipsey, 1992), substance abuse prevention (Black, Tobler, and Sciacca, 1998), and scores of others.

CHOOSING THE RIGHT IMPACT ASSESSMENT STRATEGY

Our discussion of impact assessment designs has been built around the research model of randomized experiments and has offered that design as the most rigorous of all for yielding credible conclusions about the effects of an intervention. Nevertheless, the assessment approach to be chosen in a particular circumstance depends on a variety of contextual factors. For some types of programs, randomized experiments are simply inapplicable. In other circumstances, time, funds, and skills may preclude an experimental approach. With proper care, the other designs described in this chapter can be used effectively though with somewhat diminished confidence. In the next three chapters, we present examples of all these approaches, detailing their advantages and limitations.

SUMMARY

❖ Impact assessment is undertaken to determine whether a program has its intended effects. Such assessments may be made at any stage of program development, from preimplementation policy making through planning, design, and implementation.

❖ Underlying all impact assessment is the research model of the randomized experiment, the most convincing research design for establishing cause-and-effect relationships. The experimental model depends on a comparison of one or more experimental (intervention) groups with one or more control (nonintervention) groups. Although many impact assessments cannot make use of a strict experimental technique, all impact assessment designs compare intervention outcomes with some estimate of what has occurred or would occur in the absence of the intervention.

❖ A major task of impact assessment is to disentangle the net effects of a program from the gross effects observed. Various research designs permit researchers to estimate and sometimes counteract the influence of extraneous factors and design effects.

❖ Among the extraneous factors that can mask or enhance the apparent effects of a program are uncontrolled selection or attrition of participants and endogenous changes such as secular drift, interfering events, and maturational trends. To assess the true impact of programs, evaluators must be aware of these potential confounding factors and attempt to eliminate them or compensate for their influence.

❖ Aspects of research design that can obscure or enhance apparent net effects include stochastic effects, measurement reliability and validity, poor choice of outcome measure, the Hawthorne effect and other delivery system contaminants, missing data, and sampling bias. Careful planning of a research design can counteract the influence of most design effects.

❖ Depending on the nature of an impact assessment and the resources available, evaluators can call on a varied repertoire of design strategies to minimize the effects of extraneous factors. Different strategies are appropriate for partial- and full-coverage programs, because in full-coverage programs no untreated targets are available to use as controls.

❖ A number of design options are available for impact assessments of full- and partial-coverage programs, respectively, ranging from randomized experiments to time-series analysis. Although the various designs differ widely in their effectiveness, all can be used if proper precautions are taken.

❖ Judgmental approaches to assessment include connoiseurial assessments, administrator assessments, and judgments by program participants. Judgmental assessments are less preferable than more objective designs, but in some circumstances, they are the only impact evaluation options available.

※ Impact assessments may make use of qualitative or quantitative data. Although qualitative data are important for certain evaluative purposes, precise assessments of impact generally require carefully collected quantitative data.

※ Two key characteristics of the results of impact assessments are reproducibility and generalizability. In some situations, evaluators may need to decide which value to maximize in the research design. One approach for prospective programs is to emphasize reproducibility in the early stages of assessments and generalizability in the later stages.

※ Meta-analysis enables researchers to pool the results of many impact assessments and analyze them to explore reproducibility and generalizability empirically. The findings of meta-analyses can be useful for investigating the variability of effects among programs in particular service area and summarizing the findings of large numbers of impact evaluations.

KEY CONCEPTS FOR CHAPTER 8

Control group	A group of untreated targets that is compared with experimental groups on outcome measures in impact evaluations.
Experimental group	A group of targets to whom an intervention is delivered and whose outcome measures are compared with those of control groups.
Randomization	Assignment of potential targets to experimental and control groups on the basis of chance.

RANDOMIZED DESIGNS FOR IMPACT ASSESSMENT

This chapter describes and explains the use of randomized field experiments in impact assessments. Randomized experiments are based on comparisons between groups of targets randomly assigned either to experience some intervention or to be left "untreated." The randomized controlled experiment is the strongest research design for assessing net impacts of interventions. However, randomized experiments have their limitations, a key one being that they are applicable only to partial-coverage programs. Moreover, practical considerations of target and stakeholder cooperation, time, and costs, as well as considerations concerning human subjects, further limit their use. Nevertheless, even evaluators working in areas in which it is difficult to implement true experiments need to be familiar with them, because the logic of randomized controlled experiments is the basis for the design of all types of impact assessments and the analysis of the data from them.

This chapter provides an exposition of the basic ideas behind randomized experiments. Inasmuch as the logic of randomized experiments underlies all types of impact assessments, these ideas are important for all of the other impact assessment research designs.

UNITS OF ANALYSIS

At the outset, a note on units of analysis is important. Social programs may be designed to affect a wide variety of targets, including individuals, families, neighborhoods and communities, organizations such as schools and business firms, and political jurisdictions from counties to whole nations. In this and the next chapter, individual persons are generally used as examples of program targets to facilitate the exposition of important points. This usage should not be taken to imply that impact assessments are conducted only when persons are the intended intervention targets. The logic of impact assessment remains constant as one moves from one kind of unit to another, although the costs and difficulties of conducting field research may increase with the size and complexity of units. For instance, the confounding factors that affect individual students

Dawn Blasko, Ph.D.

also influence students in classes; hence, whether one works with individual students or classes as the targets of an educational intervention, the same formal design considerations apply. Of course, the scale of field operations is considerably increased as one shifts from students to classes as targets. The samples in the two cases are composed of students and classes, respectively; however, gathering data on a sample of 200 student units is usually easier and considerably less costly than accumulating similar data on the same number of class units.

The choice of units of analysis is determined by the nature of the intervention and the target units to which it is delivered. A program designed to affect communities through block grants to local municipalities requires that the units studied be municipalities. An impact assessment of block grants that is conducted by contrasting two municipalities has a sample size of two—completely inadequate for many statistical purposes, even though observations may be made on large numbers of individuals within each of the two communities.

The evaluator attempting to design an impact assessment should begin by identifying the units designated as the targets of the intervention in question and hence to be specified as units of analysis. In most cases, defining the units of analysis presents no ambiguity; in other cases, the evaluator may need to carefully appraise the intentions of program designers. In still other cases, interventions may be addressed to more than one type of targets: A housing subsidy program, for example, may be designed to upgrade both the dwellings of individual poor families and the housing stocks of local communities. Here the evaluator may wish to design an impact assessment that consists of samples of individual households within samples of local communities, a design

that is intended to estimate the net impacts of the program on individual households and also on the housing stocks of local communities.

EXPERIMENTS AS AN IMPACT ASSESSMENT STRATEGY

As we noted in Chapter 7, randomized experiments and other comparative designs can only be employed to assess the impacts of partial-coverage programs. Partial-coverage programs are those that either are to be tested on a trial basis or, for whatever reasons, are reaching only a portion of the eligible target population. Only in these circumstances is it possible to make appropriate comparisons between persons who are receiving the intervention and comparable persons who are not.

The Concept of Control and Experimental Groups

The net outcomes of an intervention can be conceptualized as the difference between persons who have participated in the program (the experimental group or groups) and *comparable* persons who have not (the control or comparison groups). If perfect comparability is achieved, the same extraneous confounding factors will be present in both groups; overall, both would be subject to the same degree to endogenous changes such as secular drift and the other extraneous confounding factors discussed in Chapter 7. Hence, if the two groups are perfectly comparable, the only differences between them will be caused by the intervention itself and by design effects, of which stochastic effects are the most important. Depending on the ways in which data are collected from the experimental and control groups, some design effects may be identical for the two groups. Stochastic effects, however, always cause differences to appear between the groups.

On the basis of the formula developed in the last chapter, a project's net effects can be expressed in terms of intervention and control groups as follows:

$$
\begin{bmatrix} \text{Net} \\ \text{effect} \end{bmatrix} = \begin{bmatrix} \text{Gross} \\ \text{outcome} \\ \text{for an} \\ \text{intervention} \\ \text{group} \end{bmatrix} - \begin{bmatrix} \text{Gross} \\ \text{outcome} \\ \text{for a} \\ \text{comparable} \\ \text{control group} \end{bmatrix} \pm \begin{bmatrix} \text{Design} \\ \text{effects and} \\ \text{stochastic} \\ \text{error} \end{bmatrix}
$$

A critical element in estimating net effects is identifying and selecting comparable experimental and control groups. Comparability between experimental and control groups means, in ideal terms, that the experimental and control groups are identical except for their participation or nonparticipation in the program under evaluation. More specifically, comparability requires the following:

Identical composition: Experimental and control groups contain the same mixes of persons or other units in terms of their program-related and outcome-related characteristics.

Identical predispositions: Experimental and control groups are equally disposed toward the project and equally likely, without intervention, to attain any given outcome status; in other words, selection effects should be identical in both groups.

Identical experiences: Over the time of observation, experimental and control groups experience the same time-related processes: maturation, secular drifts, interfering events, and so on.

Implementing Control Group Evaluations

Although perfect comparability could theoretically be achieved by matching each target in an experimental group with an identical target in a control group, this is clearly impossible in program evaluations. No two individuals, families, or other units are identical in all respects. An experimental biologist might attempt to achieve comparability in experiments by using animals from the same litter, but such matching is not possible for the evaluator, because even identical adult twins are not identical in their lifetime experiences and certainly are not available in sufficient numbers to be the sole basis for impact assessment.

Fortunately, one-to-one comparability is not necessary. It is only necessary for experimental and control groups to be identical in aggregate terms and in respects that are relevant to the intended effects of the program being evaluated. It may not matter at all for an impact evaluation that experimental and control group members differ in place of birth or vary slightly in age, as long as such differences do not influence the outcome variables. On the other hand, differences between experimental and control groups that are related to their assignment to their respective conditions are both relevant and especially important. Any characteristic that is related both to placement as an experimental or a control and to the intended outcome of the intervention can cause errors in estimates of net effect.

One of the important implications of these observations is that impact assessments require more than just a few cases. The larger the number of units studied (given the methods of selection we will discuss), the more likely experimental and control groups are to be statistically equivalent. Studies in which only one or a few units are in each group rarely, if ever, suffice for impact assessments because the odds are that any division of a small number of units will result in differences between them. (Important exceptions to this statement will be discussed in Chapter 9.)

For interventions that are likely to have small or variable effects, both experimental and control groups must be quite large. For example, in the Transitional Aid to Released Prisoners (TARP) experiments testing the impact of unemployment insurance eligibility on recidivism among ex-felons, the experimental groups contained close to 1,500 and the control groups nearly 2,500 ex-felons (Rossi, Berk, and Lenihan, 1980; see also Exhibits 8-E and 8-G). On the basis of previous evaluation evidence, it was expected that the intervention's effects would be small and quite variable from individual to individual so a large sample size was necessary to provide adequate statistical power. Conversely, if very large effects are produced by an intervention, they can be detected with a much smaller number of targets in the experimental and control groups.

Although we have so far characterized control groups as consisting of targets who receive no intervention, this is not always the case. More often, targets in control groups receive existing programs or alternative interventions. For example, the control group in an evaluation testing the effectiveness of a nutrition program may consist of persons who are following a variety of nutritional practices, some of their own devising and others directed by their doctors. What this means is that the impact of a program is estimated relative to whatever mix of interventions is experienced by the control targets.

There are basically four approaches to configuring comparable control and experimental groups. First, there is the randomized experiment method (Boruch, 1997), discussed in this chapter. Second, participants in programs may be contrasted with nonparticipants who have been selected for comparability in important respects—the nonrandomized comparison groups method. Third, participants may be compared with nonparticipants while controlling statistically for measured differences between participants and nonparticipants—the statistical controls method. Finally, one may pursue a mixed strategy in which randomized or nonrandomized controls and statistical controls are used together. The last three approaches are discussed in Chapter 9.

We should note that some evaluators distinguish between the terms *control group* and *comparison group*, the former denoting a group formed through random allocation of targets and the latter a group assembled nonrandomly. We do not follow this usage in most of this chapter because, in practice, the distinction is often only a matter of degree. Hence, we will use the term control group to refer to both control and comparison groups, except in discussions in which the distinction is important.

For the sake of convenience in exposition, the next few sections discuss randomized experimental designs in which only one intervention is being tested for impact. However, an important variation of the experimental design consists of comparing two or more programs in a systematic way. In this case, there may be several experimental groups—for example, a number of groups that are each following a particular nutritional regimen—with the net effects of each estimated relative to the others being tested. The designs to be discussed in this chapter can easily be extended to involve the simultaneous testing of several alternative interventions (or combinations of interventions). Indeed, there is much to be gained in the way of useful information for policymakers and project managers if evaluations of several interventions are undertaken comparatively, so that a given intervention is compared not only to a control condition in which no intervention is made but also to alternative interventions. Multiple-intervention impact assessments provide more information on such issues as how best to modify interventions, alone or in combination, to maximize effects at a given level of funding. These complex designs are discussed in more detail later in the chapter.

Using Randomization to Establish Comparability

The best way to achieve comparability between experimental and control groups is to randomly allocate members of a target population to the two groups, allowing chance to decide whether a person (or other unit) is offered a program or is left untreated. It is important to note that "random" in this sense does not mean haphazard or capricious. On the contrary, randomly allocating targets to experimental and control groups requires taking extreme care to ensure that every unit in a target population has the same chance as any other to be selected for either group. This requires the application of some explicit chance-based procedure to the assignment process, for example, a random number table, roulette wheel, roll of dice, or the like.

Because the resulting experimental and control groups differ from one another only by chance, whatever influences may be competing with an intervention to produce outcomes are present in both groups to the same extent, except for chance fluctuations. For example, because of randomization, persons who would be more likely to seek out the program if it were offered to them on a free-choice basis are equally likely to be in the experimental as in the control group. Hence, both groups should have the same proportion of persons favorably predisposed to the intervention. The confounding factor of self-selection, therefore, cannot affect whatever outcome differences are observed between the groups because it has not influenced which group the targets are actually assigned to.

Of course, even though target units are assigned randomly, the experimental and control groups will never be exactly comparable. For example, by chance more women may end up in the control group than in the experimental group. But if the random assignment were made over and over, these fluctuations would average out to zero. The expected proportion of times that a difference of any given size on any given characteristic will be found in a long series of randomizations can be calculated from appropriate statistical models. Any given difference in outcome among randomized experimental and control groups, therefore, can be compared to what is expected on the basis of chance (i.e., the randomization process). Statistical testing thus lets a judgment be made as to whether a specific difference is likely to have occurred simply by chance or whether it is unlikely by chance and, hence, more likely represents the effect of the intervention. Because the intervention in a well-run experiment is the only difference other than chance between experimental and control groups, such judgments become the basis for discerning the existence of a net effect. The statistical procedures for making such calculations are quite straightforward and may be found in any text dealing with statistical inference.

Randomization Is Not Random Sampling

It is important not to confuse *randomization* (i.e., random assignment), in the sense used here, with *random sampling*. Whereas randomization means taking a set of units and assigning each unit to an experimental or control group by means of some randomizing procedure, random sampling consists of *selecting* units in an unbiased manner to form a representative sample from a population. Thus, researchers might use random sampling to select a representative group for study from a target population and then use random assignment to allocate each member of the sample to experimental or control conditions. Although the use of random samples to form a set of targets that is then randomized to form experimental and control groups is a highly recommended procedure, many randomized experiments are conducted using sets of targets that have not been selected by random sampling (i.e., that do not necessarily represent a given population). This latter procedure, of course, may not be a sensible course to follow because of the potential loss of generalizability.

Randomization Procedures

Randomization is technically easy to accomplish. Tables of random numbers are included in most elementary statistics or sampling textbooks. Larger tables of random numbers are also available in published form. Many computer statistical packages contain subroutines that generate random numbers.

Even some of the better hand calculators have random-number generators built into them. Flipping coins or rolling (fair) dice are also effective ways of randomizing (see Boruch, 1997, and Boruch and Wothke, 1985, for discussions of how to implement randomization).

The Logic of Randomized Experiments

A typical randomized experimental design can be represented by the following modification of our basic impact assessment formula:

$$\text{Net effects} = \begin{bmatrix} \text{Scores on} \\ \text{postintervention} \\ \text{outcome} \\ \text{measures for} \\ \text{randomized} \\ \text{experimental} \\ \text{group} \end{bmatrix} - \begin{bmatrix} \text{Scores on} \\ \text{postintervention} \\ \text{outcome} \\ \text{measures for} \\ \text{randomized} \\ \text{control} \\ \text{(unexposed)} \\ \text{group} \end{bmatrix} \pm \begin{bmatrix} \text{Design} \\ \text{effects and} \\ \text{stochastic} \\ \text{error} \end{bmatrix}$$

Note that this representation assumes only postintervention measurement on outcome measures. Later in this chapter we consider what is to be gained or lost by employing after-only measures versus having measures before and after an intervention.

Exhibit 8-A presents a schematic view of a simple before-and-after randomized controlled experiment, indicating the logic behind the estimates of net effects that can be computed. Of course, the differences between the experimental and control groups, $E - C$, necessarily contain the stochastic effects described in Chapter 7. Hence, it would be necessary to apply tests of statistical inference to judge whether, in any particular case, the value of $E - C$ is likely to be due to stochastic error. Conventional statistical tests for before-and-after experiments include t tests, analysis of variance, and analysis of covariance (with the pretest as the covariate).

EXHIBIT 8-A   Schematic Representation of a Randomized Experiment

| | Outcome Measures | | |
	Before Program	After Program	Difference
Experimental group	E1	E2	E = E2 − E1
Control group	C1	C2	C = C2 − C1

Net effects of program = E − C, where

E1, C1 = measures of outcome variable before the program is instituted, for experimental and control groups, respectively

E2, C2 = measures of outcome variable after program is completed, for experimental and control groups, respectively

E, C = gross outcomes for experimental and control groups, respectively

Note that the schematic presentation in Exhibit 8-A defines effects as differences between before- and after-intervention measures of outcome. As we have mentioned earlier, for some types of outcomes, a preintervention measure is not possible to define. There are statistical advantages to having both before and after measures, however, and estimates of effects can be more precise when before measures are used to hold constant each individual target's starting point prior to the intervention. The critical measurements, of course, are the postintervention outcome measures for both experimentals and controls.

Examples of Randomized Experiments in Impact Assessment

Exhibit 8-B describes a randomized experiment to test the effectiveness of an intervention to change the poor eating habits of schoolchildren. Several of the experiment's features are relevant here. First, note that schools were the unit of analysis and, correspondingly, entire schools were assigned to either the experimental or control conditions. Second, note that a number of output measures were employed,

covering the multiple nutritional objectives of the intervention. It is also important that statistical tests were used to aid in judging whether the net effects, in this case the experimental group's lower intake of overall calories and calories from fat, were simply a chance difference.

Exhibit 8-C describes a randomized experiment testing the effectiveness of case management provided by former psychiatric patients relative to that provided by the usual mental health personnel. This example illustrates the use of experimental design to compare the effects of a service innovation with customary service. It thus does not address the question of whether case management has effects relative to a control condition of no case management but, rather, evaluates whether a different approach would have better effects than current practice. Another interesting aspect of this impact assessment is the sample of clients who participated in the experiment. Although a representative group of clients eligible for case management was recruited, 25% declined to participate (which, of course, is their right), leaving some question as to whether the results of this experiment can be generalized to all eligible clients. This is rather typical of service

▒ EXHIBIT 8-B   CATCH: A Field Experiment on a Demonstration Program to Change the Dietary Habits of Schoolchildren

According to the Recommended Dietary Allowances, Americans on average consume too many calories derived from fats, especially unsaturated fats, and have diets too high in sodium. These dietary patterns are related to high incidences of coronary diseases and obesity. The Heart, Lung and Blood Institute, therefore, sponsored a randomized field experiment of an intervention designed to bring about better nutritional intake among school children, the Child and Adolescent Trial for Cardiovascular Health (CATCH).

CATCH was a randomized controlled field trial in which the basic units were 96 elementary schools in California, Louisiana, Minnesota, and Texas, with 56 randomly assigned to be intervention sites and 40 to be controls. The intervention program included training sessions for the food service staffs informing them of the rationale for nutritionally balanced school menus and providing recipes and menus that would achieve that goal. Training sessions on nutrition and exercise were given to teachers, and school administrations were persuaded to make changes in the physical education curriculum for students. In addition, efforts were made to reach the parents of participating students with nutritional information.

An analysis of the lunches served in the intervention and control schools showed that by the end of the three-year trial, the total calories provided in lunch meals declined in the intervention schools whereas there was a slight increase in the control schools, with a statistically significant difference between the two. Similar statistically significant differences favoring intervention schools were found with respect to the percentage of calories obtained from total fat and saturated fat. On the downside, there were no decreases in the cholesterol or sodium content of meals served in the intervention schools.

Importantly, the researchers found that participation in the school lunch program did not decline in the intervention schools, nor was participation lower than in the control schools. At baseline the participation rates were 72% for the intervention schools and 74% for the control schools; at the end of the experiment the rates were 70% and 74%, respectively.

Measured by 24-hour dietary intake interviews with children at baseline and at the 1994 follow-up, children in the intervention schools were significantly lower than children in control schools in total food intake, calories derived from fat and saturated fat, but no different with respect to intake of cholesterol or sodium. Because these measures include all food over a 24-hour period, they demonstrate changes in food patterns in other meals as well as school lunches. On the negative side, there was no significant lowering of the cholesterol levels in the blood of the students in intervention schools.

The CATCH study is strong evidence that the nutritional content of school lunches can be changed by relatively modest interventions with food service personnel, bolstered by nutrition education for the children. Whether both are essential to achieve change unfortunately is unknown.

SOURCE: Adapted from R. V. Luepker, C. L. Perry, S. M. McKinlay, P. R. Nader, G. S. Parcel, E. J. Stone, L. S. Webber, J. P. Elder, H. A. Feldman, C. C. Johnson, S. H. Kelder, and M. Wu, "Outcomes of a Field Trial to Improve Children's Dietary Patterns and Physical Activity: The Child and Adolescent Trial for Cardiovascular Health (CATCH)," *Journal of the American Medical Association* 275 (March 1996): 768-776.

EXHIBIT 8-C   Assessing the Incremental Effects of a Service Innovation

A community mental health center in Philadelphia customarily provides intensive case management to clients diagnosed with a major mental illness or having a significant treatment history. Case managers employ an assertive community treatment (ACT) model and assist clients with various problems and services including housing, rehabilitation, and social activities. The case management teams are composed of trained mental health personnel working under the direction of a case manager supervisor.

In light of recent trends toward consumer-delivered mental health services, that is, services provided by persons who have themselves been mentally ill and received treatment, the community mental health center became interested in the possibility that consumers might be more effective case managers than nonconsumers. Former patients might have a deeper understanding of mental illness because of their own experience and may establish a better empathic bond with patients, both of which could result in more appropriate service plans.

To investigate the effects of consumer case management relative to the mental health center's customary case management, a team of evaluators conducted a randomized field experiment. Initially, 128 eligible clients were recruited to participate in the study; 32 declined and the remaining 96 gave written consent and were randomly assigned to either the usual case management or the experimental team. The experimental team consisted of mental health service

consumers operating as part of a local consumer-run advocacy and service organization.

Data were collected through interviews and standardized scales at baseline and one month and then one year after assignment to case management. The measures included social outcomes (housing, arrests, income, employment, social networks) and clinical outcomes (symptoms, level of functioning, hospitalizations, emergency room visits, medication attitudes and compliance, satisfaction with treatment, quality of life). The sample size and statistical analysis were planned to have sufficient statistical power to detect meaningful differences, with especial attention to the possibility that there would be no meaningful differences, which would be an important finding for a comparison of this sort. Of the 96 participants, 94 continued receiving services for the duration of study and 91 of them were located and interviewed at the one-year follow-up.

No statistically significant differences were found on any outcome measures except that the consumer case management team clients reported somewhat less satisfaction with treatment and less contact with their families. While these two unfavorable findings were judged to warrant further investigation, the evaluators concluded on the basis of the similarity in the major outcomes that mental health consumers were capable of being equally competent case managers as nonconsumers in this particular service model. Moreover, this approach would provide relevant employment opportunities for former psychiatric patients.

SOURCE: Adapted from Phyllis Solomon and Jeffrey Draine, "One-Year Outcomes of a Randomized Trial of Consumer Case Management," *Evaluation and Program Planning*, 1995, 18(2): 117-127.

settings—there are almost always a variety of reasons why some appropriate participants in an impact assessment cannot or will not be included. Even when included, of course, there may be other reasons why final outcome measures cannot be obtained. In the experiment described in Exhibit 8-C, the evaluators were fortunate that only 2 of 96 original participants were lost to the study because they failed to complete service and only 3 were lost because they could not be located at the one-year follow-up.

Exhibit 8-D describes one of the largest and best known field experiments relating to national policy ever conducted in the evaluation field. This was an experiment to determine whether providing income support payments to poor, intact (i.e., two-spouse) families would cause them to reduce the amount of their paid employment, that is, create a work disincentive. The study was the first of a series of five, each varying slightly from the others, run by the Office of Economic Opportunity and the Department of Health, Education and Welfare (later, its successor agency, the Department of Health and Human Services) to test various forms of guaranteed income and their effects on the work efforts of poor and near-poor persons. All five of the experiments were run over relatively long periods, the longest involving more than five years; all had difficulties maintaining the cooperation of the initial groups of families involved; and all found that the income payments created a slight work disincentive, especially for teenagers and mothers with young children—those in the secondary labor force (Mathematica Policy Research, 1983; Robins et al., 1980; Rossi and Lyall, 1976; SRI International, 1983).

Despite their power to sustain the most valid conclusions about the net effects of inter-ventions, randomized experiments account for a relatively small proportion of impact assessments. Political and ethical considerations may rule out randomization, particularly when interventions simply cannot be withheld without violating ethical or legal rules (although the idea of experimentation does not preclude delivering some alternative intervention to a control group). Despite the obstacles to randomized evaluation designs, there is a clear consensus on their desirability for impact assessment (Cook and Campbell, 1979; Cronbach, 1982; Mohr, 1995) and a growing literature on how to enhance the chances of success (Boruch, 1997; Dennis, 1990; Dunford, 1990). Moreover, many examples of the application of experimental design to impact assessment, such as those cited in this chapter, demonstrate their feasibility under appropriate circumstances.

Nonetheless, randomized field experiments are challenging to implement; costly if done on a large scale; and demanding with regard to the time, expertise, and cooperation of participants and service providers that are required. They are thus generally conducted only when circumstances are especially favorable, for instance, when a scarce service can be allocated by a lottery or equally attractive program variations can be randomly assigned, or when the impact question has especial importance for policy. Dennis and Boruch (1989) identified five threshold conditions that should be met before a randomized field experiment is undertaken (summarized by Dennis, 1990):

■ The present practice must need improvement.

■ The efficacy of the proposed intervention must be uncertain under field conditions.

※ EXHIBIT 8-D The New Jersey-Pennsylvania Income Maintenance Experiment

In the late 1960s, when federal officials concerned with poverty began to consider shifting welfare policy to provide some sort of guaranteed annual income for all families, the Office of Economic Opportunity (OEO) launched a large-scale field experiment to test one of the crucial issues in such a program: the prediction of economic theory that such supplementary income payments to poor families would be a work disincentive.

The experiment was started in 1968 and carried on for three years, administered by Mathematica, Inc., a research firm in Princeton, New Jersey, and the Institute for Research on Poverty of the University of Wisconsin. The target population was intact families with income below 150% of the poverty level whose male heads were between 18 and 58. The eight experimental conditions consisted of various combinations of income guarantees, pegged to what was then the current "poverty level" and the rates at which payments were taxed (adjusted to earnings received by the families). For example, in one of the conditions a family received a guaranteed income of 125% of the then-current poverty level, if no one in the family had any earnings. If their plan then had a tax rate of 50% and someone in the family received earned income, their payments were reduced 50 cents for each dollar earned. Other conditions consisted of tax rates that ranged from 30% to 70% and guarantee levels that varied from 50% to 125% of the

poverty line. A control group consisted of families who did not receive any payments.

The experiment was conducted in four communities in New Jersey and one in Pennsylvania. A large household survey was first undertaken to identify eligible families, then those families were invited to participate. If they agreed, the families were randomly allocated to one of the experimental groups or to the control group. Families in the experimental groups reported their earnings each month and, if eligible for transfer payments, a check was mailed to them.

The participating families were interviewed in great detail prior to enrollment in the program and at the end of each quarter over the three years of the experiment. Among other things, these interviews collected data on employment, earnings, consumption, health, and various social-psychological indicators. The researchers then analyzed the data along with the monthly earnings reports to determine whether those receiving payments diminished their work efforts (as measured in hours of work) in relation to comparable families in the control groups.

Although about 1,300 families were initially recruited, by the end of the experiment 22% had discontinued their cooperation. Others had missed one or more interviews or had dropped out of the experiment for varying periods. Fewer than 700 remained for analysis of the continuous participants. The findings were that experimental group families decreased their work effort by about 5%.

SOURCE: Adapted from D. Kershaw and J. Fair, *The New Jersey Income-Maintenance Experiment,* vol. 1 (New York: Academic Press, 1976).

- There should be no simpler alternatives for evaluating the intervention.

- The results must be potentially important for policy.

■ The design must be able to meet the ethical standards of both the researchers and the service providers.

Some of the conditions that facilitate or impede the use of randomized experiments to assess impact are discussed in a later section of this chapter.

Near Experiments: Conditions of "Ignorability"

The desirable feature of randomization is that it is a sure way of achieving unbiased allocation of eligible targets to the experimental and control groups. Unbiased allocation requires that the probability of ending up in either the experimental or control group is identical for all participants in the study. Correspondingly, biased assignment occurs when individuals with certain characteristics have a higher probability than others of being selected for either group. In constituting experimental and control groups from a population with equal proportions of men and women, for example, an assignment procedure would be biased if members of one sex or the other were more likely to be in either the experimental or the control group.

There are several alternative ways of obtaining experimental and control groups that are close to those resulting from randomization, although each has some drawbacks. In addition, there are conditions under which it can be argued that groups have differences, but that such differences can be ignored as potential producers of bias.

Perhaps the most commonly used substitute for randomization is systematic assignment from serialized lists, a procedure that can often accomplish the same end as randomiza-

tion, provided that the lists are not ordered in some way that results in a bias. For example, in allocating high school students to experimental and control groups, it might be sensible to place all those with odd ID numbers into the experimental group and all those with even ID numbers into a control group. As long as odd and even numbers were not originally assigned to differentiate among students according to some characteristic, the result will be statistically the same as random assignment. Of course, if the school has given odd ID numbers to female students and even numbers to males, this systematic bias would create experimental and control groups that each contained only one sex. Before using such systematic selection procedures, therefore, researchers must establish how the agency that generated the list accomplished serialization and judge whether the numbering process might produce unwanted systematic differences between various sections of the list.

Sometimes ordered lists of targets have subtle biases that are difficult to detect. For example, an alphabetized list might tempt one to assign, say, all persons whose last names begin with D to the experimental group and those whose last names begin with H to the control group. In a New England city, this would result in an ethnically biased selection—many names of French Canadian origin begin with D (e.g., DeFleur), whereas very few Hispanic names begin with H. Similarly, numbered lists may contain age biases if numbers are assigned sequentially. The federal government assigns Social Security numbers sequentially, for instance, so that individuals with lower numbers are generally older than those with higher numbers.

There are also circumstances in which biased allocation may be "ignorable" (Rog, 1994; Rosenbaum and Rubin, 1983). Occasionally, unplanned interventions occur in situations that can be regarded as unbiased and hence equivalent to a randomized experiment. An example from a study of flood effects on the growth of housing and population stocks illustrates a plausibly valid "natural" experiment. Hydrologic engineers have marked off the flood plains of most American rivers into regions characterized by the expected frequency of floods. Thus, the "ten-year flood plain" includes those regions in a river basin in which floods are expected to occur, on average, once in every decade. Although each year the areas within the ten-year flood plain have a one-in-ten chance of experiencing a flood, whether or not a flood occurs in a particular year in a particular spot can be regarded as a random event. Neighborhoods built on flood plains can thus be divided into "experimentals" (those in which floods actually occurred during, say, a two-year period) and "controls" (those in which no floods occurred). Because both sets of neighborhoods had the same probability of experiencing floods, they constitute natural experimental and control groups. Growth trends in the two groups can then be compared to estimate the impact of floods on the growth of housing stocks and population.

Of course, floods are events that can be understood as the effects of known natural processes and thus are not truly random events. But because those processes do not "select" some particular flood plains more than others, floods may be regarded for our purposes as virtually random events. In addition, our knowledge of the processes that create floods gives no indication that the kinds of housing and population located in the flood plains affect the chances of floods occurring in those places over any given period of time. Note, however, that the validity of this approach depends heavily on whether the hydrologists have correctly

marked out the ten-year flood plain. Because such maps are made partly on the basis of historical experience and partly on the basis of knowledge about the behavior of rivers in various terrains, the flood plain contours are subject to error.

Another circumstance frequently encountered involves using overcapacity targets as controls. For example, in a Minneapolis test of the effectiveness of a program to keep children in their families who might be placed in foster care, those children were placed in a no-intervention control group who could not be served by the family counseling program because the counseling agency was at full capacity at the time of referral (AuClaire and Schwartz, 1986). The "ignorability" assumption made was that when a child was referred had little or nothing to do with the child's prospects for reconciliation with his or her family.

Whether natural or unplanned events in fact are unbiased or have biases that can be safely ignored must be judged with close scrutiny of the circumstances of those events. Indeed, most circumstances that often are called "natural experiments" cannot be regarded as such in the strict sense of the term. If there is any reason to suspect that the events in question were likely to affect units (persons, communities, etc.) with certain characteristics more than others, then the conditions for a virtual experiment do not exist unless those characteristics can be confidently declared irrelevant to the intervention and outcomes to be studied. For example, communities that have fluoridated their water supplies cannot be regarded as an experimental group to be contrasted with those who have not, because communities that adopt fluoridation likely have distinctive characteristics, for example, lower average age and more progressive government, that cannot be regarded as irrelevant and represent bias in the sense used here. Similarly, families that have purchased townhouses cannot be regarded as appropriate controls for those who have purchased freestanding homes, because the very act of making such purchases is an indicator of other potential differences between the two groups.

Data Collection Strategies for Randomized Experiments

Under some conditions, the outcome variable can only be measured postintervention so that no pretest is possible. A program designed to help impoverished high school students go on to college, for instance, can be judged definitively only by whether experimentals go on to college more frequently than controls, a measure that can be taken only after the intervention. Such cases aside, the general rule is that the more measurements of the outcome variables made before and after the intervention, the better the estimates of net effects will be. Multiple longitudinal measurements increase measurement reliability and provide more information on which to build estimates of net outcomes. Measures taken before an intervention provide estimates of the preexperimental states of the experimental and control groups and are useful for making adjustments for preexisting differences between the two and for measuring how much of a gain the intervention effected. For example, preintervention measures of earnings for experimentals and controls in a vocational retraining project would enable researchers to make better estimates of the degree to which earnings improve as a result of training and at the same time would offer a variable to hold constant in the analysis of outcomes.

Periodic measurements taken during the course of an intervention are also useful. Such series allow evaluators to construct useful descriptive accounts of how an intervention works over time. For instance, if a vocational retraining effort is found to produce most of its effects during the first four weeks of a six-week program, this finding might lead to the suggestion that shortening the training period would cut costs without seriously curtailing the project's effectiveness. Likewise, multiple, periodic measurements can lead to a fuller understanding of how targets react to services. Some reactions may be slow-starting and then accelerate later; others may be strong initially but soon trail off to preintervention levels. For example, motorists' response to the 55-mile-per-hour speed limit is reputed to have consisted of an initial slowing down, followed by a gradual return to higher speeds. Being able to plot reactions to interventions allows evaluators to fine-tune programs for fuller effectiveness.

Thus, there are two compelling reasons for taking many measures before, during, and after an intervention. First, the more measures taken, the higher the reliability of composite measures. Second, interventions can be expected to have their effects over time; hence, longitudinal series can allow the evaluators to examine the way the intervention works over time.

ANALYZING RANDOMIZED EXPERIMENTS

Simple Randomized Experiments

The analysis of simple randomized experiments can be quite straightforward. Conducted properly, randomization produces experimental and control groups that are statistically equivalent. Hence, a comparison of outcomes in the two groups provides estimates of net effects. A comparison of these estimates, in turn, with the chance expectation derived from a statistical model then provides a means for judging whether those effects are larger than the chance fluctuations likely to appear when there really are no differences due to the intervention. Exhibit 8-E provides an example of the analysis conducted on a simple randomized experiment. The results are analyzed first by a simple comparison between experimentals and controls and then by means of a more complex multiple regression model.

Complex Randomized Experiments

It is common for impact assessment to involve tests of several variants of an intervention or several distinct interventions in a complex design. In the New Jersey-Pennsylvania Income Maintenance experiment (Exhibit 8-D), eight variations were tested, differing from one another in the amount of income guaranteed and the tax penalties on family earnings. These variations were included in the experiment to examine the extent to which work effort depended on the degree of work disincentive believed to be embodied in different payment schemes. A critical evaluation question was whether the work response to payments would vary with (a) the amount of payment offered and (b) the extent to which earnings from work reduced those payments.

Complex experiments along these lines are especially appropriate for testing new policies, because it may not be clear in advance exactly what form a new policy should or will take. A range of program variations provides more opportunity to cover the particular policy that might be adopted and hence increases the generalizability of the impact assessment. In addition, testing variations can provide information that helps guide program construction to optimize the effects and efficiency.

Exhibit 8-F, for example, describes a field experiment conducted on welfare policy in Minnesota. Two program variants were involved in the experimental conditions, both with more generous financial benefits to welfare clients who became employed and one with mandatory employment and training activities and one without. If these two versions of the program had proved equally effective, it would clearly be more cost-effective to implement the program without the mandatory employment and training activities and their associated administrative costs. However, the largest effects were found for the combination of financial benefits and mandatory training. This information allows policymakers to consider the trade-offs between the incrementally greater effects on income and employment of the more elaborate and expensive version of the program and the smaller, but still positive effects of the lower cost version of the program.

Under some circumstances, evaluators may be concerned that the administrative procedures proposed for a new program might compromise an otherwise effective intervention. The income maintenance experiments (Exhibit 8-D), for example, were criticized for requiring monthly income reports from each of the participating families (Rossi and Lyall, 1976). Because the welfare system ordinarily does not require such frequent reports from families receiving benefits, critics argued that this amounted to a stricter "means test" than that required by ordinary welfare regulations, and hence was potentially more demeaning. Where such concerns are serious, variations in the administrative procedures can be included in the experimental design to test their effects. Had the evaluators in the income maintenance

✍ EXHIBIT 8-E   Analysis of Randomized Experiments: The Baltimore LIFE Program

The Baltimore LIFE experiment was designed to test whether small amounts of financial aid to persons released from prison would help them make the transition to civilian life and reduce the probability of their being arrested and returned to prison. The financial aid was configured to simulate unemployment insurance payments, for which most prisoners are ineligible since they cannot accumulate work credits while imprisoned.

Persons released from Maryland state prisons to return to Baltimore were randomly assigned to either an experimental or control group. Those in the experimental group were told they were eligible for 13 weekly payments of $60 as long as they were unemployed. Those in the control group were told that they were participating in a research project but were not offered payment. Researchers periodically interviewed the participants and monitored the arrest records of the Baltimore Police Department for a year beyond each prisoner's release date. The arrest records yielded the results over the postrelease year shown in Table 8-E1.

table, where the differences between the experimental and control groups in arrest rates are shown for various types of crimes. For theft crimes in the postrelease year the difference of –8.4 percentage points indicated a potential intervention effect in the desired direction. The issue then became whether 8.4 was within the range of expected chance differences, given the sample sizes (n). A variety of statistical tests are applicable to this situation, including chi-square, t tests, and analysis of variance. The researcher used a one-tailed t test, since the direction of the differences between the groups was given by the expected effects of the intervention. The results showed that a difference of –8.4 percentage points or larger would occur by chance less than five times in every hundred experiments of the same sample size (statistically significant at $p \leq .05$). The researchers concluded that the difference was large enough to be taken seriously as an indication that the intervention had its desired effect, at least for theft crimes.

TABLE 8-E1:   Arrest Rates in the First Year After Release

Arrest Charge	Experimental Group (n = 216)	Control Group (n = 216)	Difference
Theft crimes (e.g., robbery, burglary, larceny)	22.2%	30.6%	–8.4
Other serious crimes (e.g., murder, rape, assault)	19.4%	16.2%	+3.2
Minor crimes (e.g., disorderly conduct, public drinking)	7.9%	10.2%	–2.3

The findings shown in the table are known as *main effects* and constitute the simplest representation of experimental results. Since randomization has made the experimental and control groups statistically equivalent except for the intervention, the arrest rate differences between them are assumed to be due only to the intervention plus any stochastic variability.

The substantive import of the findings is summarized in the last column on the right of the

The remaining types of crimes did not show differences large enough to survive the *t*-test criterion. In other words, the differences between the experimental and control groups were within the range where chance fluctuations were sufficient to explain them according to the conventional statistical standards ($p > .05$).

Given these results, the next question is a practical one: Are these differences large enough in a policy sense? In other words, would it be worthwhile to adopt the LIFE intervention as a social program? Would a reduction of 8.4 percentage points in theft crimes justify the payments and accompanying administrative costs? To answer this last question, the Department of Labor conducted a cost-benefit analysis (discussed in Chapter 11 in this volume) that showed that the benefits far outweighed the costs.

A more complex and informative way of analyzing the theft crime data using multiple regression is shown in Table 8-E2. The question posed is exactly the same as in the previous analysis, but in addition, the multiple regression model takes into account the fact that many factors other than the payments might also affect arrests. The multiple regression analysis statistically controls those other factors while comparing the proportions arrested in the control and experimental groups.

over the two years of the experiment: Some prisoners were released at times when it was easy to get jobs, whereas others were released at less fortunate times. Adding the unemployment rate at time of release to the analysis reduces the variation among individuals due to that factor and thereby purifies estimates of the intervention effect.

Note that all the variables added to the multiple regression analysis of Table 8-E2 were ones that were known from previous research to affect recidivism or chances of finding employment. The addition of these variables strengthened the findings considerably. Each coefficient indicates the change in the probability of postrelease arrest associated with each unit of the independent variable in question. Thus, the −.083 associated with being in the experimental group means that the intervention reduced the arrest rate for theft crimes by 8.3 percentage points. This corresponds

TABLE 8-E2: Multiple Regression Analysis of Arrests for Theft Crimes

Independent Variable	Regression Coefficient (b)	Standard Error of b
Membership in experimental group	−.083*	.041
Unemployment rate when released	.041*	.022
Weeks worked the quarter after release	−.006	.005
Age at release	−.009*	.004
Age at first arrest	−.010*	.006
Prior theft arrests	.028*	.008
Race	.056	.064
Education	−.025	.022
Prior work experience	−.009	.008
Married	−.074	.065
Paroled	−.025	.051
Intercept	.263	.185

$R^2 = .094*$
$N = 432$

*Indicates significance at $p \le .05$.

In effect, comparisons are made between experimentals and controls within each level of the other variables used in the analysis. For example, the unemployment rate in Baltimore fluctuated

closely to what was shown in Table 8-E1. However, because of the statistical control of the other variables in the analysis, the chance expectation of a coefficient that large or larger is much reduced

(continued)

▧ **EXHIBIT 8-E** Continued

to only two times in every hundred experiments. Hence the multiple regression results provide more precise estimates of net effects. They also tell us that the unemployment rate at time of release, ages at release and first arrest, and prior theft arrests are factors that have a significant influence on the rate of arrest for these ex-prisoners and, hence, affect program outcome.

SOURCE: Adapted from P. H. Rossi, R. A. Berk, and K. J. Lenihan, *Money, Work and Crime: Some Experimental Evidence* New (York: Academic Press, 1980).

▧ **EXHIBIT 8-F** Making Welfare Work and Work Pay: The Minnesota Family Investment Program

A frequent criticism of the Aid to Families With Dependent Children (AFDC) program is that it does not encourage recipients to leave the welfare rolls and seek employment because AFDC payments are typically more than could be earned in low-wage employment. The state of Minnesota received a waiver from the federal Department of Health and Human Services to conduct an experiment that would encourage AFDC clients to seek employment and allow them to receive greater income than AFDC would allow if they succeeded. The main modification embodied in the Minnesota Family Investment Program (MFIP) increased AFDC benefits by 20% if participants became employed and reduced their benefits by only one dollar for every three dollars earned through employment. A child care allowance was also provided so that those employed could obtain child care while working. This meant that AFDC recipients who became employed under this program had more income than they would have received under AFDC.

Over the period 1994 to 1996, some 15,000 AFDC recipients in a number of Minnesota counties were randomly assigned to one of three conditions: (1) An MFIP experimental group receiving more generous benefits and mandatory participation in employment and training activities; (2) an MFIP experimental group receiving only the more generous benefits and not the mandatory employment and training; and (3) a control group who continued to receive the old AFDC benefits and services. All three groups were monitored through administrative data and repeated surveys. The outcome measures included employment, earnings, and participation in education and training services.

An interim report covering 18 months and the first 9,000 participants in the experiment reported findings indicating that the demonstration was successful. MFIP experimental families were more likely to be employed and, when employed, had larger incomes than control families. Furthermore, those in the experimental group receiving both MFIP benefits and mandatory employment and training activities were more often employed and earned more than the experimental group receiving only the MFIP benefits.

SOURCE: Cynthia Miller, Virginia Knox, Patricia Auspos, Jo Anna Hunter-Manns, and Alan Orenstein, *Making Welfare Work and Work Pay: Implementation and 18-Month Impacts of the Minnesota Family Investment Program* (New York: Manpower Demonstration Research Corporation, 1997).

experiments configured an experimental group that operated under the ordinary income-reporting rules of the welfare system, the validity of the criticisms of the monthly reporting requirement could have been examined directly.

Of course, evaluators cannot endlessly proliferate experimental interventions to test every conceivable variation of a proposed program. For the income maintenance experiments, Kershaw and Fair (1976) proposed the concept of "policy space" as the basis for determining which program variations should be subject to testing. Policy space is the set of program alternatives that is likely to be politically acceptable if found effective and then considered by policymakers for implementation. Experimental assessment of innovative program concepts, in this view, should concentrate primarily on those variations that are clearly within the policy space defined by policymakers and administrators, perhaps extending a bit beyond, but not too far. In the income maintenance experiment, for instance, families of full-time students were excluded on the grounds that Congress would be very unlikely to make that group eligible, even though their income levels may have been well below the poverty line.

Analyzing Complex Experiments

As might be expected, complex randomized experiments require correspondingly complex modes of analysis. Although a simple analysis of variance may be sufficient to obtain an estimate of overall effects, the greater number of experimental groups and the amount of descriptive information typically collected on participants allow more elaborate forms of analysis. Sophisticated multivariate analysis, for instance, can provide greater precision in estimates of net effects and permit evaluators to pursue analytical themes not ordinarily

available in simple randomized experiments. Exhibit 8-G provides an illustration of how a complex randomized experiment was analyzed through analysis of variance and causal modeling.

LIMITATIONS ON THE USE OF RANDOMIZED EXPERIMENTS

Randomized designs were initially formulated for laboratory and agricultural field research. Although their inherent logic is highly appropriate for the task of assessing the impact of social programs, they are nonetheless not applicable to all program situations. In this section, we review some of their limitations.

Programs in Early Stages of Implementation

As some of the examples in this chapter have shown, randomized experiments on demonstration programs can yield very useful information for purposes of policy and program design. However, once a program design has been adopted and implementation is under way, the impact questions randomized experiments are so good at answering are not usually appropriate to ask until the program is stable and operationally mature. In the early stages of program implementation, various features of a program often need to be changed for the sake of perfecting the intervention or its delivery. Although a randomized experiment can contrast program outcomes with those for untreated targets, the results will not be very informative if the program has changed during the course of the experiment. If the program has changed appreciably before outcomes are

⚶ **EXHIBIT 8-G**   Analyzing a Complex Randomized Experiment: The TARP Study

Based on the encouraging findings of the Baltimore LIFE experiment described in Exhibit 8-E, the Department of Labor decided to embark on a large-scale experiment that would use existing agencies in two states to administer unemployment insurance payments to ex-felons. The objectives of the proposed new program were the same: Making ex-felons eligible for unemployment insurance was intended to reduce the need for them to engage in crime to obtain income. The payments in that sense were intended to compete with illegal activities as a source of income and to provide for income during a transition period from prison life to gainful employment.

The new set of experiments, called Transitional Aid to Released Prisoners (TARP), was also more differentiated in that it included varying periods of eligibility for benefits and varying rate schedules by which payments were reduced for every dollar earned in employment ("tax rates").

The main effects of the interventions are shown in the analyses of variance in Table 8-G1. (For the sake of simplicity, only results from the Texas TARP experiment are shown.) The interventions had no effect on property arrests: The experimental and control groups differed by no more than would be expected by chance. However, the interventions had a very strong effect on the number of weeks worked during the postrelease year: Ex-felons receiving payments worked fewer weeks on the average than those in the control groups and the differences were statistically significant. In short, it seems that the payments did not compete well with crime but competed quite successfully with employment!

Overall, these results seem to indicate that the experimental interventions did not work in the ways expected and indeed produced undesirable effects. However, an analysis of variance of this sort is only the beginning of the analysis. The results suggested to the evaluators that a set of counterbalancing processes may have been at work. It is well known from the criminological literature that unemployment for ex-felons is related to an increased probability that they will be rearrested and subsequently returned to prison. Hence, the researchers postulated that the unemployment benefits created a work disincentive represented in the fewer weeks worked by participants receiving more weeks of benefits or a lower "tax rate" and that this should have the effect of increasing criminal behavior. On the other hand, the payments should have reduced the need to engage in criminal behavior to produce income. Thus, a positive effect of payments in reducing criminal activity may have been offset by the negative effects of less employment over the period of the payments so that the total effect on arrests was virtually zero.

To examine the plausibility of this "counterbalancing effects" interpretation of the findings of the experiment, a causal model was constructed, as shown in Figure 8-G1. In that model, negative coefficients are expected for the effects of payments on employment (the work disincentive) and for their effects on arrests (the expected intervention effect). The counterbalancing effect of unemployment, in turn, should show up as a negative coefficient between employment and arrest, indicating that fewer weeks of employment are associated with

※ EXHIBIT 8-G   Continued

TABLE 8-G1: Analysis of Variance of Property-Related Arrests (Texas data)

A. Property-related arrests during postrelease year

Experimental Group	Mean Number of Arrests	Percent Arrested	n
26 weeks payment, 100% tax	.27	22.3	176
13 weeks payment, 25% tax	.43	27.5	200
13 weeks payment, 100% tax	.30	23.5	200
No payments, job placement[a]	.30	20.0	200
Interviewed controls	.33	22.0	200
Uninterviewed controls[b]	.33	23.2	1,000
ANOVA F value =	1.15	.70	
p value =	.33	.63	

B. Weeks worked during postrelease year

Experimental Group	Average Number of Weeks Worked	n
26 weeks payment, 100% tax	20.8	169
13 weeks payment, 25% tax	24.6	181
13 weeks payment, 100% tax	27.1	191
No payments, job placement	29.3	197
Interviewed controls	28.3	189
ANOVA F value = 6.98		
p value = < .0001		

a. Ex-felons in this intervention group were offered special job placement services (which few took) and some help in buying tools or uniforms if required for jobs. Few payments were made.
b. Control observations made through arrest records only; hence no information on weeks worked.

more arrests. The coefficients shown in Figure 8-G1 were derived empirically from the data using a statistical technique known as three-stage least squares (more generally, structural equation modeling). As shown there, the hypothesized relationships appear in both the Texas and Georgia data.

This complex experiment, combined with sophisticated multivariate analysis, therefore, shows that the net effects of the intervention were negligible but also provides some explanation of that result. In particular, the evidence indicates that the payments functioned as expected to reduce criminal behavior but that a successful program would have to find a way to counteract the accompanying work disincentive with its negative effects.

(continued)

❧ EXHIBIT 8-G Continued

Texas Estimates

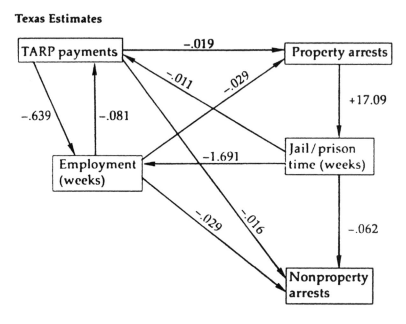

Georgia Estimates

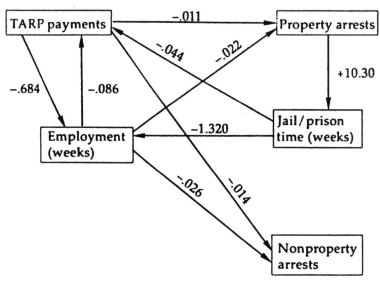

Figure 8-G1
SOURCE: Adapted from P. H. Rossi, R. A. Berk, and K. J. Lenihan, *Money, Work and Crime: Some Experimental Evidence* (New York: Academic Press, 1980).

measured on the participants, the effects of the different variants of the intervention are all mixed together in the experimental results, and there is no easy way to determine what effects are produced by any given form of the intervention.

For example, in a program that starts out providing group therapy but, in refining its services, ends up giving individual counseling, the overall results of an experiment would only indicate the effects of being in the program group relative to the control group. Because clients would not be randomly assigned to group versus individual counseling, that comparison would be contaminated by selection bias, and it would be difficult to determine the relative effectiveness of the different versions of the intervention. Moreover, if incremental program changes were adopted gradually over a period of time, it might not even be possible to establish just what conditions each participant experienced. Expensive field experiments, therefore, are best reserved for tests of firmly designed interventions that will be consistently implemented during the course of the experiment. An example of this strategy is a California experiment testing the effectiveness of a family preservation program designed to avert placement of abused or neglected children in foster or institutional homes by providing intensive services to the children and their families. A full-scale randomized experiment was started only after the agencies involved had two years of experience with running the program (Yuan, 1990).

Ethical Considerations

A frequent obstacle to the use of randomized experiments is that some stakeholders have ethical qualms about randomization, see-ing it as arbitrarily and capriciously depriving control groups of positive benefits. The reasoning of such critics generally runs as follows: If it is worth experimenting with a program (i.e., if the project seems likely to help targets), it is a positive harm to withhold potentially helpful services from those who need them. To do so is therefore unethical. The counterargument is obvious: Ordinarily, it is not known whether an intervention is effective; indeed, that is the reason for an experiment. Because researchers cannot know in advance whether an intervention will be helpful, they are not depriving the controls of something known to be beneficial.

Sometimes an intervention may present some possibility of positive harm, and decision-makers may be reluctant to authorize randomization on those grounds alone. In some utility pricing experiments, for instance, there was a good chance that household utility bills would increase in some of the experimental groups. The researchers countered this argument by promising experimental households that any such overages would be reimbursed after the study was over. Of course, this promise of reimbursement changes the character of the intervention, possibly fostering irresponsible usage of utilities.

The most compelling ethical objections generally involve the conditions of control groups. If conventional services are known to be effective for their problems, it would generally be unethical to withhold those services for the purposes of testing an alternative to conventional services. We would not, for instance, deprive schoolchildren of mathematics instruction so that they could constitute a control group in an experiment testing a new math curriculum. In such cases, however, the important question is not whether the new curriculum is better than no instruction but, rather, whether it is better than current practices. The appropriate experimental comparison, therefore, is between the new curriculum and the control condition of current instructional practice with no student going without credible instruction.

When program resources are scarce and fall well short of demand, random assignment to control conditions can present an especially difficult ethical dilemma. This procedure amounts to randomly selecting those relatively few eligible targets who will receive the program services. If the intervention cannot be given to all who qualify, it can be argued that randomization is an equitable method of deciding who is to get it, because all targets have an equal chance. And, indeed, if there is great uncertainty about the efficacy of the intervention, this may be quite acceptable. However, when service providers are convinced that the intervention is efficacious, as they often are despite the lack of experimental evidence, they may object strongly to allocating service by lot and insist that the neediest targets receive priority. As will be discussed in the next chapter, this is a situation to which the regression-discontinuity design is well adapted, although it may be very problematic for randomized designs.

Differences Between Experimental and Actual Intervention Delivery

A third limitation is that intervention delivery in experimental conditions may be different in critical ways from intervention delivery when the program is implemented. Many major, large-scale field experiments, for example, have used money payments as interventions (e.g., the income maintenance experiment described in Exhibit 8-D). With such standardized and easily delivered interventions, researchers can be relatively certain that the experimental intervention will be similar to that of a fully implemented program, because there are only a limited number of ways in which checks can be delivered. However, more labor-intensive, high-skill interventions (job placement services, counseling, teaching, etc.) are likely to be delivered with greater fidelity to the designers' intentions in a field experiment than when they are implemented as a program. Indeed, as we saw in Chapter 6, the very real danger that interventions will deteriorate in implementation is one of the principal reasons for monitoring programs.

This possibility argues for at least two rounds of experiments: a first round in which interventions are tested in their purest form, and a second round in which effective methods of service delivery through public agencies are tested and compared. The two stages of experiments in the Department of Labor's program to provide unemployment insurance benefits to released prisoners described in Exhibits 8-E and 8-G used this strategy. The first stage consisted of the small-scale experiment in Baltimore involving 432 prisoners released from the Maryland state prisons. The researchers selected the prisoners before release, provided them with payments, and observed their work and arrest patterns for a year. As may be recalled from Exhibit 8-E, the results showed a reduction in theft arrests over the postrelease period for experimental groups receiving unemployment insurance payments for 13 weeks.

The much larger second-stage experiment was undertaken in Georgia and Texas with 2,000 released prisoners in each state (Exhibit 8-G). In this experiment, payments were administered through the Employment Security Agencies in each of the states, and the tracking of the released prisoners over the postrelease year was accomplished jointly by the state prison systems and employment security agencies. The second-stage experiment was close to the system of administration that would have been put into place if the program had been enacted through federal legislation. The second-stage results, however, found the payments to be ineffective when administered under existing Employment Security Agency rules.

Time and Cost

An influential obstacle to the use of randomized experiments is that they are usually costly and time-consuming, especially large-scale multisite experiments. Ordinarily, they should not be undertaken to test program concepts that lie outside any conceivable policy space and so will never be considered, or to test established programs when there is not significant policy interest in evidence about impact. Moreover, experiments should not be undertaken when information is needed in a hurry. To underscore this last point, it should be noted that the New Jersey-Pennsylvania Income Maintenance experiment (Exhibit 8-D) cost $34 million (in 1968 dollars) and took more than seven years from design to published findings. The Seattle and Denver income maintenance experiments took even longer, with their results appearing in final form long after income maintenance as a policy had disappeared from the national agenda (Mathematica Policy Research, 1983; Office of Income Security, 1983; SRI International, 1983).

Generalizability and Validity

Because randomized experiments require such tight controls on interventions and the selection of participants, they are likely not to

have very high generalizability or external validity. No field experiment evaluating a social program has ever been conducted using a sample of clients drawn from the entire population of the United States. The administrative complexities of running national experiments have seemed too severe a burden for the designers to attempt such a study. In practice, although randomized field experiments may vary in scale, they generally are best reserved for testing services that can be standardized and easily transferred to operating agencies, and for which a relatively small number of sites or locales can be evaluated with reasonable confidence of broader external validity.

Integrity of Experiments

Finally, we should note that the integrity of a randomized experiment is easily threatened. Although randomly formed experimental and control groups are "statistically equivalent" at the start of an evaluation, nonrandom processes may threaten their equivalence as the experiment progresses. Differential attrition may introduce differences between experimentals and controls. In the income maintenance experiments, for example, families in the experimental groups who received the less generous payment plans and families in the control groups were more likely to stop participating. Also, administrative procedures for arranging the intended intervention and control conditions may fail so that the comparison between them does not actually represent program effects (Exhibit 8-H provides an example of an experiment compromised in this way).

Also, it is difficult to deliver a "pure program." Although an evaluator may design an experiment to test the effects of a given intervention, everything that is done to the experi-

EXHIBIT 8-H A Compromised Impact Assessment: The New Jersey Family Cap Experiment

In the early 1990s, New Jersey asked for a waiver to AFDC rules to remove what was thought to be an incentive in the AFDC regulations that encouraged women to have additional children to increase their AFDC payments. New Jersey proposed to change its AFDC policy to establish a "family cap" prohibiting any payment increases for children conceived by an AFDC recipient after her first enrollment in the program. The Department of Health and Human Services agreed to the request but insisted that the effectiveness of the program be evaluated through a randomized experiment. The family cap went into effect in 1992 covering all AFDC families with the exceptions noted below. The new regulations were widely publicized in the state's mass media and were carefully explained to ongoing and newly enrolled AFDC participants.

A research team from Rutgers University designed a randomized experiment in which some 6,000 AFDC families were randomly assigned to either an experimental group, whose additional children would not lead to payment increases, and a control group operating under the old AFDC rules in which grants were increased for children born while on AFDC ten or more months after enrollment. Case workers who were assigned to control group families were instructed to explain that the new family cap rules did not apply to them and letters were also sent to each family with that information. The evaluation plan was to track births and abortions occurring in the experimental and control groups through administrative data, including Medicaid records and periodic interviews. Comparisons between experimental and control families would then be used to determine if the family cap policy led to fewer additional births.

About two years into the experiment, the Rutgers researchers found that more than 20 families in the control group to whom a child had been born had been denied AFDC payment increases. In addition, a survey conducted of families in the experiment found that almost half of the women in the control group believed that their grants would not be increased if they had additional children, that is, they believed that they were subject to the family cap rules.

Apparently, the implementation of the research design had been compromised. Caseworkers failed to treat control families as intended and the control families did not understand that they were exempted from the family cap rules. Possibly the wide publicity given to the family cap simply overwhelmed whatever information was communicated to the control group families. It is also possible that not enough effort was made to communicate to caseworkers the special rules that applied and to ensure that participants knew about those rules. Most likely, both processes were at work.

The implementation of the randomized experiment was judged to have failed. As a consequence, no impact estimates could be made for the family cap program.

SOURCE: Adapted from M. J. Camasso, C. Harvey, and R. Jaganathan, *An Interim Report on the Impact of New Jersey's Family Development Program* (New Brunswick, NJ: Rutgers University School of Social Work, 1996).

mental targets becomes part of the intervention. For example, the TARP experiments (Exhibit 8-G) were supposed to test the effects of modest amounts of postprison financial aid, but the aid was administered by an existing state agency and hence that latter's procedures became part of the intervention. Indeed, there are few, if any, large-scale randomized social experiments that have not suffered some dilution. Of course, even if randomization is compromised to some extent, the results of a randomized experiment, properly analyzed, may still be superior in credibility to the nonrandomized designs discussed in the next chapter.

SUMMARY

❧ Randomized experiments are the flagships of evaluation. They generally provide the most credible conclusions about the impact of social programs. Policymakers, stakeholders, and the general public are most likely to treat findings emerging from true experiments respectfully, because they are familiar with at least the outlines of such designs from an awareness of the way laboratory studies are conducted.

❧ The designs and analysis procedures of all impact assessments are kin to those of true experiments; thus, an appreciation of experiments is important for anyone undertaking impact evaluations or using their results.

❧ The choice of units of analysis in impact assessments is determined by the nature of the intervention and the targets to which the intervention is directed.

❧ Randomized experimental designs are applicable only to partial-coverage programs in which there are sufficient untreated targets from which to draw a control or comparison group.

❧ The ideal experiment isolates the effect of the intervention being evaluated by ensuring that experimental and control groups are exactly comparable except for the intervention received. Strictly comparable groups are identical in composition, experiences over the period of observation, and predispositions toward the program under study. In practice, it is sufficient that the groups, as aggregates, are alike with respect to any characteristics that could be relevant to the intervention outcome.

❧ Randomization is a technique for ensuring comparability of experimental and control groups by distributing extraneous factors equally across the groups. Although stochastic effects will create some differences between any two groups, statistical procedures enable researchers to estimate the likelihood that observed differences are due to chance rather than to the intervention being studied.

❧ Assuming a well-run experiment, the estimate of an intervention's net effects can be expressed as the experimental group's score on a postintervention measure minus the control group's score, plus or minus stochastic effects.

※ Surrogate procedures, such as existing target lists or naturally occurring events, can sometimes substitute for randomization so long as the resulting assignments to experimental and control groups are free of biases relevant to the intervention and the expected outcome.

※ Although postintervention measures of outcome are critical in impact assessments, measures taken before and during an intervention, as well as repeated measurements afterward, increase measurement reliability and the precision of estimates of net effects and enable researchers to reconstruct how the intervention worked over time.

※ Simple randomized experiments are analyzed by means of a comparison of the outcomes of the experimental and control groups, together with statistical procedures for determining whether any observed differences are likely to be due to chance variations.

※ More complex research designs can compare a number of variations of an intervention and can be especially appropriate for testing new policies when the exact form of the intervention has not been firmly established. This type of design can also be used to study variations in the mode of intervention delivery.

※ Despite their rigor, randomized experiments have several limitations when applied to social programs:

1. They may not be useful in the early stages of program implementation when interventions may change in ways not allowed for in the experiment.

2. Randomization is sometimes perceived by stakeholders as unfair and even unethical because of the differential intervention given to experimental and, especially, control groups.

3. The way in which intervention is delivered in the experimental condition may not resemble intervention delivery in the implemented program.

4. Experiments are costly and time-consuming.

5. Because experiments require tight controls, the results may be low in generalizability and external validity.

KEY CONCEPTS FOR CHAPTER 9

Constructed control designs	Impact assessments in which there is no random assignment of program participants and nonparticipating targets. Rather, the groups are equated by matching or statistical procedures on characteristics that may be associated with program outcomes.
***Ex ante* designs**	Impact designs planned and begun prior to delivery of the program to the intervention group.
***Ex post* designs**	Impact designs undertaken subsequent to the delivery of the program to the intervention group, including secondary analyses making use of a quasi-experimental analytical approach.
Matching	Constructing control groups by finding targets identical in relevant respects to persons in experimental groups.
Statistical control designs	Impact designs without random assignment of program participants and nonparticipants. Rather, the groups are statistically equated, usually by some multivariate statistical procedure, so that they resemble each other as much as possible on characteristics associated with program outcomes.
Selection modeling	Creation of a multivariate statistical model to "predict" the probability of selection into intervention or comparison groups in a quasi-experiment. The results of this analysis are used to configure a control variable for selection bias to be incorporated into a second-stage statistical model investigating net effects of intervention on outcome.
Regression-discontinuity designs	Quasi-experimental impact assessment in which the selection procedure for intervention is based on whether an observed value on an appropriate quantitative scale is above or below a designated cutting point.
Generic controls	Established measures of social processes, such as published test norms, that are used as comparisons with the outcomes of interventions.
Cross-sectional designs	Studies in which data are collected at one point in time.
Specification error	Error in impact estimation arising out of the use of an inappropriate or incomplete statistical model.

CHAPTER 9

QUASI-EXPERIMENTAL IMPACT ASSESSMENTS

As we have indicated, relatively few impact assessments are "true experiments," employing randomly assigned experimental and control groups; more frequently, evaluators must rely on nonrandomized designs. In this chapter, we discuss designs for assessing program outcomes in which control or comparison groups are identified or constructed by nonrandom means. These designs are commonly used whenever there is partial program coverage and it is not possible to randomize targets into groups that participate and do not participate in the program. One way this is done is to construct experimental and comparison groups by matching program partici- pants as closely as possible to nonparticipants on characteristics that may be associated with the impact of the program. A second way is to statistically equate participating and nonparticipating targets on measured characteristics that may be related to program outcomes. Although the two procedures are different, the logic behind them is the same. Sometimes evaluators use reflexive controls (which we discuss in Chapter 10) instead of constructed controls, even when there are sufficient untreated targets to serve as either matched or statistical controls. In general, however, it is foolish to trade off the strength of constructed control designs for weaker, reflexive control im- pact assessments.

As we discussed in Chapters 7 and 8, a randomized field experiment is the most scientifically credible impact assessment de- sign, but there are sometimes practical or ethi- cal problems associated with its application to social programs. In such cases, there are vari- ous nonrandom designs that the evaluator may turn to. In this chapter, we expand our discus- sion of these designs and examine their advan- tages and disadvantages, both in terms of their utility in reaching firm conclusions on the net

effects of programs and the practical consider- ations relevant to their use.

QUASI-EXPERIMENTAL IMPACT ASSESSMENT

In the evaluation lexicon, the term *quasi-ex- periment* is used to describe impact designs that do not involve randomly assigned comparison groups (Campbell and Stanley, 1966; Cook and Campbell, 1979). The most common of these designs involves constructing control or comparison groups in an attempt to approximate a randomized design. This is done either by matching participating and nonparticipating targets or by statistical adjustment of participants and nonparticipants in an attempt to make them equivalent on relevant variables. In both cases, the goal is to be able to compare the program participants with nonparticipants that resemble them on those characteristics and experiences related to the evaluation's outcome measures.

As we have emphasized, quasi-experimental comparison group designs are most appropriately used for estimating the impact of partial-coverage programs when random assignment cannot be undertaken. The usual reason for this situation is that assignment to intervention and control conditions is not within the evaluator's capability or because of political, ethical, or other considerations that lead program staff, sponsors, or other powerful stakeholders to oppose randomization. In quasi-experimental designs, targets receiving the program are compared with some selected group of targets or potential targets who do not receive the program. To the extent that the latter resemble the program group on relevant characteristics and experiences, or can be statistically adjusted to resemble it, then net effects can be assessed with a reasonable degree of confidence.

A quasi-experimental design may also result when an evaluation that starts out as a randomized experiment does not end up that way. Consider, for example, the impact assessment of the New Orleans Homeless Substance Abusers Project, a residential adult resocialization project for homeless alcohol and drug abusers (Devine, Wright, and Brody, 1995). The impact assessment was designed as a random-

ized experiment, but fewer than one-third of the eligible clients were actually assigned randomly. Program staff subverted the randomization procedure by following the assignment it generated only when it yielded what they viewed as a "good" client for the program; otherwise, they ignored it. In addition, attrition from treatment and data collection further undermined the intended randomized design. Because the intervention and comparison groups that resulted did not fulfill the requirements of a randomized experiment, the evaluators were obligated to treat this situation as a quasi-experimental design. They thus applied statistical adjustments in an attempt to establish sufficient equivalence between the groups to draw a defensible conclusion about program impact.

It should be recognized, therefore, that there is almost always some chance that a randomized experiment will break down before the final data are collected and have to be treated as a quasi-experiment. It is thus wise for the evaluator to plan an experimental design as a quasi-experiment as well. There are too many instances in which unanticipated occurrences of uncontrolled selection or participant attrition have reduced true experiments to quasi-experiments to be sanguine about the likelihood of keeping randomly selected groups intact.

When a randomized experiment cannot be done, a quasi-experiment is generally the most convincing alternative and they are certainly undertaken more frequently. Nevertheless, in quasi-experimentation it will always be arguable to some degree whether the comparison group is sufficiently comparable to the intervention group on all relevant characteristics and experiences to provide an unbiased estimate of net program effects.

As noted in Chapter 7, generally neither quasi-experiments nor randomized experiments can be undertaken when evaluating full-coverage programs. An exception occurs when there is variation in the intensity or "dosage" of the interventions to which targets are exposed. For example, although all patients in a mental hospital may receive some psychotherapy, some may have therapy once a week, others three times a week, and still others on a daily basis. Assessment of outcomes after equating these groups to the extent possible allows a reasonable estimate of the impact of psychotherapy or, at least, more versus less of it. We consider this approach to nonuniform full-coverage programs in Chapter 10.

Measuring Impacts in Quasi-Experimental Evaluations

The basic formula for impact assessment in quasi-experiments looks very similar to that shown earlier for randomized experiments. The critical difference is that it contains an additional term representing uncontrolled pre-intervention differences between the intervention and control groups, highlighting the central problem of how properly to take selection bias into account:

$$
\begin{bmatrix} \text{Net} \\ \text{effect} \end{bmatrix} = \begin{bmatrix} \text{Gross} \\ \text{outcome} \\ \text{for an} \\ \text{intervention} \\ \text{group} \end{bmatrix} - \begin{bmatrix} \text{Gross} \\ \text{outcome} \\ \text{for a} \\ \text{constructed} \\ \text{control group} \end{bmatrix} \pm
$$

$$
\begin{bmatrix} \text{Uncontrolled} \\ \text{difference} \\ \text{between} \\ \text{intervention} \\ \text{and control} \\ \text{groups} \end{bmatrix} \pm \begin{bmatrix} \text{Design} \\ \text{effects and} \\ \text{stochastic} \\ \text{error} \end{bmatrix}
$$

Whether a specific quasi-experiment will yield unbiased estimates of net effects, therefore,

depends largely on the extent to which the design minimizes critical differences between the intervention and control groups. When there is a possibility that one or more relevant differences exists between the members of the intervention and comparison groups, as there typically is in quasi-experiments, then it is also a possibility that these differences—*not the intervention*—cause all or part of the observed effects.

To illustrate, suppose a state program to increase agricultural productivity uses an intensive educational campaign involving agricultural agents, pamphlets, and informal meetings to instruct farmers how to increase production by using fertilizers properly. A number of agricultural districts are chosen as the targets to be exposed to the campaign. A constructed control group of agricultural districts is selected to match the participating districts with respect to a number of characteristics that might affect agricultural productivity. The districts may be matched, say, with respect to average rainfall, average size of farm holdings, crops planted, and average amount of capital equipment per holding—all measures available in existing data sources. But there might be other, perhaps unknown, differences that are strongly related to crop yield. Perhaps the districts in which officials volunteer for the project are more progressive in relation to innovations or more inclined to take risks. To the extent that such districts have also adopted other practices that influence crop yields, a selection bias is at work that will tend to mask the estimated effects of the program.

Unknown or unintended selection effects are not the only possible contaminating differences between an intervention group and its control group. Administrators in charge of the educational program described above, for instance, might make a biased selection in an attempt to maximize the chances of showing positive program effects. They could do this by choosing districts they know from experience are more likely to adopt agricultural innovations enthusiastically. This practice, known as "creaming," is motivated by the understandable desire of program administrators to appear to do as well as possible. An easy way to do well is to choose participants who do well! A classic statement of this principle is the response reputedly made by former Governor Lester Maddox of Georgia to a question from reporters concerning an apparent lack of progress in reforming state prisons: "We can't reform the prisons of Georgia until we are able to attract a better class of prisoners!"

In evaluations in which selection bias is at work, net effects, as computed using the formula presented above, would tend to be overestimated because a portion of the difference between the intervention group and its comparison would result from the stronger potential for positive (or, sometimes, negative) effects inherent in the persons selected for intervention.

Ex Ante Versus Ex Post Quasi-Experiments

A major distinction for quasi-experiments is related to the time points at which the evaluation is designed and its implementation is undertaken. The two important types are referred to as *ex ante* and *ex post* quasi-experiments.

Ex Ante Quasi-Experiments

In an ex ante impact assessment, the evaluators are able to plan how they will select the control group before the program is provided to the intervention group, as is commonly the case in random assignment evaluations. The opportunity in ex ante evaluations to identify and plan the data collection procedures for *both* the intervention and comparison groups prior to program participation by the selected targets generally maximizes the likelihood of constructing comparison groups that are equivalent to those participants.

In ex ante evaluations, there is the opportunity to undertake a wide range of preliminary activities that can strengthen impact assessments. For example, it is possible to distinguish, from the pool of potential program participants, those targets who are most likely to become engaged in a program, to identify their characteristics, and to locate persons like them for inclusion in constructed control groups. Generally, ex ante designs also allow a greater opportunity to examine previous evaluation work in the relevant program area. This may permit potential selection effects to be identified and measures of the corresponding variables to be included in the design so that they can be used for matching or statistical adjustment.

Ex Post Quasi-Experiments

In many cases, it is not possible to construct the comparison group (or groups) before the program is delivered to the participants in the intervention group of the impact design. The comparison group then has to be constructed ex post, that is, after the start, if not the termination, of the intervention. Perhaps the most common reasons for ex post quasi-experiments are that the decision to undertake an evaluation is made after a program has already enrolled all the targets it is able to serve or insufficient time is allowed for the evaluation to enroll a fresh group and follow them to termination of services and as far beyond as necessary.

Ex post designs using constructed controls have a long history in the evaluation of program impact. More than 40 years ago, for instance, Freeman and Weeks (1956) undertook an ex post constructed control evaluation of a psychotherapeutically oriented residential delinquency program for boys known as Highfields. Although there were discussions about undertaking an evaluation from the start of Highfields, it was not designed and put in place until several cohorts had graduated from the school and been in the community for a couple of years.

The design was an ex post matched control evaluation. Rather than wait for a new cohort of delinquent youths to enter the program, complete it, and be released to the community for long enough for the interesting outcome variables to be measured, a large nearby "training school," called Annandale, was used to provide the control. Annandale served boys of about the same age and from the same communities as Highfields. However, Highfields treated only a small number of boys at a time and the Annandale group was very much larger than the Highfields one. Accordingly, data on Annandale residents were searched to find individuals similar to each Highfields "graduate" in age, race, place of residence, parents' marital status, and several other variables. Despite the size of the Annandale study group, exact matches for all the boys in the Highfields experimental group could not be found. Consequently, the constructed control group matched the Highfields boys on the majority of the control variables but not all of them. Given this limitation, the recommended procedure would be to use statistical controls rather than matching if this study were done today.

CONSTRUCTING COMPARISON GROUPS IN QUASI-EXPERIMENTAL EVALUATIONS

Like randomized experiments, quasi-experiments using constructed controls require that a substantial part of the target population not receive the program under evaluation. The several variations on the quasi-experimental approach are designed to account for the different circumstances confronting evaluators as they design their impact assessments. The major distinction among quasi-experiments concerns the ways in which comparison groups are developed to minimize the selection bias that results from the uncontrolled (i.e., nonrandom) assignment of targets to the one or more experimental and comparison groups. The following sections discuss the four most common types of quasi-experimental designs with constructed controls.

Constructing Control Groups by Matching

Up to the 1970s, most ex ante quasi-experiments were undertaken by matching. The design generally called for an intervention group, composed of targets exposed to the program, and a "parallel" control group, a set of unexposed targets chosen purposely to match the intervention group in essential ways. In this design, the intervention group is typically specified first and the evaluator is then faced with the task of identifying (or "constructing") an appropriate set of matched controls. Below are some examples of the use of such matched control or comparison groups:

• In 1994, Kids Voting USA administered a civics curriculum that was used by 2.3 million K-12 students in 20 states and the District of Columbia. One of its objectives was to have students discuss political issues with their parents to reinforce the classroom instruction and increase the parents' awareness of the election and likelihood of voting. To assess the effects, voter turnout in areas where the program was implemented was compared with that in nearby areas that did not use the program. Census data, voter registration, and voting statistics were used to match areas with regard to racial, socioeconomic, and partisan characteristics. It was not always possible to find matching areas because boundaries for political units like precincts or counties did not always align well with school district boundaries, but reasonably matched comparisons were found for communities in 15 of the 21 states in which the program was implemented (Simon and Merrill, 1998).

• The Ilderton Motor Project, based in South London, gives youths who have committed auto theft and other vehicle-related crimes an opportunity to work on cars and learn about how they function and are maintained. The effectiveness of this program in reducing reoffending was evaluated by comparing arrest data for 35 probationers who attended the project and a matched group of 40 probationers who did not. The youths in the comparison group were selected so that their offense careers were similar to the program youths up to the point the latter started the Ilderton project. This was found to yield groups that were also similar in age and proportion previously sentenced to custody (Wilkinson, 1997).

• The Washington State Family Independence Program (FIP) was approved under federal waivers in 1988 as an alternative to Aid to Families With Dependent Children (AFDC). It was intended to increase the self-sufficiency of welfare families by providing education and training along with incentives for employment. Transitional child care and medical services were also extended to those who obtained a job and left welfare, and a variety of administrative changes were made to provide a more supportive and less stigmatizing program environment than traditional welfare. The FIP evaluation examined effects on education and training, employment status, and welfare receipt. Data on these outcomes for the clients of five welfare offices that implemented FIP were compared with that of five offices that continued to operate the AFDC program that were selected as similar to the FIPs offices. Statistical controls were also used to adjust for differences that occurred despite the matching (Long and Wissoker, 1995).

In recent decades, matching has been supplanted and supplemented to a considerable extent by the use of statistical controls. In such cases, as we will expand on later in this chapter, rather than match ex ante, information on relevant variables is collected on both the intervention and comparison groups, and the functional equivalent of matching is accomplished through statistical analysis. However, matching on at least some variables continues to be relatively common in impact assessments involving comparison of small numbers of aggregate units, such as schools or communities, and when targets are drawn from specialized populations with distinctive clinical, personal, or situational characteristics such as in the evaluation of medical and health-related interventions (where matching is often referred to as "case control" design).

Procedures for Devising Matched Controls

Devising an appropriate control group by matching is not a mechanical task; it must be based on prior knowledge and theoretical understanding of the social processes in question. Such knowledge instructs the evaluator about the specific ways in which a matched control group should resemble the intervention group. For example, we would draw on prior knowledge about the factors that affect crop yields to select agricultural districts for a constructed control group in an assessment of a project designed to increase such yields. Likewise, in constructing appropriate control groups for an evaluation of the effects of a program to increase the mathematics competence of secondary school students, we would use prior knowledge concerning the characteristics of individuals and settings that affect learning (e.g., school organization and students' sex, age, intelligence, and family background).

Identifying Characteristics for Matching

Information relevant for constructing control groups may often be found in the literature published within the substantive areas related to the program. An evaluator of an educational program thus should consult research about what variables affect learning in the subject area at issue. An evaluator designing a study of a family planning campaign should consult the literature on factors influencing fertility, and so on. Special attention should be paid to identifying variables that are potentially related to self-selection processes. For example, in studying a job training program for unemployed youths, it might be important to match intervention and comparison groups with regard to the youths' attitudes toward training and assessments of its value in obtaining employment (Chen, 1990).

Although one might be tempted to construct control groups using any and all factors mentioned in the relevant research literature, some degree of restraint is advisable. Using more than a few variables for constructing matched controls is not usually very efficient, nor is it necessary. In general, the pertinent characteristics will tend to be intercorrelated and, therefore, somewhat redundant. If an evaluator for an educational intervention matches students on the basis of intelligence measures, for instance, the individuals will also be fairly well matched on parents' educational background, because intelligence and parental education are rather strongly related.

When there is little prior knowledge about the variables that are influential in a particular substantive area of intervention, some general guides may be followed in selecting variables on which to match. Over the decades, social scientists have identified various features of individuals, families, communities, or other units that affect many areas of human behavior. A brief list of such general control variables is given in Exhibit 9-A.

Note that the characteristics shown in Exhibit 9-A can be thought of as "nested." That is, characteristics for individuals may also be used to characterize higher units by forming averages, measures of dispersion, or other aggregate descriptive measures. For example, an individual may be characterized by his or her calendar age, a family by the average age of its members, a factory by the average age of its employees (or the proportion between certain ages), and a city by the average age of its inhabitants (or by the proportion of persons who are in the economically productive age group).

※ EXHIBIT 9-A   Characteristics Useful in Devising Constructed Control Groups

A. Characteristics of individuals
   Age
   Sex
   Educational attainment
   Socioeconomic status (income, wealth, property ownership)
   Tenure (land and/or home ownership)
   Marital status
   Occupation (occupational prestige)
   Ethnicity (race, cultural group, language group, national origin)
   Intellectual functioning (IQ, cognitive ability, knowledge)
   Labor force participation
B. Characteristics of families (or households)
   Life-cycle stage
   Number of members
   Number of children
   Socioeconomic status (household income or wealth, occupations of members, etc.)
   Housing arrangements
   Ethnicity
C. Characteristics of organized units (schools, classes, unions, etc.)
   Size differentiation
   Levels of authority
   Number of subunits
   Number of distinctly different roles (occupations)
   Industry class
   Growth rate
   Budget
D. Characteristics of communities (territorially organized units)
   Industry mix
   Governmental organization
   Population size
   Territorial size
   Growth rate
   Population density
   Location in relation to other territorial units
      (parts of metropolitan area, independent city, town, etc.)

Perhaps the best way to use the characteristics shown in Exhibit 9-A is to regard them as constituting a checklist designed to remind the evaluator of variables that are likely candidates for consideration in constructing control groups that are matched to intervention groups on important general social characteristics. For example, in assessing the impact of an anti-smoking educational campaign directed toward preadolescent schoolchildren, an experimental group of schools could be matched with a constructed control group of schools that are comparable in the socioeconomic status of parents, students' intellectual functioning, city size, and location.

Although they have been found to be generally useful, the characteristics in Exhibit 9-A are not adequate substitutes for a priori knowledge directly relevant to the phenomenon being studied, nor are they necessarily appropriate to all social programs. For example, a program that is designed to lower rates of fertility among unmarried adolescents is best evaluated using constructed controls chosen on the basis of an understanding of adolescents' motivations for engaging in sexual behavior, becoming pregnant, and so on. The objective would be to have comparison youths that match the treated ones as closely as possible on all the variables related to their proclivity to bear children.

Matching Procedures

Matching is accomplished by selecting units for control groups whose characteristics resemble the major relevant features of those units exposed to the program. Thus, if a particular school is chosen as the target in an intervention, a matched control group can be one or more schools whose demographic profiles mirror those of the participating school. An alternative is to select from one or more schools those children who are similar to the target participants. The options are thus either *individual* or *aggregate* matching.

In individual matching, the effort is to draw a "partner" for each target student from the unexposed pool of students. For example, if age,

sex, number of siblings, and father's occupation were deemed the relevant matching variables, the roster of unexposed children would be scrutinized to locate the closest equivalent child for pairing with a given child in the intervention group. Criteria of closeness may be adjusted to make matching possible—for example, matching so the exposed and unexposed children are within six months of age, even though a smaller difference within the pairs may be more desirable. Exhibit 9-B provides an illustration of individual matching.

The second approach is aggregate matching. In this case, individuals are not matched case by case, but the overall distributions in the intervention and control groups on each matching variable are made to correspond. For instance, the same proportions of children by sex and age would be found in the intervention and comparison groups, but this result may have been obtained by including a 12-year-old girl and an 8-year-old boy in the comparison group to balance the aggregate distribution of the experimental group, which included a 9-year-old girl and an 11-year-old boy. Exhibit 9-C gives an example of aggregate matching.

Individual matching is usually preferable to aggregate matching, especially when several characteristics are used simultaneously as matching criteria. The drawbacks to individual matching are that it is more expensive, time-consuming, and difficult to execute for a large number of matched variables, although computer-based matching procedures can facilitate the process. Also, matching by individuals can sometimes result in a drastic loss of cases. If matching persons cannot be found for individuals in the intervention group, those unmatched individuals have to be discarded as data sources. In some situations, the proportion of unmatched individuals can become so large that the exposed targets for which matches are

⚔ **EXHIBIT 9-B**   Studying the Effects of "Inclusive" Education Using Individually Matched Controls

Students with severe disabilities have traditionally been taught in self-contained special education classrooms, but current policy debates focus on whether more "inclusive" arrangements in general education settings might not be preferable. One particular interest is whether inclusive schools facilitate the social development of students with severe disabilities. An important part of the rationale for inclusive education has come from research showing poor social relationships between students with and without disabilities in traditional special education arrangements.

To assess the effects of inclusive education on the social relationships of intermediate students with severe disabilities, a team of researchers devised an impact assessment using students in junior high classrooms on the island of Oahu in Hawaii. In Oahu, disabled students in some schools receive special education support within general education classrooms while, in other schools, they are taught in self-contained classrooms on the school campus with special education supports provided within those classrooms.

Each of the eight disabled students in regular junior high classrooms was matched with a student in a special education classroom on age, gender, level of disability, adaptive communication behavior, and adaptive social behavior. Statistical analyses for matched pairs revealed no significant differences between students in the two groups. These groups were then compared on outcome measures relating to the students' friendship networks and the character of their interaction with peers without disabilities. The results showed that the students in general education classrooms interacted more frequently with peers without disabilities across a greater range of activities and settings, received and provided higher levels of social support, and had larger friendship networks and more durable relationships with peers without disabilities.

SOURCE: Adapted from Craig H. Kennedy, Smita Shikla, and Dale Fryxell, "Comparing the Effects of Educational Placement on the Social Relationships of Intermediate School Students With Severe Disabilities," *Exceptional Children*, 1997, 64(1):31-47.

available are no longer representative of the population to which the intervention is applied.

In addition, if the variables on which the matching is done have low reliability, there are some circumstances in which serious statistical artifacts may be produced. This is especially likely to occur when the individuals selected for the matches come from different tails of their respective distributions on those variables.

Suppose, for instance, that students are being matched on teachers' ratings of scholastic aptitude and those ratings have modest reliability. If the intervention group for a remedial program comes from poor schools and tends to have low scores, and they are matched with students from better schools who tend to have higher scores, most matches will be found for the higher-scoring intervention targets and the lower-scoring members of the potential control

---

※ EXHIBIT 9-C   Evaluation of a Family Development Program Using Aggregate-Matched Controls

---

A program was started in Baltimore to serve poor families living in public housing by providing integrated services with the hope of helping families escape from long-term poverty. Services included access to special educational programs for children and adults, job training programs, teenage programs, special health care access, and child care facilities. To the extent possible, these services were delivered within the LaFayette Courts public housing project. Case managers assigned to the housing project helped families choose services appropriate to them. The special feature of this program was its emphasis

on serving families rather than individuals. In all, 125 families were enrolled.

To constitute a comparison group, 125 families were chosen from a comparable public housing project, Murphy Homes. The impact of the family development program was then assessed by contrasting the enrolled families with the Murphy Homes sample. After a year of enrollment, the participating families were shown to be higher in self-esteem and sense of control over their fates, but positive impacts on employment and earnings had not yet occurred.

SOURCE: Adapted from Anne B. Shlay and C. Scott Holupka, *Steps Toward Independence: The Early Effects of the Lafayette Courts Family Development Center* (Baltimore: Johns Hopkins University, Institute for Policy Studies, 1991).

---

individuals. Under these circumstances, comparisons between these groups on subsequently measured outcome variables may show spurious differences unrelated to program effects (Campbell, 1996; Campbell and Boruch, 1975; Hsu, 1995).

However carefully matching may be done, there is always the possibility that some critical difference remains between experimentals and selected controls that is related to the outcome variables. In an important methodological study, Fraker and Maynard (1984) compared the estimates of net effects derived from a randomized control group with those derived from control groups constructed by individual matching. The program in question was the supported work experiment in which unemployed youths, AFDC mothers, and some hardcore unemployed males were provided with jobs. Using a computer, researchers constructed control groups by drawing individuals from the Current Population Survey files who matched the program recipients on age, sex, and prior earnings. Because a randomized experiment had also been done, an unbiased estimate of the net effects of the supported work intervention was available for comparison with the results using the matched controls.

Several methods of making individual matches were employed, but all gave estimates of net effects that were wide of the mark. At least in this research, matching proved to be a poor substitute for randomized controls. Subsequent reanalysis of these data by Heckman and Hotz (1989) using more sophisticated analytical methods showed that, when properly modeled, the matched comparison groups could yield results quite close to those derived from randomized experiments. Heckman and Hotz emphasized the necessity of choosing control variables related to the selection biases and using an appropriate statistical model of how selection effects are related to outcome.

A variation on constructing a control group by matching is to select a sample of units from the same population as the intervention targets and to match on some important variables while controlling other relevant differences statistically. This method will become clearer after the use of statistical controls is described in the next section.

Equating Groups by Statistical Procedures

Statistical procedures, rather than matching, are now generally used in both ex ante and ex post quasi-experimental evaluations as the primary approach to dealing with selection bias and other unwanted differences between groups. Because of their widespread use, we will go into detail about the logic behind them. We start our exposition by using a simple example, centering the discussion on the cross-tabulations contained in the following section.

The Logic Behind Statistical Controls

Exhibit 9-D contains the outcomes of a hypothetical quasi-experimental impact assessment of a vocational training program for unemployed men between the ages of 35 and 40. The ongoing, partial-coverage program was designed to upgrade the job skills of participants, enabling them to obtain higher-paying

jobs. Fewer than 1 in 20 of those eligible participated in the voluntary program.

The program was evaluated by taking a sample of 1,000 participants and interviewing them before and again one year after they completed vocational training. In addition, another 1,000 men of the same age group were sampled from the general population of the large metropolitan area in which the program was operating and interviewed at the time the program started and one year after it ended. Because the program was small, almost all men approached for interviews in the general sample did not participate in the program. Both samples were asked for information about current earnings. Hourly wage rates were computed for both groups from their second interviews. In addition, the interviews contained measures designed to be used as statistical controls.

In Panel I of Exhibit 9-D, the average post-training wage rates of the two groups are compared without application of any statistical controls. Those who had participated in the project were earning, on average, $5.75 per hour; those who had not participated, $6.20. Clearly, participants were earning less than nonparticipants (93% of the wage rate of nonparticipants). Had this been the outcome of a randomized experiment, the difference would have been an unbiased impact estimate. However, these unadjusted comparisons are quite misleading because participants and nonparticipants almost certainly differed on a number of earnings-related variables other than their participation in the project. The comparisons shown in Panel I are thus gross outcomes, the product of all the ways in which participants and nonparticipants differed.

Panel II of Exhibit 9-D takes one such difference into account by presenting average wage rates separately for men of two educa-

⚓ **EXHIBIT 9-D** Statistical Adjustments in an Evaluation of the Impact of a Hypothetical Employment Training Project

I. Gross outcome comparison between men 35-40 who have completed training program with sample of men 35-40 who did not attend training program

	Participants	Nonparticipants
Average wage rate	$5.75	$6.20
N =	1,000	1,000

II. Comparison after adjusting for educational attainment

	Participants		Nonparticipants	
	Less Than High School	High School	Less Than High School	High School
Average wage rate	$5.60	$6.10	$5.75	$6.50
n =	700	300	400	600

III. Comparison adjusting for educational attainment and employment at start of training program (or equivalent data for nonparticipants)

	Participants		Nonparticipants			
	Less Than High School, Unemployed	High School, Unemployed	Less Than High School, Unemployed	Less Than High School, Employed	High School, Unemployed	High School, Employed
Average wage rate	$5.60	$6.10	$5.50	$5.83	$6.00	$6.60
n =	700	300	100	300	100	500

tional levels: those who had not completed high school and those who had. Note that 70% of the program participants had not completed high school, as opposed to 40% of the nonparticipants. When we hold education constant by comparing the wage rates of persons of comparable educational attainment, the hourly wages of participants and nonparticipants approach one another—$5.60 and $5.75, respectively, for those who had not completed high school; $6.10 and $6.50 for those who had. Obviously, holding educational attainment constant diminishes the differences between the wage

rates of participants and nonparticipants because better-educated persons generally receive higher wages.

Panel III takes still another difference into account. Because all participants were unemployed at the time of enrollment in the training program, it is appropriate to compare participants with those nonparticipants who were also unemployed at the time the program started. In this panel, nonparticipants are divided into those who were unemployed and those who were not at the start of the program. This comparison showed that program participants in the project subsequently earned more at each educational level than comparable non-participants—$5.60 and $5.50, respectively, for those who had not completed high school, $6.10 and $6.00 for those who had.

In sum, when we take education and unemployment into account, the vocational training program shows some positive impact, amounting to a $0.10 increment in the wage rates of those who participated.

Note that the introduction of successive statistical controls was not a haphazard procedure. First, all the control variables introduced into this analysis concern what both treated and untreated men were like before the training program began. Obviously, only such characteristics could be related to subsequent selection into the program. Second, the use of each control measure was based on prior knowledge about the determinants of earnings, as found in previous research. In any real example, of course, additional controls would be entered, perhaps for previous employment experience, marital status, number of dependents, and race—all factors known to be related to wage rates. Again, the worth of statistical controls in impact assessments is heavily dependent on such prior knowledge.

It should be noted that studies such as this ordinarily are unable to account fully for the effects of selection and to remove them completely from estimates of net program impact. In our example, unemployed persons who participated in the program were by that very fact differentiated from those who did not—perhaps by higher levels of motivation, a difference that is difficult to measure and introduce into the analysis.

The adjustments shown in Exhibit 9-D were accomplished in a very simple way to illustrate the logic of successive statistical controls. Multivariate statistical methods are com-monly used to adjust for a number of contaminating variables simultaneously. The choice of which multivariate technique to use in particular cases depends on the nature of the problem and the kinds of variables involved. The application of such techniques to quasi-experimental data is discussed in more detail later in this chapter.

Similarities Between Matching and Statistical Procedures

Ex ante impact assessments using matched controls and those using statistical controls are conceptually quite similar. Both methods seek to obtain comparability between participants and nonparticipants and both depend heavily on prior knowledge about what characteristics might distinguish the two groups. The figures shown in Exhibit 9-D are identical in critical respects to ones that might have been generated by an evaluation using constructed controls created by matching. Each of the successive statistical controls introduced had the effect of isolating groups of unexposed persons comparable to participants from among the respondents in the general survey. The numbers of persons in each of the comparable groups are not identical, as would have been the case had controls been selected using matching procedures, but that is not important because averaging the data within each group compared holds numbers constant.

The comparisons in the bottom panel of Exhibit 9-D are, in principle, identical to those that would have been found had constructed controls been used with matching procedures, assuming the variables shown in the exhibit were used as matching variables. In short, matched and statistical controls are equivalent ways of proceeding, with statistical controls possessing some superior qualities arising from the retention of observations that might have to be discarded under matching procedures.

Multivariate Statistical Models

Whereas random assignment works by equating groups, save for chance variation, on all variables, known and unknown, measured and unmeasured, statistical procedures for equating groups are limited to variables that are known and measured. As indicated above, the logic of these procedures is to identify and measure those "control" variables that may represent important initial differences between the intervention and comparison groups, then make statistical comparisons on outcomes that summarizes over subsets of data on which the values of those control variables are the same.

Although the simple breakdowns (or stratifications) of outcome by control variables shown in Exhibit 9-D implement this logic, that approach is not workable for situations in which there are more than a few control variables. Because it depends, in essence, on matching intervention and comparison units on all the control variables, it is limited by the capability of the data to provide exact matches on however many control variables are applied.

An alternate, and more sophisticated, approach is to create a statistical representation of the overall *relationships* among the control variables and the outcome variables in a statistical model that allows inferences about the relationship of intervention to outcome that is left over after all the relationships of the control variables to the outcome have been accounted for. The advantage of this approach is that the relationships among variables can be described using the whole data set rather than requiring that intervention units and comparison units be found that match on all control variables (which often is not possible). The disadvantage

of such multivariate statistical models is that assumptions must be made about the form of the relationships among the variables in the model. In particular, the commonly used models represent those relationships as correlation coefficients or covariances, assuming a linear relationship between any two variables; that is, as the values on one variable increase, those on the other either increase or decrease proportionately. Other assumptions about the stochastic components of the variables are also generally involved. Of course, the "fit" of these assumptions to the data at issue can be tested, and this is an important step in multivariate analysis.

When multivariate statistical analysis is applied to quasi-experimental data, the object is to configure a statistical model that accounts for the initial measured differences between the intervention and comparison groups and adjusts the outcome difference between those groups to subtract the portion attributable entirely to those initial differences. Whatever difference on outcomes remains after this subtraction, if any, is interpreted as the net effect of the intervention. Of course, if there is some influential initial difference between the groups that is not measured and included in the model, its effect is not subtracted and the remaining difference is not actually the net effect of the intervention. This is why it is so important in quasi-experimental impact assessments to identify and measure all those variables on which the groups initially differ that are related to their status on the outcome variable when it is subsequently measured.

Against this background, multivariate statistical models for quasi-experimental data generally involve one or both of two different types of control variables presumed to account for the influential initial differences between the intervention and comparison group. One type has to do with those characteristics of the group members that are related to the outcome variable. If we imagine that the intervention has no effect (or that there is no intervention), these are the variables that, if measured at the beginning of the study, would "predict" the outcome. For instance, in Exhibit 9-D, educational level is such a variable. Other things equal, those with higher education at the beginning of the study would have higher wages at the end. Similarly, absent any intervention effect, those with more job experience, privileged social status, or location in favorable labor markets would be expected to have higher wages as the outcome.

The other type of control variable potentially useful for modeling quasi-experimental data has to do with the selection of individuals into the intervention versus the comparison group. This type of control variable thus relates directly to selection bias, the critical problem of quasi-experimental designs. Control variables of this type might include, for instance, how close individuals lived to the program site, how motivated they were to enroll in the program, whether they had the characteristics program personnel used to select participants, and so forth. The importance of these control variables lies in the fact that, if we could fully account for the characteristics that caused an individual to be in one group versus the other, we could statistically "match" on those characteristics and, in that way, perfectly offset the selection effect.

Of course, the variables related to selection are only useful if they also relate to outcome. If more individuals who like hamburgers are selected for the intervention group and more who like hot dogs are selected for the comparison group, this is relevant only if the outcome would be different, all other things equal, for these two groups. Many differences, of course,

are neutral with regard to the outcome variables pertinent to an intervention. The logic of identifying control variables related to selection, however, is that, if they are fully specified, they, in turn, must relate to all the differences between the groups that do relate to outcomes. If hamburger eaters are selected for one group and hot dog eaters for the other, a control variable representing that selection difference will, at the same time, carry information about any outcome-relevant difference between hamburger and hot dog eaters. Perhaps hamburger eaters tend to be younger than hot dog eaters and age is related to the outcome variable. Our hamburger-hot dog control variable carries that information into the statistical analysis and accounts for it. Control variables related to selection, therefore, are proxy variables for group differences related to outcome even when they are not themselves directly related.

In the two sections that follow, we will discuss multivariate statistical analysis using control variables presumed related to outcome, then those presumed related to selection. The latter are essentially a special case of the former, but are sufficiently distinct procedurally to warrant separate discussion.

Modeling outcome. The objective of multivariate analysis of quasi-experimental data is to configure a statistical model that is capable of "predicting" each individual's value on the outcome variable from their status on the control variables measured at the beginning of the study. If the average outcome for the intervention group is better than predicted from initial status whereas, of course, the comparison group is not, then the difference is interpreted as the net effect of the intervention. An alternate phrasing is that the analysis tries to establish whether the intervention is a significant predictor of outcome when the predictive relationship of the control variables has already been taken into account. A typical analytical procedure is to model the conjoint relationship of the control variables with the outcome measure and then add, or separately assess, the contribution of the intervention measure over and above that associated with the control variables.

The statistical procedures and models used for these purposes depend on the characteristics of the measures, the form of the relationships assumed among the variables in the model, the statistical assumptions deemed realistic, and the technical know-how and proclivities of the analyst. Most commonly, some variant of multiple regression analysis is used (Mohr, 1995; Reichardt and Bormann, 1994) or, sometimes, structural equation modeling (Loehlin, 1992; Wu and Campbell, 1996). Whatever the approach, all analyses have to be informed by knowledge of the procedures to be used and full understanding of the measures employed and their statistical properties.

Exhibit 9-E shows an application of multiple regression to data from the TARP experiments described in Exhibit 8-G (Chapter 8). It involves an ex ante analysis estimating the net impact of parole on the employment of ex-felons after their release from prison. The table in Exhibit 9-E presents summary statistics from a multiple regression analysis predicting the number of weeks from date of release to date of first employment on the basis of using prerelease variables believed to be related to the probability of obtaining work. The intervention variable, whether released on parole or not, is included in the regression equation with the control variables to determine if it makes a significant contribution to predicting outcome above and beyond the influence of the control variables.

The coefficients shown in the column marked b are unstandardized regression coefficients expressing the net number of weeks from discharge to first employment for each unit of each of the predictor variables. The coefficient for having been released on parole is −3.45 weeks, meaning that persons released on parole found their first job 3.45 weeks sooner than other persons, holding constant all the other variables in the equation. In effect, the regression coefficient for parole is an estimated net effect for parole supervision, indicating that persons released on parole went to work sooner than those who were let go without parole supervision.

The remaining variables in the equation were entered because there were good reasons to believe that the conditions they represent affect employment. Thus, for example, age, sex, ethnicity, education, marital status, having a physical disability, having arranged a job prior to release, and being returned to Houston (a prime labor market in Texas at the time) were expected to affect how quickly the released felons obtained employment irrespective of any effect of parole. Indeed, we see that some of them were useful: Males were likely to go to work more quickly than females (about 14.5 weeks sooner), the physically disabled took longer, those who returned to Houston got work faster in that very good labor market, and those who had arranged for a job prior to release also went to work sooner.

The worth of the analysis presented in Exhibit 9-E depends largely on how thoroughly the control variables used in the regression model capture the factors involved in going to work quickly that differentiated those released under parole supervision and those released without such supervision. To the extent that all those differences are represented in the model,

---

⬚ EXHIBIT 9-E   Multiple Regression Analysis of the Effects of Parole Supervision

The regression results shown in the table below are computed from the control group in one of the Transitional Aid to Released Prisoners (TARP) experiments. Because the table is concerned only with members of the control group from one of those experiments, it essentially describes a quasi-experiment equivalent to having drawn a random sample of all persons released from the state prisons of Texas over a six-month period and comparing those receiving parole supervision with the nonrandomly assigned group not receiving such supervision. (The details of the experimental intervention used in the TARP experiments are described in Exhibit 8-G.)

Regression of Number of Weeks Postrelease to First Employment on Selected Prerelease Characteristics and Parole Status

Predictor Variables	b	Standard Error
Parole supervision	−3.45*	1.25
Age (years)	.01	.08
Male	−14.45*	2.72
Black	4.45*	1.53
Chicano	4.33	2.07
Education (years)	−.16	.34
Married	−.01	1.89
Previous convictions (number)	.08	.09
Discharge payment	.00	.00
Handicap classification	7.36*	2.25
Released to Houston	−4.67*	1.44
Job arranged before release	−.20*	.06
Expected weeks to first job	2.81*	.76
Prison Behavior Code	−.03	.02
Constant	16.68*	6.50

$R^2 = .25*$
$N = 397$

*Statistically significant at $p \le .05$.

SOURCE: Unpublished tabulations from TARP control group in Texas. (For a full description of the study, see Rossi, Berk, and Lenihan, 1980.)

---

the additional relationship of parole supervision to the outcome represents a net program effect.

Modeling selection. A one-stage regression model, such as illustrated in Exhibit 9-E, is configured in terms of the relationships of the control variables with the outcome variable of interest. To be valid, it must incorporate measured values on each distinct variable that may influence outcome and on which the intervention and comparison group may differ. It may also include variables related to selection into intervention. In Exhibit 9-E, for instance, the number of previous convictions and the Prison Behavior Code (a point system related to misbehavior in prison) are influential in the administrative decision to release a prisoner under parole supervision. The regression model, however, incorporates them as outcome predictors, not as determinants of selection into intervention. Although related to selection, therefore, they are not set up in a way that optimizes the information they carry about selection effects.

An alternate approach that is becoming more commonplace is to use a two-stage regression analysis in which the first step is to model the selection bias and the second is to incorporate the results of that model as a predictor variable in a regression model predicting outcome. The second stage follows the same general form as described above and is illustrated in Exhibit 9-E except for the addition of another predictor variable directly related to selection bias. We turn our attention, therefore, to the first stage of this model, accounting directly for the differential selection of individuals into the intervention versus comparison group when groups are not formed by random assignment. This stage is generally called *selection modeling*.

Selection modeling depends on the evaluator's diligence in identifying and measuring the variables related to the process by which individuals select themselves (e.g., by volunteering) or are selected (e.g., administratively) into the intervention versus the comparison group in a quasi-experiment. These variables then become predictors in a multiple regression model in which the dependent variable is not the intervention outcome variable but, rather, group membership. That is, this first-stage model is set up to "predict" whether an individual is in the intervention group or the compari-

son group. Because group membership is a binary variable (e.g., 1 = intervention group, 0 = comparison group), regression models tailored for dichotomous dependent variables are typically used, for instance, logistic or probit regression analysis.

The resulting equation can then be used to estimate the probability that each case will be selected for the intervention or comparison group. It should be noted that this information can be very interesting in its own right as part of a program evaluation. It will reveal important factors that enhance or inhibit the likelihood that targets will participate in the program. This can have useful implications for program recruiting, referral patterns, identification of underserved groups, and the like.

Within the context of quasi-experimental impact assessment, however, the importance of the selection model is that if it provides a rather complete account of the systematic factors in the allocation to groups, it can be used to derive a control variable for subsequent statistical analysis that will properly adjust for selection bias when assessing intervention effects. This is done by using the selection model to create something called an *instrumental variable* that carries information about the selection effect. Using it as a control variable should then offset the selection effect and permit the quasi-experiment to yield an unbiased estimate of the intervention effect when, in turn, the outcome variable is analyzed in a second step.

Several variants on selection models and the full two-stage estimation of intervention effects are available. These include Heckman's econometric approach (Heckman and Hotz, 1989; Heckman and Robb, 1985), Rosenbaum and Rubin's propensity scores (1983, 1984), and instrumental variables (Greene, 1993). Useful general discussion can be found in

---

✦ EXHIBIT 9-F   Estimating the Net Effect of AA Attendance Using Two-Stage Selection Modeling

Does attendance at AA meetings affect the drinking of individuals who have problems with alcohol? It is part of the AA philosophy that the problem drinker make a voluntary commitment to participation, so self-selection becomes part of the intervention. Any attempt to assess impact by comparing problem drinkers who attend AA and those who do not, therefore, must deal with selection bias related to the distinctive characteristics of those who decide to attend. To attempt to equate the group through statistical controls, researchers in the Palo Alto Veterans Affairs Health Care System used two-stage selection modeling.

First, consideration was given to what variables were expected to predict AA participation. Based on prior research, three variables were selected: perceived seriousness of drinking (those who believe their drinking is a problem are presumed more likely to participate), tendency to cope with problems by seeking information and advice, and gender (women are presumed more likely to seek help than men). These variables were measured on sample of 218 individuals with drinking problems and used in a probit regression model to predict AA participation. As shown in the summary below, two of the variables showed significant independent relationships to attendance.

This selection model was then used to produce a new variable, lambda, which is a mathematical expression of the degree of self-selection bias that yields values for each individual. Lambda is then entered as a control variable in a second-stage regression predicting outcome, the amount of drinking measured on a Drinking Pattern scale. Two other outcome-related control variables were also included at this stage: baseline drinking scores and marital status. Finally, inclusion of the intervention variable, AA attendance (0 = no, 1 = yes), allowed assessment of its relation to the outcome variable when the other predictor variables, including the selection variable, were statistically controlled.

Humphreys, Phibbs, and Moos (1996) and Stolzenberg and Relles (1997).

As an example of a possible application, suppose we were studying the outcomes of criminal justice procedures. Accused persons proceed through a number of stages, each of which conditions the next successive stage, and it is possible to develop a fairly accurate model of how cases are moved from one stage to another. For example, district attorneys may move to the indictment stage only those robbery cases in which there are several witnesses.

In this case, the selection process by which cases are brought to the indictment stage can be modeled or incorporated statistically into the design. Another example of a circumstance in which the selection process can be modeled concerns the auditing procedures used by the Internal Revenue Service (IRS) on tax returns. The IRS uses a set of algorithms based on information contained in returns to guide their selection of returns to be audited. An evaluation of the effect of being audited on individuals' subsequent reporting practices would be

⁂ **EXHIBIT 9-F** Continued

The significant coefficient for AA attendance shows that those participating drank less at outcome than those not attending, controlling for baseline drinking and self-selection. Indeed, on the 30-point Drinking Pattern scale, the estimated net effect of AA attendance was a reduction of more than 6 points.

Stage 1: Probit Regression Predicting AA Attendance

Predictor Variable	Coefficient	Standard Error
Sex (0 = M, 1 = F)	.29	.19
Information seeking	.06*	.02
Perceived seriousness of drinking	.38*	.09
R^2 = .129		

Stage 2: Least Squares Regression Predicting Drinking Outcome

Predictor Variable	Coefficient	Standard Error
Baseline drinking	.20*	.08
Married (0 = no, 1 = yes)	−1.68	1.23
Lambda	2.10	1.98
AA attendance	−6.31*	3.04
R^2 = .084		

*Statistically significant at $p \leq .05$.

SOURCE: Adapted from Keith Humphreys, Ciaran S. Phibbs, and Rudolf H. Moos, "Addressing Self-Selection Effects in Evaluations of Mutual Help Groups and Professional Mental Health Services: An Introduction to Two-Stage Sample Selection Models," *Evaluation and Program Planning*, 1996, 19(4):301-308.

considerably improved if the evaluator constructed a model of the IRS auditing decisions based on the algorithms used by that agency.

Exhibit 9-F provides a more detailed example of the use of selection modeling, in this case, to account for the self-selection among problem drinkers for attendance at Alcoholics Anonymous (AA) meetings. There is every reason to believe that those who choose to attend AA meetings are different from those who do not in ways related to the likelihood of subsequent reductions in their drinking, the outcome of interest. Exhibit 9-F shows how one group of researchers identified control variables for selection bias and control variables for extraneous influences on outcome and incorporated them into a two-stage selection model.

Regression-Discontinuity Designs

As the discussion of selection modeling above should make clear, complete and valid data on the variables that are the basis for selection into quasi-experimental intervention and comparison groups provide the makings for a very effective statistical control variable. Suppose, now, that instead of having to try to figure out what variables were related to selection, the evaluator was given the selection variable up front and could then apply it case by case to allocate individuals into the intervention or comparison group according to their scores on that variable. In this circumstance, selection modeling would be pretty much a sure thing because there would be no uncertainty about how selection was done and the evaluator would have the measured values that determined it in hand.

A special type of constructed control quasi-experiment, referred to as a *regression-discontinuity design*, is based on this concept. Although the opportunities to use this design are somewhat limited, when applicable it provides the most rigorous quasi-experimental (nonrandomized) impact assessment that can be undertaken. Regression-discontinuity designs are appropriate for those circumstances when the evaluator cannot randomly assign targets to experimental groups but could collaborate with program personnel to divide them systematically on the basis of need, merit, or some other qualifying condition and assign the neediest, most meritorious, and so forth to the intervention condition and those less needy or meritorious to the comparison condition.

A more descriptive name for regression-discontinuity designs is *cutting point designs* because the way they work is to take some continuum of need, merit, and the like and, using measured values along that continuum, apply a cutting point such that those with scores over the cutting point go into one group and those whose scores are under the cutting point go into the other group. Thus, the selection procedures are explicit and known because the participants are chosen according to a fixed formula, as in the case of contests or eligibility tests that are worked out so that a certain score is needed to qualify for the selected group. Regression-discontinuity designs approximate randomized experiments to the extent that the known selection process is modeled properly, which is generally straightforward because it is explicit and quantitative.

For example, to estimate the effects of a program providing eligibility for unemployment insurance payments to released prisoners in California (modeled to some degree after the Baltimore LIFE experiment described in Exhibit 8-E), Berk and Rauma (1983) took advantage of the fact that program eligibility was contingent on the number of days a felon worked in prison. Ex-prisoners had to have worked more than 652 days in prison before becoming eligible for any payments, and the amount of payment was made proportional to the number of days worked. The formula applied was explicit and quantitative, the cutting point for eligibility was uniformly 652 days of work, and payments were made above that point and not below.

Comparing the rearrest rates of those given payments with those who were not, while using the hours worked in prison as a control variable (modeling selection exactly), provided an estimate of the net effect of the payments on rearrest. Regression analysis showed that ex-prisoners who were given payments were estimated to have 13% fewer arrests. This estimate is unbiased insofar as the selection process is known and accurately represented in the statistical analysis by the variable "hours worked in prison."

Although in some cases virtually equivalent to randomized experiments, regression-discontinuity designs have not been applied often, partly because not all programs have definite and precise rules for eligibility or are willing to adopt such rules for purposes of impact assessment. However, another reason for their infrequent use seems to be that they are not well understood by evaluators and, therefore, are often not applied even when appropriate. Evaluators who conduct impact assessments would profit from an investment in learning more about these designs. Source material can be found in Trochim (1984), Reichardt, Trochim, and Cappelleri (1995), Braden and Bryant (1990), Stanley (1991), Cappelleri et al. (1991), and Trochim, Cappelleri, and Reichardt (1991).

Generic Controls

In contrast to the physical sciences, only a few aggregate measures of social behavior and processes exist that can be used as generic controls—that is, measures that can serve to represent "control group" outcomes. It is not necessary for the industrial chemist to ascertain *de novo* typical BTU values for various fuels, because there are handbooks in which such values are listed, based on the pooled experiences of scores of investigators. For the social researcher, however, there are few comparable compilations. We do not know, for instance, the typical experiences of persons in urban labor markets. Even more important, we do know how such "typical" experiences change from season to season and from year to year or fluctuate with the business cycle and with the mix of workers on the market.

Among the social generic controls that do exist are demographic measures, such as age, sex, income, occupation and race; distributions of certain characteristics and processes (e.g., death rates, birth rates, sex ratios, proportions of persons in various labor force categories); and derivatives of these measures. In addition, there are published standards or norms for various psychological tests (including tests of intelligence, achievement of various skills, personality, etc.).

With proper safeguards, the information provided by these and other generic controls sometimes can be used to estimate what would ordinarily happen without an intervention. The best examples of appropriate use of generic controls are from epidemiological studies. For example, the positive effects of fluoridated water on reducing dental caries were discovered by noting that the incidence of caries varied among localities and was correlated with the amount of fluorides naturally found in the drinking water. This correlation was discovered because dental epidemiologists had a fairly firm notion of the normal rates of caries formation. Similarly, the detection of epidemics rests heavily on the epidemiologist's knowledge of ordinary incidence rates for various diseases, just as the efficacy of occupational health measures is judged against expected death rates from various causes in the general population.

A related example from the field of public health concerns comparing death rates from cancer for persons who have been in occupations with high exposures to suspected carcinogenic substances with those of persons in other occupations. For instance, it is suspected that high levels of exposure to formaldehyde among workers in medical pathology laboratories accounts for the high death rate among such workers from brain cancer. Comparisons of the expected death rates from this condition for persons of roughly the same age and sex in the general population with those of workers in medical pathology labs reveal that the death rate for the laboratory workers is several magnitudes higher than expected.

Many of the instances in which generic controls have been used successfully are ones in which selection processes are either known or unimportant, as in epidemiologists' use of morbidity rates in detecting epidemics. In the more usual cases handled by evaluators, generic controls can be quite misleading. For example, in planning the impact assessment of educational interventions, evaluators may be tempted to use the norms of achievement test publishers as generic controls. But doing so may result in serious errors; so much variance in achievement is associated with socioeconomic level, ethnic background, and similar factors that published norms are usually too general to be useful in a specific evaluation application. Thus, in evaluating whether a new teaching program is effective in educating inner-city children, it is clearly inappropriate to compare the annual gain in achievement test scores of a sample of inner-city children against the published norms for such gains from the test constructor. The ordinary rates of learning for such children are likely to differ greatly from such general norms. Similarly, it is probably a mistake to compare the earnings of 34-year-old males or females, as reported in the Bureau of the Census' Current Population Survey, to those of men or women of the same age who have just completed a vocational training course. Generic controls, in short, are usually unavailable in sufficient detail for evaluators to be confident that the standards in question are appropriate for a particular use.

We wish to stress that generic controls should be used only when other types of controls are not available, and then only with the utmost caution. They are tempting, to be sure—generic controls are inexpensive in comparison to randomized or constructed controls and the data take almost no time to collect. However, because of their questionable appropriateness, generic controls should generally be a last resort that are used with intense scrutiny of whether their sources are comparable to participants in every critical way.

SOME CAUTIONS IN USING CONSTRUCTED CONTROLS

The advantages of constructed controls for impact assessment of partial coverage programs rest entirely on their practicality and convenience in situations where high-quality randomized field experiments are not feasible. The scientific credibility of well-executed field experiments would make them the obvious choice if such designs were typically the easiest, fastest, and least expensive to implement. Unfortunately, the environment of social programs is such that randomized experiments are almost universally the most difficult, time-consuming, and expensive of the impact designs to implement well. Designing impact assessment, therefore, is generally a matter of weighing the importance of scientific rigor against the practical constraints inherent in the evaluation context. The value of quasi-experimental designs is that, when carefully done, they offer the prospect of providing credible estimates of net program effects while being relatively adaptable to program circumstances that are not inherently compatible with the requirements of social research.

A critical question, of course, is how good quasi-experimental designs typically are in producing valid estimates of net program effects. Put another way, how much risk of serious error in assessing program impact does the evaluator run when using constructed controls, for practical reasons, instead of randomly assigned controls? We would like to be able to answer this question by drawing on a body of research that compares the results of various quasi-experiments with those of randomized experiments in different program situations. Such studies are rare, however, so only a little evidence can be offered along these lines. What the few available comparisons show is what we might expect: Under favorable circumstances and carefully done, constructed control designs can yield estimates of net program effects that are comparable to those derived from randomized designs, but they can also produce wildly erroneous results.

We mentioned, earlier, the study by Fraker and Maynard (1984) comparing estimates of the effects of an employment program that were derived from control groups constructed by matching with those from a randomized experiment. They used various methods of making individual matches but none produced results that agreed very closely with those of the randomized experiment. But then Heckman and Hotz (1989) showed that using the appropriate control variables and applying a more sophisticated statistical model to that data did produce effect estimates similar to those from the experiment. A similar comparison for an employment training program was made by LaLonde (1986). In that case, results from statistical controls applied to a nonrandom design were compared with those from a randomized experiment. LaLonde also found substantial discrepancies, including a differential bias for female participants (effects overestimated by the quasi-experiment) in comparison to males (effects underestimated).

More recent evidence from different program areas has been somewhat more encouraging. Aiken et al. (1998) compared the results of different impact designs applied to a university-level freshman remedial writing program.

They found "highly similar" effect estimates from a nonequivalent (nonrandomized) comparison design with statistical controls, a regression-discontinuity design, and a randomized experiment. A simple pre-post comparison, however, substantially overestimated the net program effect.

In another comparative study, Reynolds and Temple (1995) examined different approaches to selection modeling controls for producing quasi-experimental estimates of school achievement effects from Chicago's Child-Parent Center preschool program. Two variations each of econometric modeling, latent-variable structural modeling, and ordinary least squares regression produced similar estimates of program effects. No results from a randomized design were available for this program to provide a standard, which leaves some ambiguity about how valid these estimates were despite their consistency. Comparisons with randomized studies of similar programs drawn from meta-analyses reported in the literature, however, showed generally similar results.

Broad comparisons of the effect estimates from impact assessments for sets of independent studies within the same program area also shed some light on the validity of the results using constructed controls. Lipsey and Wilson (1993) compared the mean effect size estimates reported for randomized versus nonrandomized designs in 74 meta-analyses of psychological, educational, and behavioral interventions. In many of the sets of studies included in a meta-analysis, the effect estimates from nonrandomized comparisons were very similar to those from randomized ones. However, in an equal number of cases there were substantial differences in both directions. That is, in some program areas the nonrandomized studies, on average, produced much larger effect estimates than the randomized studies, and in other program areas, they produced much smaller estimates. Heinsman and Shadish (1996) made a closer examination of the effect estimates in 98 studies over four program areas and also found that nonrandomized designs gave varied results relative to randomized designs—sometimes similar, sometimes appreciably larger or smaller.

What comparative evidence we have, therefore, indicates that, in a given application, impact assessments using constructed controls can yield effect estimates similar to those that would result from a randomized experiment, but frequently do not. Moreover, the empirical evidence at this point provides little indication of which program circumstances or which variations on quasi-experimental designs are associated with better or worse estimates. Evaluators using nonrandomized designs for impact assessment, therefore, must rely heavily on a case-by-case analysis of the particular assumptions and requirements of the selected design and the specific characteristics of the program and target population to optimize the likelihood that valid estimates of program effects will result.

Ex Ante Versus Ex Post Designs

The trade-offs involved in selecting a design with high inherent likelihood of producing a valid effect estimate and the practicalities of implementing that design successfully apply to both ex ante and ex post quasi-experiments. Given a number of equally feasible options, the design of choice is the one that requires the least amount of matching or statistical manipulation to maximize the comparability of the groups. It follows, in most cases, that ex ante quasi-experiments are preferable to ex post ones, because identifying one or more comparison groups in advance generally allows the evaluator to equate the groups more easily.

Assessing the impact of ongoing programs on current or former participants in ex post evaluations is particularly difficult for programs that have been in operation for a long period or for which there is a long interval between the onset of participation and the time when outcomes are expected. Because it is necessary to construct a comparison group representing preprogram characteristics, some of the crucial measurements may have to rely on existing records collected for other purposes or on very fallible recall. For example, in an ex post evaluation of the effects of parenting training for teenage mothers on their disciplinary practices when their children are age six and older, it might be necessary to obtain measures of preprogram parenting practices for both program participants and comparable nonparticipants. Such information is unlikely to have been recorded in any useful form and would clearly be difficult to establish by relying on the memories of the mothers involved.

The major problem in ex post evaluation of ongoing programs, however, is that it is not possible for the evaluator to have any influence on who receives the intervention or when. For programs that have only partial coverage, nevertheless, it may be possible to identify targets who have not received the intervention and, with careful analysis, arrive at estimates of impact. For example, to assess the impact of job training for the unemployed, a survey might be undertaken of persons who had participated and of their friends, relatives, and neighbors (designated by the participants). The subsequent work histories of program participants could then be compared with those of relatives and neighbors who also were unemployed at the time when the participants began the program. Such persons are likely to be similar to the participants in most aspects relevant to the program: age, residential location, attitudes, and perhaps motivations.

An Illustrative Ex Post Quasi-Experiment

Because ex post quasi-experiments are so difficult to implement, we provide a detailed example by examining the problem of designing an impact assessment of one of the oldest, ongoing, partial-coverage social programs, Vocational Rehabilitation. This program was started after World War I to provide vocational training to disabled veterans, then expanded to nonveterans, and is currently administered by the Department of Education. It serves about 100,000 disabled persons annually, most of whom have been referred by state employment security agencies or local hospitals.

Vocational Rehabilitation is a partial-coverage program because it accepts only those disabled persons whom program personnel assess as capable of being helped; indeed, more than half of the persons who apply for its services are turned away. In addition, many disabled persons never apply for services but are served by other sources, including private insurers under Workers Compensation, or through programs offered by the Social Security Administration and the Veterans Administration.

In the mid-1980s, Congress directed the Department of Education to plan an impact evaluation of the program, stating explicitly that the major issue was whether the persons served had improved in employability and earnings over what would have occurred if they

had not been served. In the report submitted by the contractor selected to undertake the planning task, and in subsequent discussions with consultants, a large number of options were considered for the evaluation design (Berkeley Planning Associates, 1988). The five options, described below, illustrate the difficulties of conducting an impact assessment of an ongoing program.

The first option considered was a randomized controlled experiment. Because of political and ethical considerations, however, this was quickly ruled out. Program personnel were expected to object strongly to randomization and be uncooperative. Indeed, in one program site in which a randomized experiment previously had been planned, program staff threatened to go out on strike. In addition, it was believed that withholding treatment randomly from persons clearly in need would be unacceptable to Congress. In general, once a program is ongoing for any length of time, it is very difficult to then begin withholding intervention from eligible participants for evaluation purposes.

The second option, comparisons between the preintervention and postintervention conditions of clients, was also ruled out because changes due to natural recovery were judged to be large and difficult to untangle from intervention effects. Many clients entered the program shortly after the onset of their disability, and the process of recovery itself would obviously improve their employment and earnings capacities.

A third option was to compare the postintervention employment and earnings of clients who successfully completed the program to those of clients who were either rejected for participation or dropped out before completion. This option was considered unsuitable because the program selected its clients on the basis of their prospects for successful rehabilitation; hence, any such comparisons would directly confound selection with outcome in ways expected to be difficult to control statistically.

A fourth option considered was to compare the outcomes for Vocational Rehabilitation clients with those of disabled persons who were clients of other rehabilitation programs. This option was rejected on the grounds that the potential effectiveness of the other programs contaminated that comparison group as a "no treatment" baseline for Vocational Rehabilitation clients. Also, it was clear that the different success rates of the several rehabilitation programs were not of central interest to Congress.

The final option was to identify comparable untreated disabled persons from among the respondents in a large, ongoing national survey. The plan was to compare the earnings and employment experiences of disabled persons identified in the Survey of Income and Program Participation who had not participated in any rehabilitation program with those of Vocational Rehabilitation clients while statistically controlling the seriousness of the disability, length of time disabled, predisability earnings, and selected demographic characteristics. Although it was not without problems, this option was recommended as the best impact assessment that could be done, given the constraints of time and resources.

Note that this sifting of alternative approaches was occasioned in the first place by the ongoing nature of the program and was dominated by the need to find an alternative that could be completed in a short period of time (two years) with the greatest possible validity. Especially important was how to compensate for the large selection bias inherent in the program. The design chosen still had selection bias problems, but they were thought to be

potentially manageable through statistical controls. In addition, the feasibility of the impact assessment depended heavily on identifying a sufficiently large number of disabled persons from the Survey of Income and Program Participation who were not participants in any program but were reasonably comparable in relevant respects to Vocational Rehabilitation clients.

Using Existing Data Sources

As the Vocational Rehabilitation example illustrates, it is sometimes possible to locate a timely data source that allows the identification of nonparticipating targets. In addition to the national Survey of Income and Program Participation, other potentially useful data sources are available to evaluators. One valuable source of existing data sets, most of high quality, is the Inter-University Consortium of Political and Social Research at the University of Michigan. Most research-oriented American universities are members of the consortium and have catalogs describing its collection of data sets.

In the case of ongoing programs that serve only a small proportion of eligible targets, it may not be important that a data source used to construct a control group identify who is not a program participant. For example, if public housing projects serve only a small fraction— say, 10%—of those eligible, then a sample of eligible households, whether or not they are participants in the program, can be used as controls. Use of such a sample would underestimate the differences between participants and controls (because 10% of the latter would be participants), but the resulting dilution may not be serious, especially when the estimated effects are large.

Using Cross-Sectional Sample Surveys in Ex Post Quasi-Experiments

Faced with the task of planning an impact assessment for an ongoing partial-coverage program *that is presumed to produce relatively long-term effects*, the only alternative open to an evaluator may be use of a cross-sectional sample survey. Note the emphasized clause in the last sentence—it is usually impractical on the grounds of cost and time to plan prospective longitudinal studies of programs that are expected to produce their effects over more than a few years.

Using a sample survey designed to obtain an unbiased sample of the target population can enable evaluators to identify exposed and unexposed targets, measure outcome variables, and collect data that may be useful in identifying unexposed targets who are comparable to targets that have received the intervention. The time of the exposure can be years or even decades in the past so that long-term effects may be studied. The outcomes measured for the exposed targets are compared with the same measures for the unexposed targets with statistical controls for those characteristics that distinguished the groups at the time of exposure. For some programs aimed at target populations that are a large proportion of the total population—for example, smokers currently constitute about 40% of U.S. adults—general sample surveys designed to produce unbiased samples of the total population may be appropriate. For programs aimed at target populations that constitute smaller proportions of the total population—for example, female heads of households with small children—special sampling strategies must be used to draw samples with enriched proportions of the desired target population.

An instructive example of an impact assessment of a large-scale ongoing program is the evaluation of the Special Supplemental Nutrition Program for Women, Infants, and Children (WIC), a federal nutrition program for poor pregnant women. Although based on administrative records rather than interviews or questionnaires, the study exemplifies how cross-sectional data may be used to estimate program impacts.

The WIC program was established in the 1970s to provide food supplements to poor pregnant women, infants, and children. Epidemiological studies had shown that children born to poor women tended to weigh less at birth, have higher risk for neonate mortality, and be more likely to incur expensive medical expenses after birth. Poor infants and children also were found to suffer from nutrition-related conditions, such as iron deficiency anemia and below-normal growth rates. The WIC program provides vouchers redeemable at participating food stores for the purchase of specific packages of food tailored to meet the nutritional needs of this target population.

We will be concerned here only with the portion of the program designed to improve pregnancy outcomes by increasing birth weights and reducing neonate mortality. Women are eligible if their household incomes are at or below 185% of the poverty level and they are at nutritional risk. Participants receive monthly vouchers for supplemental foods worth about $30, are offered instruction in proper nutrition, and are referred to clinics for prenatal care. In 1995, the program served about 1.6 million women, estimated to be more than three-fifths of the eligible population (Rossi, 1998).

The U.S. Department of Agriculture, which administers the WIC program, has commissioned several randomized field experiments of this portion of the WIC program. However, the contractors were unable to carry out the experiment successfully because significant proportions of the pregnant women enlisted in the control groups became WIC participants. The department then contracted with Mathematica Policy Research to conduct a nonexperimental impact assessment.

Because Medicaid enrollees are automatically eligible for WIC participation, the researchers selected pregnant women on Medicaid as the study population (Devaney, 1998; Devaney, Bilheimer, and Schore, 1991). By linking the birth registration records for Medicaid enrollees with the Medicaid medical payment and WIC participation records in five states, the researchers were able to identify 112,000 WIC-eligible women who gave birth during the period 1987-1988.

The analysis strategy was to contrast the birth outcomes for women who participated in WIC with those who did not, using data from the several merged files. The outcomes studied included birth weight, incidence of extremely low birth weight, and incurred Medicaid costs. In the statistical estimation models, variables that might independently affect birth outcomes were used as control variables. An especially important control variable was the adequacy of each patient's prenatal medical care as recorded in birth registration records, a measure that at least partially controls for the possibility that WIC participants care more about pregnancy outcomes.

Devaney and her colleagues found that prenatal WIC participation led to increased birth weight, ranging from an average of 51 grams in one state to 117 grams in another. Even greater gains were found for births that were not brought to full term (less than 37 weeks of gestation), ranging from 138 to 259 grams. WIC participation was also found to lower the incidence of extremely low birth weights (less than 2,500 grams). Furthermore, the estimated savings in Medicaid expenditures for mother and child in the 60 days after birth ranged from $277 to $744 across the five states. The resulting benefit-cost ratios indicated that the reduced Medicaid costs exceeded the costs of prenatal WIC benefits. Not only were prenatal WIC supplements shown to be effective, they were also cost-effective.

Devaney's studies were carefully and skillfully done and provide the best evidence available on the effects of prenatal WIC supplements. Nonetheless, there are limitations to the research inherent in the ex post, cross-sectional nature of the study. First, the findings pertain only to Medicaid recipients, and only about half of all WIC participants are also enrolled in Medicaid. Of course, this incomplete coverage can be taken as a point in favor of the findings because the pregnant women on Medicaid are likely to include those worst off in the WIC population, the group at greatest risk of adverse birth outcomes. Second, although Medicaid clients are drawn from among the very poor, they are not homogeneous in socioeconomic status. Because the Medicaid records did not contain data on household income, the researchers had to use mother's educational attainment as a proxy. Accordingly, differences in economic status between WIC recipients and nonrecipients may not have been well controlled.

The third caveat is the most serious. All the women in the study were eligible for the

WIC prenatal program. The fact that some participated and some did not may reflect differences between the two groups that would also affect pregnancy outcomes. For example, participants may have been more deeply invested in the pregnancy and hence sought out WIC participation. On the other side, some of the nonparticipating Medicaid clients may not have been deemed nutritional risks and therefore were not accepted into the WIC program. Although the inclusion of measures of the adequacy of prenatal care from birth records as a control variable tends to mitigate this criticism, it does not do so completely.

This example demonstrates how heavily ex post cross-sectional impact assessment depends on proper conceptualization of the measures of program participation used and the characteristics of exposed and unexposed targets relevant to participation. The latter can be used to model selection bias and to remove it from the estimation of effects, but for this process to be successful, the variables available for the analysis must be capable of fully specifying the selection effect.

Limitations on the Use of Cross-Sectional Surveys

Like all types of designs, cross-sectional approaches to impact assessment have both advantages and limitations. On the positive side, cross-sectional studies can usually be accomplished quickly and are therefore cost-effective methods for estimating net program effects. Also, this approach is often the only one that is practical for impact assessment of a program that takes many years to show its effects.

On the negative side, cross-sectional studies are quite vulnerable to selection biases as a result of what economists refer to as *specification errors*. Specification errors are mistakes in specifying the appropriate theoretical structure and corresponding variables that can rule out competing explanations. Such errors result in the absence from the statistical analysis of the variables needed to properly adjust for selection bias.

In the extreme, faulty specification may lead to undertaking evaluations that should not have been initiated. For example, in the analysis of the effects of parole supervision on subsequent employment (Exhibit 9-E), if an important factor in how parole boards judge whether prisoners are eligible for parole was left out, the analysis may simply be wrong. To be more specific, if it turns out that parole boards released only prisoners who undertook vocational training in prison, the effects that are claimed for parole in Exhibit 9-E may simply reflect the fact that parolees were better prepared to obtain jobs. In that case, the apparent effects of parole found in the analysis would, in actuality, be the effects of vocational training and may have nothing to do with parole supervision.

SUMMARY

❋ Several potentially valid impact assessment strategies can be used when it is not feasible to randomly assign targets to intervention and control conditions. Like randomized experiments, these quasi-experimental designs can usually only be implemented when there is partial program coverage, that is, when there are targets that are unexposed as well as exposed to the intervention.

❋ The logic behind quasi-experimental designs is essentially the same as in randomized experiments, except that the intervention and comparison groups cannot be assumed equivalent at the beginning of the study even though efforts may have been made to attain as much equivalence as possible. In quasi-experiments, therefore, the extent to which the comparison group differs from the intervention group must be assessed and appropriate procedures applied to adjust for those differences in any estimation of net program effects.

❋ Ideally, quasi-experiments should be designed prior to the implementation of a program, although ex post as well as ex ante evaluations are commonplace.

❋ In constructed control designs, either program participants and nonparticipants are matched (individually or as aggregates) or statistical procedures are undertaken to equate them. The most effective of these procedures is embodied in regression-discontinuity designs, which can be applied when it is possible to assign individuals to the intervention and comparison groups on the basis of their score on a quantitative measure of need, merit, or the like.

❋ Evaluators may have to resort to generic controls when no other controls are available, but these should be used only with great caution and careful scrutiny to ensure that the sources of this "control" data are genuinely comparable in relevant respects to participants.

❋ In general, the best quasi-experimental design is the one that requires the least amount of matching or statistical adjustment to equate the comparison and experimental groups.

Reflexive controls	Measures of the outcome variable taken on participating targets before interventions and used as control observations.
Pre-post design	A reflexive control design in which only one or a few before-intervention and after-intervention measures are taken.
Shadow controls	Expert and participant judgments used to estimate net impact.
Time-series analyses	Reflexive designs that rely on relatively long series of repeated measurements of the outcome variable taken before and after an intervention.

CHAPTER 10

ASSESSMENT OF FULL-COVERAGE PROGRAMS

In this chapter, we consider designs for assessing the impact of full-coverage programs. Of course, many programs intended to reach all targets fail to do so because of either faulty delivery or insufficient interest by eligible targets. In designing evaluations, it may be possible to treat these as partial-coverage programs and configure a comparison group. Often, however, there are not enough unserved targets available to construct comparison groups; under these circumstances, the most common option is to assess changes on outcome measures that occur between a point before targets participate in a program and some point afterward. The term reflexive controls *is used to describe impact assessments of this sort where targets serve as their own controls. Reflexive control designs generally provide only weak evaluations of impact because, in contrast to random and quasi-experimental evaluations, it is not generally possible to take certain important confounding effects into account. When it is possible to obtain a large number of pre- and post-program measurements on outcome variables, sophisticated time-series analyses can be undertaken, which usually allow for firmer assessment of outcomes. An alternative to reflexive controls is the use of* shadow controls. *Shadow controls basically consist of knowledgeable experts, administrators, or targets themselves, who judge program outcomes in the light of their experience or opinion regarding what might have occurred without the intervention. Shadow control evaluations rarely produce completely convincing findings about impact.*

Evaluators of fully or almost fully saturated programs, ones in which virtually all eligible targets participate in the program, encounter circumstances that make it very difficult to undertake impact assessments that yield credible results. In the absence of a comparison group, it is virtually impossible to take all the confounding effects into account that are likely to be influential and to produce convincing estimates of program effects. With the possible exception of some applications of time-series analyses in which there are a large number of measurements on outcome variables, evaluators undertaking assessments of full-coverage programs should expect the results to be vulnerable to criticism.

At the same time, it is essential to evaluate a myriad of full-coverage programs. Many, if not most, government-sponsored social pro-grams are mandated to cover all targets in the population; indeed, often it is the right of all eligible targets not only to participate but to receive the same intensity or array of services. Obvious examples at the national level are Medicare and Social Security for elderly per-sons and, at the local level, public safety and schooling. In these instances, there is little possibility of forming a reasonable comparison group, which necessarily means that the oppor-tunity for firm estimates of impact is limited. It is evident that in comparison with random-ized and quasi-experimental studies, the level of confidence in the effectiveness estimates of full-coverage programs generally is low. How-ever, it is not possible to simply avoid evaluat-ing such programs because decisionmakers and the public persistently and appropriately raise questions about their effectiveness.

This chapter discusses two types of designs applicable to impact assessments of full-cover-age programs: those using *reflexive controls* and judgmental assessments using what we have termed *shadow controls*. In reflexive con-trol studies, the estimation of net impact comes entirely from information on the targets at two or more points in time, at least one of which is before exposure to the program. Shadow controls are based on the assumption that it is possible for some persons to estimate the impact of programs by comparing program outcomes to their conjectures about what could be expected to occur without the program. Al-most always, judgmental approaches are sus-pect for estimating impact.

Because of the limitations of the designs discussed in this chapter, evaluators are wise to consider transforming a study of a supposedly full-coverage program into one that considers the relative effectiveness of variations in the program, perhaps consisting of differences in

the intensity or "dosage" provided different targets or even in qualitative differences in the way a program is implemented from jurisdic-tion to jurisdiction. Under such circumstances, it may be possible to use quasi-experiments that approximate those discussed in Chapter 9. We discuss this possibility first.

NONUNIFORM FULL-COVERAGE PROGRAMS

There are many cases where supposedly uni-form programs do not actually deliver the same intervention at the same strength and intensity to all targets. Nonuniform full-coverage pro-grams, in which implementation varies signifi-cantly, can be subjected to impact evaluations that assess the differential effects of variations in the program. However, it should be noted that such assessments provide estimates of the effects of the more effective variations relative to the less effective ones, and not of the effects of the program relative to no program.

The government subsidies and tax credits for child care assessed by Fuller et al. (Exhibit 10-A) provide a good example of a program that varies in level of activity from area to area. By examining the differing levels of these support programs across 36 states and making use of sophisticated statistical controls, the evalua-tors were able to estimate their effects on five indicators of the quality of child care providers despite the fact that no state was without such programs.

A classic cross-sectional study of a full-cov-erage program is the Coleman report (Coleman et al., 1966). This study assessed the impact of differences among schools in staffing levels, finances, student composition, and physical

---

⁂ EXHIBIT 10-A   Using State-Level Policy Variation to Assess the Impact of Subsidies and Tax Credits on the Quality of Child Care Centers

The 1990 federal budget bill created the first nationwide child care program with $3 billion for tax credit, voucher, and state block grants in addition to the $1.1 billion spent directly by state governments for subsidies or vouchers. But does this government investment result in higher levels of child care quality? Fuller, Raudenbush, Wei, and Holloway set out to answer this question by examining the relationship between variation in the type and amount of government support and the quality of child care providers.

They drew their data from a nationally representative sample of 2,089 child care centers across 36 states that was collected for a study conducted by Mathematica Policy Research; state-level information about subsidies, regulations, and staff training requirements; demographic indicators aggregated to the state level from the Bureau of the Census and the Children's Defense Fund; and Internal Revenue Service summaries of state-by-state utilization of the Child and Dependent Care Tax Credit and the Earned Income Tax Credit.

Using hierarchical linear modeling, the researchers examined the association of three types of state child care policies and two indicators of the inflow of tax credit subsidies to the states with five indicators of the quality of child care centers. Control variables were used to take account of the influence of family demand for child care; state-level wealth, maternal employment, and poverty rates; organizational type and structure of the child care centers, and the ethnicity of the participating children.

Government subsides to the child care centers were found to be related to staff with higher qualifications, larger teacher salaries, more formalized instructional programs, and more frequent parent participation but not to child-staff ratios. However, level of state regulation and utilization of the Child and Dependent Care Tax Credit were not independently related to the quality of the child care centers.

SOURCE: Adapted from Bruce Fuller, Stephen W. Raudenbush, Li-Ming Wei, and Susan D. Holloway, "Can Government Raise Child-Care Quality? The Influence of Family Demand, Poverty, and Policy," *Educational Evaluation and Policy Analysis,* 1993, 15(3):255-278.

---

plants on student learning. Coleman's original finding was that differences in these variables were not related very strongly to student achievement. Holding such student background variables constant, he found that students achieved no more in schools spending a great deal per capita than in schools spending considerably less. Similar findings held for student-to-teacher ratios, the adequacy of physical plants, and the training of teachers.

The Coleman report was not universally acclaimed as definitive, however. Many educators and researchers disputed the findings and produced a spate of reanalyses that tested alternative statistical models on the same data. This case again illustrates the vulnerability of one-shot surveys to criticisms on grounds of specification errors.

A final example involves the use of a simple before-and-after reflexive design (Exhibit 10-B).

> ### ◈ EXHIBIT 10-B   Estimating the Effects of Zoning Regulations on Housing and Population
>
> Using local municipal records, Shlay and Rossi ascertained the zoning regulations in force in 1960 for each census tract in a sample from the Chicago metropolitan area. A set of indexes was constructed for each tract reflecting the extent to which the zoning regulations restricted residential use of tract land, ranging from the most exclusionary use pattern, in which only single-family homes on large tracts were permitted, to the least exclusionary usage, in which any type of land use, including industrial and commercial use, was permitted.
>
> Using 1960 and 1970 census reports for housing and population characteristics, the researchers conducted a regression analysis that predicted the 1970 density of housing units in suburban tracts on the basis of 1960 density and the zoning index. Note that this analysis is reflexive in that the 1960 housing density is statistically controlled by including that variable in the regression equation. Thus, what is being studied is the difference between actual 1970 density and that expected on the basis of the 1960 density measures. The other independent variables are all measures of the zoning regulations governing land use in the tracts as of 1960.
>
> The results showed that the more restrictively a tract was zoned, the less its density grew in the period between 1960 and 1970. In short, exclusionary zoning restricted the growth in housing density in suburban tracts over and above what would be expected on the basis of their density in 1960.
>
> SOURCE: Adapted, with permission, from A. Shlay and P. H. Rossi, "Keeping Up the Neighborhood: Estimating Net Effects of Zoning," *American Sociological Review*, October 1981, 46:703-719.

Shlay and Rossi (1981) obtained data on a sample of census tracts in the Chicago metropolitan area to assess the effects of zoning regulations on population and housing growth in the tracts. This impact assessment took advantage of the considerable variation in zoning regulations from tract to tract, using the 1960 and 1970 decennial censuses as before and after measures. Using regression analysis, Shlay and Rossi arrived at estimates of the effects of zoning restrictions on the growth of housing density.

Note that the analysis shown in Exhibit 10-B depends heavily on the existence of variation from census tract to census tract in the 1960 zoning regulations. Hence, each tract serves as its own control in predicting growth in the period between censuses, and tracts are contrasted according to the amount of restriction placed on land uses in each. The researchers took into account the *maturational trends* in tract growth, such as age-related changes in individuals, by estimating such trends for the entire set of tracts and by considering zoning the cause of deviations from such maturational trends, as represented by the predicted 1970 values of housing and population stocks.

For many programs, however, there may not be significant variation to permit this approach to impact assessment, or evaluation sponsors may not be interested in the effects of program variations. In such cases, it usually becomes necessary to resort to one of the approaches described in the remainder of this chapter.

REFLEXIVE CONTROLS

When reflexive controls are used, the presumption must be made that no changes in the targets on the outcome variables have occurred in the time between observations other than those induced by the intervention. Under this presumption, any difference between preintervention status on those variables and postintervention status are deemed net intervention effects. For example, suppose that pensioners from a large corporation previously received their checks in the mail but now have them automatically deposited in their bank accounts. Comparison of complaints about late or missing payments before and after this procedure was implemented could be construed as evidence of impact, provided that it was plausible that the rate of burglaries from mailboxes, the level of postal service, and so on had not also changed.

The strongest reflexive control designs are time series consisting of a large number of observations over the time period spanning the intervention. For example, suppose that instead of just a pre- and postmeasure of pensioners' complaints, we had monthly information for, say, two years before and one year after the change in payment procedures. In this case, our degree of certainty about net effects would be higher because we would have more information on which to base our estimates about what would have happened had there been no change in the mode of check delivery. A second procedure often used is to disaggregate the outcome data by various characteristics of the targets.

For example, examining time-series data about pensioners' complaints regarding receipt of checks in high- and low-crime areas and in rural and urban areas would provide additional insight into the impact of the change in procedure.

In general, the use of reflexive controls is not recommended in circumstances in which comparison or control groups are possible. However, there may be formative evaluation situations in which reflexive controls are appropriate. For example, if a very large difference is essential for an innovative program to be widely implemented, it may be sensible to test it out with a pretest-posttest design that does not include a comparison group. Although only knowledge of the gross effect would emerge from the evaluation, if the gross effect is well below the needed change, there is no basis for continuing plans for implementation. Of course, if a sufficient gross effect is found, it becomes important to undertake a more refined evaluation to have net effect information.

Thus, reflexive controls may be applied usefully to partial-coverage programs as an economical first step, especially if there is little reason to believe that targets' scores on outcome measures would have changed without the intervention. For instance, the impact of a schoolwide nutrition education program consisting of a three-week set of lectures might be evaluated by testing students' knowledge of nutrition before and after participation. The use of reflexive controls in this circumstance is likely to provide a reasonable estimate of the effects of the program because knowledge of nutrition is unlikely to change spontaneously over such a short period, although addition of a properly constructed comparison group would increase confidence.

The impact assessment formula for reflexive designs is as follows:

$$\text{Net effect} = \begin{bmatrix} \text{Outcomes for} \\ \text{participants} \\ \text{after} \\ \text{intervention} \end{bmatrix} - \begin{bmatrix} \text{Outcomes for} \\ \text{participants} \\ \text{before} \\ \text{intervention} \end{bmatrix} \pm$$

$$\begin{bmatrix} \text{Effects} \\ \text{of other} \\ \text{processes at} \\ \text{work during} \\ \text{intervention} \end{bmatrix} + \begin{bmatrix} \text{Design} \\ \text{effects and} \\ \text{stochastic} \\ \text{error} \end{bmatrix}$$

Note that the critical term in the assessment formula represents the effects of other processes at work during intervention. This refers to all those influences that act to bring about change on the outcome variables independently from the intervention. All reflexive designs are vulnerable to such influences because of their lack of control for this class of effects and the general difficulty of developing good estimates of them without a comparison group.

There are several variations of reflexive designs that depend principally on how many measures are taken before and after the program in question has gone into effect. We will examine each of these variations in turn.

Simple Pre-Post Studies

A simple pre-post (or before and after) study is one in which one set of measurements is taken on targets before program participation and a second set is taken on the same targets after sufficiently long participation for effects to be expected. Impact is estimated by comparing the two sets of measurements.

As we have noted, the main drawback to this design is that the differences between before and after measures cannot be confidently ascribed to program effects. All the processes at work in the intervening period may affect these differences. For example, it might be tempting to assess the effectiveness of Medicare by comparing the health statuses of persons before they became eligible with the same measures taken after a few years of participation in Medicare. Such comparisons would be badly misleading for a variety of reasons. In the first place, the maturational effects of aging generally lead to poorer health on their own. In addition, retirement may change the life circumstances of the participants so drastically as to affect their health. Income changes also occur at the same time, and there are also the effects of the deaths of spouses, friends, and so on.

The particular dangers of relying on pre-post reflexive designs for behavior that is age related are demonstrated in the following illustration. Consider the evaluation of a program directed toward women of childbearing age that is designed to lower fertility. The evaluation attempts to show that participation in the program lowers the probability of conceiving, as compared to the ten-year period preceding program participation. Such comparisons would be quite misleading because fertility behavior at one point in time is not independent of prior fertility behavior. Some women will have completed their fertility at the point of program participation and would not have had any more children in any event. Others may be just beginning their families; because they have not had previous children, the birth of any child will appear as a failure of the program. In short, the processes at work producing fertility vary strongly with age, and hence a reflexive design would not yield good estimates of net program effects.

Sometimes time-related changes are more subtle. For example, reflexive controls are likely to be questionable in studies of the impact of job training programs. One of the main reasons people choose to enter such programs is that they are unemployed and are experiencing difficulties obtaining employment. Hence, at the time of entry into the program, most participants have no or very depressed income and some of them are likely to locate jobs irrespective of participation in the program. A job training program will thus appear to be successful automatically if only reflexive controls are used in its evaluation.

A second problem with reflexive controls arises out of potential changes in secular trends between the two time periods involved. If, in a program to increase crop yields, preprogram observations of farmers are made during a period of depressed yields, a comparison with yields during a subsequent period of more normal growing conditions would be misleading. Similarly, a program to reduce crime will appear more effective if it coincides with, say, efforts to increase policing. Confounding factors can also skew an assessment in the other direction: An employment training program will appear ineffective if it is accompanied by a prolonged period of rising unemployment and depressed economic conditions.

A third problem results from possible interfering events between the two points of data collection. An interfering event, as defined previously, is an unusual, one-time occurrence that affects outcome measures. Examples include natural occurrences (e.g., storms), political events, and outbreaks of other social problems. Any intervening event that might affect output measures could interfere with the validity of reflexive control designs for estimating program effects.

In general, then, simple pre-post reflexive designs usually provide findings that have a low degree of credibility. This is particularly the case when the time elapsed between the two measurements is appreciable—say, a year or more—because over time it becomes more and more likely that some process occurring during the time period may obscure the effects of the program, whether by enhancing or by diminishing them. The simple pre-post design, therefore, is appropriate mainly for short-term impact assessments of full-coverage programs attempting to affect conditions that are unlikely to change much on their own (Exhibit 10-C provides an example of such a situation).

Complex Repeated Measures Reflexive Designs

Panel studies that involve repeated measurements on the same group over a period of time can often be used to produce estimates of net intervention effects that have a fair degree of credibility. The reason is that the participation of targets will often vary over time, and the "dips and peaks" can be tied in with the shifts in outcome measures. Although such opportunities are not present in all instances, we urge evaluators to take advantage of them when possible. Fundamentally, this is the same advice we offered earlier in this chapter about taking advantage of differences in intensity or amount of intervention to convert reflexive control evaluations to comparison group quasi-experiments. Even if there is no comparison group, if variations in participation can be tied to changes in the outcome measures, the credibility of the findings is increased.

Exhibit 10-D describes an elaborate attempt by Milavsky and colleagues (1982) to estimate the impact of viewing violence on television on children's subsequent aggressive behaviors. Some exposure to television is almost universal among young children. However, the assessment was made possible by the considerable variation from child to child in the amount of viewing and the contents of the programs they viewed.

☒ EXHIBIT 10-C   A Convincing Pre-Post Outcome Design for a Program to Reduce Residential Lead Levels in Low-Income Housing

The toxic effects of lead are especially harmful to children and can impede their behavioral development, reduce their intelligence, cause hearing loss, and interfere with important biological functions. Poor children are at disproportionate risk for lead poisoning because the homes available to low-income tenants are generally older homes, which are more likely to be painted with lead paint and to be located near other sources of lead contamination. Interior lead paint deteriorates to produce microscopic quantities of lead that children may ingest through hand-to-mouth activity. Moreover, blown or tracked-in dust may be contaminated by deteriorating exterior lead paint or roadside soil containing a cumulation of lead from the leaded gasoline used prior to 1980.

To reduce lead dust levels in low-income urban housing, the Community Lead Education and Reduction Corps (CLEARCorps) was initiated in Baltimore as a joint public-private effort. CLEARCorps members clean, repair, and make homes lead safe, educate residents on lead-poisoning prevention techniques, and encourage the residents to maintain low levels of lead dust through specialized cleaning efforts. To determine the extent to which CLEARCorps was successful in reducing the lead dust levels in treated urban housing units, CLEARCorps members collected lead dust wipe samples immediately before, immediately after, and six months following their lead hazard control efforts. In each of 43 treated houses, four samples were collected from each of four locations—floors, window sills, window wells, and carpets—and sent to laboratories for analysis.

Statistically significant differences were found between pre and post lead dust levels for floors, window sills, and window wells. At the six-month follow-up, further significant declines were found for floors and window wells, with a marginally significant decrease for window sills.

Since no control group was used, it is possible that factors other than the CLEARCorps program contributed to the decline in lead dust levels found in the evaluation. Other than relevant, but modest, seasonal effects relating to the follow-up period and the small possibility that another intervention program treated these same households, for which no evidence was available, there are few plausible alternative explanations for the decline. The evaluators concluded, therefore, that the CLEARCorps program was effective in reducing residential lead levels.

SOURCE: Adapted from Jonathan P. Duckart, "An Evaluation of the Baltimore Community Lead Education and Reduction Corps (CLEARCorps) Program," *Evaluation Review,* 1998, 22(3):373-402.

The advantage of panel studies is that the measures of the intervention and outcomes (e.g., TV viewing and aggressiveness, respectively) are related to each other through time lags and not as cross-sectional correlations. Thus, aggressiveness at Time 2 is examined as a function of viewing patterns measured at Time 1. Panel studies are especially appropriate for impact assessments of full-coverage programs whose dosage varies over individuals and over time. In the case of TV viewing, all the children participated in the sense that virtually

> ## ▓ EXHIBIT 10-D Measuring the Effects of TV Violence on Children's Aggressive Behavior
>
> In an attempt to provide rigorous answers to public concern over whether the viewing of TV programs depicting violence and aggression affect children's aggressive behavior, the National Broadcasting Company (NBC) sponsored an elaborate panel study of young children in which aggressiveness and TV viewing were measured repeatedly over several years.
>
> In the main substudy, samples of elementary school classes, Grades 2 through 6, drawn from Fort Worth and Minneapolis schools, formed the base for a six-wave panel study, in which 400 male children in 59 classes were interviewed six times in the period 1970 to 1973. (Additional substudies were conducted with female elementary school children and with samples of high school students in the same cities.) At each interview wave, the children in the classes were asked to rate each other on aggressiveness using questionnaires that included such items as "Who is likely to punch and kick another child?" The questionnaires also picked up information about the socioeconomic background of the children.
>
> In addition, at every interview, the children were each asked to check those programs they had watched recently on lists of programs shown locally. The programs previously had been rated by media experts according to the amount of violence depicted in them. To check the accuracy of recall, several nonexistent programs were placed on the checklists. Additional interviews were conducted with the children's teachers and parents.
>
> The analyses undertaken related the viewing of violence on TV at one interview time with rated aggressive behavior at subsequent interview times, controlling statistically for the initial level of the children's aggressiveness. The results estimated the additional amount of aggressiveness that resulted from high levels of exposure to violence on TV programs. While the direction of effects indicated a small increment in aggressiveness associated with high levels of viewing of TV violence, that increment was not statistically significant.
>
> SOURCE: Adapted from J. R. Milavsky, H. H. Stipp, R. C. Kessler, and W. S. Rubens, *Television and Aggression: A Panel Study* (New York: Academic Press, 1982).

all viewed some TV. Nevertheless, some children viewed more programs containing violence than others and some watched more such programs at some times than at other times. Self-selection was to some degree controlled by statistically controlling the initial level of aggressiveness of the children under study.

It should be noted that the researchers in this study considered using randomized experiments to estimate the effects of viewing violent programs on subsequent aggressiveness but re-

jected that design as introducing an artificiality that would undermine the generalizability of their findings. It would be difficult, if not impossible, to recruit schoolchildren for experimentation, randomly allocate them to experimental and control groups, and then somehow prevent the controls from viewing any programs that contain aggressive or violent behavior. An experiment along those lines might be conducted for a very short period of time, on the order of a few days, but would be extremely difficult to carry out over the length of time needed to show the expected effects. In other words, the researchers opted for a less than optimal design of lower validity for estimating effects but higher generalizability.

Time-Series Evaluations

The term *panel study* usually designates research using a relatively modest number of repeated measurements taken on the same group of respondents to study the effects of a program or other types of change. In impact assessment, panel studies may not have measures of preprogram participation or status on outcome variables (as in the example in Exhibit 10-D) but only measures of exposure to program differentials and subsequent outcome status.

Repeated measures time-series designs, more generally, may involve many measurements that cover the periods before the program has been put into place as well as afterward and may not include the same respondents at each time of measurement. Extensive time-series data of some sort are often available to track changes in some of the conditions that social programs address and that, therefore, may be relevant to impact assessment. Many continuing databases compile periodic information related to phenomena of major public concern (e.g., fertility, mortality, and crime) or administrative concern (e.g., proportions of college students dropping out at the end of their first year). Such time series can provide relatively firm bases on which to build estimates of the net effects of full-coverage programs.

Most existing times series involve aggregated data such as averages or rates computed for one or more political jurisdictions. For example, the Department of Labor maintains an excellent time series that has tracked unemployment rates monthly for the country as a whole and major regions since 1948. Monthly rates are also available for major population subgroups—by sex, age, race, level of educational attainment, and so on.

When a relatively long time series of preintervention observations exists, it is often possible to model long-standing trends in the target group, projecting those trends through and beyond the time of the intervention and observing whether the postintervention period shows significant deviations from the projections. The use of such general time-trend modeling procedures as ARIMA (auto regressive integrated moving average; see Hamilton, 1994; McCleary and Hay, 1980) can identify the best-fitting statistical models by taking into account long-term secular trends and seasonal variations. They also allow for the degree to which any value or score obtained at one point in time is necessarily related to previous ones (technically referred to as *autocorrelation*). The procedures involved are technical and require a fairly high level of statistical sophistication.

Exhibit 10-E illustrates the use of time-series data for assessing the impact of raising the legal drinking age on alcohol-related traffic accidents. This evaluation is made possible by the existence of relatively long series of measures on the outcome variable (more than 200). The analysis uses information collected over the eight to ten years prior to the policy changes of interest to establish the expected trends for alcohol-related accident rates for different age groups legally entitled to drink. Comparison of the age-stratified rates experienced after the drinking ages were raised with the expected rates based on the prior trends provides a measure of net impact.

EXHIBIT 10-E   Estimating the Effects of Raising the Drinking Age From Time-Series Data

During the early 1980s, many states raised the minimum drinking age from 18 to 21, especially after passage of the Federal Uniform Drinking Age Act of 1984, which reduced highway construction funds to states that maintained a drinking age less than 21. The general reason for this was the widespread perception that lower drinking ages had led to dramatic increases in the rate of alcohol-related traffic accidents among teenagers. Assessing the impact of raising the drinking age, however, is complicated by downward trends in accidents stemming from the introduction of new automobile safety factors and increased public awareness of the dangers of drinking and driving.

Wisconsin raised its drinking age to 19 in 1984, then to 21 in 1986. To assess the impact of these changes, David Figlio examined an 18-year time series of monthly observations on alcohol-related traffic accidents, stratified by age, that was available from the Wisconsin Department of Transportation for the period from 1976 to 1993. Statistical time-series models were fit to the data for 18-year-olds (who could legally drink prior to 1984), for 19- and 20-year-olds (who could legally drink prior to 1986), and for over-21-year-olds (who could legally drink over the whole time period). The outcome variable in these analyses was the rate of alcohol-related crashes per thousand licensed drivers in the respective age group.

The results showed that, for 18-year-olds, raising the minimum drinking age to 19 reduced the alcohol-related crashes by an estimated 26% from the prior average of 2.2 per month per 1,000 drivers. For 19- and 20-year-olds, raising the minimum drinking age to 21 reduced the monthly crash rate by an estimated 19% from an average of 1.8 per month per 1,000 drivers. By comparison, the estimated effect of the legal changes for the 21-and-over group was only 2.5% and statistically nonsignificant.

The evaluator's conclusion was that the imposition of increased minimum drinking ages in Wisconsin had immediate and conclusive effects on the number of teenagers involved in alcohol-related crashes, resulting in substantially fewer than the prelegislation trends would have generated.

SOURCE: Adapted, by permission, from David N. Figlio, "The Effect of Drinking Age Laws and Alcohol-Related Crashes: Time-Series Evidence From Wisconsin," *Journal of Policy Analysis and Management,* 1995, 14(4):555-566. Copyright © 1995, John Wiley & Sons, Inc.

As noted earlier, the units of analysis in time-series data relevant to social programs are usually highly aggregated. Exhibit 10-E deals essentially with one case, the state of Wisconsin, where accident measures are constructed by aggregating the pertinent data over the entire state and expressing them as accident rates per 1,000 licensed drivers. The statistical models developed to fit such data are vulnerable to specification error just like all the other such models we have discussed. For example, if there were significant influences on the alcohol-related accident rates in Wisconsin at certain times that were not represented in the trend lines estimated by the model, then the results of the analysis would not be valid.

Simple graphic methods of examining time-series data before and after an intervention can provide crude but useful clues to impact. Indeed, if the confounding influences on an intervention are known and there is considerable certainty that their effects are minimal, simple examination of a time-series plot may identify obvious program effects. Exhibit 10-F presents the primary data for one of the classic applications of time series in program evaluation: the British Breathalyzer crackdown (Ross, Campbell, and Glass, 1970). The graph in that exhibit shows the auto accident rates in Great Britain before and after the enactment and enforcement of drastically changed penalties for driving while under the influence of alcohol. The accompanying chart indicates that the legislation had a discernible impact: Accidents declined after it went into effect and the decline was especially dramatic for accidents occurring over the weekend when we would expect higher levels of alcohol consumption. Although the effects are rather evident in the graph, it is wise to confirm them with statistical analysis; the reductions in accidents visible in Exhibit 10-F are, in fact, statistically significant.

Time-series approaches are not necessarily restricted to single cases, however. When time series exist for interventions at different times and in different places, more complex analyses can and should be undertaken. Parker and Rebhun (1995), for instance, examined the relationship of changes in state minimum age of purchase laws for alcohol with homicide rates with time series covering 1976-1983 for each of the 50 states plus the District of Columbia. Parker and Rebhun used a pooled cross-section time-series analysis with a dummy code (0 or 1) to identify the years before and after the drinking age was raised. Other variables in the model included alcohol consumption (beer sales in barrels per capita), infant mortality (as a poverty index), an index of inequality, racial composition, region, and total state population. This model was applied to homicide rates for different age groups, and raising the minimum age of purchase law was found to be significantly related to reductions in homicide for victims in the age 21-24 category.

Although the time-series analyses discussed above all use aggregated data, the general logic of time-series analyses can also be applied to disaggregated data, as in the analysis of interventions administered to single cases or small groups of persons whose behavior is measured a number of times before, after, and perhaps, during program participation. Therapists, for example, have used time-series designs to assess the impact of treatments on individual clients. Thus, a child's performance on some achievement test may be measured periodically before and after a new teaching method is used with the child, or an adult's drinking behavior may be measured before and after therapy for alcohol abuse. The logic of time-series analyses remains the same when applied to a single case, although the statistical methods applied are different because the issues of long-term trends and seasonality usually are not as serious for individual cases (Kazdin, 1982).

In general, when appropriate data are available, time-series analyses are relatively strong designs for estimating the effects of instituting uniform, full-coverage programs or the effects of making changes in such programs. We recommend them for circumstances in which appropriate statistical series exist, with the caveat that such analyses are vulnerable to specification errors.

✂ **EXHIBIT 10-F** An Analysis of the Impact of Compulsory Breathalyzer Tests on Traffic Accidents

In 1967 the British government enacted a new policy that allowed police to give Breathalyzer tests at the scenes of accidents. The test measured the presence of alcohol in the blood of suspects. At the same time, heavier penalties were instituted for drunken-driving convictions. Considerable publicity was given to the provisions of the new law, which went into effect in October 1967.

The chart below plots vehicular accident rates by various periods of the week before and after the new legislation went into effect. Visual inspection of the chart clearly indicates that a decline in accidents occurred after the legislation, which affected most times of the week but had especially dramatic effects for weekend periods. Statistical tests verified that these declines are greater than could be expected from the chance component of these data.

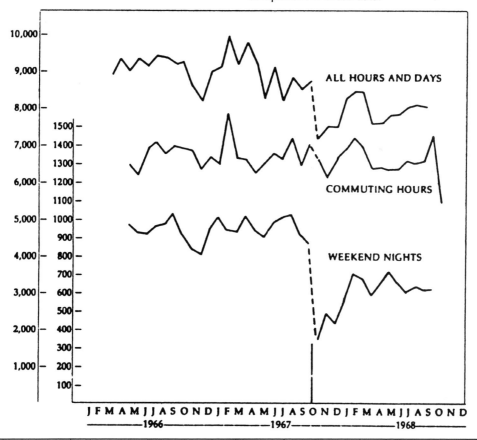

SOURCE: Adapted from H. L. Ross, D. T. Campbell, and G. V. Glass, "Determining the Social Effects of a Legal Reform: The British Breathalyzer Crackdown of 1967," *American Behavioral Scientist,* March/April 1970, 13:494-509.

SHADOW CONTROLS

When one of the more scientifically credible approaches to impact assessment is either not possible or not cost-effective, it is tempting to seek some less demanding but still reasonable alternative. The judgment of experts is one such alternative. There are persons with expertise in various human service areas on whose judgment it may be possible to rely when constructing estimates of whether a given gross outcome is sufficient indication that there has been an appreciable net impact. In addition, it is also possible to solicit judgments from program administrators or turn to the participants themselves to obtain assessments of how a program has affected them. We have termed the judgments of experts, program administrators, and participants *shadow controls*, a name chosen to reflect their role as a benchmark for comparison as well as their usual lack of a substantial evidential basis.

Shadow controls are used for a variety of reasons. Sometimes they are seen as an option to reflexive control designs for full-coverage programs, other times they are used because of their minimal costs, and still other times they are simply the traditional means used in a particular program area. In general, these judgmental assessments—even when highly trained, expert judges are used—rarely yield convincing estimates of net effects. At worst, they are highly unreliable and misestimate even gross program effects (see Exhibit 10-G). We include them in this book because of the frequency with which they are used rather than because we advocate using them.

Despite the fact that shadow controls ordinarily must be viewed with considerable skepticism, there are circumstances in which they may be justified. Although it may be sensible to spend a lot of time and money on the evaluation of prospective social programs that, if enacted, would be costly or might produce harmful unintended effects, there are many programs that are not that important. For example, it probably was justified to spend several hundred million dollars on the randomized experiments that tested the effectiveness of income maintenance programs, because a national income maintenance program would be very costly. As a matter of public policy, it may not be worth expending much money or effort on the evaluation of a program that is small (and intended to remain so) and in which the intervention is not a significant cost. In such cases, shadow controls may provide a rough estimate of impact that is sufficient for the information needs of the relevant decision-makers.

Another circumstance in which the use of shadow controls may be justified is the case of an extraordinarily and obviously successful program. For instance, suppose we found that a two-month-long vocational training program to produce drivers of heavy-duty trucks has enabled 90% of the participants (selected from among persons without such skills) to qualify for appropriate driver's licenses. Such a finding suggests that the program has been quite successful in reaching its goal of imparting vocational skills. We can make this judgment because it seems highly unlikely that so large a proportion of any group of previously unskilled persons who wanted to become truck drivers would be able to qualify for the licenses in a two-month period on their own. In this case, the shadow control estimate is based on generally held knowledge about motor vehicle licensing; if the evaluator wanted substantiation of the "shadow control" percentage, all he or she would have to do is call up the state motor vehicle licensing agency.

⚜ EXHIBIT 10-G   Evaluating Family Preservation Programs: How Shadow Controls Can Be Misleading

Family preservation programs have been initiated in many areas to provide intensive casework to families of abused or neglected children judged "at imminent risk" of being placed in foster care. These programs provide caseworkers who meet with families frequently, as much as several days per week, for periods of six to eight weeks. The function of the caseworkers is to help the families handle crises, impart proper parenting behavior, and teach strategies for coping with disciplinary difficulties.

The initial evaluations of family preservation programs were based on shadow controls. Every child in the program who, after participating, was not placed in foster care was counted as a "success" based on the assumption that they would have gone into foster care without the program. Using this estimate of outcome without service, the agencies running family preservation programs claimed startlingly high success rates, varying from 75% to 90%.

When randomized experiments were conducted, however, a very different story emerged. Those families and children who were placed in control groups and received ordinary child protective services—often meaning little or no services—were found to be no more nor no less likely to be placed in foster care than those who participated in a family preservation program. In one large experiment in Illinois, for instance, 16% of the children in control group families and 16% of those in experimental families were placed in foster care.

SOURCE: Adapted from Peter H. Rossi, "Assessing Family Preservation Programs," *Children and Youth Services Review,* 1992, 14(1):77-98.

Of course, the obverse outcomes could also lead to firm judgments. If all of the program's participants failed the license examination, that finding would be fairly clear evidence of the program's failure. Even this seemingly straightforward example, however, illustrates the risk of using shadow controls. If the evaluator did not check with the licensing agency, he or she might not know that the layperson's idea about failure rates may not be correct. It may well be, for example, that almost all applicants fail the first try and that the crucial percentage is the proportion who pass on the second attempt.

In reality, of course, the observed outcome would probably be more ambiguous—say, only 30% passing the first time. This more typical finding raises the question of whether a comparable group receiving no training would have done as well. The shadow control information available is only a rough estimate of the expected proportion who would pass without special training, and in any case there is no way of removing confounding effects from the gross outcome. In short, without a comparison group that is the equivalent of the participating targets, there is no way to estimate the net effects of the program with a high degree of certainty. Simply knowing the proportion in a program who "succeeded" and comparing that proportion to what might be expected does not provide an estimate of net program effect—hence the warning that relying on shadow controls for impact assessment is always risky.

Connoisseurial Assessments

Expert or "connoisseurial" judgments are the most common form of shadow controls. For instance, persons familiar with adult vocational education and the typical outcomes of intervention programs in that field might be asked to draw on their background to judge whether a 30% outcome in our truck driving example represents a success given the nature of the targets. Clearly, the usefulness and validity of such judgments, and hence the worth of an evaluation using them, depend heavily on the judges' expertise and knowledge of the program area.

Whenever shadow controls of any kind are to be used, their basis should be made explicit. Thus, the reasoning and assumptions on which expert judgments are made need to be described as completely as possible. If an expert makes a judgment based on his or her own direct experiences, the extent of those experiences ought to be revealed. When possible, explicit references to other evaluation studies should be given so that others can check whether the circumstances of the other interventions are comparable to those of the one under judgment. (See Nevo, 1989, for a set of rules for using experts and their judgments in evaluations.)

The actual procedures employed by experts to arrive at shadow controls vary considerably. Often, one or more well-known experts in a relevant field are hired as consultants to visit the site of a program, examine its workings closely, and write a report summarizing their assessment. Visiting experts may examine program records, observe the program in opera-

tion, conduct interviews with current and former participants, and talk to program managers, staff, and other officials. In short, all the means of informal social research may be employed.

Often the shadow control judgment of a connoisseur is a conclusion or construction based on the expert's understanding of the processes involved. The worth of the resulting assessments varies accordingly. Thus, to an expert in criminology, it may "stand to reason" that a given intervention concerning the rehabilitation of ex-prisoners will be effective, because it closely follows the leading theories in the field. However, whereas an industrial engineer's judgment concerning the effectiveness of a production process may be quite enough to justify action, the judgment of a criminologist about rehabilitation simply does not command the same standing. Unfortunately, the very reason for employing rigorous impact assessment designs in the area of social programs is that the state of knowledge in the appropriate fields is inadequate. Although it "stands to reason" that many programs will succeed, they often do not pass the more rigorous tests of the better impact assessment designs.

The worth of an expert's judgmental assessment depends on several factors. First, one must consider the general state of knowledge in the substantive fields relevant to the program. In a field where knowledge of how to achieve a particular outcome is quite advanced, an expert's appraisal may be very accurate. If little is known about an area (e.g., how to rehabilitate criminals), an expert's judgment of a particular program's effectiveness may be of little more merit than that of any informed person.

Second, one must consider how well grounded the expert is in the substantive field. An expert should be knowledgeable about the area in question and should have demonstrated that knowledge in actual accomplishments.

Third, experts should be familiar with the findings of evaluations of similar programs, especially systematic ones. For example, an expert asked to judge whether a community intervention center for released prisoners helps ex-felons obtain employment should be familiar with the many studies on the employment rates for ex-felons during the months after release. Similarly, knowledge that few studies show much influence of classroom size on achievement, whereas studies do show strong positive effects on teachers' satisfaction ratings, should make one skeptical that a program based largely on reducing class size is likely to do much for student achievement (although it may please the teachers).

Finally, because experts often rely heavily on "guided" visits to program sites, and often have more contact with program staff than with program participants, it is essential to be cautious about judgments based heavily on the reports of program staff. After all, it is only natural for a program administrator to attempt to present the program in the best possible light. Thus, one can expect the state of a program at the time of an announced visit to be better than at other periods in ways ranging from the neatness of the headquarters to possibly well-rehearsed laudatory statements from participants.

A skillful expert will base his or her judgments on data obtained from many sources. At a minimum, experts should consider the following:

1. *Administrative records.* Experts should collect information from administrative records (or have such tabulations made) on such topics as

a. Size of the program

b. Type of participants recruited

c. Attrition experience with participants

d. Postprogram experiences of participants

e. Program costs per participant who completes the program

f. Participant changes relevant to program goals, assessed by before-and-after measures

2. *Observations of program operation.* In programs that call for active work with participants (e.g., household visits, classroom sessions, media presentations), the work should be directly observed by the visiting experts.

3. *Interviews with participants.* Informal interviews with participants and/or former participants, at least some of which are spontaneous, can take up such issues as

a. Recruitment of participants

b. Motivation of participants

c. Participant satisfaction with the program

d. Participant progress toward attaining program goals

4. *Interviews with stakeholders and informants on the program's context.* Informal interviews with local officials, administrators of competing programs, administrators of important local institutions (e.g., school superintendents, members of the clergy, police chiefs), and local powerful individuals or representatives of local powerful institutions (e.g., large landlords, bankers, political officials) should cover the following topics:

a. Worth of the program

b. The extent to which the program is viewed as a help or a threat to the community

c. Interest in continuing the program when the demonstration period is over

Despite the weaknesses of connoisseurial assessments, there are circumstances in which this approach may be the only one that is feasible. This may be the case, for instance, with some full-coverage, constant-level interventions of long standing. Also, the urgency of the need for impact assessment may force evaluators to rely on expert judgments, or a lack of resources may prohibit them from mounting an impact assessment using control groups or a cross-sectional approach. Moreover, other controls may be feasible in principle but prohibitively tedious to put into practice.

When the funds allocated to evaluation are inadequate for a full-scale impact assessment, connoisseurial judgments may be resorted to on the grounds that some assessment is better than none at all. This may be particularly the case when the program is on a small scale and it would appear incongruous if the impact assessment cost a large fraction of the program costs. Under these circumstances, the "good enough" rule propounded in Chapter 7 may be invoked. Of course, a responsible connoisseurial evaluation will warn consumers of the judgmental basis for the findings.

Program Administrator Judgments

Program administrators are routinely asked to assess their progress toward fulfilling program goals. In most cases, it is doubtful that much reliance can be placed on such assessments, for fairly obvious reasons. First, undertaking a judgmental impact assessment is a difficult task under the best of circumstances. But the use of program administrator judgments is especially weak in light of the difficulty they will naturally have in adopting the attitude of skepticism toward their own work that is necessary for making hard judgments. A properly conducted impact assessment takes as its guiding hypothesis that the program has no effects, a stance that runs exactly counter to the principle that should guide the administration of a program—namely, that the intervention does have important effects on participants. To expect ordinary mortals to hold both hypotheses simultaneously is unrealistic. Furthermore, program administrators who have day-to-day responsibilities for the conduct of a program, and who often lack appropriate technical qualifications for making assessments of impact, often simply cannot devote a great deal of time and care to such assessments. In addition, there is an understandable tendency for administrators to want to put their program in the best of all possible lights, a motivation that may lead them to downplay or actively suppress negative information on effectiveness.

About the best one can expect from an administrator's judgmental assessment is reasonably accurate descriptive statements about operational procedures. One is entitled to expect that administrators will provide reliable statistical, descriptive statements about a program based on a well-kept set of administrative records. The kinds of records necessary have been described earlier in this chapter and in Chapter 6. Exhibit 10-H lists additional administrative records that can be useful for impact assessments. Clearly, all of these records are not appropriate to all programs, and this list should therefore be regarded as suggested rather than essential records.

EXHIBIT 10-H Administrative Records Useful for Project Description and as Aids in Impact Assessment

1. Participant records

    a. Socioeconomic data on participants: age, sex, location, household composition, income, occupational data

    b. Critical dates: date of entry into program, attendance record, date of leaving program

    c. Service records: exposure of participants to the program, services provided, and so forth

    d. Follow-up data: addresses of participants, including future addresses and contacts to aid in follow-up beyond participation

    e. Critical event records: records of meetings with participants, important events in participants' lives (e.g., births, deaths, residential shifts, job changes)

2. Program records

    a. Critical events in the program history: dates of start-up for important components of the program, encounters with helpful or hostile officials, periods when the program was not operational

    b. Program personnel: biographical data on program personnel, shifts in personnel, record of personnel training

    c. Changes in program implementation: problems encountered, changes instituted in program operations (including dates)

3. Financial records

    No attempt to describe such records will be made here since one can assume that the fiscal procedures typically required by program sponsors will be employed. The main issue to be emphasized is that financial records should be kept in a way that will facilitate cost-effectiveness or cost-benefit analyses, as described in Chapter 11.

Participant Judgments

Because the participants in social programs are the recipients of the services, evaluators might be tempted to rely on their accounts of how well they were served by the program as indications of net impact. Although participants can tell us many useful things, it is overly optimistic to expect that they can provide a direct assessment of program impact. The problem is that it is difficult for any individual to realistically assess what would have happened to him or her if some specific event had not occurred. Most people simply do not have the varied experiences or psychological distance from their own circumstances to be able

---

❧ EXHIBIT 10-I   The Quality of Day Care From the Perspectives of Parents

Parents tend to judge the quality of child care by different criteria than do child development specialists. One study found that parents who used better quality day care (according to experts) paid, on average, no more than parents using poorer quality services. This may indicate that parents do not value the characteristics of "quality" as highly as other characteristics of the services. Another study, for instance, provides evidence that parents may be more concerned about the location, hours, and dependability of day care arrangements than they are about aspects of quality considered important by child development professionals.

Parents appear to judge the quality of child care according to (a) whether it offers a safe and healthy environment—many parents express considerable concern about potential child abuse; (b) whether the environment promotes learning—a concern that is especially prevalent among parents of older children; and (c) convenience, including location within a 10- to 15-minute radius of home or work and hours of operation that mesh with the mother's work schedule (e.g., accommodating shift work, overtime, and other special needs).

Parents generally apply these criteria on the basis of limited knowledge about the range of their child care options. Most providers do not advertise their services, and most users do not look at alternative arrangements before placing their child in care.

SOURCE: Adapted from Ellen Kisker and Rebecca Maynard, "Quality, Cost and Parental Choice of Child Care," in *The Economics of Child Care*, ed. David M. Blau (New York: Russell Sage, 1991).

---

to construct a valid image of what their condition would be had they not participated in the program. Note that this is not a view of human beings as naive or deficient, but a recognition that assessing net impact is a comparative task and that most persons lack the breadth of experience or vantage point needed to make such comparisons for their own outcomes.

Participants' ratings of satisfaction with a program or with services, however, are informative and important in their own right. In the first place, some programs stipulate participant satisfaction as one of their goals and work to rid their procedures of the "bugs" that irritate participants. Retirement benefit programs, for instance, attempt to deliver retirement income in a way that is most satisfying to beneficiaries, including automatic bank deposits or special pick-up provisions. Public service programs may be particularly concerned with client satisfaction as an index of service-unit functioning.

As an illustration, Exhibit 10-I provides a summary of studies conducted to find out what parents considered to be quality day care arrangements for their children. Note that the perspectives of parents and those of child development experts appear to be somewhat at variance. Participant assessments of programs thus offer useful information even if they cannot replace carefully designed impact assessments.

SUMMARY

⬧ The impact of full-coverage programs is difficult to assess with confidence because the nature of such programs precludes the use of comparison groups. For programs with nonuniform coverage, evaluators sometimes are able to take advantage of variations in the intensity, type, or amount of service to approximate quasi-experimental impact assessment designs.

⬧ Full-coverage programs generally are evaluated by using reflexive controls to compare preprogram and postprogram outcome measurements. Designs range from simple before-and-after comparisons, with only one measurement before and one after program participation, to time series involving multiple measurements before and after the intervention is in place. Time-series designs are much better than simple pre-post designs for estimating net effects. In evaluations with only two measurements, it is almost impossible to differentiate net from gross effects.

⬧ An alternative to reflexive designs is the use of shadow controls. Shadow control evaluations make use of judges to estimate impact. These judges may be experts in the program area, program administrators, or program participants themselves. Although such evaluations are commonplace, they are not recommended because it is difficult to obtain valid estimates of net program effects from them. Shadow controls can be used with relative confidence only when program effects are readily apparent and there is good reason to believe that most of the gross effects can be presumed to be net effects of the program.

Costs	Inputs, both direct and indirect, required to produce an intervention.
Benefits	Net program outcomes, usually translated into monetary terms. Benefits may include both direct and indirect effects.
Net benefits	The total discounted benefits minus the total discounted costs. Also called net rate of return.
Cost-effectiveness	The efficacy of a program in achieving given intervention outcomes in relation to the program costs.
Cost-benefit analysis	Analytical procedure for determining the economic efficiency of a program, expressed as the relationship between costs and outcomes, usually measured in monetary terms.
Benefits-to-costs ratio	The total discounted benefits divided by the total discounted costs.
***Ex ante* efficiency analysis**	An efficiency analysis undertaken prior to program implementation, usually as part of program planning, to estimate net outcomes in relation to costs.
***Ex post* efficiency analysis**	An efficiency analysis undertaken subsequent to knowing a program's net outcome effects.
Accounting perspectives	Perspectives underlying decisions on which categories of goods and services to include as costs or benefits in an analysis.
Shadow prices	Imputed or estimated costs of goods and services not valued accurately in the marketplace. Shadow prices also are used when market prices are inappropriate due to regulation or externalities. Also known as accounting prices.
Opportunity costs	The value of opportunities forgone because of an intervention program.
Externalities	Effects of a program that impose costs on persons or groups who are not targets.
Distributional effects	Effects of programs that result in a redistribution of resources in the general population.
Discounting	The treatment of time in valuing costs and benefits, that is, the adjustment of costs and benefits to their present values, requiring a choice of discount rate and time frame.
Internal rate of return	The calculated value for the discount rate necessary for total discounted program benefits to equal total discounted program costs.

CHAPTER 11

MEASURING EFFICIENCY

Knowledge of the extent to which programs have been implemented successfully and the degree to which they have the desired outcomes is indispensable to program managers, stakeholders, and policymakers. In almost all cases, however, it is just as critical to be informed about how program outcomes compare to their costs. In fact, whether it is accomplished impressionistically, as in most everyday life decisions, or by formal procedures, comparison of the costs and benefits of social programs is one of the most important considerations in deciding whether to expand, continue, or terminate them.

Efficiency assessments—cost-benefit and cost-effectiveness analyses—provide a frame of reference for relating costs to program results. In addition to providing information for making decisions on the allocation of resources, they are often useful in gaining the support of planning groups and political constituencies who determine the fate of social intervention efforts.

The procedures employed in both types of analyses are often highly technical, and their applications will be described only briefly in this chapter. However, because the issue of the cost or effort required to achieve a given magnitude of desired change is implicit in all impact evaluations, all program evaluators must understand the ideas embodied in efficiency analyses, even if the technical procedures are beyond their skills.

- Policymakers must decide how to allocate funding among a variety of educational programs, ranging from basic primary educational classes for young children to vocational training efforts for adults. All have been shown to have substantial net impact in completed evaluations. How should the available educational resources be allocated?

- A government agency is reviewing national disease control programs currently in operation. If additional funds are to be allocated to disease control, which programs would show the biggest payoffs per dollar of expenditure?

- Evaluations in the criminal justice field have established the effects of various alternative programs aimed at reducing recidivism. Which program is most cost-effective to the criminal justice system? Given the policy choices, how would altering the current pattern of expenditures maximize the efficiency of correctional alternatives?

- Members of a private funding group are debating whether to promote a program of low-interest loans for home construction or to initiate work skills training for married women to increase family income. How should they decide?

These are examples of common resource allocation dilemmas faced by planners, funding groups, and policymakers everywhere. Again and again, decisionmakers must choose how to allocate scarce resources to put them to optimal use. Consider even the fortunate case in which pilot projects of several programs have shown them all to be effective in producing the desired net impacts. The decision of which to fund on a larger scale must take into account the relations between costs and outcomes in each program. Although other factors, including political and value considerations, come into play, the preferred program often is the one that produces the most impact on the most targets for a given level of expenditure. This simple principle is the foundation of cost-benefit and cost-effectiveness analyses, techniques that provide systematic approaches to resource allocation analysis.

Both cost-benefit and cost-effectiveness analyses are means of judging the efficiency of programs. As we will elaborate, the difference between the two types of analyses is the way in which the outcomes of a program are expressed. In *cost-benefit* analyses, the outcomes of programs are expressed in monetary terms; in *cost-effectiveness* analyses, outcomes are expressed in substantive terms. For example, a cost-benefit analysis of a program to reduce cigarette smoking would focus on the difference between the dollars expended on the anti-smoking program and the dollar savings from reduced medical care for smoking-related diseases, days lost from work, and so on. A cost-effectiveness analysis of the same program would estimate the dollars that had to be expended to convert each smoker into a non-smoker. (Later in this chapter we discuss the basis for deciding whether to undertake a cost-benefit or cost-effectiveness analysis.)

The basic procedures and concepts underlying resource allocation analysis stem from work undertaken in the 1930s to establish decision-making criteria for public investment activities. Early applications in the United States were to water resource development; in England, to transportation investments. After World War II, organizations such as the World Bank stimulated the application of cost-benefit analysis to both specific project activities and national programs in less-developed as well as industrialized countries. Perhaps the greatest stimulus to systematic application of cost-benefit analysis to governmental programs was the Planning, Programming, and Budgeting System (PPBS) implemented in the 1960s, an extension of the systems analysis approach then being applied in the Department of Defense. (For a review of how efficiency analyses have been applied in the federal government over the years, see Nelson, 1987.)

Cost-benefit and cost-effectiveness analyses in the social program area have their analogue in the world of business, where costs are constantly compared with income. For instance, a computer company may be concerned with the relationship of costs to income for making microcomputers compatible with those of a major competitor. Or a small restaurant owner might be concerned with whether to provide dinner music or promote her lunchtime specials to increase profits.

The idea of judging the utility of social intervention efforts in terms of their efficiency (profitability, in business terms) has gained widespread acceptance. However, the question of "correct" procedures for actually conducting cost-benefit and cost-effectiveness analyses of social programs remains an area of considerable controversy (Eddy, 1992; Zerbe, 1998). As we will discuss, this controversy is related to a combination of unfamiliarity with the analytical procedures employed, reluctance to impose monetary values on many social program outcomes, and an unwillingness to forsake initiatives that have been held in esteem for extended periods of time. Evaluators undertaking cost-benefit or cost-effectiveness analyses of social interventions must be aware of the particular issues involved in applying efficiency analyses to their specific field, as well as the limitations that characterize the use of cost-benefit and cost-effectiveness analyses in general. (For comprehensive discussions of efficiency assessment procedures, see Gramblin, 1990; Nas, 1996; Yates, 1996.)

KEY CONCEPTS IN EFFICIENCY ANALYSIS

Cost-benefit and cost-effectiveness analyses can be viewed both as conceptual perspectives and as sophisticated technical procedures. From a conceptual point of view, perhaps the greatest value of efficiency analysis is that it forces us to think in a disciplined fashion about both costs and benefits. In the case of virtually all social programs, identifying and comparing the actual or anticipated costs with the known or expected benefits can prove invaluable. Most other types of evaluation focus mainly on the benefits. Furthermore, efficiency analyses provide a comparative perspective on the relative utility of interventions. Judgments of the comparative utility of different initiatives are unavoidable, since social programs, almost without exception, are conducted under resource constraints. Almost invariably, maintaining continuing support depends on convincing policymakers and funders that the "bottom line" (i.e., dollar benefits or the equivalent) justifies the program.

An interesting illustration of decision making along these lines is a report of a large bank's support of a day care center for its employees (see Exhibit 11-A). As the report documents, despite the difficulties of undertaking efficiency analyses, and even when they are somewhat crudely done, they can provide evidence supporting the implementation of company-supported social programs. The article from which the excerpt in Exhibit 11-A is taken also discusses preventive health programs, day care centers, and lunchtime educational programs established by various businesses. In each case, knowing the bottom line in terms of the cost of benefits was the basis of the company's decisions.

In spite of their value, however, it bears emphasis that in many evaluations formal, complete efficiency analyses are either impractical or unwise for several reasons. First, the required technical procedures may be beyond the resources of the evaluation project; may call for methodological sophistication not available to the project's staff; or may be unnecessary, given either very minimal or extremely high efficacy of the intervention. Second, political or moral controversies may result from placing economic values on particular input or outcome measures, controversies that could obscure the relevance and minimize the potential utility of an otherwise useful and rigorous evaluation. Third, expressing the results of evaluation studies in efficiency terms may require selectively taking different costs and outcomes into account, depending on the perspectives and values of sponsors, stakeholders, targets, and evaluators themselves (what are referred to as *accounting perspectives*). The dependence of results on the accounting per-

---

▓ **EXHIBIT 11-A**   Cost Savings From a Bank's Child Care Facilities

In January 1987, Union Bank opened a new profit center in Los Angeles. This one, however, doesn't lend money. It doesn't manage money. It takes care of children.

The profit center is a day-care facility at the bank's Monterey Park operations center. Union Bank provided the facility with a $105,000 subsidy last year. In return, it saved the bank as much as $232,000. There is, of course, nothing extraordinary about a day-care center. What is extraordinary is the $232,000. That number is part of a growing body of research that tries to tell companies what they are getting—on the bottom line—for the dollars they invest in such benefits and policies as day-care assistance, wellness plans, maternity leaves, and flexible work schedules.

The Union Bank study, designed to cover many questions left out of other evaluations, offers one of the more revealing glimpses of the savings from corporate day-care centers. For one thing, the study was begun a year before the center opened, giving researchers more control over the comparison statistics. Union Bank approved spending $430,000 to build its day-care center only after seeing the savings projections.

Using data provided by the bank's human resource department, Sandra Burud, a child-care consultant in Pasadena, California, compared absenteeism, turnover, and maternity leave time the first year of operation and the year before. She looked at the results for 87 users of the center, a control group of 105 employees with children of similar ages who used other day-care options, and employees as a whole.

Her conclusion: The day-care center saves the bank $138,000 to $232,000 a year—numbers she calls "very conservative." Ms. Burud says savings on turnover total $63,000 to $157,000, based mostly on the fact that turnover among center users was 2.2 percent compared with 9.5 percent in the control group and 18 percent throughout the bank.

She also counted $35,000 in savings on lost days' work. Users of the center were absent an average of 1.7 fewer days than the control group, and their maternity leaves were 1.2 weeks shorter than for other employees. Ms. Burud also added a bonus of $40,000 in free publicity, based on estimates of media coverage of the center.

Despite the complexities of measurement, she says, the study succeeds in contradicting the "simplistic view of child care. This isn't a touchy-feely kind of program. It's as much a management tool as it is an employee benefit."

SOURCE: J. Solomon, "Companies Try Measuring Cost Savings From New Types of Corporate Benefits," *Wall Street Journal,* December 29, 1988, p. B1. Reprinted by permission of The Wall Street Journal, Dow Jones & Company, Inc. All rights reserved worldwide.

---

spective employed may be difficult for at least some of the stakeholders to comprehend, again obscuring the relevance and utility of evaluations.

Furthermore, efficiency analysis may be heavily dependent on untested assumptions or the requisite data for undertaking cost-benefit or cost-effectiveness calculations may not be fully available. Even the strongest advocates of efficiency analyses acknowledge that there often is no single "right" analysis. Moreover, in some applications, the results may show unacceptable levels of sensitivity to reasonable variations in the analytic and conceptual models used and their underlying assumptions.

Although we want to emphasize that the results of all cost-benefit and cost-effectiveness analyses should be treated with caution, and sometimes with a fair degree of skepticism, such analyses can provide a reproducible and rational way of estimating the efficiency of programs. Even strong advocates of efficiency analyses rarely argue that such studies should be the sole determinant of decisions about programs. Nonetheless, they are a valuable input into the complex mosaic from which decisions emerge.

Timing of Efficiency Analyses

The employment of cost-benefit and cost-effectiveness techniques is appropriate at all phases of program efforts. However, efficiency analyses are most commonly undertaken either during the planning and design phase of an initiative or after an innovative or markedly modified program has been in place for a time and there is interest in making it permanent or possibly expanding it.

In the planning and design phases, *ex ante* efficiency analyses may be undertaken on the basis of a program's anticipated costs and outcomes. Such analyses, of course, must presume a given magnitude of positive net impact even if this value is only a conjecture. Likewise, the costs of providing and delivering the intervention must be estimated by one means or another. In some cases, estimates of both the inputs and the magnitude of impact can be made with considerable confidence, either because there has been a pilot program (or a similar program in another location) or because the program is fairly simple in its implementation. Nevertheless, since ex ante analyses in

whole or in part are not based on empirical information, they run the risk of seriously under- or overestimating net benefits. Indeed, the issue of the accuracy of the estimates of both inputs and outputs is one of the controversial areas in ex ante analyses.

Ex ante cost-benefit analyses are most important for those programs that will be difficult to abandon once they have been put into place or that require extensive commitments in funding and time to be realized. For example, the decision to increase recreational facilities by putting in new jetties along the New Jersey ocean shore would be difficult to overturn once the jetties had been constructed; thus, there is a need to estimate the costs and outcomes of such a program compared with other ways of increasing recreational opportunities, or to judge the wisdom of increasing recreational opportunities compared with the costs and outcomes of allocating the resources to another social program area.

Thus, when extensive resource commitments would be required by program sponsors to initiate and maintain a program, decisions are preceded in many cases by ex ante cost-benefit analyses. Exhibit 11-B illustrates such a situation with regard to the testing of health care workers for HIV. Even though the possibility of, say, a surgeon or dentist transmitting HIV/AIDS to a patient is a matter of serious consequences and concern, testing and regulating the vast number of health care workers in this country for HIV is likely to be quite expensive. Before embarking on such a program, it is wise to develop some estimate, even if crude, of how expensive it is likely to be in relation to the number of patient infections averted. The analysis summarized in Exhibit 11-B showed that under most risk scenarios any reasonable policy option would likely be quite expensive. Moreover, there was considerable uncertainty

EXHIBIT 11-B   Ex-Ante Analysis of the Cost-Effectiveness of HIV Testing for Health Care Workers

A study by Phillips and others in 1994 examined the cost-effectiveness of alternative policies for HIV testing of health care workers, including physicians, surgeons, and dentists. The policy options considered were (a) mandatory and (b) voluntary testing, and for those who test positive, (a) exclusion from patient care, (b) restriction of practice, or (c) a requirement that patients be informed of their HIV status.

The derivation of costs in this study was based on data obtained from reviewing the pertinent literature and consulting with experts. The cost estimates included three components: (a) counseling and testing costs, (b) additional treatment costs because of early detection of HIV-positive cases, and (c) medical care costs averted per patient infection averted. Costs were estimated by subtracting (c) from (a) + (b).

Analyzing all options under high, medium, and low HIV prevalence and transmission risk scenarios, the study concluded that one-time mandatory testing with mandatory restriction of practice for a health care worker found HIV positive was more cost-effective than the other options. While showing the lowest cost of the policies considered, that option nonetheless was estimated to cost $291,000 per infection averted for surgeons and $500,000 for dentists. Given these high costs and the political difficulties associated with adopting and implementing mandatory restrictions on practice, this was not considered a viable policy option.

The analysts also found that the cost-effectiveness estimates were highly sensitive to variations in prevalence and transmission risk and to the different patterns of practice for physicians in contrast to dentists. The incremental cost per infection averted ranged from $447 million for dentists under low prevalence/transmission risk conditions to a savings of $81,000 for surgeons under high prevalence/transmission risk conditions.

Given the high costs estimated for many of the options and the uncertainty of the results, the authors concluded as follows: "Given the ethical, social, and public health implications, mandatory testing policies should not be implemented without greater certainty as to their cost-effectiveness."

SOURCE: Adapted from Tevfik F. Nas, *Cost-Benefit Analysis: Theory and Application* (Thousand Oaks, CA: Sage, 1996), pp. 191-192. Original study was K. A. Phillips, R. A. Lowe, J. G. Kahn, P. Lurie, A. L. Avins, and D. Ciccarone, "The Cost Effectiveness of HIV Testing of Physicians and Dentists in the United States," *Journal of the American Medical Association,* 1994, 271:851-858.

in the estimates possible from available information. Given the high, but uncertain, cost estimates, policymakers would be wise to move cautiously on this issue until better information could be developed.

Because of the insufficient use of ex ante analyses in the social program arena, many social programs are initiated or markedly modified without attention to the practicality of the action in cost-benefit or cost-effectiveness terms. For example, if the application of a particular dental treatment that prevents cavities costs $200 per child annually, and the treatment is estimated to reduce cavities by an average of one-half cavity per child per year, it is unlikely to gain acceptance, even if it works. After all, its cost is four or five times what dentists would charge on average for filling a single cavity. An efficiency analysis in such a case might easily dissuade decisionmakers from implementing the program.

Most commonly, efficiency analyses in the social program field take place after the completion of an impact evaluation, when the net impact of a program is known. The focus of such *ex post* cost-benefit and cost-effectiveness assessments may be on examining the efficiency of a program in either absolute or comparative terms, or both. In all cases, the analysis is undertaken to assess whether the costs of the intervention can be justified by the magnitude of the net effects.

In absolute terms, the idea is to judge whether the program is worth what it costs by comparing costs either to benefits or to outcomes in substantive terms. For example, a cost-benefit analysis may reveal that for each dollar spent to reduce shoplifting in a department store, two dollars are saved in terms of stolen goods, an outcome that clearly indicates that the shoplifting program would be economically beneficial.

In comparative terms, the issue is to determine the differential "payoff" of one program versus another—for example, comparing the reduction in arrest rates for drunken driving brought about by an educational program with that of a program that pays for taxis to take people home after they have imbibed too much. In ex post analyses, estimates of costs and outcomes are based on studies of the types

described in previous chapters on program monitoring and impact evaluations.

The Concepts of Cost-Benefit and Cost-Effectiveness Analyses

Obviously, many considerations besides economic efficiency are brought to bear in policy making, planning, and program implementation, but economic efficiency is almost always critical, given that resources are inevitably scarce. Cost-benefit and cost-effectiveness analyses have the virtue of encouraging evaluators to become knowledgeable about program costs; surprisingly, many evaluators pay little attention to costs and are unaware of the information sources they need to contact and the complexities of describing program costs. In contrast, program costs are very salient to many of the stakeholder groups important to a program's acceptance and modification; consequently, attention to costs by evaluation staff often increases cooperation and support from such groups.

A cost-benefit analysis requires estimates of the benefits of a program, both tangible and intangible, and estimates of the costs of undertaking the program, both direct and indirect. Once specified, the benefits and costs are translated into a common measure, usually a monetary unit.

Cost-benefit analysis requires the adoption of a particular economic perspective; in addition, certain assumptions must be made to translate program inputs and outputs into monetary figures. As we have noted, there is considerable controversy in the field regarding the "correct" procedures to use in converting inputs and outputs into monetary values. Clearly, the assumptions underlying the definitions of the measures of costs and benefits strongly influence the resulting conclusions. Consequently, the analyst is required, at the very least, to state the basis for the assumptions that underlie the analysis.

Often, analysts do more than that. They may undertake several different analyses of the same program, varying the assumptions made. For example, later we will discuss the need to take into account inflation (or deflation) in valuing costs and benefits that occur at different periods of time. The analyst could undertake a single study and state that an annual inflation rate of 5% was assumed, or the analyst could provide findings based on rates of 1%, 5%, and 10%. Sensitivity analyses, which alter important assumptions and estimate the consequences on program results, are a central feature of well-conducted efficiency studies. Indeed, an important advantage of formal efficiency studies over impressionistically gathered information about costs in relation to outcomes is that the assumptions and procedures are open to review and checking.

Cost-benefit analysis is least controversial when applied to technical and industrial projects, where it is relatively easy to place a monetary value on benefits as well as costs. Examples include engineering projects designed to reduce the costs of electricity to consumers, highway construction to facilitate transportation of goods, and irrigation programs to increase crop yields. Estimating benefits in monetary terms is frequently more difficult in social programs, where only a portion of program inputs and outputs may easily be assigned a monetary value. For example, it is possible to translate future occupational gains from an educational project into monetary values without incurring too much controversy. The issues are more complex in such social interventions as fertility control programs or health services projects because one must ultimately place a value on human life to fully monetize the program benefits (Jones-Lee, 1994; Mishan, 1988).

The underlying principle is that cost-benefit analysts attempt to value both inputs and outputs at what is referred to as their marginal social values. For many items, such as the cost of providing a certain medicine or the monetary benefit of outfitting new cars with engines that burn less gasoline, market prices perform this task quite well. The situation is most difficult when the good or service is not even traded.

In general, there is much more controversy about converting outcomes into monetary values than there is about inputs. Because of the controversial nature of valuing outcomes, in many cases, especially regarding human services, cost-effectiveness analysis is seen as a more appropriate technique than cost-benefit analysis. Cost-effectiveness analysis requires monetizing only the program's costs; its benefits are expressed in outcome units. For example, the cost-effectiveness of distributing free textbooks to rural primary school children could be expressed in terms of how much each 1,000 project dollars increased the average reading scores of the targeted children.

For cost-effectiveness analysis, then, efficiency is expressed in terms of the costs of achieving a given result. That is, the efficiency of a program in attaining its goals is assessed in relation to the monetary value of the resources or costs put into the program for a designated unit of outcome. For example, alternative educational interventions may be compared by measuring the costs for each of achieving a specific educational gain as measured by test scores.

An example of relating costs to gains in mathematics and reading effects among elementary school children is shown in Exhibit

✖ EXHIBIT 11-C   Cost-Effectiveness of Computer-Assisted Instruction

To assist decisionmakers in considering different approaches to improving the mathematics and reading performance of elementary school children, a cost-effectiveness study was undertaken of computer-assisted instruction (CAI) compared to three alternative interventions. The findings run counter to some conventional expectations. Although the CAI alternative did relatively well according to the cost-effectiveness criterion, it did not do as well as peer tutoring. It is somewhat surprising that a traditional and a labor-intensive approach (peer tutoring) appears to be far more cost-effective than an electronic intervention, a widely used CAI approach. Moreover, the low ranking for the option of increasing the instructional time in the classroom, the centerpiece of many of the calls for educational reform, makes it a relatively poor choice for both reading and mathematics from a cost-effectiveness perspective (see table).

To estimate the cost-effectiveness of the various alternatives, the researchers first determined the magnitude, in standard deviation units (effect sizes), of the increases on mathematics and reading achievement test scores resulting from each approach. They then determined the cost of each instructional approach and computed the achievement score effect per $100 spent per student for each approach. The results, averaging the mathematics and reading achievement findings, are presented in the table.

Average Cost-Effectiveness Ratios of Four Interventions for Two Subject Areas (average of mathematics and reading effect sizes for each $100 cost per student per subject)

Intervention	Cost-Effectiveness Ratio
Cross-age tutoring	
Combined peer and adult program	.22
Peer component	.34
Adult component	.07
Computer-assisted instruction	.15
Reducing class size	
From 35 to 30	.11
From 30 to 25	.09
From 25 to 20	.08
From 35 to 20	.09
Increasing instructional time	.09

SOURCE: Adapted from H. M. Levin, G. V. Glass, and G. R. Meister, "Cost-Effectiveness of Computer-Assisted Instruction," *Evaluation Review,* 1987, 11(1):50-72.

11-C. The analysis found that counseling by other students provided more impact per $100 than other approaches. Surprisingly, such peer counseling was more cost-effective than a high-tech, computer-assisted instruction program.

An ex ante cost-effectiveness analysis allows potential programs to be compared and ranked according to the magnitudes of their effects relative to their estimated costs. In ex post cost-effectiveness analyses, actual program costs and impact—and, hence, inputs and outputs—replace, to a considerable extent, estimates and assumptions. Moreover, retrospective analyses can yield useful insights and experiences, or methodological procedures that can be applied to future programs. However, comparisons of outcomes in relation to costs require that the programs under consideration have the same types of outcomes. If programs produce different outcomes, such as reduction in number of days in bed in the case of a medical care program and increased reading competence in the instance of an educational program, then one is still left with the difficulty of valuing the two outcomes. That is, how much is an average reduction of two bed days "worth" compared with a mean increase of 10 points on a standard reading test?

The Uses of Efficiency Analyses

Efficiency analyses, at least ex post analyses, can be considered an extension of, rather than an alternative to, impact evaluation. Since the estimation of either monetized benefits or substantive effects depends on knowledge of a program's *net* impact, it is impossible to engage in cost-benefit or cost-effectiveness calculations for programs in which impacts are unknown and inestimable. It also is senseless to do so for ineffective programs—that is, when impact evaluations discover no significant net effects. It is equally foolish to undertake efficiency analyses of ongoing or completed programs unless there are reasonable estimates of program impact.

When applied to efficacious programs, efficiency analyses are useful to those who must make policy decisions regarding the support of one program over another, or who need to decide in absolute terms whether the outcomes of a program are worth its costs, or who are

required to review the utility of programs at different points in time. Moreover, efficiency analysis can be useful in determining the degree to which different levels or "strengths" of interventions produce different levels of benefits and can be used in a formative manner to help improve program performance (Yates, 1996).

METHODOLOGY OF COST-BENEFIT ANALYSIS

To carry out a cost-benefit analysis, one must first decide which perspective to take in calculating costs and benefits. What point of view should be the basis for specifying, measuring, and monetizing benefits and costs? In short, costs to and benefits for whom? Benefits and costs must be defined from a single perspective because mixing points of view results in confused specifications and overlapping or double counting. Of course, several cost-benefit analyses for a single program may be undertaken, each from a different perspective. Separate analyses based on different perspectives often provide information on how benefits compare to costs as they affect relevant stakeholders.

Accounting Perspectives

Earlier, we referred to the need to identify an accounting perspective in estimating costs and benefits. Generally, three accounting perspectives may be used for the analysis of social projects, those of (a) individual participants or targets; (b) program sponsors; and (c) communal aggregates, or the society involved.

The *individual-target* accounting perspective takes the point of view of the units that are the program targets, that is, the persons, groups, or organizations receiving the intervention or services. Cost-benefit analyses using the individual-target perspective often produce higher benefit-to-cost results (net benefits) than those using other perspectives. In other words, if the sponsor or society bears the cost and subsidizes a successful intervention, then the individual program participant benefits the most. For example, an educational project may impose relatively few costs on participants. Indeed, the cost to targets may primarily be the time spent in participating in the project, since books and materials usually are furnished. Furthermore, if the time required is primarily in the afternoons and evenings, there may be no loss of income involved. The benefits to the participants, meanwhile, may include improvements in earnings as a result of increased education, greater job satisfaction, and increased occupational options, as well as transfer payments received while participating in the project.

The *program sponsor* accounting perspective takes the point of view of the funding source in valuing benefits and specifying cost factors. The funding source may be a private agency or foundation, a government agency, or a for-profit firm. From this perspective, the cost-benefit analysis most closely resembles what frequently is termed *private profitability analysis*. That is, analysis from this perspective is designed to reveal what the sponsor will pay to provide a program and what benefits (or "profits") should accrue to the sponsor.

The program sponsor accounting perspective is most appropriate when the sponsor must make decisive choices between alternative programs in the face of a fixed budget, that is, when there is no possibility of generating any additional funds. Under these circumstances, if, for example, the program sponsor is a county government, it may favor a vocational education initiative that includes student stipends over other programs because this type of program would reduce the costs of public assistance and similar subsidies (since some of the persons in the vocational education program would have been supported by income maintenance funds). Also, if the future incomes of the participants were to increase because of the training received, their direct and indirect tax payments would increase, and these also could be included in calculating benefits from a program sponsor perspective. The costs to the government sponsor include the costs of operation, administration, instruction, supplies, facilities, and any additional subsidies or transfers paid to the participants during the training. As another illustration, Exhibit 11-D shows a cost-benefit calculation involving the savings to the mental health system that result from providing specialized services to patients with co-occurring mental disorders and substance abuse problems.

The *communal* accounting perspective takes the point of view of the community or society as a whole, usually in terms of total income. It is therefore the most comprehensive perspective, but also usually the most complex and thus the most difficult to apply. Taking the point of view of society as a whole implies that special efforts are being made to account for secondary or indirect project effects—effects on groups not directly involved with the intervention. Moreover, in the current literature, communal cost-benefit analysis has been expanded to include equity considerations, that is, the distributional effects of programs among different subgroups. From a communal standpoint, for example, every dollar earned by a minority member who had been unemployed for six months or more may be seen as a "double benefit" and so entered into the analyses.

Exhibit 11-E illustrates the benefits that need to be taken into account from a commu-

☒ **EXHIBIT 11-D** Costs and Savings to the Mental Health System of Providing Specialized Dual Diagnosis Programs

People with serious mental disorders and co-occurring substance disorders (*dual diagnosis*) are very difficult and costly to treat in usual mental health or substance abuse services. Providing them with specialized dual diagnosis treatment programs might improve the outcomes but would add to the cost of services. However, if those improved outcomes decreased the need for subsequent mental health services they might result in savings that would offset the costs of the specialized program. Viewed from the perspective of policymakers in the mental health system, therefore, a crucial question is whether the cost to the mental health system for specialized programs for this client population will be recovered in savings to the system through reduced need for subsequent services.

To address this question, a team of evaluation researchers randomly assigned 132 patients to three specialized dual diagnosis programs and assessed both the outcomes and the costs. The "control" program was based on a 12-step recovery model and was the "usual care" condition for dual diagnosis patients in this mental health system. It involved referral to community Alcoholics Anonymous or Narcotics Anonymous meetings and associated supportive services to help the client manage the recovery process. A more intensive program option used a behavioral skills model that relied on cognitive-behavioral treatment focusing on social and independent living skills and relapse prevention. A less intensive option featured case management in which reduced caseloads allowed clinicians to

provide individualized assistance in such areas as daily living, housing, legal problems, and the like.

The behavioral skills model produced the largest positive effects on measures of client functioning and symptoms but was also the most expensive program to deliver. To further explore the cost considerations, the evaluators examined service utilization and cost data for the clients in each of the three programs for four time periods: the six months before the dual diagnosis programs began (baseline), the six months after, the 12 months after, and the 18 months after.

Mental health service costs were divided into two categories: supportive services and intensive services. Supportive services included case management, outpatient visits, medication visits, day services, and other such routine services for mental health patients. Intensive services included the more costly treatments for serious episodes, for instance, inpatient services, skilled nursing care, residential treatment, and emergency visits.

The costs of supportive services were expected to show an increase for all of the specialized dual diagnosis programs, corresponding to the extra resources required to provide them. Any significant savings to the mental health system were expected to appear as a result of decreased use of expensive intensive services. Thus, the cost analysis focused on the amount by which the costs of supportive services increased from baseline in comparison to the amount by which the costs of intensive services decreased. The table shows the results for the

☒ EXHIBIT 11-D   Continued

change in service utilization costs between the six-month baseline period and the 18 months after the program began.

As expected, the cost of supportive services generally increased after the specialized programs were implemented, except for the case management program, which actually showed a reduction in total support cost from the baseline service period. The largest increase in support costs, on the other hand, was associated with the relatively intensive behavioral skills program.

Also, as hoped, the costs for intensive services were reduced from baseline for all of the specialized programs. The greater impacts of the behavioral skills program on client functioning and symptoms, however, did not translate into corresponding decreases in service utilization and associated cost savings. Indeed, the usual-care condition of the 12-step program produced the greatest decreases in subsequent costs for intensive services. However, while the case management program did not yield such large decreases, its lower support costs resulted

in a savings-to-costs ratio that was comparable to that of the 12-step program. Additional analyses showed that these programs also generally resulted in savings to the medical system, the criminal justice system, and the families of the clients.

In terms of costs and savings directly to the mental health system, therefore, both the 12-step and the case management programs produced considerably more savings than they cost. Indeed, the cost analysis estimated that for every $1 invested in providing these programs there were about $9 in savings that would accrue over the subsequent 18 months. Moreover, the case management program could actually be implemented with a net reduction in support service costs, thus requiring no additional investment. The behavioral skills program, on the other hand, produced a net loss to the mental health system. For every $1 invested in it, there was only a $0.53 savings to the mental health system.

Average per Client Change in Costs of Services Used From Baseline to 18 Months Later, in Dollars

	12-Step Program	Behavioral Skills	Case Management
Change in mental health supportive costs (a)	+728	+1,146	−370
Change in mental health intensive costs (b)	−6,589	−612	−3,291
Ratio of (b) to (a)	9.05	0.53	8.89

SOURCE: Adapted from Jeanette M. Jerrell and Teh-Wei Hu, "Estimating the Cost Impact of Three Dual Diagnosis Treatment Programs," *Evaluation Review*, 1996, 20(2):160-180.

▓ EXHIBIT 11-E   Costs to Benefits of Correctional Sentences

The control of crime by appropriate sentencing of convicted offenders must take into account not only the costs of implementing each of the three choices typically available to judges—prison, jail, or probation sentences—but also the benefits derived. Each correctional approach generates different types of "benefits" for society. The major ones are *incapacitation* through removing the offender from the community by incarceration in a prison or jail, *deterrence* by making visible the consequences of criminal behavior to discourage potential offenders, and *rehabilitation* by resocialization and redirection of criminals' behavior. Since jail sentences are usually short, for instance, the incapacitation benefit is very small compared with the benefit from prison sentences, although, since no one likes being in jail, the deterrence benefit of jail is estimated to be about five-sixths that of prison.

Gray and associates attempted to estimate the monetary value of these different social benefits for each sentencing option (see table).

While, on average, probation sentences showed greater net benefits than jail which, in turn, showed a smaller negative benefit than prison, the relative weight given to each benefit varied according to the type and circumstances of the offense. For example, the costs of a burglary (adding loss to the victim with costs of the police investigation, arrest, and court costs) comes to about $5,000, suggesting that perhaps long prison sentences are called for in the case of recidivist burglars to maximize the incapacitation benefit. In contrast, the cost of apprehending and trying persons for receiving stolen property is less than $2,000, and a short jail sentence or even probation may be the most efficient response.

Estimated Annual Social Costs and Benefits per Offender, in Dollars, for Different Correctional Sentences (average across all offenses)

	Incapacitation Benefit	Rehabilitation Benefit	Deterrence Benefit	Costs	Net Benefits
Prison	+6,732	10,356	+6,113	−10,435	−7,946
Jail	+774	−5,410	+5,094	−2,772	−2,315
Probation	0	−2,874	+5,725	−1,675	+1,176

SOURCE: Adapted from T. Gray, C. R. Larsen, P. Haynes, and K. W. Olson, "Using Cost-Benefit Analysis to Evaluate Correctional Sentences," *Evaluation Review,* 1991, 15(4):471-481.

nal perspective. In this exhibit, Gray and associates (1991) report on an effort to integrate several studies to come out with a reasonable cost-to-benefit analysis of the efficiency of different correctional approaches. As shown in the table in Exhibit 11-E, benefits are of several different types. Although, as the article carefully notes, there are limitations to the preci-

sion of the estimates, the results are important to judges and other criminal justice experts concerned with the effects of different types of sentences.

The components of a cost-benefit analysis conducted from a communal perspective include most of the costs and benefits that also appear in calculations made from the individual and program sponsor perspectives, but the items are in a sense valued and monetized differently. For example, communal costs for a project include opportunity costs in terms of alternative investments forgone by the community to fund the project in question. These are obviously not the same as opportunity costs incurred by an individual as a consequence of participating in the project. Communal costs also include outlays for facilities, equipment, and personnel, usually valued differently than they would be from the program sponsor perspective. Finally, these costs do not include transfer payments because they would also be entered as benefits to the community and the two entries would simply cancel each other out.

Obviously, the decision about which accounting perspective to use depends on the stakeholders who constitute the audience for the analysis, or who have sponsored it. In this sense, the selection of the accounting perspective is a political choice. An analyst employed by a private foundation interested solely in containing the costs of hospital care, for example, often will take a program sponsor accounting perspective. The analyst may neglect or be uninterested in whether the cost-containment program that has the highest net benefits from a sponsor accounting perspective might actually show a negative cost-to-benefit value when viewed from the standpoint of the individual. This could be the case if the individual accounting perspective included the costs involved in having family members stay home from work because the early discharge of patients required them to provide the bedside care ordinarily received in the hospital.

Generally, the communal accounting perspective is the most politically neutral. If analyses using this perspective are done properly, the information gained from an individual or a program sponsor perspective will be included

as data about the distribution of costs and benefits. Another approach is to undertake cost-benefit analyses from more than one accounting perspective. The important point, however, is that cost-benefit analyses, like other evaluation activities, have political features.

Exhibit 11-F shows some of the basic components of cost-benefit analyses for the different accounting perspectives (the program sponsor in this case is a government agency). The list is not to be taken as complete but as an illustration only. Specific items included in real analyses vary.

Exhibit 11-G provides a simplified, hypothetical example of cost-benefit calculations for a training program from the three accounting perspectives. Again, the monetary figures are gross oversimplifications; a real analysis would require far more complex treatment of the measurement issues involved. Note that the same components may enter into the calculation as benefits from one perspective and as costs from another and that the difference between benefits and costs, or net benefit, will vary, depending on the accounting perspective used.

In some cases, it may be necessary to undertake a number of analyses. For example, if a government group and a private foundation jointly sponsor a program, separate analyses may be required for each to judge the return on its investment. Also, the analyst might want to calculate the costs and benefits to different groups of targets, such as the direct and indirect targets of a program. For example, many communities offer tax advantages to industrial corporations if they build their plants there; the intent is to provide employment opportunities for residents. Costs-to-benefits comparisons could be calculated for the employer, the employees, and also the "average" resident of the community, whose taxes may rise to take up

EXHIBIT 11-F   Components of Cost-Benefit Analyses From Different Perspectives

	Individual (targets)	Program Sponsor (government)	Communal (communities in general)
Benefits	Increase in net earnings (after taxes)	Increase in tax revenues	Increase in gross earnings (before taxes)
	Additional benefits received (e.g., direct transfers, fringe and noneconomic benefits)	Decrease in expenses of public assistance and other subsidies	Increase in other income (e.g., fringe benefits, excluding direct transfers)
		Value of work done within the project (salary and fringes at market costs)	Decrease in expenses of alternative projects no longer applicable
			Value of work done within the project (salary and fringes at market costs)
Costs	Opportunity costs (net earnings forgone)	Taxes lost	Opportunity costs (gross earnings forgone)
	Loss of direct subsidies no longer applicable (alternative social programs)	Project costs (e.g., capital, administrative, instructional, direct subsidies)	Project costs (excluding direct subsidies or transfer payments)
	Costs related to participation (e.g., fees, materials)		

the slack resulting from the tax break to the factory owners. Other refinements might be included as well. For example, we excluded direct subsidies from the communal perspective, both as a cost and as a benefit, because they probably would balance each other out; however, under certain conditions it may be that the actual economic benefit of the subsidies is less than the cost.

Measuring Costs and Benefits

The specification, measurement, and valuation of costs and benefits—procedures that are central to cost-benefit analysis—raise two distinct problems: first, identifying and measuring

all program costs and benefits, and second, expressing all costs and benefits in terms of a common denominator, that is, translating them into monetary values.

The problem of identifying and measuring costs and benefits is most acute for ex ante appraisals, where often there are only speculative estimates of costs and impact. However, data often are limited in ex post cost-benefit analyses as well. For many social interventions, the information from an evaluation (or even a series of evaluations) may in itself prove insufficient for a retrospective cost-benefit analysis to be carried out. Thus, evaluations often provide only some of the necessary information, and the analyst frequently must use additional sources or judgments.

EXHIBIT 11-G Hypothetical Example of Cost-Benefit Calculation From Different Accounting Perspectives

Benefits/Costs	
(1) Earnings improvement of trainees (before taxes)	$100,000
(2) Earnings improvement of trainees (after taxes)	80,000
(3) Value of work done in training period	10,000
(4) Project costs for facility and personnel	50,000
(5) Project costs for equipment and supplies	5,000
(6) Trainee stipends (direct transfer payments)	12,000
(7) Earnings forgone by trainees (before taxes)	11,000
(8) Earnings forgone by trainees (after taxes)	9,000
(9) Taxes lost: (7) − (8)	2,000

	Individual	Program Sponsor	Communal
Benefits	(2) 80,000	(1) − (2) 20,000	(1) 100,000
	(6) 12,000	(3) 10,000	(3) 10,000
	92,000	30,000	110,000
Costs	(8) 9,000	(4) 50,000	(4) 50,000
		(5) 5,000	(5) 5,000
		(6) 12,000	(7) 11,000
		(9) 2,000	
	9,000	69,000	66,000
B/C ratio	$\frac{92,000}{9,000} = 10.22$	$\frac{30,000}{69,000} = .44$	$\frac{110,000}{66,000} = 1.69$
Net benefit[a]	83,000	−39,000	44,000

a. Note that net social benefit can be split into net benefit for trainees plus net benefit for the government; in this case, the latter is negative: 44,000 = 83,000 + (−39,000).

The second problem in many social programs is the difficulty of translating benefits and costs to monetary units. Social programs frequently do not produce results that can be valued accurately by means of market prices. For example, many would argue that the benefits of a fertility control project, a literacy campaign, or a program providing training in improved health practices cannot be monetized in ways acceptable to the various stakeholders. What value should be placed on the embarrassment of an adult who cannot read? In such cases, cost-effectiveness analysis might be a reasonable alternative, because such analysis does not require that benefits be valued in terms of money, but only that they be quantified by outcome measures.

Monetizing Outcomes

Because of the advantages of expressing benefits in monetary terms, a number of approaches have been specified for monetizing outcomes or benefits (Thompson, 1980). Five frequently used ones are as follows:

1. *Money measurements.* The least controversial approach is to estimate direct monetary benefits. For example, if keeping a health center open for two hours in the evening reduces targets' absence from work (and thus loss of wages) by an average of ten hours per year, then, from an individual perspective, the annual benefit can be calculated by multiplying the average wage by ten hours by the number of employed targets.

2. *Market valuation.* Another relatively noncontroversial approach is to monetize gains or impacts by valuing them at market prices. If crime is reduced in a community by 50%, benefits can be estimated in terms of housing prices through adjustment of current values on the basis of prices in communities with lower crime rates and similar social profiles.

3. *Econometric estimation.* A more complicated approach is to estimate the presumed value of a gain or impact in market terms. For example, the increase in tax receipts from greater business revenue due to a reduced fear of crime could be determined by calculating relevant tax revenues of similar communities with lower crime rates, and then estimating the tax receipts that would ensue for the community in question. Such estimation may require complex analytical efforts and the participation of a highly trained economic analyst.

Econometric analysis, especially when performed with refined contemporary multivariate techniques, is a popular choice because it can account for the other influences on the variable in question (in the preceding example, taxes lost because of fear of crime). The ana-

lytical effort required to do quality econometric work is certainly complex, and the assumptions involved are sometimes troublesome. However, econometric analysis, like all good methodological procedures, requires making assumptions explicit and therefore enables others to evaluate the analytical basis of the claims made.

4. *Hypothetical questions.* A quite problematic approach is to estimate the value of intrinsically nonmonetary benefits by questioning targets directly. For instance, a program to prevent dental disease may decrease participants' cavities by an average of one at age 40; thus, one might conduct a survey on how much people think it is worth to have an additional intact tooth as opposed to a filled tooth. Such estimates presume that the monetary value obtained realistically expresses the worth of an intact tooth. Clearly, hypothetical valuations of this kind are open to considerable skepticism.

5. *Observing political choices.* The most tentative approach is to estimate benefits on the basis of political actions. If state legislatures are consistently willing to appropriate funds for high-risk infant medical programs at a rate of $40,000 per child saved, this figure could be used as an estimate of the monetary benefits of such programs. But given that political choices are complex, shifting, and inconsistent, this approach is generally very risky.

In summary, all relevant components must be included if the results of a cost-benefit analysis are to be valid and reliable and reflect fully the economic effects of a project. When important benefits are disregarded because they cannot be measured or monetized, the project may appear less efficient than it is; if certain costs are omitted, the project will seem more efficient. The results may be just as misleading if estimates of costs or benefits are either too conservative or too generous. As a means of dealing with the problem, analysts often will value everything that can reasonably be valued and then list the things that cannot be valued. They will then estimate the value that would have to be placed on the nonmonetary benefits for the project to be a "go."

Shadow Prices

Benefits and costs need to be defined and valued differently, depending on the accounting perspective used. For many programs, however, the outputs simply do not have market prices (e.g., a reduction in pollution or the work of a homemaker), yet their value must be estimated. The preferred procedure is to use *shadow prices*, also known as *accounting prices*, to reflect better than do actual market prices the real costs and benefits to society. Shadow prices are derived prices for goods and services that are supposed to reflect their true benefits and costs. Sometimes it is more realistic to use shadow prices even when actual prices are available. For example, suppose an experimental program is implemented that requires a director who is knowledgeable about every one of the building trades. For the single site, the sponsors may be fortunate to find a retired person who is very interested in the program and willing to work for, say, $30,000 per year. But if the program was shown to be a success through an impact evaluation and a cost-benefit analysis was undertaken, it might be best to use a shadow price of, say, $50,000 for the director's salary, because it is very unlikely that additional persons with the nonmonetary interests of the first director could be found (Nas, 1996).

Opportunity Costs

The concept of *opportunity costs* reflects the fact that resources generally are limited. Consequently, individuals or organizations choose from existing alternatives the ways these resources are to be allocated, and these choices affect the activities and goals of the decisionmakers. The cost of each choice can be measured by the worth of the forgone options.

Although this concept is relatively simple, the actual estimation of opportunity costs often is complex. For example, a police department may decide to pay the tuition of police officers who want to go to graduate school in psychology or social work on the grounds that the additional schooling will improve the officers' job performance. To have the money for this program, the department might have to keep its police cars an extra two months each. The opportunity costs could in this case be estimated by calculating the additional repair costs for the department's automobiles that would be incurred if the cars were replaced later. Since in many cases opportunity costs can be estimated only by making assumptions about the consequences of alternative investments, they are one of the controversial areas in efficiency analyses.

Secondary Effects (Externalities)

Projects may have external or *spillover* effects—that is, side effects or unintended consequences that may be either beneficial or detrimental. Because such effects are not deliberate outcomes, they may be inappropriately omitted from cost-benefit calculations if special efforts are not made to include them. A secondary effect of a training program, for example, might be the spillover of the training to relatives, neighbors, and friends of the participants. Among the more commonly discussed negative external effects of industrial or technical projects are pollution, noise, traffic, and destruction of plant and animal life.

For many social programs, two secondary effects are likely: displacement and vacuum effects. For example, an educational or training project may produce a group of newly trained persons who enter the labor market, compete with workers already employed, and displace them (i.e., force them out of their jobs). Project participants may also vacate jobs held previously, leaving a vacuum that other workers might fill.

Secondary effects, or externalities, may be difficult to identify and measure. Once found, however, they should be incorporated into the cost-benefit calculations.

Distributional Considerations

Traditionally, judgments of the effectiveness of social interventions are predicated on the notion that an effective intervention makes at least one person better off and nobody worse off. In economics, this yardstick is called the *Pareto criterion*. Cost-benefit analysis, however, does not use the Pareto criterion, but rather the *potential* Pareto criterion. Under this criterion, the gains must potentially compensate for the losses, with something left over. That is, it is presumed—although not necessarily tested—that if the program's impact is estimated, more targets will be better off than worse off, or, more accurately, that the "balance" between total gains and total losses will be positive. This criterion may be very difficult to satisfy in social programs, however, particularly those that rely on income transfers. Lowering the minimum wage for teenagers, for

instance, may increase their employment at the cost of reducing work opportunities for older adults.

Often the concern is not simply with winners versus losers but with movement toward equity within a target population. This is particularly true in the case of programs designed to improve the general quality of life of a group or community. The basic means of incorporating equity and distributional considerations in the cost-benefit analysis involves a system of weights whereby benefits are valued more if they produce the anticipated positive effects. Thus, if a lowered minimum wage for teenagers decreases the family incomes of the moderately disadvantaged, the dollars gained and lost could be weighted differently, depending on the degree of disadvantage to the families. Some accomplishments are worth more than others to the community, both for equity reasons and for the increase in human well-being, and should therefore be weighted more heavily.

The weights to be assigned can be determined by the appropriate decisionmakers, in which case value judgments will obviously have to be made. They may also be derived through certain economic principles and assumptions. In any case, it is clear that weights cannot be applied indiscriminately. Analysts will undoubtedly develop further refinements as they continue to deal with the issue of distributional effects.

An intermediate solution to considerations of equity in cost-benefit analyses is to first test to see whether the costs and benefits of a program meet the potential Pareto criterion. If so, calculations can be undertaken for separate subgroups in the population. Such disaggregation might be done for separate income groups, for instance, or for students with different levels of achievement. Such distributional issues are especially important in analyses of issues like the effects of schooling where costs are in part borne by taxpayers who do not receive direct benefits. Publicly supported education yields benefits primarily to those who have children in school and, disproportionately, to those who are less well off and, hence, pay lower taxes.

Discounting

Another major element in the methodology of efficiency analyses concerns the treatment of time in valuing program costs and benefits. Intervention programs vary in duration, and successful ones in particular produce benefits that are derived in the future, sometimes long after the intervention has taken place. The effects of many programs are expected to persist through the participants' lifetimes. Consequently, evaluators often must extrapolate into the future to measure impact and ascertain benefits, especially when program benefits are gauged as projected income changes for participants. In particular, ex ante appraisals often extrapolate into the future in carrying out a complete analysis. Otherwise, the evaluation would be based only on the restricted period of time for which actual program performance data are available.

Consequently, costs and benefits occurring at different points in time must be brought into a common measure or made commensurable. In other words, the time patterns for costs and benefits of a program must be taken into account. The applicable technique is known as *discounting* and consists of reducing costs and benefits that are dispersed through time to a common monetary base or adjusting them to their present values. For example, costs are usually highest at the beginning of an interven-

tion, when many of the resources must be expended; they either taper off or cease when the intervention ends. Even when a cost is fixed or a benefit is constant, increments of expenditures made or benefits derived at different points in time cannot be considered equivalent. Instead of asking, "How much more will my investment be worth in the future?" standard economic practice is to ask, "How much less are benefits derived in the future worth compared to those received in the present?" The same goes for costs. The answer depends on what we assume to be the rate of interest, or the discount rate, and the time frame chosen. Exhibit 11-H provides an example of discounting.

The choice of time period on which to base the analysis depends on the nature of the program and whether the analysis is ex ante or ex post. All else being equal, a program will appear more beneficial the longer the time horizon chosen.

There is no authoritative approach for fixing the discount rate. One choice is to fix the rate on the basis of the opportunity costs of capital, that is, the rate of return that could be earned if the funds were invested elsewhere. But there are considerable differences in opportunity costs depending on whether the funds are invested in the private sector, as an individual might do, or in the public sector, as a quasi-government body may decide it must. The length of time involved and the degree of risk associated with the investment are additional considerations.

The results of a cost-benefit analysis are thus particularly sensitive to the choice of discount rate. In practice, evaluators usually resolve this complex and controversial issue by carrying out discounting calculations based on several different rates. Furthermore, instead of

⚡ EXHIBIT 11-H   Discounting Costs and Benefits to Their Present Values

Discounting is based on the simple notion that it is preferable to have a given amount of capital in the present rather than in the future. All else equal, present capital can be saved in a bank to accumulate interest or can be used for some alternative investment. Hence, it will be worth more than its face value in the future. Put differently, a fixed amount payable in the future is worth less than the same amount payable in the present.

Conceptually, discounting is the reverse of compound interest, since it tells us how much we would have to put aside today to yield a fixed amount in the future. Algebraically, discounting is the reciprocal of compound interest and is carried out by means of the simple formula

$$\text{Preset value of an amount} = \frac{\text{Amount}}{(1 + r)^t},$$

where r is the discount rate (e.g., .05) and t is the number of years. The total stream of benefits (and costs) of a program expressed in present values is obtained by adding up the discounted values for each year in the period chosen for study. An example of such a computation follows.

A training program is known to produce increases of $1,000 per year in earnings for each participant. The earnings improvements are discounted to their present values at a 10% discount rate for five years.

Over the five years, total discounted benefits equal $909.09 + $826.45 + . . . + $620.92, or $3,790.79. Thus, increases of $1,000 per year for the next five years are not currently worth $5,000 but only $3,790.79. At a 5% discount rate, the total present value would be $4,329.48. In general, all else being equal, benefits cal- culated using low discount rates will appear greater than those calculated with high rates.

		Year		
1	2	3	4	5
$\dfrac{\$1,000}{(1 + .10)^1}$	$\dfrac{\$1,000}{(1 + .10)^2}$	$\dfrac{\$1,000}{(1 + .10)^3}$	$\dfrac{\$1,000}{(1 + .10)^4}$	$\dfrac{\$1,000}{(1 + .10)^5}$
= $909.09	= $826.45	= $751.32	= $683.01	= $620.92

applying what may seem to be an arbitrary discount rate or rates, the evaluator may calculate the program's *internal rate of return*, or the value that the discount rate would have to be for program benefits to equal program costs.

A related technique, *inflation adjustment*, is used when changes over time in asset prices should be taken into account in cost-benefit calculations. For example, the prices of houses and equipment may change considerably be- cause of the increased or decreased value of the dollar at different times.

Ethical Issues in Setting Values

It is clear that with the many consider- ations involved there can be considerable dis- agreement on the monetary values to be placed on benefits. The disputes that arise in setting these values underlie much of the conflict over whether cost-benefit analysis is a legitimate way of estimating the efficiency of programs. An interesting discussion of this matter is the article by Skaburskis (1987) in which he discusses the decision-making process in planning the BART transit system for the San Francisco Bay Area. As one illustration, in discussing the monetary values to be placed on the indirect effects of the new transportation system, he asks, "Is reduced air pollution worth 5, 10, or 15 cents to the average Bay Area resident?" (p. 605). It is the answer to this question that he says determines whether certain areas of the community are redeveloped.

Comparing Costs to Benefits

The final step in cost-benefit analysis consists of comparing total costs to total benefits. How this comparison is made depends to some extent on the purpose of the analysis and the conventions in the particular program sector. The most direct comparison can be made simply by subtracting costs from benefits. For example, a program may have costs of $185,000 and its benefits are calculated at $300,000; in this case, the net benefit (or profit, to use the business analogy) is $115,000. Although generally more problematic, sometimes the ratio of benefits to costs is used rather than the net benefit. This measure is generally regarded as more difficult to interpret and should be avoided (Mishan, 1988).

In discussing the comparison of benefits to costs, we have noted the similarity to decision making in business. The analogy is real. In particular, in deciding which programs to support, some large private foundations actually phrase their decisions in investment terms. They may want to balance a high-risk venture (i.e., one that might show a high rate of return but has a low probability of success) with a low-risk program (one that probably has a much lower rate of return but a much higher probability of success). Thus, foundations, community organizations, or government bodies might wish to spread their "investment risks" by developing a portfolio of projects with different likelihoods and prospective amounts of benefit.

Sometimes, of course, the costs of a program are greater than its benefits. In Exhibit 11-I, a cost-to-benefit analysis is presented that documents the negative results of a federal initiative to control noise. In this analysis, the costs of regulatory efforts to control the noise from motorcycles, trucks, and buses were estimated to be considerably higher than the benefits of the program. In the exhibit's table, the findings for truck and bus regulations are reported; note the negative values when benefits are subtracted from costs and the less than 1.0 values resulting when benefits are divided by costs. Of course, one can quarrel over the measure of benefits, which was simply the increase in property values resulting from a decline in decibels (dBAs) of noise. Nevertheless, according to Broder (1988), the analysis was a major reason why the Reagan administration abandoned the program.

It bears noting that sometimes programs that yield negative values are nevertheless important and should be continued. For example, there is a communal responsibility to provide for severely retarded persons, and it is unlikely that any procedure designed to do so will have a positive value (subtracting costs from benefits). In such cases, one may still want to compare the costs to benefits of different programs,

---

✎ EXHIBIT 11-I A Study of the Birth and Death of a Regulatory Agenda

---

It has long been the case that, once funded, government programs are almost impossible to eliminate. Most organizations build up constituencies over the years that can be called on to protect them if threatened. Thus, it was particularly remarkable that the federal Office of Noise Abatement and Control (ONAC) at the Environmental Protection Agency (EPA) was disbanded during the Reagan administration, thus terminating a major social regulatory program without a public outcry.

Although the halt in the spread of inefficient noise regulation is one of few examples of lasting relief from social regulation provided by the Reagan administration, a further irony is that much of the economic analysis that was at least partly instrumental was produced by the prior administration. Specifically, President Carter's Council of Economic Advisors and the Council on Wage and Price Stability, an agency disbanded by the Reagan administration, had produced several economic analyses for the public docket that were highly critical of the regulations, although it was the Reagan administration that acted on these analyses.

Cost-Benefit Analysis of Truck and Bus Noise Regulations

| | Truck Noise Regulations | | Bus Noise Regulations | |
	83 dBAs	80 dBAs	83 dBAs	80 dBAs
Benefits (a)	1,056	1,571	66.2	188.5
Costs (b)	1,241	3,945	358.8	967.3
Net benefits (a) – (b)	–185	–2,374	–292.6	–778.8
Benefit-cost ratio (a)/(b)	.85	.40	.18	.19

NOTE: dBAs = decibels. Costs and benefits are in millions of 1978 dollars except for ratios.

SOURCE: Adapted from I. E. Broder, "A Study of the Birth and Death of a Regulatory Agenda: The Case of the EPA Noise Program," *Evaluation Review,* 1988, 12(3):291-309.

---

such as institutional care compared with home care.

When to Do Ex Post Cost-Benefit Analysis

Earlier in this chapter, we discussed the importance of undertaking ex ante analyses in developing programs that result in irrevocable or almost irrevocable commitments. We also indicated that many more ex ante analyses are

called for in the social program arena than are currently performed. Too often it is only after programs are put into place that policymakers and sponsors realize that the programs' costs compared to their benefits make them impractical to implement on a permanent basis.

In the case of ex post evaluations, it is important to consider a number of factors in determining whether to undertake a cost-benefit analysis. In some evaluation contexts, the technique is feasible, useful, and a logical com-

▓ EXHIBIT 11-J Cotton Dust Regulation: An OSHA Success Story

In the late 1970s, the Occupational Safety and Health Administration (OSHA) took a major step in attempting to promote the health of workers in the textile industry, tightening its standard on cotton dust levels in textile plants. Because the OSHA cotton dust standard was widely believed to be ineffective, it became the target of a major political debate and a fundamental U.S. Supreme Court decision. However, the evidence indicates that the standard has had a significant beneficial effect on worker health, and at a cost much lower than originally anticipated. For instance, data on the relationship between exposure to cotton dust and disease incidence, as well as the disability data and the evidence based on worker turnover, suggest that the risks of byssinosis (lung disease) have been reduced dramatically. The cost of eliminating even cases classified as "totally disabled" is less than $1,500, and thus there is a strong economic basis for the enforcement of OSHA standards.

Estimated Reduction in Byssinosis Cases Associated With the Introduction of the Cotton Dust Standard

Type of Case	No. of Cases Reduced per Year, 1978-1982	Total No. of Cases Reduced per Year If Full Compliance
Byssinosis, Grades ½ and 1	3,517	5,047
Byssinosis over Grade 1	1,634	2,349
Partial disabilities	843	1,210
Total disabilities	339	487

SOURCE: Adapted, with permission, from W. K. Viscusi, "Cotton Dust Regulation: An OSHA Success Story?" *Journal of Policy Analysis and Management,* 1985, 4(3):325-343. Copyright © 1985, John Wiley & Sons, Inc.

ponent of a comprehensive evaluation; in others, its application may rest on dubious assumptions and be of limited utility.

Optimal prerequisites of an ex post cost-benefit analysis of a program include the following:

- The program has independent or separable funding. This means that its costs can be separated from other activities.

- The program is beyond the development stage, and it is certain that net effects are significant.

- Program impact and magnitude of impact are known or can be validly estimated.

- Benefits can be translated into monetary terms.

- Decisionmakers are considering alternative programs, rather than simply whether or not to continue the existing project.

Ex post efficiency estimation—both cost-benefit and cost-effectiveness analyses—should be components of many impact evaluations. In Exhibit 11-J, the impact of a program to replace machinery in cotton mills that causes an inordinate amount of dust is reported. Viscusi (1985) provides two sets of figures in the exhibit's table, showing the number of cases of byssinosis (lung disease) and of long-term disabilities that were reduced by the initiative as well as the estimated number of cases that might have been reduced given full compliance with the program. His cost data indicate that even total disabilities are prevented for less than $1,500, clearly an amount that the most conservative factory owner must acknowledge represents a saving compared to the spiraling costs of disability insurance of industrial plants. Merely presenting the information on the number of cases of lung disease that would be reduced by enforcing OSHA's standards—without demonstrating the comparatively low costs of the program—probably would not have had much impact on plant owners.

COST-EFFECTIVENESS ANALYSIS

Cost-benefit analysis allows evaluators to compare the economic efficiency of program alternatives, even when the interventions are not aimed at common goals. After initial attempts in the early 1970s to use cost-benefit analysis in social fields, however, some evaluators became uneasy about directly comparing cost-benefit calculations for, say, family planning to those for health, housing, or educational programs. As we have noted, sometimes it is simply not possible to obtain agreement on critical values—for example, on the monetary value of a life prevented by a fertility control project, or of a life saved by a health campaign—and then compare the results.

In contrast to cost-benefit analysis, cost-effectiveness analysis does not require that benefits and costs be reduced to a common denominator. Instead, the effectiveness of a program in reaching given substantive goals is related to

the monetary value of the costs. In cost-effectiveness analyses, programs with similar goals are evaluated and their costs compared. Thus, one can compare two or more programs aimed at lowering the fertility rate, or different educational methods for raising achievement levels, or various interventions to reduce infant mortality.

Cost-effectiveness analysis thus allows comparison and rank ordering of programs in terms of their costs for reaching given goals or the various inputs required for different degrees of goal achievement. But because the benefits are not converted to a common denominator, we cannot ascertain the worth or merit of a given intervention in monetary terms from such analyses. Likewise, we cannot determine which of two or more programs in different areas produces better returns. We can compare the relative efficiency of different programs only if they have the same or roughly similar goals and have the same outcome measures. In these analyses, efficiency is judged by comparing costs for units of outcome.

Cost-effectiveness analysis can be viewed as an extension of cost-benefit analysis to projects with multiple and noncommensurable goals. It is based on the same principles and uses the same methods as cost-benefit analysis. The assumptions of the method, as well as the procedures required for measuring costs and discounting, for example, are the same for both approaches. Therefore, the concepts and methodology introduced previously with regard to cost-benefit analysis can also be regarded as a basis for understanding the cost-effectiveness approach.

Cost-effectiveness analysis is a particularly good method for evaluating programs with similar outcomes without having to monetize the outcomes. Moreover, if a service or program is known to produce positive outcomes, or presumed to, cost-effectiveness analysis may be conducted in terms of costs per client served. Identifying such *unit costs* makes it possible to compare the efficiency of different programs that provide similar services or different service components within a multiservice program. Exhibit 11-K provides an example of a cost analysis of this sort for methadone treatment programs for intravenous drug abusers. Of particular interest to the evaluators was the relative magnitude of the costs per client for an add-on employment training component compared with the costs of the standard program. However, the analysis was also able to reveal differences in costs per client across programs at four separate sites.

Although some sponsors and program staff are prejudiced against efficiency analyses because they deal chiefly with "dollars" and not "people," the approach that underlies them is no different from that of any stakeholder who needs to assess the utility of implementing or maintaining a program. Our world of limited resources, though often decried, nevertheless requires setting one program against another and deciding resource allocation. Competent efficiency analysis can provide valuable information about a program's economic potential or actual payoff and thus is important for program planning, implementation, and policy decisions, as well as for gaining and maintaining the support of stakeholders.

⚜ EXHIBIT 11-K   Cost Analysis of Training and Employment Services in Methadone Treatment

Prior evaluation research has shown that vocational and employment counseling for drug users not only has positive effects on employment but also on drug use and criminality. Despite these encouraging signs, many drug treatment programs have reduced or eliminated vocational services due to changes in program emphasis or financial pressures. Against this background, a team of evaluators at Research Triangle Institute conducted cost analysis on four methadone maintenance programs with employment services components to help decision-makers explore the feasibility of a renewed emphasis on vocational services in substance abuse treatment.

The standard treatment in these programs involved methadone maintenance for intravenous drug users for as long as 12 months or more, random urine tests approximately once a month, monthly individual counseling sessions, and one to four group counseling sessions per month.

The Training and Employment Program component (TEP) of these programs included vocational needs assessment, location of existing training and employment programs suitable to the needs of methadone clients, and placement into training and jobs. Each program had an on-site vocational specialist to work with both the drug counselors and the clients to identify and address vocational issues, provide job-related services, and maintain weekly contact with each assigned client.

Findings from a randomized impact assessment of the standard methadone treatment (STD) plus TEP compared with STD only showed that the methadone clients had high rates of unemployment and lacked vocational services and that TEP helped them access such services, obtain training, and reduce their short-term unemployment.

Given these positive findings, the critical practical question is how much the TEP component added to the cost of the standard treatment program. To assess this, the evaluators examined the total costs and cost per client of TEP in comparison to the analogous costs of the standard program without TEP for each of the four program sites. The main results are summarized in the table.

The results of this analysis indicated that the cost per client of the TEP component ranged from $1,648 to $2,215, amounts corresponding to between 42% and 50% of the cost of the standard methadone treatment without TEP.

⚿ EXHIBIT 11-K Continued

Annual Total and per Client Costs of Adding Training and Employment Program (TEP) Services Compared With the Costs of Standard (STD) Services

	Program A	Program B	Program C	Program D
Personnel	$38,402	$41,681	$49,762	$50,981
Support and supplies for vocational specialists	11,969	14,467	17,053	6,443
Travel	1,211	3,035	2,625	1,870
Other overhead	7,736	14,033	2,619	2,728
Total annual TEP cost	59,318	73,217	72,060	62,022
TEP clients served	36	38	43	28
Cost per client served	$1,648	$1,927	$1,676	$2,215
Total annual STD cost	$819,202	$1,552,816	$2,031,698	$1,531,067
STD clients served	210	400	573	300
STD cost per client	$3,901	$3,882	$3,546	$5,104
Total TEP cost/total STD cost	7.2%	4.7%	3.5%	4.1%
TEP per client/STD per client	42.2%	49.6%	47.3%	43.4%

Because many methadone maintenance clients are not appropriate for training and employment services, however, a TEP component will not be applicable to the entire caseload of the standard treatment program. When the incremental costs of adding a TEP component to the total program were figured, therefore, the results showed that the TEP component added only 3.5% to 7.2% to the total program budget. In addition, the analysis showed different degrees of efficiency across programs in providing both TEP and standard services, as indicated in the varying costs per client.

SOURCE: Adapted from M. T. French, C. J. Bradley, B. Calingaert, M. L. Dennis, and G. T. Karuntzos, "Cost Analysis of Training and Employment Services in Methadone Treatment," *Evaluation and Program Planning*, 1994, 17(2):107-120.

SUMMARY

※ Efficiency analyses provide a framework for relating program costs to outcomes. Whereas cost-benefit analyses directly compare benefits to costs in commensurable (monetary) terms, cost-effectiveness analyses relate costs expressed in monetary terms to units of substantive results achieved.

※ Efficiency analyses can be useful at all stages of a program, from planning through implementation and modification. Currently, ex post analyses are more commonplace than ex ante analyses in the social program arena because reasonably sound estimates of costs and benefits prior to program implementation are often lacking. Nevertheless, ex ante analyses should be undertaken more often than they are, particularly for programs that are expensive either to implement or to evaluate. Different sets of assumptions can create a range of analyses; one thing these analyses may reveal is the improbability of achieving the desired net benefits under any sensible set of assumptions.

※ Efficiency analyses use different assumptions and may produce correspondingly different results depending on which accounting perspective is taken: that of individual targets or participants, program sponsors, or the community or society. Which perspective should be taken depends on the intended consumers of the analysis and thus involves political choice.

※ Cost-benefit analysis requires that program costs and benefits be known, quantified, and transformed to a common measurement unit; that they be projected into the future to reflect the lifetime of a program; and that future benefits and costs be discounted to reflect their present values.

※ Options for monetizing outcomes or benefits include money measurements, market valuation, econometric estimation, hypothetical questions asked of participants, and observation of political choices. Shadow, or accounting, prices are used for costs and benefits when market prices are unavailable or, in some circumstances, as substitutes for market prices that may be unrealistic.

※ In estimating costs, the concept of opportunity costs allows for a truer estimate but can be complex and controversial in application.

※ The true outcomes of projects include spillover and distributional effects, both of which should be taken into account in full cost-benefit analyses.

❈ Cost-effectiveness analysis is a feasible alternative to cost-benefit analysis when benefits cannot be calibrated in monetary units. It permits programs with similar goals to be compared in terms of their relative efficiency and can also be used to analyze the relative efficiency of variations of a program.

❈ Efficiency analyses can require considerable technical sophistication and the use of consultants. As a way of thinking about program results, however, they direct attention to costs as well as benefits and have great value for the evaluation field.

KEY CONCEPTS FOR CHAPTER 12

Primary dissemination	Dissemination of the detailed findings of an evaluation to sponsors and technical audiences.
Secondary dissemination	Dissemination of summarized, often simplified findings to audiences composed of stakeholders.
Policy significance	The significance of an evaluation's findings for policy and program development (as opposed to their statistical significance).
Policy space	The set of policy alternatives that are within the bounds of acceptability to policymakers at a given point in time.
Direct utilization	Explicit utilization of specific ideas and findings of an evaluation by decisionmakers and other stakeholders.
Conceptual utilization	Long-term, indirect utilization of the ideas and findings of an evaluation.

CHAPTER 12

THE SOCIAL CONTEXT OF EVALUATION

In the preceding chapters, we have been concerned mainly with the technical aspects of conducting systematic evaluations. From the outset, however, we have asserted our view that evaluations involve more than simply using appropriate research procedures. Evaluation research is a purposeful activity, undertaken to affect policy development, to shape the design and implementation of social interventions, and to improve the management of social programs. In the broadest sense of politics, evaluation is a political activity.

There are, of course, intrinsic rewards for evaluators, who may derive great pleasure from satisfying themselves that they have done as good a technical job as possible—like artists whose paintings hang in their attics and never see the light of day, and poets whose penciled foolscap is hidden from sight in their desk drawers. But that is not really what it is all about. Evaluations are a real-world activity. In the end, what counts is the critical acclaim with which an evaluation is judged by peers in the field and the extent to which it leads to modified policies, programs, and practices—ones that, in the short or long term, improve the conditions of human life.

In this last chapter, we examine the current status of the field of evaluation research, with emphasis on the social context of evaluations. Certainly, compared with the late 1970s, when the first edition of *Evaluation* was published, there is considerably greater sophistication today among evaluators, not only on technical matters but also on the place of evaluation research in the policy and social program arena. (For an overview of the growth and change in the field, see Chelimsky and Shadish, 1997; Haveman, 1987; Shadish, Cook, and Leviton, 1991. For a different view of change in evaluation, see Guba and Lincoln, 1989.)

At the same time, strains and tensions persist about methodological matters, the education of evaluators, and organizational arrangements for the conduct of evaluations. Moreover, there are political and ideological issues concerning the social responsibility of evaluators that continue to confront the field, disagreement on the most effective ways to disseminate findings, and differences of opinion about the best strategies for maximizing the utility of evaluations.

We acknowledge, furthermore, that each evaluation has its unique features, requiring specially tailored solutions to the problems encountered. The individuality of each evaluation makes it difficult to offer many "principles" about the conduct of evaluations. Nevertheless, the field is now mature enough that it is possible to offer reasonably sound observations about the state of the evaluation art, as well as general guidelines and advice on the conduct of the work. This chapter is based on an admixture of our own experiences and the writings of colleagues who have addressed the various interpersonal, political, and structural issues that surround doing evaluations.

With the experience of the past several decades, evaluators have become more humble about the potency of their efforts and have come to realize that social policy cannot be based on evaluation alone. Even the strongest proponents of the evaluation enterprise realistically acknowledge that its potential contributions to social policy are constrained by the range of competencies and self-interests of both the persons who undertake evaluations and the consumers of them, by diversity in styles of work and organizational arrangements, and by the political considerations and economic constraints that accompany all efforts at planned social change. Most important of all, in a democratic society, social change cannot be determined by the rule of experts but, rather, should be the outcome of processes that take into account the views of the various interests concerned.

In addition, evaluators, most of whom are convinced that social programs might improve the human condition, have been disappointed by finding out that many do not produce marked improvements and some are not effective. We have learned that designing effective programs and properly implementing them is very difficult. To many, it has not been an uplifting experience to have been the bearer of bad news.

Accordingly, evaluators have experienced the frustrations, feelings of inadequacy, and lack of self-esteem of all groups whose efforts often fall short of their hopes and aspirations. And their response has been the same as well: a great amount of introspection, a concerted effort to shift the blame to others, and an outpouring of verbal and written commentaries about the dismal state of social and human affairs, in particular the futility of developing and implementing effective and efficient interventions. Some social commentators have even blamed the reported failures of evaluation on the inability of current evaluation practices to recognize successful programs as such (Schorr, 1997).

It is evident that simply undertaking well-designed and carefully conducted evaluations of social programs by itself will not eradicate our human and social problems. But the contributions of the evaluation enterprise in moving us in the desired direction should be recognized. There is considerable evidence that the findings of evaluations do often influence policies, program planning and implementation, and the ways social programs are administered, sometimes in the short term and other times in the long term.

THE PURPOSEFULNESS OF EVALUATION ACTIVITIES

As we will discuss in a later section, evaluation practitioners are diverse in their disciplinary outlooks, their ideological and political orientations, and their economic and career aspirations. Despite this diversity, however, nearly all evaluators share a common perspective about the purposefulness of their work. The major rationale for doing applied work is to have an impact on the actions and thinking of the broad classes of persons who affect social change, and who in their policy and action roles use the findings and conclusions provided by evaluators.

Evaluation activities logically fall under the general rubric of "applied" social research. Although the boundaries separating "basic" or "academic" research from applied research are not always perfectly clear, there are qualitative differences between them (Freeman and Rossi, 1984). Some of these we have discussed or alluded to earlier, as when we noted that evaluations need to be conducted so that they are "good enough" to answer the questions under study. This pragmatic standard, of course, contrasts with that used by basic researchers, who typically strive for the "best" methodology that can be used in carrying out their research. Of course, basic research is also constrained by resources so that compromises are often necessary.

Three additional distinctions between applied and basic research are important to understand. First, basic research typically is initiated to satisfy the intellectual curiosity of the investigator and to contribute to the knowledge base of a substantive area of interest to the researcher and his or her peers. Basic research is often directed to topics that are of central concern to the discipline in question. In contrast, applied work is undertaken because it might contribute to solving a practical problem. In the evaluation field, most often the impetus for undertaking work comes not from the evaluators themselves but from persons and groups who are concerned with a particular social problem. Thus, it is imperative that the evaluator understands the *social ecology* of the evaluation field. This is the first major topic that we take up in this chapter.

Second, basic researchers generally are trained in a single disciplinary orientation to which they remain committed throughout their careers. They typically draw on a narrow band of methodological procedures, and from one study to the next address a limited substantive domain. For example, an economist may make the costs of health care her area of expertise and consistently apply econometric modeling procedures to her chosen area of study. Similarly, a sociologist might primarily use participant observation as her method of choice and devote most of her career to the study of the educational professions.

In contrast, evaluators sometimes move from one program area to another, confronting diverse questions that typically require familiarity with a range of research methods and of a variety of substantive areas. For example, one of the authors has conducted evaluations of programs concerned with nutrition, crime prevention, effects of natural disasters, child abuse and neglect, normative consensus, and various levels of education, using methods that range from randomized experiments to large-scale cross-sectional studies and the statistical analysis of archived administrative records. Some evaluators specialize in one or a few program areas, combining in a very productive way their detailed substantive knowledge with their evaluation expertise. The fact that evaluators can often be confronted with widely different subject areas raises a number of issues about the training, outlook, and theoretical perspectives of evaluators in contrast to basic researchers and, more generally, about the profession of evaluation (Shadish and Reichardt, 1987). The evaluation profession is the second major topic in this chapter.

Third, although ethical concerns are important in both basic and applied research, they loom larger and are of greater societal importance in applied work. If a basic researcher violates professional standards, his discipline may suffer, but if an applied researcher crosses the line the effects might be felt by programs, the target populations involved, and the society as a whole. Accordingly, the third major topic of this chapter will be concerned with important ethical issues encountered in applied research.

Fourth, there is a major difference in the audiences for basic and applied work, and in the criteria for assessing its utilization. Basic researchers are most concerned with their peers' responses to their studies; utilization is judged by the acceptance of their papers in prestigious journals and the extent to which the research stimulates work by others. Applied researchers judge themselves, and are judged by the sponsors of their studies, on how much of a contribution they make to the development and implementation of policies and programs and, ultimately, to the resolution of social problems. Utilization of evaluation results, and ways to maximize it, constitute our final topic.

THE SOCIAL ECOLOGY OF EVALUATIONS

The likelihood of evaluations being used depends on evaluators' recognition that the key determinants of their utilization are the social and political contexts in which the evaluations are undertaken. Consequently, to conduct successful evaluations, evaluators need to continually assess the social ecology of the arena in which they work.

Sometimes the impetus and support for an evaluation come from the highest decision-making levels: Congress or a federal agency may mandate evaluations of innovative pro-

grams, as the Department of Health and Human Services did in the case of waivers given to states for innovative reforms in income maintenance programs (Gueron and Pauly, 1991), or the president of a large foundation may insist that the foundation's major social action programs be evaluated, as in the case of the supported housing programs of the Robert Wood Johnson Foundation (Rog et al., 1995). At other times, evaluation activities are initiated in response to requests from managers and supervisors of various operating agencies and focus on administrative matters specific to those agencies and stakeholders (Oman and Chitwood, 1984). At still other times, evaluations are undertaken in response to the concerns of individuals and groups in the community who have a stake in a particular social problem and the planned or current efforts to deal with it.

Whatever the impetus may be, evaluators' work is conducted in a real-world setting of multiple and often conflicting interests. In this connection, two essential features of the context of evaluation must be recognized: the existence of multiple stakeholders and the related fact that evaluation is usually part of a political process.

The Range of Stakeholders

In undertaking their studies, evaluators usually find a diversity of individuals and groups with interest in their work and its outcomes. These stakeholders may hold competing and sometimes combative views on the appropriateness of the evaluation work and whose interest will be affected by the outcome. To conduct their work effectively and contribute to the resolution of the issues at hand, evaluators must understand their relationships with the stakeholders involved as well as the relationships between stakeholders.

The starting point for achieving this understanding is to recognize the range of stakeholders who directly or indirectly can affect the usefulness of evaluation efforts, both as evaluators go about doing their work and afterward in their responses to the product. This faces the lone evaluator situated in a single school, hospital, or social agency as well as those associated with evaluation groups in large organized research centers, federal and state agencies, or elite and community foundations.

In an abstract sense, every citizen who should be concerned with the efficacy and efficiency of efforts to improve social conditions has a stake in the outcome of an evaluation. In practice, of course, the stakeholder groups concerned with any given evaluation effort are more narrowly based, consisting of those who perceive direct and visible interests in the program. Within stakeholder groups, various stakeholders typically have different perspectives on the meaning and importance of an evaluation's findings. These disparate viewpoints are a source of potential conflict not only between stakeholders themselves but also between these persons and the evaluator. No matter how an evaluation comes out, there are some to whom the findings are good news and some to whom they are bad news.

To evaluate is to make judgments; to conduct an evaluation is to provide empirical evidence that can be used to substantiate judgments. The distinction between making judgments and providing information on which judgments can be based is useful and clear in the abstract, but often difficult to delineate in practice. No matter how well an evaluator's conclusions about the effectiveness of a program are grounded in rigorous research design and sensitively analyzed data, some stakeholders are likely to perceive the results of an evaluation to be arbitrary or capricious judgments and to react accordingly.

Very little is known about how evaluation audiences are formed and activated. Nor is it completely clear how the interests of stakeholder groups are engaged and acted on by a given evaluation outcome. Perhaps the only reliable prediction is that the parties most likely to be attentive to an evaluation both during its conduct and after a report has been issued are the evaluation sponsors and program managers and staff. Of course, these are the groups who usually have the most at stake in the continuation of the program and whose activities are most clearly judged by the evaluation report.

The reactions of beneficiaries or targets of a program are especially problematic. In many cases, beneficiaries may have the strongest stake in an evaluation's outcome, yet they are often the least prepared to make their voices heard. Target beneficiaries tend to be unorganized and scattered in space; often they are poorly educated and unskilled in political communication. Sometimes they are reluctant even to identify themselves. When target beneficiaries do make themselves heard in the course of an evaluation, it is often through organizations who aspire to be their representatives. For example, homeless persons rarely make themselves heard in the discussion of programs directed at relieving their distressing conditions. But the National Coalition for the Homeless, an organization mainly composed of persons who themselves are not homeless, will often act as the spokesperson in policy discussions dealing with homelessness.

Consequences of Multiple Stakeholders

There are two important consequences of the phenomenon of multiple stakeholders.

First, evaluators must accept that their efforts are but one input into the complex mosaic from which decisions and actions eventuate. Second, strains invariably result from the conflicts in the interests of these stakeholders. In part, these strains can be eliminated or minimized by anticipating and planning for them; in part, they come with the turf and must be dealt with on an ad hoc basis or simply accepted and lived with.

The multiplicity of stakeholders for evaluations generates strains for evaluators in three main ways. First, evaluators are often unsure whose perspective they should take in designing an evaluation. Is the proper perspective that of the society as a whole, the government agency involved, the program staff, the clients, or one or more of the other stakeholder groups? For some evaluators, especially those who aspire to provide help and advice on fine-tuning programs, the primary audience often appears to be the program staff. For those evaluators whose projects have been mandated by a legislative body, the primary audience may appear to be the community, the state, or the nation as a whole.

It is important that the issue of which perspective to take in an evaluation is not understood as an issue of whose bias to accept. Perspective issues are involved in defining the goals of a program and deciding which stakeholder's concerns should be attended to. In contrast, bias in an evaluation usually means distorting an evaluation's design to favor findings that are in accord with some stakeholder's desires. Every evaluation is undertaken from some set of perspectives, but an ethical evaluator tries to avoid biasing evaluation findings in the design or analysis.

Some schools of evaluation strongly emphasize that certain perspectives should dominate in the conduct of evaluations. The "utili-

zation-focused evaluation" approach (e.g., Patton, 1997) asserts that evaluations ought to be designed to reflect the interests of "primary users," specifying methods for determining in specific cases who they may be. The advocates of "empowerment evaluation" (e.g., Fetterman, Kaftarian, and Wandersman, 1996) claim that the aim of evaluations should be to empower marginalized groups, usually the poor and minorities, adopting their perspectives and calling for the participation of such groups in the design and analysis of evaluations. It must be emphasized that neither of these two approaches is biased, in the sense used above.

Our own views on the perspectives from which evaluations are to be conducted are more agnostic. In the Chapter 11 discussion of the different accounting perspectives for conducting efficiency analyses, we noted that there is no one proper perspective but, rather, that different perspectives may be equally legitimate. The clients' or targets' perspective cannot claim any more legitimacy than that of the program or the government agency that funds the program. The responsibility of the evaluator is not to take one of the many perspectives as *the* legitimate one, but rather to be clear from which perspectives a particular evaluation is being undertaken while explicitly giving recognition to the existence of other perspectives. In reporting the results of an evaluation, an evaluator should state, for example, that the evaluation was conducted from the viewpoint of the program administrators while acknowledging that there also exist the alternative perspectives of the society as a whole and of the client targets.

In some evaluations, it may be possible to provide several perspectives on a program. For example, from the viewpoint of a target client, an income maintenance program may be judged as falling short of providing enough dollars to satisfy basic needs, whereas from the perspective of a state legislature, the main purpose of the program is to facilitate the movement of clients off program rolls, a perspective that might view the low level of payment as a desirable incentive. From the viewpoint of income maintenance clients, a successful program may be one that provides payment levels sufficient to meet basic consumption needs of beneficiaries, whereas legislators may view a generous income maintenance program as fostering welfare dependency.

Second, the evaluator must realize that sponsors of evaluations may turn on evaluators when the results do not support the worth of the policies and programs they advocate. Although evaluators often anticipate negative reactions from other stakeholder groups, frequently they are unprepared for the responses of the sponsors of evaluations to findings that are contrary to what was expected or desired. Evaluators are in a very difficult position when this occurs. Losing the support of the evaluation sponsors, for example, may leave them open to attacks by other stakeholders, attacks they expected would be fended off by the sponsors. There are legitimate grounds for concern: Sponsors are a major source of referrals for additional work in the case of outside evaluators, and the providers of paychecks for inside ones. An illustration of the problem is provided in Exhibit 12-A, in which the findings of a study of the homeless of Chicago were severely challenged by advocacy stakeholders. (For a very different view of the same events, see Hoch, 1990.) The reactions of stakeholders in Chicago should not be taken as universal—there are many instances in which unwelcome findings are accepted and even acted on.

Third, misunderstandings may arise because of difficulties in communicating with different stakeholders. The vocabulary of the evaluation field is no more complicated and esoteric than the vocabularies of the social sciences from which it is derived. But this does not make the vocabulary of evaluation understandable and accessible to lay audiences. To take a concrete illustration, the concept of *random* plays an important role in impact assessment. Technically, the concept has a precise, nonpejorative meaning, as shown in Chapter 7. In lay language, however, random often has connotations of *haphazard, careless, aimless, casual,* and so on—all of which have pejorative connotations. To advocate the random allocation of targets to experimental and control groups means something quite precise and delimited to evaluation researchers but may connote something very different to lay audiences. Thus, evaluators use the term *random* at their peril if they do not at the same time carefully specify its meaning.

It may be too much to expect an evaluator to master the subtleties of communication relevant to all the widely diverse audiences for evaluations. Yet the problem of communication remains an important obstacle to the understanding of evaluation procedures and the utilization of evaluation results. Evaluators are therefore well advised to anticipate the communication barriers in relating to stakeholders, a topic we will discuss more fully later in this chapter.

Disseminating Evaluation Results

For evaluation results to be used, they must be disseminated to and understood by major stakeholders and the general public. For our purposes, *dissemination* refers to the set of activities through which knowledge about evaluation findings is made available to the range of relevant audiences.

✵ EXHIBIT 12-A   The Consequences of Contrary Results

In the middle 1980s, the Robert Wood Johnson Foundation and the Pew Memorial Trust provided a grant to the Social and Demographic Institute at the University of Massachusetts to develop practical methods of undertaking credible enumerations of the homeless. The two foundations had just launched a program funding medical clinics for homeless persons, and an accurate count of the homeless was needed to assess how well the clinics were covering their clients.

Our findings concerning how many homeless were in Chicago quickly became the center of a controversy. The interests of the Chicago homeless were defended and advanced by the Chicago Coalition for the Homeless and by the Mayor's Committee on the Homeless, both composed of persons professionally and ideologically devoted to these ends. These two groups were consistently called on by the media and by public officials to make assessments of the status of the Chicago homeless. Their views about homelessness in essence defined the conventional wisdom and knowledge on this topic. In particular, a widely quoted estimate that between 20,000 and 25,000 persons were homeless in Chicago came from statements made by the Coalition and the Mayor's Committee.

At the outset, the Chicago Coalition for the Homeless maintained a neutral position toward our study. The study, its purposes, and its funding sources were explained to the coalition, and we asked for their cooperation, especially in connection with obtaining consent from shelter operators to interview their clients. The coalition neither endorsed our study nor condemned it, expressing some skepticism concerning our approach and especially about the operational definition of homelessness, arguing for a broader definition of homelessness that would en-compass persons in precarious housing situations, persons living double-upped with families, single-room-occupancy renters, and so on.

When the data from Phase I were processed, we were shocked by the findings. The estimate of the size of the homeless population was many magnitudes smaller than the numbers used by the coalition: 2,344, compared to 20,000- 25,000. Because we had anticipated a much larger homeless population, our sample of streets was too small to achieve much precision for such small numbers. We began to question whether we had made some egregious error in sample design or execution. Adding to our sense of self-doubt, the two foundations that had supported most of the project also began to have doubts, their queries fueled in part by direct complaints from the advocates for the homeless. To add to our troubles, the Phase I survey had consumed all the funds that our sponsors had provided, which were originally intended to support three surveys spread over a year. After checking over our Phase I findings, we were convinced that they were derived correctly but that they would be more convincing to outsiders if the study were replicated. We managed to convince our funding sponsors to provide more funds for a second survey that was designed with a larger sample of Chicago blocks than Phase I. The street sample was also supplemented by special purposive samples in places known to contain large numbers of homeless persons (bus, elevated, and subway stations; hospital waiting rooms; etc.) to test whether our dead-of-the-night survey time missed significant numbers of homeless persons who were on the streets during the early evening hours but had found sleeping accommodations by the time our interviewing teams searched sample blocks.

When the data were in from Phase II, our calculated estimates of the average size of the nightly homeless in Chicago was 2,020 with a standard error of 275. Phase II certainly had increased the precision of our estimates but had not resulted in substantially different ones. Using data from our interviews, we also attempted to estimate the numbers of homeless persons we may have missed because they were temporarily housed, in jail, in a hospital, or in prison. In addition, we estimated the number of homeless children accompanying parents (we found no homeless children in our street searches). Adding these additional numbers of homeless persons to the average number who were nightly homeless as estimated from our Phase I and Phase II surveys, we arrived at a total of 2,722. This last estimate was still very far from the 20,000- to 25,000-person estimates of the Chicago Coalition.

Although the final report was distributed to the Chicago newspapers, television stations, and interested parties on the same date, somehow copies of the report had managed to get into the hands of the Coalition. Both major Chicago newspapers ran stories on the report, followed the next day by denunciatory comments from members of the Coalition. Despite our efforts to direct attention to the findings on the composition of the homeless, the newspapers headlined our numerical estimates. The comments from the coalition were harshly critical, claiming that our study was a serious disservice to the cause of the homeless and an attempt to lull public consciousness by severely (and deliberately) underestimating the number of homeless. Coalition comments included suggestions that the content

of the report was dictated by the Illinois Department of Public Aid, that the study was technically defective, and that our definition of the homeless omitted the thousands of persons forced to live with friends and relatives or in substandard housing conditions, or who negotiated sleeping arrangements every night.

Invited to give a presentation to the Mayor's Committee on the Homeless, I found my talk greeted by a torrent of criticism, ranging from the purely technical to the accusation of having sold out to the conservative forces of the Reagan administration and the Thompson Republican Illinois regime. But the major theme was that our report had seriously damaged the cause of homeless people in Chicago by providing state and local officials with an excuse to dismiss the problem as trivial. (In point of fact, the Illinois Department of Public Aid pledged to multiply its efforts to enroll homeless persons in the income maintenance programs the department administered.) Those two hours were the longest stretch of personal abuse I have suffered since basic training in the Army during World War II. It was particularly galling to have to defend our carefully and responsibly derived estimates against a set of estimates whose empirical footings were located in a filmy cloud of sheer speculation.

Almost overnight, I had become persona non grata in circles of homeless advocates. When I was invited by the Johnson Foundation to give a talk at a Los Angeles meeting of staff members from the medical clinics the foundation financed, no one present would talk to me except for a few outsiders. I became a nonperson wandering through the conference, literally shunned by all.

SOURCE: Adapted from Peter H. Rossi, "No Good Applied Research Goes Unpunished!" *Social Science and Modern Society,* 1987, 25(1):74-79.

Dissemination is a definite responsibility of evaluation researchers. An evaluation that is not made accessible to its audiences is clearly destined to be ignored. Accordingly, evaluators must take care in writing their reports and make provision for assuring that findings are delivered to major stakeholders.

Obviously, results must be communicated in ways that make them intelligible to the various stakeholder groups. External evaluation groups, in particular, generally provide sponsors with technical reports that include detailed and complete (not to mention honest) descriptions of the evaluation's design, data collection methods, analysis procedures, results, suggestions for further research, and recommendations regarding the program (in the case of monitoring or impact evaluations), as well as a discussion of the limitations of the data and analysis. Technical reports usually are read only by peers, rarely by the stakeholders who count. Many of these stakeholders simply are not accustomed to reading voluminous documents, do not have the time to do so, and might not be able to understand them.

For this reason, every evaluator must learn to be a "secondary disseminator." *Secondary dissemination* refers to the communication of research results and recommendations that emerge from evaluations in ways that meet the needs of stakeholders (as opposed to *primary dissemination*, which in most cases is the technical report). Secondary dissemination may take many different forms, including abbreviated versions of technical reports (often called executive summaries), special reports in more elaborate format that are issued regularly by either evaluation groups or the evaluation sponsors, memos, oral reports complete with slides, and sometimes even movies and videotapes.

The objective of secondary dissemination is simple: to provide results in ways that can be comprehended by the legendary "intelligent layperson," admittedly a figure sometimes as elusive as Bigfoot. Proper preparation of secondary dissemination documents is an art form unknown to most in the field, because few opportunities for learning are available during one's academic training. The important tactic in secondary communication is to find the appropriate style for presenting research findings, using language and form understandable to audiences who are intelligent but unschooled in the vocabulary and conventions of the field. *Language* implies a reasonable vocabulary level that is as free as possible from esoteric jargon; *form* means that secondary dissemination documents should be succinct and short enough not to be formidable. Useful advice for this process can be found in Torres, Preskill, and Piontek (1996). If the evaluator does not have the talents to disseminate his or her findings in ways that maximize utilization—and few of us do—an investment in expert help is justified. After all, as we have stressed, evaluations are undertaken as purposeful activities; they are useless unless used.

Evaluation as a Political Process

Throughout this book, we have stressed that evaluation results can be useful in the decision-making process at every point during a program's evolution and operations. In the earliest phases of program design, evaluations can provide basic data about social problems so that sensitive and appropriate services can be designed. While prototype programs are being tested, prospective evaluations may provide estimates of net effects to be expected when the program is fully implemented. After programs have been in operation, evaluations can provide considerable knowledge about accountability issues. But this is not to say that what is useful in principle will automatically be understood, accepted, and used. At every stage, evaluation is only one ingredient in an inherently political process. And this is as it should be: Decisions with important social consequences should be determined in a democratic society by political processes.

In some cases, project sponsors may contract for an evaluation with the strong anticipation that it will critically influence the decision to continue, modify, or terminate a project. In those cases, the evaluator may be under pressure to produce information quickly, so that decisions can be made expeditiously. In short, evaluators may have a receptive audience. In other situations, evaluators may complete their assessments of an intervention only to discover that decisionmakers react slowly to their findings. Even more disconcerting are the occasions when a program is continued, modified, or terminated without regard to an evaluation's valuable and often expensively obtained information.

Although in such circumstances evaluators may feel that their labors have been in vain, they should remember that the decision-making process is indeed complex and that the results of an evaluation are only one of the elements in decision making. This point was clearly illustrated as long ago as 1915 in the controversy over the evaluation of the Gary plan in New York City, described in Exhibit 12-B.

The many parties involved in a human service program, including program sponsors, managers and operators, and sometimes the participants, often have very high stakes in the program's continuation, and their frequently unsupportable but enthusiastic claims may count more heavily than the coolly objective results of an evaluation. Moreover, whereas the outcome of an evaluation is simply a single argument on one side or another, the outcome of typical American political processes may be viewed as a balancing of a variety of interests.

In any political system that is sensitive to weighing, assessing, and balancing the conflicting claims and interests of a number of constituencies, the evaluator's role is that of an expert witness, testifying to the degree of a program's effectiveness and bolstering that testimony with empirically based information. A jury of decisionmakers and other stakeholders may give such testimony more weight than uninformed opinion or shrewd guessing, but they, not the witness, are the ones who must reach a verdict. There are other considerations to be taken into account.

To imagine otherwise would be to see evaluators as having the power of veto in the political decision-making process, a power that would strip decisionmakers of their prerogatives. Under such circumstances, evaluators would become philosopher-kings whose pronouncements on particular programs would override those of all the other parties involved.

In short, the proper role of evaluation is to contribute the best possible knowledge on evaluation issues to the political process and not to attempt to supplant that process. Exhibit 12-C contains an excerpt from an article by one of the founders of modern evaluation theory, Donald T. Campbell, expounding a view of evaluators as servants of "the Experimenting Society."

Political Time and Evaluation Time

There are two additional strains involved in doing evaluations, compared with academic

✎ EXHIBIT 12-B Politics and Evaluation

This exhibit concerns the introduction of a new plan of school organization into the New York City schools in the period around World War I. The so-called Gary plan modeled schools after the new mass production factories, with children being placed on shifts and moved in platoons from subject matter to subject matter. The following account is a description of how evaluation results entered into the political struggle between the new school board and the existing school system administration.

The Gary plan was introduced into the schools by a new school board appointed by a reform mayor, initially on a pilot basis. School Superintendent Maxwell, resentful of interference in his professional domain and suspicious of the intent of the mayor's administration, had already expressed his feelings about the Gary plan as it was operating in one of the pilot schools: "Well, I visited that school the other day, and the only thing I saw was a lot of children digging in a lot." Despite the superintendent's views, the Gary system had been extended to 12 schools in the Bronx, and there were plans to extend it further. The cry for more research before extending the plan was raised by a school board member.

In the summer of 1915, Superintendent Maxwell ordered an evaluative study of the Gary plan as it had been implemented in the New York schools. The job was given to B. R. Buckingham, an educational psychologist in the research department of the New York City schools and a pioneer in the development of academic achievement tests. Buckingham used his newly developed academic achievement tests to compare two Gary-organized schools, six schools organized on a competing plan, and eight traditionally organized schools. The traditionally organized schools came out best on average, while the two Gary-organized schools averaged poorest.

Buckingham's report was highly critical of the eager proponents of the Gary system for making premature statements concerning its superiority. No sooner had the Buckingham report appeared than a veritable storm of rebuttal followed, both in the press and in professional journals. Howard W. Nudd, executive director of the Public Education Association, wrote a detailed critique of the Buckingham report, which was published in the *New York Globe,* the *New York Times, School and Society,* and the *Journal of Education.* Nudd argued that at the time Buckingham

social research, that are consequences of the fact that the evaluator is engaged in a political process involving multiple stakeholders: One is the need for evaluations to be relevant and significant in a policy sense, a topic we will take up momentarily; the other is the difference between political time and evaluation time.

Evaluations take time, especially those directed at assessing program impact. Usually, the tighter and more elegant the study design, the longer the time period required to perform

the evaluation. Large-scale social experiments that gauge the effects of major innovative programs may require anywhere from four to eight years to complete and document. The political and program worlds often move at a much faster pace. Policymakers and project sponsors usually are impatient to know whether or not a program is achieving its goals, and often their time frame is a matter of months, not years.

For this reason, evaluators frequently encounter pressure to complete their assessments

⚮ EXHIBIT 12-B Continued

conducted his tests, the Gary plan had been in operation in one school for only four months and in the other for less than three weeks. He asserted that much of the requested equipment had not been provided and that the work of the Gary schools had been seriously disturbed by the constant stream of visitors who descended to examine the program. In a detailed, school-by-school comparison, Nudd showed that in one of the Gary-organized schools 90% of the pupils came from immigrant homes where Italian was their first tongue while some of the comparison schools were largely populated by middle-class, native-born children. Moreover, pupils in one of the Gary schools had excellent test scores that compared favorably with those from other schools. When scores were averaged with the second Gary school, however, the overall result put the Gary plan well behind.

Buckingham had no answer to the contention of inadequate controls, but he argued that he was dealing, not with two schools, six schools, or eight schools, but with measurements on more than 11,000 children and therefore his study represented a substantial test of the Gary scheme. He justified undertaking his study early on the grounds that the Gary plan, already in operation in 12 Bronx schools, was being pushed on the New York schools and superintendent precipitously. As noted above, there was pressure from the mayor's office to extend the plan throughout the New York City schools and to make any increase in the education budget contingent on wholesale adoption of the Gary system. The president of the Board of Education found it advantageous to cite Nudd's interpretation of the Buckingham report in debate at the Board of Education meeting. Superintendent Maxwell continued to cite the Buckingham study as evidence against the effectiveness of the Gary plan, even a year and a half later.

SOURCE: Adapted from A. Levine and M. Levine, "The Social Context of Evaluation Research: A Case Study," *Evaluation Quarterly*, 1977, 1(4):515-542.

more quickly than the best methods permit, as well as to release preliminary results. At times, evaluators are asked for their "impressions" of effectiveness, even when they have stressed that such impressions are liable to be useless in the absence of firm results. For example, evaluators are now being asked by the mass media and legislators how effective the welfare reforms initiated by the Personal Responsibility and Work Opportunity Act of 1996 are, although for almost all states, the reforms have yet to be worked out in detail, much less been put in place. At the time of this writing (1998), no evidence exists on this topic. So great is the desire for evaluative evidence that the mass media relies on anecdotes, dramatic specific examples, and even wild guesses.

In addition, the planning and procedures related to initiating evaluations within organizations that sponsor such work often make it difficult to undertake timely studies. In most cases, procedures must be approved at several

---

✎ EXHIBIT 12-C   Social Scientists as Servants of the Experimenting Society

Societies will continue to use preponderantly unscientific political processes to decide upon ameliorative program innovations. Whether it would be good to increase the role of social science in deciding on the content of the programs tried out is not at issue here. The emphasis is rather more on the passive role for the social scientist as an aid in helping society decide whether or not its innovations have achieved desired goals without damaging side effects. The job of the methodologist for the experimenting society is not to say *what is to be done,* but rather to say *what has been done.* The aspect of social science that is being applied is primarily its research methodology rather than its descriptive theory, with the goal of learning more than we do now from the innovations decided upon by the political process. . . . This emphasis seems to be quite different from the present role as government advisors of most economists, international relations professors, foreign area experts, political scientists, sociologists of poverty and race relations, psychologists of child development and learning, etc. Government asks what to do, and scholars answer with an assurance quite out of keeping with the scientific status of their fields. In the process, the scholar-advisors too fall into the overadvocacy trap and fail to be interested in finding out what happens when their advice is followed. Certainty that one already knows precludes finding out how valid one's theories are. We social scientists could afford more of the modesty of the physical sciences, [and] should more often say that we can't know until we've tried. . . . Perhaps all I am advocating . . . is that social scientists avoid cloaking their recommendations in a specious pseudo-scientific certainty, and instead acknowledge their advice as consisting of but wise conjectures that need to be tested in implementation.

SOURCE: Quoted, with permission, from Donald T. Campbell, "Methods for the Experimenting Society," *Evaluation Practice,* 1991, 12(3):228-229.

---

levels and by a number of key stakeholders. As a result, it can take considerable time to commission and launch an evaluation, not counting the time it takes to implement and complete it. Although both governmental and private sector sponsors have tried to develop mechanisms to speed up the planning and procurement processes, these efforts are hindered by the workings of their bureaucracies, legal requirements related to contracting, and the need to establish agreement on the evaluation questions and design.

It is not clear what can be done to reduce the pressure resulting from the different time schedules of evaluators and decisionmakers. Obviously, a long-term study should not be undertaken if the information is needed before the evaluation can be completed. It may be better in such circumstances to rely on expert opinion or another of the more judgmental evaluation methods discussed in Chapter 10. At times, it is a judgment call whether it is better to have some information or no information at all. At the very least, it is important that evaluators anticipate the time demands of stakeholders, particularly the sponsors of evaluations, and avoid making unrealistic time commitments.

A strategic approach is to confine technically complex evaluations to pilot or prototype projects for interventions that are unlikely to be implemented on a large scale in the immediate future. Thus, randomized controlled experiments may be most appropriate to evaluate the worth of new programs (initially implemented on a relatively small scale) before such programs appear on the agendas of decision-making bodies.

Another strategy for evaluators is to anticipate the direction of programs and policy activities, rather than be forced to undertake work that cannot be accomplished in the time allocated. One proposal that has attracted some attention is to establish independent evaluation institutes dedicated to examining, on a pilot or prototype basis, interventions that might one day be in demand. Evaluation centers could be established that continually assess the worth of alternative social programs for dealing with social problems that are of perpetual concern or that have a high probability of emerging in the years ahead. Although this proposal has some attractive features, especially to professional evaluators, it is not at all clear that it is possible to forecast accurately what, say, the next decade's social issues will be.

Perhaps the most successful approximation of efforts to maximize the contributions of evaluation activities prior to the implementation of new initiatives is the prospective evaluation synthesis of the Program Evaluation and Methodology Division of the General Accounting Office (GAO). As Chelimsky (1987) describes in Exhibit 12-D, her division's *ex ante* activities can make important contributions to shaping social legislation. (See also Chelimsky, 1991, for a general view of how applied social research intersects with policy making.)

As things stand now, however, we believe that the tension caused by the disparities between political and research time will continue to be a problem in the employment of evaluation as a useful tool for policymakers and project managers.

Issues of Policy Significance

Evaluations, we have stressed, are done with a purpose that is practical and political in nature. In addition to the issues we have already reviewed, the fact that evaluations are ultimately conducted to affect the *policymaking* process introduces several considerations that further distinguish an evaluator's work from that of a basic researcher.

Policy Relevance and Policy Space

Policy space is that set of alternative policies that can garner political support at any given point in time. The alternatives considered in designing, implementing, and assessing a social program are ordinarily those that are within current policy space. Policy space keeps changing in response to the efforts of influential figures to gain support from other influentials and from ordinary community members. This decade's policy space with respect to crime control is dominated by programs of long and sometimes mandatory sentences for selected types of criminals. In contrast, during the 1970s it was centered on the development of community-based treatment centers as an alternative to imprisonment, on the grounds that prisons were breeding places for crime and that criminals would be best helped by being kept in close contact with the normal, civilian world.

The volatility of policy space is illustrated by the Transitional Aid to Released Prisoners

---

░░ EXHIBIT 12-D Using Evaluative Activities in the Analysis of Proposed New Programs

Many of us spend much of our time doing retrospective studies; these are and will continue to be the meat and potatoes of evaluation research. Congress asks us for them and asks the executive branch to do them, and they are needed, but these studies are not the easiest ones to insert into the political process, and they may well be the least propitious from the viewpoint of use. . . . By contrast, before a program has started, evaluators can have an enormous effect in improving the reasoning behind program purposes or goals, in identifying the problems to be addressed, and in selecting the best point of intervention and the type of intervention most likely to succeed. The tempo at which new programs are sometimes introduced presents some difficulty. . . . The pace often becomes so frantic that the lead time necessary to gear up for evaluative work is simply impossible to obtain if results are to be ready soon enough to be useful.

At the GAO we are developing a method I call the Evaluation Planning Review which is specifically intended to be useful in the formulation of new programs. We have just given it a first try by looking at a proposed program focusing on teenage pregnancy. Essentially, the method seeks to gather information on what is known about past, similar programs and apply the experience to the architecture of the new one. Senator Chaffee asked us to look at the bill he was introducing; we managed to secure four good months to do the work, and it has been a major success from both the legislative point of view and our own. From a more general, political perspective, providing understanding ahead of time of how a program might work can render a valuable public service—either by helping to shore up a poorly thought-out program or by validating the basic soundness of what is to be undertaken. True, there are questions that decisionmakers do not pose to evaluators that could usefully be posed, which seems a priori to be a problem for the framework; however, even when evaluators have been free to choose the questions, this particular type of question has not often been asked. Also, evaluators can always influence the next round of policy questions through their products.

SOURCE: Eleanor Chelimsky, "The Politics of Program Evaluation," *Society,* 1987, 25(1):26-27. Reprinted by permission of Transaction Publishers. Copyright 1987 by Transaction Publishers; all rights reserved.

(TARP) experiments, discussed in earlier chapters, which were conducted in the late 1970s to evaluate the effectiveness in reducing recidivism of providing short-term financial support to recently released felons. Whatever the merits of the Georgia and Texas TARP experiments, by the time the evaluation findings were available, federal policy space had changed so drastically that the policies emerging from those experiments had no chance of being consid-

ered. Thus, evaluators need to be sensitive not only to the policy space that exists when a research program is initiated but also to ongoing changes in the social and political context that alter the policy space as the evaluation proceeds.

Too often a prospective program may be tested without sufficient understanding of how the policy issues are seen by those decisionmakers who will have to approve the enactment of the program. Hence, even though the evaluation of the program in question may be flawless, its findings may prove irrelevant. In the New Jersey-Pennsylvania income maintenance experiment, the experiment's designers posed as their central issue the following question: How large is the work disincentive effect of an income maintenance plan? By the time the experiment was completed and congressional committees were considering various income maintenance plans, however, the key issue was not the work disincentive effect—the policy space had changed. Rather, members of Congress were more concerned with how many different forms of welfare could be consolidated into one comprehensive package, without ignoring important needs of the poor and without creating many inequities (Rossi and Lyall, 1976).

Because a major purpose of impact assessments, as with evaluative activities generally, is to help decisionmakers form and adopt social policies, the research must be sensitive to the various policy issues involved and the limits of policy space. The goals of a project must resemble those articulated by policymakers in deliberations on the issues of concern. A carefully designed randomized experiment showing that a reduction in certain regressive taxes would lead to an improvement in worker productivity may be irrelevant if decisionmakers are more concerned with motivating entrepreneurs and attracting potential investments.

For these reasons, responsible impact assessment design must necessarily involve, if at all possible, some contact with relevant decisionmakers to ascertain their interests in the project being tested. A sensitive evaluator needs to know what current and future policy space will allow consideration. For an innovative project that is not currently being discussed by decisionmakers but is being tested because

it may become the subject of future discussion, the evaluators and sponsors of the test of impact effectiveness must rely on their informed guesses about what policy issues might arise, that is, what are likely prospective changes in policy space. For other projects, the processes of obtaining decisionmakers' opinions are quite straightforward. Evaluators can consult the proceedings of deliberative bodies (e.g., government committee hearings or legislative debates), interview decisionmakers' staffs, or consult decisionmakers directly.

Interpreting evaluation results involves considerations that go beyond methodology. The fact that evaluations are conducted according to the canons of social research may make them superior to other modes of judging social programs. But evaluations provide only superfluous information unless they address the value issues of persons engaged in policy making, program planning, and management.

The weaknesses of evaluations, in this regard, tend to center on how research questions are stated and how findings are interpreted (Datta, 1980). To maximize the utility of evaluation findings, evaluators must be sensitive to two levels of policy considerations.

First, programs that address problems perceived as critical require better (i.e., more rigorous) assessments than interventions related to relatively trivial concerns. Technical decisions, such as setting levels of statistical significance and magnitude, should be informed by the nature of policy and program considerations. These are always matters of judgment and sensitivity. Even when formal efficiency analyses (Chapter 11) are undertaken, the issue remains. For example, the decision to use an individual, program, or community accounting perspective is determined by policy and sponsorship considerations. Second, evaluation findings have to be assessed according to how far they are generalizable, whether the findings are significant to the policy and to the program, and whether the program clearly fits the need (as expressed by the many factors that are involved in the policy-making process).

Policy Significance Versus Statistical Significance

An evaluation may produce results that all would agree are statistically significant and generalizable and yet be too small to be relevant to policy, planning, and managerial action (Lipsey, 1990; Sechrest and Yeaton, 1982). What the magnitude of a difference must be to have policy significance varies from field to field and from instance to instance. One formal way of providing data for such judgments is to conduct cost-benefit and cost-effectiveness analyses, as discussed in the previous chapter. Doing so allows judgments to be made on the basis of whether resources are effectively expended as compared to the costs and benefits of alternative projects, criteria that might not be appropriate for some programs. Other supplements to statistical inference tests have been proposed that involve taking into account the preponderance of evidence and replications (Browner and Newman, 1989; Goodman and Royall, 1988).

Another, more diffuse, criterion is to make judgments of the social worth of the change in outcome. Small magnitudes of change can have policy significance when the social worth of the change is high; correspondingly, large changes can have significance even when social worth is low. Thus, a program of nutritional education that reduces severe cases of malnutrition in children by only 2% undoubtedly would be regarded as policy-significant because malnutrition is regarded as a dangerous threat to children; a consumer education project that reduces the purchase of unnecessary small

household appliances by the same percentage probably would not be so regarded because consumer profligacy is not regarded as very serious. However, if the consumer education program reduced such purchases by 20%, it probably would be seen as policy-significant.

The availability of alternative interventions also needs to be taken into account. For example, in a country highly saturated with television sets and with a formal educational system that can be modified only over a long time period and through the expenditure of extensive resources, small gains from educational television may be significant for policy. The same magnitude of change would not be viewed positively if rapid changes at low cost were possible in the formal educational system.

Basic Science Models Versus Policy-Oriented Models

Social scientists often do not grasp the difference in emphasis required in formulating a model purposefully to *alter* a phenomenon as opposed to developing a causal model to *explain* the phenomenon. For example, much of the criminal behavior of young men can be explained by the extent of such behavior among males in their social network—fathers, brothers, other male relatives, friends, neighbors, schoolmates, and so on. This is a fascinating finding that affords many insights into the geographic and ethnic distributions of crime rates. However, it is not a useful finding in terms of altering the crime rate because it is difficult to envisage an acceptable public policy that would alter the social networks of young men. Short of yanking young males out of their settings and putting them into other environments, it is not at all clear that anything can be done to affect their social networks. Policy space will likely, and, it is hoped, never include population redistribution for these purposes.

In contrast, although a weaker determinant of crime, it is easier to envisage a public policy that would attempt to alter the perceived costs of engaging in criminal activities. For example, altering potential lawbreakers' subjective probabilities of being caught for committing a crime, being convicted if caught, and going to prison if convicted can be a practical basis for a program of crime control. The willingness to engage in crime is sluggishly and weakly related to these subjective probabilities: The more that individuals believe they likely will be caught if they commit a crime, convicted if caught, and imprisoned if convicted, the lower the probability of criminal behavior. Thus, to some extent the incidence of criminal acts will be reduced if the police are effective in arresting criminals, if the prosecution is diligent in obtaining convictions, and if the courts have a harsh sentencing policy. None of these relationships is especially strong, yet these findings are much more appropriate to public policy that attempts to control crime than the social network explanation discussed earlier. Mayors and police chiefs can implement programs that increase the proportion of criminals apprehended, prosecutors can work harder at obtaining convictions, and judges can refuse to plea-bargain. Moreover, dissemination of these policy changes in ways that reach the potential offenders would, in itself, have some modest impact on the crime rate. The general point should be clear: Basic social science models often ignore policy-relevance.

The Missing Engineering Tradition

Our discussion of policy-relevant and policy-significant research points to a more general lesson: In the long term, evaluators—indeed, all applied researchers—and their stakeholders must develop an "engineering tradition," something that currently is missing in most of the social sciences. Engineers are distinguished from their "pure science" counterparts by their concern with working out the details of how scientific knowledge can be used to grapple with real-life problems. It is one thing to know that gases expand when heated and that each gas has its own expansion coefficient; it is quite another to be able to use that principle to mass-produce economical, high-quality gas turbine engines.

Similar engineering problems exist with respect to social science findings. It is well known in social science theories in economics and in psychological learning theory that changing incentives can often alter behavior. In the 1980s, there developed a fair amount of consensus that the incentives involved in welfare payments under Aid to Families With Dependent Children (AFDC) fostered dependency and hindered the movement of AFDC clients off the rolls into employment. Accordingly, the Department of Health and Human Services encouraged states to modify AFDC rules to provide incentives for clients to seek and obtain employment. Several versions of incentive packages were tested in randomized experiments. The experiments tested programs in which adults on welfare were prepared through training for employment, allowed to retain some proportion of their earnings without reduction in welfare payments, and aided to find employment. The findings of the experiments were that aiding in the employment search was more effective than training and that the combination of the two strategies was the most effective (Gueron and Pauly, 1991).

We are not certain how such social science engineers should be trained, and we suspect that training models will have to await the appearance of a sufficient number of exemplars to learn from. Our hope is that the foregoing observations about the dynamics of conducting evaluations in the context of the real world of program and social policy sensitize the evaluator to the importance of "scouting" the terrain when embarking on an evaluation and of remaining alert to ecological changes that occur during the evaluation process. Such efforts may be at least as important to the successful conduct of evaluation activities as the appropriateness of the technical procedures employed.

Evaluating Evaluations

As evaluations have become more sophisticated, judging whether some particular evaluation was performed skillfully and findings interpreted properly becomes more and more difficult. Especially for laypersons and public officials, assessing the credibility of evaluations may be beyond their reach. In addition, there may often be contradictory research findings arising from several evaluations of the same program: How to reconcile conflicting evaluation claims can present problems even to evaluation experts. To meet the need for validating evaluations and for adequate communication of their findings, several approaches have been tried, as discussed below.

Quite frequently, the contracts or grants funding large-scale evaluations call for the formation of advisory committees composed of evaluation experts and policy analysts to oversee the conduct of the evaluation and provide expert advice to the evaluators and the funders. The advisory committee approach can be viewed as a way to raise the quality of evaluations and at the same time to provide greater legitimacy to their findings.

There also have been intensive reviews of evaluations, including reanalyses of evaluation datasets. For example, the National Academy of Sciences from time to time forms committees to review evaluations and synthesize their findings on topics of policy interest or significant controversy. For example, Coyle, Boruch, and Turner (1991) reviewed AIDS education evaluations with regard to their findings and also recommended improvements in the quality of such work.

Reviews such as those mentioned above typically take several years to complete and hence do not meet the needs of policymakers who require more timely information. More timely commentary on evaluations requires more rapid review and assessment. A promising attempt to be timely was funded in 1997 through a grant from the Smith-Richardson Foundation. The University of Maryland's School of Public Affairs was commissioned to convene a "blue ribbon" commission of prominent evaluators and policy analysts to review and comment on the expected considerable flow of evaluations of the reforms in public welfare undertaken under the Personal Responsibility and Work Opportunity Reconciliation Act of 1996. The Committee to Review Welfare Reform Research will issue periodic reports addressed to policymakers assessing the adequacy of the evaluations and drawing out their implications for policy. It is planned for the evaluation reviews to appear within a few months after the release of evaluation reports (Besharov, Germanis, and Rossi, 1998).

Despite these examples, we believe that the typical program evaluation is not ordinarily subject to the judgment of peers in the evaluation community. Some policymakers may have the competence to judge their adequacy, but most may have to rely on the persuasive qualities of evaluation reports. For this reason, as discussed in a later section, evaluation standards are of recurring importance in the professional associations of evaluators.

THE PROFESSION OF EVALUATION

There is no single roster of all persons who identify themselves as evaluators and no way of fully describing their backgrounds or the range of activities in which they are engaged. At a minimum, some 50,000 persons are engaged, full- or part-time, in evaluation activities. We arrived at this estimate by adding together the numbers of federal, state, county, and city governmental organizations engaged in social program development and implementation, along with the numbers of school districts, hospitals, mental hospitals, and universities and colleges, all of which are usually obligated to undertake one or more types of evaluation activities. We do not know the actual number of persons engaged in evaluation work in these groups, and we have no way of estimating the numbers of university professors and persons affiliated with nonprofit and for-profit applied research firms who do evaluations. Indeed, the actual number of full- and part-time evaluators may be double or triple our minimum estimate. It is clear that evaluators work in widely disparate social program areas and devote varying amounts of their working time to evaluation activities. At best, the role definition of the evaluator is blurred and fuzzy.

At the one extreme, persons may perform evaluations as an adjunct activity. Sometimes they undertake their evaluation activities simply to conform to legislative or regulatory requirements, as apparently is the case in many local school systems. To comply with state or federal funding requirements, schools must have someone designated as an "evaluator," and so name someone on their teaching or management staffs to serve in that capacity. Often the person appointed has no particular qualifications for the assignment either by training or by experience. Indeed, sometimes the appointee is someone who is not highly regarded as either a teacher or an administrator and is given evaluation duties as a harmless assignment.

At the other extreme, within university evaluation institutes and social science departments, and within applied social research firms in the private and nonprofit sectors, there are full-time evaluation specialists, highly trained and with years of experience, who are working at the frontiers of the evaluation field.

Indeed, the common labeling of persons as evaluators or evaluation researchers conceals the heterogeneity, diversity, and amorphousness of the field. Evaluators are not licensed or certified, so the identification of a person as an evaluator provides no assurance that he or she shares any core knowledge with another person so identified. The proportion of evaluators who interact and communicate with each other, particularly across social program areas, likely is very small. The American Evaluation Association, the major "general" organization in the field, has only a few thousand members, and the cross-disciplinary journal with the most subscribers, *Evaluation Review*, is read by only a few thousand. Within program areas, there likewise are only weak social networks of evaluators, most of whom are unaffiliated with national and local professional organizations that have organized evaluation "sections."

In brief, evaluation is not a "profession," at least in terms of the formal criteria that sociologists generally use to characterize such groups. Rather, it can best be described as a "near-group," a large aggregate of persons who are not formally organized; whose membership changes rapidly; and who have little in common with one another in terms of the range of tasks they undertake or their competencies, work sites, and outlooks. This feature of the evaluation field underlies much of the discussion that follows.

Intellectual Diversity and Its Consequences

All the social science disciplines—economics, psychology, sociology, political science, and anthropology—have contributed to the development of the field of evaluation. Persons trained in each of these disciplines have made contributions to the conceptual base of evaluation research and to its methodological repertoire. The human service professional fields have also made contributions: Persons trained in the various human service professions with close ties to the social sciences—medicine, public health, social welfare, urban planning, public administration, education, and so on— have· made important methodological contributions and have undertaken landmark evaluations. In addition, the applied mathematics fields of statistics, biometrics, econometrics, and psychometrics have contributed important ideas on measurement and analysis.

Cross-disciplinary borrowing has been extensive. Take the following examples: Although economics traditionally has not been an experimentally based social science, economists have designed and implemented a significant proportion of the large-scale, randomized field experiments of the past several decades, including the highly visible employment training, income maintenance, housing allowance, and national health insurance experiments. Sociologists and psychologists have borrowed heav-

ily from the econometricians, notably in their use of time-series analysis methods and simultaneous equation modeling. Sociologists have contributed many of the conceptual and data collection procedures used in monitoring organizational performance, and psychologists have contributed the idea of regression-discontinuity designs to time-series analyses. Psychometricians have provided some of the basic ideas underlying theories of measurement applicable to all fields, and anthropologists have provided some of the basic approaches used in qualitative fieldwork. Indeed, the vocabulary of evaluation is a mix from all of these disciplines. The list of references at the back of this book is testimony to the multidisciplinary character of the evaluation field.

In the abstract, the diverse roots of the field are one of its attractions. In practice, however, they confront evaluators with the need to be general social scientists and lifelong students if they are even to keep up, let alone broaden their knowledge base. Furthermore, the diversity in the field accounts to a considerable extent for the "improper" selection of research approaches for which evaluators are sometimes criticized. Clearly, it is impossible for every evaluator to be a scholar in all of the social sciences and to be an expert in every methodological procedure.

There is no ready solution to the need to have the broad knowledge base and range of competencies ideally required by the "universal" evaluator. This situation means that evaluators must at times forsake opportunities to undertake work because their knowledge bases may be too narrow, that they may have to use an "almost good enough" method rather than the appropriate one they are unfamiliar with, and that sponsors of evaluations and managers of evaluation staffs must be highly selective in deciding on contractors and in making work assignments. It also means that at times evaluators will need to make heavy use of consultants and solicit advice from peers.

In a profession, a range of opportunities is provided for keeping up with the state of the art and expanding one's repertoire of competencies—for example, the peer learning that occurs at regional and national meetings and the didactic courses provided by these professional associations. At present, only a fraction of the many thousands of evaluation practitioners participate in professional evaluation organizations and can take advantage of the opportunities they provide.

There also are liabilities to becoming a profession. Established professions can suffer from over-professionalization, as we know from the state of many of the practicing professions. But the near-group character of the field and its diverse roots have their consequences as well, consequences that are exacerbated by the different ways in which evaluators are educated.

The Education of Evaluators

Few people in evaluation have achieved responsible posts and rewards by working their way up from lowly jobs within evaluation units. Most evaluators have some sort of formal graduate training either in social science departments or in professional schools. One of the important consequences of the multidisciplinary character of evaluation is that appropriate training for full participation in it cannot be adequately undertaken within any single discipline. In a few universities, interdisciplinary programs have been set up that include graduate instruction in a number of departments. In these programs, a graduate student might be directed to take courses in test construction and measurement in a department of psychol-

ogy, econometrics in a department of economics, survey design and analysis in a department of sociology, policy analysis in a political science department, and so on.

Interdisciplinary training programs, however, are neither common nor very stable. In the typical graduate-training and research-oriented university, the powerful units are the traditional departments. The interdepartmental coalitions of faculty that form interdisciplinary programs tend to have short half-lives, because departments typically do not reward participation in such ventures very highly and faculty drift back into their departments as a consequence. The result is that too often graduate training of evaluators primarily is unidisciplinary despite the clear need for it to be multidisciplinary.

Moreover, even within academic departments, applied work is often regarded less highly than "pure" or "basic" research. As a consequence, training in evaluation-related competencies is often limited. Psychology departments may provide fine courses on experimental design but fail to consider very much the special problems of implementing field experiments in comparison with laboratory studies; sociology departments may teach survey research courses but not deal at all with the special data collection problems involved in interviewing the unique populations that are typically the targets of social programs. Then, too, the low status accorded applied work in graduate departments often is a barrier to undertaking evaluations as dissertations and theses. If there is any advice to be given, it is that individual students who are interested in an evaluation career must be assertive. Often the student must take the lead in hand-tailoring an individual study program that includes course offerings in a range of departments, be insistent about undertaking an applied dissertation or thesis, and seize on any opportunities within university research institutes and in the community to supplement formal instruction with relevant apprenticeship learning.

The other training route is the professional school. Schools of education train evaluators for positions in that field, programs in schools of public health and medical care produce persons who engage in health service evaluations, and so on. In fact, over time these professional schools, as well as MBA programs, have become the training sites for many evaluators.

These programs have their limitations as well. One criticism raised about them is that they are too "trade school" oriented in outlook. Consequently, some of them fail to provide the conceptual breadth and depth that allows graduates to move back and forth across social program areas, and to grasp technical innovations when they occur. Moreover, particularly at a master's level, many professional schools are required to have a number of mandatory courses, because their standing and sometimes their funding depend on accreditation by professional bodies who see the need for common training if graduates are going to leave as MSWs, MPHs, MBAs, and the like. Because many programs therefore leave little time for electives, the amount of technical training that can be taken in courses is limited. Increasingly, the training of evaluators in professional schools therefore has moved from the master's to the doctoral level.

Also, in many universities both faculty and students in professional schools are viewed as second-class citizens by those located in social science departments. This elitism often isolates students so that they cannot take advantage of course offerings in several social science departments or apprenticeship training in their affiliated social science research institutes. Students trained in professional schools, particu-

larly at the master's level, often trade off opportunities for intensive technical training for substantive knowledge in a particular program area and the benefits of professional certification. The obvious remedy is either undertaking further graduate work or seizing opportunities for additional learning of technical skills while pursuing an evaluation career.

We hold no brief for one route over the other; each has its advantages and liabilities. Increasingly, it appears that professional schools are becoming the major suppliers of evaluators, in part at least because of the reluctance of graduate social science departments to develop appropriate applied research programs. But these professional schools are far from homogeneous in what they teach, particularly in the methods of evaluation they emphasize, thus, the continued diversity of the field.

Consequences of Diversity in Origins

The existence of many educational pathways to becoming an evaluator contributes to the lack of coherence in the field. It accounts, at least in part, for the differences in the very definition of evaluation, and the different outlooks regarding the appropriate way to evaluate a particular social program. Of course, other factors contribute to this diversity, including social and political ideologies of evaluators.

Some of the differences are related to whether the evaluator is educated in a professional school or a social science department. For example, evaluators who come out of professional schools such as social work or education are much more likely than those trained in, say, sociology to see themselves as part of the program staff and to give priority to tasks that help program managers. Thus, they are likely to stress *formative* evaluations that are designed to improve the day-to-day operations of programs.

The diversity is also related to differences among social science departments and among professional schools. Evaluators trained as political scientists frequently are oriented to *policy analysis,* an activity designed to aid legislators and high-level executives, particularly government administrators. Anthropologists, as one might expect, are predisposed to qualitative approaches and are unusually attentive to target populations' interests in evaluation outcomes. Consonant with their discipline's emphasis on small-scale experiments, psychologists often are concerned more with the validity of the causal inference in their evaluations than the generalizability to program practice. In contrast, sociologists are often more concerned with the potential for generalization and are more willing to forsake some degree of rigor in the causal conclusions to achieve it. Economists are likely to work in still different ways, depending on the body of microeconomic theory to guide their evaluation designs.

Similar diversity can be found among those educated in different professional schools. Evaluators trained in schools of education may focus on educational competency tests in measuring the outcome of early-childhood education programs, whereas social work graduates focus on caseworker ratings of children's emotional status and parental reports of their behavior. Persons coming from schools of public health may be most interested in preventive practices, those from medical care administration programs in frequency of physician encounters and duration of hospitalization, and so on.

It is easy to exaggerate the distinctive outlook that each discipline and profession manifests in approaching the design and conduct of evaluations and there are many exceptions to the preference tendencies just described. Indeed, a favorite game among evaluation buffs is to guess an author's disciplinary background from the content of an article he or she has written. Nevertheless, disciplinary and professional diversity has produced a fair degree of conflict within the field of evaluation. Evaluators hold divided views on topics ranging from epistemology to the choice of methods and the major goals of evaluation. Some of the major divisions are described briefly below.

Orientations Toward Primary Stakeholders

As mentioned earlier in this chapter, some evaluators believe that evaluations should be mainly directed toward helping program managers to improve their programs. This view of evaluation sees its purpose primarily as consultation to program management to the point that the difference between technical assistance and evaluation becomes blurred. According to this view, an evaluation succeeds to the extent that programs are improved. These evaluation orientations tend also to avoid making judgments about the worth of programs on the grounds that most programs can be made to work with the help of evaluators. (See Patton, 1997, for a prominent advocate of utilization-focused evaluation.)

Others hold that the purpose of evaluations should be to help program beneficiaries (targets) to become empowered. This view of evaluation believes that engaging targets in a collaborative effort to define programs and their evaluation leads targets to become more "in charge" of their lives and leads to an increase in the sense of personal efficacy. (Fetterman, Kaftarian, and Wandersman, 1996, contains examples of this approach.)

At the other extreme of this division are the evaluators who believe that evaluators should mainly serve those stakeholders who fund the evaluation. Such evaluations take on the perspective of the funders, adopting their definitions of program goals and program outcomes.

Our own view has been stated earlier in this chapter. We believe that evaluations ought to be sensitive to the perspectives of major stakeholders. Ordinarily, the contractual requirements ruling evaluations require that primary attention be given to the evaluation sponsor's definitions of program goals and outcomes. However, such requirements do not exclude other perspectives. We believe that it is the obligation of evaluators to state clearly the perspective from which the evaluation is undertaken and to point out what other major perspectives are involved. When an evaluation has the resources to accommodate several perspectives, multiple perspectives should be used.

Epistemological Differences

The "cultural wars" that have been waged in the humanities and some of the social sciences have also touched evaluation as well. Postmodern theories of knowledge claim that positivistic epistemology has been superseded by a more relativistic view of knowledge and are reflected in evaluation with claims that social problems are social constructions and that knowledge is not absolute but that there are different "truths," each valid for the perspectives from which it derives. Postmodernists tend to favor qualitative research methods that produce rich "naturalistic" data and evaluation perspectives favoring those of the program personnel and target populations. (See Guba and Lincoln, 1989, for a foremost exponent of postmodern evaluation.)

The epistemological contrast to the postmodern position is not homogeneous in its beliefs on the nature of knowledge. Nevertheless, there is some strong consensus that truth is not entirely relativistic. For example, most believe that the definition of poverty is a social construction, but at the same time, there is the conviction that the distribution of annual incomes can be described through research operations on which most social scientists can agree. That is, whether a given income level is regarded as poverty is a matter of social judgment but the number of households at that income level can be estimated with a known sampling error. This position implies that disagreements among researchers on empirical findings are mainly matters of method or measurement error rather than matters involving different truths.

Our own position, as exemplified throughout this book, is clearly not postmodern. We believe that there are close matches between methods and evaluation problems. For given research questions, there are better methods and poorer methods. Indeed, the major message in this book is how to choose the best method for a given research question that is likely to produce the most credible findings.

The Qualitative-
Quantitative Division

Coinciding with some of the divisions within the evaluation community is the division between those who advocate qualitative methods and those who argue for quantitative ones. A sometimes pointless literature has developed around this. On one side, the advocates of qualitative approaches stress the need for intimate knowledge and acquaintance with a program's concrete manifestations in attaining valid knowledge about the program's effects.

Qualitative evaluators tend to be oriented toward formative evaluation, that is, making a program work better by feeding information on the program to its managers. In contrast, quantitatively oriented evaluators often view the field as one primarily concerned with summative evaluation and focus on developing measures of program characteristics, processes, and impact that allow program effectiveness to be assessed with relatively high credibility.

Often the polemics obscure the critical point—namely, that each approach has utility, and the choice of approaches depends on the evaluation question at hand. We have tried in this volume to identify the appropriate applications of each viewpoint. As we have stressed, qualitative approaches can play critical roles in program design and are important means of monitoring programs. In contrast, quantitative approaches are much more appropriate in estimates of net impact as well as in assessments of the efficiency of social program efforts. (For a balanced discussion of the qualitative-quantitative discussion, see Reichardt and Rallis, 1994.)

Thus, it is fruitless to raise the issue of which is the better approach without specifying the evaluation questions to be studied. Fitting the approach to the research purposes is the critical issue: To pit one approach against the other in the abstract results in a pointless dichotomization of the field. Even the most avid proponents of one approach or the other recognize the contribution each makes to social program evaluations (Cronbach, 1982; Patton, 1997). Indeed, the use of multiple methods, often referred to as *triangulation*, can strengthen the validity of findings if results produced by different methods are congruent. Using multiple methods is a means of offsetting different kinds of bias and measurement error (for an extended discussion of this point, see Greene and Caracelli, 1997).

The problem, as we see it, is both philosophical and strategic. Evaluations are undertaken primarily as contributions to policy and program formulation and modification—activities, as we have stressed, that have a strong political dimension. As Chelimsky (1987) has observed, "It is rarely prudent to enter a burning political debate armed only with a case study" (p. 27).

Diversity in Working Arrangements

The diversity of the evaluation field is also manifest in the variety of settings and bureaucratic structures in which evaluators work. First, there are two contradictory theses about working arrangements, or what might be called the insider-outsider debate. One position is that evaluators are best off when their positions are as secure and independent as possible from the influence of project management and staff. The other is that sustained contact with the policy and program staff enhances evaluators' work by providing a better understanding of the organization's objectives and activities while inspiring trust and thus increasing the evaluator's influence.

Second, there are ambiguities surrounding the role of the evaluator vis-à-vis program staff and groups of stakeholders regardless of whether the evaluator is an insider or outsider. The extent to which relations between staff members should resemble other structures in corporations or the collegial model that supposedly characterizes academia is an issue. But it is only one dimension to the challenge of structuring appropriate working relationships that confronts the evaluator.

Third, there is the concern on the part of evaluators with the "standing" of the organizations with which they are affiliated. Like universities, the settings in which evaluators work can be ranked and rated along a number of dimensions and a relatively few large evaluation organizations constitute a recognized elite subset of work places. Whether it is better to be a small fish in a big pond or vice versa is an issue in the evaluation field.

The discussion that follows, it bears emphasis, is based more on impressions of the authors of this text than on empirical research findings. Our impressions may be faulty, but it is a fact that debates surrounding these issues are commonplace whenever and wherever a critical mass of evaluators is found.

Inside Versus Outside Evaluations

In the past, some experienced evaluators went so far as to state categorically that evaluations should never be undertaken within the organization responsible for the administration of a project, but should always be conducted by an outside group. One reason "outsider" evaluations may have seemed the desired option is that there were differences in the levels of training and presumed competence of insider and outsider evaluation staffs. These differences have narrowed. The career of an evaluation researcher has typically taken one of three forms. Until the 1960s, a large proportion of evaluation research was done by either university-affiliated researchers or research firms. Since the late 1960s, public service agencies in various program areas have been hiring researchers for staff positions to conduct more in-house evaluations. Also, the proportion of evaluations done by private, for-profit research groups has increased markedly. As research

positions in both types of organizations have increased and the academic job market has declined, more persons who are well trained in the social and behavioral sciences have gravitated toward research jobs in public agencies and for-profit firms.

The current evidence is far from clear regarding whether inside or outside evaluations are more likely to be of higher technical quality. But technical quality is not the only criterion—utility may be just as important. A study in the Netherlands of external and internal evaluations suggests that internal evaluations may have a higher rate of impact on organizational decisions. According to van de Vall and Bolas (1981), of more importance than which category of researchers excels at social policy formation are those variables responsible for the higher rate of utilization of internal researchers' findings. The answer, they suggest, lies partly in a higher rate of communication between inside researchers and policymakers, accompanied by greater consensus, and partly in a balance between standards of epistemological and implemental validity: "In operational terms, this means that social policy researchers should seek equilibrium between time devoted to methodological perfection and translating results into policy measures" (p. 479). Their data suggest that currently in-house social researchers are in a more favorable position than external researchers for achieving these instrumental goals.

Given the increased competence of staff and the visibility and scrutiny of the evaluation enterprise, there is no reason now to favor one organizational arrangement over another. Nevertheless, there remain many critical points during an evaluation when there are opportunities for work to be misdirected and consequently misused irrespective of the locus of the evaluators. The important issue, therefore, is that any evaluation strikes an appropriate balance between technical quality and utility for its purposes, recognizing that those purposes may often be different for internal evaluations than for external ones.

Organizational Roles

Whether evaluators are insiders or outsiders, they need to cultivate clear understandings of their roles with sponsors and program staff. Evaluators' full comprehension of their roles and responsibilities is one major element in the successful conduct of an evaluation effort.

Again, the heterogeneity of the field makes it difficult to generalize on the best ways to develop and maintain the appropriate working relations.

One common mechanism is to have in place advisory groups or one or more consultants to oversee evaluations and provide some aura of authenticity to the findings. The ways such advisory groups or consultants work depend on whether an inside or an outside evaluation is involved and on the sophistication of both the evaluator and the program staff. For example, large-scale evaluations undertaken by federal agencies and major foundations often have advisory groups that meet regularly and assess the quality, quantity, and direction of the work. Some public and private health and welfare organizations with small evaluation units have consultants who provide technical advice to the evaluators or advise agency directors on the appropriateness of the evaluation units' activities, or both. Sometimes advisory groups and consultants are mere window dressing; we do not recommend their use if that is their only function. When members are actively engaged, however, advisory groups can be particularly useful in fostering interdisciplinary evaluation approaches, in adjudicating disputes between program and evaluation staffs, and in defending evaluation findings in the face of concerted attacks by those whose interests are threatened.

EVALUATION STANDARDS, GUIDELINES, AND ETHICS

As the field of evaluation became increasingly professionalized, many evaluators began to pressure their professional associations to formulate and publish standards that could guide them in their evaluation work and in negotiations with evaluation funders and other major stakeholders. For example, it would be useful to evaluators to be able to bolster an argument for the right to freely publish evaluation findings if they could cite a published set of practice standards that included publication rights as standard evaluation practice. In addition, almost every practicing evaluator encounters situations requiring ethical judgments. For example, does an evaluator studying a child abuse prevention program have an obligation to report his observation of child abuse in a family revealed in the course of an interview on parenting practices? Published standards or practice guidelines also provide legitimacy to those who advertise their services as practices in conformity with them.

Two major efforts have been made to provide guidance to evaluators. Under the aegis of the American National Standards Institute (ANSI), the Joint Committee on Standards for Educational Evaluation (1994) has published *The Program Evaluation Standards*, now in its second edition. The Joint Committee is made up of representatives from several professional associations, including, among others, the American Evaluation Association, the American Psychological Association, and the American Educational Research Association. Originally set up to deal primarily with educational programs, the Joint Committee expanded its coverage to include all kinds of program evaluation. The *Standards* cover a wide variety of topics ranging from what provisions should appear in evaluation contracts through issues in dealing with human subjects to the standards for the analysis of quantitative and qualitative data. Each of the several score standards is illustrated with cases illustrating how the standards can be applied in specific instances.

The second major effort, *Guiding Principles for Evaluators* (Shadish, Newman, et al., 1995), has been adopted by the American Evaluation Association. Rather than proclaim standard practices, the *Guiding Principles* sets out five principles, quite general in character, for the guidance of evaluators. The principles follow, and the full statements are presented in Exhibit 12-E.

A. *Systematic inquiry:* Evaluators conduct systematic, data-based inquiries about whatever is being evaluated.

B. *Competence:* Evaluators provide competent performance to stakeholders.

C. *Integrity/honesty:* Evaluators ensure the honesty and integrity of the entire evaluation process.

D. *Respect for people:* Evaluators respect the security, dignity, and self-worth of the respondents, program participants, clients, and other stakeholders with whom they interact.

E. *Responsibilities for general and public welfare:* Evaluators articulate and take into account the diversity of interests and values that may be related to the general and public welfare.

These five principles are elaborated and discussed in the *Guiding Principles*, although not to the detailed extent to that found in the Joint Committee's work. Just how useful such general principles may be is problematic. An evaluator who has a specific ethical problem will likely find very little guidance in any one of the general principles. (See Shadish, Newman, et al., 1995, for critical appraisals of the *Guiding Principles.*)

We expect that developing a set of practice standards and ethical principles that can provide pointed advice to evaluators will take some time. The diversity of evaluation styles will make it difficult to adopt standards because any practice so designated may contradict what some group may consider good practice. The development of standards would be considerably advanced by the existence of "case law," the accumulation of adjudicated specific instances in which the principles have been applied. However, neither the Joint Committee's *Standards* nor the American Evaluation Association's *Guiding Principles* have any mode of enforcement, the usual institutional mechanism for the development of case law.

Until such evaluation standards and ethical rules are established, evaluators will have to rely on such general principles as the profession appears to be currently willing to endorse. A useful discussion of the many issues of applied ethics for program evaluation can be found in Newman and Brown (1996).

The Leadership Role of Evaluation "Elite" Organizations

A small group of evaluators, numbering perhaps no more than 1,000, constitutes an "elite" in the field by virtue of the scale of the evaluations they conduct and the size of the organizations for which they work. They are

EXHIBIT 12-E   The American Evaluation Association's Guiding Principles for Evaluators

A. *Systematic inquiry: Evaluators conduct systematic, data-based inquiries about whatever is being evaluated.*

1. Evaluators should adhere to the highest appropriate technical standards in conducting their work, whether that work is quantitative or qualitative in nature, so as to increase the accuracy and credibility of the evaluative information they produce.

2. Evaluators should explore with the client the shortcomings and strengths both of the various evaluation questions it might be productive to ask and the various approaches that might be used for answering those questions.

3. When presenting their work, evaluators should communicate their methods and approaches accurately and in sufficient detail to allow others to understand, interpret, and critique their work. They should make clear the limitations of an evaluation and its results. Evaluators should discuss in a contextually appropriate way those values, assumptions, theories, methods, results, and analyses that *significantly* affect the interpretation of the evaluative findings. These statements apply to all aspects of the evaluation, from its initial conceptualization to the eventual use of findings.

B. *Competence: Evaluators provide competent performance to stakeholders.*

1. Evaluators should possess (or, here and elsewhere as appropriate, ensure that the evaluation team possesses) the education, abilities, skills, and experience appropriate to undertake the tasks proposed in the evaluation.

2. Evaluators should practice within the limits of their professional training and competence and should decline to conduct evaluations that fall substantially outside those limits. When declining the commission or request is not feasible or appropriate, evaluators should make clear any significant limitations on the evaluation that might result. Evaluators should make every effort to gain the competence directly or through the assistance of others who possess the required expertise.

3. Evaluators should continually seek to maintain and improve their competencies, in order to provide the highest level of performance in their evaluations. This continuing professional development might include formal coursework and workshops, self-study, evaluations of one's own practice, and working with other evaluators to learn from their skills and expertise.

(continued)

EXHIBIT 12-E Continued

C. *Integrity/honesty: Evaluators ensure the honesty and integrity of the entire evaluation process.*

1. Evaluators should negotiate honestly with clients and relevant stakeholders concerning the costs, tasks to be undertaken, limitations of methodology, scope of results likely to be obtained, and uses of data resulting from a specific evaluation. It is primarily the evaluator's responsibility to initiate discussion and clarification of these matters, not the client's.

2. Evaluators should record all changes made in the originally negotiated project plans, and the reasons why the changes were made. If those changes would significantly affect the scope and likely results of the evaluation, the evaluator should inform the client and other important stakeholders in a timely fashion (barring good reason to the contrary, before proceeding with further work) of the changes and their likely impact.

3. Evaluators should seek to determine, and where appropriate be explicit about, their own, their clients', and other stakeholders' interests concerning the conduct and outcomes of an evaluation (including financial, political, and career interests).

4. Evaluators should disclose any roles or relationships they have concerning whatever is being evaluated that might pose a significant conflict of interest with their role as an evaluator. Any such conflict should be mentioned in reports of the evaluation results.

5. Evaluators should not misrepresent their procedures, data, or findings. Within reasonable limits, they should attempt to prevent or correct any substantial misuses of their work by others.

6. If evaluators determine that certain procedures or activities seem likely to produce misleading evaluative information or conclusions, they have the responsibility to communicate their concerns, and the reasons for them, to the client (the one who funds or requests the evaluation). If discussions with the client do not resolve these concerns, so that a misleading evaluation is then implemented, the evaluator may legitimately decline to conduct the evaluation if that is feasible and appropriate. If not, the evaluator should consult colleagues or relevant stakeholders about other proper ways to proceed (options might include, but are not limited to, discussions at a higher level, a dissenting cover letter or appendix, or refusal to sign the final document).

7. Barring compelling reason to the contrary, evaluators should disclose all sources of financial support for an evaluation, and the source of the request for the evaluation.

D. *Respect for people: Evaluators respect the security, dignity, and self-worth of the respondents, program participants, clients, and other stakeholders with whom they interact.*

1. Where applicable, evaluators must abide by current professional ethics and standards regarding risks, harms, and burdens that might be engendered to those participating in the evaluation; regarding informed consent for participation in evaluation; and regarding informing participants about the scope and limits of confidentiality. Examples of such standards include federal regulations about protection of human subjects, or the ethical principles of such associations as the American Anthropological Association, the American Educational Research Association, or the American Psychological Association. Although this principle is not intended to extend the applicability of such ethics and standards beyond their current scope, evaluators should abide by them where it is feasible and desirable to do so.

2. Because justified negative or critical conclusions from an evaluation must be explicitly stated, evaluations sometimes produce results that harm client or stakeholder interests. Under this circumstance, evaluators should seek to maximize the benefits and reduce any unnecessary harms that might occur, provided this will not compromise the integrity of the evaluation findings. Evaluators should carefully judge when the benefits from doing the evaluation or in performing certain evaluation procedures should be forgone because of the risks or harms. Where possible, these issues should be anticipated during the negotiation of the evaluation.

3. Knowing that evaluations often will negatively affect the interests of some stakeholders, evaluators should conduct the evaluation and communicate its results in a way that clearly respects the stakeholders' dignity and self-worth.

4. Where feasible, evaluators should attempt to foster the social equity of the evaluation, so that those who give to the evaluation can receive some benefits in return. For example, evaluators should seek to ensure that those who bear the burdens of contributing data and incurring any risks are doing so willingly and that they have full knowledge of, and maximum feasible opportunity to obtain, any benefits that may be produced from the evaluation. When it would not endanger the integrity of the evaluation, respondents or program participants should be informed if and how they can receive services to which they are otherwise entitled without participating in the evaluation.

5. Evaluators have the responsibility to identify and respect differences among participants, such as differences in their culture, religion, gender, disability, age, sexual orientation, and ethnicity, and to be mindful of potential implications of these differences when planning, conducting, analyzing, and reporting their evaluations.

(continued)

E. *Responsibilities for general and public welfare: Evaluators articulate and take into account the diversity of interests and values that may be related to the general and public welfare.*

1. When planning and reporting evaluations, evaluators should consider including important perspectives and interests of the full range of stakeholders in the object being evaluated. Evaluators should carefully consider the justification when omitting important value perspectives or the views of important groups.

2. Evaluators should consider not only the immediate operations and outcomes of whatever is being evaluated but also the broad assumptions, implications, and potential side effects of it.

3. Freedom of information is essential in a democracy. Hence, barring compelling reason to the contrary, evaluators should allow all relevant stakeholders to have access to evaluative information and should actively disseminate that information to stakeholders if resources allow. If different evaluation results are communicated in forms that are tailored to the interests of different stakeholders, those communications should ensure that each stakeholder group is aware of the existence of the other communications. Communications that are tailored to a given stakeholder should always include all important results that may bear on interests of that stakeholder. In all cases, evaluators should strive to present results as clearly and simply as accuracy allows so that clients and other stakeholders can easily understand the evaluation process and results.

4. Evaluators should maintain a balance between client needs and other needs. Evaluators necessarily have a special relationship with the client who funds or requests the evaluation. By virtue of that relationship, evaluators must strive to meet legitimate client needs whenever it is feasible and appropriate to do so. However, that relationship can also place evaluators in difficult dilemmas when client interests conflict with other interests, or when client interests conflict with the obligation of evaluators for systematic inquiry, competence, integrity, and respect for people. In these cases, evaluators should explicitly identify and discuss the conflicts with the client and relevant stakeholders, resolve them when possible, determine whether continued work on the evaluation is advisable if the conflicts cannot be resolved, and make clear any significant limitations on the evaluation that might result if the conflict is not resolved.

5. Evaluators have obligations that encompass the public interest and good. These obligations are especially important when evaluators are supported by publicly generated funds, but clear threats to the public good should never be ignored in any evaluation. Because the public interest and good are rarely the same as the interests of any particular group (including those of the client or funding agency), evaluators will usually have to go beyond an analysis of particular stakeholder interests when considering the welfare of society as a whole.

SOURCE: American Evaluation Association, Task Force on Guiding Principles for Evaluators, *Guiding Principles for Evaluators*, New Directions for Evaluation, no. 66 (San Francisco: Jossey-Bass, 1995), pp. 19-26.

somewhat akin to those elite physicians who practice in the hospitals of important medical schools. They and their settings are few in number but powerful in establishing the norms for the field; the ways in which they work and the standards of performance in their organizations represent an important version of professionalism that persons in other settings may use as a role model.

The number of organizations that carry out national or otherwise large-scale evaluations with a high degree of technical competence is quite small. But in terms of both visibility and evaluation dollars expended, these organizations occupy a strategic position in the field. Most of the large federal evaluation contracts over the years have been awarded to a small group of profit-making research firms (such as Abt Associates, Mathematica Policy Research, and Westat, to name a few) and not-for-profit research organizations and universities (examples are Battelle Memorial Institute, the RAND Corporation, the Research Triangle Institute, the Urban Institute, and the Manpower Development Research Corporation). A handful of research-oriented universities with affiliated research institutes—the National Opinion Research Center (NORC) at the University of Chicago, the Institute for Research on Poverty at the University of Wisconsin (until recently), and the Institute for Social Research at the University of Michigan, for example—also receive grants and contracts for undertaking large-scale evaluations. In addition, the evaluation units of federal agencies that contract for and fund evaluation research, and a few of the large national foundations, include significant numbers of highly trained evaluators on their staffs. Within the federal government, perhaps the highest concentration of skilled evaluators was to be found until recently in the Program Evaluation and Methodology Division of the

GAO, where a large group of evaluation specialists has extended the activities of this key "watchdog" organization from auditing to assessing appropriate program implementation and estimating the impact of federal initiatives.

One of the features of these elite for-profit and nonprofit organizations that are the contractors for most large-scale evaluations is a continual concern with the quality of their work. In part, this has come about because of earlier critiques of their efforts, which formerly were not as well conducted technically as those done by persons in academic institutions (Bernstein and Freeman, 1975). But as they came to dominate the field, at least in terms of large-scale evaluations, and as they found sponsors of evaluations increasingly using criteria of technical competence in selecting contractors, their efforts improved markedly from a methodological standpoint. So, too, have the competencies of their staffs, and they now compete for the best-trained persons in applied work. Also, they have found it to be in their self-interest to encourage staff to publish in professional journals, participate actively in professional organizations, and engage in frontier efforts to improve the state of the art. To the extent that there is a general movement toward professionalism, these organizations are its leaders.

UTILIZATION OF EVALUATION RESULTS

In the end, the worth of evaluations must be judged by their utility. For this reason, considerable thought and research have been devoted to the use of evaluation results. As a starting point, the conventional three-way classification of the ways evaluations are used is helpful (Leviton and Hughes, 1981; Rich, 1977; Weiss, 1988).

First, evaluators prize the *direct* or *instrumental* use of their evaluations. By direct use is meant the documented and specific use of evaluation findings by decisionmakers and other stakeholders. For example, evaluators' data showing that patients of health maintenance organizations are hospitalized fewer days than patients who are treated in the ambulatory clinics of hospitals have been used by Congress and health policymakers in developing medical care programs for the poor (Freeman, Kiecolt, and Allen, 1982). More recently, the excellent field experiments conducted by the Manpower Development Research Corporation on workfare conducted under AFDC waivers (Gueron and Pauly, 1991) are influencing how the states are currently reforming welfare.

Second, utilization can be conceptual. As Rich (1977) defined it, *conceptual utilization* refers to the use of evaluations to influence thinking about issues in a general way. An example is the current effort to control the costs of delivering health and welfare services, stimulated at least in part by evaluations of the efficacy of these services and their costs-to-benefits ratios. These evaluations did not lead to the adoption of specific programs or policies but provided evidence that present ways of delivering health care were costly and inefficient.

Third, *persuasive utilization* refers to enlisting evaluation results in efforts either to support or to refute political positions—in other words, to defend or attack the status quo. For example, one of the frequent rationales used by the Reagan administration in defending the cutting of social programs was the lack of clear findings of positive impact in the evaluations of major programs. Persuasive use is

similar to speechwriters' inserting quotes into political speeches, whether they are applicable or not. For the most part, the persuasive use of evaluations is out of the hands of program evaluators and sponsors alike and will not concern us further.

Do Evaluations Have Direct Utility?

Disappointment about the extent of the utilization of evaluations apparently is due to their limited direct or instrumental use. It is clear that many evaluations initiated for their direct utility fell short of that mark. However, it is only in the past decade that the extent of direct use has been systematically studied. These recent efforts challenge the previously held belief that evaluations do not have direct utility.

One careful study (Leviton and Boruch, 1983), for example, examined the direct use of evaluations sponsored by the U.S. Department of Education. They found numerous instances in which the results of evaluations led to important program changes and even more incidents in which they were influential inputs, though not the sole inputs, in the decision-making process.

Chelimsky (1991) also cites several instances in which social science research provided critical knowledge for the development of public policy. Unfortunately, large-scale evaluations typically dominate the printed literature. The many small-scale evaluations, especially those that are diagnostic and formative, that have experienced direct use in improving programs do not ordinarily find their way into the printed literature.

Nevertheless, contrary to the views expressed in earlier editions of this book, there does seem to be a fair degree of instrumental utilization, although a pessimistic view on this point is still widely held among both evaluators and potential consumers of evaluations.

Subsequently, we will suggest means to increase the utilization of evaluations. Most of these suggestions are particularly relevant to increasing the direct use of studies. However, it is also important to appropriately value the conceptual use of evaluations.

Conceptual Use of Evaluations

No doubt every evaluator has had moments of glorious dreams in which a grateful world receives with adulation the findings of his or her evaluation and puts the results immediately and directly to use. Most of our dreams must remain dreams. We would argue, however, that the conceptual use of evaluations often provides important inputs into policy and program development and should not be compared with finishing the race in second place. Conceptual utilization may not be as visible to peers or sponsors, yet this use of evaluations deeply affects the community as a whole or critical segments of it.

By *conceptual use* we refer to the variety of ways in which evaluations indirectly have an impact on policies, programs, and procedures. This impact ranges from sensitizing persons and groups to current and emerging social problems to influencing future program and policy development by contributing to the cumulative results of a series of evaluations.

Evaluations perform a sensitizing role by documenting the incidence, prevalence, and distinguishing features of social problems. Diagnostic evaluation activities, described in Chapter 4, have provided clearer and more precise understanding of changes occurring in the family system, critical information on the

location and distribution of unemployed persons, and other meaningful descriptions of the social world.

Impact assessments, too, have conceptual utility. A specific example is the current concern with "notch" groups in the development of medical care policy. Evaluations of programs to provide medical care to the poor have found that the very poor, those who are eligible for public programs such as Medicaid, often are adequately provided with health services. Those just above them—the "notch" group—who are not eligible for public programs tend to fall in the cracks between public assistance and being able to provide for their own care. They have decidedly more difficulty receiving services, and, when seriously ill, represent a major burden on community hospitals, which cannot turn them away yet can receive reimbursement neither from the patients nor from the government. Concern with the near-poor, or notch group, is increasing because of their exclusion from a wide range of health, mental health, and social service programs.

An interesting example of a study that had considerable long-term impact is the now classic Coleman report on educational opportunity (Coleman et al., 1966). The initial impetus for this study was a 1964 congressional mandate to the (then) Office of Education to provide information on the quality of educational opportunities provided to minority students in the United States. Its actual effect was much more far-reaching: The report changed the conventional wisdom about the characteristics of good and bad educational settings, turning policy and program interest away from problems of fiscal support to ways of improving teaching methods (Moynihan, 1991).

The conceptual use of evaluation results creeps into the policy and program worlds by a variety of routes, usually circuitous, that are difficult to trace. For example, Coleman's report to the Office of Education did not become a Government Printing Office best-seller: It is unlikely that more than a few hundred people actually read it cover to cover. But journalists wrote about it, essayists summarized its arguments, and major editorial writers mentioned it. Through these communication brokers, the findings became known to policymakers in the education field and to politicians at all levels of government.

In 1967, a year after his report had been published by the Government Printing Office, Coleman was convinced that it had been buried in the National Archives and would never emerge again. Eventually, however, his findings in one form or another reached a wide and influential audience. Indeed, by the time Caplan and his associates (Caplan and Nelson, 1973) questioned influential political figures in Washington about which social scientists had influenced them, Coleman's name was among the most prominently and consistently mentioned.

Some of the conceptual utilizations of evaluations may be described simply as consciousness-raising. For example, the development of early-childhood education programs was stimulated by the evaluation findings resulting from an impact assessment of *Sesame Street*. The evaluation found that although the program did have an effect on young children's educational skills, the magnitude of the effect was not as large as the program staff and sponsors imagined it would be. Prior to the evaluation, some educators were convinced that the program represented the "ultimate" solution and that they could turn their attention to other educational problems. The evaluation findings led to the conviction that early-childhood education was in need of further research and development.

As in the case of direct utilization, evaluators have an obligation to do their work in ways that maximize conceptual utilization. In a sense, efforts at maximizing conceptual utilization are more difficult to devise than ones to optimize direct use. To the extent that evaluators are hired guns and turn to new ventures after completing an evaluation, they may not be around or have the resources to follow through on promoting conceptual utilization. Sponsors of evaluations and other stakeholders who more consistently maintain a commitment to particular social policy and social problem areas must assume at least some of the responsibility, if not the major portion, for maximizing the conceptual use of evaluations. Often these parties are in a position to perform the broker function alluded to earlier.

Variables Affecting Utilization

In studies of the use of social research in general, and evaluations in particular, five conditions appear to affect utilization consistently (Leviton and Hughes, 1981):

- Relevance
- Communication between researchers and users
- Information processing by users
- Plausibility of research results
- User involvement or advocacy

The importance of these conditions and their relative contributions to utilization have been carefully studied by Weiss and Bucuvalas (1980). They examined 155 decisionmakers in the mental health field and their reactions to

▧ EXHIBIT 12-F   Truth Tests and Utility Tests

In coping with incoming floods of information, decisionmakers invoke three basic frames of reference. One is the relevance of the content of the study to their sphere of responsibility, another is the trustworthiness of the study, and the third is the direction that it provides. The latter two frames, which we have called truth and utility tests, are each composed of two interdependent components:

Truth tests—Is the research trustworthy? Can I rely on it? Will it hold up under attack? The two specific components are

1. Research quality: Was the research conducted by proper scientific methods?
2. Conformity to user expectations: Are the results compatible with my experience, knowledge, and values?

Utility tests—Does the research provide direction? Does it yield guidance either for immediate action or for considering alternative approaches to problems? The two specific components are

1. Action orientation: Does the research show how to make feasible changes in things that can feasibly be changed?

2. Challenge to the status quo: Does the research challenge current philosophy, program, or practice? Does it offer new perspectives?

Together with relevance (i.e., the match between the topic of the research and the person's job responsibilities), the four components listed above constitute the frames of reference by which decisionmakers assess social science research. Research quality and conformity to user expectations form a single truth test in that their effects are contingent on each other: Research quality is less important for the usefulness of a study when results are congruent with officials' prior knowledge than when results are unexpected or counterintuitive. Action orientation and challenge to the status quo represent alternative functions that a study can serve. They constitute a utility test, since the kind of explicit and practical direction captured by the action orientation frame is more important for a study's usefulness when the study provides little criticism or reorientation (challenge to the status quo) than it is when challenge is high. Conversely, the criticisms of programs and the new perspectives embedded in challenge to the status quo add more to usefulness when a study lacks prescriptions for implementation.

SOURCE: Adapted, with permission, from C. H. Weiss and M. J. Bucuvalas, "Truth Tests and Utility Tests: Decision-Makers' Frames of Reference for Social Science Research," *American Sociological Review*, April 1980, 45:302-313.

50 actual research reports. Decisionmakers, they found, apply both a *truth test* and a *utility test* in screening social research reports. Truth is judged on two bases: research quality and conformity to prior knowledge and expecta-

tions. Utility refers to feasibility potential and the degree of challenge to current policy. The Weiss and Bucuvalas study provides convincing evidence of the complexity of the utilization process (see Exhibit 12-F).

Guidelines for Maximizing Utilization

Out of the research on utilization and the real-world experiences of evaluators, a number of guidelines for increasing utilization have emerged. These have been summarized by Solomon and Shortell (1981) and are briefly noted here for reference:

1. *Evaluators must understand the cognitive styles of decisionmakers.* For instance, there is no point in presenting a complex piece of analysis to a politician who cannot or will not consume such material. Thus, reports and oral presentations tailored to a predetermined audience may be more appropriate than, say, academic journal articles.

2. *Evaluation results must be timely and available when needed.* Evaluators must therefore balance thoroughness and completeness of analysis with timing and accessibility of findings. In doing so, they may have to risk criticism from some of their academic colleagues, whose concepts of scholarship cannot always be met because of the need for rapid results and crisp reporting.

3. *Evaluations must respect stakeholders' program commitments.* The usefulness of evaluations depends on wide participation in the evaluation design process to ensure sensitivity to various stakeholders' interests. Differences in values and outlooks between clients and evaluators should be explicated at the outset of a study and be a determinant of whether a specific evaluation is undertaken by a particular evaluation team.

4. *Utilization and dissemination plans should be part of the evaluation design.* Evaluation findings are most likely to be used if the evaluation effort includes "teaching" potential users the strengths and limitations of the effort, the degree to which one may expect definitive results, how the information from the evaluation can be effectively communicated by decisionmakers to their constituencies, and what criticisms and other reactions may be anticipated.

5. *Evaluations should include an assessment of utilization.* Evaluators and decisionmakers must not only share an understanding of the purposes for which a study is undertaken but also agree on the criteria by which its successful utilization may be judged. Under such conditions, however much informality is necessary, an effort should be made to judge the extent to which the uses of findings meet these expectations.

Although these guidelines are relevant to the utilization of all program evaluations, the roles of evaluation consumers do differ. Clearly, these differing roles affect the uses to which information is put and, consequently, the choice of mechanisms for maximizing utility. For example, if evaluations are to influence federal legislation and policies, they must be conducted and "packaged" in ways that meet the needs of congressional staff. For the case of educational evaluation and legislation, Florio, Behrmann, and Goltz (1979) furnished a useful summary of requirements that rings as true today as when it was compiled (see Exhibit 12-G).

EPILOGUE

There are many reasons to expect continued support of evaluation activities. First, decision-

⚒ EXHIBIT 12-G   Educational Evaluation: The Unmet Potential

The interviewees (congressional staff involved in developing educational legislation) mentioned more than 90 steps that could be taken to improve the use of educational studies in the formation of legislative policy. The most common themes, which reflect the current barriers to such use, are the ways in which research and assessment reports are presented and the failure to meet the needs demanded by the policy cycles in Congress. Staffers struck a common theme of work and information overload problems associated with the job. They rarely have time to evaluate the evaluations, let alone read through the voluminous reports that come across their desks. This was at the root of the repeated call for executive summaries in the front matter of reports, which would allow them to judge the relevance of the contents and determine whether further reading for substance was necessary. Although 16 (61%) of the staffers complained of an information overload problem, 19 also indicated that they were often forced to generate their own data relevant to political and policy questions. As one staffer put it, "We have no overload of *useful and understandable* information."

The timing of study reports and their relevance to questions before the Congress were major barriers repeatedly mentioned by congressional staff. A senior policy analyst for the Assistant Secretary of Education compared the policy process to a moving train. She suggested that information providers have the obligation to know the policy cycle and meet it on its own terms. The credibility problem is also one that plagues social inquiry. The Deputy Director of the White House Domestic Policy staff said that all social science suffers from the perception that it is unreliable and not policy-relevant. His comments were reflected by several of the staffers interviewed; for example, "Research rarely provides definitive conclusions," or "For every finding, others negate it," or "Educational research can rarely be replicated and there are few standards that can be applied to assess the research products." One went so far as to call project evaluations lies, then reconsidered and called them embellishments.

It must be pointed out that the distinctions among different types of inquiry research, evaluation, data collection, and so on are rarely made by the recipients of knowledge and information. If project evaluations are viewed as fabrications, it reflects negatively on the entire educational inquiry community. Even when policy-relevant research is presented in time to meet the moving train, staffers complain of having too much information that cannot be easily assimilated, or that studies are poorly packaged, contain too much technical jargon, and are too self-serving. Several said that researchers write for other researchers and rarely, except in congressionally mandated studies, tailor their language to the decision-making audiences in the legislative process.

SOURCE: Adapted from D. H. Florio, M. M. Behrmann, and D. L. Goltz, "What Do Policy Makers Think of Evaluational Research and Evaluation? Or Do They?" *Educational Evaluation and Policy Analysis,* 1979, 1(6):61-87. Copyright 1979 by the American Educational Research Association, Washington, DC. Adapted by permission of the publisher.

makers, planners, project staffs, and target participants are increasingly skeptical of common sense and conventional wisdom as sufficient bases on which to design social programs that will achieve their intended goals. Decades of attempts to solve the problems represented by explosive population growth, the maldistribution of resources within and between societies, popular discontent, crime, educational deficiencies among adults and children, drug and alcohol abuse, and weaknesses in traditional institutions such as the family have led to a realization that these are obstinate and difficult issues. This skepticism has, in turn, led policymakers and decisionmakers to seek ways to learn more quickly and efficiently from their mistakes and to capitalize more rapidly on measures that work.

A second major reason for the growth of evaluation research has been the development of knowledge and technical procedures in the social sciences. The refinement of sample survey procedures has provided an important information-gathering method. When coupled with more traditional experimental methods in the form of field experiments, these procedures become a powerful means of testing social programs. Advances in measurement, statistical theory, and substantive knowledge in the social sciences have added to the ability of social scientists to take on the special tasks of evaluation research.

Finally, there are the changes in the social and political climate of our times. As a society—indeed, as a world—we have come to insist that communal and personal problems are not fixed features of the human condition but can be ameliorated through the reconstruction of social institutions. We believe more than our ancestors did that societies can be improved and that the lot of all persons can be enhanced by the betterment of the disadvantaged and deprived. At the same time, we are confronted with severely limited resources for welfare, health, and other social programs. It is tempting simply to wish away unemployment, crime, homelessness—all the social ills we are too familiar with—and to believe that "moral reconstruction" will diminish the need for effective and efficient social programs. But it is catastrophically naive to think that doing so will solve our problems.

The prognosis is troublesome, in the short term at least, when we contemplate both the variety and number of concerns that require urgent action and the level of resources being committed to controlling and ameliorating them. It is clear that sensible, orderly procedures are required to choose which problems to confront first, and which programs to implement to deal with them. Our position is clear: Systematic evaluations are invaluable to current and future efforts to improve the lot of humankind.

SUMMARY

※ Evaluation is purposeful, applied social research. In contrast to basic research, evaluation is undertaken to solve practical problems. Its practitioners must be conversant with methods from several disciplines and able to apply them to many types of problems. Furthermore, the criteria for judging the work include its utilization and hence its impact on programs and the human condition.

※ Evaluators must put a high priority on deliberately planning for the dissemination of the results of their work. In particular, they need to become "secondary disseminators" who package their findings in ways that are geared to the needs and competencies of a broad range of relevant stakeholders.

※ Because the value of their work depends on its utilization by others, evaluators must understand the social ecology of the arena in which they work.

※ Evaluation is directed to a range of stakeholders with varying and sometimes conflicting needs, interests, and perspectives. Evaluators must determine the perspective from which a given evaluation should be conducted, explicitly acknowledge the existence of other perspectives, be prepared for criticism even from the sponsors of the evaluation, and adjust their communication to the requirements of various stakeholders.

※ An evaluation is only one ingredient in a political process of balancing interests and coming to decisions. The evaluator's role is close to that of an expert witness, furnishing the best information possible under the circumstances; it is not the role of judge and jury.

※ Two significant strains that result from the political nature of evaluation are (a) the different requirements of political time and evaluation time, and (b) the need for evaluations to have policy-making relevance and significance. With respect to both of these sets of issues, evaluators must look beyond considerations of technical excellence and pure science, mindful of the larger context in which they are working and the purposes being served by the evaluation.

※ Evaluators are perhaps better described as a "near-group" than as a profession. The field is marked by diversity in disciplinary training, type of schooling, perspectives on appropriate methods, and an absence of strong communication among its practitioners. Although the field's rich diversity is one of its attractions, it also leads to unevenness in competency, lack of consensus on appropriate approaches, and justifiable criticism of the methods used by some evaluators.

※ Among the enduring controversies in the field has been the issue of qualitative and quantitative research. Stated in the abstract, the issue is a false one; the two approaches are suitable for different and complementary purposes.

■ Evaluators are also diverse in their activities and working arrangements. Although there has been considerable debate over whether evaluators should be independent of program staff, there is now little reason to prefer either inside or outside evaluation categorically. What is crucial is that evaluators have a clear understanding of their role in a given situation.

■ There is reason to be concerned about the field's being dominated by a small group of elite evaluation organizations and their staffs. Although these organizations contribute to the movement toward professionalization of the field, efforts to enhance opportunities for career mobility and interaction in the profession are desirable.

■ Evaluative studies are worthwhile only if they are used. Three types of utilization are direct, or instrumental; conceptual; and persuasive. Although in the past, considerable doubt has been shed on the direct utility of evaluations, there is reason to believe they do have an impact on program development and modification. At least as important, the conceptual utilization of evaluations appears to have a definite effect on policy and program development, as well as social priorities, albeit one that is not always easy to trace.

GLOSSARY

Accessibility	The extent to which the structural and organizational arrangements facilitate participation in the program.
Accountability	The responsibility of program staff to provide evidence to stakeholders and sponsors that a program is effective and in conformity with its coverage, service, legal, and fiscal requirements.
Accounting perspectives	Perspectives underlying decisions on which categories of goods and services to include as costs or benefits in an analysis.
Administrative standards	Stipulated achievement levels set by program administrators or other responsible parties, for example, intake for 90% of the referrals within one month. These levels may be set on the basis of past experience, the performance of comparable programs, or professional judgment.
Articulated program theory	An explicitly stated version of program theory that is spelled out in some detail as part of a program's documentation and identity or as a result of efforts by the evaluator and stakeholders to formulate the theory.
Assessment of program process	An evaluative study that answers questions about program operations, implementation, and service delivery. Also known as a process evaluation or an implementation assessment.
Assessment of program theory	An evaluative study that answers questions about the conceptualization and design of a program.
Benefits	Net program outcomes, usually translated into monetary terms. Benefits may include both direct and indirect effects.
Benefits-to-costs ratio	The total discounted benefits divided by the total discounted costs.
Bias in coverage	The extent to which subgroups of a target population participate differentially in a program.
Black box evaluation	Evaluation of program outcomes without the benefit of an articulated program theory to provide insight into what is presumed to be causing those outcomes and why.

Comprehensive evaluation	An assessment of a social program that covers the need for the program, its design, implementation, impact, and efficiency.
Conceptual utilization	Long-term, indirect utilization of the ideas and findings of an evaluation.
Confounding factors	Extraneous variables resulting in observed effects that obscure or exaggerate the true effects of an intervention.
Constructed control designs	Impact assessments in which there is not random assignment of program participants and nonparticipating targets. Rather, the groups are equated by matching or statistical procedures on characteristics that may be associated with program outcomes.
Control group	A group of untreated targets that is compared with experimental groups on outcome measures in impact evaluations.
Cost-benefit analysis	Analytical procedure for determining the economic efficiency of a program, expressed as the relationship between costs and outcomes, usually measured in monetary terms.
Cost-effectiveness	The efficacy of a program in achieving given intervention outcomes in relation to the program costs.
Costs	Inputs, both direct and indirect, required to produce an intervention.
Coverage	The extent to which a program reaches its intended target population.
Cross-sectional designs	Studies in which data are collected at one point in time.
Design effects	The influence of the research methods and procedures on the estimate of the net effects of a program.
Direct utilization	Explicit utilization of specific ideas and findings of an evaluation by decisionmakers and other stakeholders.
Discounting	The treatment of time in valuing costs and benefits, that is, the adjustment of costs and benefits to their present values, requiring a choice of discount rate and time frame.
Distributional effects	Effects of programs that result in a redistribution of resources in the general population.
Efficiency assessment	An evaluative study that answers questions about program costs in comparison to either the monetary value of their benefits or their effectiveness in terms of the changes they bring about in the social conditions they address.
Empowerment evaluation	A participatory or collaborative evaluation in which the evaluator's role includes consultation and facilitation directed toward the devel-

opment of the capabilities of the participating stakeholders to conduct evaluation on their own, to use it effectively for advocacy and change, and to have some influence on a program that affects their lives.

Evaluability assessment Negotiation and investigation undertaken jointly by the evaluator, the evaluation sponsor, and possibly other stakeholders to determine if a program meets the preconditions for evaluation and, if so, how the evaluation should be designed to ensure maximum utility.

Evaluation questions A set of questions developed by the evaluator, evaluation sponsor, and other stakeholders; the questions define the issues the evaluation will investigate and are stated in terms such that they can be answered using methods available to the evaluator in a way useful to stakeholders.

Evaluation sponsor The person(s), group, or organization that requests or requires the evaluation and provides the resources to conduct it.

Ex ante designs Impact designs planned and begun prior to delivery of the program to the intervention group.

Ex ante efficiency analysis An efficiency analysis undertaken prior to program implementation, usually as part of program planning, to estimate net outcomes in relation to costs.

Experimental group A group of targets to whom an intervention is delivered and whose outcome measures are compared with those of control groups.

Ex post designs Impact designs undertaken subsequent to the delivery of the program to the intervention group, including secondary analyses making use of a quasi-experimental analytical approach.

Ex post efficiency analysis An efficiency analysis undertaken subsequent to knowing a program's net outcome effects.

Externalities Effects of a program that impose costs on persons or groups who are not targets.

Focus group A small panel of persons selected for their knowledge or perspective on a topic of interest that is convened to discuss the topic with the assistance of a facilitator. The discussion is usually recorded and used to identify important themes or to construct descriptive summaries of views and experiences on the focal topic.

Formative evaluation Evaluative activities undertaken to furnish information that will guide program improvement.

Generalizability The extent to which an impact assessment's findings can be extrapolated to similar programs or from the program as tested to the program as implemented.

Generic controls   Established measures of social processes, such as published test norms, that are used as comparisons with the outcomes of interventions.

Gross outcomes   The overall outcome subsequent to intervention, only part of which might actually be caused by the intervention.

Impact   The net effects of a program (see *net effects*).

Impact assessment   An evaluative study that answers questions about program outcomes and impact on the social conditions it is intended to ameliorate. Also known as an impact evaluation or an outcome evaluation.

Impact theory   The beliefs, assumptions, and expectations inherent in a program about the nature of the change brought about by program action and how it results in the intended improvement in social conditions. Program impact theory is causal theory: It describes a cause-and-effect sequence in which certain program activities are the instigating causes and certain social benefits are the effects they eventually produce.

Implementation failure   The program does not adequately perform the activities specified in the program design that are assumed to be necessary for bringing about the intended social improvements. It includes situations in which no service, not enough service, or the wrong service is delivered, or the service varies excessively across the target population.

Implicit program theory   Assumptions and expectations inherent in a program's services and practices that have not been fully articulated and recorded.

Incidence   The number of new cases of a particular problem or condition that arise in a specified area during a specified period of time.

Independent evaluation   An evaluation in which the evaluator has the primary responsibility for developing the evaluation plan, conducting the evaluation, and disseminating the results.

Internal rate of return   The calculated value for the discount rate necessary for total discounted program benefits to equal total discounted program costs.

Key informants   Persons whose personal or professional position gives them a perspective on the nature and scope of a social problem or a target population and whose views are obtained during a needs assessment.

Management information system (MIS)   A data system, usually computerized, that routinely collects and reports information about the delivery of services to clients and, often, billing, costs, diagnostic and demographic information, and outcome status.

Matching	Constructing control groups by finding targets identical in relevant respects to persons in experimental groups.
Measurement validity	The extent to which a measure reflects the concept it is intended to measure.
Needs assessment	An evaluative study that answers questions about the social conditions a program is intended to address and the need for the program. Needs assessment may also be used to determine whether there is a need for a new program and to compare or prioritize needs within and across program areas.
Net benefits	The total discounted benefits minus the total discounted costs. Also called net rate of return.
Net effects	The effects of an intervention that can be attributed uniquely to it, that is, with the influence of confounding effects from other sources controlled or removed. Also called net outcomes and net impact.
Opportunity costs	The value of opportunities forgone because of an intervention program.
Organizational plan	The assumptions and expectations about what the program must do to bring about the transactions between the target population and the program that will produce the intended changes in social conditions. The program's organizational plan is articulated from the perspective of program management and encompasses both the functions and activities the program is expected to perform and the human, financial, and physical resources required for that performance.
Outcome monitoring	The measurement and reporting of indicators of the status of the social conditions the program is accountable for improving.
Participatory or collaborative evaluation	An evaluation organized as a team project in which the evaluator and representatives of one or more stakeholder groups work collaboratively in developing the evaluation plan, conducting the evaluation, or disseminating and using the results.
Performance criterion	The standard against which a dimension of program performance is compared so that it can be evaluated.
Performance measurement	The collection, reporting, and interpretation of performance indicators related to how well programs perform, particularly with regard to the delivery of service (outputs) and achievement of results (outcomes).
Policy significance	The significance of an evaluation's findings for policy and program development (as opposed to their statistical significance).

GLOSSARY

Policy space	The set of policy alternatives that are within the bounds of acceptability to policymakers at a given point in time.
Population at risk	The individuals or units in a specified area with characteristics judged to indicate that they have a significant probability of having or developing a particular condition.
Population in need	The individuals or units in a specified area that currently manifest a particular problematic condition.
Pre-post design	A reflexive control design in which only one or a few before-intervention and after-intervention measures are taken.
Prevalence	The number of existing cases with a particular condition in a specified area at a specified time.
Primary dissemination	Dissemination of the detailed findings of an evaluation to sponsors and technical audiences.
Process evaluation	A form of program monitoring designed to determine whether the program is delivered as intended to the targeted recipients. Also known as implementation assessment.
Program evaluation	The use of social research procedures to systematically investigate the effectiveness of social intervention programs that is adapted to their political and organizational environments and designed to inform social action in ways that improve social conditions.
Program goal	A statement, usually general and abstract, of a desired state toward which a program is directed. Compare with *program objectives.*
Program monitoring	The systematic documentation of aspects of program performance that are indicative of whether the program is functioning as intended or according to some appropriate standard. Monitoring generally involves program performance related to program process, program outcomes, or both.
Program objectives	Specific, operationalized statements detailing the desired accomplishments of a program.
Program process theory	The combination of the program's organizational plan and its service utilization plan into an overall description of the assumptions and expectations about how the program is supposed to operate.
Program theory	The set of assumptions about the manner in which the program relates to the social benefits it is expected to produce and the strategy and tactics the program has adopted to achieve its goals and objec-

tives. Within program theory we can distinguish *impact theory*, relating to the nature of the change in social conditions brought about by program action, and *process theory*, which depicts the program's organizational plan and service utilization plan.

Proxy measure A variable used to stand in for one that is difficult to measure directly.

Quasi-experiment An impact research design in which "experimental" and "control" groups are formed by a procedure other than random assignment.

Randomization Assignment of potential targets to experimental and control groups on the basis of chance.

Randomized experiment An impact research design in which experimental and control groups are formed by random assignment.

Rate The occurrence or existence of a particular condition expressed as a proportion of units in the relevant population (e.g., deaths per 1,000 adults).

Reflexive controls Measures of the outcome variable taken on participating targets before interventions and used as control observations.

Regression-discontinuity design Quasi-experimental impact assessment in which the selection procedure for intervention is based on whether an observed value on an appropriate quantitative scale is above or below a designated cutting point.

Reliability The extent to which scores obtained on a measure are reproducible in repeated administrations (provided that all relevant measurement conditions are the same).

Reproducibility The extent to which the findings of a study can be reproduced by other researchers in replications.

Secondary dissemination Dissemination of summarized, often simplified findings to audiences composed of stakeholders.

Selection bias A confounding effect produced by preprogram differences between program participants and eligible targets who do not participate in the program.

Selection modeling Creation of a multivariate statistical model to "predict" the probability of selection into intervention or comparison groups in a quasi-experiment. The results of this analysis are used to configure a control variable for selection bias to be incorporated into a second-stage statistical model investigating net effects of intervention on outcome.

Sensitivity	The extent to which the criteria used to identify a target population result in the inclusion of individuals or units that actually have or will develop the condition to which the program is directed.
Service utilization plan	The assumptions and expectations about how the target population will make initial contact with the program and be engaged with it through the completion of the intended services. In simplest form, a service utilization plan describes the sequence of events through which the intended clients are expected to interact with the intended services.
Shadow controls	Expert and participant judgments used to estimate net impact.
Shadow prices	Imputed or estimated costs of goods and services not valued accurately in the marketplace. Shadow prices also are used when market prices are inappropriate due to regulation or externalities. Also known as accounting prices.
Social indicator	Periodic measurements designed to track the course of a social condition over time.
Social program; social intervention	An organized, planned, and usually ongoing effort designed to ameliorate a social problem or improve social conditions.
Social research methods	Procedures for studying social behavior devised by social scientists that are based on systematic observation and logical rules for drawing inferences from those observations.
Specification error	Error in impact estimation arising out of the use of an inappropriate or incomplete statistical model.
Specificity	The extent to which the criteria used to identify the target population result in the exclusion of individuals or units who do not have or will not develop the condition to which the program is directed.
Stakeholders	Individuals, groups, or organizations having a significant interest in how well a program functions, for instance, those with decision-making authority over it, funders and sponsors, administrators and personnel, and clients or intended beneficiaries.
Statistical control designs	Impact designs without random assignment of program participants and nonparticipants. Rather, the groups are statistically equated, usually by some multivariate statistical procedure, so that they resemble each other as much as possible on characteristics associated with program outcomes.
Stochastic effects	Measurement fluctuations attributable to chance.

Summative evaluation	Evaluative activities undertaken to render a summary judgment on certain critical aspects of the program's performance, for instance, to determine if specific goals and objectives were met.
Survey	Systematic collection of information from a defined population, usually by means of interviews or questionnaires administered to a sample of units in the population.
Target	The unit (individual, family, community, etc.) to which a program intervention is directed. All such units within the area served by a program comprise its target population.
Theory failure	The program is implemented as planned but its services do not produce the immediate effects on the participants that are expected or the ultimate social benefits intended or both.
Time-series analyses	Reflexive designs that rely on relatively long series of repeated measurements of the outcome variable taken before and after an intervention.
Utilization of evaluation	The use of the concepts and findings of an evaluation by decisionmakers and other stakeholders whether at the day-to-day management level or at broader funding or policy levels.

REFERENCES

Adams, B., and B. Sherman
    1978   "Sunset Implementation: A Positive Partnership to Make Government Work."
               Public Administration Review 36 (January/February): 78-81.

Affholter, D. P.
    1994   "Outcome Monitoring." In J. S. Wholey, H. P. Hatry, and K. E. Newcomer (eds.),
               Handbook of Practical Program Evaluation (pp. 96-118). San Francisco: Jossey-Bass.

Aiken, L. S., S. G. West, D. E. Schwalm, J. L. Carroll, and S. Hsiung
    1998   "Comparison of a Randomized and Two Quasi-Experimental Designs in a Single
               Outcome Evaluation." *Evaluation Review* 22(2):207-244.

American Evaluation Association, Task Force on Guiding Principles for Evaluators
    1995   "Guiding Principles for Evaluators." *New Directions for Evaluation*, no. 66 (pp. 19-26).
               San Francisco: Jossey-Bass.

Anderman, C., A. Cheadle, S. Curry, P. Diehr, L. Shultz, and E. Wagner
    1995   "Selection Bias Related to Parental Consent in School-Based Survey Research."
               Evaluation Review 19(6):663-674.

Ards, S.
    1989   "Estimating Local Child Abuse." *Evaluation Review* 13(5):484-515.

AuClaire, P., and I. M. Schwartz
    1986   *An Evaluation of Intensive Home-Based Services as an Alternative to Placement for*
               Adolescents and Their Families. Minneapolis: Hubert Humphrey School of Public
               Affairs, University of Minnesota.

Averch, H. A.
    1994   "The Systematic Use of Expert Judgment." In J. S. Wholey, H. P. Hatry, and
               K. E. Newcomer (eds.), *Handbook of Practical Program Evaluation* (pp. 293-309).
               San Francisco: Jossey-Bass.

Bausell, R. B.
    1992   "Methodologist's Corner: Sources of Evaluation Instruments." *Evaluation & the*
               Health Professions 15(4):475-490.

Berk, R. A., and D. Rauma
    1983   "Capitalizing on Non-Random Assignment to Treatment: A Regression Continuity
                Analysis of a Crime Control Program." *Journal of the American Statistical Association*
                78 (March): 21-28.

Berkeley Planning Associates
    1988   *Research Objectives and Study Questions for the Federal-State Vocation Rehabilitation
                Program.* Berkeley, CA: Berkeley Planning Associates.

Berkowitz, S.
    1996   "Using Qualitative and Mixed-Method Approaches." In R. Reviere, S. Berkowitz,
                C. C. Carter, and C. G. Ferguson (eds.), *Needs Assessment: A Creative and Practical
                Guide for Social Scientists* (pp. 121-146). Washington, DC: Taylor & Francis.

Bernstein, I. N., and H. E. Freeman
    1975   *Academic and Entrepreneurial Research.* New York: Russell Sage.

Besharov, D., P. Germanis, and P. H. Rossi
    1998   *Evaluating Welfare Reform: A Guide for Scholars and Practitioners.* College Park: School
                of Public Affairs, University of Maryland.

Bickman, L.
    1996   "Implications of a Children's Mental Health Managed Care Demonstration
                Evaluation." *Journal of Mental Health Administration* 23(1):107-118.

Bickman, L. (ed.)
    1987   *Using Program Theory in Evaluation (New Directions for Program Evaluation,* no. 33).
                San Francisco: Jossey-Bass.
    1990   *Advances in Program Theory (New Directions for Program Evaluation,* no. 47).
                San Francisco: Jossey-Bass.

Biglan, A., D. Ary, H. Yudelson, T. E. Duncan, D. Hood, L. James, V. Koehn, Z. Wright, C. Black,
D. Levings, S. Smith, and E. Gaiser
    1996   "Experimental Evaluation of a Modular Approach to Mobilizing Antitobacco
                Influences of Peers and Parents." *American Journal of Community Psychology* 24(3):
                311-339.

Black, D. R., N. S. Tobler, and J. P. Sciacca
    1998   "Peer Helping/Involvement: An Efficacious Way to Meet the Challenge of Reducing
                Alcohol, Tobacco, and Other Drug Use Among Youth?" *Journal of School Health*
                68(3):87-93.

Bloom, H. S.
    1990   *Back to Work: Testing Reemployment Services for Displaced Workers.* Kalamazoo, MI:
                W. E. Upjohn Institute.

Borman, G. D., and J. V. D'Agostino
    1996   "Title I and Student Achievement: A Meta-Analysis of Federal Evaluation Results."
                Educational Evaluation and Policy Analysis 18(4):309-326.

Boruch, R. F.
    1997   *Randomized Experiments for Planning and Evaluation: A Practical Guide.* Thousand
                Oaks, CA: Sage.

Boruch, R. F., M. Dennis, and K. Carter-Greer
    1988   "Lessons From the Rockefeller Foundation's Experiments on the Minority Female
                Single-Parent Program." *Evaluation Review* 12(4):396-426.

Boruch, R. F., and W. Wothke
    1985   "Seven Kinds of Randomization Plans for Designing Field Experiments." In
                R. F. Boruch and W. Wothke (eds.), *Randomization and Field Experimentation*
                (*New Directions for Program Evaluation,* no. 85). San Francisco: Jossey-Bass.

Boyatzis, R. E.
    1998   *Thematic Analysis: Coding as a Process for Transforming Qualitative Information.*
                Thousand Oaks, CA: Sage.

Braden, J. P., and T. J. Bryant
    1990   "Regression Discontinuity Designs: Applications for School Psychologists."
                School Psychology Review 19(2):232-239.

Bremner, R.
    1956   *From the Depths: The Discovery of Poverty in America.* New York: New York
                University Press.

Brindis, C., D. C. Hughes, N. Halfon, and P. W. Newacheck
    1998   "The Use of Formative Evaluation to Assess Integrated Services for Children."
                Evaluation & the Health Professions 21(1):66-90.

Broder, I. E.
    1988   "A Study of the Birth and Death of a Regulatory Agenda: The Case of the EPA Noise
                Program." *Evaluation Review* 12(3):291-309.

Browner, W. S., and T. B. Newman
    1989   "Sample Size and Power Based on the Population Attributable Fraction." *American
                Journal of Public Health* 79(9):1289-1294.

Bryk, A. S., V. E. Lee, and P. B. Holland
    1993   *Catholic Schools and the Common Good.* Cambridge, MA: Harvard University Press.

Bulmer, M.
    1982   *The Uses of Social Research.* London: Allen & Unwin.

Burnam, M. A., and P. Koegel
    1988   "Methodology for Obtaining a Representative Sample of Homeless Persons:
                The Los Angeles Skid Row Study." *Evaluation Review* 12(2):117-152.

Burt, M., and B. Cohen
    1988   *Feeding the Homeless: Does the Prepared Meals Provision Help?* Report to Congress on
                the Prepared Meal Provision, vols. I and II. Washington, DC: Urban Institute.

Calsyn, R. J., G. A. Morse, W. D. Klinkenberg, and M. L. Trusty
  1997   "Reliability and Validity of Self-Report Data of Homeless Mentally Ill Individuals."
          Evaluation and Program Planning 20(1):47-54.

Camasso, M. J., C. Harvey, and R. Jaganathan
  1996   *An Interim Report on the Impact of New Jersey's Family Development Program.*
          New Brunswick, NJ: Rutgers University School of Social Work.

Campbell, D. T.
  1969   "Reforms as Experiments." *American Psychologist* 24 (April): 409-429.
  1991   "Methods for the Experimenting Society." *Evaluation Practice* 12(3):223-260.
  1996   "Regression Artifacts in Time-Series and Longitudinal Data." *Evaluation and
          Program Planning* 19(4):377-389.

Campbell, D. T., and R. F. Boruch
  1975   "Making the Case for Randomized Assignment to Treatments by Considering the
          Alternatives: Six Ways in Which Quasi-Experimental Evaluations in Compensatory
          Education Tend to Underestimate Effects." In C. A. Bennett and A. A. Lumsdaine
          (eds.), *Evaluation and Experiment*, pp. 195-296. New York: Academic Press.

Campbell, D. T., and J. C. Stanley
  1966   *Experimental and Quasi-Experimental Designs for Research.* Skokie, IL: Rand McNally.

Caplan, N., and S. D. Nelson
  1973   "On Being Useful: The Nature and Consequences of Psychological Research on
          Social Problems." *American Psychologist* 28 (March): 199-211.

Cappelleri, J. C., W. M. K. Trochim, T. D. Stanley, and C. S. Reichardt
  1991   "Random Measurement Error Does Not Bias the Treatment Effect Estimate in the
          Regression-Discontinuity Design: I. The Case of No Interaction." *Evaluation Review*
          15(4):395-419.

Card, J. J., C. Greeno, and J. L. Peterson
  1992   "Planning an Evaluation and Estimating Its Cost." *Evaluation & the Health Professions*
          15(4):75-89.

Carr, J. A. (ed.)
  1991   "Counting the Homeless: The Methodologies, Policies and Social Significance
          Behind the Numbers" [Special issue]. *Housing Policy Debate* 2(3).

Chelimsky, E.
  1987   "The Politics of Program Evaluation." *Society* 25(1):24-32.
  1991   "On the Social Science Contribution to Governmental Decision-Making." *Science* 254
          (October): 226-230.
  1997   "The Coming Transformations in Evaluation." In E. Chelimsky and W. R. Shadish
          (eds.), *Evaluation for the 21st Century: A Handbook* (pp. 1-26). Thousand Oaks, CA:
          Sage.

Chelimsky, E., and W. R. Shadish (eds.)
1997   *Evaluation for the 21st Century: A Handbook.* Thousand Oaks, CA: Sage.

Chen, H.-T.
1990   *Theory-Driven Evaluations.* Newbury Park, CA: Sage.

Chen, H.-T., and P. H. Rossi
1980   "The Multi-Goal, Theory-Driven Approach to Evaluation: A Model Linking Basic
            and Applied Social Science." *Social Forces* 59 (September): 106-122.

Chen, H.-T., J. C. S. Wang, and L.-H. Lin
1997   "Evaluating the Process and Outcome of a Garbage Reduction Program in Taiwan."
            Evaluation Review 21(1):27-42.

Ciarlo, J. A., D. L. Tweed, D. L. Shern, L. A. Kirkpatrick, and N. Sachs-Ericsson
1992   "Validation of Indirect Methods to Estimate Need for Mental Health Services:
            Concepts, Strategies, and General Conclusions." *Evaluation and Program Planning*
            15(2):115-131.

Cicirelli, V. G., W. H. Cooper, and R. L. Granger
1969   *The Impact of Head Start.* Athens, OH: Westinghouse Learning Corporation and
            Ohio University.

Cohen, J.
1988   *Statistical Power Analysis for the Behavioral Sciences.* 2nd ed. Hillsdale, NJ: Lawrence
            Erlbaum.

Coleman, J. S., E. Q. Campbell, C. J. Hobson, J. G. McPartland, A. M. Mood, F. D. Weinfield, and
R. L. York
1966   *Equality of Educational Opportunity.* Washington, DC: Government Printing Office.

Coleman, J. S., T. Hoffer, and S. Kilgore
1981   *Public and Private Schools: High School and Beyond.* Chicago: National Opinion
            Research Center.

Collins Management Services
1990   *Final Report of the Head Start Evaluation Design Project.* Vienna, VA: Collins
            Management Consulting.

Cook, T. D.
1993   "A Quasi-Sampling Theory of the Generalization of Causal Relationships." In
            L. B. Sechrest (ed.), *Understanding Causes and Generalizing About Them* (*New
            Directions for Program Evaluation*, no. 57). San Francisco: Jossey-Bass.

Cook, T. D., and D. T. Campbell
1979   *Quasi-Experimentation Design and Analysis Issues for Field Settings.* Skokie, IL:
            Rand McNally.

Cook, T. D., and C. S. Reichardt (eds.)
1979   *Qualitative and Quantitative Methods in Evaluation Research.* Beverly Hills, CA: Sage.

Cordray, D. S.
    1993   "Prospective Evaluation Syntheses: A Multi-Method Approach to Assisting Policy-
                Makers." In M. Donker and J. Derks (eds.), *Rekenschap: Evaluatie-onderzoek in
                Nederland, de stand van zaken* (pp. 95-110). Utrecht, Netherlands: Centrum
                Geestelijke Volksgezondheid.

Coyle, S. L., R. F. Boruch, and C. F. Turner (eds.)
    1991   *Evaluating AIDS Prevention Programs.* Washington, DC: National Academy Press.

Cronbach, L. J.
    1982   *Designing Evaluations of Educational and Social Programs.* San Francisco: Jossey-Bass.

Cronbach, L. J., and Associates
    1980   *Toward Reform of Program Evaluation.* San Francisco: Jossey-Bass.

Culhane, D. P., and R. Kuhn
    1998   "Patterns and Determinants of Public Shelter Utilization Among Homeless Adults
                in New York City and Philadelphia." *Journal of Policy Analysis and Management* 17(1):
                23-43.

Datta, L.
    1977   "Does It Work When It Has Been Tried? And Half Full or Half Empty?" In
                M. Guttentag and S. Saar (eds.), *Evaluation Studies Review Annual.* Vol. 2
                (pp. 301-319). Beverly Hills, CA: Sage.
    1980   "Interpreting Data: A Case Study From the Career Intern Program Evaluation."
                Evaluation Review 4 (August): 481-506.

Dean, D. L.
    1994   "How to Use Focus Groups." In J. S. Wholey, H. P. Hatry, and K. E. Newcomer (eds.),
                Handbook of Practical Program Evaluation (pp. 338-349). San Francisco: Jossey-Bass.

Dennis, M. L.
    1990   "Assessing the Validity of Randomized Field Experiments: An Example From Drug
                Abuse Research." *Evaluation Review* 14(4):347-373.

Dennis, M. L., and R. F. Boruch
    1989   "Randomized Experiments for Planning and Testing Projects in Developing
                Countries: Threshold Conditions." *Evaluation Review* 13(3):292-309.

Devaney, B.
    1998   "The Special Supplemental Nutrition Program for Women, Infants and Children."
                In J. Crane (ed.), *Social Programs That Work.* New York: Russell Sage.

Devaney, B., L. Bilheimer, and J. Schore
    1991   *The Savings in Medicaid Costs for Newborns and Their Mothers From Prenatal Participation
                in the WIC Program.* Vol. 2. Alexandria, VA: U.S. Department of Agriculture Food and
                Nutrition Service.

Devine, J. A., J. D. Wright, and C. J. Brody
    1995   "An Evaluation of an Alcohol and Drug Treatment Program for Homeless Substance
                Abusers." *Evaluation Review* 19(6):620-645.

Dibella, A.
1990   "The Research Manager's Role in Encouraging Evaluation Use." *Evaluation Practice* 11(2):115-119.

Duckart, J. P.
1998   "An Evaluation of the Baltimore Community Lead Education and Reduction Corps (CLEARCorps) Program." *Evaluation Review* 22(3):373-402.

Dunford, F. W.
1990   "Random Assignment: Practical Considerations From Field Experiments." *Evaluation and Program Planning* 13(2):125-132.

Durlak, J. A., and A. M. Wells
1997   "Primary Prevention Mental Health Programs for Children and Adolescents: A Meta-Analytic Review." *American Journal of Community Psychology* 25(2):115-152.

Eddy, D. M.
1992   "Cost-Effectiveness Analysis: Is It Up to the Task?" *Journal of the American Medical Association* 267:3342-3348.

Elmore, R. F.
1980   "Backward Mapping: Implementation Research and Policy Decisions." *Political Science Quarterly* 94(4):601-616.

Fetterman, D. M., S. J. Kaftarian, and A. Wandersman (eds.)
1996   *Empowerment Evaluation: Knowledge and Tools for Self-Assessment & Accountability.* Thousand Oaks, CA: Sage.

Figlio, D. N.
1995   "The Effect of Drinking Age Laws and Alcohol-Related Crashes: Time-Series Evidence From Wisconsin." *Journal of Policy Analysis and Management* 14(4):555-566.

Fink, A.
1995   *Evaluation for Education and Psychology.* Thousand Oaks, CA: Sage.

Florio, D. H., M. M. Behrmann, and D. L. Goltz
1979   "What Do Policy Makers Think of Evaluational Research and Evaluation? Or Do They?" *Educational Evaluation and Policy Analysis* 1 (January): 61-87.

Foster, E. M., and L. Bickman
1996   "An Evaluator's Guide to Detecting Attrition Problems." *Evaluation Review* 20(6): 695-723.

Fournier, D. M.
1995   *Establishing Evaluative Conclusions: A Distinction Between General and Working Logic (New Directions for Evaluation, no. 68, pp. 15-32).* San Francisco: Jossey-Bass.

Fowler, F. L.
1993   *Survey Research Methods.* 2nd ed. Newbury Park, CA: Sage.

Fraker, T. F., A. P. Martini, and J. C. Ohls
    1995   "The Effect of Food Stamp Cashout on Food Expenditures: An Assessment of the
              Findings From Four Demonstrations." *Journal of Human Resources* 30(4):633-649.

Fraker, T., and R. Maynard
    1984   *The Use of Comparison Group Designs in Evaluations of Employment-Related
              Programs.* Princeton, NJ: Mathematica Policy Research.

Franke, R. H., and J. D. Kaul
    1978   "The Hawthorne Experiments: First Statistical Interpretation." *American Sociological
              Review* 43 (October): 623-642.

Freeman, H. E.
    1977   "The Present Status of Evaluation Research." In M. A. Guttentag and S. Saar (eds.),
              Evaluation Studies Review Annual. Vol. 2 (pp. 17-51). Beverly Hills, CA: Sage.
    1983   "A Federal Evaluation Agenda for the 1980s: Some Speculations and Suggestions."
              Educational Evaluation and Policy Analysis 5 (summer): 185-194.

Freeman, H. E., K. J. Kiecolt, and H. M. Allen III
    1982   "Community Health Centers: An Initiative of Enduring Utility." *Milbank Memorial
              Fund Quarterly/Health and Society* 60(2):245-267.

Freeman, H. E., and P. H. Rossi
    1984   "Furthering the Applied Side of Sociology." *American Sociological Review* 49(4):571-580.

Freeman, H. E., P. H. Rossi, and S. R. Wright
    1980   *Doing Evaluations.* Paris: Organization for Economic Cooperation and Development.

Freeman, H. E., and M. A. Solomon
    1979   "The Next Decade in Evaluation Research." *Evaluation and Program Planning* 2
              (March): 255-262.

Freeman, H. E., and A. Weeks
    1956   "Analysis of a Program of Treatment of Delinquent Boys." *American Journal of
              Sociology* 62 (July): 56-61.

French, M. T., C. J. Bradley, B. Calingaert, M. L. Dennis, and G. T. Karuntzos
    1994   "Cost Analysis of Training and Employment Services in Methadone Treatment."
              Evaluation and Program Planning 17(2):107-120.

Fuller, B., S. W. Raudenbush, L.-M. Wei, and S. D. Holloway
    1993   "Can Government Raise Child-Care Quality? The Influence of Family Demand,
              Poverty, and Policy." *Educational Evaluation and Policy Analysis* 15(3):255-278.

Funnell, S.
    1997   "Program Logic: An Adaptable Tool for Designing and Evaluating Programs." *Evaluation
              News and Comment: The Magazine of the Australasian Evaluation Society* 6(1):5-17.

Galster, G. C., T. F. Champney, and Y. Williams
    1994   "Costs of Caring for Persons With Long-Term Mental Illness in Alternative Residential
              Settings." *Evaluation and Program Planning* 17(3):239-248.

Gilham, S. A., W. L. Lucas, and D. Sivewright
1997   "The Impact of Drug Education and Prevention Programs: Disparity Between Impressionistic and Empirical Assessments." *Evaluation Review* 21(5):589-613.

Glasgow, R. E., H. Lando, J. Hollis, S. G. McRae, and P. A. La Chance
1993   "A Stop-Smoking Telephone Help Line That Nobody Called." *American Journal of Public Health* 83(2):252-253.

Glasser, W.
1975   *Reality Therapy.* New York: Harper and Row.

Goodman, S. M., and R. Royall
1988   "Evidence and Scientific Research." *American Journal of Public Health* 78(12): 1568-1574.

Gottfredson, D. C., C. M. Fink, S. Skroban, and G. D. Gottfredson
1997   "Making Prevention Work." In R. P. Weissberg, T. P. Gullotta, R. L. Hampton, B. A. Ryan, and G. R. Adams (eds.), *Establishing Preventive Services* (pp. 219-252). Thousand Oaks, CA: Sage.

Gramblin, E. M.
1990   *A Guide to Benefit-Cost Analysis.* Englewood Cliffs, NJ: Prentice Hall.

Gramlich, E. M., and P. P. Koshel
1975   *Educational Performance Contracting: An Evaluation of an Experiment.* Washington, DC: Brookings Institution.

Gray, P. J.
1988   "Microcomputers in Evaluation." *Evaluation Practice* 9(3):47-53.

Gray, T., C. R. Larsen, P. Haynes, and K. W. Olson
1991   "Using Cost-Benefit Analysis to Evaluate Correctional Sentences." *Evaluation Review* 15(4):471-481.

Greene, J. C.
1988   "Stakeholder Participation and Utilization in Program Evaluation." *Evaluation Review* 12(2):91-116.

Greene, J. C., and V. J. Caracelli (eds.)
1997   *Advances in Mixed-Method Evaluation: The Challenges and Benefits of Integrating Diverse Paradigm (New Directions for Evaluation,* no. 74). San Francisco: Jossey-Bass.

Greene, W. H.
1993   "Selection-Incidental Truncation." In W. H. Greene, *Econometric Analysis* (pp. 706-715). New York: Macmillan.

Grossman, J. B., and J. P. Tierney
1998   "Does Mentoring Work? An Impact Study of the Big Brothers-Big Sisters Program." *Evaluation Review* 22(3):403-426.

Guba, E. G., and Y. S. Lincoln
1987   "The Countenances of Fourth Generation Evaluation: Description, Judgment, and

Negotiation." In D. Palumbo (ed.), *The Politics of Program Evaluation* (pp. 203-234). Newbury Park, CA: Sage.

1989   *Fourth Generation Evaluation.* Newbury Park, CA: Sage.

1994   "Competing Paradigms in Qualitative Research" In N. K. Denzin and Y. S. Lincoln (eds.), *Handbook of Qualitative Research* (pp. 105-117). Thousand Oaks, CA: Sage.

Gueron, J. M., and E. Pauly
1991   *From Welfare to Work.* New York: Russell Sage.

Halvorson, H. W., D. K. Pike, F. M. Reed, M. W. McClatchey, and C. A. Gosselink
1993   "Using Qualitative Methods to Evaluate Health Service Delivery in Three Rural Colorado Communities." *Evaluation & the Health Professions* 16(4):434-447.

Hamberger, L. K., and J. E. Hastings
1988   "Skills Training for Treatment of Spouse Abusers." *Journal of Family Violence* 3(2): 121-130.

Hamilton, J.
1994   *Time Series Analysis.* Princeton, NJ: Princeton University Press.

Hamilton, Rabinowitz, and Alschuler, Inc.
1987, July   *The Changing Face of Misery: Los Angeles' Skid Row Area in Transition—Housing and Social Services Needs of Central City East.* Los Angeles: Community Redevelopment Agency.

Hatry, H. P.
1994   "Collecting Data From Agency Records" In J. S. Wholey, H. P. Hatry, and K. E. Newcomer (eds.), *Handbook of Practical Program Evaluation.* San Francisco: Jossey-Bass.

1997   *Where the Rubber Meets the Road: Performance Measurement for State and Local Public Agency (New Directions for Evaluation, no. 75, pp. 31-44).* San Francisco: Jossey-Bass.

Haveman, R. H.
1987   "Policy Analysis and Evaluation Research After Twenty Years." *Policy Studies Journal* 16(2):191-218.

Hayes, S. P., Jr.
1959   *Evaluating Development Projects.* Paris: UNESCO.

Hays, W. L.
1990   *Statistics.* 4th ed. Fort Worth, TX: Holt, Rinehart & Winston.

Heckman, J. J., and V. J. Hotz
1989   "Choosing Among Alternative Nonexperimental Methods for Estimating the Impact of Social Programs: The Case of Manpower Training." *Journal of the American Statistical Association* 84(408):862-880 (with discussion).

Heckman, J. J., and R. Robb
   1985   "Alternative Methods for Evaluating the Impact of Interventions: An Overview."
               Journal of Econometrics 30:239-267.

Hedrick, T. E., L. Bickman, and D. Rog
   1992   *Applied Research Design: A Practical Guide.* Newbury Park, CA: Sage.

Heinsman, D. T., and W. R. Shadish
   1996   "Assignment Methods in Experimentation: When Do Nonrandomized Experiments
               Approximate the Answers From Randomized Experiments?" *Psychological Methods*
               1:154-169.

Henry, G. T.
   1990   *Practical Sampling.* Newbury Park, CA: Sage.

Herman, D. B., E. L. Struening, and S. M. Barrow
   1994   "Self-Reported Needs for Help Among Homeless Men and Women." *Evaluation and
               Program Planning* 17(3):249-256.

Hoch, C.
   1990   "The Rhetoric of Applied Sociology: Studying Homelessness in Chicago." *Journal of
               Applied Sociology* 7:11-24.

Hsu, L. M.
   1995   "Regression Toward the Mean Associated With Measurement Error and the
               Identification of Improvement and Deterioration in Psychotherapy." *Journal of
               Consulting & Clinical Psychology* 63(1):141-144.

Humphreys, K., C. S. Phibbs, and R. H. Moos
   1996   "Addressing Self-Selection Effects in Evaluations of Mutual Help Groups and
               Professional Mental Health Services: An Introduction to Two-Stage Sample Selection
               Models." *Evaluation and Program Planning* 19(4):301-308.

Jacobson, N. S., and P. Truax
   1992   "Clinical Significance: A Statistical Approach to Defining Meaningful Change in
               Psychotherapy Research." In A. E. Kazdin (ed.), *Methodological Issues and Strategies
               in Clinical Research.* Washington, DC: American Psychological Association.

Jencks, C.
   1994   *The Homeless.* Cambridge, MA: Harvard University Press.

Jerrell, J. M., and T.-W. Hu
   1996   "Estimating the Cost Impact of Three Dual Diagnosis Treatment Programs."
               Evaluation Review 20(2):160-180.

Joint Committee on Standards for Educational Evaluation
   1994   *The Program Evaluation Standards.* 2nd ed. Thousand Oaks, CA: Sage.

Jones, E. M., G. D. Gottfredson, and D. C. Gottfredson
   1997   "Success for Some: An Evaluation of a Success for All Program." *Evaluation Review*
               21(6):643-670.

Jones-Lee, M. W.
    1994   "Safety and the Saving of Life: The Economics of Safety and Physical Risk." In
                R. Layard and S. Glaister (eds.), *Cost-Benefit Analysis*. 2nd ed. (pp. 290-318).
                Cambridge, UK: Cambridge University Press.

Kanouse, D. E., S. H. Berry, E. M. Gorman, E. M. Yano, S. Carson, and A. Abrahamse
    1991   *AIDS-Related Knowledge, Attitudes, Beliefs, and Behaviors in Los Angeles County*.
                Santa Monica, CA: RAND.

Kaye, E., and J. Bell
    1993   *Final Report: Evaluability Assessment of Family Preservation Programs*. Arlington, VA:
                James Bell Associates.

Kazdin, A. E.
    1982   *Single-Case Research Designs*. New York: Oxford University Press.

Kelling, G. L., T. Pate, D. Dieckman, and C. E. Brown
    1974   *The Kansas City Preventive Patrol Experiment: A Technical Report*. Washington, DC:
                Police Foundation.

Kennedy, C. H., S. Shikla, and D. Fryxell
    1997   "Comparing the Effects of Educational Placement on the Social Relationships of
                Intermediate School Students With Severe Disabilities." *Exceptional Children* 64(1):
                31-47.

Kershaw, D., and J. Fair
    1976   *The New Jersey Income-Maintenance Experiment*. Vol. 1. New York: Academic Press.

Kessler, D. A., and S. Duncan
    1996   "The Impact of Community Policing in Four Houston Neighborhoods." *Evaluation
                Review* 29(6):627-669.

King, J. A., L. L. Morris, and C. T. Fitz-Gibbon
    1987   *How to Assess Program Implementation*. Newbury Park, CA: Sage.

Kinkade, P. T., M. C. Leone, and W. N. Welsh
    1995   "Tough Laws: Policymaker Perceptions and Commitment." *Social Science Journal*
                32(2):157-178.

Kirk, R. E.
    1996   "Practical Significance: A Concept Whose Time Has Come." *Educational and
                Psychological Measurement* 56(5):746-759.

Kirschner Associates, Inc.
    1975   *Programs for Older Americans: Setting and Monitoring. A Reference Manual*.
                Washington, DC: U.S. Department of Health, Education and Welfare, Office of
                Human Development.

Kish, L.
    1987   *Statistical Design for Research*. New York: Wiley.
    1995   *Survey Sampling*. New York: Wiley.

Kisker, E., and R. Maynard
    1991   "Quality, Cost and Parental Choice of Child Care." In D. M. Blau (ed.), *The Economics of Child Care*. New York: Russell Sage.

Kraemer, H. C., and S. Thiemann
    1987   *How Many Subjects? Statistical Power Analysis in Research*. Newbury Park, CA: Sage.

Krueger, R. A.
    1988   *Focus Groups: A Practical Guide for Applied Research*. Newbury Park, CA: Sage.

LaLonde, R.
    1986   "Evaluating the Econometric Evaluations of Training Programs." *American Economic Review* 76:604-620.

Landsberg, G.
    1983   *Program Utilization and Service Utilization Studies: A Key Tool for Evaluation (New Directions for Program Evaluation, no. 20, pp. 93-103)*. San Francisco: Jossey Bass).

Lee, L. J., and J. F. Sampson
    1990   "A Practical Approach to Program Evaluation." *Evaluation and Program Planning* 13(2): 157-164.

Levin, H. M., G. V. Glass, and G. R. Meister
    1987   "Cost-Effectiveness of Computer-Assisted Instruction." *Evaluation Review* 11(1):50-72.

Levine, A., and M. Levine
    1977   "The Social Context of Evaluation Research: A Case Study." *Evaluation Quarterly* 1(4): 515- 542.

Levine, R. A., M. A. Solomon, G.-M. Hellstern, and H. Wollmann (eds.)
    1981   *Evaluation Research and Practice: Comparative and International Perspectives*. Beverly Hills, CA: Sage.

Leviton, L. C., and R. F. Boruch
    1983   "Contributions of Evaluations to Educational Programs." *Evaluation Review* 7(5): 563-599.

Leviton, L. C., and E. F. X. Hughes
    1981   "Research on the Utilization of Evaluations: A Review and Synthesis." *Evaluation Review* 5(4):525-548.

Lincoln, Y. S., and E. G. Guba
    1985   *Naturalistic Inquiry*. Beverly Hills, CA: Sage.

Lipsey, M. W.
    1990   *Design Sensitivity: Statistical Power for Experimental Research*. Newbury Park, CA: Sage.
    1992   "Juvenile Delinquency Treatment: A Meta-Analytic Inquiry Into the Variability of Effects." In T. D. Cook, H. Cooper, D. S. Cordray, H. Hartmann, L. V. Hedges,

R. J. Light, T. A. Louis, & F. Mosteller (eds.), *Meta-Analysis for Explanation: A Casebook.* New York: Russell Sage.

1993   *Theory as Method: Small Theories of Treatments (New Directions for Program Evaluation,* no. 57, pp. 5-38). San Francisco: Jossey-Bass.

1997   *What Can You Build With Thousands of Bricks? Musings on the Cumulation of Knowledge in Program Evaluation (New Directions for Evaluation,* no. 76, pp. 7-24). San Francisco: Jossey-Bass.

Lipsey, M. W., and J. A. Pollard

1989   "Driving Toward Theory in Program Evaluation: More Models to Choose From." *Evaluation and Program Planning* 12:317-328.

Lipsey, M. W., and D. B. Wilson

1993   "The Efficacy of Psychological, Educational, and Behavioral Treatment: Confirmation From Meta-Analysis." *American Psychologist* 48(12):1181-1209.

1996   *Toolkit for Practical Meta-Analysis.* Cambridge, MA: Human Services Research Institute.

Little, R. J. A., and D. B. Rubin

1987   *Statistical Analysis With Missing Data.* New York: Wiley.

Loehlin, J. C.

1992   *Latent Variable Models: An Introduction to Factor, Path, and Structural Analysis.* Hillsdale, NJ: Lawrence Erlbaum.

Long, S. K., and D. A. Wissoker

1995   "Welfare Reform at Three Years: The Case of Washington State's Family Independence Program." *Journal of Human Resources* 30(4):766-790.

Luepker, R. V., C. L. Perry, S. M. McKinlay, P. R. Nader, G. S. Parcel, E. J. Stone, L. S. Webber, J. P. Elder, H. A. Feldman, C. C. Johnson, S. H. Kelder, and M. Wu

1996   "Outcomes of a Field Trial to Improve Children's Dietary Patterns and Physical Activity: The Child and Adolescent Trial for Cardiovascular Health (CATCH)." *Journal of the American Medical Association* 275 (March): 768-776.

Lynn, L. E., Jr.

1980   *Designing Public Policy.* Santa Monica, CA: Scott, Foresman.

Madaus, G. F., and D. Stufflebeam (eds.)

1989   *Educational Evaluation: The Classic Works of Ralph W. Tyler.* Boston: Kluwer Academic Publishers.

Mark, M. M., and R. L. Shotland

1985   "Stakeholder-Based Evaluation and Value Judgments." *Evaluation Review* 9:605-626.

Martin, L. L., and P. M. Kettner

1996   *Measuring the Performance of Human Service Programs.* Thousand Oaks, CA: Sage.

Mathematica Policy Research

1983   *Final Report of the Seattle-Denver Income Maintenance Experiment.* Vol. 2. Princeton: Mathematica Policy Research.

McCleary, R., and R. Hay, Jr.
   1980   *Applied Time Series Analysis for the Social Sciences.* Beverly Hills, CA: Sage.

McFarlane, J.
   1989   "Battering During Pregnancy: Tip of an Iceberg Revealed." *Women and Health* 15(3): 69-84.

McKillip, J.
   1987   *Need Analysis: Tools for the Human Services and Education.* Newbury Park, CA: Sage.
   1998   "Need Analysis: Process and Techniques." In L. Bickman and D. J. Rog (eds.), *Handbook of Applied Social Research Methods* (pp. 261-284). Thousand Oaks, CA: Sage.

McLaughlin, M. W.
   1975   *Evaluation and Reform: The Elementary and Secondary Education Act of 1965/Title I.* Cambridge, MA: Ballinger.

Mehrens, W. A., and I. J. Lehmann
   1991   *Measurement and Evaluation in Education and Psychology.* 4th ed. Fort Worth, TX: Harcourt Brace College Publishers.

Mercier, C.
   1997   "Participation in Stakeholder-Based Evaluation: A Case Study." *Evaluation and Program Planning* 20(4):467-475.

Meyers, M. K., B. Glaser, and K. MacDonald
   1998   "On the Front Lines of Welfare Delivery: Are Workers Implementing Policy Reforms?" *Journal of Policy Analysis and Management* 17(1):1-22.

Mielke, K. W., and J. W. Swinehart
   1976   *Evaluation of the "Feeling Good" Television Series.* New York: Children's Television Workshop.

Milavsky, J. R., H. H. Stipp, R. C. Kessler, and W. S. Rubens
   1982   *Television and Aggression: A Panel Study.* New York: Academic Press.

Miles, M. B., and A. M. Huberman
   1994   *Qualitative Data Analysis: An Expanded Sourcebook.* Thousand Oaks, CA: Sage.

Miller, C., V. Knox, P. Auspos, J. A. Hunter-Manns, and A. Orenstein
   1997   *Making Welfare Work and Work Pay: Implementation and 18-Month Impacts of the Minnesota Family Investment Program.* New York: Manpower Demonstration Research Corporation.

Miller, G., and J. A. Holstein (eds.)
   1993   *Constructivist Controversies: Issues in Social Problems Theory.* New York: Aldine de Gruyter.

Millett, R. A.
   1996   "Empowerment Evaluation and the W. K. Kellogg Foundation." In D. M. Fetterman, S. J. Kaftarian, and A. Wandersman (eds.), *Empowerment Evaluation: Knowledge and Tools for Self-Assessment & Accountability* (pp. 65-76). Thousand Oaks, CA: Sage.

Mishan, E. J.
    1988   *Cost-Benefit Analysis.* 4th ed. London: Allen & Unwin.

Mitra, A.
    1994   "Use of Focus Groups in the Design of Recreation Needs Assessment Questionnaires."
                Evaluation and Program Planning 17(2):133-140.

Mohr, L. B.
    1995   *Impact Analysis for Program Evaluation.* 2nd ed. Thousand Oaks, CA: Sage.

Morgan, D. L.
    1988   *Focus Groups as Qualitative Research.* Qualitative Research Methods Series, no. 16.
                Newbury Park, CA: Sage.

Moynihan, D. P.
    1991   "Educational Goals and Political Plans." *The Public Interest* 102 (winter): 32-48.
    1996   *Miles to Go: A Personal History of Social Policy.* Cambridge, MA: Harvard University
                Press.

Muchinsky, P. M.
    1996   "The Correction for Attenuation." *Educational and Psychological Measurement* 56(1):
                63-75.

Murray, C.
    1984   *Losing Ground: American Social Policy, 1950-1980.* New York: Basic Books.

Murray, S.
    1980   *The National Evaluation of the PUSH for Excellence Project.* Washington, DC:
                American Institutes for Research.

Myers, J. L., and Well, A. D.
    1995   *Research Design and Statistical Analysis.* Hillsdale, NJ: Lawrence Erlbaum.

Nagel, S. S.
    1986   "Microcomputers and Evaluation Research" [Special issue]. *Evaluation Review* 10(5).

Nas, T. F.
    1996   *Cost-Benefit Analysis: Theory and Application.* Thousand Oaks, CA: Sage.

Nelson, R. H.
    1987   "The Economics Profession and the Making of Public Policy." *Journal of Economic
                Literature* 35(1):49-91.

Nevo, D.
    1989   "Expert Opinion in Program Evaluation." In R. F. Conner and M. Hendricks (eds.),
                International Innovations in Evaluation Methodology (*New Directions for Program
                Evaluation*, no. 42). San Francisco: Jossey-Bass.

Newman, D. L., and R. D. Brown
    1996   *Applied Ethics for Program Evaluation.* Thousand Oaks, CA: Sage.

Nowacek, G. A., P. M. O'Malley, R. A. Anderson, and F. E. Richards
1990   "Testing a Model of Diabetes Self-Care Management: A Causal Model Analysis With LISREL." *Evaluation & the Health Professions* 13(3):298-314.

Office of Income Security
1983   *Overview of the Seattle-Denver Income Maintenance Final Report.* Washington, DC: U.S. Department of Health and Human Services.

Oman, R. C., and S. R. Chitwood
1984   "Management Evaluation Studies: Factors Affecting the Acceptance of Recommendations." *Evaluation Review* 8(3):283-305.

Orshansky, M.
1969   "Perspectives on Poverty: How Poverty Is Measured." *Monthly Labor Review* 92(2): 37-41.

Palumbo, D. J., and M. A. Hallett
1993   "Conflict Versus Consensus Models in Policy Evaluation and Implementation." *Evaluation and Program Planning* 16(1):11-23.

Pancer, S. M., and A. Westhues
1989   "A Developmental Stage Approach to Program Planning and Evaluation." *Evaluation Review* 13(1):56-77.

Papineau, D., and M. C. Kiely
1996   "Participatory Evaluation in a Community Organization: Fostering Stakeholder Empowerment and Utilization." *Evaluation and Program Planning* 19(1):79-93.

Parker, R. N., and L. Rebhun
1995   *Alcohol and Homicide: A Deadly Combination of Two American Traditions.* Albany: State University of New York Press.

Patton, M. Q.
1986   *Utilization-Focused Evaluation.* 2nd ed. Beverly Hills, CA: Sage.
1990   *Qualitative Evaluation and Research Methods.* 2nd ed. Newbury Park, CA: Sage.
1997   *Utilization-Focused Evaluation: The New Century Text.* 3rd ed. Thousand Oaks, CA: Sage.

Phillips, K. A., R. A. Lowe, J. G. Kahn, P. Lurie, A. L. Avins, and D. Ciccarone
1994   "The Cost Effectiveness of HIV Testing of Physicians and Dentists in the United States." *Journal of the American Medical Association* 271:851-858.

Plantz, M. C., M. T. Greenway, and M. Hendricks
1997   *Outcome Measurement: Showing Results in the Nonprofit Sector (New Directions for Evaluation,* no. 75, pp. 15-30). San Francisco: Jossey-Bass.

Quinn, D. C.
1996   "Formative Evaluation of Adapted Work Services for Alzheimer's Disease Victims: A Framework for Practical Evaluation in Health Care." Doctoral dissertation, Vanderbilt University.

Reichardt, C. S., and C. A. Bormann
1994   "Using Regression Models to Estimate Program Effects." In J. S. Wholey, H. P. Hatry, and K. E. Newcomer (eds.), *Handbook of Practical Program Evaluation* (pp. 417-455). San Francisco: Jossey-Bass.

Reichardt, C. S., and S. F. Rallis (eds.)
1994   *The Qualitative Quantitative Debate: New Perspectives (New Directions for Evaluation,* no. 61). San Francisco: Jossey-Bass.

Reichardt, C. S., W. M. K. Trochim, and J. C. Cappelleri
1995   "Reports of the Death of Regression-Discontinuity Analysis Are Greatly Exaggerated." *Evaluation Review* 19(1):39-63.

Reineke, R. A.
1991   "Stakeholder Involvement in Evaluation: Suggestions for Practice." *Evaluation Practice* 12(1):39-44.

Reiss, A. J., Jr.
1971   *The Police and the Public.* New Haven, CT: Yale University Press.

Reviere, R., S. Berkowitz, C. C. Carter, and C. G. Ferguson (eds.)
1996   *Needs Assessment: A Creative and Practical Guide for Social Scientists.* Washington, DC: Taylor & Francis.

Reynolds, A. J., and J. A. Temple
1995   "Quasi-Experimental Estimates of the Effects of a Preschool Intervention." *Evaluation Review* 19(4):347-373.

Ribisl, K. M., M. A. Walton, C. T. Mowbray, D. A. Luke, W. S. Davidson, and B. J. BootsMiller
1996   "Minimizing Participant Attrition in Panel Studies Through the Use of Effective Retention and Tracking Strategies: Review and Recommendations." *Evaluation and Program Planning* 19(1):1-25.

Rich, R. F.
1977   "Uses of Social Science Information by Federal Bureaucrats." In C. H. Weiss (ed.), *Using Social Research for Public Policy Making* (pp. 199-211). Lexington, MA: D.C. Heath.

Riecken, H. W., and R. F. Boruch (eds.)
1974   *Social Experimentation: A Method for Planning and Evaluating Social Intervention.* New York: Academic Press.

Robertson, D. B.
1984   "Program Implementation Versus Program Design." *Policy Study Review* 3:391-405.

Robins, P. K., R. R. Spiegelman, S. Weiner, and J. G. Bell (eds.)
1980   *A Guaranteed Annual Income: Evidence From a Social Experiment.* New York: Academic Press.

Roethlisberger, F. J., and W. Dickson
1939   *Management and the Worker.* Cambridge, MA: Harvard University Press.

Rog, D. J.
1994   "Constructing Natural 'Experiments.' " In J. S. Wholey, H. P. Hatry, and
         K. E. Newcomer (eds.), *Handbook of Practical Program Evaluation* (pp. 119-132).
         San Francisco: Jossey-Bass.

Rog, D. J., K. L. McCombs-Thornton, A. M. Gilert-Mongelli, M. C. Brito, and C. S. Holupka
1995   "Implementation of the Homeless Families Program: 2. Characteristics, Strengths,
         and Needs of Participant Families." *American Journal of Orthopsychiatry* 65(4):514-528.

Rosenbaum, P. R., and D. B. Rubin
1983   "The Central Role of the Propensity Score in Observational Studies for Causal Effects."
         Biometrika 70(1):41-55.
1984   "Reducing Bias in Observational Studies Using Subclassification on the Propensity
         Score." *Journal of the American Statistical Association* 79(387):516-524.

Ross, H. L., D. T. Campbell, and G. V. Glass
1970   "Determining the Social Effects of a Legal Reform: The British Breathalyzer
         Crackdown of 1967." *American Behavioral Scientist* 13 (March/April): 494-509.

Rossi, P. H.
1978   "Issues in the Evaluation of Human Services Delivery." *Evaluation Quarterly* 2(4):
         573-599.
1987   "No Good Applied Research Goes Unpunished!" *Social Science and Modern Society*
         25(1):74-79.
1989   *Down and Out in America: The Origins of Homelessness.* Chicago: University of
         Chicago Press.
1992   "Assessing Family Preservation Programs." *Children and Youth Services Review* 14(1):
         77-98.
1997   "Program Outcomes: Conceptual and Measurement Issues." In E. J. Mullen and
         J. Magnabosco (eds.), *Outcome and Measurement in the Human Services: Cross-Cutting
         Issues and Methods.* Washington, DC: National Association of Social Workers.
1998   *Feeding the Poor: Assessing Federal Food Aid.* Washington, DC: American Enterprise
         Institute.

Rossi, P. H., R. A. Berk, and K. J. Lenihan
1980   *Money, Work and Crime: Some Experimental Evidence.* New York: Academic Press.

Rossi, P. H., G. A. Fisher, and G. Willis
1986   *The Condition of the Homeless of Chicago.* Chicago, IL and Amherst, MA: Social and
         Demographic Research Institute and NORC: A Social Science Research Institute.

Rossi, P. H., and K. Lyall
1976   *Reforming Public Welfare.* New York: Russell Sage.

Rossi, P. H., J. D. Wright, and A. Anderson (eds.)
1983   *Handbook of Survey Research.* New York: Academic Press.

Rotheram-Borus, M. J., M. Gwadz, M. I. Fernandez, and S. Srinivasan
1998   "Timing of HIV Interventions on Reductions in Sexual Risk Among Adolescents."
         American Journal of Community Psychology 26(1):73-96.

Ruggles, P.
  1990   *Drawing the Line: Alternative Poverty Measures and Their Implications for Public Policy.*
            Washington, DC: Urban Institute.

Rutman, L.
  1980   *Planning Useful Evaluations: Evaluability Assessment.* Beverly Hills, CA: Sage.

Savaya, R.
  1998   "The Potential and Utilization of an Integrated Information System at a Family and
            Marriage Counselling Agency in Israel." *Evaluation and Program Planning* 21(1):11-20.

Scheirer, M. A.
  1994   "Designing and Using Process Evaluation." In J. S. Wholey, H. P. Hatry, and K. E.
            Newcomer (eds.), *Handbook of Practical Program Evaluation* (pp. 40-68). San Francisco:
            Jossey-Bass.

Schmidt, F., and J. E. Hunter
  1996   "Measurement Error in Psychological Research: Lessons From 26 Research Scenarios."
            Psychological Methods 1(2):199-223.

Schorr, L. B.
  1997   *Common Purpose: Strengthening Families and Neighborhoods to Rebuild America.*
            New York: Doubleday Anchor.

Schuerman, J. R., T. L. Rzepnicki, and J. H. Littell
  1994   *Putting Families First: An Experiment in Family Preservation.* Hawthorne, NY:
            Aldine de Gruyter.

Schweinhart, L. J., and F. P. Weikart
  1998   "High/Scope Perry Preschool Effects at Age 27." In J. Crane (ed.), *Social Programs
            That Work.* New York: Russell Sage.

Scriven, M.
  1991   *Evaluation Thesaurus.* 4th ed. Newbury Park, CA: Sage.

Sechrest, L., and W. H. Yeaton
  1982   "Magnitudes of Experimental Effects in Social Science Research." *Evaluation Review*
            6(5):579-600.

Shadish, W. R., T. D. Cook, and L. C. Leviton
  1991   *Foundations of Program Evaluation: Theories of Practice.* Newbury Park, CA: Sage.

Shadish, W. R., D. L. Newman, M. A. Scheirer, and C. Wye (eds.)
  1995   *Guiding Principles for Evaluators (New Directions for Evaluation,* no. 66). San Francisco:
            Jossey-Bass.

Shadish, W. R., K. Ragsdale, R. R. Glaser, and L. M. Montgomery
  1995   "The Efficacy and Effectiveness of Marital and Family Therapy: A Perspective From
            Meta-Analysis." *Journal of Marital & Family Therapy* 21(4):345-360.

Shadish, W. R., Jr., and C. S. Reichardt
  1987   "The Intellectual Foundations of Social Program Evaluation: The Development of

Evaluation Theory." In W. R. Shadish, Jr. and C. S. Reichardt (eds.), *Evaluation Studies Review Annual* (pp. 13-30). Newbury Park, CA: Sage.

Shlay, A. B., and C. S. Holupka
1991   *Steps Toward Independence: The Early Effects of the Lafayette Courts Family Development Center.* Baltimore: Institute for Policy Studies, Johns Hopkins University.

Shlay, A. B., and P. H. Rossi
1981   "Keeping Up the Neighborhood: Estimating Net Effects of Zoning." *American Sociological Review* 46 (October): 703-719.

Shortell, S. M., and W. C. Richardson
1978   *Health Program Evaluation.* St. Louis, MO: C. V. Mosby.

Simon, J., and B. D. Merrill
1998   "Political Socialization in the Classroom Revisited: The Kids Voting Program." *Social Science Journal* 35(1):29-42.

Skaburskis, A.
1987   "Cost-Benefit Analysis: Ethics and Problem Boundaries." *Evaluation Review* 11(5): 591-611.

Skogan, W. G., and A. J. Lurigio
1991   *Multisite Evaluations in Criminal Justice Settings: Structural Obstacles to Success* (*New Directions for Program Evaluation*, no. 50, pp. 83-96). San Francisco: Jossey-Bass.

Smith, M. F.
1989   *Evaluability Assessment: A Practical Approach.* Norwell, MA: Kluwer Academic Publishers.

Solomon, J.
1988   "Companies Try Measuring Cost Savings From New Types of Corporate Benefits." *Wall Street Journal*, December 29, p. B1.

Solomon, M. A., and S. M. Shortell
1981   "Designing Health Policy Research for Utilization." *Health Policy Quarterly* 1 (May): 261-273.

Solomon, P., and J. Draine
1995   "One-Year Outcomes of a Randomized Trial of Consumer Case Management." *Evaluation and Program Planning* 18(2):117-127.

Soriano, F. I.
1995   *Conducting Needs Assessments: A Multidisciplinary Approach.* Thousand Oaks, CA: Sage.

Spector, M., and J. I. Kitsuse
1977   *Constructing Social Problems.* Reprinted 1987. Hawthorne, NY: Aldine de Gruyter.

SRI International
1983   *Final Report of the Seattle-Denver Income Maintenance Experiment.* Vol. 1. Palo Alto, CA: SRI International.

Stanley, T. D.
    1991   " 'Regression-Discontinuity Design' by Any Other Name Might Be Less Problematic."
                Evaluation Review 15(5):605-624.

Stephan, A. S.
    1935   "Prospects and Possibilities: The New Deal and the New Social Research."
                Social Forces 13 (May): 515-521.

Stokey, E., and R. Zeckhauser
    1978   *A Primer for Policy Analysis.* New York: Norton.

Stolzenberg, R. M., and D. A. Relles
    1997   "Tools for Intuition About Sample Selection Bias and Its Correction." *American
                Sociological Review* 62(3):494-507.

Stouffer, S. A., A. A. Lumsdaine, M. H. Lumsdaine, R. W. Williams, Jr., M. B. Smith, I. L. Janis, and
L. S. Cottrel, Jr.
    1949   *The American Soldier: Vol. 2. Combat and Its Aftermath.* Princeton, NJ: Princeton
                University Press.

Strauss, A., and J. Corbin
    1990   *Basics of Qualitative Research: Grounded Theory Procedures and Techniques.*
                Newbury Park, CA: Sage.

Suchman, E.
    1967   *Evaluative Research.* New York: Russell Sage.

Sudman, S., and N. M. Bradburn
    1982   *Asking Questions: A Practical Guide to Questionnaire Design.* San Francisco: Jossey-
                Bass.

Suen, H. K., D. Ary, and W. C. Covalt
    1990   "A Decision Tree Approach to Selecting an Appropriate Observation Reliability Index."
                Journal of Psychopathology and Behavioral Assessment 12(4):359-363.

Sylvain, C., R. Ladouceur, and J. Boisvert
    1997   "Cognitive and Behavioral Treatment of Pathological Gambling: A Controlled Study."
                Journal of Consulting and Clinical Psychology 65(5):727-732.

Terrie, E. W.
    1996   "Assessing Child and Maternal Health: The First Step in the Design of Community-
                Based Interventions." In R. Reviere, S. Berkowitz, C. C. Carter, and C. G. Ferguson
                (eds.), *Needs Assessment: A Creative and Practical Guide for Social Scientists* (pp.
                121-146). Washington, DC: Taylor & Francis.

Thompson, M.
    1980   *Benefit-Cost Analysis for Program Evaluation.* Beverly Hills, CA: Sage.

Torres, R. T., H. S. Preskill, and M. E. Piontek
    1996   *Evaluation Strategies for Communicating and Reporting: Enhancing Learning in
                Organizations.* Thousand Oaks, CA: Sage.

Trippe, C.
  1995   "Rates Up: Trends in FSP Participation Rates: 1985-1992." In D. Hall and
              M. Stavrianos (eds.), *Nutrition and Food Security in the Food Stamp Program.*
              Alexandria, VA: U.S. Department of Agriculture, Food and Consumer Service.

Trochim, W. M. K.
  1984   *Research Design for Program Evaluation: The Regression Discontinuity Approach.*
              Beverly Hills, CA: Sage.

Trochim, W. M. K., J. C. Cappelleri, and C. S. Reichardt
  1991   "Random Measurement Error Does Not Bias the Treatment Effect Estimate in the
              Regression-Discontinuity Design: II. When an Interaction Effect Is Present."
              Evaluation Review 15(5):571-604.

Turpin, R. S., and J. M. Sinacore (eds.)
  1991   *Multisite Evaluations (New Directions for Program Evaluation, no. 50).* San Francisco:
              Jossey-Bass.

United Way of America Task Force on Impact
  1996   *Measuring Program Outcomes: A Practical Approach.* Alexandria, VA: United Way of
              America.

Urban Institute
  1998   "Assessing the New Federalism: Overview and Status Report." Paper prepared for
              the Assessing New Federalism Technical Advisory Group. Washington, DC: Urban
              Institute.

U.S. Department of Justice, Bureau of Justice Statistics
  1994   *Criminal Victimization in the United States: 1973-92 Trends.* Washington, DC: U.S.
              Department of Justice, Bureau of Justice Statistics.
  1997   *Criminal Victimization 1996.* Washington, DC: U.S. Department of Justice, Bureau
              of Justice Statistics.

U.S. General Accounting Office
  1986   *Teen-Age Pregnancy: 500,000 Births a Year but Few Tested Programs.* GAO/PEMD-
              86-16BR. Washington, DC: U.S. General Accounting Office.
  1990   *Prospective Evaluation Methods: The Prospective Evaluation Synthesis.* GAO/PEMD
              Transfer Paper 10.1.10. Washington, DC: U.S. General Accounting Office.
  1995   *Mammography Services: Initial Impact of New Federal Law Has Been Positive.*
              GAO/HEHS-96-17. Washington, DC: U.S. General Accounting Office.
  1997   *Managing for Results: Analytic Challenges in Measuring Performance.*
              GAO/HEHS/GGD-97-138. Washington, DC: U.S. General Accounting Office.

van de Vall, M., and C. A. Bolas
  1981   "External Vs. Internal Social Policy Researchers." *Knowledge: Creation, Diffusion,
              Utilization* 2 (June): 461-481.

Vanecko, J. J., and B. Jacobs
  1970   *Reports From the 100-City CAP Evaluation: The Impact of the Community Action
              Program on Institutional Change.* Chicago: National Opinion Research Center.

Viscusi, W. K.
  1985   "Cotton Dust Regulation: An OSHA Success Story?" *Journal of Policy Analysis and Management* 4(3):325-343.

Weick, K. E.
  1982   *Social Psychology of Organizing.* 2nd ed. New York: McGraw-Hill.
  1984   "Small Wins: Redefining the Scale of Social Problems." In W. R. Shadish, Jr. and C. S. Reichardt (eds.), *Evaluation Studies Annual.* Vol. 12 (pp. 118-122). Beverly Hills, CA: Sage.

Weiss, C. H.
  1972   *Evaluation Research: Methods of Assessing Program Effectiveness.* Englewood Cliffs, NJ: Prentice Hall.
  1988   "Evaluation for Decisions: Is Anybody There? Does Anybody Care?" *Evaluation Practice* 9(1):5-19.
  1993   "Where Politics and Evaluation Research Meet." *Evaluation Practice* 14(1):93-106.
  1997   "How Can Theory-Based Evaluation Make Greater Headway?" *Evaluation Review* 21(4):501-524.

Weiss, C. H., and M. J. Bucuvalas
  1980   "Truth Tests and Utility Tests: Decision-Makers' Frames of Reference for Social Science Research." *American Sociological Review* 45 (April): 302-313.

Wholey, J. S.
  1979   *Evaluation: Promise and Performance.* Washington, DC: Urban Institute.
  1981   "Using Evaluation to Improve Program Performance." In R. A. Levine, M. A. Solomon, G.-M. Hellstern, and H. Wollmann (eds.), *Evaluation Research and Practice: Comparative and International Perspectives* (pp. 92-106). Beverly Hills, CA: Sage.
  1987   *Evaluability Assessment: Developing Program Theory* (*New Directions for Program Evaluation*, no. 33, pp. 77-92). San Francisco: Jossey-Bass.
  1994   "Assessing the Feasibility and Likely Usefulness of Evaluation." In J. S. Wholey, H. P. Hatry, and K. E. Newcomer (eds.), *Handbook of Practical Program Evaluation* (pp. 15-39). San Francisco: Jossey-Bass.

Wholey, J. S., and H. P. Hatry
  1992   "The Case for Performance Monitoring." *Public Administration Review* 52(6):604-610.

Wilkinson, J.
  1997   "The Impact of Ilderton Motor Project on Motor Vehicle Crime and Offending." *British Journal of Criminology* 37(4):568-581.

Winfree, L. T., Jr., F.-A. Esbensen, and D. W. Osgood
  1996   "Evaluating a School-Based Gang-Prevention Program: A Theoretical Perspective." *Evaluation Review* 20(2):181-203.

Witkin, B. R.
  1977   "Needs Assessment Kits, Models, and Tools." *Educational Technology* 17(11):5-18.
  1994   "Needs Assessment Since 1981: The State of the Practice." *Evaluation Practice* 15(1): 17-27.

Witkin, B. R., and J. W. Altschuld
    1995   *Planning and Conducting Needs Assessments: A Practical Guide.* Thousand Oaks, CA:
                Sage.

Wright, J. D., P. H. Rossi, and K. Daly
    1983   *Under the Gun: Weapons, Crime, and Violence in America.* New York: Aldine
                de Gruyter.

Wright, J. D., and E. Weber
    1987   *Homelessness and Health.* New York: McGraw-Hill.

Wu, P., and D. T. Campbell
    1996   "Extending Latent Variable LISREL Analyses of the 1969 Westinghouse Head Start
                Evaluation to Blacks and Full Year Whites." *Evaluation and Program Planning* 19(3):
                183-191.

Yates, B. T.
    1996   *Analyzing Costs, Procedures, Processes, and Outcomes in Human Services.*
                Thousand Oaks, CA: Sage.

Yuan, Y.-Y. T.
    1990   *Evaluation of AB 1562 In-Home Care Demonstration Projects.* Vols. I and II.
                Sacramento: Walter R. MacDonald and Associates.

Zerbe, R. O.
    1998   "Is Cost-Benefit Analysis Legal? Three Rules." *Journal of Policy Analysis and
                Management* 17(3):419-456.

AUTHOR INDEX

SUBJECT INDEX

ABOUT THE AUTHORS

Peter H. Rossi is Stuart A. Rice Professor Emeritus of Sociology and Director Emeritus, Social and Demographic Research Institute, at the University of Massachusetts at Amherst. He has been on the faculties of Harvard University, the University of Chicago, and Johns Hopkins University. He was Director, 1960 to 1967, of the National Opinion Research Center and has been a consultant on social research and evaluation to (among others) the National Science Foundation, the National Institute of Mental Health, the General Accounting Office, and the Rockefeller Foundation. His research centers on the application of social research methods to social issues and is currently focused on evaluating welfare reform. His recent books include *Feeding the Poor* (1998), *Thinking About Evaluation* (2nd ed., with Richard A. Berk), *Just Punishments* (1997, with Richard A. Berk), and *Of Human Bonding: Parent-Child Relations Throughout the Life Course* (1990, with Alice S. Rossi). He is past president of the American Sociological Association and the 1985 recipient of the Commonwealth Award. He has received awards from the Evaluation Research Society, the Eastern Evaluation Society, the American Sociological Association, and the Policy Studies Association. He has served as editor of the *American Journal of Sociology* and *Social Science Research*, and he is a Fellow of the American Academy of Arts and Sciences and the American Association for the Advancement of Science.

Howard E. Freeman was Professor of Sociology, University of California, Los Angeles. He was Chair of his department from 1985 to 1989, and founding director of UCLA's Institute for Social Science Research, a position he held from 1974 until 1981. He also held appointments in UCLA's Department of Medicine and School of Education. He joined UCLA in 1974 after serving as the Ford Foundation's Social Science Advisor for Mexico, Central America, and the Caribbean. Prior appointments include Brandeis University, where he was Morse Professor of Urban Studies, Harvard University, and the Russell

Sage Foundation. He published more than 150 articles and a number of monographs on the posthospital experience of mental patients, on policy issues in the delivery of health services, and on research methods. He was coeditor of the *Handbook of Medical Sociology*, now in its fourth edition, and of *Evaluation Review*. He was the recipient of the Hofheimer Prize of the American Psychiatric Association and the Myrdal Award of the American Evaluation Association and was a member of the Institute of Medicine. He also was president of Litigation Measurements, Inc., a small consulting firm that undertakes social research for attorneys. He died in 1992.

Mark W. Lipsey is Professor of Public Policy at Vanderbilt University's Peabody College where he also serves as Codirector of the Center for Evaluation Research and Methodology at the Vanderbilt Institute for Public Policy Studies. His professional interests are in the areas of program evaluation, social intervention, field research methodology, and research synthesis. The foci of his recent research are risk and intervention for juvenile delinquency and issues of methodological quality in program evaluation research. His other books include *Design Sensitivity: Statistical Power for Experimental Research* (1990) and *Toolkit for Practical Meta-Analysis* (1996, with David B. Wilson). He is a former editor in chief of *New Directions for Evaluation* and has served on the editorial boards of *Evaluation Review, Evaluation Studies Review Annual,* and *Evaluation and Program Planning*. He was the American Evaluation Association's Paul Lazarsfeld Award Recipient in 1996 and is a Fellow of the American Psychological Society.